P9-DYZ-445

CALIFORNIA STUDIES IN THE HISTORY OF ART

WALTER HORN, GENERAL EDITOR

I The Birth of Landscape Painting in China

BY MICHAEL SULLIVAN

II Portraits by Degas

BY JEAN SUTHERLAND BOGGS

III Leonardo da Vinci on Painting
A Lost Book (Libro A)

BY CARLO PEDRETTI

IV Images in the Margins of Gothic Manuscripts

BY LILIAN M. C. RANDALL

V The Dynastic Arts of the Kushans

BY JOHN M. ROSENFIELD

VI A Century of Dutch Manuscript Illumination

BY L. M. J. DELAISSÉ

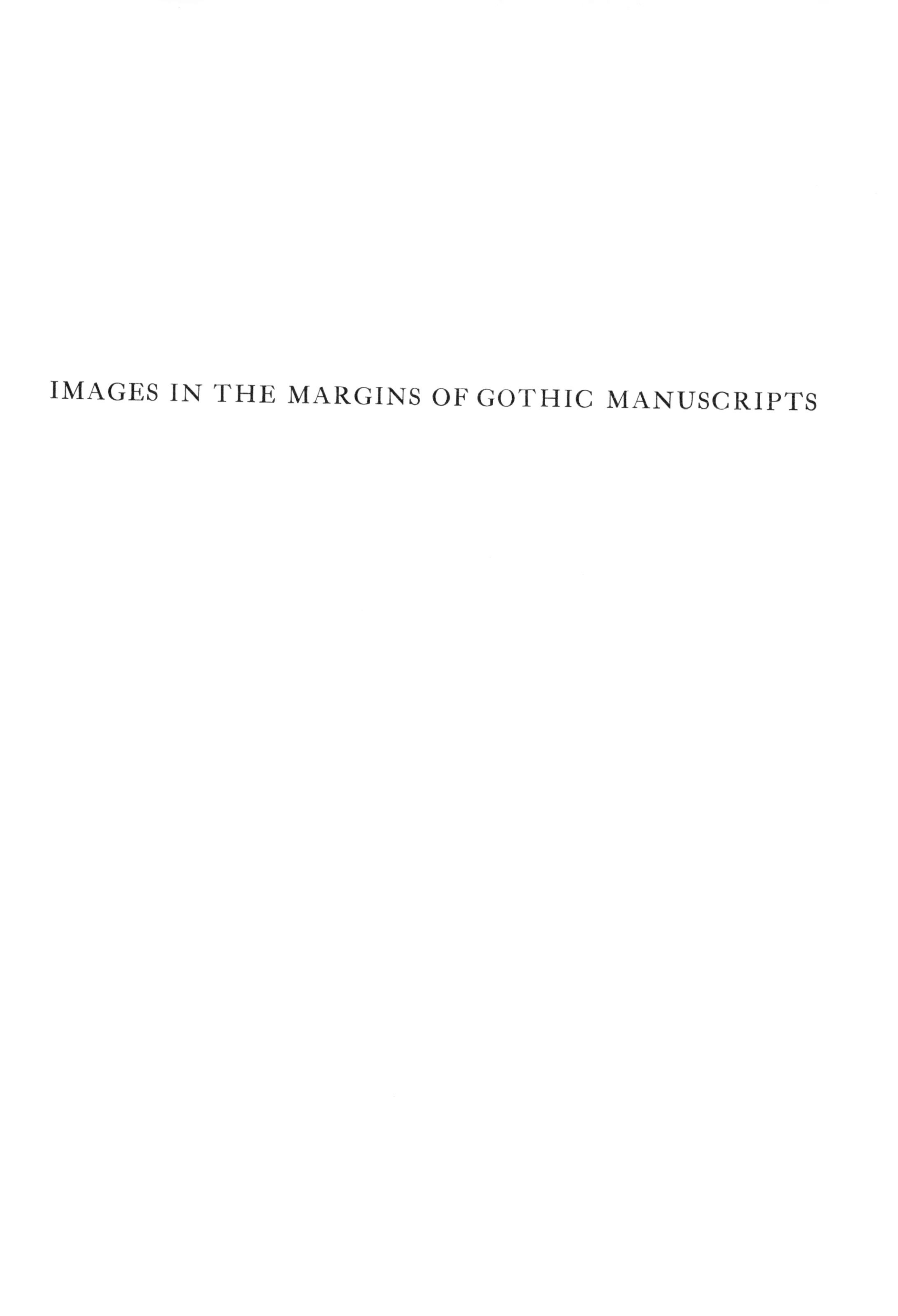

IMAGES IN THE MARGINS OF GOTHIC MANUSCRIPTS

eus in adiutori
um meum intende; domine ad
adiuuandum me festina
Gloria pri.
alleluia. hymnus.

IMAGES IN THE MARGINS OF GOTHIC MANUSCRIPTS

LILIAN M. C. RANDALL

UNIVERSITY OF CALIFORNIA PRESS
BERKELEY AND LOS ANGELES
1966

Images in the Margins of Gothic Manuscripts
is a volume in the
California Studies in the History of Art
sponsored in part by the Samuel H. Kress Foundation

University of California Press
Berkeley and Los Angeles, California
Cambridge University Press
London, England

Published with the assistance of a grant
from the American Council of Learned Societies
as a result of a contribution from the
United States Steel Foundation

Library of Congress Catalog Card Number: 65-18561
Manufactured in the United States of America

FAMILIAE

ET

JANE WOODRUFF GREENOUGH

(*in memoriam*)

PREFACE

In an article outlining the scope and function of the Index of Christian Art at Princeton, Miss Rosalie Green mentions a statement ascribed to its initiator, Charles Rufus Morey, at the inception of the project in 1917: "Only we were fools enough to get on with it."[1] In the course of preparing the present compilation of Gothic marginal illustrations, the same notion occasionally came to mind. Even though the subject represents but a fractional aspect of medieval art, it touches upon virtually every facet of contemporary thought and tradition. Herein lie its particular interest and significance, as well as its complexity.

The initial impetus for specializing in this area of research came in a course on Gothic illumination given by Professor Harry Bober at Harvard University in 1952. A term paper on marginal illustrations led to a doctoral dissertation completed under his direction in 1955. The idea for the present work grew out of my increasing awareness of the potential usefulness of a classified presentation of this material for scholars of medieval and post-medieval art and civilization.

During the past ten years my firsthand study of the widely dispersed sources here and abroad was immeasurably facilitated by grants from the American Association of University Women and the American Council of Learned Societies. From 1961 to 1963 I had the good fortune to be affiliated with the Radcliffe Institute for Independent Study as an Associate Scholar. My two-year tenure enabled me to collate the results of previous research into the present framework.

The completion of this project was further facilitated by the generous assistance of many individuals in a variety of capacities. For continued interest and support I am particularly indebted to Miss Dorothy Miner and to Messrs. L. M. J. Delaissé and H. W. Janson, who recommended the book to Walter Horn, General Editor of the California Studies in the History of Art. I should also like to express my appreciation to the following for help in obtaining information, photographs, and additional references: Messrs. G. Bonner, W. Heckscher, O. Pächt, E. Panofsky, J. Plummer, J. Porcher, H. Swarzenski, and F. Wormald, as well as to Mmes. A. Dekker, J. Gobeaux-Thonet, R. Green, O. Lorsignol, R. Schilling, and K. Smith. Special acknowledgment must also be made to the late W. S. Glazier for freely making available pertinent manuscripts from his collection.

The kindness of the keepers of manuscripts in the libraries I visited and revisited with lists of embarrassing length has put me in their permanent debt which, hopefully, may be partially repaid by some of my findings. For unlimited access to relevant material and permission to reproduce my own as well as professional photographs of original sources, I should like to thank the following persons and institutions: Arras, Bibliothèque Municipale and Musée Diocésaîn; Baltimore, Walters Art Gallery; Brussels, Bibliothèque Royale; Cambrai, Bibliothèque Municipale; Cambridge (England): Fitzwilliam Museum (by permission of the Syndics of the Museum), Trinity College (by permission of the Master and Fellows),

1. Green, R., "The Index of Christian Art," *Princeton Alumni Weekly,* LXIII, No. 19 (March 1, 1963), p. 10. In his exhortation, "Lectores, orate pro collectore," John of Bromyard expresses his sympathy with this viewpoint (*Summa Praedicantium,* British Museum, Royal MS. 17 E.IV, f. 638).

and University Library; Chantilly, Musée Condé; Copenhagen, Kongelige Bibliotek; Frankfurt, Kunstgewerbemuseum; Ghent, Bibliothèque de l'Université; The Hague, Koninklijke Biblioteek; Heidelberg, Universitätsbibliothek; Liège, Bibliothèque de l'Université; London: British Museum (by permission of the Trustees), Lambeth Palace Library; Manchester, John Rylands Library; Melbourne, National Gallery of Victoria; Metz, Bibliothèque Municipale; Munich, Bayerische Staatsbibliothek; Nancy, Bibliothèque Municipale; New Haven, Yale University Library; New York: H. P. Kraus, Metropolitan Museum of Art, New York Public Library, Pierpont Morgan Library, and Jacques Seligmann; Oxford: All Souls College; Bodleian Library, Jesus College, and Merton College; Paris: Bibliothèque de l'Arsenal, Bibliothèque Mazarine, Bibliothèque Nationale, Bibliothèque Sainte-Geneviève, and Musée Jacquemart-André; Princeton, Art Museum, Princeton University; Saint-Omer, Bibliothèque Municipale; Tournai, Bibliothèque Municipale and Trésor de la Cathédrale; Troyes, Bibliothèque Municipale; Valenciennes, Bibliothèque Municipale; Verdun, Bibliothèque Municipale; Vienna, Österreichische Nationalbibliothek.

Without the unremitting coöperation and active support of various family members, particularly of my husband, it is doubtful whether this venture could ever have been accomplished. Special thanks are also due Dr. and the late Mrs. W. B. Greenough III for help far beyond the call of duty during the summer of 1960.

For assistance in the arduous task of typing I am greatly indebted to Mrs. Irene Butterbaugh. I should also like to express my thanks to the representatives of the University of California Press for their courtesy and efficiency in preparing this volume.

LILIAN M. C. RANDALL

Baltimore, Md.

CONTENTS

INTRODUCTION 1

Selective Bibliography 21

Key to Abbreviated Manuscript References 27

List of Manuscripts According to Libraries 39

Guide to the Use of the Index 41

INDEX OF SUBJECTS 43

PLATES 237

IS THERE any thing whereof it may be said, See, this is new? it hath been already of old time, which was before us.

Ecclesiastes 1:10

Introduction

Just as the extensive domain of the Church entailed close involvement with secular affairs, religious art incorporated profane elements, often endowing them with symbolic overtones. Throughout the Middle Ages there was sporadic opposition against this fusion, or rather, lack of dividing line. The significance of St. Bernard's eloquent protest is heightened by the sparseness of comparable documentation which reflects the general tolerance toward the infiltration of *ars profana* into the sacred precinct.[4] In view of the dearth of official or private censure and countermeasures, the relative concentration of reactionary opinions voiced in the late twelfth and early thirteenth century is noteworthy. It signalizes a last determined though ineffectual effort to stem the tide of progressive secularization during this crucial transition period. In the realm of the arts the principal objections were, like St. Bernard's, against the impropriety, distraction, and unwarranted expenditure entailed in the representation of non-religious imagery.[5] The justification for depicting even simple farm animals was questioned, for instance, by Hugo de Folieto: " . . . reconnaissons qu'un cheval et un boeuf, qui dans un champ nous aident à subvenir à des besoins nécessaires, valent mieux qu'un cheval et un boeuf peints sur les murs où ils ne servent qu'à rassasier les yeux." [6] A far more explicit enumeration of grievances appears in an early thirteenth-century English tract entitled *Pictor in Carmine*.[7] Similarities of phraseology and descriptive detail show that the presumed author, the Cistercian Adam of Dore, was familiar with the diatribe of his renowned predecessor.[8] Compiled specifically to counteract the mounting propensity for profane church decoration, this work was intended to serve as a source book for artists of Scriptural types and antitypes. A most revealing testimony of the tendencies deemed particularly reprehensible at this time, the preface warrants quoting at length:

Struck with grief that in the sanctuary of God there should be foolish pictures, and what are rather misshapen monstrosities than ornaments, I wished if possible to occupy the minds and eyes of the faithful in a more comely and useful fashion. For since the eyes of our contemporaries are apt to be caught by a pleasure that is not only vain, but even profane, and since I did not think it would be easy to do away altogether with the meaningless paintings in churches, especially in cathedral and parish churches, where public stations take place, I think it an excusable concession that they should enjoy at least that class of pictures which, as being the books of the laity, can suggest divine things to the unlearned, and stir up the learned to the love of the scriptures.

For indeed—to touch but a few points out of many—which is more decent, which more profitable, to behold about the altar of God double-headed eagles, four lions with one and the same head, centaurs with quivers, headless men grinning . . . , the so-called 'logical' chimaera . . . , the fabled intrigues of the fox and the cock, monkeys playing the pipe, and Boethius's ass and lyre; or (surely) to contemplate the deeds of the Patriarchs, the rites of the Law . . . ? Is the panorama of the Old and New Testaments so meager that we must needs set aside what is comely and profitable, and, as the saying goes, make ducks and drakes of our

peinture flamande (Ghent: Librairie Néerlandoise, 1903), pp. 26-27; M. Schapiro, "From Mozarabic to Romanesque at Silos," *Art Bulletin,* XXI (1939), p. 339 and fig. 9; J. Baltrusaitis, *Réveils et prodiges, le gothique fantastique* (Paris: A. Colin, n.d.), pp. 119 ff.

4. On the edicts issued by successive Ecumenical Councils, see M. Bergenthal, *Elemente der Drolerie und ihre Beziehungen zur Literatur* (Berlin, 1936), p. 25; P. H. Michel, *La fresque romane* (Paris: P. Tisné, 1961), p. 87. A famous early medieval protest by St. Nilus is cited by H. W. Janson, *Apes and Ape Lore in the Middle Ages and the Renaissance,* Studies of the Warburg Institute, vol. 20 (London; 1952), p. 71, n. 124.

5. While according to St. Bernard greater artistic license was permissible in cathedrals than in monasteries, he deemed it deplorable that sacred images depicted in church pavements were submitted to outrageous sacrilege by soiling and spitting (Schapiro, "On the Aesthetic Attitude," p. 135). Similarly John Bromyard denounced "the gay pawmentis for meanes feet and peyntid roofs above" in his *Speculum Laicorum* (G. R. Owst, *Literature and Pulpit in Medieval England,* 2d ed. [New York: Barnes and Noble, 1961], p. 49). A mid-fifteenth century Italian reference in Archbishop St. Antonio's *Summa Theologica,* III, tit. 8, sec. 4, ch. 11 is also of note in this connection: "It seems superfluous and vain in the stories of saints or in churches to paint oddities, which do not serve to excite devotion, but laughter and vanity, such as monkeys and dogs chasing hares, and the like, or vain adornments of clothing." Professor James Ackerman kindly called my attention to this excerpt, published by C. Gilbert, "The Archbishop on the Painters of Florence, 1450," *Art Bulletin,* XLI (1959), 76.

6. E. de Bruyne, *Études d'esthétique mediéval* (Bruges: "de Tempel," 1946), II, 136.

7. M. R. James, "Pictor in Carmine," *Archaeologia,* XCIV (1951), 141-166.

8. In view of the restraint traditionally associated with Cistercianism, the enrichment in the twelfth century of Cistercian sermons with Bestiary tales is noteworthy. See J. Morson, "The English Cistercians and the Bestiary," *Bulletin of the John Rylands Library,* XXXIX (1956-1957), 146-170.

money in favour of ignoble fancies? Nay, but it is the criminal presumption of painters that has gradually introduced these sports of fantasy, which the church ought not to have countenanced so long—for it has certainly seemed to countenance what it has not ceased to tolerate with such culpable longsuffering. Therefore it is that, to curb the license of painters, or rather to influence their work in churches where paintings are permitted, my pen has drawn up certain applications of events from the Old and New Testaments . . . For the rest, it was not my business to arrange for those who supervise such matters, all that should be painted; let them look to it themselves as the fancy takes each, or as he abounds in his own sense, provided only that they seek Christ's glory, not their own . . . It has been my purpose to supplement the materials for the comely decoration already begun in many churches and to curb the faults of excessive levity by providing a supply of more excellent quality.[9]

In the present context the "few points out of many" are particularly noteworthy. Once more the author describes in detail hybrid beasts and half-men, monsters and apes, before launching into the appeal for restraint. That the blame for these representations falls on "the criminal presumption of painters" gives insight into the role assigned to the artist and corroborates the predominant laissez-faire attitude of the Church.[10] This is not to say that official control was non-existent. There were indeed periodic inspections of churches and monasteries. Undertaken for such purposes as removing elements "not required for practical needs, but for the concupiscence of the eyes," they occasionally led to violent repercussions.[11]

Other attempts at the preservation of spiritual standards were made on an individual scale. In the hope of mitigating the demoralizing influence of licentious songs, fables, and romances, for example, Gautier de Coincy, abbot of Vie-sur-Sisne (1177-1236), composed *Les miracles de la sainte Vierge,* a vernacular collection of pious tales. An indignant reference in this work to the depiction of beast epics in the very cells of the monks recalls the contemporary protest by Adam of Dore against "the fabled intrigues of the fox and the cock":

> En leurs moustiers ne font pas faire
> Sitost l'image Nostre Dame
> Com font Isengrim et sa fame
> en leurs chambres ou ils reponnent.[12]

In the course of the thirteenth century the number of protests of this type diminished as a natural consequence of developments in ecclesiastic, social, economic, and intellectual spheres. An amusing example of official control toward the end of the century records the punishment of an Arras clerk for failing to obtain episcopal permission for the construction of gargoyles on the façade of his house: "L'officiel déclare que pardevant lui Rikier-Amion, clerc, a reconnu qu'il ne pouvait, sans congé de l'évêque, établir dans sa maison de la rue des Mans, ni gargouilles, ni autres constructions débordant sur rue et qu'il s'est soumis aux réparations exigées pour ce délit." [13] The main offense is transgressing the building code, not the nature of the architectural projection. An even clearer instance of the degree of tolerance achieved toward the turn of the century is a seal commissioned by the abbot Guy de Munois. It was to represent an ape attired as abbot encircled by the inscription: "abbé de singe air main d'os serre," an ingenious reference to the ecclesiastic's position as abbé de Saint-Germain d'Auxerre from 1285 to 1309.[14]

---

9. James, "Pictor," p. 141, reproduced in conjunction with the original Latin text.

10. On the artist's role in this regard, see Schapiro, "From Mozarabic to Romanesque," p. 348. Moreover, in citing the advantages of illustration over text, Richard de Fournival remarked: "Car il est de nature de bestes et d'oisaus ke miex sont connissables paintes ke dites" (C. Segre, *Li Bestiaire d'amours di maitre Richart de Fournival e li response du Bestiaire* [Milan: P. Ricciardi, 1957], p. 7). Compare a similar view in St. Augustine's *In Joannis Evangelium Tractatus,* XXIV, No. 2 (*MPL,* XXXV, col. 1593).

11. E. Martène and U. Durand, *Thesaurus Novum Anecdotorum* (Paris, 1717), V, col. 1584. A number of other references of interest appear in Schapiro, "On the Aesthetic Attitude," pp. 135 ff.

12. Poquet, ed. (Paris: Parmantier, 1857), vv. 168-170. More explicit in their didacticism were the fables accompanied by moralizations painted in the refectory of Saint-Bênoit-sur-Loire under Abbot Arnaud in the first half of the eleventh century. (J. Adhémar, *Influences antiques dans l'art du moyen âge français* [London: Warburg Institute, 1939], p. 228).

13. A. Guesnon, *Introduction au livre rouge de la Vintaine d'Arras* (Paris: Imprimerie Nationale, 1898), p. 25.

14. Champfleury, J., *Histoire de la caricature du moyen âge et sous la renaissance* (Paris: E. Dentin, 1875), p. 31; cf. my fig. 29.

II

The license of the Church in this and other spheres did not pass without comment. From the middle of the twelfth century on, vociferous criticism was issued, particularly in England, against the dissolution of standards not only among the clergy but among members of the aristocracy as well.[15] Once more, a concentration of such commentary can be observed in late twelfth- and early thirteenth-century sources. Outstanding protagonists include John of Salisbury, Walter Map, and Nigellus Wireker, whose *Speculum Stultorum* preserves a masterly satirical view on conditions within the Church, presented through the eyes of an ass.[16] A slightly earlier and more obscure composition, also of English origin, sets forth a utopian "Order of Fair-Ease" in which the principal breaches of clerical conduct are made to serve as guiding tenets.[17] These include unlimited indulgence in food and drink abetted by free association between members of both sexes. Similar suggestions in Goliardic verse include a proposed "Missa de potatoribus."[18] A full-fledged example of pseudo-authentic ridicule is a late thirteenth-century English sermon collection based on the use of the word *nemo* in the Scriptures. By grouping his selections in an ordered sequence in which *nemo* is used as a proper name, the homilist assembled a compilation of "Nemo sermons" of ostensible plausibility.[19] A fourteenth-century account accusing prelates in the ecclesiastic courts of accepting bribes denounces the new credo "Blessed is he that cometh in the name of money."[20]

On the Continent the spirit of fomenting criticism manifested itself somewhat later in the works, for instance, of Rutebeuf and Maerlant.[21] The altercations between Church and State formed the subject of the early fourteenth-century *Roman de Fauvel,* a satire in which the leading protagonist of royal power is a horse cast in a role comparable to Nigellus Wireker's ass.[22] French royal power is also ridiculed in a lampooned text of the treaty of Montreuil concluded between Philip the Fair and Edward I in 1299. To the anonymous author's evident delight the stilted phraseology of diplomatic exchange is parodied by means of jumbled phonetics, riddles, and extensive play on words.[23] This device for critical expression, akin to *monde renversé* scenes in contemporary visual representations, was particularly popular in French medieval literature. An early example appears in Chrétien de Troyes's *Cligès* of about 1170:

> A ce me sanble que je voie
> Les chiens foir devant le lièvre
> Et la tortue chacier le bièvre . . .
> Einsi fuit le faucon por l'ane
> Et li girfau por le heiron,
> Et li gros luz por le veiron,
> Et le lion chace li cers
> Si vont les choses a anvers.[24]

Exemplified further in works such as Richard de Fournival's *Bestiaire d'Amour,*[25] the substitution of

---

15. The significance of this strain in English medieval literature is emphasized by P. Lehmann, *Die Parodie im Mittelalter* (Munich: Drei-Masken Verlag, 1922), p. 121; see also H. Reinhold, *Humoristische Tendenzen in der englischen Dichtung des Mittelalters* (Tübingen: M. Niemeyer, 1953); J. Peter, *Complaint and Satire in Early English Literature* (Oxford: Clarendon Press, 1956). Original material of interest abounds in T. H. Wright, *The Political Songs of England from the Reign of John to That of Edward III* (London: Camden Society, 1839).

16. C. Schaarschmidt, *Johannis Saresberiensis nach Leben und Studien* (Leipzig: B. G. Teubner, 1862); Walter Map, *De Nugis Curialium,* Modern Language Association Publications, vol. 32 (Cambridge, Mass., 1917); Nigel de Longchamps, *Speculum Stultorum,* introd. and notes by J. H. Mozley and R. R. Raymo, Univ. of Calif. Pubs., Eng. Stud., No. 18 (Berkeley and Los Angeles, 1960). Also of interest is A. Friedman's "Medieval Popular Satire in Matthew Paris," *Modern Language Notes,* LXXIV, No. 8 (December, 1959), 673-678.

17. Wright, *Political Songs,* p. iii.

18. T. H. Wright and J. O. Halliwell, *Reliquiae Antiquae,* (London, 1845), II, 208-210 (from British Museum, Harley MS. 2851).

19. Owst, *Literature and Pulpit,* p. 63. (See n. 5 above.) A version of the text is preserved in Cambridge, Caius College, MS. 230, f. 34 et seq. under the title: "Pars Sermonis de Nemine."

20. *Ibid.,* p. 345.

21. See G. Feger, *Rutebeufs Kritik an den Zuständen zeiner Zeit,* (Freiburg i. B.: C. A. Wagner, 1920); J. Te Winkel, *Maerlant's Werken, Beschouwd als Spiegel van de dertiende Eeuw,* 2d ed. (Ghent: J. Vuylsteke, 1892); C. F. Lenient, *La satire en France au moyen âge* (Paris: L. Hachette, 1859); E. Lommatzsch, *Gautier de Coincy als Satiriker* (Halle: M. Niemeyer, 1913).

22. Gervais du Bus, *Le Roman de Fauvel* (Paris: F. Didot, 1914-1919).

23. G. Raynaud, "Nouvelle charte de la 'Pais aus Englois (1299),'" *Romania,* XIV (1885), 280. The text appears in MS. fr. 1933 in the Bibliothèque Nationale.

24. Ed. W. Foerster (Halle: M. Niemeyer, 1888), p. 156, vv. 3849-3859.

25. See above, n. 10.

standard references in another framework was carried far beyond the bounds of reason in the vernacular satirical verse and nonsense jingles composed in north France during the second half of the thirteenth century.[26] Remarkable specimens of this genre are preserved in the *Fatrasies d'Arras*.[27]

The application of the same principle of substitution is manifest also in certain fabliaux, a typical example being the adoption of terminology appropriate to a tournament in a seduction sequel.[28] As a popular narrative form evolved in the course of the thirteenth century, the fabliaux bear closer scrutiny because of the number of points of resemblance in both form and content to Gothic marginal illustrations. Recited by jongleurs for the amusement of a predominantly lay audience,[29] the tales consisted of burlesques as well as subjects drawn from epics, romances, and observations of contemporary life. About two-thirds included moralizations in which the vicissitudes of the various social classes were sketched with unequivocal though by no means unbiased clarity, particularly in the realm of erotic extravagances. As might be expected, the nobility was generally presented in a most favorable light. The bourgeois element, on the other hand, was depicted as vacillating between the virtues of the aristocracy and the vices of the peasantry, with aspiration toward higher social status emerging as the single most reprehensible trait of the latter. Most merciless by far was the barrage of criticism directed at the regular clergy. Their pride, avarice, and debauchery, exemplified in any number of situations, provided source material for most of the tales. The fabliaux were not only anticlerical but distinctly secular in tone. By virtue of their moralization even the most outrageous travesties gained an overtone of respectability, alleviating possible qualms of conscience on the part of those for whose ears the tales were intended.[30]

In the course of the thirteenth century moralized anecdotes were being popularized in yet another sphere, namely through the *exempla* widely adopted by Franciscans and Dominicans to enliven their sermons.[31] Derived from the Scriptures as well as from fables, beast epics, and daily events, the exempla were soon incorporated into alphabetized compendia. Mostly of English origin, these compilations served as convenient reference material for preachers seeking a tale whereby to illustrate in common terms the theological context of the sermon. There is considerable evidence of the avidity for stories by the congregation:

> Langues fables et sermons cours
> Demandent; mais aval ces cours
> Larges menconges, bordes amples,
> Aiment me miex que les essemples
> Et les bons mots de l'Escriture . . .[32]

The Dominicans were particularly noted for their ability to recapture the wandering attention of inattentive auditors engrossed in gossip, games, or dozing. That this feat required the agility, prowess, and ingenuity of a jongleur had been pointed out by

26. See A. Jubinal, *Nouveau receuil de contes, dits, fabliaux, et autres pièces inédites des XIIIe, XIVe et XVe siècles* (Paris: E. Pannier, 1842), II. For illustrations derived, often very obliquely, from place names and descriptive terms in a late thirteenth-century north French account book, see L. Verriest, *Le Vieil Rentier d'Audenarde* (Brussels: Duculot, 1950). In the marginal decoration of the Ormesby Psalter (Bodleian Library, Douce MS. 366) is depicted the riddle of the farmer seeking to transport a wolf, a lamb, and some greens safely across a river (see S. C. Cockerell and M. R. James, *Two East Anglian Psalters at the Bodleian Library* [Oxford: University Press, 1926]).

27. Jubinal, *Nouveau receuil*, pp. 208 ff.

28. P. Nykrog, *Les fabliaux: Étude d'histoire littéraire et de stylistique médiévale* (Copenhagen: Munksgaard, 1957), pp. 89-90.

29. On the circulation of fabliaux in England and their censure by Oxford University officials, see G. McKnight, *Middle English Humorous Tale in Verse* (Boston: D. C. Heath, 1913), pp. x, xiv ff. An interesting account of the functions and motivations of jongleurs is preserved in *Les grandes chroniques de Hainaut:* "Sy avint aulcunes fois que jongleurs ou gouliars ou autres manières de ménestriers s'assemblent aux cours des bourgois, des princes, et des riches hommes; et sert chacun de son mestier au mieulx et au plus apertement qu'il peult pour avoir deniers, robes ou aultres joyaulx en chantant et comptant nouveaulx motz, nouveaulx ditz et nouvelles risées de diverses guises; et faignent, à la loenge des riches hommes, tout ce qu'ilz pevent faindre, affin qu'ilz leur plaisent de mielx" (J. Lefèvre, from No. XIII in the Bibliothèque du Roi, f. 441). The versatile imitativeness of jongleurs was compared with that of apes by Alexander Neckam in his *Historia Naturalis*, liber II.

30. On the rigid differenentiation of social levels in the realm of romantic lore, see Nykrog, *Les fabliaux*, p. 192.

31. Full references appear in L. Randall, "Exempla and Their Influence on Gothic Marginal Art," *Art Bulletin*, XXXIX (1957), 97-107.

32. Poquet, 378, vv. 149-153. (See n. 12 above.)

Bernard of Clairvaux long before the founding of the mendicant orders: "In the eyes of the worldly people we have the air of performing *tours de forces*. All that they desire we flee, and what they flee we desire, like those jongleurs who, head down and feet up in an inhuman fashion, stand or walk on their hands and attract the eyes of everyone." [33] An analogous simile is contained in St. Francis's definition of friars as *joculatores Dei,* a concept graphically demonstrated by him, according to an account by a contemporary, Thomas of Celano: "At times I have seen him, with my own eyes, draw a stick across his arm, in the guise of one playing a viol, and sing in French praises of the Lord." [34] The necessity for resorting to ingenious means of dispelling the lethargy of the congregation is borne out time and again in extant sermons of the thirteenth and fourteenth centuries. Among the many textual references exemplifying exasperation on this score is Caesarius of Heisterbach's account of abbot Gérard's complaint that his listeners wake only to hear "fables." To attract their full attention he must resort to a phrase such as "There was once upon a time a king called Arthur." [35] Even an outstanding preacher, the Franciscan Jacques de Vitry (d. 1240), suffered the slight of inattentiveness. A nodding female parishioner allegedly provoked the outburst: "For God's sake, if anyone has a pin, let him wake her up! Those who sleep at sermontime take good care not to sleep at table." In fact, the anticipation of feasting and gaming at the tavern after the service was one of the most common complaints in the sermons. Judging from their frequency in the exempla, lurid descriptions of Hell, demonstrating the fate of those who succumbed to these and other temptations, proved an effective stimulant (cf. figs. 270, 271, and 274).

There is ample evidence, then, of the widespread use of anecdotes to rekindle the flagging interest of the congregations in theological dogma. The effectiveness of this method in the hands of the mendicant orders is further evidenced by expressions of protest against the diminishing attendance at the services of the regular clergy as people flocked to hear the more animated sermons preached in the vernacular by Franciscans and Dominicans. The thirteenth century thus saw the diffusion on an international scale of a wide variety of anecdotic material, both in the Church and without, through exempla and fabliaux. The ground was thoroughly prepared for the artistic developments of the latter part of the century.

III

The early visual manifestations of themes popularized through fabliaux and exempla can most clearly be observed in illuminated manuscripts. Shortly after the middle of the thirteenth century extensive ornamentation begins to fill the margins in both religious and secular texts.

The emergence of this mode of decoration as a *fait accompli* has proved somewhat disconcerting. A partial explanation generally cited in this connection is the increased feeling for realism and appreciation of nature characteristic of the Gothic period. Another relevant consideration is that the profuse ornamentation which filled the initials of Romanesque and early Gothic manuscripts to the

33. Schapiro, "From Mozarabic to Romanesque," p. 344, n. 113. (See n. 3 above.) This is an excerpt from the following passage: "Nam revera quid aliud saecularibus quam ludere videmur, cum, quod ipsi appetunt in hoc saeculo, nos per contrarium fugimus: et quod ipsi fugiunt, nos appetimus? More scilicet joculatorum et saltatorum, qui capite misso deorsum, pedibusque sursum erectus, praeter humanum usum stant manibus vel incedunt, et sic in se omnium oculos defigunt. Non est hic ludus puerilis, non est de theatro, qui femineis foedisque infractibus provocet libidinem, actus sordidos repraesentat: sed est ludus jucundus, honestus, gravis, spectabilis, qui coelestium spectatorum delectare possit aspectus." (St. Bernard, *Epistolae,* LXXXVII, No. 12; *MPL,* CLXXXII, col. 217).

34. St. Francis, *Mirror of Perfection,* introd. T. Okey (London: J. M. Dent, 1934), p. XVIII (cf. my figs. 508-518). The acquisition of books is discouraged in chap. IV, "On the Novice who would fain have a Psalter . . ." (pp. 187-188), while chap. V contains the admonition: "look for proof and not price in books, edification not ornament" (p. 189).

35. This and the following example appear undocumented in Owst, *Literature and Pulpit,* p. 176, n. 4, and p. 186. (See n. 5 above.) A thirteenth-century sermon collection distinguished by the exclusion of exempla is Nicholas de Aquavilla's *Sermones Dominicales in Evangelia,* which reflects the Franciscan author's opposition to "trufas et fabulas" on the premise that preachers should instruct rather than terrify or entertain their audience (Owst, p. 236). Worth mentioning in this connection is Luther's comment: "When I was young . . . I dealt largely in allegories, and tropes, and a quantity of idle craft; but now I have let all that slip, and my best craft is to give the Scripture with its plain meaning, for the plain meaning is learning and life" (Owst, p. 313, n. 2; see M. Luther, *Works* [Philadelphia: A. J. Holman, 1932], VI, 60).

bursting point would of necessity eventually spill over into the margins.[36] One stimulus for this transferral was the enrichment of illustrative subject matter. Another was the increased demand for books from the middle of the thirteenth century on by a growing lay audience. The expansion of flourishing commercial centers effected the rise of a prosperous upper middle class to whom ownership of a profusely illustrated manuscript meant prestige as well as aesthetic pleasure. It is noteworthy that the region where marginal illumination was most fully developed in the decades preceding and following the turn of the fourteenth century coincides with one of the most active trading areas in northern Europe at this time. There was constant interchange, both commercial and cultural, between England and the provinces of particular interest in the present context, Artois, Hainaut, Picardy, Flanders, Brabant, and Liège.

The demand for books necessitated a proportionate increase in the number of professional illuminators, whose background and training inevitably wrought changes in the traditional workshop milieu.[37] Traveling about with greater mobility in response to opportunities for work, the illuminators were able to effect the rapid trans-migration of styles and ideas to the principal centers of production. The resulting homogeneity, clearly evident in miniature painting, has proved a serious impediment to the localization of manuscripts, particularly those originating on the Continent in the bordering provinces cited above. In England the problem is somewhat less acute, especially for the first part of the fourteenth century, since many of the outstanding manuscripts contain more substantial textual or stylistic evidence of origin. Yet the uniformity of manuscript production around 1300 in the regions bordering the English Channel is reflected in the still current use of the term "Channel School" to

36. A point commented on in E. M. Thompson, "The Grotesque and the Humorous in Illumination of the Middle Ages," *Bibliographica,* II, pt. VII (1896), 309 ff., and G. Haseloff, *Die Psalterillustration im dreizehnten Jahrhundert* (Kiel, 1938), p. 5.

37. The rise of lay illuminators in thirteenth-century England is cited by D. D. Egbert, *The Tickhill Psalter and Related Manuscripts* (New York: New York Public Library, and Princeton: Princeton University, Department of Art and Archaeology, 1940), pp. 3, 7-8, 80. On this subject, see also G. G. Coulton, "Medieval Faith and Symbolism," pt. I of *Art and the Reformation* (New York: Harper, 1958), pp. 73 ff.

designate the provenance of this virtually indistinguishable group.

In seeking to localize a manuscript, evidence of usage and heraldry is, of course, most useful in determining its destination. This does not coincide necessarily with its place of origin, however. Unless one of the manuscripts in question can be assigned to a specific locale, stylistic comparisons are also relatively unproductive for this period of rapid interchange, particularly in the north French and Flemish provinces. Any further device for association is therefore useful, and it is in this capacity that marginal illustrations can be made to serve. The process of iconographic classification undertaken in the present compilation discloses relationships less readily discernible in other illustrative features. While many of the cross-references in the subject index point out ideologic analogies, further specialized study, both of motifs and principles of design, will eventually reveal links facilitating the assigning of manuscripts to more circumscribed centers of illumination.

The development of marginal illumination falls into three principal phases during the hundred years spanning its full cycle. The first, from about 1250 to 1300, was characterized by inventive experimentation of a highly varied nature. Into this period fall a number of outstanding English productions,[38] among them the earliest notable exam-

38. For a consensus of scholarly views on the English origin of marginal illumination, see A. Haseloff, *Les miniatures—les vitraux—la peinture murale* in A. Michel's *Histoire de l'art,* (Paris: A. Colin, 1906), II, 349; G. Vitzthum von Eckstädt, "Eine Miniaturhandschrift aus Weigelschem Besitz," *Kunstwissenschaftliche Beiträge Gewidmet August Schmarsov* (Leipzig: Quelle und Meyer, 1907), p. 70; A. Boeckler, *Die Buchmalerei* in *Handbuch der Bibliothekswissenschaft,* ed. F. Milkau (Leipzig: O. Harrassowitz, 1931), I, 227-228; A. Byvanck, *Les principaux manuscrits à peintures de la bibliothèque royale des Pays-Bas et du musée Meermanno-Westreenianum à la Haye* (Paris: Société française de reproductions de manuscrits à peintures, 1935), V, 170; C. Gaspar and F. Lyna, *Les principaux manuscrits à peintures de la bibliothèque royale de Belgique* (Paris: Société française de reproductions de manuscrits à peintures, 1937), I, 20. This work cites the artistic homogeneity prevailing in Belgian and north French provinces (p. 22); the Netherlandish origin of marginal illumination is propounded on p. 94.

ple of full-fledged marginal illumination, a Psalter completed soon after the middle of the century in the collection of the Duke of Rutland.[39] Contemporary illumination on the other side of the Channel was characterized by relatively modest incorporation of marginal motifs. The succeeding quarter-century saw the consolidation and further expansion of earlier methods and ideas, culminating in amplified iconographic programs incorporated in the most luxurious productions of the age. Outstanding examples from this second phase include works of the East Anglian school of illumination[40] and the emergence of the *œuvre* of the renowned illuminator, Jean Pucelle.[41] The manuscripts produced by him or under his immediate supervision are characterized by their superb quality in all spheres, including a quantity of exceptionally animated *drôleries*. The latter feature was highly unusual in Parisian illumination. It reflects a northern influence on Pucelle, ultimately derived from England via Netherlandish intermediaries.[42] A clarification of this heritage must await detailed comparison of pertinent details in the manuscripts ascribed to his hand.

Pucelle's work marks one of the last creative high points of marginal illumination during the gradual *détente* in the second quarter of the fourteenth century on both sides of the Channel. Fresh ideas and methods of representations became the exception rather than the rule. After 1350 the original forms of expression characteristic of this mode of manuscript decoration persisted largely in conventionalized readaptations of earlier concepts.

In view of the abundance of extant material, it is somewhat surprising that it has escaped comprehensive study until now. Analogous artistic manifestations in choirstalls, architectural elements, textiles, and *objets d'art* such as Minnekaestchen have long since been the subject of intensive scholarly investigation.[43] One deterrent may have been the sheer volume of material involved. Although its wide dispersion is indeed a sobering thought for any potential enthusiast, access to the sources has fortunately been facilitated by the advances of technology.

The nature of published references may also account for the relative neglect of the subject. Save for the splendid facsimiles of outstanding English material, the bulk of pertinent data must be culled from catalogues of collections, exhibitions, and sales as well as from intermittent references in scholarly publications since the end of the nineteenth century. Varying considerably in length and detail, the circumstantial evidence ranges from brief allusions to "burlesque drawings" and "grotesque fancies" or phrases such as "There are also a number of interesting grotesques" to fuller accounts of themes deemed particularly noteworthy by the writer. Allowance must be made for the possibility of his disparagement of the entire subject, for differences in taste, as well as for the likelihood of inferior quality in the marginal décor. Quite naturally one finds a variety of reactions. Thus, the embellishments may strike one viewer as ludicrous, another as amusing nonsense, and yet a third (not unjustifiably in the particular instance) as "hideous and vulgar . . . too often even a reasonably good initial and border . . . is spoiled by a repulsive grotesque."[44]

Of the numerous fleeting references to grotesques or *drôleries*, many proved well worth investigating. Others led to concurrence with the statement made by Montague Rhodes James in connection with an early fourteenth-century north French Psalter: "There are also a large number of grotesques

39. E. Millar, *The Rutland Psalter* (The Roxburghe Club; Oxford: University Press, 1937).

40. M. Rickert, *Painting in Britain: The Middle Ages* (Baltimore: Pelican History of Art, 1954), pp. 137-164. See also S. C. Cockerell, *The Gorleston Psalter* (London: Chiswick Press, 1907), British Museum Add. MS. 49622.

41. Recent studies of his *oeuvre* include K. Morand, *Jean Pucelle* (Oxford: Clarendon Press, 1962), and C. Nordenfalk, "Maître Honoré and Maître Pucelle," *Apollo*, LXXIX, no. 27 (n.s.) (May, 1964), 356-364.

42. This point is discussed by E. Panofsky, *Early Netherlandish Painting* (Cambridge, Mass.: Harvard University Press, 1953), I, 31.

43. See, for example, L. Maeterlinck, *Le genre satirique dans la sculpture flamande et wallonne, Les miséricordes de stalles* (Paris: J. Schémit, 1910); F. Bond, *Wood Carvings in English Churches*, 2 vols. (London: H. Frowde, 1910); R. Koechlin, *Les ivoires gothiques français*, 2 vols. (Paris: A. Picard, 1924); B. Kurth, *Gotische Bildteppiche aus Frankreich und Flandern* (Munich: Riehn and Reusch, 1923); H. Kohlhaussen, *Minnekästchen im Mittelalter* (Berlin: Verlag für Kunstwissenschaft, 1928).

44. Rickert, *Painting in Britain*, pp. 148-149, in reference to the Luttrell Psalter, British museum Add. MS. 42130. Alluding to similar conglomerate creatures in the margins of a slightly earlier English manuscript, M. R. James states:" . . . p. 2 has knights and shields. These, and the fancy grotesques, it is no part of my plan to notice" (*The Treatise of Walter de Milemete* [Oxford: University Press (Roxburghe Club), 1913], p. xxiv).

perched on the borders. These are a very amusing and clever series but do not admit (grotesques seldom do) of detailed description." [45] Given the scope of marginal subject matter, encompassing the full range from Scriptural themes to renderings of questionable propriety, the difficulty of establishing a single all-inclusive nomenclature is readily apparent. The generic appellations most frequently used (all postmedieval) are *bas-de-page* for more elaborate compositions, *vignettes, drôleries* or their English near equivalent, drolleries, for all types of animated marginal configurations, and "grotesques" for the more beastly and monstrous apparitions in the latter category. Among the allusions in medieval texts one finds *curiositates* [46] and babewynes.[47]

The heterogeneity of the material, which is one of its chief characteristics, has also proved a deterrent to its classification. Certain aspects have been freely utilized by social and cultural historians as well as by specialists in medieval caricature and grotesquerie for over half a century.[48] To doctoral candidates the potential wealth of the subject has also been an inspiring challenge in the past few decades. The recurrence of select literary themes in the marginal representations of various media from the early Middle Ages on formed the subject, for instance, of Maria Bergenthal's *Elemente der Drolerie und ihre Beziehungen zur Literatur*.[49] Of particular interest is the discussion of the recurrence of animal motifs in late medieval proverbial lore.

A significant contribution in recent years appears in H. W. Janson's *Apes and Ape Lore in the Middle Ages and the Renaissance*.[50] The chapter entitled "The Ape in Gothic Marginal Art" is especially pertinent in the present context. After his opening statement, "The iconographer venturing into the field of Gothic *drôlerie* faces a far from enviable task," Professor Janson sets forth the problems involved in such an enterprise before proceding to define more closely the role of the ape in this sphere.[51] His approach exemplifies a method whose application to other marginal themes would prove extremely useful.

As suggested, it is indeed the iconographer whose curiosity is most likely to be aroused by the representations in the margins. Herein lies yet another reason for their relative neglect. As a genre subsidiary to the mainstream of development in major areas of Gothic painting, marginal illustrations have not without justification been relegated to a low position on the scale of artistic achievement.

---

45. *Catalogue of Manuscripts and Early Printed Books . . . of the Library of J. Pierpont Morgan* (London: Chiswick Press, 1906), I, 51.

46. See Schapiro, "On the Aesthetic Attitude," p. 134 (see n. 2 above); also H. W. Janson, *Apes and Ape Lore*, pp. 112 ff. (see n. 4 above).

47. See J. Evans, *English Art, 1307-1461*, Oxford History of English Art Series (Oxford: Clarendon Press, 1949), pp. 38 ff., and J. Baltrusaitis, *Reveils et prodiges*, p. 197 (see n. 3 above).

48. Such works include: T. H. Wright, *A History of Domestic Manners and Sentiments in England* (London: Chapman and Hall, 1862) and *A History of English Culture* (London: Truebner, 1874); J. Strutt, *Sports and Pastimes of the People of England* (London: Chatto and Windus, 1876); H. D. Traill and J. S. Mann, *Social England* (London: Cassell, 1901); J. Jusserand, *Sports et jeux dans l'ancienne France* (Paris: Plon-Nourrit, 1901) and *English Wayfaring Life*, trans. L. T. Smith, 2d ed. (London: T. F. Unwin, 1889); M. and C. H. B. Quennell, *A History of Everyday Things in England*, 3d ed. (London: B. T. Batsford, 1938), vol. I (1066-1499); Champfleury, *Histoire de la caricature* (see n. 14 above); L. Maeterlinck, *Le genre satirique dans la peinture flamande* (see n. 3 above); L. Bridaham, *Gargoyles, Chimères, and the Grotesque in French Gothic Sculpture* (New York: Architectural Book Publishing Co., 1930); J. Baltrusaitis, *op. cit.*, and *Le moyen âge fantastique*, Collection Henri Focillon, III (Paris: A. Colin, 1955).

49. See above, n. 3. Of the other dissertations known to me, I have been able to read (on microfilm) only Nora Wissgott's very generalized work, "Die Drolerie in europäischen Handschriften vom Ende des XIII. bis zu Beginn des XVI. Jahrhunderts" (Typescript, Vienna, 1933). Also of interest is a more recent Master's thesis by L. Freeman, "Formal Principles of Marginal Illustrations in Late Thirteenth- and Early Fourteenth-Century English Psalters" (typescript, Columbia, 1957). Despite repeated attempts, I have not been able to track down D. Landau, "Die Haupttypen des ornamentalen Randschmuckes in abendländischen Handschriften des 14 and 15. Jahrhunderts und deren Quellen" (Vienna, 1927), or C. Alften, "Die Entstehung der selbständigen Drolerie in England" (Berlin, 1933).

50. See above, n. 4.

51. Janson, *op. cit.*, p. 163. The difficulties inherent in the dispersion of sources had already been stated by Champfleury, (*Histoire de la caricature* [1875], p. 200). Mindful of the dangers of overinterpretation, he warned scholars delving into this "mine de détails précieux . . . de n'y pas attacher plus d'importance que les miniaturistes qui égayaient leur besogne par un trait plaisant" (p. 204).

Their interest has been primarily folkloristic.[52] To art historians their significance has been further diminished by the apparent absence of a relationship to their immediate context. Thus, marginalia fall between several fields, a position not conducive to redemption by specialists favoring what M.D. Anderson has termed the "method of strip-cultivation." [53]

Actually, the impression of haphazard spontaneity in marginal illustrations is exaggerated by their juxtaposition with representational elements of long-standing formalistic tradition. As will be seen subsequently, the distribution was not always as unsystematic as it appears. It would indeed have been atypical of the medieval mind to have discarded wholly all structure of programmatic design. Schemes governing the layout of certain pages or sections of a manuscript did exist, although their application was flexible and subject to change. This will emerge more clearly in the subsequent discussion of major underlying principles.

IV

The two hundred and twenty-six manuscripts (and portions of manuscripts) which form the basis of this compilation include both ordinary, sparsely illustrated workshop productions and luxury manuscripts of exceptional quality. About one-quarter may be assigned to the latter category. Although supplementary material can always be added to a collection such as this, the group selected here is fully representative of the types of imagery depicted in the margins of manuscripts of the period and geographic sphere defined above as critical for the full development of this form of decoration in northern Europe. Occasionally the boundaries have been extended to include works of particular note. Among them are an early thirteenth century medical treatise,[54] a mid-fourteenth century Cologne Missal,[55] and a group of manuscripts executed for members of the Bohun family after the middle of the fourteenth century.[56]

With one or two exceptions all the manuscripts have been studied in the original or, when the difficulties were insurmountable, from complete microfilms. A short-title list of the texts is useful despite the drawbacks of statistical enumeration in confirming the pronounced predilection for marginal ornament in Psalters, Hours, and Breviaries, all designed for private devotion. Another feature to emerge is the divergence of national taste, reflecting English restraint in the illustration of secular texts. The original titles may be grouped under five major headings:

Theological and Canonical Texts	*Continental*	*English*
Antiphonaries	2	
Apocalypse		1
Bibles	15	4
Breviaries	21	1
Calendrier-Obituaire	1	
Canticles of the Virgin	1	
Ceremoniale Blandiniense	1	
Decretals	1	1
Hours	31	12
Legends of Saints' Lives	1	

52. Of interest in this connection is A. Coomaraswamy's definition of folk art: "Hieratic and folk art are both alike traditional . . . Folk art preserves not merely childish or entertaining fables or crude decorative art, but a series of anything but popular invention. One may say that it is in this way, when an intellectual decadence has taken place in higher circles, that this doctrinal material is preserved from one epoch to another . . . ; the folk memory serving the purpose of a sort of ark, in which the wisdom of a former age is carried over the period of the dissolution of cultures that takes place at the close of a cycle." In "The Nature of 'Folklore' and 'Popular' Art," *Indian Art and Letters,* XI, no. 2 (1937), 81. See also on this subject S. Thompson, *Motif-Index of Folk-Literature,* 2d ed. (Bloomington, Ind. University Press, 1955-1957), 5 vols.

53. *Drama and Imagery in English Medieval Churches* (Cambridge, Eng.: University Press, 1963), p. 1.

54. M. R. James, *The Western Manuscripts in the Library of Trinity College, Cambridge* (Cambridge, Eng.: University Press, 1903), vol. III, MS. 0.1.20, p. 23, no. 1044.

55. Gaspar and Lyna, *Les principaux manuscrits,* MS. 209, p. 316, no. 128.

56. The five manuscripts from this group are listed in the appended Key under Auct. D. 4.4, Exeter 47, Riches Ps., Thott 547, and Vienna 1826.* All are fully described in M. R. James and E. Millar, *The Bohun Manuscripts* (Oxford: University Press, 1936).

Theological and Canonical Texts	*Continental*	*English*
Missals	5	1
Pontificals	2	
Psalters	44	32
Ritual	1	
Speculum Beatae Virginis	1	
Summa de Iure Canonico	1	
	128	52
Historical Works		
Compilation d'Anciennes Histoires	1	
Conquête de la Terre Sainte (Guillaume de Tyre)	1	
Historia Scholastica (Petrus Comestor)	1	
Histories of England		3
Spiegel Historial (Jacob Maerlant)	1	
Tite-Live	1	
Trésor of Baudouin d'Avesnes	1	
Trésor of Brunetto Latini	2	
Vieil Rentier d'Audenarde (account book)	1	
	9	3
Didactic, Legal, and Scientific Tracts		
Bonus Socius	1	
Corpus Iuris Civilis	1	
De Historiis Animalium (Aristotle)	1	
De Secretis Secretorum (Aristotle)		1
Du Bon Gouvernement des Rois	1	
Liber de Officiis Regum (Walter de Milemete)		1
Medical compilations	2	1
Metaphysics (Aristotle)	1	
Priscian Grammar	1	
Registrum Brevium		1
Somme le Roi (Frère Laurens)	1	
Traité de Fauconnerie of Frederick II	1	
	10	4
Romances		
Arthurian compilations	2	
La Lumière as Lais		1
Lancelot du Lac	3	
Roman de la Rose (Guillaume de Lorris and Jean de Meung)	3	
Roman de la Table Ronde	1	
Romance of Alexander	2	
Saint Graal (Robert de Borron, Gautier Map)	3	
Seven Sages of Rome	1	
Tristram	1	
Voeux du Paon (Jacques de Longuyon)	1	
	17	1
Songs and Poems		
Chansonniers	2	
Recueil de Poésies Morales	1	
	3	

These figures are misleading in one respect, namely in their implications of national productivity. On the basis of volume, the English seem to lag far behind. In terms of quantity and quality of workmanship, however, the balance is far more even than the numerical disparity indicates. Thus, a single one of the outstanding English luxury productions may contain as many marginal illustrations as appear in a score or more of less profusely ornamented manuscripts of Continental origin.

Also noteworthy in the above accounting is the relative dearth of secular texts. The sparsity of practical guides and factual treatises containing marginal illustrations is less surprising than the modest representation of Romances, which were being produced in quantity in lavish editions during the period here under consideration.[57] The pictorial enrichment apparent in the miniatures was not extended into the margins. The high proportion of private devotional books containing imaginative marginal embellishments, on the other hand, leaves no doubt as to the receptivity of the users toward diversion during the lengthy services "alorsque l'attention est fatiguée et que les paupières s'alourdissent." [58] Thus the *bêtes noires* which had so incensed St. Bernard in their elevated sculptured position had literally descended en masse into the hands of the worshipers.

From a broader aesthetic point of view, this development may be seen as a reflection of the medieval propensity for juxtaposition of contrasting elements.[59] In this conceptual approach, the incorporation of quantities of profane marginal themes into a framework diametrically opposed in spirit and content could find justification. In a surprising number of instances a *raison d'être,* even for totally inappropriate motifs, does exist.[60] The problem for the iconographer is dual, namely recognition and interpretation. It is most easily solved when the subjects in the margins are directly related to their adjoining text or miniature. Allusions to a more remote frame of reference such as local usages, prejudices, or current events are obviously far more difficult to fathom, particularly since they are often cloaked in absurd or amusing guise.[61] The search for an elucidatory denominator is thus a many-sided proposition. The fact of its existence in a few instances provides a strong incentive for further pursuit of more elusive themes. Without doubt a basis in fact, popular tradition, or the Scriptures originally linked many of the more ambiguous motifs with the text.

If we suppose that provocation by contrast underlies the exuberance of marginal illustrations in liturgical books, the absence of this motivation may explain their relative sparseness in secular texts. Whereas one might perhaps anticipate a reversal of the situation, that is, an abundance of sacred themes in a secular text, this is by no means the case. Incorporated primarily as illustrative or decorative elements, the marginal subjects generally lack in form and content the verve of their counterparts in religious texts. There are, of course, notable exceptions, such as a *Voeux du Paon* from the collection of the late William S. Glazier,[62] a *Lancelot del Lac* in the Yale University Library,[63] and an edition of the *Romance of Alexander* completed in Bruges in 1344.[64] The margins of the latter present

57. For pertinent references, see R. S. and L. H. Loomis, *Arthurian Romances in Medieval Art* (London: Oxford University Press, 1938); also H. L. D. Ward and J. Herbert, *Catalogue of Romances in the Department of Manuscripts in the British Museum* (London, 1883-1910), 3 vols.

58. A. Lecoy de la Marche, *La chaire française au moyen âge* (Paris: Didier, 1868), p. 275.

59. Allusions to this trait appear in A. Katzenellenbogen, *Allegories of the Virtues and Vices in Medieval Art* (London: Warburg Institute, 1939), pp. 75 ff. Actually, contrast was by no means synonymous with conflict, since the profane images "invite no systematic intellectual apprehension, but are grasped as individual, often irrational fantasies, as single thoughts and sensations" (Schapiro, "On the Aesthetic Attitude," p. 137). This thought also underlies a passage from Roger Bacon's *Opus Maius:* ". . . omnis creatura in se vel in suo simili, vel in universali vel in particulari, a summis coelorum usque ad terminos eorum ponitur in scriptura, ut sicut Deus fecit creaturas et scripturam, sic voluit ipsas res factas ponere in scriptura ad intellectum ipsius tam sensus literalis quam spiritualis" (ed. S. Jebb [London: W. Bowyer, 1733], II, chap. viii, p. 29).

60. For a succinct résumé on the controversies of interpretation, see Janson, *Apes and Ape Lore,* p. 42. See also M. Schapiro, "The Bowman and the Bird on the Ruthwell Cross and Other Works: The Interpretation of Secular Themes in Early Medieval Religious Art," *Art Bulletin,* XLV (1963), 351-354.

61. See, for example, L. Randall, "The Snail in Gothic Marginal Warfare," *Speculum,* XXXVII (1962), pp. 358-367.

62. J. Plummer, *Manuscripts from the William S. Glazier Collection,* Exhibition at the Pierpont Morgan Library (New York, 1959), p. 21, no. 28.

63. Formerly Phillipps MS. 130. See "Eight Mediaeval Manuscripts," *Yale University Gazette,* XXIX, No. 3 (January, 1955), 103-104; also Loomis, *Arthurian Romances,* p. 95.

64. M. R. James, *The Romance of Alexander* (Oxford: Clarendon Press, 1933).

a veritable Summa of the iconographic repertory evolved during the preceding half-century.

V

After the manuscripts had been selected for inclusion in the Index, there arose the question of sorting the iconographic content of their margins. Which themes warranted inclusion and which should be regarded as purely ornamental detail? In steering a middle course, the guiding principles here adopted were akin to those outlined by James Boswell in his biography of Samuel Johnson:

> I am justified in preserving rather too many . . . sayings, than too few; especially as from the diversity of dispositions it cannot be known with certainty beforehand, whether what may seem trifling to some, and perhaps to the collector himself, may not be most agreeable to many; and the greater the number that an author can please in any degree, the more pleasure does there arise to a benevolent mind.[65]

With these considerations in mind, the present iconographic selection consists of scenes depicting humans, animals, or hybrids in some sort of activity. These constitute the essence of marginal subject matter and provide the most valuable insight into contemporary mores and ideas. Sheer mass precluded complete listing of details such as costume, armor, household appurtenances, plant forms, and the like. Many appear in the entries under the various activities. Others are illustrated in the accompanying plates and can also be studied in the facsimile editions cited in the bibliography. For the sake of clarity as well as sanity, isolated renderings of inactive creatures have been omitted. These include a host of lions, dogs, squirrels, birds, monsters, and hybrids which constitute stereotype elements of marginal decoration.

The principal subjects are derived from four major iconographic categories: religious sources, secular literature, daily life, and parody. Viewed in a sequence of progressively disintegrating formalism, the first group comprises Scriptural incidents, the lives and passions of the saints, and apocryphal lore. While sacred themes do not rank first numerically, they represent a significant ingredient of English illumination characterized by the inclusion of extensive cycles in Psalters throughout the first quarter of the fourteenth century. Certain ones depict concentrated areas of hagiography; others contain sequences derived from a number of sources. The most notable series of Old Testament scenes appear, for instance, in the Tickhill Psalter[66] and the Psalter of Queen Isabella.[67] The Luttrell Psalter has an important group of New Testament representations.[68] A wider range, comprising in addition a long sequence of the martyrdom of saints, is found in the margins of Queen Mary's Psalter[69] and the Taymouth Hours.[70] Both these manuscripts are further distinguished by extensive series of the miracles of the Virgin, whose widespread popularity in the margins of English manuscripts is also exemplified in the Smithfield Decretals[71] and in several of a group of manuscripts produced for members of the Bohun family, referred to above.[72]

In contrast to the comprehensiveness of English cycles, sacred themes in Continental marginal illumination characteristically appear as isolated renderings of more restricted and fairly standard iconographic scope. A notable exception is the

65. *The Life of Samuel Johnson* (London: MacMillan, 1900), I, 8.

66. New York Public Library, Spencer Collection, MS. 26; see above, n. 37.

67. Munich, Bayerische Staatsbibliothek, MS. Cod. gall. 16; see D. D. Egbert, "A Sister to the Tickhill Psalter—the Psalter of Queen Isabella of England," *Bulletin of the New York Public Library*, XXXIX (1935), 762-764.

68. London, British Museum, Add. MS. 42130; see E. Millar, *The Luttrell Psalter* (London: Printed for the Trustees [of the British Museum], 1932).

69. London, British Museum, Royal MS. 2 B.VII. See G. Warner, *Queen Mary's Psalter* (London: H. Hart, 1912); see also O. Koseleff, "Representations of the Months and Zodiacal Signs in Queen Mary's Psalter," *Gazette des Beaux-Arts*, ser. 6, XXII (November, 1942), 77-88. The relation to contemporary wall paintings at Chalgrove is discussed by Rickert, *Painting in Britain*, p. 156.

70. London, British Museum, MS. Y. T. 13. W. H. J. Weale *et al.*, *A Descriptive Catalogue of Fifty Manuscripts from the Collection of Henry Yates Thompson*, 2d Ser. (Cambridge: University Press, 1902), No. 57, pp. 50-74; also *Illustrations from One Hundred Manuscripts in the Library of Henry Yates Thompson* (London: Chiswick Press, 1914), IV, pl. LI.

71. London, British Museum, Royal MS. 10 E.IV. See Sir G. Warner, *British Museum, Catalogue of Western Manuscripts in the Old Royal and King's Collections* (Oxford: University Press, 1921), I, 334. I should like to thank Mrs. Rosy Schilling for checking some of the descriptive details in this manuscript.

72. See above, n. 56.

Belleville Breviary.[73] Produced by Jean Pucelle in collaboration with several assistants soon after 1320, this manuscript inaugurated a new concept in marginal subject matter. Scenes showing the concordance of the Old and New Testament throughout the Calendar pages were followed at the major Psalm divisions by elaborate *bas-de-page* showing the Seven Sacraments flanked by personifications of the Virtues and Vices. The repetition of this scheme in a number of manuscripts produced for members of the French royal family in the course of the fourteenth century attests to its immediate success and persistent renown.

While the conception of a continuous interrelated inconographic program resembles English methods of marginal illumination, the actual placement of the Seven Sacraments is a common feature in north French and Belgian illumination as well. It is by no means unusual to find sacred themes, often related to their context, on pages marking the liturgical divisions of the manuscript or containing significant parts of the service. Thus, skulls and bones surround a text of the offices of the Dead, and the instruments of the Passion accompany the opening of the Hours of the Passion.[74] Often, too, a connection exists with the historiated initial or miniature. Thus, a marginal motif may serve to complete the narrative or furnish additional descriptive detail (fig. 619). In other instances, the choice of a marginal subject is appropriate to the use of the manuscript[75] (fig. 608). Generally, however, the fragmentary nature of representation leveled the powerful effect of hagiographic themes in sharp contrast to the profound impression achieved by the more programmatic English cycles.

The same is true of the illustrations derived from the Bestiary, the first of a series of literary sources outside the realm of the Scriptures which form the second major group of marginal subjects.[76] Once more copious sequences appear in English manuscripts, among them the afore-mentioned Psalter of Queen Isabella and Queen Mary's Psalter. It is noteworthy that with the exception of these cycles only a limited number of Bestiary themes appear over and over again in the margins of both English and Continental manuscripts. Most frequently represented are the ape pursued by hunters (figs. 39-42), the fox feigning death to attract birds (figs. 200-201), the elephant and castle (figs. 167, 169, 170), mermaids with mirror and comb or a musical instrument (figs. 497-500), the pelican in piety (figs. 552-553), and the capture of the unicorn (figs. 664-667). The compositions for these scenes were adopted without alteration from the traditional Bestiary miniatures. Minor details, such as the elephant's trunk or tail, occasionally show signs of humorous improvisation, and the capture of the unicorn is particularly noteworthy for the consistent high quality and sensitivity of its rendering (figs. 664-667).

The selectivity apparent in Bestiary themes also prevails in representations of legendary and mythological beings. Of these, centaurs and wild men far outnumber fellow-creatures such as pygmies, epifagi, or sciapodes (figs. 171, 643-644, and 686-695).[77] Adaptations of classical motifs are even rarer, so that the occasional renderings of Fortuna with her wheel or of Phyllis and Aristotle assume a special significance (figs. 554-557 and 684-685).[78]

---

73. Paris, Bibliothèque Nationale, MS. latin 10483-84. On the significance of this manuscript in the career of Jean Pucelle, see Panofsky, *Early Netherlandish Painting*, pp. 32-34, and Morand, *Jean Pucelle*, pp. 9-12, 43-45. The iconographic derivation is discussed in F. Godwin, "An Illustration to the *De Sacramentis* of St. Thomas Aquinas," *Speculum*, XXVI (1951), 609-614.

74. London, British Museum, Add. MS. 36684, ff. 83-91v, and New York, Pierpont Morgan Library, MS. 754, f. 105.

75. Franciscan saints recur, for instance, throughout the margins of two late thirteenth-century north French Psalters: Baltimore, Walters Art Gallery, MS. 45, and Paris, Bibliothèque Nationale, MS. latin 1076. For respective references, see L. Randall, "The Fieschi Psalter," *Journal of the Walters Art Gallery*, XXIII (1960), pp. 27-47, and abbé V. Leroquais, *Les psautiers manuscrits latins des bibliothèques publiques de France* (Mâcon: Protat, 1940-1941), II, No. 308, pp. 63-65.

76. A comprehensive bibliography of pertinent works is appended to T. H. White's *The Book of the Beasts* (New York: G. P. Putnam, 1954), pp. 271-281. See also F. McCulloch, *Mediaeval Latin and French Bestiaries*, Studies in Romance Lang. and Lit., No. 33 (Chapel Hill: University of North Carolina Press, 1960).

77. See R. Bernheimer, *Wild Men in the Middle Ages: A Study in Art, Sentiment, and Demonology* (Cambridge, Mass.: Harvard University Press, 1952); M. R. James, *Marvels of the East* (Oxford University Press [Roxburghe Publication], 1929).

78. On the depiction of classical motifs in English Misericords, see Bond, *Wood carvings*, I, 5-18 (see n. 43 above); other aspects of classical mythology in medieval art and literature are treated by C. Haskins, *The Renaissance of the Twelfth Century* (Cambridge, Mass.: Harvard University Press, 1927); E. Panofsky and F. Saxl, *Classical*

In the realm of fables the selection is also limited to a few consistent favorites, of which the most prevalent is the apologue of the fox and the stork, which recurs time and again, particularly in Continental manuscripts, in versions ranging from complete sequences to the most abbreviated fragments (figs. 174-181).[79]

In addition to such literary subjects popularized by oral, textual, and visual tradition, a number of marginal scenes depict episodes from the epic *Reynard the Fox.* While as a rule they appear as isolated incidents two more extensive sequences are found, not unexpectedly, in the margins of English manuscripts. The earlier, dated around 1300, is an unusual Psalter and Hours in the Walters Art Gallery, Baltimore (fig. 131).[80] The other, also an exceptional manuscript containing highly original illustrations produced some twenty years later, is a copy of the Decretals of Gratian in the British Museum (figs. 596-597).[81] Of the many other tales of adventure shown in the margins, only the more obvious have so far been identified. They include the tale of the Swan-Knight (Fig. 652),[82] the wild man's abduction of a lady (Figs. 688-691),[83] the mishaps of the blind man led by a boy (fig. 425-429),[84] and the allegory of the three living and the three dead (figs. 657-658).[85] In the margins of the Taymouth Hours are incorporated the heroic feats of Guy of Warwick and Bevis of Hampton, figures readily identifiable thanks to accompanying inscriptions.[86] If this practice had only been adopted more frequently, the iconographer's task would indeed have been simplified! One wonders, for instance, how many of the tournament scenes refer to Arthurian legends and whether some of the representations of a knight and lion may not relate to a literary figure such as Bevis of Hampton. Also enigmatic for the present are the multiple disguises adopted for references to heretics, Jews, and other controversial figures of the period.

The question of interpretation of marginal motifs frequently arises in the third iconographic group, genre themes. Future investigation will in all probability justify hitherto tenuous asumptions of symbolic meaning for some of these apparently realistic representations.[87] A large proportion, on the other hand, doubtless reflects merely the predilection for anecdotic detail, a feature particularly characteristic of north French and Flemish illumination. The possibility of hidden allusions exists

Mythology in Mediaeval Art, Metropolitan Museum Stud., IV (New York, 1933); J. Adhémar, *Influences antiques,* n. 12. For a literary rendition of the Phyllis and Aristotle theme, see Henri d'Andeli's *Le lai d' Aristote,* ed. A. Héron (Rouen: L. Gy, 1901), vv. 519-520.

79. Possible reasons for the prominence of certain fables are discussed in my article cited in n. 31 above.

80. D. Miner, *Illuminated Books of the Middle Ages and Renaissance,* Exhibition at the Baltimore Museum of Art, (Baltimore: Walters Art Gallery, 1949), MS. 102, p. 56, no. 153, pl. LVIII. F. McCulloch, "The funeral of Renart the Fox in a Walters Book of Hours," *Journal of the Walters Art Gallery,* XXV-XXVI (1962-1963), 8-27.

81. See above, n. 71.

82. A. R. Wagner, "The Swan Badge and the Swan Knight," *Archaeologia,* XCVII (1959), 129-138.

83. See R. Loomis, "A Phantom Tale of Female Ingratitude," *Modern Philology,* XIV (1916-1917), 751-755. See also H. W. Janson, "A Memento Mori," *Journal of the Warburg Institute,* III-IV (1939-1940), 248.

84. M. Roque, ed., *Le Garçon et l'Aveugle* (Paris: E. Champion, 1921).

85. K. Künstle, *Die Legende der drei Lebenden und drei Toten* (Freiburg i. B.; Herdersche Verlagshandlung, 1908).

86. Folios 7v-18. See above, n. 29. The tales are summarized in J. Ashton, *Romances of Chivalry* (London: T. F. Unwin, 1887), pp. 273-301. Both adventurers are named in a late fourteenth-century protest by William of Nassington, proctor in the ecclesiastical court of York, against the recital of such adventures in sermons. In his *Speculum Vitae,* preserved in the British Museum, Royal MS. 17 C.VIII, the pertinent passage appears on f. 2v:

> I warn you frust at the begynnyng
> That I will make na vayn carpynge
> Of dedes of armys, ne of amours,
> As dus mynstralles and jeestours
> That makys carpyng in many a place
> Of Octovyane and of Isambrase
> And of many other jeestes,
> And namly when you come to the festys.
> Ne of the lyfe of Buys of Hampton
> That was a knyght of grett renown;
> Ne of Sir Guye of Warwyke.
> All if it myght sum men lyke,
> I thinke my carpyng sall nott be,
> ffor that I hold bot vanite.

87. Much is yet to be gleaned from pre-Gothic visual and textual sources. For an account of a fascinating documented interpretation of an early twelfth-century English marginal representation of two fighting knights, see O. Pächt, C. R. Dodwell, and F. Wormald, *The St. Albans Psalter* (*Albani Psalter*) (London: Warburg Institute, 1960), pp. 149-151.

even in the numerous "obvious" representations of daily tasks and professional activities pursued by physicians, craftsmen, tradesmen, or beggars.

The prevailing emphasis in marginal "genre" scenes, however, is not on the arduous aspects of daily life but on the diversions which relieved its tedium. Musicians, acrobats, and animal trainers abound in a lively array of actions and poses (see, for example, figs. 411 and 490).[88] A wide variety of games with both male and female participants is also shown (figs. 89, 126, 206-210). Among the more strenuous forms of entertainment are wrestling and exhibitions of swordplay (figs. 736 and 739). Other amusements such as cockfights and puppet shows also drew attentive audiences (figs. 132-135, 585-586). Chess, checkers, and dice proved quieter pastimes although a heated argument, occasionally leading to bloodshed, could break out even over the gameboard (figs. 102-105).

In the round of daily activity the social levels are clearly differentiated. While the peasantry worked in the fields in seasonal tasks analogous to, and in fact derived from, traditional calendar representations of the occupations of the months,[89] members of the privileged classes engaged in the sports and games already mentioned as well as hunting, hawking, tilting, and amorous adventures (figs. 182, 316, 359, 386, 407-408). In the minority of non-satirical scenes representatives of the Church were depicted in line of duty, preaching, hearing confession, conducting Mass, bearing a sacred reliquary, or attending a funeral (figs. 1, 112, 119, 567-568).

From the realm of genre (or apparent genre) one is led directly to the fourth and most voluminous group of marginal subjects, consisting of parodies of human foibles and folly.[90] Here animals and hybrids appear in their full element. The leading role is held by the ape, who characteristically mimics human actions in the function assigned to him *similitudine hominis* (figs. 32 and 50, for example).[91] Minor parts in this world of farce were readily filled by fellow-beasts associated with equally traditional traits. Thus, the fox is cast as the sly swindler whose malice makes fools of those naïve enough to trust him (fig. 199).[92] The lion symbolizes force and courage in contrast to the fleeing hare's cowardice. Bear and wolf generally appear as scapegoats (figs. 218 and 598), while the dog faithfully serves his master with only rare outbursts of hostility. The cat directs her attention almost exclusively to the hapless mouse.

The flexible interchange of these principal characters and a quantity of assorted hybrids permitted the formulation of an infinite variety of possibilities for ridicule. While all social spheres were subjected to commentary through animal personification, the most frequent targets were representatives of the Church. The marginal illustrations, then, show that strain of violent anticlericalism already signalized as one of the main features of the fabliaux. By substitution of different creatures the dominant tone of a standard situation could be subtly altered from good-natured humor to bitter irony. Although today it is difficult to discern the precise shade of meaning in each case, the full implications were doubtless readily intelligible at the time. Certain themes are less complicated in this respect than others. Thus the connotations of a *monde renversé* scene showing the subjugation of man by a creature of inferior strength are readily apparent.[93] How-

88. On the hierarchy of musical instruments, see T. Wright, *A History of Caricature and Grotesque in Literature and Art* (London: Chatto and Windus, 1875), p. 195; also E. K. Prideaux, "The Carvings of Mediaeval Musical Instruments in Exeter Cathedral Church," *Archaeological Journal,* LXII, 2d Ser. (1915), 1-36.

89. See J. C. Webster, *The Labors of the Months* (Princeton: University Press, 1938); J. Le Sénécal, "Les occupations des mois dans l'iconographie du moyen age," *Bulletin de la Société des antiquaires de Normandie,* XXXV (1921-1923), 1-218.

90. The role of parody as a force undermining Church and society is discussed by P. Lehmann, *Die Parodie im Mittelalter* (Munich: Drei-Masken Verlag, 1922), p. 135. The psychological climate conducive to the rise of caricature and satire is outlined by R. Bernheimer, *The Nature of Representation* (ed. H. W. Janson, New York: New York University Press, 1961), p. 196. Citing Goya's *Los Caprichos* as an example, the author remarks that such work "soon abandons contact with social facts to lose itself in oppressive nightmares teeming with devils and ghouls. One is reminded of medieval *drôlerie,* marginal comment in the strictest sense, which continually mingles satire with the presentation of fantastic conceits" (p. 197).

91. Janson, *Apes and Ape Lore,* pp. 73 ff. An interesting example of the incorporation of an ape *drôlerie* in a late thirteenth-century English Psalter illustration is analyzed by M. Schapiro, "Cain's Jawbone That Did the First Murder," *Art Bulletin,* XXIV (1942), pp. 211-212.

92. See A. Meissner's "Die Bildlichen Darstellungen des Reineke Fuchs im Mittelalter," *Archiv für das Studium der neueren Sprachen und Litteraturen,* LVI (1876), 265-280; LVIII (1877), 241-260; LXXXI (1881), 199-232.

93. For the persistence of *monde renversé* themes and an extensive bibliography on the subject, see O. Odenius,

ever, when natural enemies of the animal kingdom are pitted against each other, the scene may be interpreted as a commentary on human conflicts as well (figs. 98-99, 224).

No matter how outrageous the distortion, the function of the travesties which constitute the bulk of the iconographic repertory of marginal illustrations was less overtly didactic than in analogous subjects preserved in fabliaux and exempla. An element of humor was seldom absent, in the rendering if not in the theme, and the aim was both to divert and to elevate. By means of this oblique method of presentation even the most scathing recrimination was made more palatable. If those at whom it was aimed failed to profit from the criticism, they were at least exposed to it in most conducive terms.

VI

Aside from iconographic wealth, a chief attribute of marginal illumination already mentioned is the unprogrammatic effect of its design. The combination of elements from the major categories outlined above with a host of minor decorative motifs (single birds, dragons, running hounds, and the like) inevitably created this impression. The frequent juxtaposition of unrelated themes in a totally incongruous context heightens the chaotic effect. Yet the possibility of an unrecognized underlying scheme still exists, all the more so in manuscripts where certain *mises en pages* clearly exhibit certain ideologic affinities. A dual situation of this kind is found, for instance, in the Hours of Jeanne d'Evreux in the Cloisters collection.[94] Here there are a number of *bas-de-page* obviously related to adjacent miniatures. It is by no means improbable, therefore, that a more devious rationale accounts for the depiction of seemingly realistic and humorous compositions in the margins of other pages as well.

As has already been noted, a connection between marginal motifs and their immediate context is most common (or, at least, can most readily be discerned) on pages marking the principal divisions of the text. In these instances the related subject generally appears in the lower margin, contained within the L- or C-shaped border surrounding the text. This was, so to speak, the center of the stage. In the wings were distributed other pictorial elements which, like the host of musicians accompanying the major Psalm divisions, served to illustrate the content of the page. Throughout the remainder of the manuscript, however, the array of marginalia follows no systematized dicta. Sacred and profane elements appear side by side or follow one another in rapid succession. Surprisingly enough, even the organization of the lengthy English sequences does not appear to be governed by any master plan. They are more consistent only in the choice and presentation of subject matter. For the latter they depended like the less formalistic programs of Continental manuscripts on a number of conditional factors. First and foremost was the influence of workshop tradition. Despite the dearth of sketches or pattern books preserved from this period, these were doubtless widely used. Occasionally one even finds exact duplication of hybrid creatures and other ornamental forms.[95] Another source was provided by illustrative features of earlier manuscripts. As has already been noted, Bestiary compositions, for instance, were taken over with relatively few changes. Motifs characterstic of late Romanesque and early Gothic borders and initials also persisted, for example, in the numerous representations of beasts and dragons, often shown in conflict with an armed man.

Another factor to be reckoned with in contemplating the extent and nature of a marginal program is the taste of the patron, especially when the manuscript was privately commissioned or intended for a specific purchaser. In the final analysis, however, the prime responsibility lay with the illuminator in charge of designing the over-all production. In many instances both miniatures and marginal décor were done by the same hand. In

"Mundus Inversus," *ARV,* X (1954), 142-170. For assistance in interpreting the Swedish text I should like to thank Mrs. Brita Stendhal.

94. MS. 54.1.2. See *The Hours of Jeanne d'Évreux,* introd. by J. J. Rorimer (New York: Metropolitan Museum of Art, 1957); Morand, *Jean Pucelle,* pp. 13-16, 41-42; Panofsky, *Early Netherlandish Painting,* pp. 39 ff.; *Metropolitan Museum of Art Bulletin,* XVI, No. 10 (June, 1958) for the following: R. H. Randall, "Frog in the Middle," pp. 269-275; E. Winternitz, "Bagpipes for the Lord," pp. 276-286; S. V. Grancsay, "Medieval Armor in a Prayer Book," pp. 287-292.

95. Egbert, *The Tickhill Psalter,* p. 77.

such cases it is interesting to observe the difference in style between the formal compositions and the marginal ornamentation. In contrast to the restraint imposed by the former, the margins afforded an opportunity for more spontaneous individualistic expression, whether in the realm of sacred imagery, social commentary, or fantastic invention. The ultimate success of the total production depended, like any artistic venture, on the illuminator's sensibility, skill, and aptitude for design. When the essence of these qualities was fused in the work of one man, the result was spectacular. Such was the case, for example, in a group of manuscripts produced for members of the Bar family of Lorraine soon after the turn of the thirteenth century,[96] the Gorleston Psalter, or the Pucelle Hours of Jeanne d'Evreux.[97]

When a marginal program was the work of a single individual rather than a collaborative undertaking, it is apparent not only in the stylistic uniformity but also in the repetition of idiosyncratic motifs depicted throughout certain sections of the entire course of the manuscript. Like a reiterated musical theme they strike a familiar note, giving unity to the work and alleviating its total anonymity. All are by no means interesting specimens. Many are clichés or merely monotonous products of a limited imagination. Among the more noteworthy examples are the courting couples appearing throughout the pages of a late thirteenth-century north French Psalter, with the names of the personages inscribed in accompanying rubrics. The illuminator of another north French manuscript of about the same date, an *Histoire du Graal,* specialized in centaurs, while a contemporary working on the Gorleston Psalter showed a penchant for figures disgorging themselves.[98] It may be noted in conclusion that most of such idosyncratic motifs appear in north French and Flemish margins, exemplifying once more the characteristic spontaneity already noted in the discussion of choice and grouping of marginal subject matter.

Like any other artistic vogue, marginal illumination passed from its apogee, in the first quarter of the fourteenth century, through a gradual subsiding of interest in this medium as a vehicle of expression. Retained as an integral part of late Gothic luxury illumination, its novelty had worn off and its main force been spent by the middle of the fourteenth century. Subsequent innovations were primarily in the form of improvisations on an established iconographic repertory which eventually became static to the point of formularization. It was not until the late fifteenth century that the dominant spirit of high Gothic marginal illumination was revitalized, given new impetus on a monumental scale in the works of major painters such as Hieronymus Bosch and Pieter Brueghel.

---

96. These include a two-volume Breviary of which the first is preserved in the British Museum (Y. T. MS. 8), the second in the Bibliothèque Municipale of Verdun (MS. 107); also a closely related Pontifical in the Fitzwilliam Museum in Cambridge, England (MS. 298). Published respectively in M. R. James, *A Descriptive Catalogue of the Manuscripts from the Collection of Henry Yates Thompson,* 1st Ser. (Cambridge, Eng.: Cambridge University Press, 1898), pp. 142 ff. and E. S. Dewick, *The Metz Pontifical* (London: J. B. Nichols, 1902). Another of the group, a Ritual, formerly MS. 43 in the Metz Public Library, was destroyed in 1944.

97. See above, nn. 40, 94.

98. The manuscripts referred to are: Paris, Bibliothèque Nationale, MS. latin 10435 and MS. fr. 95; London, British Museum, Add. MS. 49622. Bibliographical references appear in the appended Key.

SELECTIVE BIBLIOGRAPHY*

I. *Manuscripts*

Ameisenowa, Z., "Les principaux manuscrits à peintures de la bibliothèque Jagellione de Cracovie," *Bulletin de la Société française de reproductions de manuscrits à peintures,* XVII (1933).

Belin, Mme. T., *Les heures de Marguerite de Beaujeu* (Paris: T. Belin, 1925).

Berger, S., *La Bible française au moyen age* (Paris: Imprimerie nationale, 1884).

———, "Les manuels pour l'illustration du psautier au XIIIe siècle," *Mémoires de la Société nationale des antiquaires de France,* 6th Ser., VII (1898 [read Nov. 10, 1897]).

Billioud, J., *Trésors des bibliothèques de France,* 7 vols., Les éditions d'art et d'histoire, (Paris: G. van Oest, 1926-1946).

Birch, W. de G., and H. Jenner, *Early Drawings and Illuminations* (London: S Bagster, 1879).

Boase, T. S. R., *English Illumination of the Thirteenth and Fourteenth Centuries,* Bodleian Picture Books, No. 10 (Oxford: Oxford University Press, 1954).

Boinet, A., *Les trésors des bibliothèques de France,* 6 vols. (Paris: G. van Oest, 1925-1938).

Brassinne, J., *Psautier liègois du XIIIe siècle* (Brussels: Vromant, n.d).

British Museum, *Catalogue of Additions to Manuscripts, 1848-1853* (London, 1853). (Comp. by E. A. Bond).

———, *Catalogue of Additions to Manuscripts, 1854-1875,* 3 vols. (London, 1875-1880). (Chief compilers: E. J. Scott and G. F. Warner).

———, *Catalogue of Additions to Manuscripts, 1876-1881* (London, 1882). (Ed. by E. M. Thompson).

———, *Catalogue of the Stowe Manuscripts in the British Museum,* 2 vols. (London, 1895-1896). (Comp. by I. Jeayes).

———, *Catalogue of Western Manuscripts in the Old Royal and King's Collections,* 4 vols. (Oxford: Oxford University Press, 1921). (Comp. by G. F. Warner).

———, *Reproductions from Illuminated Manuscripts,* Series I-IV (London, 1923-1928). (Comp. and ed. by J. A. Herbert, G. F. Warner, and E. G. Millar).

———, *Schools of Illumination,* Parts I-VI (London, 1914-1930).

Burlington Fine Arts Club, *see* Cockerell, S. C.

Byvanck, A. W., "Les principaux manuscrits à peintures conservés dans les collections publiques du royaume des Pays-Bas," *Bulletin de la Société française de reproductions de manuscrits à peintures,* XV (1931).

———, "Les principaux manuscrits à peintures de la bibliothèque royale des Pays-Bas et du Musée Meermanno–Westreenianum à la Haye," *Bulletin de la Sociètè française de reproductions de manuscrits à peintures,* VIII (1924).

Caron, A., *Catalogue des manuscrits de la bibliothèque de la ville d'Arras* (Arras: A. Courtin, 1860).

Cockerell, S. C., *Burlington Fine Arts Club Exhibition of Illuminated Manuscripts* (London: Chiswick Press, 1908).

———, *The Book of Hours of Yolande de Flanders* (London: Chiswick Press, 1905).

* Additional references are cited in the footnotes.

Cockerell, S. C., *The Gorleston Psalter* (London: Chiswick Press, 1907).

Cockerell, S. C., and M. R. James, *Two East Anglian Psalters at the Bodleian Library* (Roxburghe Club; Oxford: Oxford University Press, 1926).

Cockerell, S. C., and H. Y. Thompson, *A Descriptive Catalogue of Twenty Illuminated Manuscripts (Substitutes) in the Collection of Henry Yates Thompson, nos. LXXV-XCIV* (Cambridge: Cambridge University Press, 1907).

Delaissé, L. M. J., *Miniatures médiévales* (Geneva: Edition des deux-mondes, n.d.).

Delaporte, Y., *Les manuscrits enluminés de la bibliothèque de Chartres* (Chartres: Société archéologique d'Eure et Loire, 1929).

De Ricci, S., and W. J. Wilson, *Census of Medieval and Renaissance Manuscripts in the United States and Canada,* 2 vols. (New York: H. W. Wilson, 1935-1937).

Dewick, E. S., *The Metz Pontifical (1302-1316)* (London: J. B. Nichols, 1902).

Egbert, D. D., "A Sister to the Tickhill Psalter—The Psalter of Queen Isabella of England," *Bulletin of the New York Public Library,* XXXIX (1935), 762-64.

———, *The Tickhill Psalter and Related Manuscripts* (New York: New York Public Library and Department of Art and Archaeology of Princeton University, 1940).

"Eight Mediaeval Manuscripts," *Yale University Gazette,* XXIX (1955), no. 3, 99-112.

Evans, J., *English Art, 1307-1461,* Oxford History of English Art Series, V (Oxford: Clarendon Press, 1949).

Fourez, L., "Le psautier de Louis le Hutin, 1315," *Revue belge d'archéologie de l'art,* XV (1945), 101-116.

———, "Le roman de la rose de la bibliothèque de Tournai," *Scriptorium,* I (1946-1947), 213-239.

Gaspar, C., and F. Lyna, *Les principaux manuscrits à peintures de la bibliothèque royale de Belgique,* 2 vols. (Paris: Société française de reproductions de manuscrits à peintures, 1937-1945).

Greene, B. da C., and M. P. Harrsen, *Exhibition of Illuminated Manuscripts* (New York: Pierpont Morgan Library, 1934).

Haseloff, G., *Die Psalterillustration im dreizehnten Jahrhundert* (Kiel, 1938).

Herbert, J. A., *Illuminated Manuscripts* (London: Methuen, 1911).

Hermann, J. H., *Beschreibendes Verzeichnis illuminierter Handschriften in Österreich* in *Die westeuropäischen Handschriften und Inkunabeln der Gotik und der Renaissance,* Neue Folge (Leipzig: K. Hiersemann, 1936), VII, Pt. 2.

Holländer, A., "The Sarum Illuminator and His School," *Wiltshire Archaeological and Historical Magazine* (1943), 230-262.

James, M. R., *et. al., A Descriptive Catalogue of Fifty Manuscripts from the Collection of Henry Yates Thompson,* 1st Ser. (Cambridge: Cambridge University Press, 1898). (Second series listed under Weale, W. H.)

———, *A Descriptive Catalogue of the Manuscripts in the Fitzwilliam Museum* (Cambridge: Cambridge University Press, 1895).

———, *A Descriptive Catalogue of the Manuscripts in the Library of Corpus Christi College,* I (Cambridge: Cambridge University Press, 1912).

———, *A Descriptive Catalogue of the McLean Collection of Manuscripts in the Fitzwilliam Museum* (Cambridge: Cambridge University Press, 1912).

———, *A Descriptive Catalogue of the Western Manuscripts in the Library of Queens College, Cambridge* (Cambridge: Cambridge University Press, 1905).

———, *Catalogue of Manuscripts and Early Printed Books from the Libraries of William Morris, Richard Bennett, Bertram Fourth Earl of Ashburnham, and Other Sources Now Forming Portion of the Library of J. Pierpont Morgan,* 4 vols. (London: Chiswick Press, 1906-1907).

———, *Description of an Illuminated Manuscript of the Thirteenth Century in the Possession of Bernard Quaritch* (London, 1904) (now in the Rothschild Collection).

———, *Descriptive Catalogue of Latin Manuscripts in the John Rylands Library at Manchester,* 2 vols. (Manchester: University Press, 1921).

———, *The Romance of Alexander* (Oxford: Clarendon Press, 1933).

———, *The Treatise of Walter de Milemete, De Nobilitatibus, Sapientiis, et Prudentiis Regum* (Roxburghe Club; Oxford: Oxford University Press, 1913).

———, *The Western Manuscripts in the Library of Trinity College, Cambridge,* 4 vols. (Cambridge: Cambridge University Press, 1900-1904).

James, M. R., and S. C. Cockerell, *see* Cockerell, S. C., and M. R. James.

James, M. R., and E. G. Millar, *The Bohun Manuscripts* (Roxburghe Club; Oxford: Oxford University Press, 1936).

Jeanroy, A., *Le chansonnier d'Arras* (Paris: Société d'anciens textes français, 1925).

Kohler, C., *Catalogue de manuscrits de la bibliothèque Sainte-Geneviève,* 2 vols. (Paris: E. Plon, 1893-1896).

Koseleff, O., "Representations of the months and zodiacal signs in Queen Mary's Psalter," *Gazette des Beaux-Arts,* ser. 6, XXII (1942), 77-88.

Kraus, H. P., *Catalogue No. 80* (New York, 1956).

Lejeune, R., *Histoire sommaire de la littérature wallonne* (Brussels: Office de la publicité [Collection nationale], 1942).

Leroquais, Abbé V., *Les bréviaires manuscrits des bibliothèques publiques de France,* 5 vols. (Paris, 1939).

———, *Les livres d'heures manuscrits de la bibliothèque nationale, Paris,* 2 vols. (Mâcon: Protat, 1927).

———, *Les psautiers manuscrits latins des bibliothèques publiques de France,* 3 vols. (Mâcon: Protat, 1940-1941).

———, *Les sacramentaires et les missels manuscrits des bibliothèques publiques de France,* 3 vols. (Paris, 1924).

Madan, F., *A Summary Catalogue of Western Manuscripts in the Bodleian Library at Oxford* (Oxford: Oxford University Press, 1895-1905), I-V.

Mangeart, J., *Catalogue des manuscrits de la bibliothèque de Valenciennes* (Paris: Techener, 1860).

Martin, H., *Catalogue général des manuscrits des bibliothèques publiques de France: Paris, Bibliothèque de l'Arsenal,* 8 vols. (Paris: E. Plon, 1885-1899).

———, *La miniature française du XIIIe au XVe siècle* (Paris: G. van Oest, 1923).

———, *Les peintres de manuscrits et la miniature en France,* 2d ed. (Paris: Librairie Renouard, 1927).

———, "Un caricaturiste du roi Jean (Piérart dou Tielt)," *Gazette des beaux-arts,* CIII (1909), 89-102.

Martin, H., and P. Lauer, *Les principaux manuscrits à peintures de la bibliothèque de l'Arsenal à Paris* (Paris: Société française de reproductions de manuscrits à peintures, 1929).

McCulloch, F., "The Funeral of Renart the Fox," *Journal of the Walters Art Gallery,* XXV-XXVI (1962-1963), 9-27.

Meurgey, J., *Les principaux manuscrits à peintures du Musée Condé à Chantilly* (Paris: Société française de reproductions de manuscrits à peintures, 1930).

Meyer, P., "Le psautier de Lambert le Bègue," *Romania,* XXIX (1900), 528-545.

Millar, E. G., "Bibliothèque de la National Gallery of Victoria à Melbourne," *Bulletin de la Société française de reproductions de manuscrits à peintures,* IX (1925), 20-32, pls. I-VII.

———, *English Illuminated Manuscripts from the Xth to the XIIIth Century* (Paris: G. van Oest, 1926).

———, *English Illuminated Manuscripts of the XIVth and XVth Centuries* (Paris: G. van Oest, 1928).

———, "Les principaux manuscrits à peintures du Lambeth Palace à Londres," *Bulletin de la Société française de reproductions de manuscrits à peintures,* VIII (1924); IX (1925).

———, *Souvenir de l'exposition de manuscrits français à peintures organisée à la Grenville Library* (Paris: Société française de reproductions de manuscrits à peintures, 1932).

———, *The Library of A. Chester Beatty: A Descriptive Catalogue of the Western Manuscripts,* 2 vols. (Oxford: Oxford University Press, 1927-1930).

———, *The Luttrell Psalter* (London, 1932).

———, *The Rutland Psalter* (Roxburghe Club; Oxford: Oxford University Press, 1937).

Millar, E. G., and M. R. James, *see* James, M. R., and E. G. Millar.

Miner, D., *Illuminated Books of the Middle Ages and Renaissance,* Exhibition Catalogue, Walters Art Gallery, Baltimore, Md., 1949.

Molinier, A., *Catalogue des manuscrits de la bibliothèque Mazarine* (Paris: E. Plon, 1885), I.

Morand, K., *Jean Pucelle* (Oxford: Clarendon Press, 1962).

Morel–Payen, L., *Les plus beaux manuscrits et les plus belles reliures de la bibliothèque de Troyes* (Troyes: J.–L. Paton, 1935).

Nordenfalk, C., *Gyldne Bøger; Illuminierde Middelalderlige Handskriften i Danmark og Sve-*

rige, Exhibition, Royal Library (Copenhagen, 1952).

Oechelhauser, A., *Die Miniaturen der Universitätsbibliothek Heidelberg,* 2 vols. (Heidelberg: G. Koester, 1887-1895).

Pächt, O., "A Giottesque Episode in English Medieval Art," *Journal of the Warburg and Courtauld Institutes,* VI (1943), 51-70. (*See also* Royal Academy of Arts.)

Panofsky, E., *Early Netherlandish Painting,* 2 vols. (Cambridge, Mass.: Harvard University Press, 1953).

——, *Gothic and Late Medieval Illuminated Manuscripts, with Special Reference to Manuscripts in the Pierpont Morgan Library* (New York: New York University Press, 1935).

Pierpont Morgan Library, *Review of the Activities and Acquisitions of the Library,* 1936-1940 and 1941-1948. (*See also* Greene, B. da C.; James, M. R.; and Panofsky, E.)

Plummer, J., *Manuscripts from the William S. Glazier Collection,* Exhibition, Pierpont Morgan Library (New York, 1959).

Porcher, J., *L'art religieux du moyen âge en Artois —manuscrits à peintures,* Exhibition (Arras, 1951).

——, *Les manuscrits à peintures du XIIIe au XVIe siècle,* Exhibition, Bibliothèque Nationale (Paris, 1955).

Randall, L., "The Fieschi Psalter," *Journal of the Walters Art Gallery,* XXIII (1960), 27-47.

Reid, G.-W., *Catalogue of Prints and Drawings in the British Museum (Political and Personal Satires, I: 1322-1689)* (London, 1870).

Rickert, M., *Painting in Britain: The Middle Ages* (Baltimore: Penguin Books [Pelican History of Art Series], 1954).

Royal Academy of Arts, *Flemish Art, 1300-1700,* Exhibition 1953-1954 (Manuscript section by O. Pächt).

Saunders, O., *English Illumination,* 2 vols. (Florence: Pantheon, Casa Editrice; Paris: Pegasus Press, 1928).

Schilling, R., *see* Swarzenski, G.

Sotheby and Co., *The Clumber Library: Catalogue of the Magnificent Library of the Late Seventh Duke, Removed from Clumber, Worksop,* 3d Portion (Dec. 6, 1937).

Stiennon, J., "Le manuscrit à miniatures dans le diocèse de Liège de l'art roman à la renaissance," *Art mosan et arts anciens du pays de Liège,* Exhibition (Liège, 1951).

Swarzenski, G. and R. Schilling, *Die illuminierten Handschriften und Einzelminiaturen des Mittelalters und der Renaissance in Frankfurter Besitz* (Frankfurt a. M.: J. Baer, 1929).

ter Horst, J. H., *Catalogus van de Handschriften der Koninklijke Nederlandsche Akademie van Wetenschappen, in Bruikleen in de Koninklijke Bibliotheek* (The Hague, 1938).

Thompson, H. Y. (*see also* James, M. R.; and Weale, W. H.), *Illustrations from One Hundred Manuscripts,* 7 vols. (London: Chiswick Press, 1907-1918).

——, *Thirty-two Miniatures from the Book of Hours of Joan II, Queen of Navarre* (London: Chiswick Press, 1899).

Thompson, H. Y. and S. C. Cockerell *see* Cockerell, S. C. and H. Y. Thompson.

Van den Gheyn, J., *Le psautier de Peterborough* (Haarlem: Musée des Enluminures, 1905).

Verriest, L., *Le Vieil Rentier d'Audenarde* (Brussels: Duculot, 1950).

Victoria and Albert Museum, Department of Engraving, Illustration and Design, *Catalogue of Miniatures, Leaves, and Cuttings from Illuminated Manuscripts* (London, 1923).

Vitzthum von Eckstädt, G., *Die Parisermalerei (von der Zeit des heiligen Ludwig bis zu Philip von Valois)* (Leipzig: Quelle und Meyer, 1907).

Warner, Sir G., *et al., A Descriptive Catalogue of Fourteen Illuminated Manuscripts, Nos. XCV to CVII and 79A . . . in the Library of Henry Yates Thompson* (Cambridge: Cambridge University Press, 1912).

——, *Descriptive Catalogue of Illuminated Manuscripts in the Library of C. W. Dyson Perrins,* 2 vols. (Oxford: Oxford University Press, 1920.

——, *Queen Mary's Psalter,* (London: H. Hart, 1912).

Weale, W. H., *et al., A Descriptive Catalogue of the Second Series of Manuscripts in the Collection of Henry Yates Thompson* (Cambridge: Cambridge University Press, 1902).

Willemsen, C. A., and D. Odenthal, *Über die Kunst mit Vögeln zu jagen,* 2 vols. (Frankfurt A. M.: Insel-Verlag, 1964).

Wormald, F., and P. M. Giles, "A Handlist of the Additional Manuscripts in the Fitzwilliam Museum," *Transactions of the Cambridge Bibliographical Society,* 3 (1951), 197-207, and 4 (1952), 301 ff.

II. Background

Adhémar, J., *Influences antiques dans l'art du moyen âge français* (London: Warburg Institute, 1939).

Anderson, M., *Animal Carvings in British Churches* (Cambridge: Cambridge University Press, 1938).

Baltrusaitis, J., *Réveils et prodiges, le gothique fantastique* (Paris: A. Colin, n.d.).

Barbazan, E., *Fabliaux et contes des poètes françois des XIe, XIIe, XIIIe, XIVe, XVe, siècles,* M. Méon, ed., 2d ed., 4 vols. (Paris: B. Warée, 1808).

Bergenthal, M., *Elemente der Drolerie und ihre Beziehungen zur Literatur* (diss.) (Bonn: Hohmann, 1936).

Coulton, G. G., *Medieval Panorama: The English Scene from Conquest to Reformation* (New York: Macmillan, 1938).

Courajod, L., *Les origines du style gothique* (Paris: E. Leroux, 1892).

Cronin, G., "The Bestiary and the Medieval Mind—Some Complexities," *Modern Language Quarterly* (1941), 191-198.

Denkinger, T., "Die Betterlorden in der französischen didaktischen Literatur des 13. Jahrhunderts, besonders bei Rutebeuf und im 'Roman de la Rose,'" *Franziskanische Studien,* II (1915), 63-109, 268-313.

Dept. G., *Les influences anglaise et française dans le comté de Flandre au début du XIIIe siècle* (Ghent: van Rysselberghe et Rombaut, 1928) (Ghent University, Faculté de philosophie et lettres, Recueil de travaux, fasc. 59).

Druce, G. C., "The Mediaeval Bestiaries and Their Influence on Ecclesiastical Decorative Art," *Journal of the British Archaeological Association,* XX (December, 1919), 40-82.

Evans, E. P., *Animal Symbolism in Ecclesiastical Architecture* (New York: H. Holt, 1896).

Gabelentz, H. v., *Die Lebensalter und das menschliche Leben in Tiergestalt* (Berlin: E. Steiniger, 1938).

Harvey, J., *The Gothic World (1100-1600)* (London: B. T. Batsford, 1950).

Hervieux, L., *Les fabulistes latins depuis le siècle d'Auguste jusqu'à la fin du moyen âge,* 5 vols. (Paris: Firmin-Didot, 1884-1899).

Holmes, U. T., *Daily Living in the Twelfth Century* (Madison: University of Wisconsin Press, 1952).

Koechlin, R., "La sculpture belge et les influences françaises au XIIIe et XIVe siècle," *Gazette des beaux-arts,* II (1903), 5-19, 333-348, 391-407.

Künstle, K., *Ikonographie der christlichen Kunst,* 2 vols. (Freiburg i. B.: Herder, 1926-1928).

Langlois, C. V., *La vie en France au moyen âge, de la fin du XIIe au milieu du XIVe siècle d'après des romans mondains du temps,* 4 vols. (Paris: Hachette, 1925-1928).

Lecoy de la Marche, A., *Anecdotes historiques, légendes et apologues tirées du recueil inédit d'Etienne de Bourbon, dominicain du XIIIe siècle* (Paris: Société de l'histoire de la France, 1877).

———, *L'Esprit de nos Aieux, anecdotes et bons mots tirés des manuscrits du treizième siècle* (Paris: C. Marpon, 1888).

———, *Le treizième siècle artistique* (Lille: Desdée, De Brouwer, 1889).

Lestocquoy, J., *Les dynasties bourgeoises d'Arras du XIe au XVe siècle,* Mémoires de la Commission départmentale des monuments historiques du Pas-de-Calais, V (Arras, 1945), fasc. I.

Little, A. G., "Franciscans in English Illuminated Manuscripts," Chap. IV in *Franciscan History and Legend in English Medieval Art,* (Manchester: Manchester University Press, 1937).

Loomis, R. S., and L. H., *Arthurian Legends in Medieval Art* (New York: Modern Language Association of America, Monograph Series; London: Oxford University Press, 1938).

Maeterlinck, L., *Le genre satirique dans la peinture flamande* (Ghent: Librairie Néerlandaise, 1903).

———, *Le genre satirique dans la sculpture flamande et wallonne: Les miséricordes de stalles* (Paris: J. Schémit, 1910).

Mâle, E., *L'art religieux du XIIIe siècle en France,* 5th ed. (Paris: A. Colin, 1923).

Marle, R. van, *Iconographie de l'art profane au moyen-âge et à la renaissance,* 2 vols. (The Hague: M. Nijhoff, 1931-1932).

Molsdorf, W., *Führer durch den symbolischen und*

typologischen Bilderkreis der christlichen Kunst des Mittelalters (Leipzig; K. W. Hiersemann, 1920).

Nykrog, P., *Les fabliaux: Étude d'histoire littéraire et de stylistique médiévale* (Copenhagen: E. Munksgaard, 1957).

Omont, H., *Fabliaux, dits, et contes en vers français du XIIIe siècle* (Paris: E. Leroux, 1932).

Owst, G. R., *Literature and Pulpit in Medieval England,* 2d ed. (New York: Barnes and Noble, 1961).

Robertson, D. W., *A Preface to Chaucer: Studies in Medieval Perspective* (Princeton: Princeton University Press, 1962).

Thiele, H., *Leben in der Gotik* (Munich: K. Desch, 1946).

Traill, H. D., and J. S. Mann, *Social England,* 6 vols. (London: Cassell, 1901-1904).

Waddell, H., *The Wandering Scholars* (London: Constable and Co., 1927).

Welter, J.-T., *L'Exemplum dans la littérature religieuse et didactique du moyen âge* (Paris: Occitania, 1927).

Wesselski, A., *Mönchslatein, erzählungen aus geistlichen Schriften des XIII. Jahrhunderts* (Leipzig: W. Heims, 1909).

Witkowski, G., *L'art profane à l'église, ses licenses symboliques, satiriques, et fantaisistes,* 2 vols. (Paris: J. Schémit, 1908).

III. Specialized Iconographic Studies

Blöte, J. F. D., "Der historische Schwanritter," *Zeitschrift für romanische Philologie,* XXI (1897), 176-191; XXV (1901), 1-44.

Class, E., *Auffassung und Darstellung der Tierwelt im französischen Roman de Renart* (Tübingen: G. Schnürlen, 1910).

Druce, G. C., "Some Abnormal and Composite Human Forms in English Church Architecture," *Archaeological Journal,* LXXII (1915), 135-186.

———, "The Mediaeval Bestiaries and Their Influence on Ecclesiastic Decorative Art," *Journal of the British Archaeological Association,* XX (December, 1919), 40-82.

Durrieu, P., "La légende du roi de mercie dans un livre d'heures du XVe siècle," *Monuments et mémoires Fondation Piot,* XXIV (1920), 149-182.

Faral, E., "La queue de poisson des Sirènes," *Romania,* LXXIV (1953), 433-506.

Furnivall, F. J., ed., *The Wright's Chaste Wife,* Early English Text Society, vol. XII (London: N. Trübner, 1865).

Herrmann, L., "Gallus et Vulpes," *Scriptorium,* I (1946-1947), 260-266.

Janson, H. W., "A Memento Mori Among Early Italian Prints," *Journal of the Warburg and Courtauld Institutes,* III-IV (1939-1940), 243-248.

———, *Apes and Ape Lore in the Middle Ages and the Renaissance,* Studies of the Warburg Institute, vol. 20 (London: Warburg Institute, 1952).

Koechlin, R., "Le dieu d'amour et le château d'amour sur les valves de boîtes à miroirs," *Gazette des beaux-arts,* 5th Ser., IV (1921), 279-297.

Künstle, K., *Die Legende der drei Lebenden und drei Toten,* (Freiburg i. B.: Herederschе Verlagshandlung, 1908).

Loomis, R., "A Phantom Tale of Female Ingratitude," *Modern Philology,* XIV (1916-1917), 751-755.

———, "The Allegorical Siege in the Art of the Middle Ages," *American Journal of Archaeology,* 2nd Ser., XXIII (1919), no. 3, 255-269.

Randall, L., "A Mediaeval Slander," *Art Bulletin,* XLII (1960), 25-40.

———, "Exempla as a Source of Gothic Marginal Illumination," *Art Bulletin,* XXXIX (1957), 97-107.

———, "The Snail in Gothic Marginal Warfare," *Speculum,* XXXVII (1962), 358-367.

Roque, M., ed., *Le garçon et l'aveugle* (Paris: E. Champion, 1921).

Ross, D., "Allegory and Romance on a Medieval French Marriage Casket," *Journal of the Warburg and Courtauld Institutes,* XI (1948), 112 ff.

Stechow, W., "Shooting at the Father's Corpse," *Art Bulletin,* XXIV (1942), 213-225.

Varty, K., "Reynard the Fox and the Smithfield Decretals," *Journal of the Warburg and Courtauld Institutes,* XXVI (1963), 347-354.

Wagner, A. R., "The Swan Badge and the Swan Knight," *Archaeologia,* XCVII (1959), 129-138.

Wessely, J., *Die Gestalten des Todes und Teufels in der darstellenden Kunst* (Leipzig: H. Vogel, 1876).

KEY TO ABBREVIATED MANUSCRIPT REFERENCES

Add. 10292-94 London, British Museum, Add. MS. 10292-94: Arthurian Romances, French, *ca.* 1310-20. 3 vols. $15\frac{7}{8}$ x $11\frac{1}{2}$ in. (Vitzthum, pp. 133 ff.; II, Loomis, pp. 97-98.* Fig. 106).†

Add. 17742 London, British Museum, Add. MS. 17742: Missal, Amiens use, dated 1218. $12\frac{1}{2}$ x $8\frac{1}{2}$ in. (British Museum, *Schools,* V, p. 8; Millar, *Souvenir,* no. 19).

Add. 17444 London, British Museum, Add. MS. 17444: Hours, north French (?), late thirteenth century. $3\frac{3}{4}$ x $2\frac{1}{2}$ in. (British Mus., *Cat. of Add.,* 1848-1853, p. 17).

Add. 17868 London, British Museum, Add. MS. 17868: Psalter, north French, late thirteenth century. $8\frac{3}{8}$ x $5\frac{1}{2}$ in. (British Museum, *Reprod.,* I, p. 9; Haseloff, p. 58; Vitzthum, p. 66; II, Bergenthal, p. 58. Fig. 171).

Add. 21114 London, British Museum, Add. MS. 21114: Psalter, perhaps Liège, mid-thirteenth century. $7\frac{3}{8}$ x 5 in. (Haseloff, p. 69; Meyer, p. 531).

Add. 21926 London, British Museum, Add. MS. 21926: Psalter, English, between 1262 and 1276. $9\frac{7}{8}$ x $7\frac{5}{8}$ in. (British Museum, *Reprod.,* II, p. 8).

Add. 24681 London, British Museum, Add. MS. 24681: Hours, Franco-Flemish, early fourteenth century. 5 x $3\frac{3}{8}$ in. (British Museum, *Cat. of Add.,* 1854-1875, II, p. 96. Fig. 175).

Add. 24686 London, British Museum, Add. MS. 24686: "Tenison Psalter," begun for Prince Alfonso, son of Edward I, English, before 1284. $9\frac{1}{2}$ x $6\frac{1}{2}$ in. (British Museum, *Reprod.,* III, pl. XVII; Egbert, *Tickhill Ps.,* p. 83; Rickert, pp. 139, 161; Vitzthum, pp. 130, 182. Figs. 211, 324, 377, 378, 498, 714).

Add. 28784B London, British Museum, Add. MS. 28784B: Hours, fragmentary, Belgian, late thirteenth century. $4\frac{7}{8}$ x $3\frac{1}{2}$ in. (British Museum, Postcard series B.1. Fig. 255).

Add. 29253 London, British Museum, Add. MS. 29253: Breviary, use of Saint-Pierre of Blandigny, Ghent, first quarter of fourteenth century. $7\frac{1}{2}$ x $5\frac{1}{8}$ in. (British Museum, *Cat. of Add.,* 1854-1875, II, p. 607; II, Bergenthal, p. 61. Fig. 618).

Add. 30029 London, British Museum, Add. MS. 30029: Psalter, Franco-Flemish, late thirteenth century. 6 x $4\frac{3}{8}$ in. (British Museum, *Cat of Add.,* 1876-1881, p. 23; II, Bergenthal, p. 61).

Add. 36684 London, British Museum, Add. MS. 36684: Hours (partial), executed for Marguerite de Beaujeu, Saint-Omer use(?), Franco-Flemish, after 1318. 6 x $4\frac{3}{8}$ in. (Part II = M. 754). (British Museum, *Reprod.,* II, p. 11, pl. XXI. Figs. 68, 92, 466, 570, 630).

Add. 38114-15 London, British Museum, Add. MS. 38114-15: Bible, 2 vols., north French, late thirteenth century. $11\frac{3}{8}$ x 8 in. (British Museum, *Reprod.,* IV, p. 11, pl. XIX; Millar, *Souvenir,* no. 12. Fig. 488).

Add. 38116 London, British Museum, Add. MS. 38116: Psalter, Lincoln diocese, second half of thirteenth century. $9\frac{1}{4}$ x $6\frac{1}{4}$ in. (British Mu-

* The numerals II and III refer to sections II and III of the Selective Bibliography. No Roman numeral is listed for references to section I, which comprises the main works on manuscripts.

† The figure numbers refer to illustrations in the present volume.

seum, *Reprod.*, IV, p. 11, pl. XXI-XXII; Haseloff, p. 61).

Add. 39810 London, British Museum, Add. MS. 39810: "St.-Omer Psalter," Sarum use, East Anglian, *ca.* 1330. 13⅛ x 8¼ in. (Cockerell, *Burl. F. A.*, p. 32, no. 68; Rickert, pp. 146-147, 149, 196-198; Weale, pp. 74 ff. Fig. 140).

Add. 41751 London, British Museum, Add MS. 41751: Bible, vol. II, French, late thirteenth century (vol. I = Harley 616), 15½ x 11⅜ in. (James, *Descr. Cat. of Fifty MSS.*, p. 206, no. 37. Fig. 266).

Add. 42130 London, British Museum, Add. MS. 42130: "Luttrell Psalter" for Geoffrey Luttrell, East Anglian, *ca.* 1340. 14 x 9⅝ in. (Millar, *Luttrell Ps.;* Rickert, pp. 147-149; III, Randall, "Exempla," p. 103. Figs. 73, 74, 96, 187, 230, 247, 252, 257, 263, 265, 270, 284, 340, 349, 380, 381, 415, 468, 504, 559, 675, 678, 697, 701, 732).

Add. 48985 London, British Museum, Add. MS. 48985 (formerly A. Chester Beatty MS. 60): Hours, Sarum use, English, late thirteenth century. 12¾ x 8¾ in. (Millar, *Lib. of A. C. Beatty,* II, p. 70, no. 60).

Add. 49622 London, British Museum, Add. MS. 49622 (formerly C. W. Dyson Perrins MS. 13): "Gorleston Psalter," Sarum use, East Anglian, *ca.* 1310-25. 14¾ x 9¼ in. (Cockerell, *Burl. F. A.*, p. 32, no. 67; *idem, Gorleston Ps.;* Millar, *Lib. of A. C. Beatty,* p. 50, no. 13; Rickert, p. 145; Warner, *Descr. Cat.*, I, pp. 50-56; III, Randall, "The Snail," p. 358. Figs. 50, 86, 109-111, 113, 155, 160, 218, 220, 260, 296, 308, 353, 409, 455, 477, 525, 569, 672).

Add. 50000 London, British Museum, Add. MS. 50000 (formerly C. W. Dyson Perrins MS. 11): "Oscott Psalter," English, second half of thirteenth century. 11⅞ x 7½ in. (Warner, *Descr. Cat.*, I, p. 40; III, Randall, "Exempla," p. 110).

All Souls lat. 6 Oxford, All Souls College, MS. lat. 6: Psalter, English, *ca.* 1240-1260. 12 x 8½ in. (Haseloff, pp. 61 ff.; Rickert, p. 115).

All Souls lat. 7 Oxford, All Souls College, MS. lat. 7: Psalter, Sarum use, English, *ca.* 1322-1325. 15⅝ x 10 in. (Cockerell, *Burl. F. A.*, p. 30, no. 64; Rickert, p. 116).

Arras 47 Arras, Musée Diocésain, MS. 47: Psalter and Hours, Saint-Omer calendar, north French, early fourteenth century. 10½ x 7⅝ in. (Leroquais, *Les ps.*, I, p. 50, no. 37; III, Randall, "Exempla," p. 106. Figs. 313, 485, 493, 554, 734, 735).

Arras 139 Arras, Bibliothèque Municipale, MS. 139: "Chansonnier d'Arras," probably Arras, late thirteenth century. 12½ x 8¾ in. (Jeanroy; Porcher, *Les MSS.*, p. 34, no. 63; Vitzthum, p. 127; II, Loomis, p. 92. Fig. 395).

Arras 229 Arras, Bibliothèque Municipale, MS. 229: Breviary, Saint-Vaast use, Arras, early fourteenth century. 6⅜ x 4¼ in. (Leroquais, *Les brév.*, I, p. 39, no. 23; III, Randall, "The Snail," p. 367. Figs. 45, 512).

Arras 302 Arras, Bibliothèque Municipale, MS. 302: Psalter, Saint-Vaast use, Arras, early fourteenth century. 12¾ x 9⅛ in. (Leroquais, *Les ps.*, I, p. 43, no. 29).

Arras 561 Arras, Bibliothèque Municipale, MS. 561: Bible, Mont-Saint-Eloy use, Arras, late thirteenth century. 9½ x 6¼ in. (Caron, p. 243; Vitzthum, p. 120. Fig. 456).

Arras 729 Arras, Bibliothèque Municipale, MS. 729: Breviary, Saint-Vaast use, Arras, late thirteenth century. 10 x 6⅞ in. (Leroquais, *Les brév.*, I, p. 65, no. 39; Vitzthum, pp. 128 ff.).

Arras 790 Arras, Bibliothèque Municipale, MS. 790: Bible, Arras, late thirteenth century. 20 x 14 in. (Caron, p. 386).

Arras 1043 Arras, Bibliothèque Municipale, MS. 1043: Compilation d'anciennes histoires, Arras, late thirteenth century. 12 x 7⅞ in. (Caron, p. 511).

Arsenal 603 Paris, Bibliothèque de l'Arsenal, MS. 603: Breviary, vol. II, Saint-Louis of Poissy use, Dominican, French, second quarter of fourteenth century. 9⅜ x 6¾ in. (Leroquais, *Les brév.*, II, p. 349, no. 411; Martin, *Cat. gén.*, I, p. 454).

Arsenal 5056 Paris, Bibliothèque de l'Arsenal, MS. 5056: Bible, vol. I, north French, late thirteenth century. 15⅜ x 11 in. (Martin, *Cat. gén.*, V, p. 28; Martin and Lauer, p. 18).

Arsenal 5218 Paris, Bibliothèque de l'Arsenal, MS. 5218: Gautiers Map, *Saint Graal,* written and illuminated by Piérart dou Tielt, Tournai, dated 1351. 11⅛ x 7⅝ in. (Martin, *Cat. gén.*, V, p. 162; *idem,* "Un caricaturiste." Figs. 25, 26, 563, 719).

Arsenal 6329 Paris, Bibliothèque de l'Arsenal, MS. 6329: Frère Laurens, *Somme le roi,* for Jeanne, Countess of Eu and of Guines, written by Lambert le Petit, French, dated 1311. 8½ x 6 in. (Martin, *Cat. gén.*, VI, p. 96; Martin and Lauer, p. 23; Porcher, *Les MSS.*, p. 39, no. 78; Vitzthum, p. 147).

Arundel 83 London, British Museum, Arundel MS. 83: "Lisle Psalter," East Anglian, Pts. I, II: *ca.* 1308, 1339. 13⅝ x 9 in. (British Museum, *Reprod.,* III, pls. XXII-XXV; Rickert, pp. 147-148 ff.; Vitzthum, pp. 72, 76. Fig. 338).

Ashmole 828 Oxford, Bodleian Library, MS. Ashmole 828: Arthurian Romance, French, early fourteenth century. 13¾ x 9¾ in. (II, Loomis, p. 100).

Auct. D.3.2 Oxford, Bodleian Library, MS. Auct. D.3.2: Bible, English, late thirteenth century. 10⅝ x 7¼ in. (Boase, pp. 6-7. Figs. 147, 297, 609).

Auct. D.4.2 Oxford, Bodleian Library, MS. Auct. D.4.2: Psalter, Flemish, late thirteenth century. 5⅔ x 3¼ in. (Madan, I, p. 579).

Auct. D.4.4 Oxford, Bodleian Library, MS. Auct. D.4.4: Psalter, begun for Humphrey de Bohun (d. 1373) and finished for his daughter, Mary, first wife of Henry IV, English, second half fourteenth century. 7 x 5½ in. (James and Millar, pp. 23-32).

BBR 209 Brussels, Bibliothèque Royale, MS. 209: Missal, vol. II, Cologne, mid-fourteenth century. 12½ x 8 in. (Gaspar and Lyna, I, p. 316, no. 128; Vitzthum, p. 209; II, Bergenthal, p. 63).

BBR 329-41 Brussels, Bibliothèque Royale, MS. 329-41: Saints' Lives, Cologne, first quarter of fourteenth century. 12¾ x 8¾ in. (Gaspar and Lyna, I, p. 242, no. 101; Vitzthum, p. 206; II, Bergenthal, p. 63. Figs. 226, 707).

BBR II 988 Brussels, Bibliothèque Royale, MS. II 988: Baudouin d'Avesnes, *Trésor des histoires,* 2 vols., Belgian, first half of fourteenth century. 16 x 11⅛ in. (Gaspar and Lyna, I, pp. 292, no. 118).

BBR 1175 Brussels, Bibliothèque Royale, MS. 1175: *Le Vieil Rentier d'Audenarde,* north French, after 1291. 11⅛ x 8¼ in. (Gaspar and Lyna, I, p. 192, no. 83; Verriest. Figs. 375, 465, 622, 727).

BBR 5163-64 Brussels, Bibliothèque Royale, MS. 5163-64: Psalter, Flemish, mid-thirteenth century. 11⅜ x 6⅝ in. (Gaspar and Lyna, I, p. 196, no. 84).

BBR 8469 Brussels, Bibliothèque Royale, MS. 8469: Missal, Brussels use, Belgian, early fourteenth century. 9½ x 6½ in. (Gaspar and Lyna, I, p. 239, no. 99; Vitzthum, p. 136).

BBR 9157 Brussels, Bibliothèque Royale, MS. 9157: Bible, Belgian, *ca.* 1330-1340. 14¼ x 10¾ in. (Gaspar and Lyna, I, p. 312, no. 126. Fig. 159).

BBR 9217 Brussels, Bibliothèque Royale, MS. 9217: Missal of Louis de Mâle, Flemish, third quarter of fourteenth century. 15 x 11¼ in. (Delaissé, p. 66, no. 13; Gaspar and Lyna, I, p. 344, no. 143; III, Randall, "A Med. Slander," p. 25. Figs. 577, 578).

BBR 9391 Brussels, Bibliothèque Royale, MS. 9391: Hours, Franco-Flemish, early fourteenth century. 12⅞ x 9 in. (Gaspar and Lyna, I, p. 236, no. 98; Vitzthum, p. 125. Figs. 27, 186, 241, 258, 264, 281, 399, 494, 515, 539, 568, 673).

BBR 9411-26 Brussels, Bibliothèque Royale, MS. 9411-26: *Recueil de Poésies Morales,* Franco-Flemish, late thirteenth century. 15½ x 10½ in. (Gaspar and Lyna, I, p. 202, no. 87. Figs. 271, 348, 385).

BBR 9427 Brussels, Bibliothèque Royale, MS. 9427: Breviary of Louis de Mâle, Flemish, third quarter of fourteenth century. 8½ x 6 in. (Gaspar and Lyna, I, p. 346, no. 144; III, Randall, "A Med. Slander," p. 25. Figs. 148, 174).

BBR 9433-34 Brussels, Bibliothèque Royale, MS. 9433-34: *Les Sept Sages de Rome,* Franco Flemish, second quarter of fourteenth century. 13⅞ x 9⅞ in. (Gaspar and Lyna, I, p. 310, no. 125).

BBR 9543 Brussels, Bibliothèque Royale, MS. 9543: *Li Ars d'Amour, de Vertu, et de Boneurté,* Flemish(?), late thirteenth century. 9⅝ x 6⅛ in. (Gaspar and Lyna, I, p. 205, no. 88. Fig. 396).

BBR 9961-62 Brussels, Bibliothèque Royale, MS. 9961-62: "Peterborough Psalter," East Anglian, *ca.* 1300. 11¾ x 7⅞ in. (Delaissé, p. 54, no. 10; Gaspar and Lyna, I, p. 114, no. 43; Haseloff, pp. 61 ff.; Rickert, pp. 140, 161; van den Gheyn; Vitzthum, pp. 73 ff. Figs. 117, 118, 192, 388, 729).

BBR 10228 Brussels, Bibliothèque Royale, MS. 10228: Brunetto Latini, *Trésor des Sciences,* Belgian, early fourteenth century. 11¼ x 8½ in. (Gaspar and Lyna, I, p. 174, no. 73; Vitzthum, p. 123. Fig. 71).

BBR 10607 Brussels, Bibliothèque Royale, MS. 10607: Psalter of Gui de Dampierre, Flemish, late thirteenth century. 4¼ x 3⅛ in. (Delaissé,

p. 50, no. 9; Gaspar and Lyna, I, p. 219, no. 95; Haseloff, pp. 68 ff.; Vitzthum, p. 138; III Randall, "A Med. Slander," p. 27. Figs. 194, 290, 357, 363, 381a, 410, 419, 463, 540).

BBR 11040 Brussels, Bibliothèque Royale, MS. 11040: *Romance of Alexander,* north French(?), early fourteenth century. 9¼ x 6⅞ in. (Gaspar and Lyna, I, p. 228, no. 96; Vitzthum, p. 141).

BBR 14682 Brussels, Bibliothèque Royale, MS. 14682: Psalter, Cambrai diocese, last quarter of thirteenth century. 2⅝ x 1¾ in. (Gaspar and Lyna, I, p. 216, no. 94; Haseloff, pp. 50 ff.; Vitzthum, p. 124. Fig. 685).

BBR 15001 Brussels, Bibliothèque Royale, MS. 15001: Jacob de Maerlant, *Rijmbijbel,* Limbourg(?), early fourteenth century. 15 x 8¾ in. (Gaspar and Lyna, I, p. 168, no. 71; Vitzthum, p. 138. Figs. 144, 213, 269, 295).

Bodley 264 Oxford, Bodleian Library, MS. Bodley 264: *Romance of Alexander,* illuminated by Jehan de Grise, Bruges, 1338-1344. 17⅛ x 12½ in. (James, *Rom. of Alex.;* Royal Academy, p. 151, no. 560; III, Randall, "Exempla," p. 98. Figs. 104, 127, 128, 164, 332, 356, 374, 392, 407, 408, 417, 445, 528, 560, 585, 586, 590, 599, 688, 712, 715.

Burney 275 London, British Museum, Burney MS. 275: *Priscian Grammar* and other texts, north French, early fourteenth century. 16⅛ x 11 in. (Haseloff, p. 91; Vitzthum, p. 27; II, Bergenthal, p. 53. Fig. 214).

Burney 345 London, British Museum, Burney MS. 345: Psalter, Flemish, late thirteenth century. 7 x 4⅞ in. (Figs. 188, 418, 619).

Busch 293 Rudolf Busch Collection, Auction Catalogue, Mainz, May 3-4, 1921, no. 293: Antiphonary page, French, after 1350. 18⅜ x 11⅞ in.

C.B. 61 Dublin, Chester Beatty Library, MS. 61: Psalter, Flemish, late thirteenth century. 6⅜ x 4½ in. (Millar, *Lib. of A. C. Beatty,* II, pp. 66 ff. Figs. 193, 412).

C.B. 62 Formerly in A. Chester Beatty Collection, MS. 62: *Speculum Beate Mariae Virginis,* north French, late thirteenth century. 4¾ x 3⅜ in. (Millar, *Lib. of A. C. Beatty,* II, pp. 80 ff. Figs. 333, 366).

C.B. 64 Formerly in A. Chester Beatty Collection, MS. 64: Hours, Amiens use (?), north French, early fourteenth century. 10¼ x 7¼ in. (Millar, *Lib. of A. C. Beatty,* II, pp. 103 ff.).

Cambrai 87 Cambrai, Bibliothèque Municipale, MS. 87: Hours, Reims use, northeast French, early fourteenth century. 10 x 6½ in. (Cockerell, *Burl. F. A.,* p. 141; Porcher, *Les MSS.,* p. 37, no. 69; Vitzthum, p. 146; II, Bergenthal, p. 58. Fig. 141).

Cambrai 102-103 Cambrai, Bibliothèque Municipale, MS. 102-103: Breviary, 2 vols., use of Saint-Sépulcre of Cambrai, Cambrai, late thirteenth century. 8¼ x 5⅞ in. (Haseloff, pp. 50 ff.; Leroquais, *Les brév.,* I, pp. 194 ff.; Porcher, *Les MSS.,* p. 41, no. 85; Randall, pp. 34 ff.; Vitzthum, p. 154; III Randall, "A Med. Slander," p. 27. Figs. 30, 31, 46, 77, 306, 376, 387, 501, 652, 654).

Cambrai 133 Cambrai, Bibliothèque Municipale, MS. 133: Breviary, use of Saint-Aldégonde of Maubeuge, north French, second quarter of fourteenth century. 5¼ x 4¼ in. (Vitzthum, p. 161).

Cambridge Dd.5.5 Cambridge, University Library, MS. Dd.5.5: Psalter and Breviary of Mary of Valence, second Countess of Pembroke, French, second quarter of fourteenth century. 7⅝ x 5 in. (Morand, p. 49. Figs. 67, 394, 470, 595, 720).

Chantilly 62 Chantilly, Musée Condé, MS. 62 (lat. 1423): Hours, north French, early fourteenth century. 3⅝ x 2⅝ in. (Haseloff, pp. 51 ff., 57 ff.; Meurgey, pp. 29 ff.; Vitzthum, p. 154; II, Bergenthal, p. 57. Figs. 36, 287, 517).

Chantilly 64 Chantilly, Musée Condé, MS. 64 (lat. 1671): Hours, French, second half of fourteenth century. 9½ x 7 in. (Meurgey, pp. 204 ff.; II, Bergenthal, p. 141).

Chartres 549 Chartres, Bibliothèque Municipale, MS. 549: Psalter, Tournai(?), mid-fourteenth century. 4½ x 2⅝ in. (Destroyed in World War I). (Leroquais, *Les ps.,* I, pp. 158 ff.).

Christ Church E.II Oxford, Christ Church Library, MS. E.II (92): Walter de Milemete, *De Nobilitatibus Sapientiis et Prudentiis Regum,* written for Edward III, East Anglian, *ca.* 1326-1327. 9¾ x 6¼ in. (Cockerell, *Burl. F. A.,* p. 33, no. 69; James, *Treatise;* Rickert, p. 150. Figs. 165, 320, 452, 689, 694).

Cloisters 54.1.2 New York, The Cloisters, MS. 54.1.2: Hours of Jeanne d'Evreux, illuminated by Jean Pucelle, Paris, before 1328. 3⅝ x 2⅜ in. (Morand, pp. 13 ff., 41-42; Panofsky, *Early*

Neth. Ptg., pp. 29 ff. Figs. 120, 250, 254, 277, 279, 329, 464, 510, 511, 516, 661, 693, 723).

Clumber 938 London, Sotheby's, Clumber Library Sale, Dec. 6, 1937, Lot 938: Breviary, use of Chalons-sur-Marne, French, second quarter of fourteenth century. 6½ x 4½ in.

Corpus Christi 53 Cambridge, Corpus Christi College Library, MS. 53: Psalter and Bestiary, probably Peterborough, early fourteenth century. 13⅝ x 9¼ in. (James, *Descr. Cat. of the MSS. in the Library,* I, pp. 105 ff.; Rickert, pp. 140-141, 161).

Cracow 815 Cracow, Bibliothèque Jagellione, MS. 815: Compilation of medical treatises, French, late thirteenth century. 15 x 9¼ in. (Ameisenowa, pp. 43 ff.).

Cracow 816 Cracow, Bibliothèque Jagellione, MS. 816: Compilation of medical treatises, French, late thirteenth century. 13⅞ x 9⅞ in. (Ameisenowa, pp. 39 ff. Fig. 59).

D.P. 12 Formerly C. W. Dyson Perrins Collection, MS. 12: Hours, York use, English, *ca.* 1300. 6⅞ x 4¾ in. (Warner, *Descr. Cat.,* I, p. 47).

D.P. 35 Formerly C. W. Dyson Perrins Collection, MS. 35: Hours, Metz use, Metz (?), early fourteenth century. 5 x 3½ in. (Warner, *Descr. Cat.,* I, pp. 102 ff.; III, Randall, "Exempla," p. 104).

Dijon 113 Dijon, Bibliothèque Municipale, MS. 113: Breviary, use of Saint-Bénigne of Dijon, late thirteenth century. 9⅜ x 6½ in. (Leroquais, *Les brév.,* II, pp. 23 ff.).

Douai 152 Douai, Bibliothèque Municipale, MS. 152: Breviary (Summer), northeast French, early fourteenth century. 7¼ x 5¼ in. (Leroquais, *Les brév.,* II, pp. 56 ff.).

Douai 171 Douai, Bibliothèque Municipale, MS. 171: Psalter, East Anglian, early fourteenth century. (Destroyed in World War I). (Cockerell, *Gorleston Ps.,* p. 4; Vitzthum, p. 85).

Douai 193 Douai, Bibliothèque Municipale, MS. 193: Psalter, Dominican use of Saint-Omer, north French, early fourteenth century. 4⅛ x 3¼ in.

Douce 5-6 Oxford, Bodleian Library, MS. Douce 5-6: Psalter, 2 vols., calendar of Saint-Pierre of Blandigny near Ghent, Flemish, first quarter of fourteenth century. 3¾ x 2¾ in. (Haseloff, pp. 50 ff.; Madan, IV, p. 490; Nordenfalk, p. 43; Royal Academy, pp. 150-151, nos. 558-559; III, Randall, "A Med. Slander," p. 27; III, Randall, "Exempla," p. 104. Figs. 39, 150, 215, 216, 300, 373, 420, 471, 480, 518, 700).

Douce 23 Oxford, Bodleian Library, MS. Douce 23: Psalter, Amiens use, north French, third quarter of thirteenth century. 4¾ x 3⅛ in. (Madan, IV, p. 496; Vitzthum, p. 126).

Douce 24 Oxford, Bodleian Library, MS. Douce 24: Psalter, Franco-Flemish, third quarter of thirteenth century. 4¾ x 3¼ in. (Haseloff, p. 68; Madan, IV, p. 496; Vitzthum, p. 108).

Douce 48 Oxford, Bodleian Library, MS. Douce 48: Psalter, Anglo-French, third quarter of thirteenth century. 5½ x 3¾ in. (Madan, IV, p. 503; Vitzthum, p. 88. Fig. 253).

Douce 49 Oxford, Bodleian Library, MS. Douce 49: Psalter, Flemish, third quarter of thirteenth century. 5⅜ x 3⅝ in. (Madan, IV, p. 504; Vitzthum, p. 108).

Douce 118 Oxford, Bodleian Library, MS. Douce 118: Psalter and Hours (partial) for Joffroy d'Aspremont and Isabelle de Kievraing, Metz diocese, before 1302. 9 x 6 in. (Part II = Melbourne 1254/3). (Madan, IV, p. 527. Figs. 133, 222, 319, 401, 551, 626, 705).

Douce 131 Oxford, Bodleian Library, MS. Douce 131: Psalter, English, first half of fourteenth century. 9¼ x 6⅛ in. (Boase, pp. 9-10; Madan, IV, p. 531. Figs. 135, 136, 690, 691).

Douce 366 Oxford, Bodleian Library, MS. Douce 366: "Ormesby Psalter," East Anglian, early fourteenth century. 15 x 9¾ in. (Boase, p. 9; Cockerell and James; Pächt; Rickert, pp. 143-144, 149, 162, 189; Vitzthum, pp. 75 ff.; III, Randall, "Exempla," p. 106. Figs. 239, 249, 352, 482, 513, 667).

Egerton 1151 London, British Museum, Egerton MS. 1151: Hours, English, third quarter of thirteenth century. 6¼ x 4¼ in. (British Museum, *Reprod.,* I, p. 8; Rickert, pp. 189-190; Vitzthum, p. 90).

Egerton 2781 London, British Museum, Egerton MS. 2781: Hours, English, mid-fourteenth century. 6½ x 4¼ in. (British Museum, *Reprod.,* II, pl. XV; II, Bergenthal, p. 55).

Exeter 47 Oxford, Exeter College, MS. 47: Psalter for Humphrey de Bohun, East Anglian, second half of fourteenth century. 11¼ x 7¾ in.

(Cockerell, *Burl. F. A.*, p. 35, no. 73; James and Millar, pp. 5-22; Rickert, pp. 189-190).

Fitz. 2-1954 Cambridge, Eng.: Fitzwilliam Museum, MS. 2-1954: "Bird Psalter," English, late thirteenth century. 7½ x 5⅛ in. (Figs. 60, 168, 204, 728).

Fitz. 47 Cambridge, Fitzwilliam Museum, MS. 47: Hours, English, third quarter of thirteenth century. 7¾ x 4¾ in. (James, *Descr. Cat. of the MSS. in the Fitzw. Mus.*, p. 98, no. 47).

Fitz. 48 Cambridge, Fitzwilliam Museum, MS. Fitz. J.48: "Carew-Poyntz Hours," English, second half of fourteenth century. 7⅛ x 4⅝ in. (James, *Descr. Cat. of the MSS. in the Fitzw. Mus.*, p. 100, no. 48; Rickert, p. 167).

Fitz. 242 Cambridge, Fitzwilliam Museum, MS. 242: Hours, East Anglian, *ca.* 1308. 9½ x 6 in. (Egbert, *Tickhill Ps.*, pp. 175 ff.; Rickert, p. 146; Wormald and Giles, no. 3, p. 198. Fig. 12).

Fitz. 288 Cambridge, Fitzwilliam Museum, MS. 288: Psalter and Hours, Liège, third quarter of thirteenth century. 8 x 5¼ in. (Cockerell, *Burl. F. A.*, P. 68, no. 142; Haseloff, pp. 68 ff.; Royal Academy, p. 50, no. 555; Wormald and Giles, no. 4, pp. 301 ff.).

Fitz. 298 Cambridge, Fitzwilliam Museum, MS. 298: "Metz Pontifical," for Reynaud de Bar, bishop of Metz (1302-16). 12½ x 9¾ in. (Dewick, *Metz Pont.;* III, Randall, "Exempla," p. 105, and "The Snail," p. 358. Figs. 169, 326, 354, 365, 566, 598, 635, 664, 665).

fr. 95 Paris, Bibliothèque Nationale, MS. fr. 95: Robert de Borron, *L'Histoire du graal,* Picard, late thirteenth century. 18½ x 13¼ in. (Porcher, *Les MSS.*, no. 57, p. 32; Vitzthum, p. 143; II, Baltrusaitis, p. 210; II, Loomis, pp. 95-97, 114. Figs. 72, 246, 305, 367, 368, 403, 446, 447, 459, 460, 556, 557, 582, 631, 636, 671, 708).

fr. 776 Paris, Bibliothèque Nationale, MS. fr. 776: *Tristram,* north French, late thirteenth century. 12¼ x 8½ in. (II, Loomis, p. 92. Fig. 309).

fr. 2754 Paris, Bibliothèque Nationale, MS. fr. 2754: Guillaume de Tyr, *La conquête de la terre sainte* (incomplete), north French, late thirteenth century. 16 x 11¼ in. (Porcher, *Les MSS.*, p. 32, no. 58).

fr. 6447 Paris, Bibliothèque Nationale, MS. fr. 6447: Bible and Saints' Lives, French, late thirteenth century. 14¾ x 10¾ in. (Porcher, *Les MSS.*, p. 34, no. 64; Vitzthum, p. 140).

fr. 12400 Paris, Bibliothèque Nationale, MS. fr. 12400: Frederick II, *Traité de fauconnerie,* illuminated by Simon d'Orléans, French, late thirteenth century. 14 x 9¼ in. (Porcher, *Les MSS.*, p. 45, no. 97; Vitzthum, p. 228; Willemsen. Figs. 337, 350, 472).

fr. 25526 Paris, Bibliothèque Nationale, ms. fr. 25526: Guillaume de Lorris and Jean de Meung, *Roman de la rose,* French, mid-fourteenth century. 10 x 7¼ in. (II, Adhémar, p. 289, n. 1).

G.K.S. 393 Copenhagen, Det Kongelige Bibliotek, MS. 393.2°: *Corpus Iuris Civilis,* north French, late thirteenth century. 16⅛ x 10 in. (Nordenfalk, p. 39, no. 44. Fig. 238).

G.K.S. 3384 Copenhagen, Det Kongelige Bibliotek, MS. 3384.8°: Psalter, Flemish, first quarter of fourteenth century. 3¾ x 2⅜ in. (Nordenfalk, p. 43, no. 54. Figs. 28, 49, 51, 58, 64, 69, 75, 119, 152, 184, 234, 307, 312, 322, 389, 424, 437, 439, 473, 475, 479, 481, 546, 562, 573, 580, 644, 660, 738).

Ghent 233 Ghent, Bibliothèque de l'Université, MS. 233 (8): *Ceremoniale Blandiniensis,* Saint-Pierre of Blandigny, Ghent, dated 1322. 9 x 6⅛ in. (II, Maeterlinck, *Le genre sat. dans la pture.*, p. 57).

Glazier 24 New York, William S. Glazier Collection, MS. 24 (now on deposit at the Pierpont Morgan Library): Jacques de Longuyon, *Voeux du Paon* (incomplete), Franco-Flemish, mid-fourteenth century. 9¾ x 6¾ in. (Plummer, p. 21, no. 28; III, Randall, "The Snail," p. 363. Figs. 53, 62, 63, 179, 180, 328, 341, 361, 441, 442, 449, 462, 520, 529, 531, 532, 534-538, 565, 576, 640, 641, 651, 659, 687, 692, 703, 733).

Glazier 53 New York, William S. Glazier Collection, MS. 53 (formerly C. W. Dyson Perrins MS. 14; now on deposit at the Pierpont Morgan Library): Psalter of Richard of Canterbury, use of St. Augustine's Abbey, Canterbury, English, early fourteenth century. 12¾ x 8½ in. (Plummer, p. 19, no. 26; Warner, *Descr. Cat.*, I, pp. 57-59).

Hague 10.A.14. The Hague, Meermanno-Westreenianum Museum, MS. 10.A.14: Missal, Ghent, dated 1366. 14¾ x 10½ in. (Byvanck, *Les princ. MSS...de la bib. roy.*, p. 99, no. 36. Fig. 461).

Hague 10.B.21. The Hague, Meermanno-Westreenianum Museum, MS. 10.B.21: Jacob Maerlant, *Rijmbibel,* Netherlandish, dated 1332.

14⅛ x 9¾ in. (Byvanck, *Les princ. MSS...de la bib. roy.*, p. 96, no. 35).

Hague 78.D.40 The Hague, Meermanno-Westreenianum Museum, MS. 78.D.40: Missal, use of Saint-Jean, Amiens, illuminated by Pierre de Raimbaucourt, dated 1323. 14 x 9 in. (Byvanck, *Les princ. MSS...de la bib. roy.*, p. 19, no. 6; Vitzthum, p. 153. Figs. 1, 44, 122, 190, 196, 197, 497, 614, 617, 684).

Hague XX The Hague, Koninklijke Biblioteek, Koninklijke Akademie MS. XX: Jacob Maerlant, *Spiegel Historiael,* Netherlandish, second quarter of fourteenth century. 12¾ x 9¼ in. (Byvanck, *Les princ. MSS. conservés*, p. 7; II, Maeterlinck, *Le genre sat. dans la pture.*, p. 365).

Harley 616 London, British Museum, Harley MS. 616: Bible, vol. I, French, late thirteenth century (vol. II = Add. 41751). 15½ x 11⅝ in. (Berger, *La Bible,* pp. 114, 363-366; James, *Descr. Cat. of Fifty MSS.*, pp. 207-208; Vitzthum, p. 165).

Harley 928 London, British Museum, Harley MS. 928: Hours, English, late thirteenth century. 4½ x 2⅞ in. (Vitzthum, p. 91; II, Bergenthal, p. 54).

Harley 6563 London, British Museum, Harley MS. 6563: Hours, English, first quarter of fourteenth century. 6¼ x 4 in. (Millar, *Eng. Ill. MSS. of the XIVth and XVth Cent.*, p. 85; III, Randall, "The Snail," p. 367. Figs. 35, 98, 99, 161, 162, 232, 233, 434, 435).

Heidelberg Cod. Sal. 9,51 Heidelberg, Universitätsbibliothek, MS. Cod. Sal. 9,51: Breviary, north French, dated 1288. 9½ x 6¼ in. (Oechelhauser, II, no. XII, pp. 3 ff.; Vitzthum, p. 202. Fig. 151).

Holkham 458 Norfolk, Holkham Hall, Library of Earl of Leicester, MS. 458: Aristotle, *De Secretis Secretorum,* English, *ca.* 1330. 9½ x 6¼ in. (James, *Treatise of W. de M.*, pp. xxxviii ff.).

Jacquemart 1 Paris, Musée Jacquemart-André, MS. 1: Hours for Jeanne of Savoy, Paris use, illuminated by Pucelle atelier, Paris, *ca.* 1320. 7 x 5⅛ in. (Morand, p. 47; Porcher, *Les MSS.*, p. 53, no. 108).

Jesus 40 Oxford, Bodleian Library, MS. Jesus 40: Psalter, English, early fourteenth century. 9⅜ x 6⅛ in. (Millar, *Eng. Ill. MSS. of the XIVth and XVth Cent.*, p. 83; III, Randall, "The Snail," p. 367. Figs. 272, 314).

Kraus 75/88 New York, H. P. Kraus Catalogue no. 75, no. 88: Psalter for Marguerite of Flanders and Hainaut, Flemish, *ca.* 1260-1280. 4¼ x 3⅜ in. (Kraus, pp. 95-97. Figs. 13, 85, 413, 503, 620, 650).

L.M. 13 Frankfurt, Kunstgewerbemuseum, Linelsammlung, MS. L.M. 13: Breviary, Metz (?), first quarter of fourteenth century. 5½ x 3⅞ in. (Swarzenski and Schilling, p. 62, no. 60. Fig. 231).

Lambeth 209 London, Lambeth Palace Library, MS. 209: Apocalypse, Canterbury, late thirteenth century. 10¾ x 7¾ in. (Millar, *Les princ. MSS.*, pp. 38 ff.; Rickert, pp. 122, 134. Fig. 78).

Lambeth 233 London, Lambeth Palace Library, MS. 233: "Bardolf-Vaux Psalter," East Anglian, first quarter of fourteenth century. 12⅞ x 8⅝ in. (Cockerell, *Burl. F. A.*, p. 24, no. 51; Egbert, *Tickhill Ps.*, pp. 189 ff.; Vitzthum, p. 71. Figs. 149, 422).

Lansdowne 420 London, British Museum, Lansdowne MS. 420: Psalter, English, early thirteenth century. 12⅛ x 9¾ in. (Haseloff, p. 53; Herbert, pp. 179-180).

Lansdowne 451 London, British Museum, Lansdowne MS. 451: *History of England,* English, late thirteenth century. 6⅝ x 4½ in. (II, Maeterlinck, *La genre sat. dans la pture.*, p. 366).

lat. lit. f.3 Oxford, Bodleian Library, MS. lat. liturg. f.3: Hours of Anne of Bohemia (queen of Richard II), Brussels, before 1382. 6⅜ x 4⅜ in. (Madan, V, p. 682; Royal Academy, p. 151, no. 561).

latin 1029A Paris, Bibliothèque Nationale, MS. latin 1029A: Breviary, use of Saint-Maur, Verdun, early fourteenth century. 8⅜ x 6⅛ in. (Leroquais, *Les brév.*, III, p. 10, no. 488. Fig. 134).

latin 1052 Paris, Bibliothèque Nationale, MS. latin 1052: Breviary of Charles V, Paris, before 1380. 9⅜ x 6¾ in. (Leroquais, *Les brév.*, III, p. 49, no. 511; Morand, pp. 25-26; Porcher, *Les MSS.*, p. 55, no. 111. Figs. 273, 669, 670).

latin 1076 Paris, Bibliothèque Nationale, MS. latin 1076: Psalter, north French, late thirteenth century. 7⅞ x 5⅜ in. (Haseloff, pp. 48 ff.; Leroquais, *Les ps.*, II, p. 63, no. 308; Porcher, *Les MSS.*, p. 40, no. 81. Figs. 259, 545, 608).

latin 3893 Paris, Bibliothèque Nationale, MS. latin 3893: Decretals of Gratian, French, dated 1314. 14 x 8⅝ in. (Martin, *La min.*, pl. 25; Porcher, *Les MSS.*, p. 22, no. 32; Vitzthum, p. 78).

latin 10435 Paris, Bibliothèque Nationale, MS. latin 10435: Psalter, Picard (?), late thirteenth century. 7⅛ x 5 in. (Haseloff, pp. 34 ff., 56 ff.; Leroquais, *Les ps.*, II, p. 95, no. 328; Porcher, *Les MSS.*, p. 52, no. 68; Vitzthum, pp. 153, 156 ff.; III, Randall, "A Med. Slander," p. 27. Figs. 102, 552, 717).

latin 10483-84 Paris, Bibliothèque Nationale, MS. latin 10483-84: "Belleville Breviary," 2 vols., illuminated by Jean Pucelle and his atelier, Paris, early 1320's. 9½ x 6¾ in. (Leroquais, *Les brév.*, III, p. 198, no. 599; Morand, pp. 9 ff.; Panofsky, *Early Neth. Ptg.*, I, pp. 32 ff.; Vitzthum, pp. 138 ff. Figs. 268, 567, 616, 668).

latin 13260 Paris, Bibliothèque Nationale, MS. latin 13260: Psalter and Hours, use of Saint-Amand, north French, second half of thirteenth century. 9⅝ x 5¼ in. (Leroquais, *Les livres d'heures*, II, p. 44; Porcher, *Les MSS.*, p. 41, no. 83. Figs. 116, 342).

latin 14284 Paris, Bibliothèque Nationale, MS. latin 14284: Hours, Thérouanne use, north French, late thirteenth century. 16½ x 12½ in. (Leroquais, *Les livres d'heures*, II, p. 158; Porcher, *Les MSS.*, p. 40, no. 79; III, Randall, "Exempla," p. 103, and "The Snail," fig. 3. Figs. 167, 209, 311, 639).

latin 16260 Paris, Bibliothèque Nationale, MS. latin 16260: Bible, Arras(?), late thirteenth century. 9⅞ x 6⅞ in. (Haseloff, pp. 51, 56 ff. Fig. 391).

Laud Lat. 84 Oxford, Bodleian Library, MS. Laud Lat. 84: Breviary, Franco-Flemish, early fourteenth century. 5¼ x 3¼ in. (Madan, I, p. 33. Fig. 478).

Liège, Bibliothèque de l'Université, MS. 431: Psalter, Liège, third quarter of thirteenth century 6⅝ x 4⅜ in. (Brassinne; Haseloff, pp. 70 ff.; Lejeune, p. 20; Meyer; Stiennon, pp. 88-89. Fig. 379).

M. 88 New York, Pierpont Morgan Library, MS. 88: Hours, Metz use, Metz(?), first half of fourteenth century. 6 x 4 in. (James, *Cat. of MSS.*, I, p. 74, no. 41; III, Randall, "The Snail," p. 367. Figs. 286, 505, 575).

M. 102 New York, Pierpont Morgan Library, MS. 102: "Windmill Psalter," East Anglian, late thirteenth century. 13⅛ x 8¾ in. (Cockerell, *Burl. F. A.*, p. 22, no. 47; Greene and Harrsen, p. 24, no. 45; Haseloff, pp. 61 ff.; James, *Cat. of MSS.*, p. 41, no. 19; Miner, p. 56, no. 152; Rickert, pp. 139-140, 161).

M. 108 New York, Pierpont Morgan Library, MS. 108: *Le Jeu des Echecs*, north French, late thirteenth century. 9⅝ x 7 in. (James, *Cat. of MSS.*, p. 170, no. 110).

M. 149 New York, Pierpont Morgan Library, MS. 149: Breviary, Paris, 1322-1340. 7⅝ x 5 in. (James, *Cat. of MSS.*, p. 22, no. 13).

M. 155 New York, Pierpont Morgan Library, MS. 155: Psalter, Liège(?), early fourteenth century. 6⅜ x 4¼ in. (Haseloff, pp. 70 ff.; James, *Cat. of MSS.*, p. 58, no. 29).

M. 183 New York, Pierpont Morgan Library, MS. 183: Psalter, Liège use, Liège, late thirteenth century. 6⅜ x 4½ in. (Cockerell, *Burl. F. A.*, p. 57, no. 125; Greene and Harrsen, p. 25, no. 48; Haseloff, pp. 70 ff.; James, *Cat. of MSS.*, p. 54, no. 27).

M. 494 New York, Pierpont Morgan Library, MS. 494: Bible, north French, second half of thirteenth century. 15⅜ x 11 in. (Greene and Harrsen, p. 27, no. 52).

M. 729 New York, Pierpont Morgan Library, MS. 729: Psalter of Yolande de Soissons, Amiens use, north French, late thirteenth century. 7⅛ x 5⅛ in. (Cockerell, *Burl. F. A.*, p. 65, no. 129; Greene and Harrsen, p. 29, no. 57; Miner, p. 24, no. 59. Fig. 383).

M. 730 New York, Pierpont Morgan Library, MS. 730: Psalter and Hours, Arras use, north French, late thirteenth century. 7⅛ x 5⅞ in. (Cockerell, *Burl. F. A.*, p. 64, no. 138; Greene and Harrsen, p. 30, no. 58; Haseloff, p. 35).

M. 754 New York, Pierpont Morgan Library, MS. 754: Hours (partial), executed for Marguerite de Beaujeu, Saint-Omer use(?), Franco-Flemish, early fourteenth century. 6 x 4⅜ in. (Part I = Add. 36684). (Greene and Harrsen, p. 38, no. 74; II, Baltrusaitis, p. 214. Frontispiece and fig. 261).

M. 761 New York, Pierpont Morgan Library, MS. 761; *La Lumière as Lais*, English, second half of thirteenth century. 10⅞ x 5¼ in. (De Ricci and Wilson, II, p. 1498).

M. 796 New York, Pierpont Morgan Library, MS.

796: Psalter, Amiens (?), late thirteenth century. 13¼ x 9⅜ in. (Pierp. Morgan Lib., *Review* [1936-1940], pp. 31-32. Fig. 243).

M. 812 New York, Pierpont Morgan Library, MS. 812: *Registrum Brevium and Statutes of the Realm,* English, thirteenth century. 8⅜ x 6 in. (Pierp. Morgan Lib., *Review* [1941-1948], pp. 42-43).

Marseilles 111 Marseilles, Bibliothèque Municipale, MS. 111: Hours, Thérouanne use, north French, early fourteenth century. 7¾ x 4⅜ in. (Billioud, V, pp. 165 ff.; Porcher, *L'art du m. a.,* p. 62, no. 74; *idem., Les MSS.,* p. 41, no. 82).

Maz. 34 Paris, Bibliothèque Mazarine, MS. 34: Bible, English, early fourteenth century. 15 x 9½ in. (Molinier, I, p. 12).

McLean 41 Cambridge, Eng., Fitzwilliam Museum, McLean Collection, MS. 41: Psalter, Flemish, mid-thirteenth century. 7½ x 5¼ in. (Haseloff, pp. 69 ff.; James, *Descr. Cat. of McLean Coll.,* p. 80, no. 41).

Melbourne 1254/3 Melbourne, National Gallery of Victoria, MS. 1254/3: Psalter and Hours of Joffroy d'Aspremont and Isabelle de Kievraing (partial), Metz diocese, before 1302. 9 x 6 in. (Part I = Douce 118). (Millar, *Bib. de la Nat. Gall.,* pp. 20 ff. Figs. 47, 219, 221, 301, 318, 432, 541, 550, 558, 571, 579, 591, 602, 642, 704).

Merton 0.1.3 Oxford Merton College, MS. 0.1.3: Aristotle, *De Historiis Animalium,* French, late thirteenth century. 12 x 8½ in. (Cockerell, *Burl. F. A.,* p. 42, no. 86; II, Bergenthal, p. 91. Fig. 405).

Metz 43 Metz, Bibliothèque Municipale, MS. 43: Ritual of Reynaud de Bar, bishop of Metz (1302-1316). Destroyed in 1944; four extant photographs. (Vitzthum, p. 220).

Montpellier H.196 Montpellier, Bibliothèque de la faculté de médecine, MS. H.196: *Chansonnier de Paris,* French, ca. 1300. 8 x 5½ in. (Billioud, IV, pp. 145 ff.; Porcher, *Les MSS.,* p. 20, no. 26; II, Baltrusaitis, p. 205. Fig. 208).

Munich c.g. 16 Munich, Bayerische Staatsbibliothek, MS. Cod. gall. 16: Psalter of Queen Isabella, English, 1303-1308. 11½ x 8 in. (Egbert, "A Sister to the Tickhill Psalter," and *Tickhill Ps.,* pp. 149 ff.; Rickert, p. 146; Vitzthum, pp. 70 ff.; III, Randall, "Exempla," p. 103. Figs. 42, 79, 83, 145, 170, 251, 292, 294, 496, 522, 544, 548, 662, 683, 724).

N.K.S. 41 Copenhagen, Kongelige Bibliotek, MS. Ny Kgl. Saml. 41.8°: Psalter, Flemish, early fourteenth century. 4½ x 3 in. (Nordenfalk, p. 42, no. 53. Figs. 37, 384).

Nancy 249 Nancy, Bibliothèque Municipale, MS. 249: Psalter, Franco-Flemish, early fourteenth century. 4 x 3 in. (Leroquais, *Les ps.,* I, p. 282, no. 235; III, Randall, "Exempla," p. 106. Figs. 8, 16, 100, 330, 438, 484, 574, 593, 637, 647, 713, 722).

Olschki 4 Florence, L. Olschki, Fourth International Book Fair, *Settima del libro raro e antico* (1932), no. 4: Psalter, Flemish, late thirteenth century. 6⅛ x 4½ in.

Princeton 44-18 Princeton, Art Museum, Princeton University, MS. 44-18: Hours, possibly use of Chartres, Maestricht(?), early fourteenth century. 3¾ x 2⅝ in. (Figs. 7, 207, 240, 282, 288, 304, 344, 359, 360, 400, 467, 589, 601, 655, 656).

Queens 17 Cambridge, Eng., Queens College Library, MS. 17: Psalter, English, mid-thirteenth century. 8¾ x 5⅛ in. (Cockerell, *Burl. F. A.,* p. 36, no. 74; Haseloff, pp. 61 ff.; James, *Descr. Cat. of the Western MSS.,* pp. 19 ff.).

Riches Ps. Shenley (Herts.), collection of T. H. Riches: Psalter (formerly known as the Psalter of John of Gaunt and No. XCIX in the collection of Henry Yates Thompson), Sarum use, English, *ca.* 1370(?). 6¾ x 4¾ in. (Cockerell, *Burl. F. A.,* pp. 34-35, no. 72; James and Millar, pp. 53-59; Warner, *A Descr. Cat.,* pp. 45-52).

Rothschild MS. Paris, Private Collection: Canticles of the Virgin ("Rothschild Canticles"), Flemish, *ca.* 1300. 4¾ x 3⅜ in. (James, *Descr. of an Ill. MS.;* III, Janson, *Apes and Ape Lore,* pp. 94 ff. Figs. 38, 88, 173, 345, 453, 543, 730).

Royal 1 B.XII London, British Museum, Royal MS. 1 B.XII: "Bible of William de Hales," English, dated 1254. 12⅛ x 8 in. (Holländer; Rickert, pp. 117, 133).

Royal 1 D.I London, British Museum, Royal MS. 1 D.I: "Bible of William of Devon," English, mid-thirteenth century. 12⅜ x 8 in. (British Museum, *Cat. of Western MSS.,* I, p. 15; *idem, Reprod.,* II, pl. X; Haseloff, pp. 61 ff.; Millar, *Eng. Ill. MSS. from the Xth to the*

XIIIth Cent., I, p. 95; Rickert, p. 118; Vitzthum, pp. 91 ff. Fig. 125).

Royal 2 B.VII London, British Museum, Royal MS. 2 B.VII: "Queen Mary's Psalter," English, first quarter of fourteenth century. 10⅞ x 6⅞ in. (British Museum, *Cat. of Western MSS.*, I, p. 42; Koseleff; Rickert, pp. 139 ff.; Vitzthum, pp. 77 ff.; Warner, *Queen Mary's Ps.* III, Randall, "Exempla," p. 103; Figs. 200, 201, 203, 276, 495, 627, 628, 680, 681).

Royal 3 D.VI London, British Museum, Royal MS. 3 D.VI: Petrus Comestor, *Historia Scholastica,* East Anglian, late thirteenth century. 15¾ x 10⅞ in. (British Museum, *Cat. of Western MSS.*, I, p. 377; *idem, Reprod.*, IV, pl. XXIII; Millar, *Eng. Ill. MSS. from the Xth to the XIIIth Cent.*, p. 113; Rickert, p. 139).

Royal 10 E.IV London, British Museum, Royal MS. 10 E.IV: "Smithfield Decretals" (of Gregory IX), written in Italy, illuminated in England, perhaps at St. Bartholomew's, Smithfield, London, second quarter of fourteenth century. 18 x 11¼ in. (Pächt, p. 55; Rickert, pp. 149 ff.; III, Randall, "Exempla," p. 103; III, Furnivall; III, Roque; III, Varty. Figs. 9, 20-24, 114, 163, 191, 212, 217, 228, 316, 317, 331, 351, 425-429, 596, 597, 605, 623, 679, 698).

Royal 14 B.V London, British Museum, Royal MS. 14 B.V.: *Roll-chronicle of the Genealogy of Kings of England,* English, before 1300. 13 ft. x 9½ in. (British Museum, *Cat. of Western MSS.*, II, p. 126; II, Traill and Mann, II, p. 788).

Royal 14 E.III London, British Museum, Royal MS. 14 E.III: *St. Graal,* French, late thirteenth century. 19 x 13¼ in. (British Museum, *Cat. of Western MSS.*, II, p. 140; Vitzthum, pp. 133 ff.; II, Loomis, pp. 97-98, 123).

Royal 17 E.VII London, British Museum, Royal MS. 17 E.VII: Guiart des Moulins, Bible Historiale, 2 vols., French, dated 1357. 15½ x 11¼ in. (British Museum, *Cat. of Western MSS.*, II, p. 260. Figs. 18, 19).

Royal 20 D.IV London, British Museum, Royal MS. 20 D.IV: *Lancelot du Lac,* French, early fourteenth century. 13½ x 9½ in. (British Museum, *Cat. of Western MSS.*, II, p. 378; Rickert, p. 189, n. 10; II, Bergenthal, p. 136).

Rutland Ps. Belvoir Castle, Duke of Rutland Collection: Psalter, English, mid-thirteenth century. 11⅜ x 8 in. (Cockerell, *Burl. F. A.*, p. 20, no. 43; Haseloff, pp. 61 ff.; Millar, *Rutland Ps.;* Rickert, pp. 115, 118; II, Coulton, p. 78. Figs. 40, 101, 103, 202, 321, 362, 382, 416, 433, 451, 454, 458, 502, 547, 663, 718, 731, 739).

Rylands fr. 1-2 Manchester, John Rylands Library, MS. fr. 1-2; *Lancelot du Lac,* 2 vols. Picard, *ca.* 1300. 15¾ x 11 in. (II, Loomis, p. 97. Figs. 3, 54, 523).

Rylands lat. R.16 Manchester, John Rylands Library, MS. lat. R.16: Bible, vol. I, north French, late thirteenth century. 18¼ x 13⅜ in. (James, *Descr. Cat. of Latin MSS.*, I, pp. 44-45).

Rylands lat. R.24 Manchester, John Rylands Library, MS. lat. R.24: "Missal of Henry of Chichester," English, mid-thirteenth century. 12½ x 8 in. (James, *Descr. Cat. of Latin MSS.*, pp. 73-75).

Rylands lat. R.117 Manchester, John Rylands Library, MS. lat. R.117: Psalter and Hours, Franco-Flemish, late thirteenth century. 7¾ x 5¾ in. (Haseloff, pp. 53 ff.; James, *Descr. Cat. of Latin MSS.*, pp. 217-221. Fig. 108).

Schilling MS. London, Mrs. Rosy Schilling: Calendar from a Book of Hours, Flemish, *ca.* 1300. 4¾ x 3¼ in. (Figs. 126, 588).

Seligman 11 New York, Jacques Seligmann, *Illuminated Manuscripts from the Bibliothèque of their Highnesses the Dukes d'Arenberg* (1952), no. 11: Breviary, Laon use, north French, early fourteenth century. 7 x 5⅞ in.

Spencer 2 New York, Public Library, Spencer Collection, MS. 2 (formerly H. Y. Thompson MS. 56): "De la Twyere Psalter," East Anglian, first quarter of fourteenth century. 11¾ x 8½ in. (Weale, p. 39).

Spencer 26 New York, Public Library, Spencer Collection, MS. 26: "Tickhill Psalter," English, early fourteenth century. 12⅞ x 8¾ in. (Egbert, *Tickhill Ps.;* Miner, p. 57, no. 154; Rickert, p. 146. Fig. 146).

St. Omer 5 Saint-Omer, Bibliothèque Municipale, MS. 5: Bible, vol. II, Franco-Flemish, late thirteenth century. 10⅞ x 7⅞ in. (Porcher, *L'art,* p. 63, no. 77; Vitzthum, pp. 145-146; II, Maeterlinck, *Le genre sat. dans la pture.*, pp. 36, 131. Figs. 291, 411, 486, 492, 521).

St. Omer 595 Saint-Omer, Bibliothèque Municipale, MS. 595: Aristotle, *Metaphysics,* Saint-Bertin, early fourteenth century. 13 x 8⅜ in.

Ste. Gen. 777 Paris, Bibliothèque Sainte-Geneviève,

MS. 777; *Tite-Live* of Charles V, Paris, *ca.* 1370. 18⅜ x 12⅝ in. (Kohler, p. 369. Fig. 235).

Stowe 12 London, British Museum, Stowe MS. 12: Breviary, East Anglian, 1322-1325. 11½ x 7¼ in. (British Museum, *Cat. of Stowe MSS.*, pp. 8-9; *idem., Reprod.*, II, pl. XIV; II, Bergenthal, p. 54).

Stowe 17 London, British Museum, Stowe MS. 17: Hours, Maestricht (?), *ca.* 1300. 3¾ x 2½ in. (British Museum, *Cat. of Stowe MSS.*, pp. 12-13; *idem., Reprod.*, I, p. 12, pl. XXXV; Herbert, p. 205; II, Bergenthal, p. 61. Figs. 2, 14, 15, 65, 66, 76, 80, 94, 95, 105, 112, 121, 139, 199, 267, 280, 327, 397, 406, 443, 509, 514, 524, 600, 612, 613, 615, 633, 634, 638, 646, 657, 658, 676, 677, 696, 726, 736).

Thott 547 Copenhagen, Det Kongelige Bibliotek, MS. Thott S.547.4°: Hours for Mary de Bohun, first wife of Henry IV, English, second half of fourteenth century. 7⅛ x 5⅛ in. (James and Millar, pp. 47-52; Nordenfalk, p. 61, no. 106; Rickert, p. 189, n. 10; p. 190, n. 13).

Tournai CI Tournai, Bibliothèque Municipale, MS. CI: *Roman de la Rose,* French, second quarter of fourteenth century. 10½ x 7¾ in. (Fourez, "Le roman de la rose." Fig. 587).

Tournai Ps. Tournai, Cathedral Treasury: Psalter of Louis le Hutin, Tournai, 1315. 6 x 4¾ in. (Fourez, "Le psautier de Louis le Hutin"; Vitzthum, p. 146. Figs. 43, 55 57, 124, 229, 369-372, 500, 526, 527, 533).

Trinity B.11.22 Cambridge, Trinity College Library, MS. B.11.22: Hours, Flemish, early fourteenth century. 6⅝ x 5⅛ in. (James, *Western MSS.*, I, p. 364, no. 261; Vitzthum, p. 132; III, Randall, "A Med. Slander," p. 27. Figs. 29, 93, 137, 223, 323, 335, 347, 355, 398, 421, 423, 431, 483, 508, 519, 530, 549, 553, 592, 648, 653, 725).

Trinity O.1.20 Cambridge, Eng., Trinity College Library, MS. O.1.20: Medical Tracts, English, early thirteenth century. 8 x 6 in. (James, *Western MSS.*, III, p. 23, no. 1044).

Troyes 89 Troyes, Bibliothèque Municipale, MS. 89; *Summa de Iure Canonico* of Innocent IV, French, early fourteenth century. 16 x 8¾ in. (Morel–Payen, p. 133).

Troyes 898 Troyes, Bibliothèque Municipale, MS. 898: Legal and Philosophical Tracts, French, early fourteenth century. 12 x 8¾ in. (Morel–Payen, p. 136).

Troyes 1905 Troyes, Bibliothèque Municipale, MS. 1905: Hours, French, early fourteenth century. 3¼ x 2⅜ in. (Morel–Payen, p. 124. Fig. 89).

V. and A. no. 8997E London, Victoria and Albert Museum, no. 8997E: Antiphonary page, Flemish, early fourteenth century. 19¼ x 12¾ in. (Victoria and Albert Museum, p. 8).

Valenciennes 838 Valenciennes, Bibliothèque Municipale, MS. 838: Calendrier-Obituaire, abbey of Notre-Dame-des-Prés near Douai, late thirteenth century. 16⅛ x 13½ in. (Mangeart, p. 614, no. 620. Figs. 621, 625, 629, 699).

Verdun 107 Verdun, Bibliothèque Municipale, MS. 107: Breviary, Part II, for Marguerite de Bar, Verdun use, Lorraine, before 1304. 11½ x 8 in. (Part I = Y. T. 8). (Leroquais, *Les brév.*, IV, pp. 300 ff.; Vitzthum, p. 220. Figs. 142, 156, 182, 225, 285, 302, 315, 364, 440, 444, 666, 716).

Vienna 1826* Vienna, Österreichische Nationalbibliothek, Codex 1826*: Psalter of Humphrey de Bohun, English (Salisbury?), second half of fourteenth century. 11⅜ x 7⅞ in. (Hermann, pp. 17 ff.; James and Millar, pp. 33-46; Rickert, pp. 168, 189, n. 10; 190, nn. 11, 14).

Vienna 2542 Vienna, Österreichische Nationalbibliothek, Codex 2542: *Romans de la Table Ronde,* Anglo-French, early fourteenth century. 17¾ x 13 in. (James and Millar, pp. 1 ff.).

W. 37 Baltimore, Walters Art Gallery, MS. 37: Hours, Flemish, late thirteenth century. 3½ x 2¾ in. (Miner, p. 22, no. 55. Figs. 81, 244, 339).

W. 39 Baltimore, Walters Art Gallery, MS. 39: Hours, north French, late thirteenth century. 10 x 7 in. (Miner, p. 23, no. 56).

W. 41 Baltimore, Walters Art Gallery, MS. 41: Psalter, Langres use, French, late thirteenth century. 4¼ x 3⅛ in. (De Ricci, I, p. 770, no. 82).

W. 45 Baltimore, Walters Art Gallery, MS. 45: Psalter for Leonardo de' Fieschi, north French, late thirteenth century. 7¼ x 4⅞ in. (Miner, p. 23, no. 57; Randall, pp. 27 ff.; III, Randall, "The Snail," p. 358. Figs. 61, 143, 177, 242, 248, 310, 386, 572, 611, 643).

W. 82 Baltimore, Walters Art Gallery, MS. 82: Psalter and Hours, Flemish, early fourteenth century. 6⅜ x 4⅛ in. (De Ricci, I, p. 782, no. 160; III, Randall, "A Med. Slander," p. 27. Figs. 10, 70, 82, 90, 390, 393, 581, 649).

W. 85 Baltimore, Walters Art Gallery, MS. 85: Hours, Franco-Flemish, early fourteenth century. 2¾ x 1¾ in. (Miner, p. 21, no. 49).

W. 87 Baltimore, Walters Art Gallery, MS. 87: Hours, French, early fourteenth century. 4 x 2¾ in. (De Ricci, p. 783, no. 162. Figs. 107, 436).

W. 88 Baltimore, Walters Art Gallery, MS. 88: Hours, Franco-Flemish, early fourteenth century. 4⅜ x 3¼ in. (De Ricci, I, p. 783, no. 165. Figs. 138, 189, 237, 343, 450, 469, 476).

W. 90 Baltimore, Walters Art Gallery, MS. 90: Hours, Thérouanne use, north French, first quarter fourteenth century. 5¾ x 3½ in. (Miner, p. 21, no. 51. Figs. 84, 198, 274, 298, 489).

W. 102 Baltimore, Walters Art Gallery, MS. 102: Psalter and Hours, English, *ca.* 1300 (Augustinian). 10½ x 7¼ in. (Miner, p. 56, no. 153; McCulloch, pp. 9 ff. Figs. 131, 262, 491).

W. 104 Baltimore, Walters Art Gallery, MS. 104: Hours, Franco-Flemish, early fourteenth century. 6¾ x 4¾ in. (De Ricci, I, p. 784, no. 172. Figs. 11, 123).

W. 109 Baltimore, Walters Art Gallery, MS. 109: Breviary, Franco-Flemish, late thirteenth century. 7⅜ x 4¾ in. (Miner, p. 24, no. 61. Figs. 48, 176, 206, 346, 358).

W. 110 Baltimore, Walters Art Gallery, MS. 110: Psalter, north French, early fourteenth century. 4⅜ x 3⅛ in. (De Ricci, I, p. 772, no. 93).

W. 143 Baltimore, Walters Art Gallery, MS. 143: Guillaume de Lorris and Jean de Meung, *Le Roman de la Rose,* French, mid-fourteenth century. 11½ x 7¾ in. (De Ricci, I, p. 847, no. 509. Fig. 166).

W. 759-762 Baltimore, Walters Art Gallery, MS. 759-62: Antiphonary for Cistercian convent of Beaupré near Grammont (Belgium), 4 vols., dated 1290 (vol. IV contains later additions). Vol. I: 19⅜ x 13⅝ in.; Vol. II: 19⅜ x 12⅞ in.; Vol. III: 16¾ x 12⅜ in.; Vol. IV: 19⅜ x 13⅝ in. (Formerly Chester Beatty MS. 63). (Cockerell and Thompson, p. 55; Warner, *Descr. Cat.,* II, pp. 88 ff. Figs. 153, 154, 185).

Y.T. 8 London, British Museum, Yates Thompson MS. 8: Breviary, Pt. I, for Marguerite de Bar, Verdun use, Lorraine, completed after 1302. 11½ x 8 in. (Part II = Verdun 107). (James, *Descr. Cat. of Fifty MSS.,* pp. 142 ff.; Vitzthum, p. 220; III, Randall, "The Snail," p. 358. Figs. 17, 33, 34, 91, 132, 158, 224, 227, 256, 275, 278, 289, 293, 325, 490, 506, 507, 555, 624, 682, 695, 710).

Y.T. 13 London, British Museum, Yates Thompson MS. 13 (formerly H. Y. Thompson MS. 57): "Taymouth Hours," English, first half of fourteenth century. 6½ x 4¼ in. (Rickert, pp. 149, 163, n. 54; Weale, pp. 50 ff. Figs. 205, 603, 604, 606, 607, 610, 632, 674, 686).

Y.T. 15 London, British Museum, Yates Thompson MS. 15 (formerly H. Y. Thompson MS. 62): Psalter and Hours, Franco-Flemish, late thirteenth century. 5½ x 4 in. (Weale, pp. 92 ff.).

Y.T. 19 London, British Museum, Yates Thompson MS. 19 (formerly H. Y. Thompson MS. 74): Brunetto Latini, *Trésor,* north French, first quarter of fourteenth century. 12⅜ x 8⅞ in. (Weale, pp. 145 ff.).

Y.T. 27 London, British Museum, Yates Thompson MS. 27 (formerly H. Y. Thompson MS. LXXXVI): Hours of Yolande de Flandre, Paris, *ca.* 1353. 4⅜ x 3¼ in. (Cockerell, *Book of Hours;* Cockerell and Thompson, p. 91; Morand, pp. 22-23, 41).

Y.T. 42 London, British Museum, Yates Thompson MS. 42: Psalter, Flemish, late thirteenth century. 4¼ x 2¾ in.

Y.T. 75 Whereabouts unknown, formerly Henry Yates Thompson MS. 75: Hours of Jeanne II, queen of Navarre, Paris, 1336-1348. 7 x 5¼ in. (Morand, pp. 20-21, 48-49, no. 15; Weale, pp. 151 ff.).

Yale MS. New Haven, Yale University Library: *Lancelot del Lac,* Pt. 3, Picard, late thirteenth century. 18¾ x 13½ in. (formerly Phillipps MS. 130; remainder: fr. 95). ("Eight Mediaeval Manuscripts," pp. 103-104; II, Loomis. pp. 95 ff.; III, Randall, "A Med. Slander," p. 27, and "The Snail," p. 359. Figs. 4-6, 41, 87, 97, 157, 172, 178, 183, 195, 236, 245, 299, 303, 334, 414, 457, 487, 499, 542, 561, 583, 706, 709).

LIST OF MANUSCRIPTS ACCORDING TO LIBRARIES

Arras
  Bibliothèque Municipale: MSS. 229, 302, 561, 639, 657, 725, 790, 1043
  Musée Diocésain: MS. 47

Baltimore, Walters Art Gallery: MSS. 37, 39, 41, 45, 82, 85, 87, 88, 90, 102, 104, 109, 110, 759-62 (W.) *

Belvoir Castle, Duke of Rutland Collection, Psalter (Rutland Ps.) *

Brussels, Bibliothèque Royale: MSS. 209, 329-41, 1175, 5163-64, 8469, 9157, 9217, 9391, 9411-26, 9427, 9433-34, 9543, 9961-62, 10228, 10607, 11040, 15001, II 988 (BBR) *

Cambrai, Bibliothèque Municipale: MSS. 87, 102-103, 133

Cambridge
  Corpus Christi College: MS. 53 (Corpus Christi) *
  Fitzwilliam Museum: MSS. 2-1954, 47, 48, 242, 288, 298; McLean Collection 41 (Fitz.; McLean) *
  Queens College: MS. 17 (Queens) *
  Trinity College Library: MSS. B.11.22, O.1.20 (Trinity) *
  University Library: MS. Dd.5.5 (Cambridge) *

Chantilly, Musée Condé: MSS. 62 (lat. 1423), 64 (lat. 1671)

Chartres, Bibliothèque Municipale: MS. 549 (destroyed)

Copenhagen, Kongelige Bibliotek: MSS. G.K.S. 393.2°, G.K.S. 3384.8°, N.K.S. 41.8°; Thott S. 547.4° (G.K.S., N.K.S., Thott) *

* refers to abbreviations used in Index of Subjects; unstarred references are found there cited under name of city.

Cracow Bibliothèque Jagellione: MSS. 815, 816

Dijon, Bibliothèque Municipale: MS. 113

Douai, Bibliothèque Municipale: MSS. 152, 171 (destroyed), 193

Dublin, A. Chester Beatty Library: MSS. 61, 62 (sold), 64 (sold) (C.B.) *

Florence, L. Olschki, *Settima del libro raro e antico* (1932), no. 4 (Olschki) *

Frankfurt, Kunstgewerbemuseum: MS. L.M. 13 (L.M.) *

Ghent, Bibliothèque de l'Université: MS. 233 (8)

The Hague, Koninklijke Biblioteek: MSS. 10.A.14, 10.B.21, 78.D.40, Koninklijke Akademie XX

Heidelberg, Universitätsbibliothek: MS. Cod. Sal. 9,51

Liège, Bibliothèque de l'Université: MS. 431

London
  British Museum
    Add. MSS. 10292-94, 17742, 17444, 17868, 21114, 21926, 24681, 24686, 28784B, 29253, 30029, 36684, 38114-15, 38116, 39810, 41751, 42130, 48985, 49622, 50000 (Add.) *
    Arundel MS. 83 (Arundel) *
    Burney MSS. 275, 345 (Burney) *
    Egerton MSS. 1151, 2781 (Egerton) *
    Harley MSS. 616, 928, 6563 (Harley) *
    Lansdowne MSS. 420, 451 (Lansdowne) *
    Royal MSS. 1 B.XII, 1 D.I, 2 B.VII, 3 D.VI, 10 E.IV, 14 B.V, 14 E.III, 17 E.VII, 20 D.IV (Royal) *
    Stowe MSS. 12, 17 (Stowe) *

Yates Thompson MSS. 8, 13, 15, 19, 27, 42 (Y.T.) *
Lambeth Palace Library: MSS. 209, 233 (Lambeth) *
Rosy Schilling Collection: Calendar (Schilling) *
Sotheby's, Clumber Library Sale, Dec. 6, 1937: Lot 938 (Clumber) *
Victoria and Albert Museum: no. 8997E (V. and A.) *
Malvern, C. W. Dyson Perrins Collection (formerly): MSS. 12, 35 (D.P.) *
Manchester, John Rylands Library: MSS. fr. 1-2, lat. R.16, lat. R.24, lat. R.117 (Rylands) *
Marseilles, Bibliothèque Municipale: MS. 111
Melbourne, National Gallery of Victoria: MS. 1254/3
Metz, Bibliothèque Municipale: MS. 43 (destroyed)
Montpellier, Bibliothèque de la faculté de médecine: MS. H.196
Munich, Bayerische Staatsbibliothek: Cod. gall. 16
Nancy, Bibliothèque Municipale: MS. 249
New Haven, Yale University Library, *Lancelot del Lac* (Yale MS.) *
New York
The Cloisters: MS. 54.1.2 (Cloisters) *
William S. Glazier Collection (on deposit at the Pierpont Morgan Library): MSS. 24, 53 (Glazier) *
H. P. Kraus (formerly), Catalogue no. 75: No. 88 (Kraus) *
Pierpont Morgan Library: MSS. 88, 102, 108, 149, 155, 183, 494, 729, 730, 754, 761, 796, 812 (M.) *
Public Library, Spencer Collection: MSS. 2, 26 (Spencer) *
Jacques Seligmann, *Illuminated Manuscripts from the Bibliothèque of . . . the Dukes d'Arenberg* (1952): No. 11 (Seligman) *
Norfolk, Holkham Hall, Library of the Earl of Leicester: MS. 458 (Holkham) *
Oxford
All Souls College: MSS. lat. 6, lat. 7 (All Souls) *
Bodleian Library
Ashmole MS. 828 (Ashmole) *
Auct. MSS. D.3.2, D.4.2, D.4.4 (Auct.) *
Bodley MS. 264 (Bodley) *
Douce MSS. 5-6, 23, 24, 48, 49, 118, 131, 366 (Douce) *
Lat. liturg. MS. f. 3 (lat. lit.) *
Laud Lat. MS. 84 (Laud. Lat.) *
Exeter College: MS. 47 (Exeter) *
Jesus College: MS. 40 (Jesus) *
Merton College: MS. 0.1.3 (Merton) *
Paris
Bibliothèque de l'Arsenal: MSS. 603, 5056, 5218, 6329 (Arsenal) *
Bibliothèque Mazarine: MS. 34 (Maz.) *
Bibliothèque Nationale: MSS. fr. 95, fr. 776, fr. 2754, fr. 6447, fr. 12400, fr. 25526; latin 1029A, 1052, 1076, 3893, 10435, 10483-84, 13260, 14284, 16260 (fr.; latin) *
Bibliothèque Sainte-Geneviève: MS. 777 (Ste. Gen.) *
Musée Jacquemart André: MS. 1 (Jacquemart) *
Rothschild Collection: Canticles of the Virgin (Rothschild) *
Princeton, Art Museum, Princeton University: MS. 44-18
Saint-Omer, Bibliothèque Municipale: MSS. 5, 595
Shenley (Herts.), Library of T. H. Riches, Esq.: Psalter (Riches Ps.)
Tournai
Bibliothèque Municipale: MS. CI (Tournai CI) *
Trésor de la Cathédrale: Psalter (Tournai Ps.) *
Troyes, Bibliothèque Municipale: MSS. 89, 898, 1905
Valenciennes, Bibliothèque Municipale: MS. 838
Verdun, Bibliothèque Municipale: MS. 107
Vienna, Österreichische Nationalbibliothek: MSS. 1826 *, 2542
Whereabouts Unknown: Formerly Henry Yates Thompson Collection: MS. 75 (Y.T. 75) *

GUIDE TO THE USE OF THE INDEX

A few words of explanation may serve to increase the efficacy of the index as a research tool:

Basic principles

1. Subjects are listed alphabetically according to participants. In the more complicated sections the entries are broken down into specific categories, for example, Ape and ape-child, Ape and ass, Ape and bear, with pertinent activities listed under each heading. Occasionally, as in a few of the lengthier entries under saints, the descriptions appear in order of folio number. An alphabetical sequence here would have proved unwieldy and less clear.

2. Figures holding objects are cited as "with," for example, Cleric with book. The same method is used for figures playing musical instruments, as Man with bagpipe, Man with trumpet. An entry such as Hybrid man and hare fighting with sword, club and buckler refers to the weapons used by the respective opponents.

Cross-references

1. These serve to point out analogies as well as variations on a theme. They also refer occasionally to other noteworthy motifs appearing on the same page but listed under a separate heading.

2. Additional material of possible interest is cited under key words. Thus, for instance, under Bagpipe, Bestiary, and Games are listed references to pertinent entries appearing throughout the index.

Parenthetical notations

1. Additional descriptive detail or otherwise pertinent information appears in parentheses following the folio number, as for Boar, Bestiary representation: Munich c.g. 16, f. 32 (in cycle); Giant and knight . . . (fabliau?).

2. Arabic numerals refer to the number of principal participants. Thus, Bee and dog, stinging: Stowe 17, f. 48 (2) indicates that there are two bees. Numbers written out refer to the number of secondary participants. Thus, Boar and dog, attacked by: Royal 2 B.VII, f. 145 (three) indicates that three dogs are shown attacking.

3. A possible connection between the marginal motif and its context is suggested by references to the adjoining miniature (Min.) and/or text.

4. Parenthetical figure numbers set in italic type, as (*fig. 26*), refer to illustrations in the present book.

Illustrations and captions

1. The illustrations appear in alphabetical sequence according to the order of the subject entries in the Index.

2. The captions are curtailed forms of the Index entries. When more than one motif is illustrated on a page, the subjects are listed as they appear in the margins, beginning with the most significant motif (generally shown at the foot of the page) and proceeding around the text from this point on.

3. Parentheses are used in the captions to set off motifs such as isolated birds which appear in the illustrations but are not included in the Index. In certain instances, as in the series of figures labeled "Musical instruments, parody," parentheses are also used to enclose the main heading, since the themes depicted are listed individually in the Index. In this way related subjects can be shown together as a group.

Word of warning

Because of variables in certain of the manuscripts, such as multiple pagination, lack of pagination, and state of preservation, it is advisable when ordering photographs from the respective libraries to cite both the folio number and the specific subject required.

Index of Subjects

A

Aaron *see* Moses
Abacus *see* Man with
Abbess (*see also* Hybrid abbess; Patrons: Marguerite; Virgin, miracles of)
  hand raised, blessing(?): W. 87, f. 63v (below, cock)
  with book: Douce 118, f. 125v (kneeling); W. 87, ff. 69v (winged), 102v (below, nude man climbing up border stalk)
  with gittern: Laud Lat. 84, f. 361v
  with hand bell: W. 87, f. 11
  with vielle: Laud Lat. 84, f. 361v
Abbot (*see also* Butterfly, ringing; Hybrid abbot; Hybrid man with hand bells; St. Dunstan): Add. 42130, f. 55v; BBR 1175, ff. 81, 88
  and clerics: Hague 78.D.40, ff. 109 (two, at lectern) (*fig. 1*), 155 (three; at R., winged lion)
  kneeling, praying: Cambrai 103, f. 587v
  with book: M. 754, f. 101
Abdias (Obadiah): Y.T. 13, f. 45v
Abel *see* Cain and
Abigail *see* David, life of: D. and
Abishag *see* David, life of: D. and
Abner *see* David, life of: —: D. and; —: D. and Goliath; —: D. and Joab; —: D. and Saul
Abraham *see also* Dives and Lazarus
Abraham and Isaac, sacrificing: Munich c.g. 16, f. 29v; Spencer 26, f. 6; St. Omer 5, f. 170; Y.T. 8, f. 199; Y.T. 13, ff. 25v-26
Abraham and Ishmael: Munich c.g. 16, f. 28v
Abraham and Sarah, casting forth Hagar and Ishmael, who are comforted by angel: Munich c.g. 16, f. 28v
  promise of son: Munich c.g. 16, f. 26v
  receiving the three angels: Munich c.g. 16, f. 27v
Absalom *see also* David, life of: D. and
Absalom hanged: Spencer 2, f. 69v
Achan *see* Joshua
Achilles and Hector, parody?: fr. 95, f. 345 (ape astride horse, dragging ape tied by feet)
Achisch *see* David, life of: D. and
Acorns *see* Man and pigs
Acrobat *see* Tumbler, references under
Acteon (?) *see* Hybrid man with stag horns; Man in costume as stag
Adam *cf.* Ape with fruit; *see also* Vices: Apostasy
Adam and Eve
  Creation: Add. 39810, f. 7 (of Eve) (*fig. 140*); Auct. D.4.4, f. 1 (of Eve); Munich c.g. 16, f. 9v; Spencer 26, ff. 4-4v; Stowe 17, f. 24v; Y.T. 13, ff. 19-19v
  Expulsion from Paradise: Add. 39810, f. 7 (fig. 140); Munich c.g. 16, f. 10v; Spencer 26, f. 5v; Stowe 17, f. 29 (*fig. 2*); Y.T. 13, ff. 22v-23
  Fall of: Add. 39810, f. 7 (*fig. 140*); Spencer 26, f. 5; Y.T. 13, f. 20v
  injunction to: Spencer 26, f. 5
  kneeling before Creator: Add. 39810, f. 7 (*fig. 140*)
  marriage of: Spencer 26, f. 4v
  parodied (?), ape offering fruit to ape: Glazier 24, f. 84v
  reproved: Spencer 26, f. 5v
  under tree of knowledge: fr. 6447, f. 10; latin 10483, f. 7; Spencer 26, f. 5v; Stowe 17, ff. 26v, 27; Y.T. 13, f. 20

A with half-figure of angel with trumpet: M. 761, f. 10
Adam delving
addressed by angel: Y.T. 13, ff. 23v-24
Eve spinning: Add. 39810, f. 7 (*fig. 140*); Stowe 17, f. 32 (Abel on lap, Cain playing with spindle)
Eve with distaff and spindle: Yale MS., f. 169 (Min.: Cain and Abel sacrificing) (*figs. 4-6*)
receiving spade from angel: Stowe 17, f. 31v
Adam naming creatures: Auct. D.4.4, f. 1 (in presence of Eve); Spencer 26, f. 4
Adonijah *see* David, life of
Adoration of Magi *see* Jesus Christ, life of
Adoration of Shepherds *see* Jesus Christ, life of
Aesop's fables *see* Fables
Ages of man *see* Man in bed
Agony in the Garden *see* Jesus Christ, life of
Agriculture *see* references listed under Cycles and specific activities
Ahimaaz *see* David, life of: D. and Absalom: Jonathan and
Ahimelech *see* David, life of: D. and Saul
Ahinoam *see* David, life of: D. and Abigail
Ai *see* Joshua
Alexander, episodes from Romance of: Bodley 264
combat between Cassians and Caulus: ff. 153v-154
combats between Emenidus and Porras: ff. 152, 156
death mourned by hooded men: ff. 190 (eight), 191v (four), 193 (six)
death mourned by hooded men and women: f. 191 (four, four)
death revenged by son: ff. 196v-204
Enoch's illicit bath, walled up in tower: f. 67v
enthroned, seeking cause of fire and snow, consequences: ff. 68v-69
episode of undrinkable water: ff. 183-184v
Gadifer, armed: f. 137v
in armor, astride horse: f. 66
journey in boat with followers: ff. 144-148
journey to Trees of the Sun and the Moon: f. 72v
misadventure with women who lived in the water: f. 66v
Queen Teminie: f. 97 (under tree, with three peacocks)
Alexander III *see* St. Thomas of Canterbury
Alms
given by king: Royal 10 E.IV, ff. 261-262v
given by man to cripple on hand trestles with bowl in mouth: W. 82, f. 193v
given by man to cripple on wheelbarrow: Add. 42130, f. 186v
given by man to pilgrim with bowl: G.K.S. 3384, f. 78
given by woman to cripple: Douce 118, f. 50
Altar *see* Angel at; Ape as bishop, before; Ape as cleric, before; —, patting; Cleric at; Man kneeling; Nun kneeling; Woman at; Woman praying
Amalekites *see* David, life of: D. and
Amasa *see* David, life of: D. and Joab
Amminadab and Aram: Y.T. 13, f. 32 (Genealogy of Christ)
Ammon *see* David, life of: Ammon; —: D. and Joab
Ammonites *see* David, life of: D. and
Amnon *see* David, life of: D. and Absalom, servants of
Amon: Y.T. 13, f. 51 (Genealogy of Christ)
Amos: Y.T. 13, f. 39v
Amphisbaena (?) (*see also* Man nude and dragon, astride): Royal 2 B.VII, f. 138v (2, necks interlaced); Rutland Ps., f. 82 (before nude man astride dragon's tail)
Amputation *see* Virgin, miracles of: Pope Leo; —: woodcutter
Amusements *see* Games, references listed under
Ananias *see* St. Paul
Angel *see also* Abraham and Sarah; Adam and Eve, with; Adam delving; Ape as; Hybrid angel; Jacob wrestling with; King in bed; Miniature; St. Catherine; St. Christina; St. Denis; St. Margaret; St. Mary Magdalene; St. Mary the Egyptian; St. Peter; Saints
Angel at altar, cleric conducting Mass, man kneeling: fr. 25526, f. 146
Angel, Evangelist symbol *see* Evangelist symbols, St. Matthew
Angel leading nude couple toward tower: Cambrai 87, f. 51 (saint?)
Angel nude, asleep, with arm around small lion: Rutland Ps., f. 53v
Angel with bagpipe (*see also* Angel with hand organ): Y.T. 75, f. 65v
Angel with bat wings: M. 729, f. 338 (and large gloves)
Angel with book, others with censer, candlesticks: Add. 42130, f. 102v (4; f. 103: Jesus Christ showing wounds)
Angel with censer (*see also* Pilgrim, beggar; Procession, angels): Add. 36684, ff. 69v-75

(Litany), 83; BBR 9391, f. 111 (Hours of the Virgin, Vespers; Min.: Death of the Virgin); Jacquemart 1, f. 90; M. 754, f. 64; Melbourne 1254/3, f. 48
and incense boat: BBR 329-41, f. 72 (hybrid; Min.: Clerics with reliquary); Douce 118, ff. 93v, 151; latin 10483, f. 324 (hybrid)
another with trumpet: Cambridge Dd. 5.5, f. 280 (Min.: Assumption of the Virgin)
before God the Father: Stowe 17, f. 25 (another with taper)
others with candles, incense boat, and spoon approaching church or shrine: Add. 42130, f. 103v (5)
saint at tomb: Valenciennes 838, f. 55v (at R., saint at altar) (*fig. 629*)
Angel with gittern: fr. 95, f. 1 (Min.: Trinity); Stowe 17, ff. 23 (in Creation cycle), 47, 66, 104v, 219v
Angel with gold disk (sun?): Douce 6, f. 87 (below, man praying)
Angel with hand organ: fr. 95, f. 1 (Min.: Trinity); Rylands fr. 1, f. 82 (*fig. 3*); Stowe 17, ff. 22v (in Creation cycle), 65v, 211v; W. 104, f. 28 (hybrid; another with vielle)
Angel with hand organ, others with bagpipe, mandola, psaltery, timbrel, vielles: BBR 9157, f. 4v
Angel with harp (*see also* St. Mary the Egyptian): Douce 48, f. 205v (Min.: Nativity); fr. 776, f. 1 (Min.: Trinity); Stowe 17, ff. 21v (in Creation cycle), 65v, 138v (at R., Harrowing of Hell), 173v (Litany)
another with vielle: W. 104, f. 70v
others with gittern, psaltery, trumpet, vielle: M. 183, f. 141v
Angel with mandola (*see also* Angel with hand organ): fr. 95, f. 1 (Min.: Trinity); Princeton 44-18, ff. 126, 193
Angel with psaltery (*see also* Angel with hand organ): Stowe 17, ff. 220, 270 (below, Death of Virgin)
another with bagpipe: BBR 9157, f. 1
others with trumpet, vielle: D.P. 35, f. 56v
Angel with scroll (*see also* Evangelist symbols): Auct. D.3.2, f. 360 (Gospel of St. Matthew, beginning); Stowe 17, ff. 220v (beside Annunciation), 257v (below, Flight into Egypt), 264v (Annunciation to shepherds)
Angel with shield and spear: latin 16260, f. 198
Angel with soul *see* Jesus Christ, life of: Last Judgment: Pains of Hell
Angel with timbrel (*see also* Angel with hand organ): Stowe 17, f. 129 (man playing organ)
Angel with trumpet (*see also* Jesus Christ, life of: Last Judgment: Pains of Hell): Add. 49622, f. 10v; BBR 9961-62, f. 65; BBR 10607, f. 175v (Min.: Nativity); Douce 48, f. 205v; Jacquemart 1, f. 113v (at R., man rending dragon); Lambeth 233, f. 101 (2; Ps. 68); St. Omer 5, f. 138v; W. 45, f. 279 (Offices of the Dead)
Angel with trumpet, woman kneeling at altar: Nancy 249, f. 94v
Angel with vielle: Add. 28784B, f. 7 (Min.: Virgin and Child); BBR 10607, f. 170v (at R., three birds in nest); Stowe 17, ff. 66, 174 (Litany), 187v (Min.: Harrowing of Hell), 211v, 271 (below, Assumption of the Virgin); W. 87, f. 52v; W. 104, ff. 28 (hybrid; another with hand organ), 70v (another with harp)
Angel writing: latin 10483, f. 111v (at R., church, St. Matthew?)
Angels
adoring Jesus *see* Jesus Christ, head of
fighting many-headed devils: Add. 42130, f. 101 (4, including Sts. Michael and Gabriel)
procession of: *see* Procession, angels
supporting aureole containing Jesus Christ, blessing: latin 10483, f. 213
supporting coat of arms of England: Christ Church E.II, ff. 1v, 58, 70
with instruments of the Passion *see* Jesus Christ, life of: Passion
with musical instruments (*see also* under Angel with): Y.T. 75, f. 185
Animal trainer *see* Ape and bear; — and hare; Hare and bear; Man and ape; — and bear; — and horse
Annunciation to Magi *see* Jesus Christ, life of
Annunciation to Virgin *see* Virgin, life of
Anselm *see* Virgin, miracles of
Ant, Bestiary representation (in cycle): Munich c.g. 16, f. 26; Royal 2 B.VII, ff. 95v-96
Antelope
Bestiary representation (in cycle): Munich c.g. 16, f. 10; Royal 2 B.VII, ff. 87v-88
pursued by ape and fox: Hague 78.D.40, f. 64v
pursued by boar: Hague 78.D.40, f. 53v
pursued by centaur: Hague 78.D.40, f. 130
pursued by fox: Hague 78.D.40, f. 98v
with gittern *see* Ass with pipe

A

Ants and grasshoppers, fable: Trinity B.11.22, f. 125
Ape *see also* Hybrid ape; Obscaena; St. Mary the Egyptian
Ape and ape-child (*see also* Procession, funeral of fox): latin 14284, f. 47v (at R., running hare)
approached by ape with staff, three young on back: Royal 10 E.IV, f. 152
approached by man (Bestiary variant?): Douce 5, f. 115v
approaching ape-child in crib: Hague 78.D.40, f. 22v (large bird aiming beak at ape's hindquarters; at R., second ape with paddle doing laundry?)
bearing in arms: M. 183, f. 85v (at L., ape with club and buckler; Ps. 68)
begging *see* Ape as beggar
Ape and ass (*see also* Ape and owl, as falconer)
astride: N.K.S. 41, f. 154v
in procession *see* Procession, ape
singing at lectern: Glazier 24, f. 48 (2)
Ape and bear (*see also* Ape with pitcher; Man and woman, throwing fruit)
astride: Harley 928, f. 12
as bishop, holding document, approaching kneeling ape: Douce 6, f. 128v
bear tied to post, with whip: W. 102, f. 29v (line ending)
with hammer and shield: Douce 49, f. 65v (bear or lion; Min.: Flagellation; Ps. 52)
confronted, ape pleading(?) with raised hands, open mouth: Harley 6563, ff. 75v-76
confronted, ape talking, gesturing: Royal 10 E.IV, f. 66v
pulling rope attached to bear cub(?) held by bear(?): G.K.S. 3384, f. 227
pursued by, ape in tree, bear standing against trunk while second bear devours ape on ground: Royal 10 E.IV, f. 151v (*fig. 9*)
pursued by, ape pulling wheelbarrow containing three young, ape with two young in arms in tree (Bestiary variant?): Y.T. 13, ff. 183v-185
school of apes observed by chained bear: Stowe 17, ff. 108v-109
tilting, astride beasts: Christ Church E.II, f. 51v
training, bear chained, goat with pipe, boar with tabor: Arsenal 5218, f. 88
training, bear chained to tree: Royal 10 E.IV, ff. 154, 155v
training(?), holding on chain: C.B. 62, f. 196v
training with horn, bear doing handstand: M. 729, f. 265
Ape and beast
fighting with club and buckler: Tournai Ps., f. 215
fighting with spear: G.K.S. 3384, f. 301v
kissing: Douce 6, f. 113 (ape with dish, standing by tub)
rending: G.K.S. 3384, f. 235 (above, man with triangle)
shooting: Tournai Ps., ff. 234, 236; W. 87, ff. 39v-40
tilting, astride cat and fox: M. 729, f. 346
Ape and bees, pursued by, holding horn: Add. 10293, f. 1 (two, hovering over hindquarters)
Ape and beggar *see* Beggar crippled
Ape and bird (*see also* Ape and cock; — and crane; Ape as cleric; — as falconer; — as physician; Ape seated; Ape with bagpipe; Bandyball; Man with pipe and tabor)
crawling toward: G.K.S. 3384, f. 102v (man with pipe and tabor); W. 90, f. 50v (falcon?)
feeding with spoon from bowl: Douce 6, f. 86v
holding: Tournai Ps., ff. 50v, 239v; W. 45, f. 161
holding, offering round object to hybrid bishop: Tournai Ps., f. 76v
hunting with bow and arrow: Add. 29253, f. 351v; Add. 49622, f. 195; Arsenal 5218, ff. 15 (second ape holding string tied to ape's ankle), 81 (*fig. 563*); Bodley 264, f. 57v; Cambrai 102, f. 275v; Cambrai 103, f. 421; Douai 193, f. 101; Princeton 44-18, ff. 71v-72; Stowe 17, ff. 54v-55, 189v-190; Tournai Ps., ff. 94v, 144; W. 45, f. 273; W. 85, f. 79v; W. 110, f. 44v; Y.T. 27, f. 1 (at L., hare with trumpet)
hunting with club: Bodley 264, f. 54v; Douce 118, f. 35v (forked stick); Glazier 24, f. 98v; Y.T. 8, f. 202
hunting with crossbow: Add. 30029, f. 12v (stork/duck)
hunting with lure: Arsenal 5218, f. 1
hunting with lure, accompanied by ape with tabor: BBR 9391, f. 112v
patting *see* Ape as cleric
patting, imitating woman holding falcon and lure: Nancy 249, f. 150 (*fig. 8*)
pulling tail of: M. 754, f. 1v
snaring with clapnet: Fitz. 298, f. 32v; G.K.S. 3384, f. 225v; Tournai Ps., ff. 124v, 196v; W. 82, f. 75v (*fig. 10*)

snaring with decoy: Add. 29253, f. 416v (below, bandyball, apes); BBR 9391, f. 94v; BBR II 988, v. II, f. 165v; Cambrai 102, f. 8; Chartres 549, f. 42v; Douce 5, f. 110; Douce 6, ff. 51, 90 (ape with knife; at R., birdcage, tree, fox tied to stake, examined by five birds in air and on ground; *cf.* Woman and bird, snaring); Fitz. 298, f. 45; G.K.S. 3384, ff. 225v (3), 294v; Harley 78.D.40, f. 23v (2, one holding owl); Laud lat. 84, f. 359; Princeton 44-18, ff. 71v-72 (above, owl), 95v-96, 201v-202 (*fig.* 7); Rothschild MS., f. 133v; Stowe 17, ff. 54v-55 (2); Tournai Ps., ff. 24 (2), 27, 230; W. 45, f. 41v (above, two birds in nest); W. 104, f. 28 (2) (*fig. 11*)
and birdcage: M. 754, f. 54 (bird aiming beak at hindquarters); W. 88, f. 142; W. 90, f. 119v
and clapnet: Tournai Ps., ff. 124v, 196v (*see above,* —, snaring with clapnet)
snaring with net: Arsenal 5218, f. 1; G.K.S. 3384, ff. 8v, 127; Hague 78.D.40, f. 132 (at L., birdcage containing two birds); latin 1029A, f. 23v; Nancy 249, f. 195v
stealing from nest: Christ Church E.II, f. 38v; Douce 5, f. 202
stealing from nest by scaling ladder, second ape with book: Douce 6, f. 99v (3)
stepping on tail of, pointing up at squirrel: Stowe 17, f. 100
Ape and bishop
blessed by: Douce 5, ff. 117v (with book), 132 (3, one seated on hill or in water and beaten by other two)
kneeling before, with book (*see also* Ape and hybrid bishop): Douce 6, f. 102v (bird aiming beak at ape's hindquarters)
Ape and boar
astride backwards, biting tail of: Stowe 17, f. 35
astride, blowing large spoon like trumpet: Stowe 17, f. 173v
hunting: Add. 49622, f. 8; Hague 78.D.40, ff. 50v, 101v, 125
hunting with club: Hague 78.D.40, f. 148v; Rothschild MS., f. 127
leading on rope, with staff: Stowe 17, f. 263v
Ape and bull, offering cup to: Glazier 24, f. 150
Ape and butterfly (*cf.* Hybrid ape and)
holding in hand: latin 10483, f. 28v
pursuing: Bodley 264, f. 67; Laud Lat. 84, f. 293
with hood (blue): Bodley 264, f. 45v
with hood (red), second ape with churn: Arsenal 5218, f. 40
shooting: Arsenal 5218, f. 75; Royal 14 E.III, f. 89
snaring with decoy: G.K.S. 3384, f. 9v
Ape and camel, astride: Chantilly 64, f. 30; Y.T. 19, f. 18 (2, with swords and shields)
Ape and cat
fishing, catch stolen by (*cf.* Ape and fox): Hague 78.D.40, ff. 44, 105
hanging: W. 88, f. 47v
shooting: Harley 928, f. 97v (cat or fox on tall tower)
stalking: Harley 928, f. 44v (cat with mouse)
Ape and centaur *see* Centaur and ape
Ape and child (*cf.* Ape and ape-child)
by fire, cradle nearby: Douce 6, f. 87v
holding: Add. 29253, f. 36
mother looking in empty cradle: Stowe 17, ff. 189v-190
pursued by dog and distraught mother with distaff and spindle: Add. 10292, f. 76 (at R., ape-child in cradle tended by ape) (*fig. 106*)
Ape and cleric *see* Ape balancing, on pole; Cleric and ape
Ape and cock (*see also* Ape as cleric, before altar; Ape as falconer; — as physician; Ape astride)
astride, tilting with ape astride goose: Y.T. 8, f. 176
pulled by, in cart: Y.T. 8, f. 192v (2)
with stick, encouraging cockfight: Douce 118, f. 125
Ape and crane (*cf.* Ape and stork; Ape with basket on back)
astride: Add. 24686, f. 12; Rothschild MS., f. 110 (hare with trumpet); Trinity B.11.22, f. 165v
bridled crane: Douce 5, f. 211v
with spear and shield, charging nude man: Rutland Ps., ff. 66v-67 (ostrich?)
exposing hindquarters to *see* Obscaena, beak aimed
fighting: Rothschild MS., ff. 165, 171v (pygmy astride ape)
holding beak open: Y.T. 75, f. 36
seated in chair, receiving document with red seal in crane's beak: Kraus 75/88, f. 19v (ape/cleric?) (*fig. 13*)
shooting: Add. 24686, f. 11; Cambrai 133, f. 392; Ghent 233, f. 27; latin 3893, f. 98 (at R., bird aiming beak at hindquarters of man)

A

Ape and dog
as tumbler, dog with hurdy-gurdy: Harley 6563, f. 42
astride: G.K.S. 3384, f. 194v
approaching man astride dog: Tournai Ps., f. 207 (at R., ape with fruit)
pulling fox, followed by second ape: Trinity B.11.22, f. 22
pulling harrow: W. 88, f. 85v
tilting at quintain: N.K.S. 41, f. 181
tilting with ape astride hare: Princeton 44-18, ff. 151v-152
with buckler, riding toward ape with buckler astride hare: Princeton 44-18, ff. 50v-51 (above, nude man with pipe and tabor)
with distaff and spindle, accompanied by ape with spindle and reel, ape with harp: Rylands fr. 1, f. 82
with fruit: Glazier 24, f. 151v
with shield and spear, charging hybrid ape (female) with book: Princeton 44-18, ff. 203v-204
with shield and spear, charging three apes: Princeton 44-18, ff. 202v-203
attacking hare: Trinity B.11.22, f. 19
biting neck of: Add. 36684, f. 47
biting tail of: Douce 5, f. 207; Glazier 24, f. 71v (dog irate, swinging pan or flabellum)
dancing, dog with pipe and tabor, hare with trumpet: Hague 78.D.40, f. 21
fishing, catch stolen by: BBR II 988, vol. II, f. 193v (dog or fox)
leading on rope: BBR II 988, vol. II, f. 229v (at R., ape with ?pipe)
leading on rope, with trumpet: lat. lit. f. 3, f. 95v (2, three)
pursued by: M. 754, f. 102v; Y.T. 8, f. 272
ridden by: Harley 6563, f. 6v
seated, receiving document from dog with javelin (*cf.* Ape and crane, seated): Trinity B.11.22, f. 20 (*fig. 508*)
tilting on foot: Tournai Ps., f. 190 (pig's head on ape's shield)
training: G.K.S. 3384, ff. 227, 268
Ape and dragon
as physician, ministering to cowering dragon: Arsenal 5218, f. 15
astride, plunging sword into jaws of (Samson parody?): Arsenal 5218, f. 176v
bitten in head by: G.K.S. 3384, f. 229
confronting with club: W. 39, f. 30
fighting with ax: G.K.S. 3384, f. 268v
fighting with club, buckler: G.K.S. 3384, f. 170v
fighting with scourge: M. 754, f. 47v (dragon or dog)
shooting: Cambrai 103, f. 400v (flames issuing from dragon's mouth); G.K.S. 3384, f. 193; W. 110, f. 136v
Ape and elephant, astride behind castle, with switch: Stowe 17, f. 36
Ape and fish
eating: Stowe 17, f. 161
eating, placing another in hindquarters: Stowe 17, f. 83
Ape and fox (*see also* Ape as king, with trumpet; Fox, Bestiary representation; Hybrid ape with vielle)
as cleric patting bird, fox reaching for cock on column by altar: Cambrai 103, f. 384
as falconer, followed by: Royal 14 E. III, f. 294
as physician, ministering to: Cambrai 102, f. 294
as pilgrim astride horse, approaching ape shooting fox or cat on castle: Harley 928, f. 97v
astride backwards, beating tabor: Fitz. 242, f. 55v (*fig. 12*)
astride, tilting with ape astride cock: Hague 78.D.40, f. 44v
back to back with: latin 3893, f. 347
defending castle against ass, hares, foxes: Stowe 17, ff. 243v-244
fishing, catch stolen by: Arras 229, f. 655; BBR II 988, vol. II, f. 193v (dog?); Cambrai 103, f. 313
hunting antelope: Hague 78.D.40, f. 64v
leading on rope: Cambrai 102, f. 5v (at L., hybrid beast with spear)
ridden by: Add. 49622, f. 218v
seated with bowl, fox looking over ape's shoulder: BBR II 988, vol. II, f. 262v (at R., ape as cleric and bird)
tilting, astride dragons backwards: M. 729, f. 389
wrestling: Y.T. 8, f. 179
Ape and giant, receiving bowl from: G.K.S. 3384, f. 37
Ape and goat (*see also* Ape as falconer)
astride: Harley 6563, f. 91v; Rothschild MS., f. 176; Y.T. 8, f. 172v
applauding cockfight (*cf.* Ape and cock): latin 1029A, f. 27 (*fig. 134*)
backwards: BBR 9961-62, f. 14 (at L., man shooting owl) (*fig. 388*); Cambridge Dd. 5.5, f. 403

backwards with sword and buckler, shot by man: Stowe 17, ff. 213v-214
fighting ape astride boar, with sword and buckler, spear with impaled fowl: Stowe 17, f. 82
fighting pig astride goat: M. 729, f. 311
tilting at quintain: Melbourne 1254/3, f. 61
tilting with ape, basket as helmet: G.K.S. 3384, f. 229v
wearing doctor's cap: Add. 49622, f. 218v
with horn: Douce 118, f. 163; Melbourne 1254/3, f. 26v; Y.T. 8, f. 280v
with trumpet: Royal 2 B.VII, f. 194v
with whip: BBR 9157, f. 411v
bearing on shoulders, goat with bagpipe: Rothschild MS., f. 158
confronted, seizing by horns: W. 88, f. 94
feeding with spoon from gold bowl: Douce 5, f. 129 (ape in female dress)
holding, knife in hand: Stowe 17, f. 88v (Min.: Flagellation)
Ape and goose, astride, tilting with ape astride snail (*cf.* Ape and cock): Cambrai 103, f. 95
Ape and hare (*see also* Ape fishing, hare)
approaching burrow with axe: Trinity B.11.22, f. 137v (hare looking out)
as falconer, hunting astride dog: Douce 366, f. 147v
as falconer, hunting astride lion, gold owl on wrist: fr. 776, f. 18 (at R., ape with spear)
as king, borne by two hares toward tent of ape-queen: Y.T. 8, ff. 295v-296 (*figs. 33-34*)
astride, tilting at quintain: G.K.S. 3384, f. 279
astride, tilting with ape astride dog: Princeton 44-18, ff. 151v-152
confronted: Douce 5, f. 143
conversing with: Tournai Ps., f. 57
conversing with hare-cleric reading book: Y.T. 8, f. 293v
fighting with spear: Add. 29253, f. 41
holding: Tournai Ps., f. 60
hunting astride collapsing horse: Add. 49622, f. 65
hunting astride dog, as falconer: Douce 366, f. 147v
hunting astride hybrid horse with bird's head, wearing coif, with club: Add. 49622, f. 135
hunting astride lion, as falconer, gold owl on wrist: fr. 776, f. 18 (at R., ape with spear)
hunting astride lionesque beast, with spear and shield: Princeton 44-18, ff. 151v-152
hunting, carrying hare on stick over shoulder: Nancy 249, f. 4v (*fig. 16*)
hunting hare and stag with hounds: Glazier 24, f. 69 (two hounds)
hunting with bow and arrow: Add. 49622, ff. 8, 46v, 90v; Christ Church E.II, f. 33 (hare also with bow and arrow); Stowe 17, ff. 147v-148; W. 82, f. 210v
hunting with club (*see above,* —, hunting astride hybrid horse): BBR 329-41, f. 72
hunting with club, horn, astride dragon backwards: Royal 14 E.III, f. 140 (at L., owl)
hunting with horn, hound: BBR 9433-34, f. 1 (at R., hare with vielle); fr. 25526, f. 31v
hunting with sack: G.K.S. 3384, f. 63v; W. 82, f. 210v (hare with purse around neck)
hunting with spear: Arsenal 5218, f. 70v; Melbourne 1254/3, f. 119v
prodding with pole: Douce 5, f. 5v (at L., unicorn; at R., stork with frog; October)
pulling ears of: Trinity B.11.22, f. 42v (hanging by ears?); Y.T. 8, f. 291v
pumping bellows for hare at organ: Add. 49622, f. 67v
pursuing: G.K.S. 3384, ff. 81, 99v (at L., scribe)
ridden by: Y.T. 8, ff. 198 (with club), 298v (hare with horn, preceded by hound)
shot by: Christ Church E.II, f. 33 (ape hunting stag)
standing on nose of, holding purse or flask: Cloisters 54.1.2, f. 69v
trained by: Add. 49622, f. 84
Ape and horse
astride (*see also* Ape and hare, hunting astride; Ape as falconer, astride): Add. 49622, f. 142 (horse collapsing)
charging hybrid beast with shield: Royal 2 B.VII, f. 139v (ape with shield and spear)
dragging second ape tied by feet (Hector and Achilles parody?): fr. 95, f. 345
fighting snail, with spear: BBR 9391, f. 94; W. 90, f. 194
leading coach containing two female apes, with spear: Douce 6, f. 200v
man training horse to kick buckler with hind legs: Douce 5, f. 98v
plowing: W. 88, f. 85v
riding away from ape: Y.T. 15, f. 307v
tilting at hooded head issuing from border: W. 110, f. 36v

tilting with ape astride horse: W. 90, f. 75; Yale MS., f. 126
with club, wearing coif: Add. 49622, f. 125 (horse with bird's head)
with spear, followed by hound: W. 90, f. 203
beating: Add. 49622, f. 142
falling off: Douce 5, f. 20v
standing on, aiming stick backwards between legs: Stowe 17, f. 124
standing on, with sword and buckler: Glazier 24, f. 80v

Ape and hybrid beast
astride: W. 88, f. 122v
charging with spear and shield: Royal 2 B.VII, f. 139v (hybrid beast with shield)
singing from book (reciting?), ape with switch (*cf.* School, attended by apes): Glazier 24, f. 76

Ape and hybrid bishop (*see also* Obscaena, sword aimed; Obscaena, exposing)
fighting, with sword and buckler: Add. 30029, f. 55
praying or confessing to: Douce 5, ff. 22, 71; Princeton 44-18, ff. 63v-64
pursuing: latin 16260, f. 536 (hybrid bishop with two bells; at L., nude hybrid man with knife)

Ape and hybrid dragon, astride backwards, hunting hare with club and horn: Royal 14 E.III, f. 140

Ape and hybrid king, approaching: fr. 776, f. 117v

Ape and hybrid man (*see also* Ape playing organ; Hybrid man pruning)
arguing: All Souls lat. 6, f. 13 (man/lion)
astride nude hybrid man, with spear and stool basket: Glazier 24, f. 73v
astride, with club and buckler, shot by second hybrid man: Stowe 17, ff. 223v-224
biting beak of: M. 108, f. 134v
conversing: Tournai Ps., ff. 64v, 84
doing handstand, hybrid man with spear: Cambrai 103, f. 356v
fighting with club: G.K.S. 3384, f. 181v; Tournai Ps., f. 34
fighting with stick and buckler: Tournai Ps., f. 52v
fighting with swords and bucklers: Add. 49622, f. 68v; G.K.S. 3384, f. 274v; Stowe 17, ff. 40v-41
pointing to place in book read by hybrid man, with staff: Add. 10293, f. 1
shooting: G.K.S. 3384, f. 115v; Tournai Ps., f. 89
shot by: Add. 36684, f. 14v; Stowe 17, ff. 32v-33

Ape and hybrid woman
astride, with crested helmet, spear, shield: M. 796, f. 67v
beckoning to, in tall boots, hood: latin 14284, f. 48
stroking cheek of: W. 759, f. 32v

Ape and knight
as knight, astride horse, charging knight: Stowe 17, f. 94v (below, cock and hen mating) (*fig. 15*)
astride hybrid bird, tilting with: Stowe 17, f. 121v
confronted, ape with weighted club(?), knight with sword and shield: Douce 5, f. 135
doing handstand before nude helmeted knight pleading: Douce 5, f. 37v
fighting knight on horse (in initial) defended by two dragons: Yale MS., f. 272v (2)
fighting with club and basket, knight with spear: Douce 6, f. 152
pleading for mercy, knight unsheathing sword: Add. 49622, ff. 136, 137v
showing hindquarters to knight charging on horse, brandishing falchion: W. 90, f. 78v (*fig. 298*)
with basin, catching blood dripping from head of monster held by knight: Douce 5, f. 167v
with club, beating on head, sword flying out of knight's hand: Douce 5, f. 121
with sword and shield, challenging knight on horse with spear and shield: Stowe 17, ff. 79v-80 (*fig. 14*)

Ape and lion
astride as falconer: fr. 776, f. 18 (pursuing hare); W. 90, f. 34
astride with banner: Y.T. 8, f. 276 (f. 275v, ape with trumpet)
astride with club, pursuing wild man astride stag: Bodley 264, f. 95
astride with switch: latin 14284, f. 38
confronted: Fitz. 298, f. 2v
ape chained: Melbourne 1254/3, f. 7
seated: W. 109, f. 316
fighting with sword and buckler: BBR II 988, vol. II, f. 266
held on leash by man: BBR 9157, f. 4v (two apes)
holding on leash, lion fighting with another: Hague 78.D.40, f. 152v
pulling tail of lion with sheep between paws,

others poking hindquarters, pulling sheep's tail: Royal 17 E.VII, f. 1 (*figs. 18, 19*)
pursuing: Hague 78.D.40, f. 83v (at R., dog pursuing hare)
rending (David or Samson parody?): Y.T. 8, f. 197v (*fig. 17*)
with vielle, lion dancing: Add. 49622, f. 35

Ape and man *see* Man and ape

Ape and mermaid, doing handstand on tail of mermaid suckling her child: Add. 24686, f. 13

Ape and merman with pipe, dancing: Glazier 24, f. 137v

Ape and nun *see* Nun and ape

Ape and offspring *see* Ape and ape-child

Ape and owl (*cf.* Ape pruning border; Ape with arrow)
aiming lure at: Arundel 83, f. 40v (Ps. 52)
as falconer
owl flying off: Stowe 17, f. 270
owl on branch nearby: Fitz. 298, f. 136v
owl on fist: Add. 42130, f. 13
owl on perch: G.K.S. 3384, f. 13
owl on wrist, astride
ass: M. 812, f. 34 (inscription: "Pay me no less than an owl and an ape and an ass")
dog, pursuing hare: Douce 366, f. 147v
goat: Add. 42130, f. 38
lion, pursuing hare: fr. 776, f. 18
as physician, ministering to: Cambrai 87, f. 138; Chantilly 62, f. 36v (patting its head); Laud lat. 84, f. 193
conversing, owl perched on fist: Royal 10 E.IV, f. 49v
holding, trapping birds: Hague 78.D.40, f. 23v
hunting with club: Arundel 83, f. 40v
kneeling before mitered owl, receiving crosier from second ape: W. 82, f. 184
pursuing with lure, owl astride hare: Douce 366, f. 147v
shooting: Douce 366, f. 41v; Ghent 233, f. 10; G.K.S. 3384, f. 188
threatening with sword: Hague XX, f. 95v
with wheelbarrow containing three apes, drawn by owl: Trinity B.11.22, f. 206v

Ape and parrot *see* Lover, conversing

Ape and peacock, astride: BBR 10607, f. 177 (at L., Jonah issuing from whale) (*fig. 290*)

Ape and peacock, fighting with club and buckler: Douce 118, f. 31v

Ape and pedlar, robbing (*Roman de Renart* episode): Royal 10 E.IV, ff. 149-151 (*figs. 20-24*)

Ape and pig (*cf.* Ape and sow)
astride, as bishop: G.K.S. 3384, ff. 55v (with flabellum), 229 (with slingshot)
astride, tilting at quintain: G.K.S. 3384, f. 194v (at L., ape astride dog, with club and shield)
tilting, astride goats: M. 729, f. 311
tilting, astride quadrupeds: Christ Church E.II, f. 51v

Ape and pygmy *see* Pygmy

Ape and ram (*see also* Ape with fruit, and knife)
astride: G.K.S. 3384, f. 222
backwards: BBR 9961-62, f. 14 (owl nearby)
hunting stag: Hague 78.D.40, f. 1
with horn: Douce 118, f. 163
with rake and shield, tilting with ape on stilts with switch and shield: W. 82, f. 205v
holding basket behind two rams butting: Hague XX, f. 3v
warding off with basket: Arsenal 5218, ff. 25v, 55 (*fig. 25*)

Ape and sciapode, confronted: Christ Church E.II, f. 44v

Ape and sheep, accompanying woman: G.K.S. 3384, f. 141v

Ape and sheep, holding, eating bone(?): BBR 9961-62, f. 74

Ape and snail
as physician, ministering to: Cambrai 103, f. 313
astride, tilting with ape astride goose: Cambrai 103, f. 95
fighting with spear: BBR 9391, f. 94 (astride horse) (*fig. 27*); W. 90, f. 194 (above, ape with book)
fighting with sword: Add. 49622, f. 210v; BBR II 988, vol. II, f. 273
shooting: Add. 49622, f. 214v; BBR II 988, vol. II, f. 268 (hybrid ape; at L., hybrid knight fighting snail with sword and buckler)

Ape and sow, as physician, ministering to: Bodley 264, f. 168

Ape and squirrel (*see also* Ape and bird, stepping; Ape as bishop, pursuing; Ape as cleric, gesturing)
pursuing with ax, squirrel with nut in tree: Harley 6563, ff. 81v-82
pursuing with club: fr. 776, f. 10

Ape and stag
astride: G.K.S. 3384, f. 90v; Melbourne 1254/3, f. 25 (belled cap)

shot by man: G.K.S. 3384, f. 112v
with sword and buckler, fighting hybrid snail with bow: Y.T. 8, f. 200v
hunting: Chartres 549, f. 70v; Glazier 24, f. 69; Hague 78.D.40, ff. 24v, 56, 57, 87v, 92, 95v, 100, 123, 124v, 132v
astride ram: Hague 78.D.40, f. 1
stag and hare: Christ Church E.II, f. 51v; Glazier 24, f. 69
stag, boar, hare: Add. 49622, f. 8
in tree, observing two hounds pursuing stag: Burney 275, f. 143
kneeling before: Douce 6, f. 121v
waving clapnet at: Douce 5, f. 120
Ape and stork (*cf.* Ape and crane; *see also* Ape vomiting; Ape with mortar and pestle; Obscaena, beak)
aiming slingshot at: Add. 30029, f. 63
as physician, ministering to: Fitz. 298, f. 81
astride bridled stork: Douce 5, f. 211v
astride, tilting at quintain: G.K.S. 3384, f. 26
astride with spear, confronting ape astride cock: Tournai Ps., f. 211
bitten by, holding up Host before altar: Tournai Ps., f. 166v
fighting with club: Douce 6, f. 164v
fighting with spear and buckler, astride ape with paw on stool: Tournai Ps., f. 121v
fighting with stick and buckler: G.K.S. 3384, f. 93
fighting with sword and buckler: Melbourne 1254/3, f. 4
shooting: BBR II 988, vol. II, f. 238 (hybrid ape); Cambrai 133, f. 392; Princeton 44-18, ff. 37v-38; W. 82, f. 169 (hybrid stork)
wrestling with, second ape applauding: Tournai Ps., f. 208v
Ape and swan, holding swan seated in gold basin: Douce 6, f. 53
Ape and unicorn, astride: W. 82, f. 175
confronting hare with spear: Douce 5, f. 68v
fighting squirrel astride antelope (ibex?): Y.T. 19, f. 3
fighting with club and buckler: Melbourne 1254/3, f. 28
pursued by hunter and hound: W. 82, f. 62v (*fig. 391*)
standing on back of: Douce 5, f. 177 (*fig. 216*)
Ape and wild man *see* Man and woman, dancing in pairs; Wild man and lion
Ape and woman *see* Woman and ape
Ape as angel: Add. 36684, f. 46v (Min.: Adoration of Magi)
Ape as armorer, cutting and hammering plates: Bodley 264, f. 84 (at R., smith by forge)
Ape as baker
looking out of oven: M. 754, f. 47
man carrying burning oven on back: G.K.S. 3384, f. 67
with four loaves on tray: M. 754, f. 48 (below, ape aiming pole at hindquarters in oven)
Ape as barber (dentist?): Yale MS., f. 1
Ape as beggar
crippled, with ape-child in arms: BBR II 988, vol. II, f. 265v
(fool?) with peaked belled hood, confronting bearded hybrid man with bat wings: Melbourne 1254/3, f. 9v
with basket *see* Ape with basket
Ape as bishop (*see also* Bishop parodied; Procession, ape; Stag, on hind legs): Add. 49622, f. 96; G.K.S. 3384, f. 301v; latin 14284, f. 53v; W. 102, f. 74
and cleric with book: G.K.S. 3384, f. 80; Royal 1 D.I, f. 5
astride devil, with bone(?): Douce 6, f. 9v (at R., man gesturing; at L., man with fowl impaled on spear)
astride man, fighting ape with sword and shield: Add. 10292, f. 1
astride pig: G.K.S. 3384, ff. 55v (with flabellum), 229 (with slingshot)
before altar composed of stool basket, holding up calf's head, attended by cat with asperge: Trinity B.11.22, f. 4 (*fig. 29*)
confronting human head, in border, sticking out tongue: W. 87, f. 46
conversing with ape: Add. 49622, f. 96
in procession *see* Procession, ape
pursuing squirrel disappearing into its house, gesture admonishing silence: Add. 30029, f. 62v
with asperge *see* Procession, ape
with bagpipe approaching ape wearing doctor's cap, seated holding flabellum: W. 87, ff. 37v-38 (above, woman emptying jar)
with book, singing: fr. 95, f. 343v (2)
with chalice: Douce 118, f. 18
with churn, stirring with crosier: Add. 30029, ff. 19, 89 (stork plunging head into large jar, Fable reference?), 122v

- with cloven foot: G.K.S. 3384, f. 108 (above, bishop's head, man praying)
- with processional cross: Glazier 24, f. 59
- with trumpet, staff: Melbourne 1254/3, f. 16v

Ape as blacksmith (*cf.* Ape as armorer): BBR II 988, vol. II, f. 217v; G.K.S. 3384, f. 27 (*fig. 28*); Rothschild MS., f. 169 (above, two apes turning grindstone) (*fig. 88*)

Ape as cleric (*see also* Ape playing jawbone; Ape with Host)
- ape (female) confessing: Hague 78.D.40, f. 59v
- at lectern, seated, receiving ape-cleric with document: latin 16260, f. 302v
- at lectern, singing; at R., ape on bier surrounded by six tapers: fr. 25526, f. 66v (2)
- at school *see* School
- beating with switch ape with book: Douce 6, f. 115 (at R., kneeling ape with clasped hands)
- before altar surmounted by cock, book: Cracow 815, f. 132v
- confronting monster in line ending: Douce 5, ff. 29 (*fig. 700*), 74
- gesturing at back of squirrel: Christ Church E.II, f. 43v
- patting bird, fox-cleric reaching for cock on column by altar: Cambrai 103, f. 384 (*fig. 30*)
- praying: latin 14284, f. 30 (at R., hybrid cleric); Y.T. 8, f. 287v (second ape with book)
- with animal's head on gold pole before two apes gesturing and aiming stick at hindquarters: Douce 6, f. 123v (above, nude man with cape, spear, trumpet; f. 124, mitered ape holding head of animal, beckoning)
- with asperge and situla, bird bowing before him: BBR II 988, vol. II, f. 262v (at L., ape and fox)
- with asperge and situla, pointed at by hybrid man: Cloisters 54.1.2, f. 72v
- with book: BBR II 988, vol. II, f. 259; latin 14284, f. 8 (and nun with book); Y.T. 8, f. 287v (before him ape praying)
- with document *see above, —* at lectern, seated
- with harp, seated: latin 14284, f. 21v
- with horn, confronting woman wearing chaplet, warding off gesture: Douce 118, f. 87

Ape as doctor *see* Ape as physician

Ape as falconer (*see also* Ape and owl): Add. 49622, f. 209v; BBR II 988, vol. II, f. 232; Cambrai 103, ff. 411, 421 (*fig. 31*); Fitz. 298, ff. 86v, 115v; Hague 78.D.40, f. 19v; Nancy 249, ff. 97-97v; Tournai Ps., ff. 132v, 154; W. 85, f. 79v; Y.T. 8, f. 269v (2)
- ape with fruit: Tournai Ps., f. 195
- astride (*cf.* Ape astride)
  - cock: Melbourne 1254/3, f. 44v
  - goat: Lambeth 75, f. 1 (at R., man aiming bow at hare; peacock) (*fig. 32*)
  - horse: Trinity B.11.22, f. 26v; Y.T. 8, f. 182 (seated backwards); Y.T. 15, f. 307v (riding away from gesturing ape)
  - ibex or goat: latin 14284, f. 10v (at L., ape seated)
  - lion: W. 90, f. 34
  - unicorn: Douce 118, f. 19
- followed by fox: Royal 14 E.III, f. 140
- hare with bagpipe, ape with trumpet: Douce 5, f. 1v
- holding owl and rat (ferret?): Olschki 4, f. 52v
- hybrid man with krummhorn, second hybrid man with pipe and tabor: Tournai Ps., f. 132v
- seated: W. 45, f. 161 (below, semi-nude man with book)
- seated on bench with woman: Stowe 17, f. 62

Ape as fool *see* Ape as beggar

Ape as glove-seller(?), handing glove to ape, another glove on table before him: G.K.S. 3384, f. 179 (at R., hare running)

Ape as king
- borne by two hares toward tent of ape-queen: Y.T. 8, ff. 295v-296 (*figs. 33-34*)
- dancing(?): W. 87, f. 51v
- enthroned
  - ape seated before him: Princeton 44-18, f. 122v
  - ape standing on tree playing jawbone with tongs: Princeton 44-18 f. 53
  - ape tied with rope around neck dragged before him: Nancy 249, f. 66v
  - ape with spear bringing document with red seal: Douce 6, f. 157v
  - with harp (David parody? *Cf.* Ape as cleric, with harp): Douce 118, f. 101v
- seated at lectern, two apes before him, one with book: fr. 25526, f. 48v
- with asperge and situla: fr. 25526, f. 58 (below, cockfight; man in tree)
- with bagpipe: Stowe 17, f. 9v
- with hybrid man drinking: W. 87, f. 60
- with trumpet, man with pipe and tabor, fox dancing: Cambrai 103, f. 529

A

Ape as knight (*cf.* Apes tilting)
astride horse, fighting knight: Stowe 17, f. 94v
astride hybrid woman: M. 796, f. 67v
with spear, shield: BBR 10607, f. 40
Ape as moneylender (?), at table strewn with coins, approached by man with sack: G.K.S. 3384, f. 40v
Ape as monk *see* Ape as cleric
Ape as pardoner with document bearing red seal: Princeton 44-18, f. 109
Ape as pedlar with wares: Harley 6563, f. 100 (*fig. 35*)
Ape as philosopher(?), eating with spoon from bowl before female ape: G.K.S. 3384, f. 28v (domed cap)
Ape as physician
with urinal: Auct. D.3.2, f. 193 (at R., man pouring green liquid into bowl); BBR 9157, f. 1; BBR II 988, vol. II, f. 213; M. 149, f. 422; Rylands fr. 2, f. 212 (*fig. 523*); Vienna 1826*, f. 54; W. 104, f. 45v
with urinal, ministering to
ape: Y.T. 8, f. 191
ape pointing to purse: Add. 49622, f. 178
ape with hand organ, another with pipe and tabor: Cambridge Dd.5.5, f. 239
ape with staff and stool basket; ape-physician in gold robe: Cambrai 103, f. 301
bird: C.B. 64, f. 89; Liège 431, f. 68; Royal 10 E.IV, f. 52
cock: Stowe 17, f. 198
dragon cowering before him: Arsenal 5218, f. 15
falcon: FR. 12400, f. 1
fox, feeling pulse: Cambrai 102, f. 294
hybrid man: W. 104, f. 23v (hybrid ape)
hybrid woman: latin 14284, f. 12
man: Fitz. 298, f. 25 (feeling pulse); Yale MS., f. 1
man crippled: Y.T. 8, f. 273v
man kneeling before him: Melbourne 1254/3, f. 125
nun with stool basket: Stowe 17, f. 51 (Franciscan)
owl: Add. 30029, f. 23 (owl with stool basket around neck); Cambrai 87, f. 138; Chantilly 62, f. 36v (*fig. 36*); Laud lat. 84, f. 193; Troyes 898, f. 253; W. 88, f. 143
snail (gold): Cambrai 103, f. 313 (second ape fishing) (*fig. 47*)
sow: Bodley 264, f. 168
stork, feeling pulse: Fitz. 298, f. 81
woman: Add. 49622, ff. 94 (kneeling), 105 (with coin); Douce 5, f. 156; latin 10435, f. 12v; Princeton 44-18, f. 33v
with urinal, seated, tied to his seat: Royal 10 E.IV, f. 50
Ape as pilgrim: Glazier 24, f. 53 (2)
approaching ape ringing bell: Verdun 107, f. 93v
astride horse, approaching ape shooting fox (cat?) on tall tower: Harley 928, f. 97v
Ape as queen in tent, two hares approaching, bearing ape-king on litter: Y.T. 8, ff. 295v-296 (*figs. 33-34*)
Ape as Saracen fighting beast: Add. 30029, f. 97v
Ape as schoolmaster (?) (*cf.* School; Schoolmaster)
seated with staff, nude man hiding in border foliage: M. 754, f. 75
seated with switch, ape suppliant before him: Tournai Ps., f. 45v
Ape as scribe: Douce 6, f. 84v (writing left-handed); G.K.S. 3384, f. 293; Hague 78.D.40, f. 124 (3, with cleric-scribe)
Ape as tailor(?), with shears, cutting cloth: Hague 78.D.40, f. 119v
Ape as Templar(?), with switch: Glazier 24, f. 172v
Ape as tumbler
doing handstand: Bodley 264, f. 41; fr. 25526, f. 23v; Nancy 249, f. 9v
ape with bagpipe: Stowe 17, f. 35v
apes applauding: Tournai Ps., f. 8 (two)
dog with hurdy-gurdy: Harley 6563, ff. 42v-43
hybrid woman looking on: W. 85, ff. 2v-3
man with tabor: Cloisters 54.1.2, f. 76
turning somersault: Trinity B.11.22, f. 7; Y.T. 8, f. 297v (on chair for man)
Ape astride (*cf.* Ape as falconer)
ape *see* Ape and stork; Apes fighting; Wrestling, apes
ape, on shoulders of: W. 88, ff. 35v-36 (pointing at man on stilts); W. 90, f. 107
ape/unicorn, with spear and shield: G.K.S. 3384, f. 242
ape with switch, seated backwards: M. 754, f. 114
ass *see* Ape and ass; Ape and owl, as falconer
bear: Harley 928, f. 12
bear tied to post: W. 102, f. 29v (line ending)
bear, with mace and shield: Douce 49, f. 65v
bird, tilting with ape astride bird: Cracow 815, ff. 11v, 269v
wearing cardinal's hat and papal tiara: W. 45, f. 166

  with spade and distaff: Cambrai 102, f. 283v
bird with shield and spear, approaching nude man exposing buttocks: Rutland Ps., ff. 66v-67 (ostrich?)
broom: G.K.S. 3384, f. 300v
camel: Chantilly 64, f. 30
cock
  confronting ape astride duck, both with spears: Y.T. 8, f. 176
  confronting ape astride stork with spear and shield: Tournai Ps., f. 211
  with spear and buckler, confronting ape astride stork whose beak he holds open: Y.T. 75, f. 36
  with trumpet: Melbourne 1254/3, f. 6
crane: Add. 24686, f. 12; Douce 5, f. 211v; Rothschild MS., f. 110; Trinity B.11.22, f. 165v
devil *see* Ape as bishop, astride
dog *see* Ape and dog; Apes tilting
dragon *see* Ape and dragon, astride
elephant: Stowe 17, f. 36
fox *see* Ape and fox, astride
goat *see* Ape and goat, astride
goose *see* Ape and goose
hare *see* Ape and hare, astride
hobbyhorse: G.K.S. 3384, f. 86v (*fig. 49*)
horse *see* Ape and horse, astride; Ape as falconer, astride; Ape as knight
horse, seated backwards: Add. 36684, ff. 46 (aiming spear at hybrid man), 96; Y.T. 8, f. 182
hybrid beast: W. 88, f. 122v
hybrid bird, tilting with knight: Stowe 17, f. 121v
hybrid dragon, seated backwards with club and horn: Royal 14 E.III, f. 140
hybrid man (nude), with spear and stool basket: Glazier 24, f. 73v (at L., knight)
ibex(?) *see* Ape as falconer, astride
keg pulled by four apes toward building: Bodley 264, f. 82 (at R., man with club astride keg pulled by two apes)
lion *see* Ape and lion, astride
lionesque beast *see* Ape and hare, hunting
man (*see also* Ape as bishop, astride): Cambridge Dd. 5.5, f. 307v; Glazier 24, f. 131v (man nude, saddled)
ostrich (?) *see* Ape and crane, astride
peacock: BBR 10607, f. 177 (at L., Jonah issuing from whale) (*fig. 290*)
pig *see* Ape as bishop, astride
ram *see* Ape and ram
snail *see* Ape and goose
stag *see* Ape and stag
stork *see* Ape and stork; *above*, —, astride cock
sword (Arthurian reference?) M. 754, f. 57
unicorn *see* Ape and unicorn
Ape at altar *see* Ape as bishop; Ape as cleric; Ape with Host
Ape at lectern (*see also* Ape as cleric)
  with book: BBR 9391, f. 125v
  with fellow-ape: W. 88, f. 52 (book on lectern); fr. 25526, f. 48v (crowned; before him two apes, one with book)
Ape at school *see* School
Ape baking *see* Ape as baker
Ape balancing
  ape on nose, standing in water: M. 754, f. 36
  basins on short sticks (two): Arsenal 5218, f. 66; Bodley 264, ff. 64 (butterfly, owl nearby), 66; Cambrai 87, f. 144v; C.B. 64, f. 15 (three); lat. lit. f. 3, f. 87; Laud Lat. 84, ff. 67, 297 v, 300v; M. 754, f. 41; N.K.S. 41, f. 105v (*fig. 37*)
    ape with bagpipe: C.B. 64, f. 52v
    ape with hand organ: Ashmole 828, f. 1
    dog looking on: Tournai Ps., f. 27
    hare looking on: W. 104, f. 31v
    man with vielle, ape with bagpipe: Add. 24686, f. 17v (*fig. 324*)
  on back of horse, standing with sword and buckler: Glazier 24, f. 80v
  on bowl (gold) atop pole held by man, with fruit: Trinity B.11.22, f. 211
  on hands *see* Ape as tumbler
  on head of nude man: W. 88, f. 96v
  on pole held by cleric and man, seizing cleric's crosier: W. 88, f. 127v
  on seesaw: Rothschild MS., f. 131v (2) (*fig. 38*)
  on shoulders of ape: W. 88, f. 117; W. 90, f. 107
  swan in gold bowl: Douce 6, f. 53
  sword: G.K.S. 3384, f. 218v
Ape bathing(?) in tub: M. 754, f. 15 (2); Melbourne 1254/3, f. 6v (2)
Ape beaten *see* Centaur and; School
Ape beating ape (*see also* Ape as cleric): G.K.S. 3384, f. 79v (or beating dog between them)
  with club: Y.T. 8, f. 217v
  with switch: Cambridge Dd.5.5, f. 211; fr. 95, f. 66v
Ape beating laundry(?) with paddle, bird aiming beak at hindquarters; (*cf.* Man washing; Woman —) Hague 78.D.40, f. 22v
Ape begging *see* Ape as beggar
Ape, Bestiary representation (*see also* Ape with wheelbarrow)
  pursued by hunters, with offspring: Munich c.g.

A

16, f. 20 (in Bestiary cycle) (*fig. 42*); Royal 2 B.VII, ff. 107v-108 (in Bestiary cycle); Trinity B.11.22, f. 72
trapped by imitating man stepping into drawers: fr. 25526, f. 147
trapped by man with tarred boots: Add. 30029, f. 91v; Cambridge Dd. 5.5, f. 65; Douce 5, ff. 112, 115v, 191v (ape in tree), 195v (ape caught); Douce 6, f. 179 (ape in tree, encouraged by man with club; above, another ape, fox); Douce 48, f. 191; latin 13260, f. 29v; Rothschild MS., f. 172v; Royal 2 B.VII, ff. 106-106v (in Bestiary cycle); Stowe 17, f. 70 (ape in tree); Trinity B.11.22, f. 215v; W. 88, ff. 74, 167; Yale MS., f. 203 (*fig. 41*)
with offspring in arms, on back (curtailed reference?): M. 183, f. 85v; Rothschild MS., f. 127 (at R., tree); Royal 10 E.IV, f. 152; Rutland Ps., f. 88 (at L., large horned bird) (*fig. 40*); W. 102, f. 76
Ape biting *see* Ape and boar; — and dog; — and hybrid man; Ape with pitcher; — with staff
Ape blowing pipe with pinwheel attached to end *see* Windmill, toy
Ape bowling *see* Bowls, apes
Ape chained or tied (*cf.* Ape tied, references under; Ape with fruit; Bear; Lion chained; *see also* Man and ape, training; Man and bear, dancing): Add. 29253, f. 61 (ball and chain); BBR II 988, vol. II, f. 172 (on ball); Princeton, 44-18, f. 147v (ball and chain); Trinity B.11.22, f. 28
to border stalk, wearing collar: BBR 9961-62, f. 65
to post, man balancing two basins on sticks: W. 90, f. 137v
to post, man training horse to kick buckler: Bodley 264, f. 73 (three children pointing at ape) (*fig. 374*); Melbourne 1254/3, ff. 7 (opposite lion) (*fig. 318*), 39
Ape-child *see* Ape and ape-child
Ape chopping down small tree with ax: W. 87, f. 27
Ape chopping firewood with ax: BBR II 988, vol. II, f. 217v
Ape climbing border stalk: Bodley 264, f. 54v (hare observing); Cloisters 54.1.2, f. 174; M. 754, f. 64v; W. 82, ff. 52 (at L., man carrying horse), 181v, 193v
Ape climbing spear (*cf.* Ape with sword): M. 754, f. 40
Ape climbing tree: Fitz. 298, f. 36
Ape confessing, kneeling before ape-cleric: Hague 78.D.40, f. 59v (female)
Ape conversing with ape (*cf.* Hybrid bishop and ape): Tournai Ps., f. 161v
Ape cooking (*cf.* Ape with churn)
roasting fowl on spit: Stowe 17, f. 176 (above, man with mortar and pestle)
stirring pot: Add. 36684, f. 143
stirring pot on fire: Douce 6, f. 73v (2, stork on chimney); G.K.S. 3384, ff. 21v (second ape begging food), 48 (second ape holding two round objects), 111v
Ape crawling: Fitz. 298, f. 119 (attached to wheel by rope); Glazier 24, f. 172v
Ape crippled (*see also* Ape as beggar)
on hand trestles: BBR II 988, vol. II, f. 212v; Douce 6, f. 54v (hybrid man with handbells); Trinity B.11.22, f. 115
with fruit: fr. 95, f. 343
Ape dancing (*see also* Ape and dog; Ass with pipe): Add. 36684, ff. 24 (2), 46v (4); G.K.S. 3384, f. 228 (2); Glazier 24, ff. 60 (3), 79 (2); M. 754, f. 11 (4); W. 88, ff. 136 (2, wrestling?), 158 (2, wrestling?)
ape with bagpipe: Fitz. 298, f. 3v (2); Tournai Ps., ff. 218v, 249
ape with hurdy-gurdy: Bodley 264, f. 81
ape with pipe and tabor: Tournai Ps., f. 19
apes with harp and vielle: Royal 2 B.VIII, ff. 179v-180 (4)
hybrid animal with vielle, winged cap: Douce 118, f. 17
hybrid man with pipe and tabor, two-faced man with two trumpets: M. 754, f. 11 (4)
hybrid woman with shawm: W. 85, f. 89v
man with pipe and tabor: W. 87, f. 29v
man with vielle: Laud Lat. 84, f. 40v
merman with pipe: Glazier 24, f. 137v
opposite man wearing boar's head: Chantilly 64, ff. 69, 69v
with ape, holding ribbons: W. 82, f. 193 (man with ?tambourine issuing from border, hare standing behind with one paw on man's shoulder)
Ape defecating *see* Obscaena, defecating
Ape disputing with ape: W. 88, f. 172v
Ape drinking (*see also* Man with mortar and pestle)
bringing two cups to hybrid beast: Glazier 24, f. 70
drawing wine from keg: Bodley 264, f. 94v (4);

fr. 25526, f. 76 (two apes playing dice, another drinking)
seated on oven: M. 754, f. 35
with two cups: Tournai Ps., f. 7
Ape driving cart drawn by three horses: Add. 42130, f. 162
Ape eating (*cf.* Ape with fruit): Add. 30029, ff. 65, 146v (from bowl with spoon)
Ape feeding ape: Ashmole 828, f. 62; G.K.S. 3384, f. 28v (female feeding male)
Ape fighting
ape *see* Apes fighting; — tilting
beast *see* Ape and beast
crane *see* Ape and crane
hybrid man *see* Ape and hybrid man
knight *see* Ape and knight
lion *see* Ape and lion
man *see* Man and ape
pig *see* Ape and pig
snail *see* Ape and snail
stork *see* Ape and stork
Ape fishing: Douce 118, f. 14v; Melbourne 1254/3, f. 70v (*fig. 46*); W. 88, f. 93
ape behind him with pot, another ape cutting open fish on table: Riches Ps., f. 1 (at R., ape blowing fire under large pot, ape with dish; Ps. 1)
ape pushing him in water: Douce 118, f. 67v
ape rowing boat at R.: Hague 78.D.40, f. 44
ape trapping birds at L., ape as falconer: Arsenal 5218, f. 1 (woman extending hand to fishing ape)
basket in right hand: latin 10483, f. 14
bird looking on: Stowe 17, ff. 51v-52
catch stolen by cat: Hague 78.D.40, ff. 44 (*fig. 44*), 105
catch stolen by fox: Arras 229, f. 655 (*fig. 45*); BBR II 988, vol. II, f. 193v; Cambrai 103, f. 313 (*fig. 47*); Cracow 815, f. 11
eating fish: Douce 118, f. 127v
hare on end of line: Stowe 17, f. 253
wearing jester's cap: Douce 118, f. 128v
winged hybrid man aiming spear at hindquarters: Melbourne 1254/3, f. 16
Ape, funeral of *see* Ape as cleric, at lectern
Ape hanging from border-stalk: M. 754, f. 88v (upside down); W. 87, f. 80 (by rope around neck)
Ape hawking *see* Ape as falconer
Ape holding top of small tree: M. 754, f. 77
Ape hung by neck from beak of hybrid beast: Glazier 24, f. 44v
Ape hunting (*see also* Ape and bird; — and boar; — and hare; — and owl; — and stag; Ape pursuing, references under; Ape shooting): Lat. lit. f. 3, f. 95v
Ape in basket *see* Man with basket
Ape in boat *see* Ape rowing
Ape in tree *see* Ape, Bestiary representation; Ape playing jawbone; Man and ape, conversing; St. Mary the Egyptian
Ape in tub *see* Ape bathing
Ape juggling three knives, ass with vielle at R.: W. 109, f. 20 (*fig. 48*)
Ape kissing beast *see* Ape and beast
Ape kneeling (*see also* Hybrid bishop and ape)
before ape: Tournai Ps., ff. 123v (ape-cleric?), 202v (confessing? head patted by seated ape)
before bare buttocks *see* Obscaena, revering
Ape on column (idol?): Stowe 17, f. 123v
Ape on hobbyhorse: G.K.S. 3384, f. 86v (*fig. 49*)
Ape on roof of church: Douce 6, f. 122v (at L., two women with basket containing child covered with red flowers)
Ape on see-saw *see* Ape balancing
Ape on stilts *see* Stilts
Ape on swing *see* Ape swinging
Ape picking pears *see* Man and woman, throwing fruit
Ape playing
bandyball *see* Bandyball
bellows with tongs: Nancy 249, f. 83v
checkers or chess *see* Checkers
dice *see* Dice
jawbone with bow, hybrid woman dancing: Cambrai 102, f. 188v (ape-cleric?)
jawbone with plectrum, sticking out tongue: Bodley 264, f. 112 (below, man and woman playing chess) (*fig. 104*)
jawbone with tongs, standing in tree before ape-king: Princeton 44-18, f. 53
organ, hybrid man with pipe and tabor: M. 729, f. 306
ram's head with spoon: Douce 6, f. 53
tug-of-war *see* Tug-of-war
vielle with rake: Cambrai 87, ff. 55v, 117, 154; Chantilly 62, f. 88v; Laud Lat. 84, f. 138
Ape plowing with horse, two oxen: Add. 49622, f. 15v (*fig. 50*)
Ape pointing to mouth (parody of David?): Glazier 24, f. 132v

Ape praying or confessing to bishop: Princeton 44-18, ff. 63v-64
Ape pruning border foliage
with ax: Douce 5, f. 161 (owl on branch)
with knife: Rylands fr. 1, f. 212
with pole: G.K.S. 3384, f. 75
with sword: Douce 5, f. 155v; G.K.S. 3384, f. 46
Ape pulling ape's leg: Douce 5, f. 77
Ape pumping bellows for man playing organ: Add. 49622, f. 117
Ape pursuing *see* Ape and butterfly; — and hare; — and hybrid bishop; — and lion; — and squirrel; *also* Ape hunting, references under; Ape shooting, references under
Ape putting on boots *see* Ape, Bestiary representation
Ape raising right foot, examining it: W. 88, f. 127
Ape reading *see* Ape as cleric, with book; Ape with book
Ape rending *see* Ape and beast; — and lion
Ape revering buttocks *see* Obscaena, revering
Ape riding *see* Ape astride, references under
Ape ringing bell on bell rope: Add. 36684, f. 132 (seated on pot); Douce 118, f. 35v (at R., crow); Glazier 24, f. 81a v; M. 754, f. 18 (2); St. Omer 5, f. 137 (bell suspended from church tower with cock as weathervane); Verdun 107, f. 93v (ape-pilgrim approaching); W. 85, f. 87
Ape rowing boat: Hague 78.D.40, f. 44 (at L., ape fishing); Stowe 17, f. 76v (3)
Ape sawing carcass of animal: G.K.S. 3384, f. 118v (2)
Ape scratching hindquarters (*see* Ape with fruit) W. 761, f. 175v
Ape seated (*see also* Ape with arrows; — with book; — with psaltery)
cloak flying out to sides: Add. 42130, f. 189v
on head of man with hands clasped, with pipe and tabor: M. 754, f. 53
on head of nude man without arms or feet, M. 754, f. 50v
receiving document *see* Ape and crane; Ape and dog
receiving three apes, one kneeling, second with staff, third followed by bird: fr. 25526, f. 27
with jawbone or comb, scratching head (*cf.* Ape playing): W. 37, f. 111
Ape shooting *see* Ape and beast, shooting; Ape and bird, hunting; Ape and butterfly, shooting; Ape and cat, —; Ape and crane, —; Ape and dog, —; Ape and dragon, —; Ape and hare, hunting; Ape and hybrid man, shooting; Ape and owl, —; Ape and snail, —; Ape and stork, —
Ape singing *see* Ape and hybrid beast; Ape as bishop, with book; Ape as cleric, at lectern
Ape spinning: G.K.S. 3384, f. 60 (above, blacksmith) (*fig. 51*); M. 754, f. 20v (hybrid man and two dogs with reels); Stowe 17, ff. 5 (March), 92 (f. 91, ape winding wool)
Ape standing on chair, another looking out of oven holding baker's tray: M. 754, f. 47
Ape stealing child *see* Ape and child
Ape stirring pot *see* Ape cooking
Ape swimming: Douce 6, f. 153 (2; at R., beggar with ape in basket on back) (*fig. 52*)
Ape swinging: Add. 36684, ff. 16, 31; G.K.S. 3384, f. 333
ape beckoning with bowl: G.K.S. 3384, f. 39
from bar: M. 754, f. 92v
from border stalk: Lat. lit. f. 3, f. 9v
from border stalk by one hand, holding sprig of gold leaves in other: latin 10483, f. 17v
on rope suspended from border: Glazier 24, f. 126v (*fig. 53*)
propelled by second ape pulling rope: W. 82, f. 190
Ape threshing: Hague 78.D.40, f. 22
Ape tied *see* Ape and horse, astride, dragging; Ape as king, enthroned; Ape chained; Man and horse, training; Man and woman, on horseback
Ape tilting *see* Ape and beast; — and dog; — and fox; — and horse, astride; — and pig; Apes tilting; Quintain, tilting
Ape trained *see* Man and ape, training
Ape trapped *see* Ape, Bestiary representation
Ape trapping *see* Ape and bird, snaring; Man and ape, trapped
Ape tumbling *see* Ape as tumbler
Ape turning grindstone: Rothschild MS., f. 169 (2; below, ape as blacksmith) (*fig. 88*)
Ape two-faced, wearing tall pointed ecclesiastical hat, blowing two trumpets: Melbourne 1254/3, f. 128
Ape urinating into jug: Stowe 17, f. 68v
Ape vomiting green liquid into basin: Douce 6, f. 109v (second ape pinching beak of stork with pliers)
Ape weaving (?): G.K.S. 3384, ff. 11v, 138v
Ape whipping top *see* Top-whipping

Ape winding rope tied between two stakes: Douce 6, f. 153 (*fig. 52*)
Ape winding wool *see* Ape with reel
Ape with arrow in mouth: M. 149, f. 293v (f. 294, owl)
Ape with arrows (two) seated on column flanked by two apes pierced with arrows (Eros parody?): Hague 78.D.40, f. 28
Ape with asperge and situla (*see also* Ape as cleric; Procession; School): Yale MS., ff. 267, 298v
Ape with ax
  approaching burrow from which hare looks out: Trinity B.11.22, f. 137v
  chopping down small tree: W. 87, f. 27
  chopping firewood: BBR II 988, vol. II, f. 217v; Glazier 24, f. 163v
  pruning *see* Ape pruning
  whetting(?) on table: Trinity B.11.22, f. 63 (2)
Ape with bagpipe: Add. 49622, f. 43v; Stowe 17, f. 157v; W. 110, f. 36v; Yale MS., f. 14
  ape balancing two basins on sticks: Add. 24686, f. 17v (man with vielle) (*fig. 324*); C.B. 64, f. 52v
  ape dancing: Fitz. 298, f. 3v (two); G.K.S. 3384, f. 228 (man with vielle); Tournai Ps., f. 218v (two)
  ape tumbling: fr. 25526, f. 3v (handstand); Stowe 17, f. 35v
  ape with hand organ, another with pipe and tabor, with ape-physician: Cambridge Dd. 5.5, f. 239
  ape with shawm, basket on back containing apes: fr. 95, f. 237 (2)
  ape with trumpet (*see also* Woman nude, and goat): Tournai Ps., f. 204v
  apes fighting with swords and bucklers: Tournai Ps., f. 3
  apes playing with hood: Tournai Ps., f. 235 (three apes)
  apes tilting on foot, ape with pipe and tabor: Tournai Ps., f. 247
  as bishop, approaching ape-physician seated with stick and rattle: W. 87, ff. 37v-38
  dog with pipe and tabor: Tournai Ps., f. 31
  dog with staff: Douce 6, f. 191v
  hybrid couple dancing: Tournai Ps., f. 89
  hybrid woman dancing: Douce 118, f. 21v
  lion dancing: Tournai Ps., f. 216v (at R., ape with bird on brow)
  supporting bent trumpet played by hybrid man: Tournai Ps., f. 207v
Ape with ball, playing (*cf.* Handball): Harley 6563, f. 76v
Ape with basket (*cf.* Beggar)
  beckoning to man holding fish: G.K.S. 3384, f. 156 (above, man with basket and eel)
  containing small yellow round objects (picked off border?): latin 10483, f. 20 (one hand on border stalk)
  picking gold balls off border: Douce 6, f. 48
Ape with basket on back containing
  ape: W. 82, f. 195 (hybrid ape); W. 87, f. 41 (with staff)
  apes with bagpipe and trumpet: fr. 95, f. 237
  apes, with staff, confronting one-legged man with bagpipe: fr. 95, f. 64v
  cranes: Y.T. 8, f. 171v
Ape with bell *see* Ape ringing; Ape with hand bells
Ape with bell tied to stick: Melbourne 1254/3, f. 72v (at L., hybrid man with sword and buckler)
Ape with belled peaked hood: W. 87, f. 39v
Ape with bellows (*see also* Ape playing; — pumping): M. 754, ff. 69v (blowing fire), 104v (the same); W. 87, f. 69
Ape with bone *see* Apes, seated
Ape with book (*see also* Ape as cleric; School): Add. 36684, ff. 125 (2), 132v; BBR 9157, f. 181; G.K.S. 3384, f. 305; M. 155, f. 119; M. 754, f. 17v; Princeton 44-18, f. 109; W. 45, f. 129; W. 90, ff. 77, 194 (seated on chair, pointing to page in book)
  at lectern: BBR 9391, f. 125v
  at lectern, crowned; before him two apes, one with book: fr. 25526, f. 48v
  following man with book, approaching two apes reading: Bodley 264, f. 96
  reading: Arras 47, f. 7; BBR II 988, vol. II, f. 244 (seated in chair); Bodley 264, f. 96 (2, following man with book); Yale MS., f. 40v
  seated before ape with switch: W. 88, f. 38v
  seated before hybrid man playing psaltery with rake: M. 754, f. 46v
Ape with bow: W. 87, f. 33
Ape with bowl (nest?) containing bird (*cf.* Bird in nest; Man and dragon, astride, with bowl): Tournai Ps., f. 165
Ape with buckets (two) on pole over shoulder; Add. 29253, f. 210v; Douce 5, f. 5v; Trinity B.11.22, f. 53
Ape with castle *see* Castle

A

Ape with censer, magpie(?) aiming beak at hindquarters: Douce 118, f. 122
Ape with churn, stirring (*cf.* Ape cooking): Add. 30029, ff. 19, 60v, 89; Nancy 249, ff. 62v, 159v, 186v; Rothschild MS., f. 111v
ape holding out bowl: M. 754, f. 18
ape pursuing butterfly with red hood: Arsenal 5218, f. 40
as bishop, stirring with crosier: Add. 30029, f. 122v
crowned bird aiming beak at hindquarters: Add. 36684, f. 24
Ape with cloak flying out to sides, seated: Add. 42130, f. 189v
Ape with coin (*see also* Ape as moneylender; Fables: woman with jug)
another ape adjusting coif, two coins on ground (small gold balls): Cambrai 133, f. 258v
apes (two) prodding him with pole: Douce 6, f. 35 (above, knight with sword and shield)
Ape with cornet, hybrid man with mandola: Royal 2 B.VII, f. 192v
Ape with crossbow
aiming at ape with hoop: Hague 78.D.40, f. 19v
aiming at ape with staff: Hague 78.D.40, f. 22
Ape with cup *see* Ape and bull; Ape drinking
Ape with distaff and spindle (*see also* Ape and dog, astride; Hare as cleric): Douce 6, f. 118v (above, woman with basket of eggs on head, hare; proverb?); Glazier 24, f. 39; Laud Lat. 84, f. 152v (wearing coif); Rylands fr. 1, f. 82 (ape winding wool) (*fig. 54*); Stowe 17, ff. 30v, 114, 133v, 140v, 216, 242v (f. 243, falconer and woman on horseback), 259v; Trinity B.11.22, f. 102v
Ape with double pipe: Tournai Ps., ff. 1 (at R., siren), 196 (another with vielle), 221v (another with pipe and tabor)
Ape with eel and basket: G.K.S. 3384, f. 157
Ape with egg (*cf.* Proverbs: eggs)
behind man sitting on basket of eggs holding one up to sun, second ape eating egg: Douce 6, f. 93a v
blowing fire, three eggs on ground: Trinity B.11.22, f. 216
bowling with eggs: W. 82, f. 192v (3)
exchanging three eggs with ape: Douce 6, f. 116
hovering over basket of eggs: Glazier 24, f. 105v
in basket containing eggs, empty hood on stick: Stowe 17, f. 256v
sitting on: M. 149, ff. 243v, 261v, 386v (f. 387, bird)
throwing into basket: Trinity B.11.22, f. 41 (at side, knight with gold shield)
with dish containing three eggs in lap, holding one up: Douce 6, f. 24v
Ape with falcon *see* Ape as falconer
Ape with fish *see* Ape and fish; Ape fishing
Ape with flabellum *see* Ape as bishop with bagpipe
Ape with fruit (comprises all round objects variously colored; *cf.* Hare with; Hybrid beast with; Patrons; St. Francis): Add. 17444, f. 119v; Add. 17742, f. 7 (wearing hood); Add. 49622, f. 59v; Arras 47, f. 71v; Arras 139, f. 25 (above, man with vielle); Ashmole 828, f. 58; BBR 5163-64, f. 24v (blue ball, in other hand holding sprig with three more blue balls on it); BBR 9391, ff. 92, 125v; BBR 14682, f. 22v; C.B. 61, f. 156v (Ps. 109); Cambrai 133, f. 258v; Christ Church E.II, f. 31v; Cloisters 54.1.2, f. 35; Douce 5, ff. 164v, 221v (above, owl); Douce 6, f. 71v (below, ape with book); Douce 118, f. 31v (ape chained); Douce 366, f. 24v; fr. 95, ff. 120 (gold), 226 (*cf.* Knight and woman, charged) (*fig. 708*), 338v, 343 (with crutch, staff); fr. 25526, f. 33; Glazier 24, ff. 81a, 109v; latin 1029A, f. 18v; latin 3893, ff. 1, 129v, 209v, 281v; latin 10483, f. 158v; latin 10484, f. 245; M. 149, ff. 156, 198, 234v, 351, 401; M. 730, f. 34v; M. 761, f. 77v; M. 796, ff. 36, 76v, 90v, 95; Royal 1 B.XII, f. 3v; Rutland Ps., ff. 10v, 12; Tournai Ps., f. 207; Trinity B.11.22, f. 155 (at L., spider in web) (*fig. 648*); W. 45, f. 51v (wafer?); W. 85, f. 23v; W. 102, f. 77v (*fig. 131*); W. 104, f. 2v (hare with horn, hybrid man with shawm)
and basket, throwing round object at second ape: Cambridge Dd. 5.5, f. 253
and knife: Glazier 24, f. 86 (below, ram looking up)
and staff: Ashmole 828, f. 1; Bodley 264, f. 36 (stooping, displaying hindquarters); fr. 95, ff. 226 (*fig. 708*), 343 (and crutch)
as falconer: Tournai Ps., f. 195
as pilgrim: Y.T. 27, f. 87v
astride dog: Glazier 24, f. 151v
balancing on bowl set on pole held by man: Trinity B.11.22, f. 211

  female with long hair, tailed: Christ Church E.II, f. 31
  hooded: W. 102, f. 77v
  hybrid, with head of woman, crowned: Add. 50000, f. 101
  man pointing at: BBR 9391, f. 97
  offering fruit(?) to nude man (Adam and Eve parody?) Jacquemart 1, f. 14
  offering fruit to protesting ape (Adam and Eve parody?): Glazier 24, f. 84v
  pursued by man: Cambridge Dd. 5.5, f. 217v (holding two green objects; above, man with basket picking ?fruit off border)
  scratching hindquarters: Add. 50000, f. 101; fr. 95, f. 268; Hague XX, f. 105; latin 3893, f. 118v; Rylands fr. 2, f. 212; Rylands lat. R. 24, f. 147v
Ape with garland (green) crowning ape: M. 754, f. 72v
Ape with gameboard: Add. 36684, f. 148v
Ape with gittern: Laud Lat. 84, f. 295v
  ape dancing: Laud Lat. 84, f. 144v
  ape with trumpet: Douce 5, f. 41v
  hare with pipe and hand bell: Egerton 1151, f. 7
Ape with glove *see* Ape as glove-seller(?)
Ape with *godendag* (Flemish sword) and shield: Melbourne 1254/3, f. 11v
Ape with hand bells: BBR II 988, vol. II, f. 259 (hybrid ape); G.K.S. 3384, f. 145; Harley 6563, f. 58
  confronting hybrid abbot: Glazier 24, f. 107v
  issuing from mouth of hybrid beast: W. 87, f. 31v
Ape with hand organ: Ashmole 828, f. 1; Laud Lat. 84, f. 65; M. 729, f. 306
Ape with harp (*see also* Ape and dog, astride)
  ape with vielle, four apes dancing: Royal 2 B.VII, f. 180
  as cleric, seated: latin 14284, f. 21v
  as king, enthroned (David parody?): Douce 118, f. 101v
  dog dancing: Stowe 17, f. 245
  hare dancing: Royal 14 E.III, f. 3
  holding short red stick(?): Fitz. 2-1954, f. 145
Ape with hood
  another ape trying to get his head in: Tournai Ps., f. 235
  tossing to ape: Tournai Ps., ff. 115 (*fig. 55*), 236 (3; at L., ape with bagpipe; below, dragon) (*fig. 56*)
Ape with horn, bear tumbling: M. 729, f. 265
Ape with Host at altar, bitten by stork: Tournai Ps., f. 166v
Ape with hurdy-gurdy, three apes dancing: Bodley 264, f. 81
Ape with jawbone or comb, seated on hillock, scratching head (*cf.* Ape playing): W. 37, f. 111
Ape with knife
  and fruit: Glazier 24, f. 86 (below, ram looking up)
  holding goat: Stowe 17, f. 88v (Min.: Flagellation)
  juggling three knives, ass with vielle: W. 104, f. 20
  pruning border foliage *see* Ape pruning
Ape with lantern: Glazier 24, f. 54v
Ape with lure *see* Ape and bird, hunting; Apes fighting
Ape with mandola: G.K.S. 3384, f. 167
Ape with mirror: Cambridge Dd. 5.5, f. 388; Chartres 549, f. ?; D.P. 12, f. 76; Fitz. 2-1954, f. 152v (*fig. 60*); M. 754, f. 20 (another in drawers); Nancy 249, f. 274 (reflection shown)
  and comb: fr. 25526, f. 133v; Tournai Ps., f. 219v (before him beseeching man kneeling); W. 85, f. 89 (combing hair; above, hybrid woman)
  scratching hindquarters: fr. 12400, f. 20
Ape with mortar and pestle: Tournai Ps., f. 73 (at R., stork looking on) (*fig. 57*); W. 87, f. 104 (seated on hillock); W. 90, f. 204v
Ape with papal tiara (*cf.* Ape, two-faced)
  pursued by crowned centaur: Douce 118, f. 10 (hybrid)
  tilting astride bird with ape wearing cardinal's hat astride bird: W. 45, f. 166
Ape with pillar sundial *see* Goat with astrolabe
Ape with pipe: M. 729, f. 265 (bear tumbling); W. 37, f. 92
Ape with pipe and tabor: Add. 49622, ff. 71, 211; Bodley 264, f. 20v; Melbourne 1254/3, f. 102
  ape dancing: Tournai Ps., f. 19
  ape with bagpipe, apes tilting: Tournai Ps., f. 247
  dancing on shoulders of man with bagpipe: Stowe 17, f. 31
  seated on head of man with hands clasped: M. 754, f. 53
Ape with pitcher, spilling, biting it (proverb?): Rothschild MS., f. 178 (bear reaching for honeypot in tree, beam falling on his head)

A

Ape with pot (three-legged) held high: Cambridge Dd. 5.5, f. 246
Ape with processional cross *see* Ape as bishop; Procession
Ape with psaltery, seated in chair, cowled: latin 14284, f. 21v
Ape with purse: Add. 49622, f. 178 (pointing to, before ape-physician); M. 754, f. 52v (below, two beasts supporting gameboard; *cf.* Proverbs, gameboard)
Ape with rake (*see also* Ape playing vielle): Glazier 24, f. 91v; M. 754, ff. 14, 74v (before ?stool basket, confronting hare running out of sack; nun with club, man brandishing psaltery)
Ape with reel: G.K.S. 3384, f. 60 (above, fishmonger); M. 754, f. 22
and spindle: Glazier 24, f. 39
and spindle, hybrid woman (nude) with distaff and spindle: Stowe 17, ff. 43v-44
ape spinning, shorn sheep below: Stowe 17, ff. 91v-92
ape winding distaff: Arsenal 5218, f. 75
ape with distaff and spindle: Hague 78.D.40, ff. 19, 121v; Rylands fr. 1, f. 82 (*fig. 54*)
ape with spindle: Nancy 249, f. 80
man and woman, both with reels: Add. 36684, f. 102
woman with distaff and spindle: Douce 6, f. 48
Ape with rock *see* Ape with stone
Ape with shawm: Add. 29253, f. 54; M. 149, f. 471
and bagpipe, with basket on back containing apes: fr. 95, f. 237
displaying genitals: Add. 49622, f. 120v
Ape with shears, cutting cloth: Hague 78.D.40, f. 119v (tailor?)
Ape with spear (*see also* Ape and horse; — and snail; Ape astride bird; Ape climbing; Man nude and stag): W. 85, f. 88; W. 90, f. 93v (preceding falconer on horse)
Ape with spindle *see* Ape with distaff; — with reel
Ape with staff: BBR 10607, f. 228
and fruit *see* Ape with fruit
biting beak of bird-headed man: M. 108, f. 134v
Ape with stone held to ear, putting (? *cf.* Dog with stone): W. 104, f. 8
Ape with stool basket: Douce 6, f. 50
Ape with switch (Disciplina?; *see also* Apes fighting; School): fr. 95, f. 66v; Hague XX, f. 4 (5); W. 87, f. 35
and shield, on stilts, tilting with ape astride ram with rake and shield: W. 82, f. 205v
ape kneeling before him: Hague 78.D.40, f. 29
ape with book seated before him: W. 88, f. 38v
beating ape: G.K.S. 3384, f. 79v (or beating dog between apes); Y.T. 8, f. 217v
Ape with sword (*see also* Ape fighting, references under; Ape pruning; Ape with *godendag*)
climbing border stalk (*cf.* Ape climbing): Melbourne 1254/3, f. 11 (above, patrons: Joffroy d'Aspremont and Isabelle de Kievraing) (*fig. 550*)
seated: Trinity B.11.22, f. 199v (*fig. 335*)
straddling sword (Arthurian reference? *Cf.* Man, nude, armless): M. 754, f. 57
Ape with tablet *see* Ape as scribe
Ape with tabor: G.K.S. 3384, f. 202v; Tournai Ps., f. 203; Trinity B.11.22, f. 131
Ape with tabor, astride fox backwards: Fitz. 242, f. 55v
Ape with tambourine *see* Apes fighting, with swords
Ape with top *see* Top-whipping
Ape with trumpet (*see also* Apes tilting, astride ram; Ass with pipe; Woman and lion, astride): Douce 49, f. 103 (Min.: Crucifixion); Glazier 24, ff. 100, 126; Hague XX, f. 155; Melbourne 1254/3, f. 30v; W. 37, f. 92; W. 87, f. 107
ape with bagpipe (*see also* Woman nude, and goat): Tournai Ps., f. 204v
astride goat: Royal 2 B.VII, f. 194v
directed by ape: Tournai Ps., f. 108
held against hindquarters of ape: Yale MS., f. 147
stag hunt in upper margin: Ashmole 828, f. 13
two-faced, wearing tall pointed ecclesiastical hat: Melbourne 1245/3, f. 128 (two)
Ape with vielle (*see also* Ape playing): Add. 17868, f. 32; BBR 329-41, f. 67; Cambrai 87, ff. 55v, 117; Fitz. 298, f. 26v; Laud Lat. 84, f. 235v (at L., hawk); Stowe 17, f. 144v (f. 145, couple under tree); Vienna 2542, f. 158
ape dancing: Laud Lat. 84, ff. 307v-308
ape doing handstand: Nancy 249, f. 9v
ape with double pipe: Tournai Ps., f. 196
ape with harp, four apes dancing: Royal 2 B.VII, ff. 179v-180
centaurs fighting with whips and bucklers: Add. 17868, f. 143
lion dancing: Add. 49622, f. 35

man/dog dancing: W. 88, f. 85
man nude dancing: W. 37, ff. 165v-166
standing on second vielle: M. 754, f. 14
Ape with wheelbarrow
containing ape: Bodley 264, ff. 98v (two), 133v; G.K.S. 3384, f. 296v
containing ape with belled cap drinking (proverb?): G.K.S. 3384, f. 145v (*fig. 58*)
containing apes (3), drawn by owl: Trinity B.11.22, f. 206
containing apes (3), pursued by bear (Bestiary variant?): Y.T. 13, ff. 183v-185
containing apes (3), second ape pulling on long rope: Arras 1043, f. 7
Ape with whip *see* Ape with switch
Ape wrestling *see* Wrestling
Ape writing *see* Ape as scribe
Apes attacking castle *see* Castle
Apes dancing *see* Ape dancing
Apes fighting
as bishop astride man, with sword and shield against ape: Add. 10292, f. 1
astride apes moving in opposite directions, with swords and bucklers: Glazier 24, f. 99v
astride dog with spear and shield against ape astride dragon with switch: Douce 6, f. 184
with clubs and bucklers: Cambridge Dd. 5.5, f. 403; Tournai Ps., ff. 16v, 100v, 157v, 201v
with dagger: Douce 5, f. 159v
with flails: G.K.S. 3384, f. 79v (in center, dog)
with lures and bucklers: Lat. lit. f. 3, f. 70v
with spear and sword: M. 155, ff. 7v-8
with swords and bucklers: BBR II 988, vol. II, f. 228; Cambrai 103, f. 364; Cambridge Dd. 5.5, f. 299; fr. 95, f. 249v; fr. 25526, f. 30v; G.K.S. 3384, f. 171; Hague 78.D.40, f. 152; Lat. lit. f. 3, f. 70; Tournai Ps., ff. 3, 78v, 205v
with swords and bucklers astride apes moving in opposite directions: Glazier 24, f. 99v
with swords and shields astride apes, flanked by apes with tambourine and trumpet: Royal 2 B.VII, ff. 175v-176
with war hammers and shields: Melbourne 1254/3, f. 31
Apes performing play(?): Hague 78.D.40, f. 153 (2 beckoning to small ape gesturing in center before table or raised platform; at R., two apes)
Apes, seated back to back, holding large bones: M. 754, f. 49
Apes tilting, astride (*see also* Quintain, tilting)
apes: Nancy 249, f. 101
birds: Cambrai 102, f. 283v (with distaff and shovel); Cambrai 103, f. 400v; Cracow 815, ff. 11v (with distaff and spear), 269v; W. 45, f. 166 (wearing cardinal's hat and papal tiara; above, hybrid man with pipe and tabor) (*fig. 61*)
dog and fox, with distaff and broom, tongs and bellows: Hague 78.D.40, f. 154
dog and fox, with fowl impaled on lances: Hague 78.D.40, f. 126v
dog and hare: Tournai Ps., f. 160v
dog and horse: Princeton 44-18, ff. 151v-152
dog and unicorn: Seligman 11, p. 23
dog, wearing basket as helmet: G.K.S. 3384, f. 229v (second ape on foot)
fox and cock: Hague 78.D.40, f. 44v
goats, hare with trumpet and squirrel with pipe: Arras 729, f. 142
goat-types: M. 729, f. 311
goose and cock: Y.T. 8, f. 176
goose and snail: Cambrai 103, f. 95
horses: Hague 78.D.40, f. 94; W. 90, f. 75; Yale MS., f. 126
ibex and stag, with arrows: Hague 78.D.40, f. 90v (in center, ape with shield)
ram and fox: Hague 78.D.40, ff. 73v, 86 (fowl impaled on lances)
ram with long fork and shield, second ape seated on border foliage with long fork: W. 82, f. 194v (flanked by apes with trumpets)
ram with rake and shield, second ape with broom and shield on stilts: W. 82, f. 205v
snail *see above,* —, goose
unicorn and lion: G.K.S. 3384, f. 259
Apes tilting on foot: Glazier 24, f. 88; Royal 10 E.IV, f. 75v; Tournai Ps., ff. 61v (fox rampant on shield), 98, 210v, 247 (accompanied by two apes with bagpipe and pipe and tabor)
Apocalyptic vision *see* St. John the Evangelist, vision of
Apostles (*see also* Jesus Christ and disciples; Jesus Christ, life of; Prophets; Virgin and apostles; individual names listed under St.—): Cambrai 87, f. 93v (12); Y.T. 27, f. 125
Apothecary (*cf.* Man with mortar and pestle): Cracow 816, f. 101v (3) (*fig. 59*)
Apple *see* Ape with fruit; Hedgehog; Hybrid man with club; Man balancing on table; Siren holding; Virgin and Child, seated

A

April *see* King with branches; Man and woman, parting; Man with branch; Quintain, balancing, ape seated
Aram and Amminadab: Y.T. 13, f. 32 (Genealogy of Christ)
Arbalest *see* Castle attacked by knights
Archangels: Add. 42130, f. 101 (3, trampling devils; at R., Gabriel); Stowe 17, f. 144 (Michael?)
Archer (*see also* references under Man and [name of weapon], hunting; Man and [name of prey], shooting):
  attacked by ape astride stag: G.K.S. 3384, f. 112v
  fighting knight: fr. 95, f. 32 (2, two)
  shooting hindquarters of man: BBR 9391, f. 93; BBR 10607, f. 17
Archery
  man shooting at hillock, second man gesturing: Hague 78.D.40, f. 10
  men shooting at animal-head target: Trinity B.11.22, f. 33v (2)
  men shooting at bird on pole held by woman: Hague 78.D.40, f. 159 (3)
  men shooting at cock and bird on low shrub: Royal 2 B.VII, f. 161 (2)
  men shooting at stop-butt: Add. 42130, f. 147v (5 and instructor)
Aristotle *see* Phyllis and
Ark *see* Noah
Armorer *see* Ape as armorer; Blacksmith
Arrow *see* Ape with; Apes tilting astride ibex; Hare hanging; Hybrid ape with
Arthurian legends, references to (?) *see* Ape with sword
Artisan *see* specific occupation, e.g., Blacksmith
Artois *see* Patron: Joffroy d'Aspremont
Asahel *see* David, life of: Abner and; —: Asahel
Ascension *see* Jesus Christ, life of
Asinus *see* Cleric nude, disputing
Asp, Bestiary representation: Royal 2 B.VII, ff. 125v-126 (in cycle)
Asperge and situla *see* Ape with; Bishop at church door; Bishop with; Cat with; Cleric with; Fox with; Procession
Ass (*see also* Balaam; Cleric nude, disputing; Hybrid ass; Pilgrim astride)
  and ape, ridden by: N.K.S. 41, f. 154v
  and apes (2) singing at lectern containing scroll with musical notations: Glazier 24, f. 48 (*fig. 62*)
  and bear, fighting with hammers and shields: M. 729, f. 255v
  and hare under trees: Hague 10 A.14, f. 144 (2, three)
  and hare, with foxes attacking castle defended by apes: Stowe 17, ff. 243v-244
  and hybrid man, shot by: Jacquemart 1, f. 88
  and man
    carried by (fable or proverb): G.K.S. 3384, f. 82; Glazier 24, f. 32
    driven by: Y.T. 8, f. 254
    driven by, to windmill, loaded with sack: Bodley 264, f. 81; Stowe 17, f. 89v; Valenciennes 838, f. 55 (*fig. 699*)
    ridden by, fighting man astride dog: Bodley 264, f. 50
  and stag under tree bearing golden fruit: Hague 10 A.14, f. 106v
  and woman, driven by, accompanied by child: Yale MS., f. 85v
  and woman, ridden by, sack over her shoulder, holding distaff and spindle: Arsenal 5218, f. 20 (at side, two apes on stilts)
  as bishop: G.K.S. 3384, f. 301v
  as cleric (*see also* Obscaena, revering): Add. 10294, f. 1; Chantilly 64, ff. 28, 28v (with book; below, ?cleric gesturing)
  as physician (with urinal) before hybrid man with stool basket around neck: Glazier 24, f. 76v (*fig. 63*)
  as schoolmaster before three fowl: Chantilly 64, ff. 89, 89v
  Bestiary representation (in cycle): Munich c.g. 16, f. 44; Royal 2 B.VII, ff. 105v-106 (wild ass)
  climbing into fenced enclosure *see* Proverbs: ass
  dancing, man with pipe and tabor: Chantilly 64, ff. 119, 119v
  head of
    impaled on spear of knight: W. 90, f. 146
    in bowl held by hybrid man: fr. 25526, f. 95v
    nude headless man stooping to pick it up: Glazier 24, f. 109v
  playing bellows with jawbone, merman fishing: M. 729, f. 268
  pulling cart *see* Man in cart
  ridden by bishop seated backwards: Yale MS., f. 104v
  with ax (polearm?): Glazier 24, f. 44v
  with bagpipe: W. 85, f. 93
  with gittern: Glazier 24, f. 72v
  with lyre (harp): Douce 131, f. 20; W. 85, f. 85
  with mortar and pestle: W. 87, f. 77

with pipe (*see also* Procession, funeral of fox): fr. 25526, f. 68 (and tabor); Royal 2 B.VII, f. 193
with pipe, dogs with vielle, mandola, psaltery, timbrel, hand organ, flask and cup; goat with pipe and tabor, two apes with trumpets, antelope(?) with gittern; ape, dogs, hares wearing bells around ankles dancing: BBR 9157, f. 1
with processional cross *see* Procession, ape-cleric with asperge
with trumpet: Royal 2 B.VII, f. 194v (cat with tabor); W. 85, f. 92
with vielle: BBR 10607, f. 130v; M. 754, f. 89; W. 109, f. 20 (at L., ape juggling three knives) (*fig. 48*)

Assumption of Virgin *see* Virgin, life of

Astronomer
looking up at stars: Stowe 17, f. 205v (hybrid; below, ape with sword and buckler) (*fig. 65*)
with telescope: Douce 6, f. 127 (doctor's cap; below, bishop, ape with crosier); G.K.S. 3384, f. 126 (*fig. 64*)

August *see* Man reaping; Obscaena, defecating: ape

Avarice *see* Dives; Hybrid woman with coins; — with purse; Jesus Christ, life of: Last Judgment: Pains of Hell: miser; Man hoarding; Man with abacus; Treasure chest; Woman hoarding

Ax *see* Ape with; Ass with; Hare with; Hybrid man with; Man and snail, fighting with; Man nude and snail; Man with; Man with claw feet; Wild man with

B

Baal *see* Gideon

Babel, confusion of tongues brought to: Munich c.g. 16, f. 24v

Babel, tower of, constructed (*cf.* Man building): Munich c.g. 16, f. 24v

Backgammon(?): Add. 42130, f. 76v (king and woman); Stowe 17, f. 268v (two men disputing, bleeding) (*fig. 66*)

Badger *see* Fox and

Bagpipe *see* Ape as bishop; Ape with; Ape with basket; Ass with; Cat with; Centaur with; Devil with; Dog with; Hare with; Hybrid man with; Man and dog; Man with; Merman with; Shepherd; Stag with

Baker baking bread in oven (*cf.* Oven, references under): Cambridge Dd.5.5, f. 280 (2) (*fig. 67*); Douce 6, f. 181 (2, one with tray containing two loaves); Harley 6563, f. 66
carrying oven (flaming) on back, ape retrieving rolls: G.K.S. 3384, f. 67 (*fig. 69*)
carrying tray containing six loaves on back: Y.T. 27, f. 70a v
carrying tray on back; above, hybrid beast with oven: Add. 36684, f. 48 (*fig. 68*)
hybrid woman with tray containing loaf: M. 754, f. 6v
man bringing basket (*Wright's Chaste Wife* sequence?): Royal 10 E.IV, ff. 145-145v
nude hybrid man pulling bread out of oven: Add. 36684, f. 67
with woman assisting: W. 88, f. 14v (December)
woman kneading dough: Add. 36684, f. 152; Nancy 249, f. 195; Stowe 17, f. 211

Bakery(?), pavilion with triple wheat-sheaf sign; two men behind table filled with loaves: Bodley 264, f. 204 (at R., men cooking, roasting meat before inn)

Balaam blindfolded astride ass: St. Omer 5, f. 159v (at L., Jew before cave)

Balancing *see* Ape; Fish; Hare; Hybrid cleric; Hybrid man; Man; Merman; Sciapode; Sheep; Woman

Ball game *see* Hybrid man with ball; Handball; Man and ape, aiming

Banana(?) *see* Hybrid man with basket

Bandyball (with target)
apes: Add. 29253, f. 416v (above, ape snaring bird with decoy); Add. 30029, f. 141; Cambrai 102, f. 3; Douce 5, f. 67; G.K.S. 3384, ff. 183, 240v; Hague 10 A.14, f. 167; Tournai Ps., ff. 142v, 213, 214v; W. 82, f. 209v (*fig. 70*); Y.T. 8, f. 194v
centaur: fr. 95, f. 347v
hybrid men (*cf.* Duck flying): Cambrai 103, f. 187 (at R., apes fighting with swords and bucklers)
men: Add. 38114, f. 1; Arras 47, f. 196v; Arras 729, ff. 8, 156; Arras 1043, f. 155; BBR 9411-26, f. 139v; BBR 9961-62, f. 14; BBR 10228, f. 6 (*fig. 71*); BBR II 988, vol. I, f. 1; Cambrai 103, f. 438v; Chantilly 64, ff. 90, 90v; Douce 6, f. 156v; fr. 95, f. 321 (*fig. 72*) Hague 78.D.40, ff. 11 (man and cleric), 39v; M. 108, f. 131

B

(trimmed); M. 729, f. 333v (above, peacock); M. 796, f. 90v (6); Princeton 44-18, ff. 80v-81, 188v, 201; Rothschild MS., f. 117v; St. Omer 5, f. 240v; Trinity B.11.22, ff. 35, 123v; Vienna 2542, f. 155; W. 88, ff. 22, 178v; W. 90, f. 31v; Yale MS., f. 183v

Bandyball (without target), men: Royal 10 E.IV, f. 95; W. 88, f. 40v; Y.T. 27, f. 120

Banquet (*see also* Virtues: Temperance; Woman at table): Add. 36684, f. 40
- king and men (2) at table, servants bringing food (Dives?): fr. 25526, f. 96 (f. 95v, pilgrim and two men with staffs)
- king and men (2) at table, servant kneeling with cup: Royal 2 B.VII, f. 185 (f. 184v, two servants bearing dishes, led by man with vielle)
- man at table, servant: Douce 6, f. 66v (at L., huge knight with sword astride dragon)
- men (3) and woman, three servants bearing dishes out of building at R.: Royal 2 B.VII, ff. 199v-200
- men (3), cupbearer kneeling; men with mandola and vielle: Royal 2 B.VII, ff. 202v-203
- men (4), man with harp seated, four men dancing: Royal 2 B.VII, ff. 203v-204
- Sir Geoffrey Luttrell at table, with wife, two Dominicans, two men, woman: Add. 42130, f. 208 (two men serving; ff. 206v-207v, preparation of food) (*figs. 73-74*)

Baptism *see* Jesus Christ, life of; Sacraments; St. John the Baptist; St. Paul; St. Thomas of Canterbury

Baptismal font *see* Font

Barber (*cf.* Man combing; Man cutting hair): G.K.S. 3384, f. 51 (cutting ape's hair) (*fig. 75*)

Bardolf-Vaux arms on banner suspended from trumpet blown by angel: Lambeth 233, f. 101 (f. 44, Vaux arms)

Barons of Love *see* Lover

Basilisk: Harley 6563, f. 80v; Stowe 17, f. 267v (f. 268, man with sword and buckler)

Basket *see* Ape and goat, astride, tilting; Ape with; Apes tilting, astride dog; Beggar with; Devil with; Eel; Fox with; Hybrid snail with; Hybrid woman with; Lion with; Man and hare, hunting; Man and ram; — and unicorn, warding off; Man in; Man with; Proverbs: eggs; —: woman; Quintain, tilting at hybrid knight; Saracen with; Virgin and Child, leading; Man and woman, fighting; Woman with

Bat: Add. 42130, f. 164 (below, centaur); Fitz. 242, f. 52; fr. 12400, f. 75v; latin 3893, ff. 146, 151v (butterflies?)
- Bestiary representation (in cycle): Munich c.g. 16, f. 51; Royal 2 B.VII, ff. 91v-92
- confronting bull: M. 796, f. 59v
- confronting pelican: Chantilly 64, ff. 113, 113v

Bathhouse approached by two nude women; at R., man and woman in tub embracing: Bodley 264, f. 75

Bathing *see* Ape; Hare and offspring; Hybrid man with water buckets; Jesus Christ, life of; Man; Man and woman; Woman

Bathsheba *see* David, life of: D. and Bathsheba;—: D. and Solomon

Battlement, knights shooting from: Holkham 458, f. 44

Bat wings *see* Angel with; Ape as beggar; Eagle; Hybrid man with; Man with

Bear (*see also* Ape and; Ass and; Centaur and; Fables: bears; Goat with astrolabe; Handball; Hare and; Horse and; Hybrid man and; Lion and; Man and; St. Mary the Egyptian): Add. 39810, f. 7 (*fig. 140*); Yale MS., f. 183v
- Bestiary representation: Munich c.g. 16, f. 34 (in cycle)
- chained: Nancy 249, f. 245; Stowe 17, f. 108v (f. 109, school of apes) (*fig. 634*)
- head emerging from cave in ground: Fitz. 242, f. 55v (lion? Min.: Crucifixion) (*fig. 12*)
- held at bay by two hounds: Royal 10 E.IV, f. 155
- intercourse: Merton 0.1.3, f. 120v (erased; at R., birds' intercourse)
- reaching for honeypot in tree, beam falling on his head (proverb?): Rothschild MS., f. 178 (ape biting, spilling pitcher; proverb?)
- trained by: Add. 49622, ff. 71v, 109v
- tumbling: Fitz. 242, f. 49; Harley 6563, f. 42 (f. 41v, boar with harp); M. 729, f. 265 (ape with horn)
- under tree: Add. 29253, f. 22 (3)
- with doe and hedgehog: Fitz. 242, f. 55v (Min.: Crucifixion) (*fig. 12*)
- with pipe, second bear pursuing nude man in tree: Rutland Ps., ff. 52v-53
- with taper(?): Cloisters 54.1.2, f. 36v

Beast (*cf.* Monster; *see also* Ape and; Knight with head of; Man and; Procession, funeral of fox)

astride cat, tilting with ape(?) astride cock: M. 729, f. 346 (trimmed)
balancing in mouth horizontal bar with taper at either end: Douce 5, f. 39 (line ending, head only; below, man with crook) (*fig. 480*)
head of, with ax in mouth, four gold coins(?) on ground: M. 754, f. 80
with crosier: Lansdowne 420, f. 87
with distaff, hybrid man with distaff: M. 754, f. 93v
with oven on pole in mouth: Add. 36684, f. 48 (below, baker with tray containing loaves on back)
with spoon: M. 729, f. 258v
with stag horns: BBR 9157, throughout (also hybrid men with stag horns throughout)

Beating *see* Ape with switch; Beggar, blind; Lover, beaten; Man and woman, beaten by; Man beating; School, attended by apes; *Wright's Chaste Wife*

Beaver
Bestiary representation: BBR 9411-26, f. 138v (variant: two-legged animal; man juggling); BBR 10607, f. 39; Douce 118, f. 107v; fr. 776, f. 160 (dog?); latin 16260, f. 29 (cat washing itself?); Munich c.g. 16, f. 15 (in cycle) (*fig. 79*); Rothschild MS., f. 181v; Royal 2 B.VII, ff. 101v-102 (in cycle)
in water, grasping board: Lambeth 209, f. 7v (added) (*fig. 78*)

Becket, Thomas *see* St. Thomas of Canterbury

Bed *see* Ape and child; King in; Man and woman in; Men making

Bee
and ape with horn, stinging: Add. 10293, f. 1 (2)
and dog, stinging: Stowe 17, f. 48 (2) (*fig. 80*)
and hare, stinging: W. 37, f. 158v (f. 159, Capricorn) (*fig. 81*)
Bestiary representation (in cycle): Munich c.g. 16, f. 57 (beekeeper, two beehives) (*fig. 83*)
man releasing three bees from sack: Stowe 17, f. 148 (catching in sack?)

Beehive
flanked by pelican in piety and two birds: Merton 0.1.3, f. 52v
with swarm of bees: Add. 42130, f. 204; Douce 6, f. 136v (at R., hooded veiled figure beating tabor)

Beggar (*see also* Ape as; Centaur with vielle; Hybrid man as): Add. 49622, f. 62; Chantilly 64, ff. 91, 91v; Cloisters 54.1.2, f. 20v; M. 754, f. 56
and ape *see* Beggar, crippled
and child: Bodley 264, f. 133v (2, four)
in arms, with bowl: Y.T. 27, f. 79v
in sling on back: D.P. 12, f. 76 (with vielle); fr. 95, f. 106v (with harp, monster with gittern); St. Omer 5, f. 133 (below, Jonah) (*fig. 291*); W. 90, f. 160 (approaching dog)
in sling on pole: Cloisters 54.1.2, f. 33
led by dog: Cambrai 103, f. 339 (2)
on back, with staff and rosary: Add. 42130, f. 53
and dog: Cloisters 54.1.2, f. 147v; Trinity B.11.22, f. 213v; W. 88, f. 18
followed by gesturing boys: Cambridge Dd. 5.5, f. 364 (2)
led by (blind?): Bodley 264, f. 77v (dog with bowl in mouth); Douce 6, f. 98v (woman giving coin; above, Christ in clouds, blessing); Fitz. 298, f. 108v; W. 82, f. 207 (at R., beggar with basket on back containing ape)
and hybrid man in initial, patting: Cloisters 54.1.2, f. 85
and man (youth), both gesturing: BBR 9411-26, f. 90
blind, cheated by boy, beating him (*Le Garçon et l'Aveugle*): Royal 10 E.IV, ff. 217v-220v (*figs. 425-429*)
crippled (*cf.* Man crippled): Chantilly 64, ff. 100, 100v; Douce 5, f. 157
crippled(?) in wheelbarrow: Cloisters 54.1.2, f. 81v (below, snail)
crippled(?) in wheelbarrow pushed and pulled by two apes, holding gold cup and wearing belled hood: Douce 6, f. 136v
in horsecart approaching city: W. 82, f. 193v (man giving coin)
supporting miniature: Cloisters 54.1.2, f. 142 (2; Min.: St. Louis ministering to sick)
with basket on back containing (*cf.* Man with basket)
ape: Douce 5, f. 74; Douce 6, f. 153 (man ringing bell attached to peak of beggar's hood) (*fig. 52*); G.K.S. 3384, f. 105 (below, man holding up ?food); W. 82, f. 207 (at L., beggar with dog, ape blowing pipe with pinwheel attached) (*fig. 82*)
child: Bodley 264, f. 133v (two); G.K.S. 3384, f. 75v; Hague 78.D.40, f. 42v (at R., beggar exposing hindquarters); Melbourne 1254/3, f. 22v

preceded by child, wearing drawers, carrying bowls: latin 3893, f. 207v
with dog and bowl, approaching woman with churn: Add. 10294, f. 1
with dog and staff, child in sling on back: W. 90, f. 160
with staff: fr. 25526, ff. 68 (2; at R., hare winding wool), 92v (2)
with bowl (*cf.* Virtues: Charity): Cloisters 54.1.2, ff. 142 (2), 154
and rattle: Cloisters 54.1.2, f. 130 (hybrid; leper?)
and staff: Cambridge Dd. 5.5, f. 364 (2); Nancy 249, f. 68v (2); W.90, f. 142v
astride: Y.T. 27, f. 27
standing on monster: Cloisters 54.1.2, f. 149
with harp: fr. 95, f. 106v (child in sling on back, monster with gittern); Y.T. 8, f. 198v
with sling *see above,* — and child
with vielle *see above,* — and child
Beggarwoman with bowl and rattle (leper?): Cloisters 54.1.2, f. 20 (astride monster backwards); Y.T. 27, f. 21v (seated on old hybrid man)
Bell *see* Ape as pilgrim; Ape ringing; Bird with; Butterfly ringing; Cleric with; Horse, leg of; Hybrid bishop with bells; Hybrid man ringing; Man ringing; Man with shawm; Mermaid with hand bells; Pygmy and crane
Bellows *see* Ape and hare, pumping; Ape playing; Cleric with; Devil and man, seated; Dog and hare, blowing; Dominican playing; Franciscan playing; Hare with; Hybrid bishop blessing; Hybrid man playing; Hybrid man with; Jew with; Man and ape, playing; Man with; Tinker; Wild man with; Winged head-dress, worn by monster with
Bells for falcon: fr. 12400, f. 108
Bells worn by dancing animals *see* Ass with pipe
Benedictine *see* Cleric
Benjamin *see* David, life of: D. and
Bessus (Brunehilde?) martyred: Bodley 264, f. 42v
Bestiary *see* Ant; Antelope; Ape; Asp; Ass; Bat; Bear; Beaver; Bee; Boar; Bonnacon; Caladrius; Camel; Cattle; Centaur; Cinomolgus; Cock; Cockatrice; Crane; Crocodile; Crow; Cycles; Dog; Dromedary; Eagle; Elephant; Epifagus; Fox; Goat; Griffin; Halcyon; Hart; Hedgehog; Hoopoe; Horse; Hydra; Hyena; Ibex; Ibis; Leopard; Lion; Mandrake; Manticora; Ostrich; Owl; Panther; Parandrus; Partridge; Peacock; Pelican; Peridexion; Phoenix; Pigeon; Salamander; Serpent; Serra; Sheep; Siren; Stag; Stork; Swallow; Swan; Terrobuli; Tiger; Turtledove; Unicorn; Viper; Weasel; Whale; Wolf; Yale
Betrayal *see* Jesus Christ, life of
Bevis of Hampton, adventures of: Royal 10 E.IV, ff. 80-88; Y.T. 13, ff. 7v-12v
Bier (*cf.* Funeral, references under): Add. 49622, f. 92v (six lit tapers); fr. 25526, f. 128 (attended by cleric and man; at R.; lectern with book)
Bird (*see also* Ape and; Butterfly in cart; Cat and; Centaur and; Centauress; Cleric and; Dog and; Fox and; Hare and; Hybrid bird; Knight and; Lion and; Man and; Man nude and; Man nude and fox; Obscaena, beak; Stag, tail bitten; Wild man and; Woman and; Woman nude and man; specific entries under species)
and hybrid woman holding out round object: Add. 17868, f. 104 (siren?)
and snail, confronted: Add. 49622, f. 209v (below, ape-falconer)
and wivern, attacked by: All Souls lat. 6, f. 13
as bishop, with devil's head in beak: Melbourne 1254/3, f. 13 (serpent coiled around adjacent border stalk)
as cleric: Royal 1 D.I, f. 350v
flying from nest containing two young: W. 45, f. 178 (below, hybrid man with gittern)
flying out of oven (proverb?): Add. 36684, f. 20v
flying toward nest: Cambrai 103, f. 118
flying toward nest containing eggs: Cambrai 102, f. 394v (nest flanked by beasts); W. 45, f. 201v (hen, five eggs)
flying toward nest containing young: Add. 24681, ff. 20 (?magpie; below, dog hunting stag; Min.: Annunciation), 77 (Min.: Pentecost), 100 (Min.: Noli me tangere); BBR 10607, ff. 51 (3 magpies; Ps. 30), 170v (at L., angel with vielle); Douce 5, f. 202 (ape climbing border stalk toward nest); Douce 118, f. 121v; W. 45, ff. 10v, 162 (below, ape snaring birds), 205, 217, 219v
in building (church?): Rutland Ps., f. 18
in cage: Kraus 75/88, f. 114v; M. 149, f. 1v
in nest (*see also* Ape with bowl; Man and dragon, astride with bowl; Pelican): Add. 21114, f. 105v; Add. 29253, f. 41v (Ps. 52);

C.B. 62, f. 120v; Cambrai 102, ff. 195v, 324, 340v, 387, 427, 436v (at R., lion), 497; Cambrai 103, ff. 153, 272v; Douce 6, f. 29 (at L., man holding nest; below, man with ax chopping supporting branch); Douce 118, f. 58v; latin 3893, f. 13; latin 13260, f. 29v; M. 754, ff. 13v (*frontispiece*), 57v, 93v (nest of bricks? beast and hybrid man with distaffs); Melbourne 1254/3, f. 102v; W. 45, ff. 41v (below, ape snaring birds), 44v (with hare's ears), 197 (above, lion with hare's ears); W. 87, f. 93
hunted by man with stick, birdcage: Trinity B.11.22, f. 199v
in tree: Douce 118, f. 160 (5); fr. 12400, f. 18 (3, and owl)
shot by man: Douce 118, f. 95
in tree (*see also* King as falconer): Melbourne 1254/3, f. 93v; W. 88, ff. 79 (2, at R., dog), 137 (leaping dog); W. 759, f. 99v (2)
in water: M. 754, f. 54
intercourse: Merton 0.1.3, ff. 24v, 120v
looking out of oven (*cf. above,*—, flying out): Add. 36684, f. 58v
pecking breast (*cf.* Pelican in piety): Douce 366, ff. 71v, 109; M. 754, f. 66 (hybrid knight with spear)
snared *see* Ape and bird, snaring; Man and bird, snaring; Wild man and bird
with bell, second bird with sword: Add. 21926, f. 208v
with distaff *see* Hybrid man with
with hare's ears in nest containing eggs (*cf.* Dragon with): W. 45, f. 44v
with horseshoe in beak: latin 1076, f. 16v (ostrich variant?); Stowe 17, f. 120v (*fig. 736*)
with lantern on head, second bird with lantern hung from beak: M. 754, f. 89v
with reel, hybrid woman and second bird with reels, hybrid woman spinning: M. 754, f. 21v
with sprig of green in beak: latin 13260, ff. 116v (Min.: Trinity), 119 (below, dog pursuing hare with green sprig in mouth)
with worm in beak: Stowe 17, f. 120v (f. 121, two men wrestling); W. 45, ff. 6v, 12v, 14v, 159, 165v, 202v (twig?); W. 87, f. 15v (above, man with scroll)
Birdcage *see* Ape and bird, snaring; Man and bird, feeding; —, hunting; Woman with
Birdcage, two birds below, dog pursuing hare and stag: M. 754, f. 42
Birds in pond: fr. 12400, ff. 13v, 14, 20, 23, 51, 52v, 68v
Birds, various species: Add. 39810, f. 7 (*fig. 140*); Add. 24686, throughout; Bodley 264, throughout; Fitz. 2-1954, throughout; fr. 12400, throughout (mostly water fowl)
Bishop (*see also* Ape and hybrid bishop; Ape as; Ass as; Bird as; Cardinal and cleric; Centaur as; David, life of: D. crowned; Fox as; Goat, head of; Hybrid abbot; Hybrid bishop; Jesus Christ, life of: Last Judgment: Pains of Hell: devil with; Lion as; Man nude as; Merman as; Procession; Sacraments; Virgin, miracles of; Wolf as): Add. 42130, ff. 31, 85; Kraus 75/88, f. 200 (*fig. 85*); latin 1076, f. 116v; W. 87, f. 61v (below, fox with bull's head)
and ass, astride backwards, blessing and holding up ass's tail, followed by man pointing: Yale MS., f. 104v (*fig. 87*)
and bear, pointing at: Douce 5, f. 198v
and boy with asperge: Trinity B.11.22, f. 141
and cleric (*see also below,* — at church door; — with book)
at tomb: Harley 6563, ff. 58v (f. 59, female mourner)
hearing confession of: Add. 49622, f. 131v
preaching to, cleric kneeling: BBR 10607, f. 119
receiving book from, cleric kneeling: fr. 25526, f. 159 (at L., cardinal?)
and devil *see below,*—as devil;—on stilts
and dog: Add. 42130, f. 84 (dog jumping through hoop)
and dragon: latin 10483, ff. 13v (blessing, with asperge), 63 (blessing or warding off)
and king with reliquary: latin 14284, f. 25
and man *see* Man and bishop
and monster, astride: Cambrai 87, f. 86v
and nun
fighting with swords and bucklers: Add. 30029, f. 90
hearing confession of: Add. 49622, f. 102v
kneeling before: Add. 49622, f. 117 (*fig. 86*)
and pilgrim *see* Pilgrim
and pope: Add. 49622, f. 207
and snail, conversing: Melbourne 1254/3, f. 118v
and woman: G.K.S. 3384, f. 281 (confronted); Princeton 44-18, f. 40 (blessing); Yale MS., ff. 315, 326 (kissing)
as devil (*cf.* Bishop wearing; Bishop with book,

head): G.K.S. 3384, f. 215 (with cloven hoof, cleric with crosier)
at church door, dedicating: Fitz. 298, ff. 1 (cleric with cross, acolyte with asperge and situla), 9 (knocking at door, deacon with book, acolyte with asperge and situla) (*fig. 566*)
at tomb with asperge, two men, cleric: Harley 6563, f. 58v (f. 59, female mourner)
blessing (*see also above,* — and ass; — and dragon; — and woman; Pilgrim; School attended by apes): Fitz. 2-1954, f. 154; Stowe 17, f. 140 (Min.: abbot blessing female patron)
hybrid beast exposing hindquarters: W. 88, f. 106
man blowing bellows like trumpet, standing on his shoulders: Cloisters 54.1.2, f. 104
dedicating church *see above,* — at church door
head of *see* Man nude holding
in wheelbarrow *see* Jesus Christ, life of: Last Judgment: Pains of Hell: devil with wheelbarrow
investing man (half-figure) with miter and crosier: Yale MS., f. 133v (hybrid)
nude (*see also below,*—with book)
armless (*cf.* Man nude, armless): M. 796, f. 79
carried off by devil: Cambrai 87, f. 73
climbing border stalk (*cf.* Ape climbing): W. 87, ff. 6, 67v
with cloven hooves: Add. 36684, f. 109
on stilts, devil reaching for him with forked stick: W. 90, f. 153 (*fig. 84*)
parodied by ape, ass, dogs, goats ram (*cf.* references after Bishop, main entry) G.K.S. 393, f. 301v
preaching, cleric praying: BBR 10607, f. 119
wearing bellows on head, crosier terminating in cloven hoof: Y.T. 27, f. 38
winged, praying: W. 87, f. 104
with asperge: latin 10483, f. 13v
with book
book attached to tail of hybrid man with gold chalice: W. 88, f. 176
head shaped like cloven hoof: Cloisters 54.1.2, f. 203v
nude save for cape: W. 90, f. 88 (above, nude man with rope tied to rock)
with censer: M. 754, f. 81v (hybrid man, nude and armless, hooved, exposing hindquarters)
with cloven hoof, cleric with crosier: G.K.S. 3384, f. 215
with crucifix staff: Add. 42130, f. 45
with hand bells *see* Procession, funeral
with harp: Cloisters 54.1.2, f. 83
with pipe and tabor before nude man dancing: W. 102, f. 76
with reliquary, bearing with king: latin 14284, f. 25
with scroll "Ecce psalmus trinitatis": Melbourne 1254/3, f. 103
Blacksmith (*see also* Ape as): BBR 1175, f. 24v; G.K.S. 3384, f. 60 (ape spinning) (*fig. 51*)
forging helmets and scale armor: Bodley 264, ff. 164v-165
forging horseshoe: Add. 49622, ff. 144v, 154v, 193; Bodley 264, f. 107 (at L., shoeing horse); Harley 6563, ff. 68v-69
forging sword, carving plates of metal (Tubalcain): Munich c.g. 16, f. 19v
hammering on anvil: Add. 36684, ff. 100v-101; Bodley 264, ff. 84 (2, by forge), 171v (by forge); Rothschild MS., f. 169 (ape) (*fig. 88*)
polishing and sharpening sword on grindstone: Bodley 264, f. 113v
Bladder *see* Man nude, balancing
Bleeding of man by physician: Add. 42130, f. 61
Blessed (*see also* Jesus Christ, life of: Last Judgment: Pains of Hell): St. Omer 5, f. 138v
Blind *see* Beggar; Man; Samson
Blindfolded *see* Balaam; Hybrid men fighting, one; Jew
Blindman's buff (*cf.* Man with hood)
man with hood over head, others swinging hoods at him: Bodley 264, ff. 70v, 98, 130 (knotted hoods); Clumber 938, f. 108; fr. 25526, ff. 26v, 39; Hague 78.D.40, ff. 14, 25; Y.T. 8, f. 92
man with hood over head, women swinging knotted hoods at him: Bodley 264, f. 130v
Boar (*see also* Ape and; Hare and; Man and; Procession; Woman and)
and antelope, pursuing: Hague 78.D.40, f. 53v
and bear, with harp, bear tumbling: Harley 6563, ff. 41v-42
and crow, pecked on back by (*cf.* Fables: sheep and crow): Rothschild MS., f. 124
and dog
attacked by: Royal 2 B.VII, f. 145 (three)
pursued by: Hague 78.D.40, ff. 120v (two), 133 (three); latin 13260, f. 96v; M. 729, f. 323
with bagpipe, dog dancing: Y.T. 8, f. 201v
with distaff *see below,* —, with distaff
and dragon, pursued by: Lansdowne 451, f. 66

and knight, charging kneeling knight dropping sword: Add. 49622, f. 151
and siren, shot by: W. 45, f. 108v
and stag, astride with vielle: fr. 25526, f. 25v
as king, labeled "Stephanus": Lansdowne 451, f. 70v
Bestiary representation: Munich c.g. 16, f. 32 (in cycle)
head of *see* Centaur as knight, charging; Detached limbs, hand; Man in costume as boar
with distaff and spindle, dog winding wool on reel, hare disappearing into burrow: M. 88, f. 162v
with hand organ: Harley 6563, f. 41 (f. 40v, cat with bagpipe)
with harp, bear tumbling: Harley 6563, ff. 41v-42
with mattock *see* Procession, funeral of fox
with tabor: Arsenal 5218, f. 88
with vielle, astride stag: fr. 25526, f. 25v
Boat (*see also* Sailboat; St. Mary the Egyptian; Sea battle; Swimming)
knights tilting in: Royal 2 B.VII, ff. 158v-159 (2)
men in: Douce 118, f. 36
pulled by swan, containing knight and horse: Cambrai 103, f. 314
pulled by swan, containing men (4): Nancy 249, f. 140v
pulled by woman with rope around neck, containing man (or corpse) with bleeding neck (Fabliau?): Nancy 249, f. 236
rowed by ape: Hague 78.D.40, f. 44 (at L., ape fishing); Stowe 17, f. 76v (three)
rowed by men (4), pulled by two men, preceded by snail: Add. 42130, f. 160
wolf and lamb, man with greens preparing to cross river in boat (riddle): Douce 366, f. 89
Bob-cherry: Royal 2 B.VII, f. 166v (4 men)
Bohun, Mary de: Thott 547, f. 1 (patroness)
Bone *see* Apes seated; Dogs fighting
Bonnacon, Bestiary representation: Munich c.g. 16, f. 33 (in cycle)
Book *see* Ape and hare, conversing; Ape and hybrid man, pointing; Ape as cleric with; Ape with; Bishop with; Cleric with; Fox as cleric; Fox with; Hybrid cleric with; Hybrid fox as cleric; Hybrid man with; Jew with; Man and bird, reading; Man at lectern; Merlin; Nun, Franciscan, with; Patroness; School; Woman with
Boot *see* Ape, Bestiary representation; Man biting; Man with shoe; Woman with pitcher
Border supported by (*cf.* Initial; Miniature)
man: fr. 2754, f. 1 (two); Rutland Ps., ff. 17, 21, 21v (contortionist), 30 (with gold ball), 34v (man running, pointing up), 35 (in water waist-deep)
woman: Rutland Ps., f. 46 (above, dog)
Bourges, Jew of *see* Virgin, miracles of
Bow and arrow *see* Arrow, references under
Bowls, played by
apes: Cambrai 103, f. 411; G.K.S. 3384, ff. 15, 307; Tournai Ps., ff. 58, 181, 185v; Trinity B.11.22, ff. 5v, 118v
apes and man: Add. 29253, f. 66v (3, one ape holding up hood)
apes with eggs: G.K.S. 3384, f. 98v; W. 82, f. 192v (*fig. 90*)
man: BBR 9411-26, f. 121; M. 754, f. 19v
man nude: M. 754, f. 65v
men: Bodley 264, f. 63 (4); Cambridge Dd. 5.5, ff. 46, 294; D.P. 35, f. 51; Fitz. 298, f. 103 (3); fr. 95, f. 61v (3) (*fig. 557*); Hague 78.D.40, f. 10 (2 and cleric); Montpellier H.196, f. 231v; Nancy 249, f. 134v (two opposing teams); Royal 20 D.IV, f. 187 (2); Tournai Ps., ff. 12 (2), 234 (2); Troyes 1905, f. 171 (4) (*fig. 89*); Y.T. 8, ff. 37v (4) (*fig. 91*), 199v (2); Yale MS., f. 293 (4)
Brabant, Mahaut de *see* Patroness
Bricks *see* Bird in nest
Bride between two youths, followed by three bridesmaids, men with hand organ and pipe, approaching groom and friend standing before church with priest and acolyte: Bodley 264, f. 105
Brothel(?), two men approaching: Bodley 264, f. 91v
Brunehilde (Bessus?) martyred: Bodley 264, f. 42v
Builders *see* Man building
Building supported by man: Trinity B.11.22, f. 56v
Bull: Add. 42130, f. 159v; W. 37, ff. 22v (running), 36v, 54 (right front leg raised), 59 (running)
and ape, offered cup by: Glazier 21, f. 150
and bat, confronting: M. 796, f. 59v
and man
baited by: Royal 2 B.VII, f. 144v (with dog)
confronting man with horn: fr. 25526, f. 114
pulling up hill: Rutland Ps., f. 103
rope around neck tied to ankles of man with tankard (proverb?): Add 36684, f. 54v (*fig. 92*)

B

and woman, milking (proverb?): Trinity B.11.22, f. 118v (*fig. 93*)
Evangelist symbol: *see* Evangelist symbols, St. Luke
sitting: W. 37, f. 25v (f. 26, man aiming bow at bull, hybrid knight with sword and buckler)
wearing hair shirt, standing upright, with bell and forked stick: M. 812, f. 111v
with horn *see* Procession, funeral of fox
Bullfinch: Fitz. 2-1954, ff. 51v (and duck), 65v (and stork), 83v (and woodpecker); W. 82, ff. 42, 179v, etc.
Bullock *see* Gideon
Butcher (*see also* Man and pig; Man at table): Trinity B.11.22, f. 25v; W. 45, f. 91v
Butterfly (*see also* Ape and; Centaur and; Cleric and; Dog and; Hybrid man and; Knight and; Man and; Man nude and; Man plowing; Pea pods; Stork and; Woman and): Add. 36684, throughout; Cambridge Dd. 5.5, throughout; Fitz. 2-1954, f. 123v (below, stag); fr. 25526, throughout; Glazier 24, ff. 38v, 164v, 166; Hague 78.D.40, throughout; M. 149, throughout; M. 754, throughout; Y.T. 8, f. 254v; Y.T. 75, throughout)
flanked by woman with two gold sticks, man with hands raised: BBR 9433-34, f. 1
in cart: Add. 36684, f. 109
in cart drawn by bird: M. 754, f. 52 (2)
ringing bell on long rope: M. 754, f. 85v (abbot's skull, abbot praying)
stork reaching for: Arras 790, f. 190v
with taper *see* Procession
Buzines *see* Double pipe, references under

C

Cacus and Hercules: Ste. Gen. 777, f. 7
Caedmon *see* Jesus Christ, life of
Cage *see* Birdcage; Hares caged
Caiaphas (*see also* Jesus Christ, life of: before): Y.T. 13, f. 114 (before group of Jews)
Cain
and Abel
as children *see* Adam delving; Eve spinning
binding wheat sheaves, guarding sheep: Munich c.g. 16, f. 13v
sacrificing: Add. 39810, f. 7 (*fig. 140*); Munich c.g. 16, f. 28v; Stowe 17, f. 79 (*fig. 94*); Y.T. 13, ff. 24v-25
slaying of A. with jawbone of ass (*see also* Vices: Hate): Add. 39810, f. 7 (*fig. 140*); Stowe 17, f. 80v (*fig. 95*); Y.T. 13, f. 28
birth of: Munich c.g. 16, f. 11v
curse of: Munich c.g. 16, f. 14v; Stowe 17, f. 81
plowing: Munich c.g. 16, f. 14v
slain by Lamech: Add. 39810, f. 7 (*fig. 140*); Munich c.g. 16, f. 15v
Caladrius, Bestiary representation (in cycle): Munich c.g. 16, f. 58; Royal 2 B.VII, ff. 89v-90
Calendar derivations (possibly) *see* Baker; Butcher; Falconer; Hybrid man beating; — raking; Man and pig; — and sheep; — and woman, breaking; — weeding; Man by fire; Man picking grapes; — plowing; — pruning; — raking; — reaping; — scything; — sowing; — spading; — threshing; — tying; Man with pickax
Calipers *see* Man with
Cambrai, cleric of *see* Virgin, miracles: cleric of
Cambrai, Notre-Dame of, coat of arms: BBR 1175, ff. 158, 160v, 161 (Virgin and Child)
Camel (*see also* Man and): BBR 9217, f. 205 (below, man approaching woman); Douce 6, f. 129v; Fitz. 242, f. 53; fr. 12400, f. 98; Harley 928, f. 55; Merton 0.1.3, f. 33; Trinity B.11.22, f. 149
and ape, ridden by: Chantilly 64, f. 3
and boar, confronted: Royal 10 E.IV, f. 152v
and dragon, necks interlaced: Rutland Ps., f. 14v
and hybrid man, confronted: Cambrai 102, f. 275v
and man (nude), pursuing: Rothschild MS., f. 131
head of: W. 41, f. 304v
with hand bells *see* Procession, funeral of fox
Campaspe *see* Phyllis and Aristotle
Cancer *see* Virgin, miracles of: cleric cured
Candle *see* Taper, references under
Candlestick *see* Cleric at lectern; Man and squirrel, confronting; Procession
Cannibalism *see* Cynocephalus; Man nude, eating
Cannon(?), dragon on wheels: Add. 42130, f. 184
Cannon fired: Christ Church E.II, f. 70v (at castle door by knights): Holkham 458, f. 44v
Canterbury *see* Patron: Richard of; St. Dunstan; St. Thomas of
Capricorn: Jacquemart 1, f. 77v (below, hybrid knight with spear and shield); W. 37, ff. 159

(f. 158v, bee stinging hare) (*fig. 81*), 179 (possibly); W. 87, f. 89v
Carcass *see* Ape sawing; Corpse, references under
Cardinal (*see also* Apes tilting astride birds; Pope)
and cleric, astride horses, approaching bishop and two clerics before church: fr. 25526, f. 154
and cleric, kneeling; at R., two men pointing at king on throne: fr. 25526, f. 159
cleric kneeling before bishop, presenting book: fr. 25526, f. 158
hybrid, conversing with merman/bishop: fr. 25526, f. 148v
standing with pilgrim; at R., four riders departing: fr. 25526, f. 154v
Carmel, Mount of: Y.T. 13, f. 194 (hill with many holes shown; clerics' heads issuing from six, a stream from a seventh; on top, Virgin and Child, both with apples)
Carpenter(?) straddling bench, with plane(?): W. 88, f. 73 (2)
Cart *see* Ape driving; Butterfly in; Man with tabor; Snail pulling
Caryatids *see* Border; Initial; Miniature
Casket (Minnekaestchen?), man working on; at R., woman observing: Nancy 249, f. 27
Castle (*see also* Cock with rope; Elephant; Giant; Hybrid man with; Knights fighting; Lover in)
attacked by apes, defended by apes: Tournai Ps., f. 105
attacked by cat with crossbow, defended by mice with stones: Harley 6563, ff. 72v-73
attacked by dogs, defended by hares: Verdun 107, f. 137v
attacked by foxes, defended by apes: Stowe 17, ff. 243v-244
attacked by giant, defended by knights (fabliau): Royal 10 E.IV, f. 111v (in center, woman and devil; story continued f. 112)
attacked by hares with catapult, crossbow, ax, defended by knights with crossbow, rocks: Fitz. 298, f. 41 (*fig. 354*)
attacked by knights
defended by knight with ax: Arras 561, f. 108v (2, with ladder)
defended by knights with rocks: fr. 25526, f. 155v
with arbalest: Christ Church E.II, ff. 68v-69
with cannon: Christ Church E.II, f. 70v
attacked by mice with catapult, defended by cat: Harley 6563, ff. 71v-72 (*figs. 98, 99*)
borne by two apes on pole: Tournai Ps., f. 212v
combat between two castles: Royal 10 E.IV, f. 92v
occupied by men and women, messenger kneeling before gate (*Jeu des Dames* sequence): Y.T. 13, f. 76
occupied by women observing combat of knights in initial: Yale MS., f. 18 (*fig. 97*)
Castle of Love, attacked by knights, defended by women: Add. 42130, f. 75v (women casting flowers) (*fig. 96*); BBR 9961-62, f. 91v (women casting flowers); Royal 10 E.IV, f. 18v
Cat (*see also* Ape fishing, catch; Beast astride; Castle, attacked by; —, attacked by mice; Centaur and; Procession, funeral of fox): Cloisters 54.1.2, ff. 134v, 155, 204v
and ape, hanged by (*see also* Ape as bishop, before altar; *below*, Cat and mouse, holding): W. 88, f. 47v
and bird, beating quilt(?) with sticks: Trinity B.11.22, f. 56
and dog, biting tail of: Cambrai 102, f. 336v
and dog, confronted: W. 109, f. 122
and fox stalking mouse and cock (*cf. below*, Cat and mouse, holding): M. 729, f. 262
and hare, baited by with mouse: Nancy 249, f. 234v (*fig. 100*)
and hare, fighting: Trinity B.11.22, f. 7 (cat?)
and hybrid mouse, stalking snail with head of mouse: fr. 776, f. 117v (at R., woman looking on)
and mouse
baited by hare with mouse on string: Nancy 249, f. 234v (*fig. 100*)
confronting dancing mouse: Tournai Ps., f. 7
hanged by: Rutland Ps., f. 61 (four) (*fig. 101*)
holding in mouth: Add. 42130, f. 13; Arras 729, f. 164v (at L., hybrid bishop; at R., man with vielle); Arras 790, f. 169; BBR II 988, v. I, f. 162 (reaching for); Chartres 549, f. 116v; Cloisters 54.1.2, ff. 143, 175; Douai 171, f. 83v; Douai 193, f. 197; Douce 5, f. 44; Douce 118, f. 134v; Douce 131, f. 20; Douce 366, f. 131; Egerton 1151, f. 9v (followed by cleric); Fitz. 298, f. 69v; fr. 25526, ff. 23v (ape doing handstand), 146v; Harley 928, f. 44v (stalked by ape); Harley 6563, f. 43v (with psaltery); Jacquemart 1, f. 101v (hybrid cat); L.M. 13, f. 15; M. 108, f. 135v; M. 796, f. 80; Rothschild

C

MS., f. 181; Stowe 17, ff. 75v, 129v; Tournai Ps., f. 135; Y.T. 8, f. 178; Y.T. 15, f. 314v; Y.T. 19, f. 18 (at R., fox with cock in mouth); Y.T. 27, f. 30a (line ending); Yale MS., f. 113
holding in paws: Add. 42130, f. 190
killed by, with spear: Harley 6563, ff. 74v-75
pouncing on: W. 85, f. 49v
pursuing: Cambrai 102, f. 331v (below, fox running with sheep in mouth); Douce 131, f. 20; Jacquemart 1, f. 16v
shooting, mouse with spear and shield: Harley 6563, ff. 73v-74
stalking (*see also* Cat and fox; — and hybrid mouse): Rutland Ps., f. 60 (mouse on top of wheat sheaf, eating)
playing with spindle *see* Cat with spindle
stealing fish *see* Ape fishing; Man fishing
with asperge *see* Ape as bishop, before altar
with bagpipe: Harley 6563, f. 40v
with churn: Rothschild MS., ff. 137v, 148
with hand bell: Trinity B.11.22, f. 156v
with psaltery: Harley 6563, f. 43v (mouse in mouth)
with spindle held by
cleric with distaff astride hooded man: Cloisters 54.1.2, f. 51
nun (Dominican?) with distaff: Stowe 17, f. 34
with tabor (*see also* Procession, funeral of fox): fr. 25526, f. 151v (second cat with vielle); Royal 2 B.VII, f. 194v (ass with trumpet)
with trumpet: W. 45, f. 85v
with vielle: fr. 25526, f. 151v (second cat with tabor); Harley 6563, f. 40
with wings, shot by hybrid man: Stowe 17, f. 174
wrestling with cat: latin 16260, f. 4v
Catapult (*see also* Castle attacked; Hybrid man with): Holkham 458, f. 43; M. 754, f. 73 (below, man with spear and hybrid woman)
Catapult, wound by man: Bodley 264, f. 201 (sequence of revenge of Alexander's death)
Cattle, Bestiary representation: Munich c.g. 16, f. 41 (in cycle)
Cave *see* Fox as pilgrim; Jew with book; Man nude in
Celestial globe *see* Goat with astrolabe
Censer *see* Angel with; Ape with; Bishop with; Cock with; Dog and hare, with book; Hybrid man with; Man with; Saints, unidentified, male; Siren with
Centaur (*see also* Hybrid centaur; Hybrid knight and; Hybrid man as falconer; Obscaena, pole; —, shooting; St. George)
and antelope, pursuing: Hague 78.D.40, f. 130
and ape
beating: fr. 95, f. 330v
pursuing: Douce 118, f. 10 (centaur crowned, ape with papal tiara); Hague 78.D.40, f. 143 (with spear, both with winged caps)
shooting: Add. 49622, ff. 66, 78; Cracow 815, f. 321; Hague 78.D.40, f. 133v (winged headdress, ape exposing hindquarters); Melbourne 1254/3, ff. 71-70v (ape fishing); Royal 20 D.VI, f. 150v (ape exposing hindquarters)
and bear
killing with sword: Christ Church E.II, f. 35v
threatening (motioning to?) with club: fr. 776, f. 11v
and bird, shooting: Arras 1043, f. 179v; Burney 275, f. 464; Douce 24, f. 73v; Douce 118, f. 1 (dog pursuing hare); Egerton 1151, f. 88v (followed by hare); Fitz. 47, f. 72v; W. 88, f. 160v; Y.T. 8, f. 174 (at R., wild man)
and boar, shooting: Hague 78.D.40, f. 134
and butterfly, shooting: Douce 366, f. 38
and cat, confronted, each raising one front leg: Add. 50000, f. 66v
and crow, shooting: latin 16260, f. 234v
and dog (calf?), aiming ax at: Arras 47, f. 64v
and dog, pulling tail of: St. Omer 5, f. 134 (knight/centaur; at R., woman with two rakes by fire)
and dragon (*cf. below,* — and monster)
fighting with sword and buckler: BBR 5163-64, f. 139v
shooting: Hague 78.D.40, f. 86v (winged cap)
and fish, fighting: Lansdowne 420, ff. 58, 67
and goat, shooting: W. 37, ff. 105v-106
and hare, fighting with sword and shield, hare with spear and buckler: Fitz. 298, f. 17v
holding on left arm: W. 88, f. 103
hunting with bow and arrow: Add. 17868, f. 32v
hunting with bow and horn: fr. 776, f. 9v
hunting with horn and hound: St. Omer 5, f. 132v
shooting: Add. 49622, f. 42v; Egerton 1151, f. 38; Hague 78.D.40, f. 12v; W. 104, f. 32v (also shooting lion); W. 110, f. 72v
and hawk, shooting: fr. 95, f. 319

and hybrid beast in tree, shooting: Rutland Ps., f. 102 (centaur depicted as man issuing from rear part of horse)
and hybrid king, fighting with sword and shield: Cambrai 103, f. 153 (at R., David and Goliath; bird in nest)
and hybrid knight
  fighting: St. Omer, ff. 184 (with bow and battleax), 235v
  shooting: Jacquemart 1, f. 53
and hybrid man
  confronted: Cambrai 103, f. 168 (at R., hybrid man with club, pelican in piety)
  shooting: Arras 1043, f. 177v; Cambrai 102, f. 8v; Chantilly 62, f. 141v; fr. 776, f. 284; Rylands 117, f. 9; Royal 1 D.I, f. 232; W. 37, ff. 60v-61 (bald)
  with gittern, hybrid man dancing: Add. 17868, f. 143; Arras 47, f. 7v; fr. 95, f. 43
and knight
  charging, unsheathing sword, knight with spear: Arras 1043, f. 174
  charging with sword, knight confronted by snail: fr. 776, f. 176v
  fighting snail: W. 45, f. 23
  killed by, with spear: Chantilly 62, f. 14v
  shooting: Cambrai 102, f. 391 (knight kneeling) (*fig. 387*); Hague 78.D.40, f. 14v; latin 14284, f. 38v (knight issuing from border)
  shooting, knight astride cock backward: Arras 47, f. 211
and knight-centaur, fighting with three arrows and sword and shield: Jacquemart 1, f. 51
and lion
  fighting with sword and buckler: W. 88, f. 49v
  pursuing with spear and shield: Hague 78.D.40, f. 70v
and man
  charging with spear, man kneeling with sword and shield: fr. 776, f. 133
  fighting with sword and shield: fr. 95, ff. 13v (man nude, with club), 52; St. Omer 5, ff. 16, 226v (man with spear and shield)
  fighting with swords and bucklers: Hague 78.D.40, f. 13v (at L., centaur with handbells)
  shooting man (nude): fr. 95, ff. 190v (large bird pecking man's eye), 380 (man pleading); Rutland Ps., ff. 33v-34; W. 102, ff. 89v-90
  shooting, man with sword and buckler: Arras 47, f. 221
  shooting men wrestling: W. 102, ff. 82v-83
  with ax, attacked by man with sword and shield: St. Omer 5, ff. 272v-273 (at R., seminude knight fighting lion with spear)
and monster
  fighting horned monster, with sword and buckler: latin 13260, f. 19v (centaur with fishtail)
  shooting: Chantilly 64, ff. 83, 83v; St. Omer 5, f. 41 (monster winged)
and parrot, shooting: fr. 95, f. 319
and pygmy *see* Pygmy
and ram *see* Obscaena, pole aimed
and siren, fighting with sword and shield and crossbow: Hague 78.D.40, f. 68
and snail (*see also below,*—as knight, charging)
  fighting with knight, with spear and shield: W. 45, f. 23
  shooting: Christ Church E.II, f. 55
and stag
  hunting with club, horn, two hounds: Cambrai 102, f. 252v
  hunting with spear, hound: Cambrai 102, f. 3v
  shooting: Cracow 815, f. 5; Hague 78.D.40, ff. 33v, 78, 88, 110v; St. Omer 5, f. 239 (pursued by hybrid man with poleax); Y.T. 8, f. 317
and stork, shooting: Hague 78.D.40, f. 23 (winged cap); Royal 1 D.I, ff. 258v, 259
and wild man
  astride dog with club and spear, fighting with bow: W. 37, ff. 155v-156 (wild man or hybrid ape)
  creeping toward: Y.T. 8, f. 174 (centaur shooting bird)
  fighting with sword and buckler and club: Hague 78.D.40, f. 31v
as bishop, supporting turreted tabernacle containing altar with chalice: latin 1076, f. 32v
as cleric
  bearded (pilgrim?): W. 102, f. 16
  singing from book: fr. 95, f. 138v
  with staff, approached by dog with belled collar: Melbourne 1254/3, f. 11 (*fig. 550*)
as falconer: Melbourne 1254/3, f. 54 (with ?ecclesiastical hat)
as knight
  charging boar's head (huge): Add. 42130, f. 187
  charging hare emerging from burrow with spear: Harley 6563, ff. 106v-107

charging snail, with spear: Cambrai 102, f. 337v
fighting centaur, with bow and arrow, spear and shield: Hague 78.D.40, f. 28v (at R., lion with trumpet)
fighting centaur, with swords and shields: fr. 95, f. 108; Hague 78.D.40, f. 102v, Y.T. 8, f. 188v
fighting centauress, with spears and shields: Cambrai 103, f. 489v
fighting dragon: Hague 78.D.40, f. 77 (with spear); latin 1076, f. 148v (with sword)
fighting knight astride horse, with swords: fr. 95, f. 99v
fighting lion, with sword: fr. 95, f. 86v
fighting man (nude), with spear and shield, polearm: St. Omer 5, f. 125
fighting monster (five-headed), with spear and shield: Cambrai 103, f. 511 (five heads: beast, bird, three human) (*fig.* 77)
pulling dog's tail: St. Omer 5, f. 134 (at R., woman with two rakes by fire)
shooting flying dragon with three dragon's heads issuing from tail: Cambrai 102, f. 409v
shot by hybrid man: Cambrai 103, f. 511
tilting: Hague 78.D.40, ff. 85v (2), 139 (2)
tilting at quintain: Hague 78.D.40, f. 30v
with pot on head and wheat sheaf (?) fighting knight/centaur with bellows and tongs: Hague 78.D.40, f. 138
with shield bearing emblem of female head, brandishing sword: latin 1076, f. 158v
with sword and shield, attacked by mermaid with spear and buckler: Royal 2 B.VII, f. 135v
with sword raised as though about to cut off own tail: St. Omer 5, f. 115v
with sword, shown with monster's head: latin 1076, f. 154v
as physician, with urinal; fr. 95, f. 314v
as skeleton, with vielle before centaur/skeleton dancing: Hague 78.D.40, f. 160v
Bestiary representation (in cycle): Munich c.g. 16, f. 11 (centauress grasping beard of centaur)
bridled *see* Hybrid man as falconer
charged by St. George with sword and buckler: Cambrai 102, f. 447
dancing: Jacquemart 1, f. 113v (above, angels with trumpets, man rending dragon)
centaur with bagpipe: fr. 776, f. 152
centaur with trumpet: Hague 78.D.40, f. 89v
merman (winged headdress) with pipe and tabor: Jacquemart 1, f. 133v
drinking, centauress with distaff and spindle: Hague 78.D.40, f. 102
kissing centauress: fr. 95, f. 345
playing bandyball *see* Bandyball
playing vielle with tongs, centaur with hand bells: Hague 78.D.40, f. 90
shooting (*see also* Centaur and [name of prey], shooting): Add. 42130, f. 164 (above, bat); W. 37, f. 34v; W. 85, f. 37
centaur with pot as crown, sword and shield: Hague 78.D.40, f. 38v (winged headdress)
centauress (winged): Hague 78.D.40, f. 147 (at L., lion)
with arrow: W. 37, f. 35; W. 102, f. 82v
with bagpipe
centaur dancing: fr. 776, f. 152
centaur with trumpet, fox dancing: Cambrai 102, f. 423
with double pipe: fr. 95, f. 343
with garland held high: W. 90, f. 115
with gittern, hybrid man dancing: Add. 17868, f. 143 (at R., hybrid man with vielle); Arras 47, f. 7v; fr. 95, f. 43
with hand bells: fr. 95, f. 59 (2); Hague 78.D.40, f. 24
centaur playing vielle with tongs: Hague 78.D.40, f. 90
centaur with trumpet: Hague 78.D.40, f. 92v (both winged)
with hand organ: W. 88, f. 59
with harp
centaur with gittern: fr. 95, f. 43
centaur with vielle: fr. 95, f. 24 (both hooded)
playing to hybrid woman with coif: Arras 47, f. 54v
with head of beast in hand (*cf.* Knight with): fr. 95, f. 153v
with mirror and comb: Douce 366, f. 29
with pipe and tabor: Hague 78.D.40, ff. 29v (winged headdress), 85 (centauress with vielle), 134v (centauress with hand bells)
with pot on head (*cf. above,* — as knight with; Pot worn): W. 88, f. 183
with psaltery: fr. 95, f. 61v (*fig. 557*); Stowe 17, f. 12 (November); W. 88, f. 116v (winged, hooded)
with shawms (trumpets?): fr. 95, f. 343 (2)
with sword and shield (*see also above,* — as knight; Centaurs): BBR 5163-64, f. 139v

with trumpet: Arras 47, f. 33v; Hague 78.D.40, f. 17; M. 102, f. 47v; Rutland Ps., f. 53v
ape (crippled), with fruit: fr. 95, f. 343 (above, proverb: eggs hatched by man) (*fig. 582*)
centaur dancing: Hague 78.D.40, f. 89v
centaur with bagpipe, fox dancing: Cambrai 102, f. 423
centaur with hand bells: Hague 78.D.40, f. 92v (both winged)
men tilting: fr. 776, f. 271v (two)
with vielle: Douce 24, f. 117; W. 88, f. 62
beggar in drawers listening: St. Omer 5, f. 243v
centaur with harp: fr. 95, f. 24
centaur with vielle: Hague 78.D.40, f. 12v
hybrid man dancing: Add. 17868, f. 143

Centauress (*see also* Centaur drinking; — fighting; — kissing; — with pipe and tabor; Centaurs fighting)
and child, suckling (*cf.* Mermaid and offspring): Rutland Ps., f. 58v (at L., half-figure of nude man and man's face looking on)
and children on lap, holding red and gold balls: Rutland Ps., f. 111 (two children)
shooting three birds in nest: M. 730, f. 147
with distaff and spindle: Hague 78.D.40, ff. 14 (at L., blindman's buff), 102 (centaur drinking)
with spear and shield fighting knight/centaur with spear and shield: Cambrai 103, f. 489v
with trumpet and hand bells: Hague 78.D.40, ff. 43v (2), 84v

Centaurs fighting
one (centauress) with distaff and broom, the other with pot as helmet and bellows and tongs: Hague 78.D.40, f. 10v
with ax, sword, and buckler: Y.T. 15, f. 169
with bow and arrow, spear and shield: Hague 78.D.40, f. 58 (winged headdress)
with club and bow: Y.T. 8, f. 197
with pot as helmet and bird impaled on spear, the other with spear and shield: Hague 78. D.40, f. 71
with spears and shields: Hague 78.D.40, ff. 47v (winged headdresses), 97v
with sword and spear: fr. 776, f. 4
with swords and shields: fr. 95, f. 33v; Hague 78.D.40, f. 15; Y.T. 8, f. 313
with whip and buckler: Add. 17868, f. 143 (at L., ape with vielle)

Centaurs tilting (*cf.* Centaur as knight): fr. 95, ff. 78, 242v; W. 104, f. 5v

Chaladrius *see* Caladrius

Chalice *see* Centaur as bishop; Hybrid man with; Man and stork, offering; Man nude, armless; Man with; Nun, kneeling; Sacraments: Order; St. Donatus; St. Mary the Egyptian; Woman with

Chantecler *see* Cock

Chapel *see* St. Mary the Egyptian

Charity *see* Virtues

Charlemagne: BBR 1175, f. 93v

Chartres *see* Virgin, miracles of: clerk

Checkers
apes: M. 754, f. 55v
man and woman: Add. 42130, f. 76v (man crowned; backgammon?); Bodley 264, ff. 60, 92 (second couple with morris board)
men disputing, bleeding: Stowe 17, f. 268v (backgammon?)

Checkers or chess
ape and cleric: latin 13260, f. 55v
apes: W. 88, f. 186
man and woman: BBR 9411-26, f. 127; Bodley 264, f. 92v; Cloisters 54.1.2, f. 191; fr. 25526, f. 5 (above, couple embracing); latin 10435, f. 61 (woman with falcon, couple flanked by dogs) (*fig. 102*); M. 754, f. 33v (*see* Man with harp: man and woman); Princeton 44-18, ff. 11, 137 (falconer), Royal 2 B.VII, f. 198v (f. 199, two cupbearers)

Cheese and fish, food for falcons: fr. 12400, f. 98

Cherry *see* Bob-cherry; Man and thief

Chess
King Alexander and man: Bodley 264, f. 145v
man and woman: Stowe 17, f. 141
ape playing jawbone with plectrum at R.: Bodley 264, f. 112 (*fig. 104*)
flanked by peacocks: Bodley 264, f. 121v
men: BBR 9411-26, f. 127; Bodley 264, f. 126; G.K.S. 3384, f. 133
devil reaching for one player in drawers, tearing his hair: Stowe 17, f. 111v (*fig. 105*)
disputing: Add. 10292, f. 1; fr. 95, f. 261v (one in drawers); W. 88, f. 53v
one bald, in drawers, with sack or stone under arm: W. 102, f. 29 (line ending)
one in drawers: Rutland Ps., f. 78v (form of chess?) (*fig. 103*)

Chevalier au Cygne *see* Man with harp, before swan; Swan

Chickens (*see also* Fowl, references under)

C and cock, feeding: Douce 118, f. 98v; Glazier 24, f. 31
and fox, pursued by *see* Fox and cock
and woman, fed by: Add. 42130, f. 166v
intercourse: All Souls Lat. 6, f. 13; Laud Lat. 84, f. 299v; Merton 0.1.3, f. 130v (cock looking on)
Child *see* Ape and (*fig. 106*); Beggar and; Cleric with book, wearing; Dog and (*fig. 107*); Fox and; Hybrid woman and; Lion and (*fig. 108*); Man and bear, training: woman; Man giving food; Man with basket containing; Puppet show; Virgin and; Virgin, miracles of: dead; Wild man and; Woman and
Childbirth *see* Virgin, miracles of: woman in
Christ Child *see* St. Christopher; Virgin and Child; Virgin, miracles of
Christ in Majesty *see* Jesus Christ, life of
Church (*see also* Ape ringing bell; Bishop at; Bride; Cardinal and cleric; Cleric leaving; Confession; Crosier; Hare balancing; Man and woman, directed; Man building; Nun and man, receiving; Procession: angels; —: ape-bishop; —: clerics; —: funeral, coffin borne by men; —: funeral of fox; Sacraments; St. Dunstan, ff. 242, 243v, 246v; St. Mary the Egyptian, ff. 285v, 289v, 290)
parodies of *see* references under Bishop; Cleric
with cock as weathervane, entered by three men; sun in cloud, rain pouring down: Cambrai 87, f. 61 (ground: rabbit burrow supported by man issuing from border)
Churn *see* Ape as bishop with; Ape with; Cat with; Man with; Woman with
Cinomolgus *see* Man and bird, hunting bird (or eggs); —, hunting with sling
Circumcision *see* Jesus Christ, life of
Cistercian(?) *see* Scribe, cleric; Woman with book, seated
Clarisse *see* Nun, Franciscan
Classical motifs *see* specific subjects, e.g., Cacus and Hercules
Claw feet *see* Hybrid horse with; Hybrid man with; Man with; Man nude with; Man nude, tailed, with
Clementia *see* Patroness: Marie of Viane
Cleric (*see also* Abbot and clerics; Ape and hare; Ape as; Ass as; Bird as; Centaur as; Hare and; Hybrid cleric; Jesus Christ, life of: Last Judgment: Pains of Hell; Ram as; Sacraments; St. Mary the Egyptian; Sheep as; Virgin, miracles of; Wolf as)
and angel at altar conducting Mass, man kneeling: fr. 25526, f. 146
and ape (*see also* Ape balancing, on pole; Cleric with book): Add. 49622, f. 86v
beseeching ape with sword and shield: G.K.S. 3384, f. 80
playing checkers (or chess): latin 13260, f. 55v
and bird
catching in net: Add. 42130, f. 63
pointing at: Melbourne 1254/3, f. 16v (bird flying toward him); W. 85, f. 72 (two; clerics in tan, black surplice)
and bishop *see* Bishop and cleric; Bishop as devil
and butterfly, painting *see* St. Dunstan
and cat, following: Egerton 1151, f. 9v (cat pursuing mouse)
and child *see* Cleric with book, wearing
and devil *see* Jesus Christ, life of: Last Judgment: Pains of Hell: devil
and dog *see* Dog disappearing
and fox *see below*, — and hare, carrying
and hare
carrying tied to stick over shoulder, hound on leash: Add. 49622, f. 145v (above, cleric warning fox off duck) (*fig. 110*)
pelting with stone: Rothschild MS., f. 141
and hermit, pulling him out of cave: Royal 10 E.IV, f. 118v (with crosier)
and hybrid man
astride, hybrid man with book: W. 88, f. 166 (at R., hybrid woman)
confronting, hybrid man with book: W. 88, ff. 162, 174
conversing: C.B. 62, f. 201v
and hybrid woman
beseeching, hybrid woman nude with distaff and spindle: Add. 49622, f. 146v
pointing at, with spoon: W. 88, f. 37v
and man (*see also below*, — at altar; — kneeling; Man nude and cleric)
astride, drinking: Cloisters 54.1.2, f. 31
astride hooded man, with distaff: Cloisters 54.1.2, f. 51 (below, cat playing with spindle)
feeling brow of: W. 88, f. 122
kneeling before man on horse: W. 759, f. 44v (erased; at L., cleric kneeling)
singing from scroll: G.K.S. 3384, f. 138 (2)
slashing shoulder of old bearded man in

drawers with sword: Add. 49622, f. 40 (*fig. 111*)
and nun (*see also* Fox and geese; Man nude with wheelbarrow; Man with wheelbarrow; Obscaena, defecating, —, exposing)
carrying over shoulder, depositing on ground: Bodley 264, f. 98v
confronted (heads only): M. 754, f. 32v
dancing: Royal 2 B.VII, f. 176v (4; f. 177, cleric with mandola, nun with psaltery)
embracing: Princeton 44-18, f. 192v
embracing, offering red fruit to, woman with skirts raised: BBR 9433-34, f. 29 (Franciscans?)
hearing confession of: Stowe 17, f. 191 (f. 190v, two men pointing) (*fig. 112*)
intercourse: Add. 10294, f. 1 (two nuns looking on); Add. 49622, f. 98v (partly erased)
offering heavy purse to: Add. 49622, f. 115
playing club-ball *see* Club-ball
playing dice *see* Dice
turning somersaults: Bodley 264, f. 98v (2, two)
and ram, astride as falconer (*see also* Ram on column): Douce 118, f. 31
and snail, fighting with spears: M. 754, f. 84
and squirrel as pet (*cf.* Man and squirrel): Nancy 249, f. 221
and Templar, beheaded by: Glazier 24, f. 90 (*fig. 659*)
and woman (*see also above,* — and hybrid woman; — and nun; *below,* — kneeling; — with book; Hermit; Woman and Dominican; Woman dancing on man's shoulders)
administering Host to: Douce 6, f. 99v (holding gold chalice)
confessing: W. 109, f. 286
embracing: Royal 10 E.IV, f. 127
man turning and pointing at them: Princeton 44-18, ff. 187v-188
youth crowned leaning out of tower, gesturing: latin 14284, f. 31
emptying purse before (*cf.* Man and woman, emptying): Add. 49622, f. 142v
in stocks *see* Virgin, miracles of: sacristan (*fig. 114*)
kneeling before, woman holding heart and arrow: Princeton 44-18, f. 76 (Frau Minne? *cf.* Man and woman, kneeling before Frau Minne)
observing two women with garlands on heads pointing at wine-keg under trees (fabliau?): W. 109, ff. 39 (*fig. 115*), 64
playing bellows with distaff, woman dancing barefoot: Stowe 17, f. 38
seated, reading to, from book: latin 13260, f. 130 (at R., two clerics with books, seated) (*fig. 116*)
talking to, woman seated with book: latin 14284, f. 69v (at L., school of apes, bishop) (*fig. 639*)
as falconer, astride ram: Douce 118, f. 31
as illuminator *see* St. Dunstan
as scribe *see* Scribe
at altar
conducting Mass: fr. 25526, ff. 83 (2), 146 (man kneeling, angel looking on); Nancy 249, f. 147 (2)
kneeling: W. 88, f. 77v (at side, man with trumpet)
men kneeling: fr. 25526, f. 61 (2, two)
at baptismal font: Verdun 107, f. 91v (3)
at lectern containing book: Add. 49622, f. 68 (*fig. 109*); BBR 9391, f. 125v; Hague 78.D.40, f. 41v (3, 4 in two groups before two lecterns) (*fig. 122*); Melbourne 1254/3, ff. 17v (two tapers in candlesticks), 89v
at lectern, singing: Stowe 17, f. 117 (Min.: Anointing of Christ)
at organ: BBR 9961-62, f. 66 (above, woman with birdcage) (*figs. 117, 118*)
at school *see* School
beating half-nude cleric kneeling before him with book: Douce 118, f. 112v
Benedictine, with pet dog and squirrel: Nancy 249, f. 221
carrying reliquary *see* Reliquary
conducting Mass *see* above, — at altar
dancing *see below,* — nude
Dominican *see* Dominican, parodied
drinking
astride man: Cloisters 54.1.2, f. 31
blessing: Add. 21114, f. 92
Franciscan *see* Franciscan
head of, unshaven stubble on face: M. 761, f. 143
in wheelbarrow *see below,* — with wheelbarrow
kneeling (*see also above,* — and man; — and woman; — at altar; *below,* — with book)
before cross: Melbourne 1254/3, f. 99
before crowned woman nude save for wimple: Add. 49622, f. 63
praying, man with hands raised: M. 761, f. 17

C

leaving church, man on balcony pouring liquid on him: Royal 10 E.IV, f. 91 (below, woman receiving garland from man)
nude: W. 104, f. 28 (at L., apes snaring birds; school attended by apes) (*fig. 11*)
by fire, stirring pot: W. 88, f. 70v
dancing, nude man with vielle: W. 759, f. 99
disputing with cleric drawing dagger saying "Tu es asinus": Rutland Ps., f. 37 (in short cape)
on stairway, balancing mirror (stone?) on foot: M. 754, f. 61 (below, hybrid man with catapult)
seated, burying head in arms: Add. 42130, f. 54 (below, Moses with Tablets of the Law) (*fig. 504*)
with ladder on head, armless (*cf.* Man nude, armless): M. 754, f. 72
with switch: M. 754, f. 4
on column
flanked by four hybrid men: Royal 1 D.I, f. 1 (four groups of two; above, peacock and man shooting hare) (*fig. 125*)
with club and shield: Stowe 17, f. 123v (white robe, brown hood)
playing bellows with tongs: Trinity B.11.22, f. 20 (*fig. 508*)
playing games *see* references under specific games
playing grill with spoon: Cloisters 54.1.2, f. 129
playing organ: BBR 9961-62, f. 66 (above, woman with birdcage) (*figs. 117, 118*)
praying
kneeling: M. 761, f. 17 (before him, man with hands raised)
seated on hillock: W. 88, f. 82 (at L., man nude save for loincloth, wielding club)
preaching
to men and women, cleric seated at base of pulpit: G.K.S. 3384, f. 132v (*fig. 119*)
to storks (St. Francis reference?): BBR 10607, f. 27v
reading inscription "Ke prestres dessent estre sobres e chastes": M. 761, f. 130 (with book)
ringing bell on bell rope: BBR 9411-26, f. 133v (above, man seized by devil); Chantilly 64, f. 16v; Fitz. 288, f. 189; G.K.S. 3384, f. 134 (bell suspended from horn of grotesque)
singing: Add. 49622, f. 197; Stowe 17, f. 117 (2, at lectern; Min.: Anointing of Christ)
three-faced: Christ Church E.II, f. 36 (half-figure, holding ?rod) (*fig. 452*)
vomiting or spitting water: G.K.S. 3384, f. 54 (cleric? Above, bearded head, man spearing eel with fork)
with asperge: W. 87, f. 9 (below, ram butting border foliage)
with asperge and situla (*cf. below,* — with stool basket): Add. 17868, f. 39v (and bishop with book); Y.T. 27, ff. 36v (Dominican), 87a
with basket and rod: Y.T. 27, f. 49 (stool basket?)
with bell *see above,* — ringing; *below,* — with hand bell; — with purse
with bellows, long rope attached to handle held by man and woman: M. 754, f. 36
with book: Add. 21114, f. 36v; Cambridge Dd. 5.5, f. 211; Cloisters 54.1.2, ff. 151, 155; Fitz. 2-1954, f. 55; fr. 776, f. 92v (2); latin 1076, f. 156v; Royal 10 E.IV, ff. 4-6 (unidentified story)
ape marking place in book: Chantilly 64, ff. 109, 109v
held open by second cleric: Chantilly 62, f. 208v (white dove hurtling down toward leaf in border)
holding, hybrid man (cleric?) in initial playing bellows with plectrum: Cloisters 54.1.2, f. 149
kneeling: latin 1076, f. 85
kneeling, presenting book to bishop: fr. 25526, f. 158 (at L., cardinal)
nun with book: BBR 10607, f. 112 (border terminals); W. 104, f. 74 (*fig. 123*) (2 Franciscans, 2 Dominicans, 2 ?Cistercians, 2 hybrid nuns)
seated (*see also above,* — reading): latin 13260, f. 130 (2; at L., woman and cleric seated with books) (*fig. 116*)
seated, pointing at falconer: fr. 12400, f. 1
stag horns on head: W. 87, f. 43v
wearing gold robe, before him child with book: Princeton 44-18, f. 58
woman holding out arms to, tempting: Y.T. 8, f. 196
with bowl containing stork aiming beak at mouth of man above: G.K.S. 3384, f. 9
with coffin *see* Jesus Christ, life of: Last Judgment: Pains of Hell: miser
with crosier, bishop with cloven hoof: G.K.S. 3384, f. 215
with cross and banner, barefoot: Stowe 17, f. 168v

with distaff, seated (*cf.* Nun, Dominican, with distaff): Cloisters 54.1.2, f. 51 (cat playing with spindle) (*fig. 120*); Stowe 17, f. 113 (at L., squirrel) (*fig. 121*)
with gittern: Laud Lat. 84, f. 351v
nun with vielle: BBR 9433-34, f. 29 (flanking butterfly; Franciscans?)
woman dancing on his shoulders: C.B. 62, f. 156
with hand bells and horn: Add. 21114, f. 93
with mandola, nun with psaltery: Royal 2 B.VII, f. 177
with processional cross *see* Procession, Dominicans
with psaltery *see* Man with horn
with purse (bell?), swinging by cord: G.K.S. 3384, f. 85
with reliquary *see* Reliquary
with shawm *see* Hare and man, tapping
with shears: M. 754, f. 95
with stool basket and stick (parody of cleric with asperge and situla?): Cloisters 54.1.2, ff. 38, 51v; Y.T. 27, f. 49 (stool basket?)
with switch *see above,* — nude; Man in costume as boar
with sword, cutting border stalk (*cf.* Ape, pruning; Hybrid bird, — ; Hybrid man, — ; Man, —): Add. 42130, f. 54 (below, Moses with Tablets of the Law) (*fig. 504*)
with taper *see* Procession, Dominicans
with trumpet
hare with pipe and tabor: Melbourne 1254/3, f. 56
woman dancing: Trinity B.11.22, f. 20 (*fig. 508*)
with wheelbarrow containing cleric embracing woman, followed by devil (*cf.* Man with wheelbarrow): Princeton 44-18, ff. 169v-170
Clermont *see* Virgin, miracles of: St. Bon
Club-ball
apes: Douce 6, f 96v (2; ball [stone?] resting on stick)
clerics and nuns: Bodley 264, f. 22 (3, 3; at L., nude man with wheelbarrow containing clerics and nuns approaching church) (*figs. 127-128*)
hybrid woman: W. 88, f. 78
man: Y.T. 27, f. 120
man and ape: G.K.S. 3384, f. 120v (ball resting on stick)
man and woman: Douce 6, f. 148 (below, ass wearing cape)
man nude, hooved: M. 754, f. 40v
men: Arras 729, f. 156; BBR 8469, f. 14v (erased); Cambridge Dd. 5.5, f. 236; Chantilly 64, ff. 90, 90v; G.K.S. 3384, f. 26v; Royal 10 E.IV, f. 94v; Royal 14 B.V; Schilling MS., September (*fig. 126*); Trinity B.11.22, f. 16v; W. 88, ff. 25, 43v, 193 (f. 192v, hybrid cleric preparing to catch ball)
men and women: fr. 25526, ff. 34v, 48; G.K.S. 3384, f. 64; Hague 78.D.40, f. 40v
women: Montpellier H. 196, f. 112 (4)
Clubkayles
ape(s): Douce 6, f. 131v (2), 153v (1); G.K.S. 3384, f. 118v; Hague 78.D.40, f. 29 (3); Tournai Ps., ff. 28v (*fig. 124*), 118, 135, 227v, 230v
men (2): Add. 42130, f. 199 (ninepins?): BBR 9217, f. 54v; Douce 6, f. 159v; G.K.S. 3384, f. 43v; latin 3893, f. 273; Royal 2 B.VII, f. 167; Royal 10 E.IV, f. 99
Coach containing
five ladies, drawn by two horses driven by man: Douce 131, f. 43
four queens drawn by five horses: Add. 42130, ff. 181v-182 (five retainers, one handing pet dog to coach occupant)
two female apes, drawn by horse ridden by ape, ape with spear following: Douce 6, f. 200v (*fig. 129*)
Cobweb *see* Spider
Cock (*see also* Ape and; Ape as cleric; — as physician; Ape ringing bell; Fox and; Hare and; Knight and; Man and; Man nude and; Man playing; Owl and; Procession, funeral of fox
and hen (*cf.* Chickens): Douce 118, f. 98v (two); M. 796, f. 127; Rutland Ps., f. 100v
feeding: Douce 118, f. 98v (two); Glazier 24, f. 31 (*fig. 641*)
intercourse: All Souls Lat. 6, f. 13 (surrounded by chicks); Bodley 264, f. 99v; Merton 0.1.3, f. 130 (at L., cock); Stowe 17, f. 94v
and hybrid knight with sword and buckler, confronted: Melbourne 1254/3, ff. 113v-114
and St. Peter, confronted: BBR 10607, f. 129
and serpent, fighting: Royal 2 B.VII, f. 187v
and wild man, ridden by: Glazier 24, f. 45
as weathervane, shot by man (*see also* Ape ringing bell; Church with): Royal 10 E.IV, f. 89 (on windmill; at L., giant in armor; at R., castle; fabliau)

C

at lectern, singing, stalked by fox: Add. 50000, f. 146v (Ps. 97) (*fig. 130*)
Bestiary representation (cockfight): Munich c.g. 16, f. 55 (in cycle)
crowing: Douce 118, f. 85v; Fitz. 2-1954, f. 150; Fitz. 288, f. 189 (two; above; man shooting bird; at R., cock crowing; Offices of the Dead); M. 796, f. 85
eating gold pellet (*cf. below,* — raising head): Douce 118, f. 162v
on column (*see also* Ape as cleric): McLean 41, f. 2 (Ps. 1)
on hat *see* Dog and hare, beside
on stilts: Bodley 264, f. 91
raising head to catch pellet in air (*cf.* Cock eating): Melbourne 1254/3, ff. 92, 124
with censer *see* Procession, funeral of fox (*fig. 131*)
with rope in beak, other end attached to small castle (*cf.* Wild man and lion): Glazier 24, f. 62v
with spear: M. 754, f. 3v (heads of cleric and man issuing from basket; man crawling out of oven)
Cockatrice: Christ Church E.II, f. 69; Rutland Ps., f. 81 (confronting ?eagle)
Cockfight: Add. 21926, f. 26 (Ps. 1); Bodley 264, f. 99v (two pairs); Chantilly 62, ff. 18v, 111v; Chantilly 64, ff. 64, 64v; Douce 23, f. 14; Douce 118, ff. 90, 140 (gold pellets on ground); Fitz. 242, f. 3; fr. 25526, ff. 7v, 58 (at R., man in tree), 143; Glazier 24, f. 35; Hague 78.D.40, f. 23; Melbourne 1254/3, ff. 32, 67; Rothschild MS., f. 108; Royal 2 B.VII, f. 142v; W. 88, f. 73v
ape astride goat applauding: latin 1029A, f. 27 (*fig. 134*)
ape with stick, encouraging: Douce 118, ff. 125, 165v
Bestiary representation: Munich c.g. 16, f. 55 (in cycle)
children looking on: Bodley 264, f. 50
hen (crowned) looking on from tower (*cf.* Knights tilting, queen): Douce 131, f. 42v (*figs. 135, 136*)
woman (man?) holding spindle between cocks: Douce 118, f. 7v (*fig. 133*)
Cocks confronted: Douce 366, f. 128; Fitz. 288, f. 90 (Min.: St. Peter martyred); G.K.S. 3384, f. 257; Jacquemart 1, f. 73v; latin 3893, f. 241v; M. 754, f. 15; W. 37, ff. 109v-110; W. 88, f. 57v; Y.T. 8, f. 335 (at R., woman with distaff and spindle) (*fig. 132*)
Coffin, open, containing corpse (*cf.* Corpse; Jesus Christ, life of: Crucifixion; —: Deposition; Man nude, with Saracen headdress; Procession, funeral): Add. 42130, f. 157v (Ps. 87:6)
Coin *see also* Ape as moneylender; — as physician, ministering to woman; Man tearing hair; Physician and man, ministering to; Woman with; *also* references under Man hoarding; Miser; Purse
Coin, gold, disgorged by head of monster into basin: Douce 6, f. 157v (at R., ape-king receiving message from ape-messenger)
Coinmaker(?) with hammer: Cambridge Dd. 5.5, f. 217v; Trinity B.11.22, f. 192v
Cologne *see* Virgin, miracles of: cleric of
Colossians *see* St. Paul
Column *see* Ape on; Cleric on; Cock on; Lion as king; Man with calipers; Proverbs: man biting; Ram on; Scribe, prophet
Comb *see* Detached limbs, hand with; Hybrid ape sawing; Man with; Mermaid with mirror and; Siren with mirror; Woman with mirror, and
Confession *see* Ape confessing; Bishop and cleric; — and nun; Cleric and woman; Dominican and nun; Franciscan and —; Hybrid bishop
Confirmation *see* Sacraments
Constantinople *see* Procession, men
Construction *see* Babel, tower of; Man building church
Contortionist
female: Princeton 44-18, ff. 39, 146
balancing on hands, applauded by devil-grotesque: Rutland Ps., f. 65
balancing on hands, hybrid man balancing on her calves: C.B. 62, f. 23
hybrid man with trumpet: Jacquemart 1, f. 26
man with bagpipe: fr. 95, ff. 205, 262 (second woman dancing)
man with hand bells: Princeton 44-18, f. 175
man with vielle: Princeton 44-18, f. 158
male (*see also* Tumbler, references under): Add. 49622, f. 62v; BBR II 988, vol. II, f. 214v; latin 14284, f. 15; Princeton 44-18, f. 146; Rutland Ps., f. 90v
balancing basin on angled stick: Cloisters 54.1.2, f. 45v
bird perched on knee: C.B. 62, f. 179v
hanging from border: latin 14284, f. 22

with cymbals: Rutland Ps., f. 73
with hoop: Bodley 264, f. 64v
with pipe and tabor: W. 88, f. 176v
Cooking *see* Dinner and kitchen scenes, references under
Corinthians *see* St. Paul
Corpse (*see also* Crow; Hyena; Jesus Christ, life of: Last Judgment: Pains of Hell; Magpie; Physician and man with; Skeleton; Solomon, judgment of)
beckoning to three men: Y.T. 13, f. 123 (f. 122v, Descent into Limbo)
dragged from tower by knight: M. 812, f. 33
in open coffin: Add. 42130, f. 157v (Ps. 87, v. 6)
laid out by two men, third man holding his nose: Trinity B. 11.22, f. 55v (two angels with soul; Physician) (*fig. 137*)
Costume *see* Man in
Council *see* Sacraments: Penitence
Courtship *see* Man and woman, pertinent entries under
Covetous *see* Jesus Christ, life of: Last Judgment: Pains of Hell
Cow and lion, pursued by: Hague 78.D.40, f. 53
Cow playing spoon with rake: G.K.S. 3384, f. 208 (two men with hand organ and triangle, dog dancing)
Cowardice *see* Knight and hare; — and snail; Man and hare; — and snail
Crab pierced by hybrid man with spear: M. 796, f. 87
Cradle *see* Ape and child; Hybrid man and child; Woman and child
Crane (*see also* Ape and; Epifagus and; Man and; Physician and; Pygmy and; *cf.* Stork): Fitz. 2-1954, ff. 137, 141v, 142
and hare, fighting: Fitz. 298, f. 117v (crane with hare's ears)
and snail, pouncing on: BBR 10607, f. 240v; Rutland Ps., f. 81v; Yale MS., f. 25
Bestiary representation: Cambrai 102, f. 338v; Munich c.g. 16, f. 47 (in cycle); Royal 2 B.VII, ff. 123v-124 (in cycle); W. 37, ff. 95v, 96; W. 88, f. 154v (*fig. 138*)
eating pellet: Rutland Ps., ff. 26 (six more above in air), 90
pecking face of grotesque: Yale MS., f. 128
with frog in beak (stork?): Burney 275, f. 143; Yale MS., f. 203
with swan, falcon, duck: Add. 39810, f. 7 (*fig. 140*)
Creation of
air and water: Spencer 26, f. 3; Stowe 17, f. 21v; Y.T. 13, f. 17v
animals: Add. 39810, f. 7 (*fig. 140*); Spencer 26, f. 4; Stowe 17, f. 24 (*fig. 139*); Y.T. 13, ff. 18-18v
fowl: Spencer 26, f. 3v
Heaven and earth: Spencer 26, f. 3; Stowe 17, f. 20
man: Add. 39810, f. 7; Munich c.g. 16, f. 9v; Spencer 26, ff. 4-4v; Stowe 17, f. 24v; Y.T. 13, ff. 19-19v
sun, moon, stars: Munich c.g. 16, f. 8v; Spencer 26, f. 3v; Stowe 17, f. 22v
Creator between two cherubims: Add. 39810, f. 7 (*fig. 140*)
Cripple (crippled) *see* Ape; Ape as physician. . . ministering to man; Beggar; Hunchback; Hybrid man; Knight; Man; Man with bagpipe, crippled; —, woman dancing; Man with wheelbarrow; Pilgrim; St. Dunstan, f. 197; Woman; Woman and
Crocket *see* Man with
Crocodile, Bestiary representation: Munich c.g. 16, f. 17 (in cycle); Royal 2 B. VII, ff. 102v-103 (in cycle)
Crosier *see* Beast with; Dog with; Man with bellows
Cross *see* Jesus Christ, life of: bearing; —: Resurrection; Merman with pectoral; Processional cross
Cross, Eleanor (?): Add. 42130, f. 159v
Crossbow *see* Ape with; Hybrid bird with; Knight with; Man and bird, hunting with; Man with
Crow (*see also* Centaur and; Hare with pipe; Man and; Parrot; Raven)
at lectern, inscription reading "Corvix cantat": M. 812, f. 27v
Bestiary representation (in cycle): Munich c.g. 16, f. 52; Royal 2 B.VII, ff. 129v-130
eating from sack, another chased off by dog, man sowing: Add. 42130, f. 170v
pecking boar on back (*cf.* Fables: sheep): Rothschild MS., f. 124
pecking corpse (Bestiary reference; *cf.* Noah, references to raven): latin 3893, f. 95v (chest of nude man); W. 82, f. 70v (eye of head hidden in border foliage); W. 102, f. 77v (eye of nude man; Min.: Crucifixion)

Crown of thorns *see* Jesus Christ, life of: bearing cross; —: Passion, references under
Crucifix staff, borne by bishop: Add. 42130, f. 45
Crucifixion *see* Jesus Christ, life of
Crutches *see* Cripple, references under
Cuckoo (?): Fitz. 2-1954, f. 63
Cup *see* Ape with; Banquet: king; Detached limbs, hand with pitcher; Hybrid woman with hand bell; Man with
Cupid *see* Eros, references under
Cutpurse apprehended by soldier: Add. 49622, f. 153 (*fig. 409*)
Cycles (specific subjects or references to same appear under individual headings; *see also* Sacraments; Vices; Virtues)
agricultural scenes: Add. 42130, ff. 170-173v
Alexander: Bodley 264, ff. 66-69, 144-148, 152-156, 183-184v, 196v-204
Bestiary: Munich c.g. 16, ff. 9-64; Royal 2 B.VII, ff. 85v-130v
Bevis of Hampton: Y.T. 13, ff. 8v-12
Cain and Abel: Munich c.g. 16, ff. 11v-28; Stowe 17, ff. 79-81; Y.T. 13, ff. 24v-28
Creation: Munich c.g. 16, ff. 8v-9v; Spencer 26, ff. 3-6; Stowe 17, ff. 20-29; Y.T. 13, ff. 17v-19v
David: Munich c.g. 16, ff. 7v-123v; Spencer 26, ff. 6v-109; Y.T. 13, ff. 7v-30
Enyas: Y.T. 13, ff. 60v-67v
Florent and Octavian: Royal 10 E.IV, ff. 119-125
Guy of Warwick: Royal 10 E.IV. ff. 80v-88; Y.T. 13, ff. 12v-17
Jacob: Munich c.g. 16, ff. 33v-44v
Jesus Christ and Virgin Mary, scenes from lives of: Add. 42130, ff. 86-100v; Y.T. 8, ff. 86, 88v, 232v-244; Y.T. 13, ff. 88v-103v, 110v-150
Jesus Christ, genealogy of: Y.T. 13, ff. 31-34
Jeu des Dames see Jeu des Dames, references under
Joseph: Munich c.g. 16, ff. 36v-45v; Royal 10 E.IV, ff. 6v-28v; Y.T. 8, ff. 207-212; Y.T. 13, ff. 124-125v
Joshua: Munich c.g. 16, ff. 69v-78v
kitchen and banquet scenes: Add. 42130, ff. 206v-208
Old and New Law represented by prophets and apostles (calendar pages):
Daniel and Andrew: Y.T. 27, f. 4; Y.T. 75, f. 5v
David and John: latin 10484, f. 2v; Y.T. 27, f. 2; Y.T. 75, f. 4v
Ezekiel and Simon: Y.T. 27, f. 10; Y.T. 75, f. 8v
Haggai and James the Less: Y.T. 27, f. 9; Y.T. 75, f. 8
Hosea and Philip: Y.T. 27, f. 5; Y.T. 75, f. 6
Isaiah and James the Greater: Y.T. 27, f. 3; Y.T. 75, f. 5
Jeremiah and Peter: latin 10484, f. 2; Y.T. 27, f. 1; Y.T. 75, f. 4
Joel and Matthew: Y.T. 27, f. 8; Y.T. 75, f. 7v
Malachi and Thaddeus: latin 10483, f. 6; Y.T. 27, f. 11; Y.T. 75, f. 9
Micah and Bartholomew: Y.T. 27, f. 7; Y.T. 75, f. 7
Zechariah and Matthias: latin 10483, f. 6v; Y.T. 27, f. 12; Y.T. 75, f. 9v
Zephaniah and Thomas: Y.T. 27, f. 6; Y.T. 75, f. 6v
Prophets and Apostles (*cf. above,* —, Old and New Law): Y.T. 13, ff. 34v-53
Reynard the fox: Royal 10 E.IV, ff. 53v-57; W. 102, ff. 73-81
Saints: Royal 2 B.VII, ff. 233v-318; Y.T. 13, ff. 182v, 189v-194v
Samson: Munich c.g. 16, ff. 89v-94v; Royal 10 E.IV, ff. 29-38
Solomon: Spencer 26, ff. 109v-112
Virgin, miracles of (*see also above,* —, Jesus): Fitz. 48, ff. 152v-188v; Royal 2 B.VII, ff. 204v-232; Royal 10 E.IV, ff. 192-228v; Thott 547, ff. 1-28v
Cymbals *see* Contortionist, male; Hare with; Hybrid man with; Man with
Cynocephalus
devouring human arm and leg: Rutland Ps., f. 83v (at R., monster pointing)
with human leg under arm, holding dragon's tail: Rutland Ps., f. 98
with large rock: Royal 10 E.IV, f. 159 (2, confronted)

D

Dagon *see* Samuel, life of: Philistines
Damned *see* Jesus Christ, life of: Last Judgment: Pains of Hell
Dancing *see* Ape; — with harp; Centaur with bagpipe; Cleric and nun; Dog; Dog and hare; Fox; Hare; Hybrid man; Lover embracing; Man and woman; Man with bagpipe, dog; — with gittern; — with pipe; — with vielle;

Men; Merman; Nun, Franciscan; Woman; Woman nude; Women
Danger *see* Lover
Daniel (*see also* Man nude, and lion)
and Andrew, Apostle (Old and New Law): Y.T. 27, f. 4; Y.T. 75, f. 5v
before Nebuchadnezzar, vision in dream: St. Omer 5, f. 115v
David (*see also* Jesus Christ and; Man nude, and lion): BBR 9391, ff. 48v, 109; BBR 10607, f. 103v; Y.T. 13, f. 35v
David, life of
Abner and Asahel, slaying: Munich c.g. 16, f. 23v
Abner and Joab, killed by: Munich c.g. 16, f. 123v; Spencer 26, f. 58
Abner and Rizpah, reproached by Ish-bosheth: Spencer 26, f. 55
Abner feasting at Hebron: Spencer 26, f. 57
Abner, flight of, smiting Asahel, gathering children of Benjamin, with Joab: Spencer 26, ff. 52-54
Abner with sons of Ish-bosheth: Munich c.g. 16, f. 121v
Adonijah exalting himself, banquet: Spencer 26, f. 105
Ammon and Tamar: Spencer 26, ff. 75-76
Ammon at feast, slain by servants of Absalom: Spencer 26, ff. 76-76v
Asahel buried: Spencer 26, f. 54v
David and Abigail
at Ziklag with Ahinoam: Spencer 26, f. 41
going to Hebron with Ahinoam: Spencer 26, f. 51
marriage: Spencer 26, f. 41
David and Abishag, lying with: Spencer 26, f. 104v
David and Abner
protesting innocence of slaying, mourning: Spencer 26, ff. 58-59v
question of landrights: Spencer 26, ff. 55v, 56v-57
David and Absalom
A. before Talmai: Spencer 26, f. 77v
A. brought before D. by Joab, return home, fire set to Joab's fields, Joab at A.'s house: Spencer 26, ff. 78-79
A. saved by Hushai, with father's concubines: Spencer 26, ff. 86-86v
advised by Ahitophet and Hushai to pursue D.: Spencer 26, ff. 86v-87v
D. approaching Mahanaim, Ahitophel hanging himself: Spencer 26, f. 90
D. ascending Mount Olivet, Hushai sent to A.: Spencer 26, ff. 83v-84
D. kissing A., A. with servants, conversing with people, journey to Hebron, sacrifice of A., news brought to D., departure of D. from Jerusalem: Spencer 26, ff. 79v-82v
D. receiving news of A.'s death, mourning, reproached by Joab, addressing multitude: Spencer 26, ff. 91v-93
Jonathan and Ahimaaz receiving message, escaping capture, leaving well, warning David: Spencer 26, ff. 88-89v
servants of A. slaying Amnon, news reported to D.: Spencer 26, ff. 76v-77v
with men of Gilead, preparing for battle: Spencer 26, ff. 90v-91
David and Achish
appointed keeper of head of: Spencer 26, f. 42
booty brought to D.: Spencer 26, f. 41v
coming before, feigning madness: Spencer 26, f. 29v
coming before, joining Philistines: Spencer 26, f. 44v
David and Ahimelech
requesting bread from: Spencer 26, f. 28v
requesting spear or sword from, receiving sword of Goliath: Spencer 26, f. 29
David and Amalekites
combat, victory over, spoils sent to elders of Judah: Spencer 26, ff. 45-46v
news of Saul's death, crown offered to D., messenger beheaded: Spencer 26, ff. 49-50v
David and Ammonites, attacking under Joab's leadership: Spencer 26, ff. 69-70
David and Bathsheba
seeing from tower: BBR 15001, f. 63 (*fig. 144*)
seeing from tower, lying with, news of conception: Spencer 26, ff. 70v-71
Uriah before D., slain by Joab: Spencer 26, ff. 71-72
wedding of: Spencer 26, f. 72v
David and Benjamin, servants in combat with: Spencer 26, f. 54v
David and elders of Israel, anointed king by: Spencer 26, f. 61v
David and fool: BBR 9391, f. 31v (Ps. 52)
David and Goliath (*cf.* Man and giant)
battle of Israelites and Philistines: Spencer 26, ff. 10-11

beheading of: Cambrai 103, f. 153; Spencer 26, f. 14
combat: Add. 10293, f. 1; Add. 24686, f. 11; Add. 49622, ff. 8, 204v; Arras 302, f. 7; Auct. D.3.2, f. 195 (*fig. 147*); BBR 9961-62, f. 14 (*fig. 388*); BBR 9427, f. 14 (*fig. 148*); Corpus Christi 53, f. 1; Fitz. 2-1954, f. 1; Glazier 53, f. 6; Lansdowne 431, f. 43v; M. 183, f. 54v; Nancy 249, f. 210; Spencer 2, f. 15; Spencer 26, ff. 11-13v; Stowe 17, f. 72; Verdun 107, f. 149v (*fig. 142*); Vienna 1826*, f. 7 (lion couchant); W. 45, f. 16 (*fig. 143*)
parody of (?) *see* Knight and hare, fighting
with head of, acclaimed by women of Israel: Spencer 26, f. 17 (at R., Saul) (*fig. 146*)
with head of, before Saul and Abner: Spencer 26, ff. 15-17
with head of, pursued by Philistines: Spencer 26, f. 14v
David and Hanum, sending servants to, maltreatment of servants reported to D.: Spencer 26, ff. 67v-68v
David and Ish-bosheth
combat and preambles to: Spencer 26, ff. 51v-52
demanding return of Michal from I.: Spencer 26, f. 56
I. slain: Spencer 26, ff. 59v-60
receiving head of I., murderers slain, head buried in Abner's tomb: Spencer 26, ff. 60v-61
David and Israelites *see* Israelites
David and Jebusites: Spencer 26, f. 62
David and Joab (*see also* David and Absalom)
attack of Syrians and children of Ammon: Spencer 26, ff. 69v-70
command to number people of Israel, consequences: Spencer 26, ff. 103-104
dispute with men of Judah, Amasa slain by J., abandoned: Spencer 26, ff. 96-98v
slaying of Uriah: Spencer 26, f. 72
warned by J. of Abner: Spencer 26, f. 57v
David and John, Apostle (Old and New Law): Y.T. 27, f. 2; Y.T. 75, f. 4v
David and Jonathan: Spencer 26, ff. 16-16v
encounter in wilderness of Zith: Spencer 26, f. 34v
Saul's attempt to murder D.: Spencer 26, ff. 20v-22, 26v-27v
David and Joram: Spencer 26, f. 66
David and men of Jabesh-gilead: Spencer 26, f. 51
David and men of Judah, anointed king by (*cf.* D. and Joab): Spencer 26, f. 51
David and Mephibosheth: Spencer 26, f. 67
David and Micah: Munich c.g. 16, f. 36
David and Michal
receiving in marriage: Spencer 26, f. 20v
reproached by, for uncovering himself before handmaidens: Spencer 26, f. 64v
David and Moab, coming before, leaving: Spencer 26, ff. 30-30v
David and musicians with bagpipe, harp, trumpet, vielle, woman with psaltery: Vienna 1826*, f. 85
David and Nathan (*see also below,* D. and Solomon, promise)
hearing parable of ewe lamb from, D. admitting sin: Spencer 26, ff. 72v-73
proposal to build house for ark, forbidden by Lord: Spencer 26, ff. 64v-65
siege of Rabbah, D. crowned king of Rabbah: Spencer 26, ff. 74-74v
David and Samson: Add. 29253, f. 309v
David and Samuel
anointed by: Spencer 2, f. 15; Spencer 26, f. 7
coming before: Spencer 26, f. 24v
S. raised by witch of Endor, Saul seeking counsel: Spencer 26, ff. 42v-44
together with Saul, prophets: Spencer 26, f. 26
David and Saul
at camp of S., with Abishai, Abner, Ahimelech, reconciliation and parting: Spencer 26, ff. 39-40v
at Keilah, departure of D.: Spencer 26, ff. 33v-34
D. appointed captain of thousand men: Spencer 26, f. 17v
D. in wilderness of Maon, pursued into cave by S., cutting skirt off S. on latrine, leaving cave, swearing allegiance: Spencer 26, ff. 35v-37v
flight of D., anger of S. before Doeg and Ahimelech, slaying of priests of Nob: Spencer 26, ff. 31-32
flight of D. to Samuel, pursuit: Spencer 26, ff. 24v-26
harping before S., with ass: Spencer 26, ff. 8, 9v
javelin cast at D.: Spencer 26, ff. 17v, 22v
Jesse sending laden ass to S. by D.: Spencer 26, f. 9
Merab offered in marriage: Spencer 26, ff. 18-20
messenger of S. before Jesse: Spencer 26, f. 8v
murder attempts and plots, aid from Jonathan and Michal: Spencer 26, ff. 20v-24
S. and witch of Endor, raising of Samuel, S. seeking counsel: Spencer 26, ff. 42-44

S. beheaded, hung with son, burned, buried by men of Jabesh-gilead: Munich c.g. 16, ff. 118v, 119v; Spencer 26, ff. 47v-49

S. enthroned, calling for harpist: Spencer 26, f. 7v

S. enthroned, messenger sent to Jesse: Spencer 26, f. 8v

David and Shimei, meeting on bridge of Jordan, saving life of S.: Spencer 26, ff. 94-94v

David and Solomon

anointed by, news of: Spencer 26, f. 106v

presenting as king: Spencer 26, f. 107

promise of S.'s rule, Nathan's reminder to D. and Bathsheba: Spencer 26, ff. 105-106

receiving as infant: Spencer 26, f. 73v

S. anointed by Zadok, charged by D.: Spencer 26, ff. 107v-108v

David and Ziba, food brought by, Z. granted Mephibosheth's possessions, division of same: Spencer 26, ff. 85, 95

David crowned by two bishops: Y.T. 13, f. 29v

David, death and burial of: Spencer 26, f. 109

David, famine, giving up sons of Saul to Gideonites, death and burial of sons, end of famine: Spencer 26, ff. 100v-102

David harping: Add. 49622, f. 173; Chantilly 62, f. 79; Christ Church E.II, f. 1 (Solomon with scroll); Douce 118, f. 137; Fitz. 2 1954, f. 1; M. 183, f. 13; Munich c.g. 16, f. 35v; Y.T. 13, f. 30

before Saul: Spencer 2, f. 15; Munich c.g. 16, f. 8; Spencer 26, f. 9v

in Jesse's house: Spencer 26, f. 8

seated on cloud, cleric and patron couple kneeling before him: Cambrai 87, f. 30 (*fig. 141*)

David in cave at Adullam: Spencer 26, f. 30

David in Jerusalem, enlarging city, building palace with aid of Hiram's artisans: Spencer 26, ff. 62v-63

David issuing from water: BBR 9391, f. 39 (Ps. 68) (*fig. 241*)

David kneeling at altar, with book: BBR 9391, f. 98

David kneeling before hybrid man with tall gold hat, processional cross: BBR 9391, f. 16 (Ps. 26)

David kneeling before man bending bow at eagle(?): BBR 9391, f. 24 (Ps. 38)

David nude, crowned, with spear, lion at his feet: Lambeth 233, f. 15 (*fig. 149*)

David, parody of (?) *see* Ape and lion; Harp, references under

David slaying lion: Munich c.g. 16, f. 36

David tending sheep: W. 45, f. 16

lion attacking ram, David rending lion: Munich c.g. 16, f. 7v (*fig. 145*); Spencer 26, f. 6v (D. also slaying bear)

David with slingshot: Y.T. 13, f. 27v (ff. 28v-29, D. and Goliath)

Death of Virgin *see* Virgin, life of

December *see* Man and pig; — and woman baking; Man with hand organ

Defecating *see* Obscaena

Delilah *see* Samson

Dentist(?), man extracting man's tooth: Cloisters 54.1.2, f. 80v (*cf.* Ape as barber)

Deposition *see* Jesus Christ, life of

Descent into Limbo *see* Jesus Christ, life of: Harrowing

Despair (Discordia) *see* Hybrid man drinking, hybrid women; Man nude, tearing hair; Man tearing hair; Vices; Woman tearing hair

Detached limbs

arm and leg, two grotesques disputing over: Rutland Ps., f. 83v

foot, man's head, hindquarters of animals and birds: Merton 0.1.3, ff. 80v, 84v, 100v

hand: W. 41, f. 277v

blessing(?) *see* Hare nibbling

emerging from sleeve, picking flowers: M. 754, f. 86v (imitated by hare)

emerging from sleeve, two legs and tail attached: W. 37, f. 89v

gloved, attached to dragon's body, holding dish filled by liquid gushing from border stalk: M. 155, f. 146

gloved, blessing, issuing from trouser leg: Cloisters 54.1.2, f. 93

with battleax, serving as dragon's head: W. 37, f. 187v

with boar's head issuing from dragon's mouth: Cloisters 54.1.2, f. 44

with comb: G.K.S. 3384, f. 188

with spear aimed at running hare: Douce 118, f. 117v

with tankard, hand with goblet below: Cloisters 54.1.2, f. 58v (below, hybrid man by fire)

with urinal: G.K.S. 3384, f. 192

head of beast *see* Centaur with; Knight with

head of bishop *see* Man nude, holding

head of leaves *see* Hybrid man with

head of man (*see also* Man, head of; Man headless; Man nude, headless; — holding; Man with): Glazier 24, f. 51
emerging from glove: W. 41, ff. 222v, 228v
held by woman: Bodley 264, f. 28 (mirror?)
in bowl: W. 41, f. 247v (possibly reference to St. John the Baptist cited in Litany on f. 248)
in oven *see* Man, head of
lifted off neck by man: Cloisters 54.1.2, f. 120
old, held by seated man: Jacquemart 1, f. 57
pierced by arrow: W. 41, f. 288v
three-faced: C.B. 62, f. 181v; Douce 6, f. 125 (bald; line ending)
head of monster *see* Ape and knight, with basin; Knight with head of beast
leg amputated (his own), eaten by nude man: Glazier 24, f. 50v
legs (2): M. 754, ff. 2v (below, bishop's head, hybrid abbot); 3 (on one leg, bishop's head)
miscellaneous: Add. 36684, throughout; M. 754, throughout

Devil (*see also* Angels fighting; Bishop as; Bishop, head of; Bishop on stilts; Bishop with book; — with censer; Chess, men; Cleric with wheelbarrow; Jesus Christ, life of: Last Judgment: Pains of Hell; Lion and; Man horned; Man nude, hoofs; Man with head of; — with wheelbarrow; St. Margaret; St. Mary the Egyptian, f. 269; Virgin, miracles of: cleric assailed; —: hermit; —: woman)

Devil and dragon, holding by neck: Rutland Ps., f. 10v

Devil and goat, astride with spear and shield (*see also* Hare and man, tapping): Douce 118, f. 44v

Devil and hybrid bird, astride backwards: Arras 47, f. 64

Devil and hybrid bishop, shooting: Melbourne 1254/3, f. 14

Devil and hybrid man
attacked by, with sword and buckler: Royal 2 B.VII, f. 139
conversing with: Rutland Ps., f. 77v

Devil and knight (nude save for helmet), killing with spear (*cf.* Man nude and monster): fr. 95, f. 309

Devil and lion, biting tail of: Rutland Ps., f. 32v

Devil and man
attacked by, with two swords: fr. 95, f. 199v (devil has body of nude man, head of devil)
seated in chair, pulled toward tower by man, three men pointing at devil: Bodley 264, f. 68
seated on head of man working bellows on fire under St. Lawrence in miniature: Burney 345, f. 69 (Ps. 51) (*fig. 619*)
with scourge, astride nude man: fr. 95, ff. 61v, 209v

Devil and woman
astride woman walking on all fours, followed by pointing man: Rutland Ps., f. 62
carrying on shoulders nude woman tearing hair: fr. 95, f. 226v

Devil, nose pinched with pincers by St. Dunstan: Add. 42130, f. 54v

Devil playing spoon with bow: G.K.S. 3384, f. 225 (at R., man fighting Saracen)

Devil with bagpipe and scourge: W. 102, f. 82 (Min.: Doubting Thomas)

Devil with bagpipe, another with scourge: BBR 10607, f. 77 (terminal border figures)

Devil with basket *see* Jesus Christ, life of: Last Judgment: Pains of Hell

Devil with branches (2), sticking out tongue (*cf.* Man sticking out tongue): Rutland Ps., f. 23v (below, man/monster)

Devil with pipe and tabor, two devils roasting man in fire (Pains of Hell): fr. 25526, f. 85

Devil with scourge (*see also* Jesus Christ, life of: Last Judgment: Pains of Hell): Burney 345, f. 69 (standing on head of man working bellows under St. Lawrence on grill in initial of Ps. 51) (*fig. 619*); W. 85, f. 98 (with staff, wooden leg)

Devil with triangle, hybrid man with vielle: Douce 5, f. 19 (Jewish cap)

Devil with vielle: BBR 10607, ff. 159, 189v; Rutland Ps., f. 54v

Devil's head on nude man (*cf.* Devil and man, attacked): fr. 95, f. 199v

Dice (*see also* Jesus Christ, life of: Crucifixion; —: Last Judgment: Pains of Hell, gamblers)
ape weighing(?): G.K.S. 3384, f. 22v (above, hare with purse) (*fig. 152*)
apes: Douce 5, f. 138v (*fig. 150*); Douce 6, f. 139 (one, casting); fr. 25526, f. 76 (two other apes drinking); Harley 6563, f. 100v (1); latin 14284, f. 29 (disputing; at R., hooded ape beckoning, another ape pointing up); M. 754, f. 55v (2, one seated, one throwing dice? at gameboard)

- cleric and nun: Heidelberg Cod. Sal. 9,51, f. 272v (his hand on her breast) (*fig. 151*)
- man holding triangle on stand over gameboard, five dice at side: Douce 6, f. 158
- man holding two dice: Douce 5, f. 155
- men: Bodley 264, ff. 64 (2, one has removed his hood), 109v (group of seven men, two hoods on ground; at R., man holding hood beside man reaching into purse); Stowe 17, f. 269; Y.T. 8, f. 183
  - one in drawers: fr. 95, f. 261v (disputing); Royal 10 E.IV, f. 92v (flanked by two huge men shooting at one another; above, owl on perch)
  - one nude: Royal 2 B.VII, f. 167v

Dinner and kitchen scenes *see* Ape cooking; Banquet; Man cooking; Woman cooking

Discipline *see* Ape with switch; Cleric beating; School

Discordia *see* Despair, references under

Distaff (and spindle) *see* Ape with; Apes tilting astride birds; Beast with; Boar and dog with; Cleric with; Dolphin; Franciscan with; Hare with; Hybrid Franciscan; Hybrid man with; Man and hybrid man, seated; Man with; Mermaid with; Merman and hybrid woman with; Nun, Dominican: Pig with; St. Margaret; Squirrel with; Stork as woman; Woman with

Dives and Lazarus (*see also* Banquet): BBR 15001, f. 309 (death of) (*fig. 269*); Harley 6563, ff. 10v-11, 11v-12 (half erased); W. 759, ff. 60 (feast) (*fig. 153*), 90 (death of Dives) (*fig. 151*)

Doctor *see* Physician

Doctor preaching from pulpit: Stowe 17, f. 181 (three men, two women seated on ground)

Document *see* Ape and crane, seated; Ape as king, enthroned; Ape and dog, seated; Knight receiving; Man with message

Doe (*see also* Stag drinking)
- and hedgehog, bear: Fitz. 242, f. 55v (Min.: Crucifixion) (*fig. 12*)
- couchant: Cloisters 54.1.2, f. 184v; Fitz. 242, f. 55v (at R., bear, hedgehog); W. 45, f. 7v; W. 85, f. 96 (with bell collar)
- hunted by hybrid man with horn and hound: W. 45, f. 164v
- shot by hybrid queen: Cambrai 102, f. 394v (doe?)
- stalked by fox (wolf?): Lambeth 233, f. 64 (at R., magpie)

Doeg *see* David, life of: — and Saul, flight of D.

Dog and antelope(?), pursuing: Lambeth 233, f. 148v; Tournai Ps., f. 85 (2)

Dog and ape *see* Ape and dog

Dog and bee, stung by (*cf.* Hare and bee): Stowe 17, f. 48 (two)

Dog and beggar *see* Beggar and dog

Dog and bird
- leaping at gold bird in tree: W. 88, f. 137
- looking at gold birds (2) in tree: W. 88, f. 79
- pursuing: C.B. 62, f. 197 (another pursuing hare, both issuing from lion/fish)

Dog and boar *see* Boar and dog

Dog and bull tied to post, baiting, urged on by two men: Royal 2 B.VII, f. 144v (3)

Dog and butterfly, confronting with shawm: Glazier 24, f. 164v

Dog and cat
- confronted: W. 109, f. 122
- tail bitten by: Cambrai 102, f. 336v

Dog and centaur *see* Centaur and dog

Dog(?) and child, stealing off with: W. 87, f. 34 (*fig. 107*)

Dog and cleric *see* Dog disappearing

Dog and dragon
- barking at dragon in tree (reference to fable of fox and raven?): W. 88, f. 112
- biting tail of: Rutland Ps., f. 74 (wolf? above, lion)

Dog and fox
- confronted, dog with bone wearing low domed hat, fox with ax and dagger: Harley 6563, ff. 53v-54
- pursuing: Add. 49622, f. 87v; Cambrai 102, f. 4 (2, foxes or wolves); C.B. 62, f. 146; Hague 78.D.40, ff. 118v (2), 173 (fox pursuing ram); lat. lit. f. 3, f. 92v; W. 90, f. 28
- ridden by ape, pulling fox, followed by second ape: Trinity B.11.22, f. 22
- singing from book, fox with asperge: Harley 6563, ff. 22v-23
- with pipe and tabor, fox with pipe: fr. 25526, f. 80

Dog and hare (*see also* Hare and dog; Hare with basket)
- approaching, bearing pot, hare lying in burrow: Cambrai 103, f. 43v
- astride, confronting dog astride man/snail: Y.T. 8, f. 294

D

barking at hare behind gold border leaf: Jacquemart 1, f. 8
beside hare with book, venerating cock on man's hat: Verdun 107, f. 8v
biting ear of: Y.T. 19, f. 21v
blowing bellows, hare playing organ: Add. 49622, ff. 88v, 116v (*fig. 155*)
confronting hare/pilgrim: BBR 9157, f. 463; Fitz. 298, f. 129
crowned, in tent, commanding attack of castle defended by hares: Y.T. 8, f. 137v (*fig. 156*)
dancing, hare with vielle: Arsenal 6329, f. 14
fighting with spear and shield: Tournai Ps., f. 142v
hunting
  hare tied to stick across shoulder: Douce 5, f. 177
  stalking: Yale MS., ff. 108, 169
  with horn, two hounds: Tournai Ps., f. 195v
playing organ, hare blowing bellows: Add. 49622, f. 106v
pursued by: V. and A. 8997E (2)
pursuing: All Souls lat. 7, f. 7; Ashmole 828, ff. 19, 71; Arras 229, f. 553; BBR 8469, f. 7v; BBR 9961-62, f. 74; Bodley 264, ff. 17v, 69, 89 (2, three), 110, 189 (2, two); C.B. 62, f. 197 (another pursuing bird, both issuing from lion/fish); Cloisters 54.1.2, ff. 73v, 123v; D.P. 35, f. 56v; Fitz. 298, ff. 62, 103v; G.K.S. 3384, ff. 16v, 23v, 43, 197v; Glazier 24, ff. 26 (two), 65 (two), 66v; Hague 10.B.21, f. 153; Hague 78.D.40, throughout; Jacquemart 1, ff. 7, 35v, 52; Lambeth 233, f. 81v; latin 14284, f. 63 (Ps. 1); M. 88, f. 144v (2); M. 102, f. 53 (line ending); M. 155, ff. 54v, 159v; M. 494, f. 1 (2); M. 729, ff. 40, 141, 196, 258v, 260, 261, 263, 338; M. 754, ff. 38, 42 (and stag), 59v, 98; M. 796, ff. 47 (at L., man with winged headdress shooting stag; Ps. 52), 74v, 76, etc.; Melbourne 1254/3, ff. 8, 25v, 45, 48v, 51v (2), 60, 78v (dog pursued by stag), 104v, 133 (2), 135 (2); Merton 0.1.3, f. 6; Montpellier H. 196, f. 232; Rothschild MS., ff. 169 (*fig. 88*), 180v; Royal 1 D.I, f. 5; Rutland Ps., f. 14v; Rylands fr. 1, f. 82 (*fig. 54*); Schilling MS., August; Tournai Ps., ff. 5, 6, 11, 12, 18 (2), 21v, 60, 82v (at R., dog cheering), 150, 251; W. 37, ff. 66v-67, 98v-99, 113v-114; W. 45, ff. 6v, 34, 90v, 121, 141, 141v, 144; W. 82, ff. 15, 42, 52 (biting), 171 (2), 194v; W. 90, throughout; W. 109, f. 20; W. 110, f. 136v; Y.T. 19, f. 20
pursuing hare disappearing into burrow (*cf.* Hare disappearing): Douce 118, ff. 14, 134, 139; Fitz. 288, f. 58 (Min.: martyrdom of St. Lambert); fr. 25526, ff. 141, 143v; Jacquemart 1, f. 86; lat. lit. f. 3, ff. 37v (two), 72, 79; latin 10435, f. 88v; M. 729, f. 342 (hood?); Melbourne 1254/3, f. 22
pursuing hare emerging from beast's mouth: M. 754, f. 82v
pursuing hare emerging from burrow: latin 13260, f. 55v; M. 88, f. 96
pursuing hare with small hare on stick across shoulder (*cf. above, —,* hunting): Yale MS., f. 286 (*fig. 157*)
pursuing hares in and out of blue hood: Add. 49622, ff. 148, 202v, 212
reading from one book: BBR II 988, vol. II, f. 216v
shot by: Royal 10 E.IV, f. 57v (in *Roman de Renart* sequence)
stalking three hares in cage: M. 754, f. 69
tilting, astride hare and man/snail: Y.T. 8, f. 294 (*fig. 158*)
with book, hare with censer and staff: BBR 9157, f. 419v (*fig. 159*)
with vielle, hare dancing: Add. 49622, f. 86v
with vielle, hare with hand bells, lion dancing: fr. 25526, f. 94v

Dog and hybrid knight *see* Hybrid knight and dog
Dog and hybrid man *see* Dog with pot
Dog and hybrid lion, astride: W. 88, f. 81
Dog and lion *see* Lion and dog
Dog and man *see* Man and dog
Dog and pygmy *see* Pygmy and crane
Dog and queen *see* Coach
Dog and ram, astride, tilting with second dog astride ram: fr. 776, f. 92v (gold lances)
Dog and siren *see* Siren fighting
Dog and snail
  as knight, fighting: Cambrai 102, f. 337v
  attacking with spear and shield: Trinity B.11.22, f. 8v
  lying across door of tower on which sits snail: Add. 49622, f. 146
Dog and stag
  biting: Douce 48, f. 214 (2; Min.: Presentation); fr. 12400, f. 18v (surrounded by vultures); lat. lit. f. 3, ff. 71, 71v (traced from recto), 84; Trinity B.11.22, f. 20
  confronted: Douce 118, f. 157

pursuing: Add. 24681, ff. 20 (Min.: Annunciation), 53 (Min.: Presentation); Ashmole 828, ff. 37, 58; Bodley 264, f. 54v; Burney 275, f. 143 (ape in tree observing); Cambrai 102, ff. 232, 427; Cambrai 103, ff. 1 (hybrid man shooting hare), 208; Cloisters 54.1.2, f. 65; Douce 118, throughout; Fitz. 242, f. 29 (also hare); G.K.S. 3384, throughout; Hague 78.D.40, throughout; Hague XX, f. 208 (3); Jacquemart 1, ff. 95v, 118; Lambeth 233, f. 148v (Ps. 101); latin 13260, f. 19v; M. 155, ff. 1 (2; above hybrid man shooting bird), 31 (4), 50 (3), 114v, 152; M. 754, f. 42 (also hare); Melbourne 1254/3, f. 29; Merton 0.1.3, f. 1; Royal 1 D.I, f. 5; Royal 20 D.IV, f. 225v; Schilling MS. (February); St. Omer 5, f. 11 (pouncing on); Stowe 17, f. 102v; Trinity B.11.22, f. 20 (*fig. 508*); W. 45, ff. 11v (2), 32v (2); W. 82, ff. 31 (two), 87v (2, holding at bay reclining stag; *see* Man and stork, hunting); W. 90, ff. 137v (below, falconer, ape, man balancing two basins), 191; W. 761, f. 142 (erased); Y.T. 8, ff. 184, 290; Y.T. 15, f. 75v

Dog and unicorn *see* Unicorn and dog

Dog and wild man *see* Wild man and dog

Dog and wolf(?) *see* Dog and fox, pursuing

Dog as cleric (*see also* Dog and fox, singing; Dominican, parodied): Cloisters 54.1.2, f. 52v (below, hooded hybrid man)

Dog as Dominican *see* Dominican, parodied

Dog as king *see* Dog and hare, crowned

Dog as knight, fighting snail: Cambrai 102, f. 337v

Dog as pardoner: Harley 6563, f. 23v (f. 24, squirrel with nut)

Dog as pet (*see also* Patroness; Patrons)

of cleric (Benedictine): Nancy 249, f. 221 (also, pet squirrel)

of hybrid man drinking: Cloisters 54.1.2, f. 204

of man (*see also* Man and dog, holding): latin 10483, f. 139v; W. 37, f. 48 (patting): W. 88, ff. 56, 90v

of queen *see* Coach

of woman: BBR 9427, f. 62v (below, falconer); Douce 6, f. 33v; Kraus 75/88, f. 80v; Nancy 249, f. 71 (seated); Princeton 44-18, f. 112 (at R., couple embracing); Royal 2 B.VII, f. 200v; Trinity B.11.22, ff. 12v, 31, 76

of woman with hoop: Hague 78.D.40, f. 21v

Dog as pilgrim: Royal 10 E.IV, f. 55 (in *Roman de Renart* sequence)

hare as pilgrim: BBR 9157, f. 463

shot by hare (in *Roman de Renart* sequence): Royal 10 E.IV, f. 57v

Dog asleep: Rutland Ps., f. 13

Dog, Bestiary representation, hunting beasts and birds: Munich c.g. 16, f. 24 (in cycle)

Dog biting (licking?) right hind leg: Jacquemart 1, f. 131

Dog bitten by bees *see* Dog and bee

Dog climbing into jug: W. 88, f. 17v (beside man with churn)

Dog dancing (*see also* Ass with pipe; Hare with vielle; Hybrid man with —; Man playing jawbone; Man with harp; — with horn; — with pipe and tabor; — with triangle; Woman with vielle): Cambrai 102, f. 316 (second dog with bagpipe)

Dog disappearing into burrow (*cf.* Hare): Melbourne 1254/3, ff. 22, 94 (hare? pursued by dog), 105, 117v, 120v

Dog disappearing under robe of surprised cleric(?): Melbourne 1254/3, f. 59v (2)

Dog drinking from puddle: M. 149, f. 295v

Dog, funeral of *see* Procession, funeral of

Dog in basket *see* Man with wheelbarrow

Dog jumping across stream *see* Man with harp, man and woman

Dog playing handball *see* Handball

Dog playing organ *see* Dog and hare, playing

Dog running along border stalk: W. 45, ff. 45 (2), 74

Dog running into hood (*cf.* Hare and dog, pursued by): BBR II 988, vol. II, f. 226v; Melbourne 1254/3, f. 42 (blue hood, held by hand) (*fig. 221*)

Dog tied to post: Rothschild MS., f. 177

Dog winding wool, boar with distaff and spindle, hare disappearing into burrow (*see also* Ape spinning): M. 88, f. 162v

Dog with bagpipe (*see also* Man with bagpipe, blown; Procession, funeral of fox): Add. 30029, f. 44; fr. 25526, f. 30 (another with pipe and tabor, hare dancing, lion with hand bells); Trinity B.11.22, f. 20v

dog dancing: Cambrai 102, f. 316

hare with hand organ: Metz 43, photograph

hare with timbrel: BBR 9157, f. 415v

hare with trumpet: Y.T. 8, f. 183v

Dog with bell collar: All Souls lat. 6, f. 13

Dog with bone (*see also* Dog and fox, confronted; Dogs fighting): Add. 36684, f. 34 (at L., hybrid man shoveling water; proverb?); Cloisters 54.1.2, ff. 22 (back to back with hare) (*fig. 510*), 123; lat. lit. f.3, ff. 30v, 76v, 77v; M. 754, f. 66v; Royal 10 E.IV, f. 64v

Dog with book, hare with censer and staff (*cf.* Dog and hare, reading): BBR 9157, f. 419v

Dog with crosier: Lansdowne 420, ff. 77, 86v

Dog with hand bells (*see also* Hare with harp): Douce 5, f. 180v (at R., hybrid man with psaltery)

Dog with hand organ *see* Ass with pipe

Dog with hurdy-gurdy, ape tumbling: Harley 6563, f. 42

Dog with mandola *see* Ass with pipe

Dog with pipe and tabor: Add. 49622, f. 82 (*fig. 160*)
- ape dancing, hare with trumpet: Hague 78.D.40, f. 21
- ape with bagpipe: Tournai Ps., f. 31
- devilish creature dancing: M. 729, f. 260 (at L., dog pursuing hare; fox, Bestiary representation)
- fox with pipe: fr. 25526, f. 80
- hare dancing, second dog with bagpipe, lion with hand bells: fr. 25526, f. 30
- winged, winged lion with trumpet: Hague 78.D.40, f. 17v

Dog with pot on head confronting hybrid man: BBR 9217, f. 169

Dog with psaltery *see* Ass with pipe

Dog with reel *see* Ape spinning; Dog winding wool

Dog with staff (beggar?): fr. 95, f. 24

Dog with stone (ape?): Royal 10 E.IV, f. 159 (2, throwing stones at one another?) (*fig. 163*)

Dog with tabor: Add. 49622, f. 23v

Dog with timbrel *see* Ass with pipe

Dog with trumpet (*see also* Man and knight, bending): Douce 131, f. 20; M. 769, f. 148v (above, hare with horn, dog dancing); Melbourne 1254/3, f. 84v; W. 87, f. 24v

Dog with vielle *see* Ass with pipe; Dog and hare, with vielle

Dogs fighting: latin 13260, f. 1 (two pairs); Nancy 249, f. 193v; Princeton 44-18, f. 30 (owl in tree; f. 29v, woman running toward them with distaff); Yale MS., f. 267

Dogs fighting over bone (proverb?): Cambrai 87, f. 65; Chantilly 62, f. 170v; Laud Lat. 84, f. 51

Dogs, intercourse: Merton 0.1.3, ff. 24v (at L., hare; at R., birds' intercourse), 137v (at R., pigs' intercourse)

Dogs tilting: fr. 776, f. 92v (astride rams); Nancy 249, f. 193v (f. 193, knights tilting)

Dogs, winged, pursuing stag (*cf.* Dog and stag, pursuing): Hague 78.D.40, f. 54

Dolphin
- beside woman with distaff on huge shell: Glazier 24, f. 107 (Venus reference?) (*fig. 733*)
- eating smaller fish (proverb?): Glazier 24, f. 163 (dolphin?)

Dominican (*see also* Sacraments: Eucharist; Woman with book): latin 10484, f. 263

Dominican and Franciscan parodied by wolf and fox kneeling before crowned lion seated on column with scroll reading "Jalusie, orgueul, envie": Hague 78.D.40, f. 26

Dominican and nun, hearing confession of: Stowe 17, f. 191

Dominican and woman
- embracing woman kneeling before him, her head under his hood: W. 143, f. 69v
- tilting, his lance broken: Yale MS., f. 100v (astride horses)

Dominican nun *see* Nun, Dominican

Dominican, parodied by dogs ("Domini canes")
- dog-cleric holding two branches: Christ Church E.II, f. 69v (*fig. 165*)
- dog in Dominican garb pursued by three dogs: W. 143, f. 72v (*fig. 166*)
- playing bellows with tongs: Trinity B.11.22, f. 20
- preaching: Bodley 264, f. 79 (from pulpit) (*fig. 164*); Y.T. 13, f. 182v
- saint, female: Add. 28784B, throughout
- with asperge and situla: Y.T. 27, f. 36v
- with staff: latin 16260, f. 587v

Dominicans: Stowe 17, f. 180; W. 45, f. 89v
- and Franciscans flanking building, praying: Lansdowne 451, f. 108v (text: advent of orders to England in 1216 and 1214, respectively)
- at table with Sir Geoffrey Luttrell and company: Add. 42130, f. 208 (2)
- with reliquary: latin 10483, f. 184 (in foreground, two cripples); latin 10484, f. 218v (in foreground, two cripples; preceded by three clerics with tapers and processional cross, followed by four Dominicans, one with book)

Donkey *see* Ass

Double pipe *see* Ape with; Centaur with; Hare with; Hybrid man with; Hybrid man with distaff and broom; Man two-faced; Man with; Merman with

Double trumpet *see* Man with; Merman with

Doubting Thomas *see* Jesus Christ, life of
Dove *see* Cleric with book, held; Noah; Peridexion; Sacraments (Holy Spirit)
Dragon (*see also* Ape and; Boar and; Hybrid knight and; Hybrid man and; Hybrid man with vielle, bitten; Hybrid woman and; Knight and; Lion and; Man and; Obscaena, beak aimed at genitals; St. George; St. Michael)
 and knight/centaur with spear, biting: fr. 95, fr. 113v
 and snail, biting: Add. 49622, f. 200
 and wildcat, attacked by: Royal 2 B.VII, f. 188
 as king, labeled "Edelbert": Lansdowne 451, f. 68
 biting own neck: W. 37, f. 82
 biting right front leg: W. 37, f. 62v
 breathing fire (*see also* Man nude and dragon; Merman as knight, with sword and buckler): Add. 50000, f. 40; W. 37, f. 131v
 coiled around border stalk supported by woman: M. 729, f. 253v
 crowned *see* Man, two-torsoed
 feeding gold balls to dragon: G.K.S. 393, throughout
 spitting liquid: Douce 6, f. 75 (man with basin below); M. 754, f. 68v (at R., nude man crawling on all fours)
 with bell attached to neck growling at man giving directions: latin 10483, ff. 46v-47
 with gold balls in mouth: latin 10483, throughout
 with hare's ears (*cf.* Bird with): W. 45, f. 95v (below, falcon, running hare)
 with shawm (*see also* Man and woman before Eros): Trinity B.11.22, f. 30
Dragonfly (*see also* Hybrid man and): Add. 42130, f. 210 (hybrid); Harley 6563, ff. 8, 8v (perhaps), 21 (perhaps)
Dragons biting one another: Royal 2 B.VII, ff. 136v, 180v-181
Draughts *see* Checkers
Drill *see* Man with
Drinking *see* specific references, e.g., Ape drinking; Dog drinking
Drinking, variations on theme of: Add. 36684, ff. 19v-20
Dromedary, Bestiary representation: Munich c.g. 16, f. 43 (in cycle)
Drowning *see* Virgin, miracles of
Drum *see* Man with snare drum; Tabor, references under
Drusiana *see* St. John the Evangelist
Duck (*see also* Man and)
 and frog, eating: Rothschild MS., f. 148
 flying: fr. 12400, ff. 25 (6), 25v (4), 26v (7), 76 (3, pursued by two hawks)
 flying over water: W. 87, f. 19v (above, hybrid man with curved stick)
 struck by hawk *see* Falcon and duck
 swimming: fr. 12400, f. 6 (several, with herons); M. 88, f. 156v
Ducking stool occupied by woman (scold?) with distaff and spindle (at base, man with raised mallet): Rutland Ps., f. 86 (*fig. 731*)
Ducks feeding on worms and bread (?): fr. 12400, f. 15

E

Eagle
 Bestiary representation: Munich c.g. 16, f. 28; Royal 2 B.VII, ff. 92v-93
 confronting one-legged nude man: Christ Church E.II, f. 55
 double-headed: Rutland Ps., f. 38
 double-headed with bat wings: M. 729, ff. 261v, 273 (*fig. 583*)
 Evangelist symbol *see* Evangelist symbols, St. John
 pecking hair of seated man: Cloisters 54.1.2, f. 176 (eagle? below, hybrid prophet with scroll gesturing)
 shot by hybrid man: BBR 9391, f. 24 (David kneeling)
Earthquake *see* Moses and Aaron
Eating *see* Dinner and kitchen scenes, references under; Man with cup
Ebbo *see* Virgin, miracles of
Ecclesia (?): Douce 118, f. 30; W. 87, f. 10v
Ecclesia and Synagogue *see* Synagogue; *cf.* Cycles: Old and New Law
Ecclesiastics *see* Abbess; Abbot; Bishop; Cleric; Dominican; Franciscan; Nun
Edelbert, inscription accompanying crowned dragon: Lansdowne 451, f. 68
Eden *see* Adam and Eve
Edward III
 astride horse, page adjusting stirrup: Christ Church E.II, f. 14v

E

confronting bishop with hand raised: Christ Church E.II, f. 29
confronting queen: Christ Church E.II, ff. 31v, 35, 38, 45, 45v
Eel (*see also* Ape with basket; Man and; Man with bagpipe, hybrid bird); Fitz. 2-1954, f. 65v (Ps. 68; below, stork and bullfinch)
entering basketwork trap in stream passing by water mill: Add. 42130, f. 181
issuing from water, one eel biting nude buttocks: Add. 36684, f. 147 (3)
Egg *see* Ape with; Bowls; Horse walking; Hybrid man with stone; Knight and owl; Lion and bird, eating; Man with; Merman with stone; Proverbs; Quintain, tilting at: hybrid knight
Eleanor cross(?) supported by hybrid man: Add. 42130, f. 159v
Elders with book, gittern, harp, shawm, vielle (*see also* David, life of: D. and): M. 796, f. 1
Eleazar (*see also* Samuel, life of: ark): Y.T. 13, f. 46v
Elephant (*see also* Man and stag, hunting with club; Man nude, with trumpet; Procession, funeral of fox)
and castle, Bestiary representation: Christ Church E.II, ff. 49, 59; Fitz. 242, f. 22; Royal 2 B.VII, f. 118v (in cycle); W. 760, f. 152; Y.T. 8, f. 206
occupied by knights: Munich c.g. 16, f. 22 (in Bestiary cycle) (*fig. 170*); Y.T. 8, f. 206
attacked by archer on ground: Fitz. 298, f. 26 (*fig. 169*)
attacked by hybrid knight with sword: latin 14284, f. 18 (*fig. 167*)
attacked by man with sword: Rothschild MS., f. 168v
attacked by men with crossbow and spear, knights surrendering(?): Royal 10 E.IV, f. 43v (two)
confronting knight with spear: Royal 2 B.VII, f. 119 (in Bestiary cycle)
knight with sword kneeling before elephant: St. Omer 5, f. 145v
occupied by man with trumpet, ape aiming bow at him: W. 102, f. 28 (line ending)
parodied(?) by hybrid man bearing on back castle occupied by two birds: Fitz. 2-1954, f. 25v (*fig. 168*)
ridden by ape: Stowe 17, f. 36
with two lions, unicorn: Y.T. 13, f. 188
without castle (Bestiary representation?): Fitz. 47, f. 171 (line ending); M. 102, f. 162 (line ending)
Eleven thousand Virgins *see* St. Ursula
Eli *see* Samuel, life of
Elisabeth of Mulbarton *see* St. Omer
Elkanah *see* Samuel, life of: going to Shiloh
Emmaus *see* Jesus Christ, life of: supper at
Emperor, saints before *see* St. Fabian; St. Lawrence; St. Pancras; St. Paul; St. Peter
Emperor's crown(?) worn by hybrid man accompanied by hybrid king: Jacquemart 1, f. 118v
Endor, witch of *see* David, life of: D. and Samuel
Enema (*see also* Obscaena, bellows)
ape administering to ape: Tournai Ps., f. 29v (enema? possibly eating feces)
woman administering to man: Royal 10 E.IV, f. 67v; W. 88, f. 81v
England, arms of, held by angels: Christ Church E.II, ff. 1v, 58, 70v
Entombment *see* Jesus Christ, life of
Enyas slaying wildman, sequence (fabliau): Y.T. 13, ff. 60v-67v
Ephesians *see* St. Paul
Ephraim *see* Joseph (Old Testament), life of: Jacob's journey
Epifagus: Glazier 24, f. 89 (hand in mouth of grotesque); Rothschild MS., f. 142; Rutland Ps., f. 57
and crane, confronting with club and buckler: Add. 17868, f. 158
and dog with bow, confronting with club: Add. 17868, f. 166v
fighting epifagus, with swords and shields: Add. 17868, f. 156 (*fig. 171*)
fighting hybrid man, with sword and buckler, mace and shield: Cambrai 102, f. 244v
fighting lion: Rutland Ps., f. 78 (epifagus?)
Eros *see* Ape with arrows; Lover; Man and woman before; Woman before
Esau *see* Isaac and
Esrom: Y.T. 13, f. 31v (genealogy of Christ sequence)
Eucharist *see* Sacraments
Eulalia *see* Virgin, miracles of: nun
Evangelist *see under* Sts. John, Luke, Mark, Matthew
Evangelist symbols (*see also* Procession, angels)
St. John (symbol: eagle): Add. 42130, f. 50v;

Arundel 83, f. 14; Auct. D.3.2, f. 91v (beginning of Gospel of St. John)
St. Luke (symbol: bull): Add. 36684, f. 71v (Litany) (*fig. 630*); Add. 42130, f. 50; Arundel 83, f. 14; Auct. D.3.2, f. 379 (beginning of Gospel of St. Luke)
St. Mark (symbol: lion): Add. 36684, ff. 71v (Litany) (*fig. 630*), 96; Add. 42130, f. 49; Arundel 83, f. 14; Auct. D.3.2, f. 371v (beginning of Gospel of St. Mark); BBR 1175, f. 62
St. Matthew: (symbol: angel): Add. 36684, f. 71v (Litany) (*fig. 630*); Add. 42130, f. 49v; Arundel 83, f. 14; Auct. D.3.2, f. 360 (beginning of Gospel of St. Matthew)
Eve (*see also* Adam and; Siren holding)
reproved by God: Y.T. 13, f. 21v (in Creation cycle)
spinning (*see also* Adam delving): Y.T. 13, f. 23v (in Creation cycle)
Evil-Tongue *see* Lover, receiving
Ewer *see* Knight with; Procession, ape; Woman with
Execution *see* Cat and mouse; Geese; Hare and dog; — and man; King enthroned; Saint, name of (martyred); Thomas, Earl of Lancaster
Exemplum, man (or Grania?) astride goat (*see also* Man with handbells; Men dancing): Douce 366, f. 72 (approaching king) (*fig. 352*); Royal 10 E.IV, f. 156 (at R., hare under tree) (*fig. 351*)
Expulsion *see* Adam and Eve
Extreme Unction *see* Sacraments
Ezekiel
and Simon, Apostle (Old and New Law): Y.T. 27, f. 10; Y.T. 75, f. 8v
before him vision of haloed seraphim, wounds in hand and feet: Y.T. 13, f. 41v

F

Fables (*see also* Man and doe)
ants and grasshoppers: Trinity B.11.22, f. 123
bears pursuing two apes, one in tree, one on ground (variant of Aesop's fable of friend in need?): Royal 10 E.IV, f. 151v (2)
fox and stork, Part I: Add. 24681, f. 87 (*fig. 175*); BBR 9427, f. 62v (*fig. 174*); Dijon 113, f. 48; Jacquemart 1, f. 112v (at R., hybrid man, crippled); latin 14284, f. 21; W. 45, f. 147; W. 109, f. 210v
fox and stork, Part I, variant
flat board instead of bowl: lat. lit. f. 3, f. 40
hybrid bird instead of stork: M. 754, f. 26; W. 85, ff. 48v, 50v
hybrid man holding flat dish, stork eating: G.K.S. 3384, f. 173v
man nude with bird's head bending over flat dish: W. 90, f. 129v
monster dipping beak into dish held by man: G.K.S. 3384, f. 7
stork aiming beak at dish held by man eating: Douce 6, f. 161
stork drinking from shallow bowl held by man: Douce 6, f. 125 (at L., stag also bending down)
stork/grotesque instead of stork: Kraus 75/88, f. 45v
woman with ewer and basin, dragon bending down: C.B. 62, f. 76
fox and stork, Part II: Add. 30029, ff. 71, 72, 77v, 89 (above, ape/bishop stirring churn); BBR 9427, f. 62v (*fig. 174*); Dijon 113, f. 48; Douce 5, f. 35 (abridged); Douce 6, f. 92 (abridged) (*fig. 181*); Douce 118, ff. 88v (two storks), 118v (two storks); Fitz. 288, f. 145v (two storks); Fitz. 298, f. 145 (two storks); G.K.S. 3384, f. 29v; Glazier 24, ff. 101v (*fig. 180*), 110v (*fig. 179*); lat. lit. f. 3, f. 38; Melbourne 1254/3, ff. 30v (two storks), 134 (two storks); Rothschild MS., f. 115; Rutland Ps., f. 34; W. 45, f. 104 (*fig. 177*); W. 109, f. 82 (*fig. 176*); Yale MS., f. 27v (*fig. 178*)
fox and stork, Part II, variant
hybrid bird instead of stork: M. 754, f. 49v
man offering tall jar to head of bird: W. 85, f. 52
mouse and fox before tall jar: Trinity B.11.22, f. 102
stork/dragon; hare upright against jar: latin 14284, f. 12v
stork on rim of tall jar resting on beak of second stork issuing from border: W. 85, f 52
two dragons plunging heads in tall jar: lat. lit. f.3, f. 21v

F

fox, raven, and cheese (*cf.* Dog and dragon, barking): Add. 24681, ff. 54v, 65 (variants); BBR 10607, f. 88; Fitz. 298, f. 87; Princeton 44-18, f. 134; Rothschild MS., f. 116 (*fig. 173*); Yale MS., f. 238 (*fig. 172*)
sheep and crow: BBR 9427, f. 14; BBR 9961-62, f. 14 (*fig. 388*)
wolf and stork (*cf.* Stork and hybrid man, inserting): latin 10435, f. 140; Marseilles 111, f. 137v; W. 45, f. 145v (hybrids)
woman with jug on head (*cf.* Proverbs: woman with basket; *see also* Man and sheep, milking; Man with jug, on head): BBR 10607, f. 183; Cambridge Dd. 5.5, f. 264 (second woman with basket on head; at L., man with finger held to nose, holding ?sack); Douce 5, f. 2v (at R., ape with coin and jug, hybrid woman with large gold wings); Douce 6, f. 49 (2, one holding out coin); Royal 10 E.IV, f. 29v (on stilts, holding child)

Fabliaux (and possible Fabliaux) *see* Ape and pedlar; Bevis of Hampton; Castle, attacked by giant; Cleric and woman, observing; Florent and Octavian; Giant; Guy of Warwick; *Jeu des Dames,* references under; King, exploits of; Knight and horse, climbing; Knight performing; Knights fighting; Man and giant; — and knight, shooting; — and lion, carried by; — and woman, presenting; Man blind, references under; Man with chalice; — with sores; Nun and man; Phyllis and Aristotle; Swan; Sword tied; Wild man; Windmill, woman; Winged headdress, worn by man with coiled rope; Woman pulling boat; *Wright's Chaste Wife*

Fair-Welcome *see* Lover

Faith *see* Virtues

Falchion *see* Man and dragon, fighting with

Falcon (*see also* Man and; Operation): fr. 12400, throughout (text illustrations)

Falcon and bird, striking: Douce 5, f. 185; fr. 12400, ff. 15, 16; W. 45, f. 40v (above, man fighting snail); Yale MS., f. 174v

Falcon and dog, striking: M. 754, f. 13v (*frontispiece*)

Falcon and duck, striking: Add. 38114, f. 53; Add. 39810, f. 7; Christ Church E.II, f. 50v (three women hawking); fr. 12400, ff. 76, 85, 115v (*see* Man swimming); Harley 6563, f. 7v; latin 10483, f. 214; Royal 2 B.VII, f. 151; Rutland Ps., f. 81v

Falcon and fox, striking: fr. 12400, f. 25

Falcon and hare
confronted: Rylands fr. 1, f. 212
running off in opposite direction: W. 45, f. 95v (above, dragon with hare's ears)
striking: BBR II 988, vol. II, f. 285; fr. 12400, f. 79; Harley 6563, f. 7; latin 10483, f. 214 (at R., group of men, man shooting owl; Min.: Isaiah's vision)
with dead hare: Chantilly 64, ff. 112, 112v

Falcon and hen with chicks, striking: Chantilly 64, ff. 104, 104v

Falcon and heron, striking: Royal 2 B.VII, ff. 157, 190

Falcon and lizard, striking: fr. 12400, f. 122

Falcon and stork
in nest on chimney, striking: Bodley 264, f. 128
striking: fr. 12400, ff. 68, 85

Falcon feeding, observed by five others tied to posts: Bodley 264, f. 127v

Falcon, houses for raising of: fr. 12400, ff. 96, 96v

Falcon, jesses for, types and use: fr. 12400, ff. 173-185v

Falcon on perch: Bodley 264, f. 128 (men holding two broad perches occupied by three and four falcons, respectively); fr. 12400, ff. 87-94, 121v-131v (in training), 150-153; W. 45, f. 103; Y.T. 13, f. 75

Falconer (*cf.* Ape as; Cleric as; Hybrid king as; Hybrid man as; Hybrid woman as; Man and; Woman as): Add. 38114, f. 4v (2, one with dog); Add. 49622, f. 125v; BBR 10607, ff. 90, 95v; BRR II 988, v. I, f. 100v; Burney 345, f. 3; Cambridge Dd. 5.5 ff. 13 (knight), 199 (at R., butterfly), 299; C.B. 62, f. 89v (standing on neck of hybrid man); Chartres 549, f. 249v (dog bringing bird); Christ Church E.II, f. 1 (5); Cloisters 54.1.2, ff. 5v (May), 106v; Douce 6, ff. 51, 92, 133; Douce 118, ff. 56, 138v; Fitz. 298, f. 16v; fr. 95, f. 261v (with lure); fr. 12400, throughout; G.K.S. 3384, ff. 50, 89, 96, 158, 171 (below, two apes fighting with swords and bucklers), 223v, 267, 290v (above, man with crook); latin 10483, ff. 79, 114; latin 14284, f. 64; M. 155, f. 13v; Olschki 4, f. 219; Princeton 44-18, ff. 3v-4, 78 (under tree, bird in tree), 136v; Rothschild MS., ff. 108, 134 (*fig. 543*); Schilling MS. (May); W. 39, f. 24; W. 45, f. 17v;

W. 82, f. 184; W. 85, f. 6v; W. 88, ff. 8 (May), 179; W. 90, ff. 6v (May), 114, 137v; Y.T. 8, f. 300; Y.T. 27, f. 117
Falconer and ape, astride horse, preceded by ape with spear: W. 90, f. 93v
Falconer and companions by fire, storks in nest on chimney looking up at striking hawk: Bodley 264, f. 128 (flanked by men holding falcon perches)
Falconer and duck, hunting astride horse: Add. 24686, f. 14v
Falconer and hare, hunting: Chantilly 64, ff. 112, 112v (hare dead); Glazier 24, f. 26; Princeton 44-18, ff. 197-198
with horn, hounds astride horse: BBR 9157, f. 1 (also hunting stag)
with hounds: W. 761, f. 186 (erased)
Falconer and lion, astride, charging second falconer astride lion: Hague 78.D.40, f. 96
Falconer and skeleton, conversing: latin 3893, f. 169v
Falconer and stag *see* Falconer and hare, hunting with horn
Falconer and woman (*see also* Falconer crowned)
astride horses: M. 796, f. 106
astride horses, hawk striking duck in water: Royal 2 B. VII, f. 151 (two women)
attendant holding horse: BBR 9961-62, f. 72v
conversing: Bodley 264, f. 138
embracing: BBR 10607, f. 15 (Ps. 4; Min.: white lapdog); Stowe 17, f. 59 (under tree, falcon in tree)
hawking together: Verdun 107, f. 12
kissing: Yale MS., f. 104v (half-figures)
playing checkers or chess: Princeton 44-18, f. 137
riding off together as rejected suitor offers ring to monster: latin 14284, f. 35
seated: Bodley 264, f. 43v
with mirrors: St. Omer 5, f. 193 (at R., stork)
woman with lap dog: BBR 9157, f. 1 (at R., man crowned with garland, couple embracing, man with vielle, woman dancing)
woman with mirror: fr. 2754, f. 1 (2, one on foot, one on horse)
Falconer astride horse: Add. 38114, f. 137; Add. 42130, ff. 41, 159, 163; Douce 6, f. 12v; Douce 118, ff. 83, 135v; G.K.S. 3384, f. 158; Harley 6563, f. 10; Melbourne 1254/3, f. 23v; Royal 2 B.VII, ff. 156v (2), 157 (hawk striking heron); Stowe 17, f. 101 (crowned); Trinity B.11.22, f. 103 (2); W. 88, f. 7v (May); Y.T. 8, f. 7 (crowned; retainer playing harp; at R., two women with harp and vielle, two others dancing); Y.T. 19, f. 28
Falconer crowned
and two companions on horseback, falcon striking heron: Royal 2 B.VII, ff. 189v-190
astride horses, woman with lapdog: Stowe 17, f. 243
nude, tailed: Yale MS., f. 363 (*fig. 183*)
Falconer parodied *see* Ape as; Hare and snail; Hybrid man as; Man and ass, astride; — and goat, astride; — and owl, with owl
Falconer seated: Verdun 107, f. 26 (at R., man with handbells issuing from border; at L., lion with vielle) (*fig. 182*)
Falconer seated, falcon on wrist; at L., two falcons (with jesses) on ground: Bodley 264, f. 119
Falconry, accoutrements of and preoccupations with: fr. 12400, throughout
False-Seeming *see* Lover
Fear of God *see* Sacraments: Marriage
Feast *see* Banquet
February *see* Dog and stag, pursuing; Man by fire; Man cooking, stirring; Man sliding; Man with bowl; Mermaid with fish; Woman with taper
Feeding *see* Ape; Dragon; Hybrid man; Magpie; Man; Woman and child, suckling
Ferret *see* Ape as falconer, holding; Hybrid man with horn; Man with; Rabbit burrow; Serpent, crawling; Stork and rat; Wild man with; Woman and hare
Fight over pants *see* Proverbs
Figure supported by man: Douce 6, f. 110v (on foliate base)
Finch (?): Fitz. 2-1954, f. 70
Fire *see* Hybrid man by; Man balancing basins; Man by; Man cooking; Man nude, by; St. Margaret; Windmill, woman; Woman and child by; Woman cooking
Firewood *see* Woman cooking; Woodchopping, references under
Fish (*see also* Ape with; Dolphin; Eel; Hybrid bird with large; Hybrid man and; Man and; Mermaid with; Merman and; Stork and): Add. 36684, throughout; Lansdowne 420, throughout
and beast, fighting: Lansdowne 420, ff. 52, 58v
and centaur, fighting: Lansdowne 420, ff. 58, 67
balancing crowned lion's head on nose: Lansdowne 451, f. 43v

F

in pond: fr. 12400, f. 54
swimming in and out of oven (proverb?): M. 754, ff. 14, 59
symbol of St. Landrade: Add. 29253, f. 361
with pig's head *see* Skull
Fishing *see* Ape; Hybrid man; Man and frog; Man; Merman
Fishmonger (*cf.* Man and fish)
chopping fish on blocks (*cf.* Ape fishing, ape behind): G.K.S. 3384, f. 49 (above, woman's head in line ending) (*fig. 184*)
selling fish to woman and boy: W. 759, f. 108 (*fig. 185*)
Fitzpayn, Joan *see* Patroness
Flabellum *see* Ape as bishop with bagpipe; Pot worn on head by man
Flagellation *see* Jesus Christ, life of
Flail *see* Switch, references under
Flanders, arms of (*cf.* Patroness: Margaret of): Kraus 75/88, f. 63
Flaying *see* Hare and man
Flight into Egypt *see* Jesus Christ, life of
Florent and Octavian, fabliau: Royal 10 E.IV, ff. 119-125 (lioness carrying off two infants, suckling them; baptism of children)
Flowers *see* Man picking; Woman picking
Flute, transverse, played by man: Cloisters 54.1.2, f. 174
Fly: Stowe 17, f. 64 (2, large)
and swallow: Rothschild MS., f. 157
attacked by man with spear: Add. 49622, f. 7v
Font, baptismal (*cf.* Sacraments: Baptism): Cloisters 54.1.2, f. 141; Royal 10 E.IV, f. 125; Verdun 107, f. 91v (three clerics)
Fool (*see also* Ape as beggar; David, life of: D. and; Man and goat, astride): Burney 345, f. 70 (Ps. 52) (*fig. 188*); Cambridge Dd. 5.5, f. 236; Douce 118, f. 42v; G.K.S. 3384, f. 98 (f. 97v, beginning of Ps. 52)
before David: BBR 9391, f. 31v (Ps. 52) (*fig. 186*)
begging: Y.T. 19, f. 26
parodied by hare: Tournai Ps., f. 92 (below, Ps. 52 initial: Fool) (*fig. 229*)
pointing to eyes: Add. 21114, f. 106
with belled cap and bauble: Add. 42130, f. 167 (Ps. 91:7) (*fig. 187*)
with belled cap and bauble of horsehair (or tail): Add. 42130, f. 54v
with harp: Douce 6, f. 70 (fool?)
with vielle: Glazier 24, f. 56 (below, cat)
Fortitude *see* Sacraments: Confirmation; Virtues
Forge *see* Blacksmith, references under
Fortune *see* Wheel of
Fountain (*cf.* Spout; *see also* Woman by)
lion spout, duck in water shot by man with crossbow: Christ Church E.II, f. 65
male head spouting liquid through tube into basin held by woman below: G.K.S. 3384, f. 9
Fowl *see* Chickens; Cock; Creation of; Duck; Fox and; Geese; Hen; Man and geese; School
Fox (*see also* Ape as physician; Fables; Falcon and; Hybrid fox; Man and woman, embracing; Procession, fox; —, funeral of fox; *Roman de Renart*)
Fox and antelope, pursuing: Hague 78.D.40, f. 98v
Fox and ape *see* Ape and fox
Fox and badger, befouling den of: latin 14284, f. 34v
Fox and bird (*see also* Fox and cock; — and fowl; Fox, Bestiary; Fox with trumpet)
confronted: W. 45, f. 243 (hooded; above, hare running)
pursuing, running up border stalk (*cf.* Dog running): W. 45, f. 230
stealing birds from nest: Cambrai 103, f. 499; M. 730, f. 217
Fox and cat *see* Fox and cock, stalking; —, stealing
Fox and child, stealing off with: W. 87, f. 34 (fox?)
Fox and cock (*see also* Ape as cleric, patting; Hybrid woman and fox; Man and —, pursuing; Procession, funeral of fox; Woman and fox)
dragged on long rope by: BBR II 988, vol. II, f. 263v
pursuing: Cracow 815, f. 132v; Hague 78.D.40, f. 149; lat. lit. f. 3, ff. 50v-51 (three hens), 91; latin 10483, f. 97v (at R., woman with jar or basket, hand raised); Liège 431, f. 198v
pursuing, catching: Princeton 44-18, ff. 189-189v
stalking: Add. 38116, ff. 15 (cock singing), 35 (the same); Add. 50000, f. 146v (cock singing at lectern; Ps. 97) (*fig. 130*); Cloisters 54.1.2, f. 178v; fr. 776, ff. 1, 270v; W. 37, ff. 107v-108
stalking, walking beside; cat walking beside mouse: M. 729, f. 262
stealing (*cf.* Fox and goose; Procession: funeral of fox; *Roman de Renart:* fox and goose. Possibly also allusion to fable or proverb): BBR 9157, ff. 334v, 417, 428v; BBR 9961-62, ff. 14 (*fig. 388*), 34; BBR II 988, vol. I, ff. 148, 218, 281, and vol. II, f. 115; Burney

275, f. 336; Cambrai 102, ff. 7v (fox-type with bird), 289v; Chantilly 64, f. 24; Cloisters 54.1.2, f. 46; Cracow 815, f. 132v; Douai 193, f. 202v; Fitz. 2-1954, f. 6; fr. 25526, f. 115 (second fox with stolen sheep); Hague 78.D.40, f. 22; Harley 6563, ff. 60v-61; latin 10483, f. 97v; St. Omer 5, f. 89; W. 45, ff. 75 (owl looking on), 137v (above, cat); 139 (below, hare), 196, 214v; W. 88, f. 155 (confronting woman with paddle) (*fig. 189*); Y.T. 19, f. 18 (at L., cat with mouse)

stealing, pursued by (*see also* Man and fox, pursuing; Man nude and fox; Woman and—)

barking dog: Add. 49622, f. 87v; Arras 229, f. 574v; C.B. 62, f. 146 (tail bitten by dog); Cambrai 103, f. 393v

hybrid woman with distaff and spindle: Add. 49622, f. 35

woman with distaff and spindle: Hague 78.D.40, f. 31 (*fig. 190*)

Fox and doe *see* Doe

Fox and dog *see* Dog and fox

Fox and fish *see* Ape fishing, catch stolen by fox

Fox and fowl

observing: fr. 12400, f. 14 (duck, swan, storks in water; below, wolf)

preaching to: Add. 49622, ff. 47 (mitered with crosier), 49v, 128, 143v (mitered, with crosier); Egerton 2781, f. 53; Harley 6563, ff. 14v-15, 54v-55; Royal 2 B.VII, f. 157v (mitered, with crosier) (*fig. 203*); Royal 10 E.IV, 49v (mitered, with crosier; at R., woman beating with distaff a fox escaping with goose; in *Roman de Renart* sequence); Rutland Ps., f. 98v (mitered) (*fig. 202*); Stowe 17, f. 84 (as cleric or pilgrim, with staff) (*fig. 199*)

Fox and geese *see Roman de Renart:* fox and geese (*fig. 191*)

Fox and goat (*see also* Fox as cleric; Fox with trumpet)

astride: Add. 49622, f. 152v

pursuing: Troyes 89, f. 163v

stealing: Cambrai 103, f. 6 (pulling up stake to which goat is tied)

Fox and goose

stealing (*cf.* Fox and cock, stealing; *Roman de Renart:* fox and goose): Add. 42130, ff. 31, 66v; M. 812, f. 35

pursued by hybrid woman with distaff and spindle, goose saying "quec": Add. 49622, f. 149v

pursued by two men, one with club: Royal 2 B.VII, f. 160

pursued by woman with distaff: Royal 2 B.VII, f. 158

warned away from, by cleric(?): Add. 49622, f. 145v (below, cleric with hare tied to stick across shoulder, dog on leash)

Fox and hare (*see also* Castle; Fox as pilgrim; Fox with trumpet; *Roman de Renart:* fox and hare; —: fox and wolf)

confronted: BBR 9961-62, f. 94 (hare holding left ear down) (*fig. 192*)

confronting as palmer, hare as suppliant: Fitz. 298, f. 34

fighting, with battleax, sword: Y.T. 8. f. 171

fighting with swords and shields: Y.T. 8, f. 181

hunting: Y.T. 8, f. 195v (with hound, pipe, and tabor)

hunting man (*see also* Man and hare): W. 109 f. 168

reading over hare's shoulder (*cf.* Man and stork): BBR 10607, f. 86 (*fig. 194*); C.B. 61, f. 61 (*fig. 193*); Yale MS., f. 133v (*fig. 195*)

stalking: fr. 12400, f. 79

Fox and hermit *see* Fox as pilgrim

Fox and horse, astride, with shield and white standard marked with gold cross: W. 90, f. 26 (at R., dog and hare running)

Fox and ibex, pursuing: Hague 78.D.40, f. 29v

Fox and knight *see* Knight and fox

Fox and lion (*see also* Lion as king; *Roman de Renart*): Add. 38116, f. 48 (looking back at)

Fox and man *see* Man and fox

Fox and offspring: Trinity B.11.22, f. 102v

Fox and ram

as clerics with scrolls before lectern: Hague 78.D.40, f. 25 (at R., archer; at L., hybrid man with trumpet) (*fig. 196*)

fighting with swords and bucklers: Hague 78.D.40, f. 32

pursuing: Hague 78.D.40, ff. 5, 20, 26v, 54v, 106v, 137v, 149, 173 (pursued by dog)

Fox and raven *see* Fables: fox, raven, and cheese

Fox and sheep

borne on shoulders by: M. 729, f. 279 (goat?)

stealing (*cf.* Fox and cock; — and goose): BBR 9157, f. 1 (pursued by hybrid man with club); Bodley 264, f. 52; Cambrai 102, ff. 21 (at L., another sheep tied to stake), 331v; fr.

F

25526, f. 115 (second fox with stolen cock); Melbourne 1254/3, f. 25v; Nancy 249, f. 269
Fox and snail, pushing on wheelbarrow: Cambrai 102, f. 273
Fox and stag *see* Fox with basket
Fox and stork (*see also* Fables)
looking up at: Add. 38114, f. 187v
running away from: W. 90, f. 159v
Fox and wild man *see* Wild man and fox
Fox and wolf *see* Fox with trumpet; Lion as king; *Roman de Renart;* Wrestling
Fox and woman *see* Woman and fox
Fox (dog?) as beggar: Douce 118, f. 8
Fox as bishop (*see also* Fox and fowl; Procession, funeral of fox): Glazier 24, f. 56v
confronting beseeching woman: Y.T. 8, f. 185
with scroll: Douce 118, f. 12v
Fox as cleric (*see also* Ape as cleric; Fox and fowl; — and ram; Hybrid fox; Procession, fox-cleric): BBR II 988, vol. II, f. 240; Fitz. 2-1954, f. 56v; G.K.S. 393, f. 326v
at lectern: Troyes 898, f. 97
hybrid bishop pointing at hybrid woman: latin 14284, f. 13v
with book, goat with processional cross: BBR 9157, f. 1
Fox as Franciscan preaching to six-headed pig-grotesque (*see also* Lion as king): Glazier 24, f. 31 (below, cock and three hens feeding)
Fox as knight, with shield and white standard marked with gold cross, astride horse: W. 90, f. 26 (at R., dog and hare running) (*fig. 198*)
Fox as palmer, hare as suppliant: Fitz. 298, f. 34
Fox as physician (*see also Roman de Renart:* fox and lion; —: fox and wolf): All Souls lat. 6, f. 13; Chantilly 64, f. 39
Fox as pilgrim: Fitz. 2-1954, f. 125v; W. 85, f. 2; W. 87, f. 35v; Y.T. 8, f. 208
before hermit's cave, gesticulating: Fitz. 298, f. 51
confronting hare: Douce 366, f. 89; Fitz. 298, f. 44; Royal 10 E.IV, f. 53v (hare aiming arrow at fox; in *Roman de Renart* sequence)
hybrid woman pointing the way: latin 14284, f. 13v
Fox as tradesman, selling pardons (?): W. 109, f. 82
Fox astride *see* Ape and fox, ridden by; Fox and goat; — and horse
Fox at lectern *see* Fox and cock; Fox as cleric
Fox attacking castle *see* Castle
Fox befouling badger's den: latin 14284, f. 34v
Fox, Bestiary representation (*see also* Ape and bird, snaring with decoy; Woman and bird, snaring): Cracow 815, f. 146; Douce 5, f. 56 (at R., man with club and horn; above, dog pursuing hare); Douce 6, f. 190v (at L., man shooting old hybrid man); Douce 118, ff. 56v, 102v, 121; fr. 776, f. 24v (at R., ape shooting two heads issuing from border); latin 3893, f. 267v; M. 729, f. 260 (dog pursuing hare, another dog with pipe and tabor); M. 730, line endings, throughout; Melbourne 1254/3, f. 69v (ape charging with club and buckler); Munich c.g. 16, f. 13; Nancy 249, f. 130v; Royal 2 B.VII, ff. 99v-100 (*figs. 200, 201*); Stowe 17, f. 207; W. 87, f. 38v; Y.T. 8, f. 173v
Fox dancing
ape as king with trumpet, man with pipe and tabor: Cambrai 103, f. 529
centaurs with bagpipe and trumpet: Cambrai 102, f. 423 (two)
hybrid ape with vielle, hybrid man with bagpipe: Cambrai 102, f. 324
hybrid man with hand organ: Jacquemart 1, f. 121
man with bagpipe: W. 88, f. 113v
Fox disappearing into hole in hill, cock in mouth, pursued by woman with distaff: Royal 10 E.IV, f. 40 (2? urged on by two men)
Fox, funeral of *see* Procession, funeral of fox
Fox, intercourse: Merton 0.1.3, ff. 135v (dogs?), 144
Fox preaching *see* Fox and fowl
Fox running: Douce 6, ff. 40v (at L., hybrid man supporting miniature depicting man and woman with falcon), 105v
Fox running along border stalk (*cf.* Dog running): W. 45, ff. 105 (above, magpie), 116v
Fox with asperge, dog singing from book: Harley 6563, ff. 22v-23
Fox with ax and dagger, dog with bone: Harley 6563, ff. 53v-54 (*figs. 161-162*)
Fox with bagpipe: lat. lit. f. 3, f. 35v
Fox with basket on back containing four men, confronting stag: Y.T. 8, f. 269
Fox with book (*see also* Fox as cleric; Procession: hares): L.M. 13, f. 42; lat. lit. f. 3, f. 78 (at R., bird flying toward him); W. 45, f. 68 (below, stork, apes wrestling or dancing)
Fox with celestial globe *see* Goat with astrolabe

Fox with fruit (*cf.* Ape with; Hare with; Squirrel with nut): Stowe 17, f. 120v (*fig. 736*)
Fox with harp: Fitz. 2-1954, f. 158 (*fig. 204*)
Fox with horn: Fitz. 2-1954, f. 18v (cowled); W. 102, f. 4 (fox?)
Fox with stag horns (green): Arras 790, f. 194v
Fox with standard showing arms of Flanders: Kraus 75/88, f. 40v
Fox with trumpet: W. 45, f. 245v
bird flying toward fox: lat. lit. f. 3, f. 92
bird pecking ear: lat. lit. f. 3, f. 8v
bird pecking tail: lat. lit. f. 3, ff. 47v, 53
hare with pipe, wolf with tabor, goat with harp: latin 1029A, f. 32v
Fox with wheelbarrow containing snail: Cambrai 102, f. 273
Franciscan (*see also* Ass as; Cleric and nun, embracing; Hybrid Franciscan; Lion as king; Woman with book)
and nun, hearing confession of: Add. 42130, f. 74
kneeling, praying: latin 1076, f. 153v (above, St. Francis and man worshiping)
playing bellows with distaff, Franciscan nun dancing: Stowe 17, f. 38
playing plate with fork, ape exposing hindquarters: Y.T. 27, f. 48
preaching to audience of five: fr. 25526, f. 120
seated: W. 45, ff. 279v (below, stork), 282v (below, stork, man with bagpipe wearing garland on head)
with distaff and spindle: Stowe 17, f. 113 (at L., squirrel)
with processional cross: G.K.S. 3384, f. 227 (f. 226v, Ps. 101, Min.: Sts. Clare and Francis)
Franciscan nun *see* Nun, Franciscan
Franciscans and Dominicans *see* Dominicans
Franciscans sent out into the world, shown in turreted building: Y.T. 13, f. 181 (*fig. 205*)
Frau Minne *see* Cleric and woman, kneeling; Man and woman, kneeling before; —, standing before
Frederick II, seated, two men with falcons wearing jesses kneeling before him: fr. 12400, f. 16
Frog *see* Crane with; Man and; Stork and
Frog-in-the-middle (*cf.* Man balancing on one foot): Bodley 264, ff. 65 (3 boys), 97v (4 girls), 130v (5 boys), 168 (4 boys); Cloisters 54.1.2, f. 16 (2 boys, 2 girls; Min.: Annunciation); Douce 6, f. 97v (2 boys, 2 girls) (*fig. 210*); latin 14284, ff. 9 (variant? 3 boys, center one balancing on one leg; at R., boy with one bare foot), 63 (Ps. 1) (*fig. 209*); Montpellier H.196, f. 88 (8 boys) (*fig. 208*); Nancy 249, ff. 105, 184 (variant? 3 boys, 1 girl looking expectant, each with hand in lap of girl holding ?apple); Princeton 44-18, f. 181 (at L., cleric gesturing) (*fig 207*); Royal 20 D.IV, f. 194 (at L., hybrid man with hand bells); Stowe 17, f. 142v (4 boys); Trinity B.11.22, ff. 24, 144 (variant? 2 boys aiming hoods at boy with hood in center. *Cf.* Blindman's buff); W. 109, f. 53 (4 boys) (*fig. 206*); W. 761, f. 196v (erased); Y.T. 8, f. 222v (4 boys)
Fruit *see* Ape with; Fox with; Hare with
Fulica, Bestiary representation: Royal 2 B.VII, ff. 109v-110
Funeral *see* Ape as cleric, at lectern; Bier; Hare, funeral of; Procession, funeral; Virgin, life of: Death of
Funerary chapel *see* St. Mary the Egyptian, f. 290

G

Gabriel *see* St. Michael
Galatea, image carved by Pygmalion: Tournai CI, f. 319
Galatians *see* St. Paul
Gallows *see* Hanging, references under
Gambler *see* Dice; Jesus Christ, life of: Last Judgment: Pains of Hell, gamblers
Game, unidentified, showing two men with cylindrical pole, another pointing at fourth man crouching, preparing to throw stone(?) at pole: Add. 42130, f. 197v
Gameboard, man aiming small round object (coin?) at (*see also* Ape with purse; Hybrid man with chess board; Men fighting with club; Proverbs): G.K.S. 3384, f. 133
Games, sports, and pastimes *see* Archery; Backgammon(?); Balancing; Bandyball; Blindman's buff; Bob-cherry; Bowls; Checkers; Chess; Club-ball; Clubkayles; Cockfight; Dancing; Dice; Frog-in-the-middle; Handball; Hockey; Hot cockles; Leapfrog; Man bending; Man sticking out tongue; Man with hood; Morris board; Musical chairs; Pitch-in-the-hole; Puppet show; Putting; Quin-

tain; Ringtoss; Seesaw; Skating; Stilts; Strike-the-pot; Swimming; Swordplay; Tilting; Top-whipping; Tug-of-war; Wrestling
Garçon et l'Aveugle, Le (*cf.* Beggar, blind): Royal 10 E.IV, ff. 217v-220v (*figs. 425-429*)
Garden of Eden *see* Adam and Eve
Gargoyle(?) *see* Spout
Garland *see* Ape with; Centaur with; Hybrid cleric with; Hybrid man with; Man and woman, holding; —, kneeling
Gaza *see* Samson
Geese (*see also* Fox and; Goose)
  flying in formation: fr. 12400, f. 12 (5)
  pulling large black box toward furnace: Royal 10 E.IV, f. 128v
Genealogy of Christ *see* Jesus Christ, genealogy of
Genesis *see* specific subjects
Genitals *see* Obscaena, exposing; —, handling; Nun and man
Giant (*see also* Knight and; Man with bagpipe, dragging; Man and)
  and knight, slain by, with sword: Add. 24686, f. 17 (at L., lion with man in jaws; Ps. 7:1-2) (*fig. 211*); Royal 10 E.IV, ff. 125v-126v (fabliau?)
  before castle occupied by men in full armor (fabliau?): Royal 10 E.IV, f. 89 (in center, archer aiming at cock on windmill) (*fig. 212*)
  nude save for mantle, with club, holding lion's head (Hercules?): G.K.S. 3384, f. 106 (above, man seizing club)
Giants(?) and men engaged in sea battle, in two ships: Royal 10 E.IV, f. 19
Gideon
  asking Lord for sign of fleece: Munich c.g. 16, f. 84v
  bringing gift to angel: Munich c.g. 16, f. 82v
  casting down altar of Baal, cutting down grove, slaying second bullock: Munich c.g. 16, f. 83v
  giving men trumpets and lamps: Munich c.g. 16, f. 86v
Gittern *see* Ass with pipe; Centaur with; Hybrid man with; Hybrid woman with; Man with; Mermaid with; Woman with
Globe *see* Goat with astrolabe; Hybrid bird standing; Woman praying
Gloves *see* Ape as glove-seller(?); Detached limbs, hand; Proverbs: ape
Goat (*see also* Ape and; Bishop, parodied; Centaur and; Fox and; Hare and man, tapping; Hybrid man and; Knight and; Lion and; Man and; Man nude, and lion, astride; Woman nude, and; Woman with spade)
  and owl: Rutland Ps., f. 63
  Bestiary representation: Munich c.g. 16, f. 40 (2, face to face; in cycle) Rothschild MS., ff. 139v (2 butting, between them ape or nude man), 161v (2 butting)
  head of, mitered: Lansdowne 420, f. 74v
  playing jawbone with rake: Cloisters 54.1.2, f. 22 (*fig. 510*); Y.T. 27, f. 88
  running: W. 85, f. 38
  standing by foliate border: W. 85, f. 86v
  standing on hind legs, feeding from tree or border foliage: BBR 10607, f. 156v; BBR 15001, f. 9 (Min.: Drunken Noah) (*fig. 213*); Douce 5, f. 147 (*fig. 373*); Douce 118, ff. 51 (two kids suckling), 62, 112, 159v; Fitz. 242, f. 29 (hare at foot of tree); Harley 6563, f. 79; M. 796, ff. 39v, 51; Melbourne 1254/3, ff. 66v, 71v, 72, 115, 122; Royal 10 E.IV, f. 154v; W. 37, f. 27v; W. 85, f. 29v; W. 90, f. 150; W. 109, f. 141
  with astrolabe, fox with celestial globe, ape with pillar sun-dial, ram and bear with sextant: Burney 275, f. 390v (*fig. 214*)
  with bagpipe: M. 729, f. 275; Rothschild MS., f. 158 (another goat seated on shoulders of ape); Y.T. 8, f. 173
  with harp, hare with pipe, fox with trumpet, wolf with tabor: latin 1029A, f. 27
  with pipe (*see also* Ass with pipe)
    boar with tabor, ape training bear: Arsenal 5218, f. 88
    pygmy(?) listening: Rutland Ps., f. 49v
  with processional cross, fox-cleric with book (*cf.* Procession, fox-cleric): BBR 9157, f. 1
  with trumpet, hare hiding: Princeton 44-18, ff. 137v-138
Goats butting *see* Goat, Bestiary
Goats separated from sheep: Munich c.g. 16, f. 16v
God the Father, enthroned, flanked by angels with censer and taper (*see also* Adam and Eve; Creation; Jesus Christ, life of: Trinity; Patron): Stowe 17, f. 25
Godendag see Ape with; Man and woman, beaten by
Goldfinch: Add. 42130, f. 73; Christ Church E.II, f. 55; Fitz. 298, ff. 37v (shot by man), 78v (shot by hybrid hare)
Goldsmith *see* St. Dunstan, f. 250

Goliath *see* David, life of: D. and
Goose (*see also* Apes tilting, astride; Fox and; Geese; Hawk; Proverbs: goose): Fitz. 2-1954, f. 87v
Gothic monument (Eleanor cross?): Add. 42310, f. 159v
Grania(?) *see* Exemplum
Grapes *see* Hybrid man picking; Knight and thief; Man picking; Man treading
Grasshopper *see* Fables: ants
Grave *see* Man digging
Grey, Richard *see* Patrons
Griffin (*see also* Knight and; Man and): Add. 42130, f. 160v; Jacquemart 1, f. 61
  and dragon, biting: Royal 2. B.VII, f. 140
  and dragon, confronting with man's head in claws: Rutland Ps., f. 59
  and lion, confronted: Christ Church E.II, f. 14; Royal 2 B.VII, f. 145v (springing at)
  Bestiary representation: Munich c.g. 16, f. 31 (in cycle)
Grill *see* Cleric playing; Man —
Grindstone *see* Ape turning; Blacksmith polishing; Man and dog, holding; Man turning
Grotesques, outstanding examples (*see also* under Hybrid [name of creature]): throughout Add. 36684, Add. 42130, M. 754, Royal 2 B.VII, and W. 102
Grouse(?): Fitz. 2-1954, f. 77
Gull: Fitz. 2-1954, f. 75v
Guy of Warwick, adventures of (fabliau): Royal 10 E.IV, ff. 80v-88; Y.T. 13, ff. 12v-17

H

Hagar *see* Abraham and Sarah
Haggai and James the Less, Apostle (Old and New Law): Y.T. 27, f. 9; Y.T. 75, f. 8
Hainaut, arms on banner held by knight/merman (*see also* Patroness: Margaret): Kraus 75/88, f. 190v
Hair *see* Ape with mirror and comb; Barber; Knight and woman, holding; Man nude, tearing; Man tearing; Man with comb; Mermaid tearing; Woman nude, tearing; Woman tearing; — washing; — with mirror and comb; — with mirror, arranging hair
Halcyon, Bestiary representation: Munich c.g. 16, f. 49 (in cycle)
Hammer *see* Coinmaker; Hybrid man and lion, holding; Hybrid man with; Initial supported by man seated; Man building church; Man with; Men fighting with; St. Dunstan, f. 250; War hammers, references under
Hammock strung up by two men: Add. 42130, f. 200
Hand *see* Detached limbs
Head *see* Detached limbs
Handball
  apes: fr. 25526, ff. 3 (2), 103 (3); latin 3893, f. 187v (3); Tournai Ps., ff. 226 (ape aiming ball at hindquarters of ape), 227v (2), 239v (2, arguing)
  bear and hybrid man: Tournai Ps., f. 236
  dogs (apes?): Royal 10 E.IV, f. 159 (pilgrims? 2, in robes, purses at waist)
  hybrid men: M. 155, ff. 165v-166 (2)
  hybrid women: Jacquemart 1, f. 58 (2)
  man and woman: Douce 5, f. 123 (*fig. 215*); Harley 6563, f. 36; Nancy 249, ff. 71v, 140
  men: Douce 6, f. 135 (*fig. 336*); Royal 10 E.IV, f. 98v; Trinity B.11.22, f. 12; W. 88, ff. 59v (3), 70 (2)
Hand bells *see* Ape with; Cat with; Centaur with; Cleric with; Dog with; Hare with; Hybrid ape with; Hybrid man with; Hybrid woman with; Man with; Procession
Hand organ *see* Angel with; Ass with pipe; Boar with; Centaur with; Hare with; Hybrid cleric with; Hybrid man with; King with; Man with; Woman with
Hand trestles *see* Cripple, references under
Hanging *see* Ape; Cat and mouse; Fox and geese; Hare and dog, capturing; Hare and man, dragging; Joshua; Man; Vices: Despair; Virgin, miracles of: Ebbo
Hannah *see* Samuel, life of: going to Shiloh
Hanum *see* David, life of: D. and
Hare (*see also* Rabbit burrow)
Hare and ape *see* Ape and hare; Ape as king; Obscaena, eating
Hare and ass *see* Ass and hare
Hare and bear, training: Add. 49622, ff. 71v (*fig. 218*), 109v
Hare and bee, stung by (*cf.* Dog and bee): W. 37, f. 158v (f. 159, Capricorn)
Hare and bird, shooting: Add. 49622, f. 85
Hare and boar
  hunting with dog: Merton 0.1.3. f. 111v
  running in opposite directions: M. 155, f. 37

H

Hare and cat *see* Cat and hare
Hare and centaur *see* Centaur and hare
Hare and cleric, pelted with stone by: Rothschild MS., f. 141
Hare and cock, astride, tilting at quintain: Melbourne 1254/3, f. 5
Hare and crane *see* Crane and hare
Hare and crow *see* Hare with pipe
Hare and dog (*see also* Castle; Dog and hare; Hare and snail; Hare with bagpipe)
astride: Add. 49622, f. 140; D.P. 12, f. 92 (holding pennant with three streamers); W. 85, ff. 46 (above, stag head issuing from border), 74 (with horn; above, lion's head issuing from border); Y.T. 8, ff. 183v (with trumpet), 331 (with horn)
hunting *see* Hare and stag; Hare hunting
tilting *see* Hares tilting
tilting at quintain: Melbourne 1254/3, f. 5
capturing, bringing before ape-judge, driving in cart to gallows, hanging: Royal 10 E.IV, ff. 62v.-64 (hare thumbing nose at hanged fox) (*fig. 217*)
carrying on shoulders: Y.T. 18, f. 255
carrying on stick across shoulder: Add. 49622, f. 161v (two, dead, second hare shooting another dog); Douce 5, f. 177 (*fig. 216*); Douce 6, f. 164v
dragging on ground, dog tied with rope: Cambrai 102, f. 284v
eating gold pellet, dog watching: Douce 118, f. 163v
feeding gold pellet to: Douce 118, f. 161
fighting: Y.T. 8, f. 181 (with swords and bucklers)
fighting, seated on shoulders of men, with sword and shield, battleax: Fitz. 298, f. 17
hunted by, borne on stick across shoulder: Douce 5, f. 177 (at R., ape standing on back of unicorn; above, man and woman kissing) (*fig. 216*)
hunting: Fitz. 298, f. 35v; Nancy 249, ff. 212, 254; Troyes 89, f. 163v (accompanied by goat with horn); V. and A. 8997E; W. 104, f. 168 (and man); Y.T. 8, ff. 275, 325v
pouncing on: fr. 95, f. 254 (*cf.* Phyllis and Aristotle); latin 1076, ff. 101v, 146v
pursued by, into burrow (*cf.* Hare disappearing): Douce 118, ff. 124, 134, 139; fr. 25526, ff. 141, 143v; Jacquemart 1, f. 86; lat. lit. f. 3, ff. 37v (two), 72, 79; latin 10435, f. 88v; M. 729, f. 342 (hood?); Melbourne 1254/3, f. 22 (*fig. 219*)
pursued by, into hood (*cf.* Dog running; Hare running): Add. 49622, f. 202v (four; blue hood) (*fig. 220*)
pursuing: Fitz. 298, ff. 29, 35v; Glazier 24, f. 46; M. 729, ff. 256v-257, 258; M. 754, ff. 83, 92v; Nancy 249, ff. 212 (2), 254; W. 45, f. 46 (hare with green sprig in mouth); Y.T. 8, ff. 325v, 343v
seated on shoulders of men, fighting with sword and shield, battleax: Fitz. 298, f. 17
shooting: Add. 49622, ff. 161v, 173v; Douce 366, f. 12 (hare/crane); Harley 6563, ff. 96v-97; Royal 10 E.IV, ff. 57v (dog-pilgrim), 62; Y.T. 8, f. 256
sprinkling, with asperge and situla: Fitz. 298, f. 129v (dog or wolf)
threatening: Add. 49622, ff. 88, 119 (with stick); Douce 366, f. 128 (with sword and mace); Nancy 249, f. 120 (with club); Verdun 107, f. 129 (with club)
thumbing nose at *see above, —,* capturing
tilting, astride man/snail, dog astride hare (*see also* Hare and cock): Y.T. 8, f. 294 (*fig. 158*)
trying before hare-judge *see above, —,* capturing
tying dog's tail to border stalk: BBR II 988, vol. II, f. 287v
tying dog up *see above, —,* capturing
with censer, dog with book: BBR 9157, f. 419v
with horn, dog dancing: M. 796, f. 148v (below, dog with trumpet)
with spear, dog's head impaled: M. 729, f. 233
Hare and dragon, astride: C.B. 62, f. 58v (above, woman)
Hare and falcon in tree, confronted (*see also* Falcon and hare): Rylands fr. 1, f. 212
Hare and fox *see* Fox and hare; Procession: fox-cleric
Hare and hare-child *see* Hare and offspring
Hare and hybrid man *see* Hybrid man and hare
Hare and hybrid woman *see* Hybrid woman and hare
Hare and knight *see* Knight and hare
Hare and lion (*see also* Hare and man, wrestling; Hare with club; Hybrid knight and hare)
astride: latin 14284, f. 28v
astride with sword and buckler fighting man/snail with bow: Verdun 107, f. 89 (*fig. 225*)
confronted: Add. 38115, f. 27; Fitz. 298, f. 136 (man/lion); M. 729, f. 355; Royal 3 D.VI,

f. 234 (hare with trumpet); W. 88, ff. 53 (lion with single horn like unicorn, piercing tree trunk), 68v (in center, tree); Y.T. 8, f. 278
confronted over gameboard: Add. 36684, f. 44v
devoured by: Trinity B.11.22, f. 155v (*fig. 223*)
frightened by lion's roar, falling over backwards: M. 88, f. 61
hunting with horn, astride dog: W. 85, f. 46
hunting with spear: Y.T. 8, f. 283 (*fig. 224*)
pursued by: Arras 1043, f. 155 (manticora?); Fitz. 298, ff. 21, 127v
Hare and man (*see also* Castle; Man and hare; Man nude and hare; Tailor and hare)
astride: Verdun 107, f. 105
nude man: Fitz. 298, f. 53 (with whip, bridle; Phyllis and Aristotle parody?); Metz 43, two photographs; Y.T. 8, f. 261v (with trumpet)
with bagpipe: Fitz. 298, f. 112
beheading: Fitz. 298, f. 49v; Royal 10 E.IV, f. 61v
carrying bound man over shoulder: BBR 10607, f. 150; Bodley 264, f. 81v; Chartres 549, f. 216v; Nancy 249, f. 1v; Trinity B.11.22, f. 28; Y.T. 8, f. 288 (tailor); Yale MS., f. 94v (another dog seizing second man)
dragging man clutching hood: Fitz. 298, f. 38 (tailor?)
dragging to gallows (*cf.* Hare and dog, capturing): Royal 10 E.IV, f. 61
fighting with clubs and shields: Fitz. 298, f. 104v
fighting with shield and club against man shooting at him: Fitz. 298, f. 11v
flaying: Fitz. 298, f. 74 (2)
following, man with horn, hound: W. 109, f. 168
frightening: Trinity B.11.22, f. 114v
hunting with bow, horn (*see also* above, —, carrying): Harley 6563, ff. 97v-98
hunting with horn, hound biting nude hindquarters of man: M. 729, f. 268
killing (*cf.* Hare and man, shooting): Verdun 107, f. 96v (with club); Y.T. 8, f. 327 (with sword)
kissing: Fitz. 298, f. 37
leading on rope: Fitz. 298, ff. 3, 66v
leading to prison: Fitz. 298, ff. 48 (?tailor with ?hood, hands tied), 104
shoeing goose *see* Proverbs: goose
shooting: Royal 10 E.IV, f. 57v
shooting with crossbow: Bodley 264, f. 81v (at R., man in tree, shot, carried off on stick across shoulder by hare)
tapping shoulder of man (cleric?) with shawm: Melbourne 1254/3, f. 2 (at R., devil leading goat)
threatening: Fitz. 298, ff. 21v (with rod), 49v (with sword, man kneeling), 304 (with switch), 310, 322
wrestling: Glazier 24, f. 65 (hare with lion's tail; below, two dogs pursuing two hares)
Hare and man/snail, astride, fighting with dog astride hare: Y.T. 8, f. 294
Hare and mouse (rat?) on leash, baiting cat: Nancy 249, f. 234
Hare and offspring (*see also* Tailor and hare, approaching)
bearing offspring to hare in bed: fr. 25526, f. 58v (at L., two apes wrestling)
bearing swaddled young to hare in canopied tub: Y.T. 8, f. 264 (*fig. 227*)
Hare and owl, pounced on by: M. 796, f. 69v
Hare and pig *see* Hare winding wool
Hare and ram astride dogs, tilting: Arras 790, f. 169
Hare and snail
butting: Douai 193, f. 213v
fighting with club and shield: Fitz. 298, f. 123
issuing from snail shell, confronting hybrid beast: Cambrai 102, ff. 9, 316
with asperge and processional cross: Y.T. 8, f. 282 (snail with bearded human head)
Hare and stag
hunting astride dog: Royal 14 B.V. (roll); W. 85, f. 74
shooting: Y.T. 8, f. 256
Hare and stork
approaching with battleax: Fitz. 298, f. 139
confronted: Ashmole 828, f. 43
fighting with club: Fitz. 298, f. 117v (stork with hooked beak, hare's ears)
Hare and tailor *see* Tailor and hare
Hare and unicorn *see* Man and unicorn, holding
Hare and wolf (dog?), sprinkling with asperge from situla: Fitz. 298, f. 129v
Hare as cleric (*see also* Procession, funeral of dog)
with book, confronting ape gesticulating: Y.T. 8, f. 293v
with book, confronting bishop/snail: Y.T. 8, f. 298
with book on lectern, flanked by hybrid bishop and hybrid king: BBR 329-41, f. 54 (at R., female ape with distaff and spindle) (*fig. 226*)

H

with processional cross: Melbourne 1254/3, f. 131v
Hare as fool (?), biting round object: Tournai Ps., f. 92 (below, Min.: Fool; Ps. 52) (*fig. 229*)
Hare as pardoner with sealed document, fox as pilgrim: Royal 10 E.IV, f. 53v (in *Roman de Renart* cycle)
Hare as pilgrim: BBR 9157, ff. 428 (at R., cock), 463 (with dog-pilgrim); Fitz. 298, ff. 129 (conversing with dog); G.K.S. 3384, f. 256v
Hare astride *see* Ape and hare; Hare and cock; — and dog; — and lion; — and man; — and man/snail
Hare at funeral *see* Procession, funeral; —, hares
Hare at lectern *see* Hare as cleric
Hare at school *see* School
Hare attacking castle *see* Castle
Hare balancing crocket on ears: St. Omer 5, f. 136 (at L., two hybrid men)
Hare bathing *see* Hare and offspring
Hare before burrow: M. 102, f. 127 (line ending)
Hare dancing (*see also* Ass with pipe): Add. 49622, ff. 86v (dog with vielle), 154v (hybrid ape with pipe and tabor)
Hare dead *see* Dog and hare, hunting; Falcon and hare; Hare, funeral of; Man and hare, carrying
Hare disappearing into burrow (*see also* Dog and hare, pursuing hare): Douce 118, ff. 111v (bird biting tail), 154; Harley 6563, ff. 33, 55v; lat. lit. f.3, f. 33; latin 10483, f. 214; M. 88, ff. 162v (at R., dog winding wool, boar with distaff and spindle), 169; Melbourne 1254/3, f. 132v (f. 133, two dogs pursuing hare)
Hare disappearing into burrow, emerging: fr. 25526, f. 84 (several)
Hare emerging from burrow: *see* Hare running out of
Hare fighting *see* Centaur and hare; Crane and hare; Hare and man; — and ram; — and snail; — with ax; Hares; Hybrid hare
Hare, funeral of: Add. 49622, f. 164 (two lighting tapers at bier, three others mourning)
Hare hanging from pole resting on two forked sticks: M. 754, ff. 78v (2; above, hybrid king; below, spear aimed at hares), 79 (arrow flying from bow in direction of f. 78v)
Hare hunting (*see also* Hare and bird; — and boar; — and dog; — and lion; — and man; — and stag)
with bow and arrow, horn: Harley 6563, ff. 20-20v
with horn, astride dog: W. 85, ff. 46 (stag's head issuing from border), 74 (lion's head issuing from border)
with spear, horn, hounds on leash: lat. lit. f. 3, f. 95v (2)
Hare in basket (*see also* Man with basket, Proverbs: woman with basket): W. 45, f. 106
Hare in cage: M. 754, f. 69 (3, dog before cage); Nancy 249, f. 275 (3, ?dog jumping at cage)
Hare issuing from snail shell, confronting hybrid beast: Cambrai 102, ff. 9, 316
Hare juggling (?) two knives: latin 16260, f. 335v
Hare kissing (?) hare (*cf.* Hare and man, kissing): W. 88, f. 78v
Hare nibbling leaf, looking at hand issuing from border, blessing (? ; *cf.* Hare running with leaf): Melbourne 1254/3, f. 41v
Hare picking flowers (*cf.* Man picking): M. 754, f. 86v (three gloved hands doing the same)
Hare playing organ
ape pumping bellows: Add. 49622, f. 67v
hare pumping bellows: Fitz. 298, f. 79v
Hare reading *see* Hare with book
Hare ringing bell on bell rope (*see also* Procession, funeral of fox): Add. 36684, f. 113; Douce 118, f. 124v; Nancy 249, f. 42
Hare running (*see also* Dog and hare, pursuing; Hare disappearing; Hare with purse; Rabbit burrow): W. 37, ff. 55v (f. 56, large bird), 57 (f. 57v, nude man with club), 123, 133v
from hand with spear: Douce 118, f. 117v
into hood: Melbourne 1254/3, ff. 97, 118, 131; W. 87, f. 109 (blue hood)
out of blue hood (*cf.* Dog running; Hare and dog, pursued by): Douce 118, ff. 97 (hood supported by hand) (*fig. 222*), 113, 158v
out of burrow: Arsenal 5056, f. 1 (hybrid man shooting stag); Harley 6563, ff. 33v, 56, 56v; M. 88, ff. 168v, 189 (at R., man digging grave; text: Offices of the Dead); M. 754, f. 14v (looking out)
out of sack: M. 754, f. 64v (2, white sack)
confronting ape with rake standing before (stool?) basket: M. 754, f. 74v (nun with club, man brandishing psaltery)
horse with vielle: M. 754, f. 87 (another hare, vielle)
up steps of post mill: M. 754, f. 62
with leaf in mouth: W. 37, ff. 75, 85

Hare threshing: G.K.S. 3384, f. 88 (2)
Hare tilting *see* Hare and ram; Hares; Quintain
Hare winding wool on reel: fr. 25526, ff. 68 (at L., two beggars, one with basket on back containing child), 68v (at L., Crucifixion), 74, 102v (pig with distaff and spindle)
Hare with asperge *see* Fox and geese
Hare with asperge and situla *see* Hare and dog, sprinkling
Hare with ax: Cloisters 54.1.2, f. 23
aiming at border stalk (*cf.* Pruning, references under): latin 3893, f. 170
fighting headless hybrid man wearing tall ecclesiastical hat: Add. 49622, f. 13v
Hare with bagpipe (*see also* Hare with harp): Add. 24681, f. 49; Add. 30029, f. 105; Add. 49622, f. 192; Cambrai 103, f. 479v (at R., female saint beheaded); Douce 6, f. 33v; Rothschild MS., f. 180v (dog pursuing hare); W. 45, f. 82; W. 85, f. 93
dog dancing: Cambrai 102, f. 13v
exposing hindquarters to ape with staff: Arsenal 5218, f. 15
seated on man's shoulders: Fitz. 298, f. 112
Hare with bellows: D.P. 35, f. 56v (2)
Hare with bellows held against hand organ, bow aimed at hare from above: M. 754, f. 88
Hare with book (*see also* Hare as cleric)
and hybrid bird with book: M. 754, f. 74
with dog, venerating cock on man's hat: Verdun 107, f. 8v
Hare with bundle of green rods on back: Y.T. 8, f. 202v
Hare with censer, dog with book: BBR 9157, f. 419v (*fig. 159*)
Hare with club (*see also* Hare and dog, threatening): W. 85, f. 69v (f. 69, knight killing lion)
Hare with cymbals, hybrid man with trumpet: Rutland Ps., ff. 53v-54
Hare with distaff and spindle (*see also* Hybrid man with): fr. 25526, f. 104; Glazier 24, f. 59v (hybrid man drinking); latin 3893, f. 235
Hare with double pipe: Christ Church E.II, f. 56
Hare with fox trap (?): Trinity B.11.22, f. 44v
Hare with fruit (*cf.* Ape with; Hare as fool): Bodley 264, f. 36v; Vienna 2542, f. 274; W. 88, f. 78v (confronting hare)
Hare with hand bells (*see also* Procession, funeral of dog): M. 149, f. 417
dog with vielle, lion dancing: fr. 25526, f. 94v
man ringing bell on rope: Nancy 249, f. 42
man with hurdy-gurdy: fr. 25526, f. 8v
Hare with hand organ: Add. 36684, f. 56
dog with bagpipe: Metz 43, photograph; Y.T. 8, f. 184v
Hare with harp: Yale MS., ff. 1, 209
dog with hand bells, another hare with bagpipe, man balancing basins on sticks: Trinity B.11.22, f. 6v
man playing cock with tongs: Stowe 17, f. 92v (*fig. 514*)
merman dancing: Fitz. 298, f. 14
Hare with horn (*see also* Hare hunting)
and pipe: Fitz. 2-1954, f. 13
wearing cape: Fitz. 2-1954, f. 139
woman dancing: Bodley 264, f. 20v
Hare with knives *see* Hare juggling
Hare with pipe: Rutland Ps., f. 100; W. 45, f. 154 (above, owl)
and hand bell, ape with gittern: Egerton 1151, f. 7
and horn: Fitz. 2-1954, f. 13
and tabor: Harley 6563, f. 44; Melbourne 1254/3, f. 56 (cleric with trumpet)
black bird (crow?) singing: Add. 38114, f. 67v
fox with trumpet, wolf (?) with tabor, goat with harp: latin 1029A, f. 23v
Hare with processional cross (*see also* Procession, fox-cleric; —, funeral of dog): Douce 118, f. 38v
Hare with psaltery: Add. 36684, f. 104v; BBR 10607, f. 96v (at L, hybrid man with pipe); Kraus 75/88, Cat. p. 96; W. 85, f. 17
Hare with purse around neck, running (proverb? *Cf.* Hare running): G.K.S. 3384, f. 22v (*fig. 152*); M. 812, f. 28 (half-snail, licking round object)
man pushing or holding back hare: Douce 6, f. 96v
pursued by ape with sack: W. 82, f. 210v
Hare with reel, pig with distaff and spindle: fr. 25526, f. 102v
Hare with slingshot, confronting knight (David and Goliath parody?): Fitz. 298, f. 7
Hare with tabor (*see also* Hare with pipe and): latin 1029A, f. 32v
Hare with taper (*see also* Hare, funeral of; Procession, funeral of dog): BBR 9157, f. 329
Hare with timbrel
ass with mandola: BBR 9157, f. 1
dog with bagpipe: BBR 9157, f. 415v
Hare with trumpet (*see also* Procession, funeral of dog): Cloisters 54.1.2, f. 166v; Fitz. 298, f.

23; G.K.S. 3384, f. 195; Hague 78.D.40, f. 115; Melbourne 1254/3, ff. 95v, 103v, 104, 125v, 134v; W. 85, f. 34 (hare?); W. 87, f. 59
ape dancing, dog with pipe and tabor: Hague 78.D.40, f. 21
confronting lion: Royal 3 D.VI, f. 234
confronting man with horn and spear: Melbourne 1254/3, f. 121v
dog with bagpipe: Y.T. 8, f. 183v
hybrid man with handbells: Cambrai 102, f. 335v
hybrid man with pipe and tabor: W. 45, f. 94v
hybrid man with vielle: Melbourne 1254/3, f. 100v
Hare with vielle: Arras 790, f. 146v (hybrid); M. 812, f. 35v
dog dancing: Arsenal 5218, f. 14; Y.T. 8, f. 284
Hare costume *see* Man in costume as
Hares
attacking castle *see* Castle
caged *see* Hare in cage
confronted, one eating around red object (*cf.* Hare with fruit): W. 88, f. 114v
fighting with swords and bucklers, three hares looking on: Nancy 249, f. 118
into burrow *see* Hare running; Rabbit burrow
kissing (?): W. 88, f. 78v
tilting: Nancy 249, f. 224v
tilting, astride dogs: BBR 9157, f. 1; Royal 10 E.IV, f. 70 (with sword and lance, baskets as shields) (*fig. 228*)
winged: Hague 78.D.40, throughout
Harp *see* Angel with; Ape as cleric with; Ape dancing; Ape with; Beggar with; Bishop with; Boar with; Centaur with; David harping; Fox with; Goat with; Hare with; Hybrid man with; Jubal; Lion with; Man with; Mermaid with; Merman with; Stag with; Woman with
Harpy: M. 796, f. 117v; W. 102, f. 58v (with sword, confronting hybrid man)
Harrow *see* Ape and dog, astride, pulling; Man harrowing; — sowing; Man with
Harrowing of Hell *see* Jesus Christ, life of
Hart, Bestiary representation: Munich c.g. 16, f. 19 (in cycle)
Harvesting *see* Man picking grapes; — reaping; — scything; — threshing; Man with wheat sheaf
Hawk (*cf.* Falcon)
flying over goose and goslings; gooseherd waving club and hood: Add. 42130, f. 169v
shot by centaur: fr. 95, f. 319
striking hen and chicks: Chantilly 64, ff. 104, 104v
Hawking *see* Falconer
Haywain, man driving three horses, three men pushing: Add. 42130, f. 173v (*fig. 230*)
Head *see* Detached limbs
Hebrews *see* Moses
Hector and Achilles parody(?) Ape astride horse dragging ape tied by feet: fr. 95, f. 345
Hedge sparrow: Fitz. 2-1954, f. 145v
Hedgehog: Glazier 24, f. 69v; Lambeth 209, f. 8 (added); M. 729, f. 258; W. 90, f. 148v
and bear, doe: Fitz. 242, f. 55v (Min.: Crucifixion) (*fig. 12*)
in Bestiary cycle: Munich c.g. 16, f. 12; Royal 2 B.VII, ff. 97v-98
with apples on spines: Add. 36684, f. 59; Add. 38114, f. 4v; Add. 39810, f. 7 (*fig. 140*); Fitz. 47, ff. 49, 161 (line endings); L.M. 13, f. 41v (*fig. 231*); Nancy 249, ff. 216, 237 (ibex leaping away, frightened?); Rothschild MS., f. 176 (at foot of tree, another hedgehog climbing tree); Royal 14 E.III, f. 140; Verdun 107, ff. 8, 13; W. 760, f. 152; Y.T. 27, f. 51v
Hell *see* Dives and Lazarus; Jesus Christ, life of: Last Judgment: Hell-mouth; —: Pains of Hell
Helmet *see* Man nude and hare, hunting with spear; — and monster; Knight and woman kneeling before
Hen and chicks (*see also* Chickens; Fox as Franciscan): Hague 78.D.40, f. 31 (at L., woman with distaff and spindle pursuing fox with cock; at R., stag) (*fig. 641*)
fed by woman: Add. 42130, f. 166v
struck by hawk: Chantilly 64, ff. 104, 104v
Hen crowned, in tower, observing cockfight (*cf.* Knights tilting, queen): Douce 131, f. 42v (*fig. 135*)
Hen flying toward nest containing five eggs (*cf.* Bird flying): W. 45, f. 201v
Hercules
and Cacus: Ste. Gen. 777, f. 7 (*fig. 235*)
man nude save for mantle, with club, holding lion's head: G.K.S. 3384, f. 106 (Hercules? above, man seizing club) (*fig. 234*)
man wearing lionskin, blowing trumpet, holding white sack: C.B. 64, f. 89 (Hercules?)
Heretic *see* Jesus Christ, life of: Last Judgment: Pains of Hell

Hermit (*see also* Virgin, miracles of: abbess; —hermit): Add. 49622, f. 161
confronting monstrous reptile/insect: Rothschild MS., f. 184
gesturing to woman pointing at small bird on her head: Harley 6563, ff. 95v-96
in chapel, conversing with knight: Trinity B.11.22, f. 207
pleading with indignant woman: Harley 6563, ff. 67v-68 (*figs. 232-233*)
sinning, repenting: Royal 10 E.IV, ff. 113v-117, 129-136v
Herod (*see also* Jesus Christ, life of: before; —: Massacre; Salome): Add. 29253, f. 387; Royal 2 B.VII, f. 235v (giving orders to three soldiers)
Heron (*see also* Falcon and)
shot by man: Fitz. 298, f. 51v
swimming, diving for fish: Melbourne 1254/3, f. 55v
Hoarding *see* Man hoarding
Hobbyhorse, ridden by ape: G.K.S. 3384, f. 86v
Hockey: Royal 10 E.IV, f. 95 (two men); W. 88, f. 40v (two men)
Hogs *see* Man and pigs; Pig
Holly growing out of tail of hybrid beast: Add. 42130, f. 174v
Holofernes *see* Judith; Vices: Cruelty
Holy Communion administered by cleric (*see also* Sacraments: Eucharist): Add. 49622, f. 13
Holy Ghost: Add. 24681, f. 90v (Min.: Baptism of Christ); Add. 36684, f. 70v (Litany)
Holy Ghost, gifts of *see* Sacraments; St. Margaret, f. 161v
Honey *see* Bear reaching
Hood (*see also* Ape and butterfly; Ape with; Blindman's buff; Dice, men; Dog and hare, pursuing hare; Dog running into: Hare running; Man and butterfly, pursuing with; Man with bagpipe, half-nude; Tailor and hare, pierced by; Woman and butterfly)
empty, with body and legs of animal: W. 37, f. 104v (brown)
four heads under, issuing from hybrid man (proverb?): Cambrai 103, f. 356v
two heads under (proverb? *cf.* Man and woman, heads under): Chantilly 64, ff. 131, 131v (blue)
Hoop *see* Man with
Hoopoe, Bestiary representation: Royal 2 B.VII, ff. 94v-95 (in cycle)
Hope *see* Virtues
Horeb *see* Moses, smiting
Horn *see* Ape with; Fox with; Hare with; Hybrid man and hare, hunting with; Hybrid man with; Lion with; Man with; Samson, blind; Squirrel
Horse (*see also* Ape and; Coach; Dominican and woman; Fox and; Haywain; King and; Knight and; Knight and woman, charged by; Man and; Man plowing; Procession, funeral of fox; Virgin, miracles of: woman saved; Windmill)
and bear, leaping at one another: Royal 2 B.VII, f. 130v
Bestiary representation: Munich c.g. 16, f. 45 (in cycle)
grazing: Add. 39810, f. 7 (*fig. 140*); Melbourne 1254/3, f. 85
head of: Lansdowne 420, f. 75v
intercourse: Merton 0.1.3, f. 111v
leg of, pulling bell rope: M. 754, f. 94
riderless, with golden saddle: M. 155, f. 145v
shoed *see* Blacksmith
walking on eggs (droppings?): Stowe 17, f. 153v (nude man aiming trumpet at horse's hindquarters)
with vielle: M. 754, f. 87; Trinity B.11.22, f. 185v
Horseshoe *see* Ostrich with
Hosea and Philip, Apostle (Old and New Law): Y.T. 13, f. 38v; Y.T. 27, f. 5; Y.T. 75, f. 6
Host *see* Ape with; Holy Communion; Sacraments: Eucharist
Hot cockles: Bodley 264, ff. 52 (three men, three women), 97 (six women), 132v; Cambridge Dd. 5.5, f. 280 (two men, one woman; at L., two men putting bread in oven; Min.: Death of the Virgin); Fitz. 298, f. 98 (unfinished); Trinity B.11.22, f. 143v (three men); Y.T. 8, f. 92 (three men, one with sack over head); Y.T. 75, ff. 39 (three men, two women; Min.: Annunciation), 146 (three men; f. 145v, Min.: Nativity)
Houses for raising of falcons: fr. 12400, ff. 96, 96v
Human quintain *see* Quintain, balancing
Hunchback: Jesus 40, f. 88v
Hunting *see* references under specific agents, e.g., Ape and bird; Ape and stag; *also* Ox with club
Huque bleue see Hood
Hurdy-gurdy *see* Ape with; Dog with; Man with
Hybrid abbess: W. 85, f. 85v

H

and bishop, kneeling before: BBR 10607, ff. 107v-108
and hybrid bishop, two hybrid men by water: M. 754, f. 61v
and snail, blessing snail with stag's head: Douce 118, f. 12
and snail, holding: W. 87, f. 73v (winged; f. 73, knight with tankard)
Hybrid abbot (*see also* Ape with hand bells; Man nude, holding; Man with harp; Procession, funeral of dog): Glazier 24, f. 85
back turned to book on lectern: M. 754, f. 2v
with spindle: Glazier 24, f. 53v (above, nude man holding bishop's head)
Hybrid angel
with censer, trumpet: latin 16260, f. 5v (2, Genesis, I)
with gittern: W. 104, f. 32v
with hand organ, vielle: W. 104, f. 28 (2) (*fig. 11*)
with trumpet: Add. 24686, f. 16v
Hybrid ape
and bird, shooting: Bodley 264, f. 57v
and butterfly, holding: M. 149, ff. 235, 267, 298v (f. 299, hare)
half-snail: Y.T. 8, ff. 292, 298
sawing comb: Add. 49622, f. 146
with arrow, throwing at second ape: Bodley 264, f. 66
with book, charged by ape with spear and shield astride dog: Princeton 44-18, ff. 203v-204 (female)
with hand bells: BBR II 988, vol. II, f. 259
with mirror, combing hair: W. 102, f. 60
with papal tiara, pursued by crowned centaur: Douce 118, f. 10
with pipe and tabor, hare dancing: Add. 49622, f. 154v
with trumpet: W. 45, f. 101v
with vielle: M. 155, f. 49
with vielle, fox dancing, hybrid man with bagpipe: Cambrai 102, f. 324
Hybrid ass
half-bird in nest (proverb?): W. 45, f. 44v (eggs in nest; hybrid bird with hare's ears?)
with stag horns: W. 87, f. 48v
Hybrid beast (grotesque): Add. 42130 and Christ Church E.II, remarkable specimens throughout
three-faced: C.B. 62, f. 181v
with fruit (*cf.* Ape with): Christ Church E.II, f. 68
with pipe and tabor: Stowe 12, f. 334v
with platform shoes: W. 88, ff. 106v, 159v (hybrid woman)
with spoon: Glazier 24, f. 37v
with vielle, winged headdress, ape dancing: Douce 118, f. 17
Hybrid bee: M. 761, ff. 38, 39
Hybrid bird (*see also* Devil and; Ape and knight; Man and)
pruning border stalk with knife (*cf.* Man pruning): fr. 95, f. 321
standing on globe: M. 754, f. 38v (at R., fish, stag)
with bagpipe, hybrid man dancing: latin 14284, f. 63v
with bone in beak W. 87, f. 64 (at R., stork biting border stalk)
with book, two hares with books, nude armless hybrid man: M. 754, f. 74
with crossbow: M. 754, f. 64v
with distaff *see* Hybrid man with distaff and spindle
with hare's ears, in nest containing eggs (proverb?): W. 45, f. 44v (hybrid ass?)
with large fish in beak: M. 754, f. 53
Hybrid bishop (*see also* Ape and bird, holding; — and hybrid bishop; Cat and mouse, holding; Hare as cleric; Man and; Man and snail, astride; Obscaena: kissing; —: sword): Add. 42130, ff. 175, 192; Ashmole 828, f. 99v; Cloisters 54.1.2, ff. 124, 167v, 171; Christ Church E.II, f. 49; Douce 5, f. 138v (*fig. 150*); Douce 23, f. 14; Glazier 24, ff. 49v, 161, 164, 169v; Harley 6563, f. 68; Lambeth 233, ff. 18v, 23, 129v, 148, 188v, 215; latin 3893, throughout; latin 16260, f. 292v (below, woman with distaff and spindle); M. 754, ff. 33, 46 (2); W. 37, ff. 86v, 180, 181v; W. 45, f. 5v; W. 85, f. 85v; Yale MS., f. 23v
and ape, hearing confession of: Princeton 44-18, ff. 63v-64
and ape with back turned, conversing with: Tournai Ps., f. 96
and bird, gesturing before: Add. 17868, ff. 96, 97v (with book); Stowe 17, ff. 41v-42
and devil, shot by: Melbourne 1254/3., f. 14
and hare (*see also below,* — with vielle)
conversing: Tournai Ps., f. 93v
with book, before hare-cleric: Y.T. 8, f. 298 (half-snail)
and hybrid cleric

confronting stork: Tournai Ps., f. 87
hybrid cleric kneeling before him: latin 14284, f. 23
hybrid cleric with asperge and situla: Add. 17868, f. 39v (with book)
hybrid cleric with book: Fitz. 288, f. 159v (Min.: Harrowing of Hell)
and hybrid knight gesticulating: Arras 1043, f. 190 (with book)
and hybrid peacock, aiming crook at: W. 87, ff. 2v-3 (f. 3, ape kneeling)
and hybrid woman, winding wool for, on reel (*see also below,* — blessing): Douai 152, f. 118
and man astride horse, fighting with spear and shield, war hammer and shield: Melbourne 1254/3, f. 65
and snail
confronting: Add. 49622, f. 194v
conversing with, holding processional cross: Melbourne 1254/3, f. 27v
with bellows, turning his back on man/snail: Melbourne 1254/3, f. 14
at lectern: W. 88, f. 32v
blessing: Add. 10294, f. 1; Cloisters 54.1.2, ff. 37 (bellows on head), 104 (blowing bellows in initial); Douce 118, ff. 148v, 172v
hybrid couple: BBR 329-41, f. 198v
hybrid woman praying: latin 14284, f. 56v
investing bishop: Yale MS., f. 133v (2) (*fig. 236*)
issuing from tail of hybrid king: W. 88, f. 184v
singing from book: fr. 95, f. 343v (2)
three-faced, with two trumpets: W. 88, f. 185v
winged: W. 87, f. 104 (praying); Yale MS., f. 25
with ax: M. 812, f. 25 (half-snail)
with bagpipe, hybrid nun (Dominican) dancing: Stowe 17, f. 49
with bellows *see above,* — and snail; — blessing
with bells (three) attached to band around neck: Jacquemart 1, f. 3
with book: Cloisters 54.1.2, f. 195
with book, head shaped like cloven hoof (*see also above,* — and hybrid cleric; — and hybrid knight; — singing): Cloisters 54.1.2, f. 203v
with distaff *see* Hybrid man with distaff and spindle
with hand bells (*see also* Procession, funeral): latin 16260, f. 536 (at R., ape gesturing)
with hand organ: Add. 10293, f. 1
with harp: Cloisters 54.1.2, f. 83
with pipe and tabor: Cloisters 54.1.2, f. 80
with trumpet, buckler: Douce 118, f. 165
with vielle, hare dancing: Stowe 17, f. 169v (f. 170, hybrid man aiming bow at hare)
Hybrid cat with mouse in mouth: Jacquemart 1, f. 101v
Hybrid centaur
and dog, pursuing: W. 88, f. 140 (bishop's head issuing from tail)
and stag, shooting: W. 104, f. 5v (at R., lion)
Hybrid cleric: W. 85, f. 84
and dragon, beard pulled by: C.B. 62, f. 214
and hybrid bird, head pecked by: Add. 42130, f. 179v
and hybrid bishop *see* Hybrid bishop and
and hybrid man, confronting: Arras 1043, f. 180v (with book); W. 88, f. 136v (hybrid man wearing hood)
and hybrid nun, both with book: W. 104, f. 74
and hybrid woman (*see also below,* — with garland)
confronted, hybrid woman with mirror and comb: Arras 229, f. 449v
confronted, hybrid woman with purse(?): W. 104, f. 70v
pointing at: latin 14284, f. 13v (fox as cleric?)
and lion, frightened by: Fitz. 298, f. 9v (cleric/snail)
and nun praying, woman/snail with crosier: M. 754, f. 12v (2, with crosiers)
and nun with book: W. 87, f. 16v
as physician: fr. 2754, f. 164v (with urinal)
balancing two basins on sticks: M. 754, f. 53v
flanking text: G.K.S. 393, f. 301v (7)
playing bellows with distaff: Stowe 17, f. 38 (woman dancing) (*fig. 509*)
praying: fr. 25526, f. 62 (2, with bishop, pope); Glazier 24, f. 119v
singing from book (*cf.* Hybrid bishop): fr. 95, f. 138v (cleric/centaur)
with asperge and situla: Add. 17868, f. 39v (hybrid bishop with book); Cloisters 54.1.2, f. 51v (hybrid man pointing)
with basket and stick (parody of asperge and situla? *cf.* Bishop with): Cloisters 54.1.2, ff. 38 (below, hybrid man holding head of man, hybrid man with cup), 51v; Y.T. 27, f. 49 (stool basket)
with book (*see also* Hybrid man with hand bell): Add. 17868, ff. 75, 77v; BBR 9217, f. 116; Cloisters 54.1.2, ff. 55, 155; Jacquemart 1, f. 85v (at L., hybrid man with shield); latin

H

10483, f. 8v; M. 155, f. 3v; Rylands fr. 1, f. 82 (*fig. 54*); Stowe 17, f. 203v (Dominican; below, butterfly)
book placed on lectern attached to body: W. 88, ff. 26v (at R., ape), 173 (*fig. 237*)
book placed on lectern, hand issuing from tail: W. 88, f. 32v (with crosier)
confronting amused hybrid man: Arras 1043, f. 180v
confronting hybrid nun with book: W. 104, f. 74
confronting hybrid woman, pointing at: latin 14284, f. 13v (fox as cleric?)
ringing two bells on bell ropes: M. 754, f. 58 (above, cockfight)
with garland: M. 155, ff. 113v-114 (hybrid woman with scroll), 165v-166 (hybrid woman with ?apple)
with hand organ: W. 87, f. 21
with harp: Cloisters 54.1.2, f. 166 (*fig. 516*)
with pan(?), beating with spoon: Cloisters 54.1.2, f. 129
with staff: Melbourne 1254/3, f. 11
with switch *see* Man in costume as boar
with vielle, hybrid man issuing from tail dancing: W. 88, f. 63v
Hybrid clerics: G.K.S. 393, f. 301v (*fig. 238*)
Hybrid cock issuing from shell bitten by hybrid hare: W. 45, f. 16v (above, fox)
Hybrid devil with trumpet: W. 87, f. 6v
Hybrid dog with processional cross (*see also* Hybrid hare; Hybrid man and; Hybrid man with gittern, with winged headdress): fr. 25526, f. 67 (below, man shooting bird)
Hybrid Dominican with book: Stowe 17, f. 203v (below, butterfly)
Hybrid dragon *see* Ape and
Hybrid elephant: Cloisters 54.1.2, f. 133; G.K.S. 3384, f. 111 (*fig. 479*)
Hybrid falconer *see* Hybrid man as
Hybrid fox (?) as cleric, pointing at hybrid woman: latin 14284, f. 13v
Hybrid Franciscan
and hybrid nun (Dominican) with mirror, making advances to(?): Add. 28784B, f. 3
and hybrid nun with distaff, confronting with spindle: Add. 28784B, f. 10
with book: Stowe 17, f. 57
Hybrid hare (*see also* Hybrid bird with hare's ears; Hybrid stag)
and bird (goldfinch), shooting: Fitz. 298, f. 78v
and dog/snail, fighting: Add. 49622, f. 179v
and hybrid cock issuing from shell, biting: W. 45, f. 16v (above, fox)
and hybrid dog, pursued by: W. 37, f. 176v
half-dog, running: W. 37, f. 21v (f. 22, small hare)
with vielle: Arras 790, f. 146v
Hybrid horse (ass?) with claw feet: W. 102, f. 58
Hybrid Jew: Add. 17868, f. 49v; W. 39, f. 33
confronting bird with back turned, one finger pointing up: Add. 17868, f. 136
shooting owl: Add. 17868, f. 86
Hybrid king (*see also* Ape and; Centaur and; Hare as cleric; Pope admonishing; Rabbit burrow): Douce 23, f. 14; Jacquemart 1, f. 118v (2, one with ?emperor's crown); Lambeth 233, ff. 41v, 77, 124v; W. 45, f. 244; W. 85, f. 115; W. 90, throughout
and butterfly, shooting: Cloisters 54.1.2, f. 76v
and unicorn, hunting with horn, hound: Cambrai 103, f. 172
as falconer: latin 14284, f. 24 (with retainer); Yale MS., f. 363
playing jawbone with plectrum: Cloisters 54.1.2, f. 54 (*fig. 511*)
pointing at bishop with crosier issuing from tail: W. 88, f. 184v
with club over shoulder: W. 37, f. 105
with horn: W. 87, f. 16 (dog with horn issuing from tail)
with trumpet: M. 155, ff. 151, 159v
with vielle: W. 85, f. 87v
Hybrid knight (*see also* Capricorn; Centaur and; Centaur as knight):
and bird, shooting: W. 88, f. 104v (at R., hare; at L., dog)
and centaur, fighting with battleax and bow: St. Omer 5, f. 184
and centaur/knight astride horse, fighting: St. Omer 5, f. 235v
and cock, confronting with sword and buckler: Melbourne 1254/3, ff. 113v-114
and dog, astride with spear: Melbourne 1254/3, f. 1v (knight/snail)
and dog, pulling tail of: St. Omer 5, f. 134 (knight/centaur; at R., woman with two rakes, by fire)
and dragon
bitten by, bending crossbow at: M. 155, ff. 87v-88

fighting with bent, forked sword: Princeton 44-18, f. 167
fighting with spear: Fitz. 2-1954, f. 23v
fighting with sword: Add. 49622, f. 21; Cambrai 102, f. 340 (killing); Douce 5, ff. 44, 80
and hare
fighting with spear and shield: Jacquemart 1, f. 39v
fighting with sword and shield, lion at side: Princeton 44-18, ff. 75v-76
under tree, confronting with bent sword and buckler: Princeton 44-18, ff. 99v-100 (owl in tree)
and hybrid beast, fighting with spear: St. Omer 5, f. 235v
and hybrid man
bending crossbow at: M. 155, ff. 155v-156
charged by, with polearm: Cloisters 54.1.3, f. 59
fighting with spear: latin 10483, f. 40
fighting with spear and shield, club and buckler: M. 155, ff. 162v-163
shooting: Add. 17868, f. 80; latin 13260, f. 96v
shot by: Jacquemart 1, f. 118v (with spear and shield)
and hybrid Saracen, fighting: Burney 275, f. 166
and hybrid woman, disarmed by, her spear ornamented with garland, several flowers in air: Stowe 17, ff. 226v-227
and hybrid woman, fighting with bow and sword: St. Omer 5, f. 130 (hybrid knight in drawers, with lion's tail)
and knight, pointing at hybrid man with bat wings, fighting with sword and shield: M. 796, f. 75v
and lion
fighting with club and buckler: Cambrai 102, f. 354 (at L., man fighting snail with spear and shield)
fighting with spear: M. 754, f. 56v (lion with aillettes, sword)
fighting with sword: Cambrai 102, ff. 340v, 342 (aided by knight), 352 (2, with sword and spear); W. 88, f. 123
and man, fighting with sword and buckler (issuing from border): latin 14284, ff. 19, 33
and man (woman?) astride bird, tilting, breaking lance of: Cambrai 103, f. 272v
and man with garland, bending crossbow at: M. 155, ff. 86v-87 (f. 87, below, woman with vielle)
and merman/knight, fighting with sword and bellows, sword and shield: Princeton 44-18, ff. 191v-192 (*fig. 240*)
and monster
fighting with crossbow: St. Omer 5, f. 128 (behind hybrid knight, bearded nude hybrid man crawling on all fours)
fighting with sword: Douce 6, f. 54v
fighting with sword and buckler: Cambrai 102, f. 470v
killed by, with spear: fr. 95, f. 309
and snail
fighting with spear: Add. 49622, f. 179 (snail labeled "limasconn"); BBR 329-41, f. 198v; BBR 9391, f. 39 (*fig. 241*); Royal 2 B.VII, f. 148 (two)
fighting with sword and buckler: BBR II 988, vol. II, f. 268 (at R., hybrid ape shooting same snail); latin 3893, f. 176v
fighting with sword and shield: Douai 193, f. 72; G.K.S. 3384, f. 224v
and stork, fighting: G.K.S. 3384, f. 237v (at R., hare)
and unicorn, charging with spear: latin 3893, f. 243v
tilting at quintain: Melbourne 1254/3, f. 40v
with battleax, followed by dog: Add. 21926, f. 151
with harp: Stowe 17, f. 61v
with head of man in one hand, sword in other (*cf.* Centaur with head; Knight with head): St. Omer 5, ff. 11, 145v
with mortar and pestle: W. 88, f. 84
with spear in one hand, round object in the other: Melbourne 1254/3, f. 15v (knight/merman)
with sword aimed at head issuing from his posterior: W. 88, f. 116
with sword and buckler: Arras 1043, f. 132v
with wheelbarrow drawn by semi-nude man: W. 88, f. 39v
Hybrid knights
extending right hands toward each other: Jacquemart 1, f. 97v
fighting with bow and arrow, sword: Royal 2 B.VII, f. 137v
fighting with spear and sword: M. 754, f. 48 (one, armless)
fighting with swords: Christ Church E.II, f. 31
tilting: Jacquemart 1, f. 36
Hybrid man and ape (*see also* Ape and; Hybrid man with pipe and tabor; — with tabor)
fighting with sword and buckler: Bodley 264, f. 55v (ape hiding behind large shield)

H

shooting: M. 155, ff. 26v-27 (hybrid ape with sword and buckler); Tournai Ps., f. 2 (at R., large bird)
Hybrid man and ass, shooting: Jacquemart 1, f. 88
Hybrid man and bear, training: W. 85, f. 31v
Hybrid man and beast
fighting with ax: Royal 2 B.VII, f. 169
fighting with club: Royal 2 B.VII, f. 168v
fighting with club and buckler: Hague 10.B.21, f. 20v
unsheathing sword before: Tournai Ps., f. 20v
Hybrid man and beggar *see* Beggar and hybrid man
Hybrid man and bird
confronting, hands clasped in prayer: fr. 776, f. 133
conversing with: M. 155, f. 5 (another hybrid man praying before woman in initial); W. 88, f. 117v
hunting with bow, club, and spear: Add. 17868, throughout
hunting with crossbow: W. 88, f. 174v (parrot?)
hunting with slingshot: Ghent 233, f. 93v
shooting: BBR 11040, f. 4; Douce 5, f. 110; latin 3893, f. 197v; latin 16260, f. 234v; Laud Lat. 84, f. 131; M. 155, ff. 1 (below, three dogs pursuing stag), 46v-47, 75v-76; W. 45, f. 147; W. 88, f. 135; Y.T. 19, f. 1
Hybrid man and boar, hunting with bow and arrow: Burney 275, f. 293
Hybrid man and butterfly
hunting with lure: Arsenal 5218, f. 50
shooting: Cloisters 54.1.2, f. 76v (crowned); Douce 366, f. 38 (*fig. 239*)
Hybrid man and camel, confronting: Cambrai 102, f. 275v
Hybrid man and centaur *see* Centaur and hybrid man; Centaur with gittern
Hybrid man and child in swaddling clothes, woman bending over cradle, suckling child: Y.T. 75, f. 50 (old hybrid man)
Hybrid man and cock, confronting with sword and buckler: Add. 17868, f. 72
Hybrid man and crab, piercing with spear: M. 796, f. 87
Hybrid man and crane, confronting with battleax: Fitz. 47, f. 72v
Hybrid man and devil, fighting with sword and buckler: Royal 2 B.VII, f. 139
Hybrid man and doe
carrying on shoulders (proverb or fable, *cf.* Man and ass; Man and horse): Cloisters 54.1.2, f. 120; Y.T. 27, f. 92
hunting with horn and hound: W. 45, f. 164v
Hybrid man and dog (*see also* Hybrid man with bagpipe; — with pipe and tabor)
confronting with club: Cloisters 54.1.2, f. 31v
fighting with ax: fr. 95, f. 39 (two-legged dog)
fighting with club and buckler: W. 88, f. 32
playing like bagpipe: Cloisters 54.1.2, ff. 34v (f. 35, hybrid man with dog-headed bagpipe, two old men dancing), 166 (man with ball in mouth dancing on "bagpiper's" head)
seizing: Cloisters 54.1.2, f. 120v
threatening with club: Cloisters 54.1.2, ff. 104 (spoon?), 209
training: W. 88, f. 154
Hybrid man and dog/unicorn, astride, wearing jester's cap: Douce 118, f. 79v
Hybrid man and dragon
bitten by: fr. 95, ff. 1, 281v (bearded, horned; satyr?); Jacquemart 1, f. 55v (f. 56, hybrid man dancing)
confronting: Add. 42130, f. 53v; latin 10483, f. 20v (with bagpipe)
conversing with: M. 155, ff. 91v-92
fighting with club: Cloisters 54.1.2, f. 124v; M. 155, ff. 155v-156, 157v; Royal 1 D.I, f. 246v
fighting with club and basket, flames (red tongue?) issuing from dragon's mouth: Jacquemart 1, f. 51
fighting with club and pitcher: Add. 42130, f. 177
fighting with club and shield: W. 85, f. 43v
fighting with flail: latin 10483, f. 284
fighting with knife: M. 754, f. 23v (at L., nude man with knife)
fighting with spear: Cloisters 54.1.2, f. 135
fighting with stick and buckler: Cloisters 54.1.2, f. 67
fighting with sword and buckler: Holkham 458, f. 20; latin 16260, f. 556; M. 155, ff. 70v-71; Royal 2 B.VII, f. 136; W. 88, f. 118
fighting with sword and large leaf: M. 155, f. 149
fighting with sword and shield: latin 10484, ff. 100v, 231v; Fitz. 2-1954, f. 38v
killing with spear: W. 88, ff. 112v, 131v
seated on, beating with club to which key is attached at lower end: Add. 42130, f. 166
seizing: W. 45, f. 262 (below, hybrid woman tearing hair)
shooting: latin 14284, f. 12v; M. 155, ff. 13v-14, 85v-86, 156v-157; W. 37, ff. 79v-80

two-torsoed, fighting crowned dragon in tree, with sword and shield: Rutland Ps., f. 72

Hybrid man and dragonfly, sticking out tongue at (*cf.* Hybrid man sticking out tongue): Add. 42130, f. 36v (bald) (*fig. 349*)

Hybrid man and eagle, shooting: BBR 9391, f. 24 (David kneeling before him)

Hybrid man and falcon, shooting: Rylands fr. 2, f. 212; W. 45, f. 106 (above, hare in nest)

Hybrid man and fish, holding: Add. 36684, f. 96v; Jacquemart 1, f. 122v (fishing); M. 729, f. 254v

Hybrid man and fly *see* Hybrid man and dragonfly; — and insect

Hybrid man and fox, with vielle, fox sitting up: Add. 17868, f. 163

Hybrid man and goat, hunting
- with bow: Cambrai 103, f. 421v (second hybrid man shooting stag); W. 37, ff. 105v-106 (goat?)
- with spear: Jacquemart 1, f. 51v

Hybrid man and hare (*see also* Hybrid man and falcon; Hybrid man drinking; Hybrid man with pipe and tabor; Rabbit burrow)
- astride lion, shooting: Verdun 107, f. 89 (man/snail)
- confronting: Cloisters 54.1.2, f. 174v (man/lion)
- confronting, unsheathing sword: Stowe 17, f. 27v
- fighting with club: Add. 17868, f. 67v
- fighting with club and buckler: Add. 17868, f. 160 (wearing ?cardinal's hat)
- fighting with club and shield: W. 37, ff. 49v-50
- fighting with club and shield, spear: Fitz. 298, f. 63v
- fighting with sword and buckler, spear and shield: Stowe 17, f. 175v
- fighting with sword, club and shield: BBR 329-41, f. 47
- fighting with swords and bucklers: BBR 329-41, f. 50v
- headless, fighting hare with ax: Add. 49622, f. 13v (wearing tall ecclesiastical hat)
- holding: Stowe 17, f. 160v (f. 161, ape eating fish)
- hunting with bow and arrow (*see also* Hybrid man and hare, astride): Add. 17868, ff. 33v, etc.; Arundel 83, f. 26v (Ps. 26); Cambrai 103, f. 1 (at L., two hounds pursuing stag); fr. 776, f. 126; Lambeth 233, f. 82v; M. 155, ff. 51v-52; Stowe 17, ff. 18, 151v-152; W. 45, f. 163v; W. 88, f. 178 (*fig. 450*)
- hunting with horn: Add. 49622, f. 106v (and two hounds); Royal 1 D.I, f. 353v
- hunting(?) with horn, back turned on dog pursuing hare: M. 754, f. 132v
- hunting with horn, club, and hound: Y.T. 8, f. 296v
- ridden by: Fitz. 298, f. 15
- running after: W. 88, f. 142v (man/dog)

Hybrid man and harpy with sword, confronting: W. 102, f. 58v

Hybrid man and hybrid bird, shooting (*see also* Hybrid man with distaff and spindle): latin 14284, f. 33

Hybrid man and hybrid bishop, fighting with swords and bucklers: Stowe 17, f. 160

Hybrid man and hybrid dog, fighting with club and buckler: W. 88, ff. 56v-57

Hybrid man and hybrid knight
- conversing: fr. 776, f. 176v
- winged, with spear, fighting with sword and shield: St. Omer 5, f. 137

Hybrid man and hybrid snail (wolf/snail), confronted: latin 16260, f. 116v

Hybrid man and hybrid woman (*see also* Hybrid man with bagpipe; — with pipe)
- beseeching, hybrid woman astride horse, charging with club: Jacquemart 1, f. 123
- blessed by hybrid bishop: BBR 329-41, f. 198v
- bombarded with flowers by: latin 10435, f. 38v
- chucked under chin by: C.B. 62, f. 117
- confronted, hybrid woman aiming spear (arrow?), hybrid man with garland (*cf.* Man and woman, before Frau Minne): M. 155, ff. 158v-159 (upper margin, knights tilting)
- confronted, with distaff and spindle, sword and shield: W. 87, ff. 40v-41
- embracing: Christ Church E.II, f. 38v; Cloisters 54.1.2, f. 94
- fighting with clubs and shields: Add. 28784B, f. 11v
- fighting with sword and shield, pot and spoon: Douce 366, f. 109
- half-sheep, aiming arrow at hybrid woman with basket and reel: latin 14284, f. 4
- kissing: Add. 10294, f. 1; Add. 49622, f. 197; BBR 10607, ff. 33v (man with pipe and tabor), 129 (above, St. Peter, cock); fr. 95, throughout (heads only), f. 30 (winged); latin 10435, throughout; St. Omer 5, f. 22v; W. 82, f. 208v; W. 85, f. 4v; Yale MS., f. 257v (heads)

H

offering garland to: Jacquemart 1, f. 19v (hybrid woman surprised, aghast?)
pointing at, with spindle: Cloisters 54.1.2, f. 139v
shooting basket held by: latin 14284, f. 4
shot by: W. 87, ff. 35v-36 (hybrid man with sword and buckler)
threatening with club: latin 14284, f. 39
Hybrid man and insect (fly?), hunting with spear (*cf.* Hybrid man and butterfly; — and dragonfly): Harley 6563, ff. 8v-9 (Saracen?)
Hybrid man and knight *see* Knight and hybrid man
Hybrid man and knight/merman *see* Hybrid man with shawm, prodded
Hybrid man and knight's head issuing from tail, piercing with spear: W. 88, f. 86 (man with stone seated on knight's head)
Hybrid man and lion
fighting with club: BBR 209, f. 171v
fighting with mace and shield: Cambrai 102, f. 344
fighting with spear: Cambrai 102, f. 150 (bird sitting on lion's back)
fighting with sword and shield: Y.T. 8, f. 340; Y.T. 15, f. 324v
holding under arm, brandishing hammer, dragon biting lion's tail: Cloisters 54.1.2, f. 36
leading on leash, with club: Jacquemart 1, f. 52v
unsheathing sword before: Add. 28784B, f. 13
Hybrid man and man
aiming sword at face of (*see also* Man and hare, hunted by): BBR 10607, f. 150
fighting with sword and buckler: Jacquemart 1, f. 23
nude, fighting with club and basket, gold pot on head; man nude, with lance and bellows, red pot on head: W. 88, f. 175
shooting: latin 14284, f. 8 (man with club and shield); W. 37, ff. 54v-55 (man nude, physician?) (*fig. 244*)
threatening with spear: Add. 49622, f. 16v (man old, semi-nude)
Hybrid man and merman *see* Merman with stone
Hybrid man and monster (*see also* Hybrid man with pipe): Hague 10.B.21, f. 20v (shooting); Rutland Ps., f. 86v (with pipe, monster dancing)
Hybrid man and monster/man, shooting: Add. 21114, f. 121
Hybrid man and nun, fighting with spears: Jacquemart 1, f. 78
Hybrid man and owl, shooting (*see also* Hybrid man as falconer): Add. 17868, f. 86 (Jewish cap); Douce 366, f. 41v; G.K.S. 3384, f. 295v
Hybrid man and peacock, shooting: Melbourne 1254/3, ff. 37v-38
Hybrid man and ram, charged by: Cambrai 103, f. 393v; W. 88, f. 101v (horned, warding off with shield)
Hybrid man and sheep
carrying on shoulders (*cf.* Man and sheep): M. 155, f. 117v; W. 45, f. 91v (below, ?butcher at table on which rests ax) (*fig. 242*)
holding out gold bowl to (baiting?): Douce 5, f. 129 (at R., woman urging on running sheep)
Hybrid man and siren *see* Siren bitten
Hybrid man and snail
confronted: BBR II 988, vol. I, f. 211v; Y.T. 27, f. 103
fighting with slingshot and buckler: Douce 366, f. 38 (*fig. 239*)
fighting with spear: Add. 49622, f. 13; Douce 5, f. 88v (and shield)
fighting with stick: BBR 9391, f. 92 (at L., knight killing dragon, ape with fruit)
fighting with sword: Add. 49622, f. 10; Vienna 1826*, f. 85 (and shield); W. 45, ff. 4v, 103 (and buckler)
holding, shield in left hand: W. 87, f. 3v
with basket containing three snails: Chantilly 64, f. 34 (man/snail)
Hybrid man and stag
hunting with bow and arrow: Add. 49622, f. 10; Arsenal 5056, f. 1 (in center, hare emerging from burrow); BBR 9961-62, f. 34 (at L., man on horse); BBR 10607, f. 132; Cambrai 103, f. 421v (second hybrid man shooting two goats); latin 14284, f. 2; Stowe 17, ff. 55v-56
hunting with club, horn, hounds: M. 155, ff. 110v-111
hunting with mock crosier, mock horn, hound: Cloisters 54.1.2, f. 20v
hunting with spear, shield, hound: St. Omer 5, f. 1v
killing with sword: W. 45, f. 280v (carrying buckler)
Hybrid man and stork *see* Stork and hybrid man
Hybrid man and stork/dragon, strangling: Melbourne 1254/3, f. 12v
Hybrid man and unicorn
confronting with club: W. 87, ff. 107v-108

  - hunting with bow and arrow: G.K.S. 3384, f. 209v
  - hunting with horn and hound: Cambrai 103, f. 172 (crowned)
  - hunting with spear, holding wicker trap (*cf.* Hybrid man with pyx; — with trap): Cloisters 54.1.2, f. 177 (below, hare)
- Hybrid man and woman with hands raised, confronting with upright spoon (*see also* Hybrid man with distaff and spindle; — with mandola): M. 754, f. 52
- Hybrid man as abbot *see* Hybrid abbot
- Hybrid man as beggar: Arras 47, f. 55v
  - with bowl and rattle (leper?): Cloisters 54.1.2, f. 130
  - with dog and staff: W. 88, f. 18
  - with crutch: W. 90, f. 28
- Hybrid man as bishop *see* Hybrid bishop
- Hybrid man as blacksmith, hammering on anvil: Add. 36684, ff. 100v-101
- Hybrid man as cleric *see* Hybrid cleric
- Hybrid man as falconer (*see also* Hybrid man with claw feet): BBR 10607, f. 166; BBR II 988, vol. II, f. 274v; Christ Church E.II, ff. 38v, 50v; Douce 366, f. 38 (at L., squirrel with nut) (*fig. 239*); G.K.S. 3384, f. 304v; Hague 10.B.21, ff. 118, 153; Jacquemart 1, f. 79v; Kraus 75/88, f. 93; Lambeth 233, f. 52v; Royal 20 D.VI, f. 150v; St. Omer 5, f. 231v (at R., centaur wearing bridle, bit, with whip); W. 45, ff. 59v, 158v (below, hare); W. 87, f. 8v; W. 761, f. 253v
  - crowned, nude, with long tail: Yale MS., f. 363
  - with owl on wrist, three-legged pot on head: M. 796, f. 49v (*fig. 243*)
- Hybrid man as illuminator, painting border: Jacquemart 1, f. 51v
- Hybrid man as king *see* Hybrid king
- Hybrid man as physician (with urinal): Add. 42130, f. 47; BBR II 988, vol. II, f. 174; Cloisters 54.1.2, f. 63v (possibly); Douce 23, f. 109; fr. 95, ff. 64v (in center, dog with belled collar, staff), 113v, 314v; fr. 2754, f. 164v (cleric); fr. 25526, ff. 53 (at L., Resurrection), 63 (lower margin, man and woman in bed); latin 1052, f. 7; latin 1076, f. 7 (Ps. 1); W. 37, f. 38v; W. 45, f. 233 (above, sun behind cloud); W. 87, ff. 1v (f. 2, dragon), 41v, 104v; W. 104, ff. 10v (men tilting astride goats), 32v
  - before hybrid woman: Cloisters 54.1.2, f. 143
  - confronting nude man exposing hindquarters to sun, two hybrid birds (one as abbot): M. 754, f. 73v
  - conversing with hare: W. 104, f. 97v
  - hybrid woman praying: W. 104, f. 51
  - nude, tailed: W. 102, f. 86v
  - with stool basket on head: Exeter 47, f. 96v
- Hybrid man as pilgrim: W. 88, f. 155v
- Hybrid man as scribe *see* Scribe
- Hybrid man asleep, with trumpet(?) in lap: Cloisters 54.1.2, f. 50
- Hybrid man astride dog/unicorn, wearing jester's cap: Douce 118, f. 79v
- Hybrid man balancing basins on sticks: Add. 28784B, f. 11v (second hybrid man with hand bells); Cloisters 54.1.2, ff. 45v, 150v; Stowe 17, f. 180v; W. 88, f. 166v; Y.T. 27, f. 125v
- Hybrid man balancing sword on nose: Glazier 24, f. 42v (beside nude man inserting hand in monster's mouth)
- Hybrid man, bald
  - preparing to catch arrow flying at him: W. 37, f. 190v
  - with large ears (Panatios reference?): W. 37, f. 192v
- Hybrid man beating down acorns with club (*cf.* Man and pigs): Add. 49622, f. 108v
- Hybrid man biting his tail: Vienna 1826*, f. 100
- Hybrid man by fire, working bellows (*see also* Detached limbs, hand with tankard): Douce 6, f. 102v
- Hybrid man chopping down tree with ax: W. 88, f. 75 (beside man with rope)
- Hybrid man cooking: W. 88, ff. 128v (stirring pot), 129 (roasting meat on spit)
- Hybrid man crippled
  - pointing at hybrid man with sword: Cloisters 54.1.2, f. 129
  - with crutch: Hague 78.D.40, f. 26
  - with drums: Y.T. 27, f. 20 (two)
  - with hand trestles: Christ Church E.II, f. 43v (old); Douce 366, f. 34v; Jacquemart 1, f. 112v (old; at L., fable of fox and stork, Part I)
  - with keg on back, crutch: Cloisters 54.1.2, f. 123
- Hybrid man crowned *see* Hybrid king
- Hybrid man dancing (*see also* Centaur with gittern; — with vielle; Hybrid man with rebec; — with vielle; Mermaid with vielle): Jacquemart 1, f. 111v

H

Hybrid man drinking (*see also* Fables: fox and stork, Part I, variant: man nude; Hybrid man with cup; — with shawm): BBR 10607, f. 94; fr. 95, f. 159v (2); W. 82, f. 193; W. 87, f. 60 (below, ape as king)
from bowl, red jug in hand: Fitz. 2-1954, f. 168v
from bowl, refilling from pitcher: Yale MS., f. 361v
from sprout, refilling from pitcher: Jacquemart 1, f. 79
handing cup to second hybrid man: N.K.S. 41, f. 105v (*fig. 37*)
hare with distaff and spindle: Glazier 24, f. 59v
hybrid women (3) tearing hair, looking in mirror, putting coins in chest (Vices: Gluttony, Despair, Vanity, Avarice): fr. 95, f. 134 (*fig. 671*)
with ewer on head, cup in hand: Y.T. 75, f. 36
with lap dog: Cloisters 54.1.2, f. 204
Hybrid man eating with spoon from bowl set on stool: W. 88, f. 91 (2)
Hybrid man feeding hybrid man: Jacquemart 1, f. 18v (with pellets); W. 82, f. 209v (from bowl)
Hybrid man fishing, holding fish in hand: Jacquemart 1, f. 122v
Hybrid man headless *see* Hare with ax; Hybrid men; Man and hybrid man, shooting; Man, headless, hybrids
Hybrid man, hooded, pulling lips sideways, confronting hybrid man grasping oak tree issuing from body: (*cf.* Woman pulling): Christ Church E. II, f. 31v
Hybrid man horned (Moses reference?): Add. 42130, f. 150; Douce 118, f. 155
shot by man: fr. 95, f. 311 (satyr?)
with asperge and situla: Jacquemart 1, f. 88v (at R., hybrid beast)
Hybrid man juggling with three knives: BBR 5163-64, f. 41v
Hybrid man kissing *see* Hybrid man and hybrid woman; Hybrid men
Hybrid man nude
armless (*see also* Obscaena, exposing hindquarters): M. 754, f. 74
on stilts, aiming sword at head issuing from tail: W. 102, f. 56
tailed: W. 102, ff. 86v (as physician), 87v
wearing shoes, dog with basket on head, and blowing trumpet issuing from own tail: W. 88, f. 175v
with sword, piercing his throat: latin 16260, f. 536
with trumpet, holding serpent: Douce 118, f. 73
Hybrid man picking
flowers, putting into basket: Stowe 17, f. 203
fruit off border: BBR 10607, f. 95v
fruit off tail into basket: Rutland Ps., f. 45v
grapes off vine into basket, with knife: Christ Church E.II, f. 33v
Hybrid man playing
bellows with crutches: Rothschild MS., f. 110v
bellows with plectrum (in initial) before cleric with book: Cloisters 54.1.2, f. 149 (hybrid ?cleric)
bellows (vielle?) with rake: W. 88, f. 90
bellows with rod or scourge: Jacquemart 1, ff. 102, 123 (man dancing); M. 88, f. 175v
bellows with tongs: Arras 229, f. 187v (*fig. 512*); Bodley 264, f. 42v; Douce 366, f. 24 (*fig. 513*); M. 796, f. 104v; Tournai Ps., ff. 208v, 251; Vienna 1826*, ff. 85v (tongs held behind back), 143
cock with tongs: Stowe 17, f. 92v (hare with harp) (*fig. 514*)
dog like bagpipe: Cloisters 54.1.2, ff. 34v, 166 (man balancing on his head) (*fig. 516*)
fish with distaff: Stowe 17, f. 241
grill with rod or scourge: latin 10483, f. 114v
jawbone: latin 14284, f. 7v; Y.T. 27, f. 113v
jawbone with plectrum: Cloisters 54.1.2, f. 54 (crowned, dog dancing) (*fig. 511*)
jawbone with rake: Princeton 44-18, f. 118v; Y.T. 27, f. 103v (bearded, with goat's ears)
jawbone with tongs: Princeton 44-18, f. 107v
pot with spoon, hybrid man with pipe: Jacquemart 1, f. 55
psaltery with rake: M. 754, f. 46v (ape with book seated before him)
vielle with rake: W. 104, f. 30v (at R., hare)
wheat sheaf with rake: BBR 9391, f. 113v (*fig. 515*)
Hybrid man pointing to eye, holding mirror: Exeter 47, f. 124
Hybrid man praying; M. 155, f. 5 (second hybrid man conversing with bird); W. 88, f. 60v (addressed by man)
Hybrid man pruning
border stalk with ax: Cambrai 102, f. 232; Jacquemart 1, ff. 114v 115 (at R., hare); latin 3893, f. 219v
border stalk with sickle: BBR 329-41, f. 47; Jacquemart 1, f. 106

border stalk with sword: W. 82, f. 182v (at L., ape bending bow)
pointed end of hood on head issuing from border: Fitz. 298, f. 70v
Hybrid man putting *see* Hybrid man with stone
Hybrid man raking: W. 88, f. 124
Hybrid man reaping: M. 754, f. 64 (aided by beast with rake in mouth)
Hybrid man ringing bell with two short poles: Add. 30029, f. 137v
Hybrid man sawing border stalk; at L., winged hybrid woman holding broken ends of stalk (*cf.* Hybrid man pruning): Bodley 264, f. 58
Hybrid man seated, arms folded, legs crossed, arrow flying at him from R.: W. 87, f. 26v
Hybrid man shooting hybrid man: Bodley 264, f. 59; Hague 10.A.14, f. 26 (second hybrid man with sword); latin 1076, f. 41 (2, one with buckler, one with two swords); M. 155, ff. 7v-8; W. 760, f. 100 (erased)
Hybrid man shoveling water (proverb?): Add. 36684, f. 33v (cleric? below, man plowing) (*fig. 466*)
Hybrid man sticking out tongue
at dragonfly: Add. 42130, f. 36v (bald)
at female head: latin 10483, f. 47v
at hybrid man with club and buckler: Jacquemart 1, f. 30
at hybrid men: Cloisters 54.1.2, f. 140 (two)
two-torsoed: Add. 42130, f. 175v
Hybrid man supporting border stalk (*cf.* Initial): Add. 42130, f. 178v
Hybrid man tailed *see* Hybrid man nude
Hybrid man threshing, hybrid men with winnowing basket and rake: Cloisters 54.1.2, f. 32
Hybrid man tilting *see* Quintain, tilting at: hybrid knight
Hybrid man tumbling, doing handstand: W. 88, f. 195v (bishop's head issuing from tail)
Hybrid man two-faced
with psaltery: latin 3893, f. 201
with triple-pointed hat: Add. 42130, f. 206v
with two trumpets: Douce 118, f. 59v; fr. 95, f. 261; Holkham 458, f. 16 (four legs); W. 88, f. 108 (conical cap)
Hybrid man two-torsoed (*see also* Hybrid man and dragon, two-torsoed; Hybrid man sticking out tongue): fr. 776, f. 167v (shot by man); M. 729, f. 260v (mitered single head): M. 183, f. 69v (Ps. 51)
Hybrid man two-torsoed, bodies fighting one another with clubs: Add. 42130, f. 211
Hybrid man vomiting or spitting blood: Lambeth 233, f. 218
Hybrid man walking on sword: M. 754, f. 67
Hybrid man wearing pot on head *see* Pot
Hybrid man wearing winged headdress *see* Winged headdress
Hybrid man with asperge and situla: Cloisters 54.1.2, f. 189; Jacquemart 1, f. 88v (at R., hybrid beast)
Hybrid man with ax (*see also* Centaur and stag; Hybrid man pruning)
brandishing: Arsenal 5056, f. 1 (at R., dog pursuing hare); Jacquemart 1, ff. 82v (arms issuing from hat), 84v (at R., bald man)
chopping down tree, man with rope beside him: W. 88, f. 75
cutting off second leg, seated on back of old man screaming, holding other amputated leg (*cf.* Knight with sword, kneeling): Y.T. 27, f. 106v
fighting dog (two-legged): fr. 95, f. 39
fighting hybrid man with crossbow: Jacquemart 1, f. 121v
Hybrid man with bagpipe (*see also* Hybrid man playing dog; Man with cymbals, men): Arras 1043, f. 7; Bodley 264, ff. 91, 105; Burney 275, f. 359v; Cloisters 54.1.2, ff. 49, 63v, 143, 174; Kraus 75/88, ff. 9 (with stag horns, hare on his head, dog barking at) (*fig. 650*), 93; Lambeth 233, ff. 33v, 150; latin 10483, f. 20v (before dragon); latin 10484, f. 270; latin 16260, f. 536; Stowe 17, f. 116; W. 88, ff. 149v, 152, 161, 181
ape with vielle, fox dancing: Cambrai 102, f. 324
dog dancing: M. 183, f. 248v
head of bishop issuing from hindquarters: W. 88, f. 95
head of man blowing trumpet issuing from hindquarters: Add. 42130, f. 185v
head of man wearing pot issuing from hindquarters: W. 88, f. 189v
hybrid man swinging from border: Cloisters 54.1.2, f. 143
hybrid man with gittern: Arundel 83, f. 33v
hybrid man with mandola: Royal 2 B.VII, f. 192
hybrid man with transverse flute: Bodley 264, f. 12v
hybrid man with triangle: Arras 229, f. 35v
hybrid woman dancing: Stowe 17, f. 115

man dancing: Rutland Ps., f. 56v
woman dancing
issuing from border: BBR 10607, f. 13v
on his shoulders: Cloisters 54.1.2, f. 38; W. 82, f. 169
on shoulders of second hybrid man: Cloisters 54.1.2, f. 49
woman with hand organ: M. 754, f. 5v
Hybrid man with ball: Add. 38114, f. 134 (2); W. 45, f. 98 (two; hare running off)
Hybrid man with basket (*see also* Hybrid man picking)
containing three birds: Y.T. 27, f. 28v
containing three snails: Chantilly 64, f. 34 (man/snail)
holding out banana(?): Jacquemart 1, ff. 60v (to hybrid man with ?coin), 103v
Hybrid man with bat wings (*see also* Hybrid knight and knight; Hybrid man with transverse flute): Burney 275, f. 120; M. 761, f. 34
Hybrid man with bellows (*see also* Hybrid man playing)
blowing like trumpet (*cf.* Hybrid bishop blessing; Hybrid man with broom; Man with bellows): Glazier 24, f. 62v; latin 10483, f. 37; W. 88, f. 107v
with man seated by fire: Add. 49622, f. 138v
Hybrid man with book: Add. 10293, f. 1; Cloisters 54.1.2, ff. 61, 85 (about to be beheaded by hybrid man with sword); M. 754, ff. 1v, 34; Y.T. 27, f. 15
Hybrid man with bow and arrow: Yale MS., f. 85v
Hybrid man with broom, blowing like trumpet (*cf.* Hybrid man with bellows): W. 88, f. 170
Hybrid man with castle *see* Elephant and castle, parodied (?)
Hybrid man with catapult, operating: M. 754, f. 61
Hybrid man with censer: BBR 329-41, f. 72
Hybrid man with chalice: Cloisters 54.1.2, ff. 44v (balancing base in mouth), 160 (seen from back); Jacquemart 1, f. 141; W. 88, f. 176 (bishop with book issuing from posterior)
Hybrid man with chessboard, holding: Holkham 458, f. 17v (2)
Hybrid man with claw feet (*cf.* Man nude, with; Man with): W. 110, f. 66v
and falchion: W. 102, f. 51
and trumpet, man and dog(?) dancing: Bodley 264, f. 43v
Hybrid man with claw foot, hoof, cleaving head of hybrid man, with sword: W. 102, f. 54
Hybrid man with club
biting apple(?): Jacquemart 1, f. 87v (at R., hybrid man gesturing ?in fear)
confronting hybrid man with hands crossed on chest: W. 37, ff. 39v-40
Hybrid man with coffin *see* Procession, funceral
Hybrid man with coin(?) *see* Hybrid man with basket, holding
Hybrid man with comb *see* Hybrid man with mirror
Hybrid man with cymbals, another with psaltery, mermaid dancing: fr. 25526, f. 38
Hybrid man with distaff (*see also* Man and hybrid man, seated on)
and broom in mouth (*cf.* Hybrid man with broom): Hague 10.A.14, f. 26
and spindle (*see also* Hybrid man and hybrid woman): Arras 229, f. 525 (at R., hybrid man); Cloisters 54.1.2, ff. 152, 196 (below, skull with veil); W. 88, f. 196v
hybrid bird with distaff and spindle, bird with distaff: M. 754, f. 21
woman with reel, beast with distaff and spindle, hare, hybrid bishop, and man each with distaff: M. 754, f. 20v
beast with distaff, bird in nest: M. 754, f. 93v
Hybrid man with double pipe: Add. 38114, f. 313v; Add. 42130, f. 174; Jacquemart 1, ff. 54, 90v; lat. lit. f. 3, f. 120; Royal 2 B.VII, f. 194; W. 45, f. 135; Yale MS., f. 260v
hybrid woman with trumpet: Tournai Ps., f. 97
with winged headdress, second hybrid man with hand organ: Royal 2.B.VII, f. 193v
Hybrid man with egg, looking at, against sun (*cf.* Proverbs: eggs): latin 14284, f. 51
Hybrid man with finger at nose: Cloisters 54.1.2, f. 162
Hybrid man with fish *see* Hybrid man and fish
Hybrid man with flail and winnowing basket: Y.T. 13, f. 185v
Hybrid man with garland: M. 155, ff. 152v (on head), 158v-159 (hybrid woman aiming arrow at him; upper margin, knights tilting)
Hybrid man with gittern: Bodley 264, f. 17; latin 13260, f. 1; W. 45, ff. 87v, 178 (above, bird flying from nest); W. 88, ff. 141v, 179v
hybrid man with bagpipe: Arundel 83, f. 33v
hybrid man with harp: M. 729, f. 223v
hybrid man with psaltery: Arundel 83, f. 63v
hybrid woman dancing: fr. 776, f. 102; M. 729, f.

40 (at R., lion, nude man with spear and shield walking away)
owl looking on: Ghent 233, f. 28
with winged headdress, hybrid dog with trumpet: W. 45, f. 85v
Hybrid man with hammer: Jacquemart 1, f. 110v
hammering nail into border: Douce 6, f. 73v
hammering nail into his tail: Cambridge Dd.5.5, f. 190v
Hybrid man with hand bell, hybrid cleric with book, abbot (nude save for headdress) ringing bell on rope: M. 754, f. 9v
Hybrid man with hand bells (*see also* Hybrid man balancing basins): Add. 42130, f. 176; Cloisters 54.1.2, ff. 22 (three in each hand), 92 (beating with stick), 157v (three, on strings); G.K.S. 3384, f. 292 (*fig. 573*); M. 155, f. 152; W. 87, f. 9v; W. 88, ff. 20v, 21v, 190v
hare with trumpet: Cambrai 102, f. 335v
hybrid man with trumpet: Add. 42130, f. 41
hybrid woman with trumpet: fr. 95, f. 52v
wearing jester's cap: Douce 118, f. 79 (beggar?)
wearing loincloth, body in position of Christ on the cross: W. 102, f. 57
woman dancing: BBR 10607, f. 185
Hybrid man with hand organ (*see also* Fox dancing; Hybrid man with double pipe): Bodley 264, f. 3; Burney 275, f. 336; Chantilly 62, f. 103v; Royal 2 B.VII, f. 194; Royal 14 E.III, f. 3; Stowe 17, ff. 13 (December), 28; W. 87, f. 21; W. 88, ff. 59, 64; Y.T. 27, f. 105v
confronting hybrid man with stick: W. 88, f. 163v
hybrid man with vielle: Holkham 458, f. 18v
man with harp: Arundel 83, f. 55v (Ps. 80)
Hybrid man with harp: Cloisters 54.1.2, f. 166 (cleric? at R., hooded hybrid man with back turned); M. 754, f. 38; W. 85, f. 44
hybrid man with gittern: M. 729, f. 223v
hybrid man with shawm, two centaurs fighting with spears and shields: W. 104, f. 11
hybrid man with trumpet: Royal 2 B.VII, f. 191v
hybrid man with vielle: W. 104, ff. 5v, 25
hybrid men with shawm and hand bells, mermaid dancing: Add. 38114, f. 1 (2)
man playing bellows with rake, man dancing: W. 104, f. 14v (f. 15, woman dancing)
Hybrid man with head of (*cf.* Knight with head of)
animal and club, holding: G.K.S. 3384, f. 99v
ass in bowl: fr. 25526, f. 96
bull, bearing taper (St. Luke?): W. 87, f. 23v
bull, winged, bearing basket or pot: W. 87, f. 82v (below, serpent coiled around border stalk)
dog, winged: W. 87, f. 88 (serpent coiled around border stalk)
king, holding: W. 87, f. 47v
leaves, with staff, in brown cloak: Add. 38114, f. 317
man bald, holding: W. 87, f. 70v
Hybrid man with horn (*see also* Hybrid man and hare, hunting; — and stag; — and unicorn)
and club: Fitz. 2-1954, f. 138v
directing man to hunt stag: Yale MS., f. 257v
ferret(?) emerging: Glazier 24, f. 134
hare dancing: W. 759, f. 90
Hybrid man with infant in swaddling clothes, pointing at(?) woman snaring birds (*cf.* Hybrid man and child): Bodley 264, f. 21v
Hybrid man with jug (*cf.* Hybrid woman with jug; Man with —; Woman with —)
breaking jug over head of second hybrid man with jug (proverb?): Add. 42130, f. 153
emptying: W. 87, f. 49v (leaves on hat)
emptying on kneeling semi-nude man below: Cloisters 54.1.2, f. 178v
Hybrid man with krummhorn, second hybrid man with pipe and tabor, ape as falconer: Tournai Ps., f. 132v
Hybrid man with ladder on back: M. 754, f. 15v
Hybrid man with mandola: Bodley 264, f. 42v; Cloisters 54.1.2, ff. 57, 166 (*fig. 516*); Douce 131, f. 42v (*fig. 135*); Jesus 40, f. 8; St. Omer 5, f. 125; W. 87, f. 65v
ape with cornet: Royal 2 B.VII, f. 192v
hybrid man dancing or holding his ears: Jacquemart 1, f. 124v
hybrid man with bagpipe: Royal 2 B.VII, f. 192
woman dancing: Christ Church E.II, f. 51v
Hybrid man with mirror: Add. 42130, f. 145; Stowe 17, f. 251 (peacock's tail); W. 82, f. 195; W. 760, f. 182
and comb: fr. 95, f. 295v (at L., disdainful beast) (*fig. 246*); W. 82, f. 182v (combing hair)
bearded, hand to brow: Cloisters 54.1.2, f. 197
pointing to eye: Exeter 47, f. 124 (robed figure with grotesque bird's head. Related to adjacent miniature showing St. Mark writing?)
Hybrid man with mortar and pestle: W. 88, f. 151v
Hybrid man with Negroid head: Jacquemart 1, f. 3v (dragon's body)
Hybrid man with papal tiara: Douce 5, f. 66 (pulled by man above); Glazier 24, f. 174 (unsheathing sword); latin 3893, through-

out; latin 10483, f. 169; Y.T. 8, f. 305v (half-snail confronting hare with bird's beak wielding club and buckler)
Hybrid man with pipe: Cloisters 54.1.2, f. 25; W. 88, ff. 143v, 144 (issuing from posterior of hybrid man with shawm)
and shawm (krummhorn?): Jacquemart 1, f. 74
hybrid man playing pot with spoon (*cf.* Man playing spoon; Woman playing): Jacquemart 1, f. 55
hybrid woman dancing: latin 3893, f. 357v
monster dancing: Rutland Ps., f. 86v
woman dancing: latin 14284, ff. 6v, 50v
Hybrid man with pipe and tabor (*see also* Ape as falconer, hybrid): Bodley 264, f. 67; Cloisters 54.1.2, ff. 94, 148 (drum on back); Glazier 24, f. 156v; M. 754, f. 11; W. 45, f. 285 (at R., grotesque); W. 88, f. 26; W. 104, f. 12v (man shooting second hybrid man)
ape playing organ: M. 729, f. 306
ape snaring birds in net: W. 82, f. 75v
apes tilting: W. 45, f. 166
dog dancing: W. 45, f. 76v
hare with trumpet: W. 45, f. 94v
hybrid man with bird's head, web foot, and hoof at R.: Christ Church E.II, f. 51
hybrid man with krummhorn: Tournai Ps., f. 132v (ape as falconer)
hybrid man with psaltery: M. 155, ff. 119v-120
hybrid man with trumpet: W. 104, f. 70v
hybrid man with vielle, hare dancing: W. 104, f. 24v
hybrid woman dancing: W. 45, f. 174v (above, pelican in piety)
man dancing: Add. 38114, f. 67v; Arras 1043, f. 149v (at R., hybrid man aiming bow at dancer)
Hybrid man with pitchfork, peaked belled cap: Melbourne 1254/3, f. 15
Hybrid man with pot on head *see* Pot worn
Hybrid man with psaltery (*see also* Hybrid man playing; Hybrid man with cymbals; — with pipe and tabor): Cloisters 54.1.2, f. 149; W. 88, f. 133v
hybrid man nude, with sword: M. 754, f. 9
hybrid man with gittern: Arundel 83, f. 63v
hybrid man with shawm: M. 729, f. 303 (at R., owl, hybrid man); W. 88, f. 67 (issuing from hindquarters)
hybrid man with vielle: BBR 329-41, f. 162 (at L., owl); Royal 2 B.VII, f. 193 (hybrid woman with psaltery)
man carrying harrow: W. 88, f. 100v
Hybrid man with pyx, placing hat on head issuing from posterior: Cloisters 54.1.2, f. 183 (at R., seated man; above, man whipping top) (*fig. 661*)
Hybrid man with rake: W. 88, f. 124
Hybrid man with rebec, hybrid man dancing: Add. 42130, f. 149
Hybrid man with reel, two apes with reels (*see also* Ape spinning): M. 754, f. 29 (2)
Hybrid man with reliquary: W. 45, f. 49
Hybrid man with ring (quoit?) holding with second hybrid man, both with winged headdresses: Hague 10.A.14, f. 26
Hybrid man with sack (large, gold), carrying on shoulder: W. 88, f. 194
Hybrid man with scroll: Cloisters 54.1.2, ff. 113, 158; M. 754, f. 83v (as beard)
Hybrid man with scythe, nude man with scourge: M. 754, f. 6
Hybrid man with shawm: Burney 275, f. 359v; Cloisters 54.1.2, ff. 96v, 159; W. 41, f. 113v; W. 45, f. 18; W. 104, f. 2v (ape with fruit, hare with horn)
dog dancing: Jacquemart 1, f. 22
hybrid man drinking: Jacquemart 1, f. 25
hybrid man with harp: W. 104, f. 11
hybrid man with pipe issuing from posterior: W. 88, f. 144
hybrid man with psaltery: M. 729, f. 303 (at R., owl, hybrid man); W. 88, f. 67
hybrid woman dancing: latin 14284, f. 59
prodded by knight/merman in water with spear: Cambrai 103, f. 519
seated on hybrid man: Cloisters 54.1.2, f. 86
woman balancing on shoulders: Cloisters 54.1.2, f. 150
Hybrid man with shield, hybrid cleric with book: Jacquemart 1, f. 83v
Hybrid man with sickle *see* Hybrid man pruning
Hybrid man with slingshot: Cloisters 54.1.2, f. 41
Hybrid man with spade: Add. 36684, f. 34 (shoveling water; proverb?); W. 88, f. 169v
Hybrid man with spear: Douce 23, f. 14 (and shield); M. 754, ff. 4, 5; Yale MS., f. 167 (and shield)
Hybrid man with spindle, pointing at hybrid woman: Cloisters 54.1.2, f. 44v

Hybrid man with spoon (*cf.* Hybrid man eating; — playing; Hybrid man with pipe)
and long-handled pan: Jacquemart 1, f. 83v (at L., stork)
held upright, confronting woman throwing up her hands: M. 754, f. 52

Hybrid man with stag horns (Acteon? *cf.* Man with): BBR 9157, throughout (also beasts with stag horns); Cloisters 54.1.2, f. 193v; Kraus 75/88, f. 9 (with bagpipe); latin 16260, ff. 2, 447

Hybrid man with stick (bone?), biting: Cloisters 54.1.2, f. 27

Hybrid man with stone
aiming at grass mound pointed at by ape (*cf.* references under Putting stone): Add. 49622, f. 54
hanging upside down: Cloisters 54.1.2, f. 107v (egg?)

Hybrid man with stool basket around neck, ass-physician with urinal: Glazier 24, f. 76v

Hybrid man with stool basket on head, holding urinal: Exeter 47, f. 96v

Hybrid man with sword, stabbing himself (*cf.* Hybrid man nude): Jacquemart 1, ff. 57 (in chest), 62 (in head); Yale MS., f. 223 (in side) (*fig.* 245)

Hybrid man with tabor: Cloisters 54.1.2, f. 76 (ape doing handstand); Douce 118, f. 115v; W. 82, f. 75v

Hybrid man with tambourine: Royal 2 B.VII, f. 195v (2)

Hybrid man with thumb in mouth, holding his head (*cf.* Hybrid man with finger): Cloisters 54.1.2, f. 153v

Hybrid man with transverse flute: Cloisters 54.1.2, f. 174; latin 10483, f. 28v (bat wings as ears; below, hybrid woman with mandola[?]; at R., man with bagpipe standing on beast); latin 10484, f. 264 (monster)

Hybrid man with trap (small), placing it over tiny nude figure (*cf.* Hybrid man and unicorn; Hybrid man with pyx): Y.T. 27, f. 115v

Hybrid man with triangle: Cloisters 54.1.2, f. 60; Stowe 17, f. 105v
hybrid man with bagpipe: Arras 229, f. 35v
hybrid man with vielle: Yale MS., f. 194v

Hybrid man with trumpet (*see also* Hybrid man alseep; — two-faced): C.B. 62, f. 108v; Douce 118, ff. 89, 100, 152v; Douce 366, f. 72; Jacquemart 1, f. 111; W. 45, f. 171v; W. 82, f. 191v; W. 88, ff. 83v, 90, 108, 130; Yale MS., f. 260 (2)
bird sitting on his head: Douce 118, f. 116
held to ear: Douce 118, f. 78
hybrid man with hand bells: Bodley 264, f. 41
hybrid man pulling extremely long nose with both hands: C.B. 62, f. 213v (parodying trumpeter?)
looking through: Melbourne 1254/3, f. 47; Stowe 17, f. 205v
man with pipe and tabor: Maz. 34, f. 123
nude, holding serpent: Douce 118, f. 73
(two), with necks entwined: Cracow 815, f. 269v
wearing double-peaked belled cap: Melbourne 1254/3, f. 20v
wearing winged headdress: Royal 2 B.VII, f. 196 (second hybrid man with vielle); Yale MS., f. 74
with claw feet: Bodley 264, f. 43v (man and ?dog dancing)
with pot on head: W. 88, f. 77v
woman dancing, bending over backwards to ground: Jacquemart 1, f. 26

Hybrid man with vielle (*see also* Hybrid man with hand organ; — with triangle; — with trumpet, wearing): M. 155, f. 3; M. 796, f. 68; Melbourne 1254/3, f. 25v; St. Omer 5, f. 62; W. 37, f. 126v; W. 39, f. 125; W. 88, ff. 48, 62, 63v, 113; Yale MS., f. 306
ape below: Arras 139, f. 25
bitten in rear by dragon: Jacquemart 1, f. 55v (f. 56, hybrid man dancing)
dog dancing: fr. 776, f. 246; Rylands fr. 1, f. 82 (*fig.* 54); W. 45, f. 12v (hybrid dog)
fox sitting up, front paws raised: Add. 17868, f. 163
hare dancing, hybrid man with pipe and tabor: W. 104, f. 24v
hare with cymbals: Rutland Ps., ff. 53v-54
hybrid man dancing: Arras 1043, f. 161v; fr. 776, f. 102; Jacquemart 1, ff. 55v-56 (bitten by dragon); W. 37, ff. 77v-78; W. 88, ff. 48, 126
hybrid man looking on: W. 88, f. 162v
hybrid man with harp: W. 104, ff. 5v, 25 (confronting dog)
hybrid man with pipe and tabor, hare dancing: W. 104, f. 24v
hybrid man with psaltery: BBR 329-41, f. 162 (at L., owl); Royal 2 B.VII, f. 193
hybrid man with shawm: latin 3893, f. 122
hybrid man with trumpet: W. 104, f. 70v

H

hybrid men fighting with bow and arrow, sword and buckler: Cambrai 103, f. 56
man dancing: fr. 776, f. 102; W. 88, ff. 71, 134
man nude, tumbling: latin 3893, f. 208v (at R., nude man or woman running)
merman dancing: W. 88, f. 50
shot by nude man: Auct. D.3.2, f. 193
swan below: latin 3893, f. 196v
wearing winged headdress: St. Omer 5, f. 132v

Hybrid man with water buckets on pole across shoulder: Y.T. 27, f. 23 (two)

Hybrid man with whistle(?): Cloisters 54.1.2, f. 166 (at R., man dancing with ball in mouth) (*fig. 516*)

Hybrid man with winged headdress *see* Winged headdress, references under

Hybrid man with yoke around neck: Cloisters 54.1.2, f. 31

Hybrid men
embracing: W. 88, ff. 139v, 185 (kissing)
fighting
one blindfolded piercing opponent with spear: Arras 47, f. 37
with ax and shield, sword and shield: Royal 2 B.VII, f. 134v
with ax, crossbow: Jacquemart 1, f. 121v
with bow and arrow, club and buckler: M. 155, ff. 159v-160; W. 37, ff. 124v-125
with bow and arrow, sword and buckler: Cambrai 103, f. 56 (at R., hybrid man with vielle)
with club and buckler, spear and buckler: Fitz. 298, f. 1
with club, sword: Royal 2 B.VII, ff. 138, 144
with club, sword and buckler: M. 155, ff. 156v-157; M. 754, f. 71
with clubs: Cloisters 54.1.2, ff. 31v, 64, 105; W. 88, f. 111
with clubs and bucklers: Add. 17868, f. 34, etc.; W. 88, ff. 61v, 64v-65
with clubs, sticking out tongues at one another (*cf.* Hybrid man sticking out tongue; Hybrid men —): Hague 10.B.21, f. 2
with falchion and buckler, spear and shield: Stowe 17, ff. 229v-230
with falchion and sword: Burney 275, f. 293
with falchions and shields: W. 109, f. 186
with pitchers, one breaking pitcher over other's head: Add. 42130, f. 153
with spear (against unarmed opponent): Rutland Ps., f. 82v
with spears and bucklers: Christ Church E.II, f. 46
with spears and shields: Douce 118, f. 177
with sword and shield, spear: M. 155, ff. 89v-90
with swords: Add. 42130, f. 180
with swords and bucklers: Add. 42130, f. 49; Arras 229, f. 614; BBR 10607, f. 232v; Douce 118, f. 133v; Fitz. 298, f. 1 (*fig. 566*); fr. 25526, f. 51; Jacquemart 1, ff. 13v, 53v, 109, 117v, 136; latin 10483, f. 16; M. 155, ff. 162v-163; Royal 2 B.VII, ff. 132, 134; Stowe 17, ff. 111v-112 (*fig. 105*); W. 37, ff. 75v-76; W. 760, f. 113v; W. 761, f. 218v
with war hammers and square shields: Christ Church E.II, f. 46
headless, with swords, holding a bleeding human head between them: Stowe 17, f. 73 (2)
kissing, embracing: W. 88, ff. 139v, 185
sticking out tongues at each other (*see also above,* — fighting with clubs): fr. 25526, f. 162 (below, man hunting hare with club)

Hybrid nun: Fitz. 298, ff. 85v (2), 86v; W. 90, f. 108v
Dominican, dancing before hybrid bishop with bagpipe: Stowe 17, f. 49
Dominican, unsheathing sword before hybrid man with bow and arrow: Stowe 17, ff. 200v-201
with book, nun and six clerics, each with book: W. 104, f. 74 (2) (*fig. 123*)

Hybrid peacock *see* Hybrid bishop and

Hybrid pope (*see* Hybrid ape with papal tiara; Hybrid man —)

Hybrid queen: Add. 42130, ff. 82, 175; Cambrai 102, f. 394v (shooting ?doe)

Hybrid Saracen confronting lion, unsheathing sword: Cloisters 54.1.2, f. 79

Hybrid sheep (with bird's head; *see also* Hybrid woman with basket): Add. 42130, f. 204v (*fig. 247*)

Hybrid snail (*see also* Cat and hybrid mouse; Dog and hare, astride; Hare issuing; Hybrid hare and dog/snail; Hybrid man with papal tiara)
hare/snail with purse around neck (*cf.* Hare with purse): M. 812, f. 28 (licking round object)
knight/snail, confronting hybrid knight with lance: Add. 30029, f. 105
man/snail, confronting hare with asperge and processional cross: Y.T. 8, f. 282

with basket on back containing three small snails: Chantilly 64, f. 34
Hybrid stag
and hybrid hare with sword and buckler, astride beasts, charging: Royal 2 B.VII, f. 141 (with shield)
with head of Christ between antlers: Trinity B.11.22, f. 149v
Hybrid stork
drinking from pond: M. 754, f. 4
fighting hybrid man with Jewish cap: Fitz. 2-1954, ff. 52, 83v
playing psaltery(?): M. 754, f. 4
with fish in beak: lat. lit. f. 3, throughout
Hybrid unicorn: Add. 42130, f. 179; Glazier 24, f. 63v; latin 10483, ff. 20 (wearing scarf), 31v
Hybrid woman (*see also* Ape as physician; Cleric and; Hybrid bishop; Hybrid fox; Hybrid knight and; Hybrid man and; Knight and; Man and)
and bird, holding out round object to: Add. 17868, f. 104 (siren?)
and child: Stowe 17, f. 102v; W. 88, f. 152v
and child (nude), threatening with sword: Add. 28784B, f. 14
and dragon
confronting with sword and shield dragon with seven beasts' heads issuing from tail (Apocalyptic reference?): W. 45, f. 256v (*fig. 248*)
pursuing with spear and shield: latin 10483, f. 18v
and fox, pursuing with distaff and spindle: Add. 49622, ff. 35 (fox with cock), 149v (fox with goose which says "quec"); BBR 209, f. 12 (fox with cock)
and hare
hair arranged by: Jacquemart 1, f. 11 (hare kissing or biting her brow), 117; Y.T. 75, f. 25
pursuing with sword and shield, hare with spear: Glazier 24, f. 92
and hybrid ape, confronting with horn: W. 45, f. 262v
and hybrid physician, praying before: W. 104, f. 51
and rat(?) with spear and shield, shooting: Douce 118, f. 13
and snail, holding: W. 87, f. 73v (winged)
and stork with eel, shooting: Stowe 17, ff. 82v-83
as falconer: Burney 275, f. 184 (at R., lion); Chantilly 62, f. 149
dancing
ape (ape-cleric?) playing jawbone with bow: Cambrai 102, f. 188v
ape with bagpipe: Douce 118, f. 21v
horned: W. 87, f. 100v
praying: Chantilly 62, f. 59 (Min.: Nativity); W. 104, f. 51 (before hybrid physician)
spinning *see* Bird with reel
tearing hair (Despair? *cf.* Man tearing hair): Cloisters 54.1.2, f. 172v; fr. 95, ff. 134 (*fig. 671*), 267v (2); W. 45, f. 262 (supporting initial; above, hybrid man seizing dragon)
two-bodied, winged, gold bird on head: W. 88, f. 160
washing hair: Cloisters 54.1.2, ff. 45 (below, hybrid woman holding up wide shallow basin), 87 (below, hybrid Saracen with bucket on head); Y.T. 27, f. 50v (over basin)
with bagpipe: Bodley 264, f. 50; Douce 131, f. 42v (*fig. 135*); Glazier 24, f. 48v; W. 87, f. 11v (stag horns as wings)
with basket and reel, warding off arrow of man/goat: latin 14284, f. 4 (half-sheep)
with basket, wearing large basket upside down on head: latin 10483, f. 108v
with book: Add. 42130, f. 192v; W. 88, f. 141 (at R., grotesque)
with churn: latin 14284, f. 65 (at R., hybrid man pointing)
with coins in sack, emptying into chest (Avarice?): fr. 95, f. 134 (*fig. 671*)
with distaff and spindle (*see also above,* — and fox): fr. 25526, f. 153; Glazier 24, f. 26v; Jacquemart 1, f. 114; latin 14284, ff. 34, 63v (at L., hybrid woman with ?paddle or ?knife working on skein hung in forked tree); latin 16260, f. 592v; Stowe 17, ff. 43v, 70, 114v, 133 (2, beating one another), 195; W. 87, f. 80v; W. 88, f. 31v; W. 759, f. 169
ape kneeling before her: W. 88, f. 138v
confronting merman: Cloisters 54.1.2, f. 106
man with reel: W. 82, f. 192v (*fig. 90*)
with gittern: Cambrai 102, f. 284v (at R., cock)
with hand bell: latin 10483, f. 287v
with hand bell and trumpet, hybrid woman filling cup from ewer: Bodley 264, f. 68v
with hand bells (three) on band around neck, wearing white veil (*cf.* Hybrid man with hand bells): Jacquemart 1, f. 52

with jug, emptying, pointing at bird-headed dragon with three gold pellets in beak (*cf.* Hybrid man with jug): W. 87, f. 27v
with mandola *see* Hybrid man with transverse flute
with mirror (Vanity?): fr. 95, f. 134 (*fig. 671*); fr. 2754, f. 198; latin 16260, f. 306 (at R., squirrel with nut); Y.T. 27, f. 47d (f. 47v, hybrid woman with purse, Avarice?)
with mirror
and comb: Cloisters 54.1.2, f. 123 (combing hair; below, hybrid man looking up); Douce 366, f. 29 (*fig. 249*); fr. 25526, f. 49 (below, Christ before Herod); latin 10483, f. 253; Y.T. 27, f. 61v (hag)
arranging hair (*cf.* Hybrid woman and hare): G.K.S. 3384, f. 110 (*fig. 580*); Glazier 24, f. 28v
hand to face: Cloisters 54.1.2, f. 149
hybrid man with apple(?) exposing hindquarters: W. 88, f. 149
with ring(?), before gesticulating hybrid man: fr. 776, f. 24v
with offspring, holding, with two red balls in hands: Rutland Ps., f. 80
with ointment jar (*cf. above,* — with jug): Jacquemart 1, f. 63 (text: Litany)
with parrot on hand: Bodley 264, f. 58
with platform shoes: W. 88, ff. 106v (hybrid beast), 159v
with pole, chain and ball attached to one end: W. 87, f. 31
with psaltery, hybrid man with vielle: Royal 2 B.VII, f. 193
with purse (Avarice?): Y.T. 27, f. 47v (f. 47d, hybrid woman with mirror)
with pyx, mouse escaping from it (*cf.* Hybrid man with pyx): Cloisters 54.1.2, f. 20v (below, man preparing to catch mouse in hat?) (*fig. 250*)
with rake, basket: Y.T. 13, f. 186
with rattle (leper?): Cloisters 54.1.2, f. 123
with reel *see* Bird with; *above,* Hybrid woman with basket
with shawm, ape dancing: W. 88, f. 89v
with stag horns as wings, bagpipe: W. 87, f. 111v
with sword and buckler: W. 87, f. 101
with trumpet: W. 87, f. 46v
hybrid man with double pipe: Tournai Ps., f. 97
hybrid man with hand bells: fr. 95, f. 52v
with vielle: Lambeth 233, f. 64
hybrid man dancing: Tournai Ps., f. 51
hybrid woman dancing: latin 14284, f. 34
woman dancing: Princeton 44-18, f. 196
Hydra, Bestiary representation: Munich c.g. 16, f. 17 (in cycle); Royal 2 B.VII, f. 104 (in cycle)
Hyena
Bestiary representation: Royal 2 B.VII, ff. 103-103v (in cycle)
devouring corpse in coffin: Merton 0.1.3, f. 33
Hypocrite *see* Jesus Christ, life of: Last Judgment: Pains of Hell: devil with

I

Ibex
and hedgehog: Nancy 249, f. 237 (leaping away from)
Bestiary representation: Munich c.g. 16, f. 19 (in cycle) (*fig. 251*); Royal 2 B.VII, ff. 104v-105 (in cycle)
pursued by fox: Hague 78.D.40, f. 29v
ridden by ape: latin 14284, f. 10 (at L., ape seated)
ridden by nude man: Add. 38115, f. 50v
Ibis, Bestiary representation: Royal 2 B.VII, ff. 98v-99 (in cycle)
Idol *see* Ape as cleric, patting bird; Ape on column; Jesus Christ, life of: Flight into Egypt; Lion as king; Ram on column; St. Lucy
Illuminator (*see also* Painter)
cleric painting butterfly, man kneeling before him (*see* St. Dunstan for other episodes in sequence): Royal 10 E.IV, f. 248 (St. Dunstan)
hybrid man painting border: Jacquemart 1, f. 51v
old man with scroll reading "Nicolaus me fecit qui illuminat librum": Douce 118, f. 142 (holding ?stool in other hand; bird aiming beak at hindquarters)
seated, working; behind him double page hung across horizontal bar (*cf.* Scribe): fr. 25526, f. 77v (at L., scribe)
Implements for healing leg wounds of falcon: fr. 12400, ff. 105-107v
Incense boat *see* Angel with censer; Siren with censer
Infant *see* Child, references under; Hybrid man with

Initial supported by (*cf.* Border; Miniature)
centaur and hybrid man with swords: Arras 1043, f. 128
hybrid falconer: W. 88, f. 66
hybrid man: BBR 5163-64, f. 33; BBR II 988, vol. I, f. 92v; Douce 6, f. 40v; G.K.S. 3384, f. 267v; Jacquemart 1, f. 76; latin 14284, f. 44v; M. 155, ff. 1, 11 (with spear), 37; M. 183, ff. 13, 69v; Stowe 17, ff. 251v-252; W. 37, ff. 30v, 64v, 140, 148, 191v; W. 82, ff. 87v (winged), 184, 185, 190; Yale MS., throughout
hybrid woman tearing her hair (*cf.* Hair, references under): W. 45, f. 262 (above, hybrid man seizing dragon)
knight: Arras 1043, f. 190v (on shoulders of hybrid knight); St. Omer 5, f. 208v
man: Add. 39810, f. 7 (in drawers) (*fig. 140*); Cloisters 54.1.2, f. 109v; Douce 5, f. 161; Douce 6, ff. 84v, 139v, 141v; latin 1076, f. 66; latin 10483, f. 214 (bald); latin 10484, f. 16v; M. 155, ff. 37, 114v; Royal 1 B.XII, f. 3v; W. 82, ff. 31, 75v, 175, 208v, 210v; W. 109, f. 141; W. 110, f. 22 (wreath on head); Yale MS., throughout
in position of Christ on the cross (*cf.* Hybrid man with hand bells, wearing): St. Omer, f. 137
seated on mason with hammer: St. Omer 5, f. 138v
turning somersault: Marseilles 111, f. 129
with bagpipe: N.K.S. 41, f. 132
woman: N.K.S. 41, f. 132
Inn
man leading horse pulling cart toward: BBR 1175, f. 8v
man offering cup to knight before inn: Bodley 264, f. 158v
men roasting meat on spit before inn; at L., two horses and rider with whip approaching with cart containing cask, bundle, and shields (*cf.* Tournament): Bodley 264, f. 83v
Inscriptions *see* Cleric reading; Crow at lectern; Illuminator, old man; Isaiah with scroll; King with scroll; Lion as king; Man and goat, astride; Man with harp; Patron; Procession, men with trumpets; Proverbs: ass; Snail, labeled; Stork with scroll; Zechariah with scroll
Insect *see* name of specific insect, e.g., Ant; Fly
Instruments of Passion *see* Jesus Christ, life of: Passion
Intercourse *see* Bear; Bird; Chickens; Cleric and nun; Dogs; Fox; Horse; Man and woman; Nun and man; Pig; Sheep
Ire(?) *see* Hybrid man with sword
Isaac
and Esau, sending for venison, receiving same: Munich c.g. 16, ff. 30v, 33
blessing Jacob: Munich c.g. 16, f. 31
sacrifice of: Munich c.g. 16, f. 29v; Spencer 26, f. 6; St. Omer 5, f. 170; Y.T. 8, f. 199; Y.T. 13, ff. 25v-26
Isabelle de Kievraing *see* Patroness
Isaiah: Y.T. 13, f. 36v
and James the greater, Apostle (Old and New Law): Y.T. 27, f. 3; Y.T. 75, f. 5
executed by Manasseh: Y.T. 13, ff. 49v-50
with scroll reading "Ecce virgo concipiet": Melbourne 1254/3, ff. 65v, 77v; Y.T. 13, f. 60 (Min.: Annunciation)
Ish-bosheth *see* David, life of: D. and
Ishmael *see* Abraham and
Israel, elders of *see* David, life of: D. and elders; Moses before Pharaoh
Israelites *see* David, life of: D. and Goliath; Joshua; Moses and Aaron; Samuel, life of
Israelites and Philistines (in cycle of life of David)
battling: Spencer 26, ff. 10-11, 20, 22, 32-33, 65v, 102v
combat with Ish-bosheth, flight of Abner: Spencer 26, ff. 63v-64
Philistines despoiled, booty brought to Achish: Spencer 26, ff. 41-41v
Philistines smitten by David at Baal-perazim: Spencer 26, ff. 63v-64
preparations for war: Spencer 26, f. 41v
Saul's sons slain: Spencer 26, f. 47

J

Jabal separating sheep from goats: Munich c.g. 16, f. 16v
Jabesh-gilead *see* David, life of: D. and men of; —: D. and Saul
Jacob
and Esau: Exeter 47, f. 33v
and Isaac, blessed by: Munich c.g. 16, f. 31
and Joseph, journey to Egypt: Munich c.g. 16, f. 44v

J

and Joseph, receiving coat of many colors, tearing hair: Munich c.g. 16, f. 36v
and Solomon: Y.T. 13, f. 30v
approaching two shepherds: Y.T. 8, f. 204v
blessing Ephraim and Manasseh, embalmed: Munich c.g. 16, f. 45v
pouring oil on stone at Bethel: Munich c.g. 16, f. 33v
Shechem with Dinah, on a bed: Exeter 47, f. 33v
Schechemites agreeing to circumcision, slain by Simeon and Levi: Exeter 47, f. 33v
with staff, sunrise at Penuel: Munich c.g. 16, f. 34v
wrestling with angel: Exeter 47, f. 33v; Munich c.g. 16, f. 33v
Jael and Sisera, bringing butter to, slaying: Munich c.g. 16, f. 80v
January *see* Janus; Man cooking, roasting; Man vomiting; Man with bucket
Janus at table: Cloisters 54.1.2, f. 1v (January); W. 88, f. 3v (January); W. 90, f. 2v (January)
Jar *see* Ointment jar, references under; *cf.* Jug, references under
Jawbone *see* Ape as king; Ape playing; Cain and Abel, slaying; Hybrid man playing; Man —; Mermaid —; Ram —; Samson
Jay: Add. 42130, f. 51 (with ?crow, parrot, robin); Fitz. 2-1954, ff. 73, 149 (jay?)
Jealousy *see* Lover
Jeanne II of Navarre *see* Patroness
Jebusites *see* David, life of: D. and
Jechonias: Y.T. 13, f. 49
Jephthah and daughter, rending garments before: Munich c.g. 16, f. 87v
Jeremiah: Y.T. 13, f. 34v
and Peter, Apostle (Old and New Law): Y.T. 27, f. 1; Y.T. 75, f. 4
seated before collapsing towers: Y.T. 8, f. 237
Jericho *see* Joshua, siege of
Jerusalem *see* David, life of: D. in; Jesus Christ, life of: entry
Jesse, tree of (*see also* David, life of: D. and Saul; —: D. harping; —: Jesse): Corpus Christi 53, f. 1
Jesses for falcons, types and uses of (*see also* Falconer seated): fr. 12400, ff. 173-185v
Jesus Christ and David: Add. 42130, f. 160v (giving unction to; Ps. 88, v. 21); Stowe 17, f. 81 (David?)
Jesus Christ and disciples, preaching to: St. Omer 5, f. 251v (five; Gospel of St. Mark); Y.T. 13, ff. 100 (five, at table with Virgin); 113 (twelve), 131 (ten, at table with Virgin)
Jesus Christ and Virgin, seated at table: Y.T. 13, ff. 100 (with five disciples), 131 (with ten apostles)
Jesus Christ, genealogy of: Y.T. 13, ff. 31 (Judas), 31v (Esrom), 32 (Aram and Amminadab), 33 (Naazon), 33v (Solomon), 34 (Josaphat)
Jesus Christ, head of: Add. 41751, f. 162 (*fig. 266*); W. 87, f. 64v (f. 65, pelican in piety), 69v (saint?); W. 102, f. 29 (line ending)
adored by angels: Christ Church E.II, f. 32 (2; at sides, knight, cleric)
between antlers of stag (St. Hubert reference?): Douce 6, f. 113 (*fig. 594*); Trinity B.11.22, f. 149v (hybrid stag); W. 82, f. 31 (stag with bagpipe)
Jesus Christ, life of (*see also* Lover: Nature kneeling; Virgin, life of)
Adoration of Magi: Add. 42130, f. 88; fr. 25526, ff. 45, 142
Herod enthroned giving edict to messenger: Y.T. 13, ff. 93v-94
Magi approaching shepherds pointing the way: Add. 42130, f. 87v (*fig. 252*)
Magi on horseback, arriving before Herod: Y.T. 13, ff. 90v-92
Magi wakened by angel: Y.T. 13, f. 94v
man kneeling, holding camel on rope: Douce 48, f. 211v (Min.: Adoration of Magi) (*fig. 253*)
man with scourge, guarding horses of Magi: Y.T. 75, f. 55v (Min.: Adoration of Magi)
Adoration of shepherds: Y.T. 13, f. 90
Agony in the Garden: Y.T. 8, f. 237v; Y.T. 13, f. 128v
Annunciation to Magi: Add. 49622, f. 9
Annunciation to shepherds: Add. 24681, f. 44 (Min.: Nativity); Add. 28784B, f. 6v (*fig. 255*); Add. 42130, f. 87 (f. 86v, Nativity) (*fig. 257*); BBR 15001, f. 129v (Min.: Nativity); fr. 25526, ff. 46v, 97; Stowe 17, ff. 264v-265; Thott 547, f. 14v; Y.T. 8, f. 204v (*fig. 256*); Y.T. 13, f. 89v (rams butting)
angel with trumpet: Douce 48, f. 209 (Min.: Annunciation to shepherds; below, man and hound pursuing wolf with sheep in mouth)
shepherd dancing, others with bagpipe and kettledrums on back played by child: Y.T. 75, f. 53 (Min.: Annunciation to shepherds)

shepherds in field, one with bagpipe: latin 10483, f. 242v (Min.: Nativity)
shepherds tending flock, one with bagpipe, dog: Cloisters 54.1.2, f. 62 (3; Min.: Annunciation to shepherds) (*fig. 254*)
appearing in aureole held by two angels before kneeling worshipers: latin 10483, f. 213
Ascension: Add. 39810, f. 120; Add. 42130, f. 96; fr. 25526, f. 28; Y.T. 13, f. 131v
at Gethsemane: Y.T. 13, f. 111
Baptism: Y.T. 13, f. 104
bathing of Christ child (*see also* Woman and child; — and Christ child); Douce 118, f. 135 (angel with taper issuing from cloud)
bearing cross: fr. 25526, ff. 50v, 69v; latin 1076, f. 28 (*fig. 259*); Y.T. 8, f. 243v; Y.T. 27, f. 70v
hands grasped by man with winged headdress holding crown of thorns, three nails: Add. 42130, f. 93 (followed by man, St. John, and the Virgin)
man with hammer supporting miniature of Christ bearing cross: Cloisters 54.1.2, f. 61v
Virgin Mary following: BBR 9391, f. 161 (*fig. 258*)
beaten with sticks, seated with hands bound: Y.T. 13, f. 120v
before Caiaphas: Y.T. 8, f. 241v; Y.T. 13, f. 119v
before Herod: Add. 42130, f. 91v; fr. 25526, f. 49 (above, hybrid woman with mirror and comb); Y.T. 8, f. 242v
before Pilate: Y.T. 8, f. 242; Y.T. 27, f. 44v
Betrayal: Add. 39810, f. 120; Add. 42130, f. 91; fr. 25526, ff. 50, 87v; M. 183, f. 213; Y.T. 8, f. 241; Y.T. 13, f. 116
burial of St. Martha, attended by St. Fronton: latin 10484, f. 262
Caedmon leading ass, Apostles Peter and John with books: Y.T. 13, f. 113v
Caiaphas before group of Jews: Y.T. 13, f. 114
Circumcision: Add. 42130, f. 89; Stowe 17, f. 125
Crucifixion (*see also* Hybrid man with hand bell; Initial supported by man; Man kneeling; Skeletons): Add. 39810, f. 120; Add. 42130, f. 94; Add. 49622, f. 199 (*fig. 260*); Cambrai 87, f. 77v; fr. 25526, ff. 52, 68v (at R., hare winding wool on reel); Harley 6563, f. 38v; M. 754, f. 105 (above, open coffin; below, instruments of Passion) (*fig. 261*); M. 761, f. 3v; W. 102, f. 56v (parody of?) (*fig. 262*); Y.T. 8, f. 244; Y.T. 13, f. 121v (in miniature; below, two dice players quarreling); Y.T. 27, f. 74v
Deposition: Add. 42130, f. 94v (*fig. 263*); BBR 9391, f. 100v (in min.; below, Nicodemus with ointment jar pointing at tomb) (*fig. 264*): fr. 25526, ff. 53v, 71v; Stowe 17, f. 116v; Y.T. 13, f. 123v; Y.T. 27, f. 80v
disputing with Jews: Y.T. 13, f. 99
Doubting Thomas: fr. 22256, f. 76v (at L., *Noli me tangere*); Princeton 44-18, f. 87v; Verdun 107, f. 90v (*fig. 285*); Y.T. 8, f. 267v; Y.T. 13, f. 130
Entombment: Add. 39810, f. 120; Add. 42130, f. 95 (*fig. 265*); fr. 25526, ff. 52v (at R., lion), 66; Y.T. 27, f. 86v
Entry into Jerusalem: Add. 42130, f. 90; Y.T. 8, f. 232v; Y.T. 13, ff. 114v-115
expulsion of money-changers from temple: Y.T. 13, f. 110v
Flagellation: Add. 39810, f. 120; Add. 42130, f. 92v; fr. 25526, ff. 55, 56v, 81v; M. 761, f. 72v (Text: Passion of our Lord); Y.T. 8, f. 243; Y.T. 13, f. 120; Y.T. 27, f. 58v
Flight into Egypt: Add. 24681, f. 57v (in initial; at R., Joseph leading ass); Add. 42130, f. 88v; Cloisters 54.1.2, f. 83 (*fig. 279*); fr. 25526, ff. 45v, 88v; Stowe 17, ff. 257v-258; Y.T. 13, ff. 95 (warned by angel), 95v (flight), 96 (fall of idols), 96v (Herod in pursuit), 97 (three ships burned); Y.T. 75, f. 61 (Herod's men approaching sower)
giving unction to David: Add. 42130, f. 160v (Ps. 88, v. 21)
Harrowing of Hell: Princeton 44-18, f. 87; Stowe 17, f. 138v (f. 139, Coronation of the Virgin) (*fig. 267*); Y.T. 13, f. 122v
imprisoned by two soldiers, body covered with bleeding wounds: fr. 25526, f. 49v
in aureole supported by two angels, standing, blessing: latin 10483, f. 213 (at L., group of kneeling worshipers) (*fig. 268*)
in Majesty (*see also* Lover: Nature kneeling): Add. 42130, ff. 41v, 51, 103
flanked by kneeling abbess and bishop (Patrons: Marguerite and Renaud de Bar): Y.T. 8, f. 31
flanked by stag, scratching head with right hind leg, and peacock: Maz. 34, f. 5
Journey to Emmaus: M. 183, f. 180 (at L., *Noli me tangere*); Y.T. 13, f. 127v

J

Last Judgment: Add. 49622, ff. 45, 161; BBR 15001, f. 309 (*fig. 269*); latin 1052, f. 261 (*fig. 273*); Stowe 17, f. 38v (extension of initial)

angels with trumpets escorting thirteen souls: Add. 42130, f. 101v (3)

blessed ascending ladder: Spencer 2, f. 259 (two clerics led by angel); Thott 547, f. 32v (Min.: Last Judgment; below, Solomon beside a king in a coffin, a queen, a pope, and others; at R., Hell mouth)

blessed received by St. Peter: Y.T. 13, f. 138v

corpses rising from tombs: Add. 49622, f. 217; Douce 118, f. 147v; Jesus 40, f. 150 (wrestling pickaback) (*fig. 272*); Melbourne 1254/3, f. 35; Thott 547, f. 32v; Y.T. 13, f. 136; Y.T. 27, f. 107v

Hell mouth: Add. 39810, f. 7 (*fig. 140*); Add. 49622, f. 181v; Thott 547, f. 32v (Min.: Last Judgment); Vienna 1826*, f. 141 (Min.: Last Judgment)

containing bell: M. 754, f. 72 (below, nude armless cleric with ladder on head, hybrid man with pot on head, man straddling pole)

containing devil standing, pointing up at king in tree charged by unicorn, black and white beasts at base: Stowe 17, f. 84v

containing men: Add. 49622, f. 181v (four)

containing soul kneeling, clothed man reaching out ?to save him: Add. 49622, f. 191

containing two queens and woman, devil casting in cleric: Spencer 2, f. 259

devil with fork propelling last of three souls into: Y.T. 13, f. 148

devil with wheelbarrow containing three nude men approaching; at R., devil with stick: W. 90, f. 194v (above, cleric with coffin, angel with haloed soul in lap; at L., devil leading miser) (*fig. 274*)

guarded by devil: Y.T. 13, f. 142 (second devil casting in bound souls)

nude soul with hands clasped looking into: Add. 42130, f. 157v (Ps. 87, v. 4) (*fig. 270*)

intercession of the Virgin and St. John the Evangelist, two angels with crown of thorns and three nails: Y.T. 13, f. 137

Jesus Christ seated on aureole showing wounds, before him Virgin kneeling and group of shrouded figures: Y.T. 13, f. 137v

Jesus Christ with Resurrection cross: Y.T. 13, f. 136v

Pains of Hell (*cf.* Devil)

angel with sword driving away five sinners roped together, held by devil: Y.T. 13, f. 139

covetous, soul bound in chair, in flames; two devils holding his head, inserting silver into his mouth: Y.T. 13, f. 149

devil leading two souls on chain; at R., devil before smoking Hell mouth: fr. 25526, f. 59

devil mocking and carrying off souls: Add. 39810, f. 7 (several) (*fig. 140*)

devil on beam from which two souls hang over fire, one by feet, the other by tongue: Y.T. 13, f. 142v

devil roasting man in fire: fr. 25526, f. 85 (2; at R., devil with pipe and tabor)

devil with basket on back containing man, accompanied by second devil, six men in caldron over fire: fr. 25526, f. 71

devil with basket on back containing three men, second devil dragging hypocrite by feet with rope: Y.T. 13, f. 140v

devil with long scroll, nine sinners, second devil holding chain: Y.T. 13, f. 138

devil with bishop on back: Cambrai 87, f. 73

devil with nude man on back, bearing toward caldron over fire: BBR 9391, f. 102 (Min.: Harrowing of Hell)

devil with scourge reaching for prostrate man: BBR 9411-26, f. 133v (below, cleric pulling bell rope) (*fig. 271*)

devil with soul on back: Y.T. 13, f. 141 (2)

devil with wheelbarrow containing bishop, king, others, pulled by horned monster with bagpipe: St. Omer 5, f. 138v (one leg, crutch; at side, four trumpeting angels, group of blessed; Min.: Last Judgment)

devil with whip astride nun, pulling rope tied around necks of cleric and pope: Spencer 2, f. 259

dragon devouring head of bound soul lying on ground: Y.T. 13, f. 144v

false palmer, soul as pilgrim with hat, staff, begging bowl seated on flaming mound, devil casting white stones(?) at him: Y.T. 13, f. 150

gamblers, two souls seated in flames, between them diceboard with three dice and two heaps of gold and silver coins: Y.T. 13, f. 149v

heretic, soul turned on spit over fire by devil, second devil with bellows: Y.T. 13, f. 144

hypocrite dragged by feet by devil with rope, second devil with basket containing three men: Y.T. 13, f. 140v
merrymakers, three in flames, devil with lure fanning fire; second devil prodding soul with fork; two other devils pulling soul in opposite directions: Y.T. 13, ff. 145v-146
miser led by devil, second devil with wheelbarrow containing three nude men approaching Hell mouth; at R., devil with stick: W. 90, f. 194v (at R., cleric with coffin; angel with haloed soul in lap)
murderer in ground up to shoulders, surrounded by flames, attacked by dragon, toad, snake, lizard: Y.T. 13, f. 145
proud man, soul standing in flames, head pierced by flanking devils: Y.T. 13, f. 148v
robbers, three souls pursued by two hounds toward devil, torn to pieces: Y.T. 13, ff. 146v-147v
soul standing in dark river: Y.T. 13, f. 143v (5)
usurer in caldron over fire, devil inserting gold roll into his mouth: Y.T. 13, f. 143
Last Supper: Add. 42130, f. 90v; Y.T. 8, f. 235 (*fig. 275*); Y.T. 13, f. 116v
Longinus delivered by St. Michael: Y.T. 13, f. 127
Marriage at Cana: Y.T. 13, ff. 99v-100
Mary Magdalene prostrate with ointment jar, anointing feet: Royal 2 B.VII, f. 300 (*fig. 276*)
Massacre of Innocents: Add. 28784B, f. 4v (in miniature; below, mother with dead child); C.B. 64, f. 85v; Chantilly 64, f. 81v (woman with bleeding head of child); Cloisters 54.1.2, f. 69 (Min.: Adoration of Magi) (*fig. 277*); fr. 25526, ff. 44v, 81; Stowe 17, ff. 261v-262 (angels bearing soul to heaven); Y.T. 13, f. 98 (f. 97v, Herod giving command to soldiers); Y.T. 75, f. 189
miracles *see* Jesus Christ, miracles of (*fig. 278-280*)
mocking of: Add. 42130, f. 92; BBR 9391, f. 158v (*fig. 281*); Chantilly 62, f. 135v; fr. 25526, ff. 28v (seated with orb, approached by hooded man with club), 55v, 82; Princeton 44-18, f. 57 (*fig. 282*); Troyes 1905, f. 19 (*fig. 283*); Y.T. 13, f. 119 (Min. above showing same subject)
nailed to cross: Add. 42130, f. 93v; Y.T. 13, f. 121
Nativity: Add. 29253, f. 392v; Add. 42130, f. 86v (*fig. 284*); fr. 25526, ff. 46, 97v; latin 14284, f. 242v (Min.; in margin, shepherds, one with bagpipe)
Nicodemus *see above,* Deposition
Noli me tangere: Add. 49622, f. 208; fr. 25526, f. 76v (at L., Doubting Thomas); latin 10484, f. 255v; M. 183, f. 180 (at R., Journey to Emmaus); Princeton 44-18, f. 92; Verdun 107, f. 90v (*fig. 285*)
on Mount of Olives: Y.T. 13, f. 118 (dove flying down)
Passion, instruments of: Add. 42130, f. 102 (held by five angels); fr. 25526, f. 29v (held by two angels; Jesus seated on rainbow showing wounds; Virgin and St. John the Evangelist); M. 88, f. 179 (on shield held by two angels) (*fig. 286*); M. 754, f. 105 (at R., Crucifixion; Hours of the Passion) (*fig. 261*); Y.T. 13, f. 137 (two angels with crown of thorns and three nails; intercession of the Virgin and St. John; in Last Judgment cycle)
Pentecost: Add. 39810, f. 120; Add. 42130, f. 96v; Add. 49622, f. 178v; fr. 25526, f. 37v; Y.T. 13, f. 132
Pietà: Y.T. 13, f. 123v
Pilate commanding soldiers to watch sepulcher: Y.T. 13, f. 124v
preaching: fr. 25526, f. 21v (three men seated on ground); Y.T. 13, f. 103v
Presentation in Temple: Add. 42130, f. 89v; fr. 25526, ff. 47, 139v; Y.T. 8, f. 289; Y.T. 13, f. 99
Resurrection: Add. 36684, f. 74v; Add. 39810, f. 120; Add. 42130, f. 95v; Add. 49622, f. 198v; BBR 9391, f. 101 (Min.: Entombment); Chantilly 62, f. 155 (*fig. 287*); fr. 25526, ff. 53 (at R., hybrid physician), 72; Y.T. 27, f. 96v
Jesus Christ with Resurrection cross: Y.T. 13, f. 136v
news reported to Apostles by Mary Magdalene, tomb found empty by Peter and John: Y.T. 13, ff. 128v-129
saint kneeling before: Douce 48, f. 198v
seated, showing wounds: Add. 42130, ff. 43v, 103 (on rainbow); fr. 25526, f. 29v (on rainbow; Virgin, St. John the Evangelist, and two angels with instruments of Passion)
sought by Mary and Joseph in Jerusalem: Y.T. 13, f. 98v

J

Supper at Emmaus: Princeton 44-18, f. 88v (*fig. 288*); Verdun 107, f. 92; Y.T. 13, f. 128 (f. 129v, news reported to four Apostles by two Apostles)
Temptation: Add. 28784B, f. 7v; Stowe 17, f. 7v; Stowe 17, f. 110v; Y.T. 8, f. 194; Y.T. 13, ff. 111v-112v
Three Maries at the tomb: Add. 39810, f. 120; latin 10483, f. 375v (Min.: Resurrection); Princeton 44-18, ff. 90v-91 (censing angel); Y.T. 13, f. 126
Trinity: Add. 42130, f. 44; Add. 49622, f. 207; Cambrai 87, f. 230 (at R., St. John the Evangelist, writing); M. 754, f. 22v
Veronica with sudarium: Y.T. 27, f. 44v (Min.: Annunciation)
washing of feet: Y.T. 8, f. 236v (*fig. 289*); Y.T. 13, f. 117
with Host (*see also* Lover: Nature kneeling): BBR 9961-62, f. 65 (half-figure)
with orb, blessing: Corpus Christi 53, f. 1

Jesus Christ, miracles of
conversion of adulteress: Y.T. 13, ff. 100v-101v
draught of fishes: Y.T. 8, f. 249v (*fig. 278*); Y.T. 13, f. 130v
feeding of five thousand: Y.T. 8, f. 216; Y.T. 13, f. 102
healing the blind: Stowe 17, f. 135 (*fig. 280*); Y.T. 13, f. 103
healing sick woman: Y.T. 13, f. 102v
Joseph of Arimathea offering gold to Sidonia for sudarium, imprisoned, delivered by Christ: Y.T. 13, ff. 124, 125-125v
raising of corpse: latin 10484, f. 262
raising of Lazarus: Y.T. 13, f. 115v
wheat field *see* Jesus Christ, life of: Flight into Egypt

Jeu des Dames see Castle, occupied by men; Woman and boar; — and hare; — and stag; — as falconer

Jew (*see also* Devil with triangle; Hybrid Jew; Jesus Christ, life of: Caiaphas before; Judas; Siren with vielle; Virgin, life of: death of; Virgin, life of: miracles of: Jew; Virgin, life of: woman selling
on podium, addressing three men, two women: Stowe 17, f. 181 (Jew?)
with bellows, aiming at hybrid woman praying: Douce 118, f. 17v
with book, before cave, blindfolded Balaam riding off on ass: St. Omer 5, f. 159v

Joab *see* David, life of: Abner; —: D. and Joab
Joachim *see* Virgin, life of
Joatham: Y.T. 13, ff. 51v-52
Job: Thott 547, f. 43 (text: Offices of the Dead)
Joel: Y.T. 13, f. 40v
Joel and Matthew, Apostle (Old and New Law): Y.T. 27, f. 8; Y.T. 75, f. 7v
Joffroy d'Aspremont *see* Patron
Jonah in jaws of whale (*cf.* Man and fish, emerging): BBR 10607, f. 177 (*fig. 290*); St. Omer 5, f. 133 (at L., hybrid man; at R., beggar with child in sling on back, staff) (*fig. 291*); Vienna 1826*, f. 57v (addressed by God; Ps. 68); W. 102, f. 30v (St. Margaret?)
Jonathan *see* David, life of: D. and; —: D. and Saul; Samuel, life of
Jongleur *see* Man balancing; — juggling; Man with (specific objects)
Joram (*see also* David, life of: D. and): Y.T. 13, f. 53
Jordan *see* St. Mary the Egyptian, ff. 272-273
Josaphat: Y.T. 13, ff. 34 (in genealogy of Christ sequence), 52v
Joseph (New Testament) (*see also* Jesus Christ, life of: Flight into Egypt; St. Anastasia): W. 39, f. 102 (with basket, staff; Min.: Presentation); Y.T. 13, ff. 125 (imprisoned), 125v (delivered by Jesus)
Joseph (Old Testament):
and lamb, slaying, cloak shown to father: Munich c.g. 16, f. 36v (*fig. 292*)
Benjamin detained: Munich c.g. 16, f. 43v
brought before Pharaoh to interpret dream: Munich c.g. 16, f. 38v; Royal 10 E.IV, f. 8
building in Egypt: Y.T. 8, f. 213 (two men)
cup discovered in Benjamin's sack: Munich c.g. 16, f. 43v; Royal 10 E.IV, f. 23
dream of: Royal 10 E.IV, f. 7
imprisoned after Potiphar's wife's advances: Exeter 47, f. 34 (taking hand of butler; baker at side); Munich c.g. 16, f. 37v; Royal 10 E.IV, ff. 16v-17
in well: Royal 10 E.IV, ff. 9v (cast into), 12 (drawn out of); Y.T. 8, f. 207 (flanked by ten men, rider with purse approaching from R.) (*fig. 293*)
Jacob examining cloak: Royal 10 E.IV, f. 13
Jacob's journey to Egypt, blessing Ephraim and Manasseh, embalming of Jacob: Munich c.g. 16, f. 45v

Moses digging up bones of *see* Moses
released from prison: Royal 10 E.IV, f. 17v
removing garments: Royal 10 E.IV, f. 9
sold to merchants: Exeter 47, f. 34
storing of grain: Y.T. 8, f. 210v (man with sack entering building)
with brothers: Munich c.g. 16, ff. 39-42v; Royal 10 E.IV, f. 8v; Y.T. 8, f. 212
with Jacob: Munich c.g. 16, f. 44v
with Potiphar and Potiphar's wife: Exeter 47, f. 34; Royal 10 E.IV, ff. 15-16
Joshua
five kings discomfited, hanged: Munich c.g. 16, ff. 76v, 78v
Israelites at Ai: Munich c.g. 16, f. 75v
marriage of Salmon and Rahab: Munich c.g. 16, f. 71v
receiving Achan's garment, A.'s belongings burned: Munich c.g. 16, ff. 72v, 73v
siege of Jericho: Munich c.g. 16, f. 70v
worshiping before angel, losing shoe: Munich c.g. 16, f. 69v
Josiane (in series of adventures of Bevis of Hampton): Royal 10 E.IV, ff. 80-88; Y.T. 13, ff. 7v-12v
Jousting *see* Tilting, references under
Jubal (Tubal?) writing music on column, with harp? and organ beside him: Munich c.g. 16, f. 17v (shown twice) (*fig. 294*)
Judah: Y.T. 13, f. 31 (in genealogy of Christ sequence)
Judah, men of *see* David, life of: D. and Joab; —: D. and men of
Judas (*see also* Jesus Christ, life of: Betrayal; Vices: Despair)
hanged: Arras 47, f. 191v (Min.: Betrayal); Y.T. 13, f. 122 (f. 121v, addressed by two men)
receiving payment, pointing to mouth, with three Jews: Y.T. 8, f. 238v
Judge *see* Ape as king, enthroned; Hare and dog, capturing; St. Agnes; St. Faith; St. Felix; St. Juliana; St. Nicasius; St. Quintin; St. Saturninus and St. Sisinnius; St. Tiburtinus; St. Valentine; St. Vincent; St. Vitalis; Solmon, judgment of
Judith, with servant, leaving city: BBR 15001, f. 106v (Min.: Holofernes beheaded) (*fig. 295*)
Jug *see* Ape urinating; Fables: woman with; Man nude, urinating; Man with; Pitcher, references under; Woman with
Juggling *see* Ape; Hare; Hybrid man; Jongleur, references under; Man; Woman
July *see* Man scything; Siren with vielle
June *see* Man and bird, snaring with decoy and birdcage; Man chopping wood; Man with wheat sheaf
Jurdan *see* Virgin, life of: arrival
Justice *see* Virtues

J

K

Keg *see* Ape astride; Man drinking; Men tilting at; Quintain, tilting, man nude
Kettledrums *see* Man with
Key *see* Lover, kneeling; Man and monster, astride
King (*see also* Alexander; Ape as; Boar as; Dragon as; Edward III; Exemplum; Frederick II; Hybrid king; Jesus Christ, life of: Last Judgment: Pains of Hell; Knight performing; Lion as; Man with harp, before swan; Merlin; Merman as; Nun and man, embracing; St. Agatha; St. Alban; St. Andrew; St. Bartholomew; St. Cecilia; St. Chrysogonus; St. Clement; St. Cosmas and St. Damian; St. Edmund; St. Edward; St. Lucy; St. Maurice; St. Thomas, Apostle; St. Thomas of Canterbury; St. Tiburtinus; Siren, conversing; Virgin, miracles of: king's soul): C.B. 62, f. 176; Douce 118, f. 134
King and ape, pointing at apes wrestling pickaback: M. 754, f. 17v
King and bishop, with reliquary: latin 14284, f. 25
King and horse, astride: Add. 10293, f. 1; Add. 49622, f. 125 (with pipe and tabor, horse seated) (*fig. 296*)
King and hybrid woman, giving command to: latin 14284, f. 40
King and jester: Exeter 47, f. 34 (five pairs shown alternately; Ps. 52)
King and man, giving command to: latin 10484, f. 17 (seated on hybrid man)
King and queen *see* Edward III, confronting
King and queen kissing: Douce 6, f. 163 (heads; below, ?surprised man); Yale MS., f. 360v (winged heads)
King and stag, hunting: Royal 10 E.IV, ff. 229 (beginning of St. Hubert sequence), 255v-256v (in sequence of three living and three dead); Yale MS., f. 209

K

King and wild man (*cf.* Knight and wild man)
hunting, astride horse, with retainers horn, and hounds: Royal 2 B.VII, ff. 172v-173
pursuing wild man with abducted lady: Bodley 264, f. 69v (astride stag) (*fig. 688*)
King and woman
conversing: Bodley 264, f. 121v
kneeling before, crowned by: Yale MS., f. 110v
playing backgammon(?): Add. 42130, f. 76v
King as falconer: Melbourne 1254/3, f. 80v (f. 81, bird in tree); Y.T. 8, f.7
King at table *see* Banquet
King beckoning: BBR 10607, f. 43v (Ps. 26; Min.: Beheading of St. John the Baptist; below, two women, one with harp)
King confronting king, one with glove, one with scepter: Christ Church E.II, f. 36v
King defecating (Saul?): Add. 10294, f. 1
King dethroned *see* Vices; Imprudence
King drinking: Douce 118, f. 15 (below, knight holding severed head)
King enthroned (*see also* Cardinal and cleric, kneeling)
holding up sword, man beheaded, two others menaced by man with sword: Spencer 2, f. 90
receiving cup from kneeling attendant: Royal 2 B.VII, f. 188v
with orb and sword: Melbourne 254/3, f. 24
with sword, before him man between two soldiers: fr. 25526, f. 14v
King, exploits of (unidentified tale): Royal 10 E.IV, ff. 290v-299
King, geometric configuration: Auct. D.3.2, f. 136 (*fig. 297*)
King giving alms: Royal 10 E.IV, ff. 261-262v
King, head of *see* Man, head of, three-faced
King in bed, angel descending, gold cross in cloud: Stowe 17, f. 128v
King kneeling
before hybrid man with tall gold hat and processional cross: BBR 9391, f. 16
crowned by woman: Yale MS., f. 110v
praying: Melbourne 1254/3, ff. 34v (at *prie-dieu*), 109
King playing backgammon(?) with woman: Add. 42130, f. 76v
King pointing to initial showing man beheaded: W. 85, f. 5v
King sticking out tongue (*cf.* Sticking out tongue, references under): Exeter 47, f. 117v
King with branches, holding, woman winding wreath, basket on ground: W. 88, f. 7 (April)
King with hand organ: Arras 47, f. 52
King with reliquary *see* King and bishop
King with scepter (*see also* King confronting): BBR 10607, f. 142v
King with scroll: Douce 118, ff. 111 (kneeling; inscription "Deus deus meus rex"), 177v (old, with staff; "vere languores nostros ?eripe")
King with sword (*see also* King enthroned): Douce 118, f. 25 (and shield); M. 102, f. 141 (stabbing himself; Ps. 136:17-18)
King with vielle, hybrid man dancing: W. 90, f. 157
Kingfisher: Add. 42130, f. 61
Kissing *see* Bishop and woman; Falconer and —; Hybrid men; King and queen; Man and woman
Knife *see* Ape juggling; Ape with; Hare juggling; Hybrid man —; Man —; Man pruning; Man with, references under: Woman juggling): Add. 36684, ff. 144v-145 (scattered in margins)
Knife grinder: Add. 42130, f. 78v (two men turning grindstone, third holding knife)
Knight (*see also* Ape and; Ape as; Boar and; Castle; Centaur and; Centaur as; Corpse; Elephant and castle occupied by; Fox as; Hybrid knight; Initial; Man and; Merman as; Obscaena; Patron; Siren confronting; Virgin, miracles of): Christ Church E.II, throughout
Knight and ape, charging with falchion: W. 90, f. 78v (ape showing hindquarters) (*fig. 298*)
Knight and ass, with head of ass on spear: W. 90, f. 146
Knight and beast *see* Knight with head of
Knight and bird
fighting with sword and buckler: G.K.S. 3384, f. 227v (stork?)
shooting: fr. 95, f. 74; Princeton 44-18, f. 145
tilting at head of: Douce 118, f. 102
Knight and butterfly, aiming sword at: Bodley 264, f. 41
Knight and cock
astride backwards, shot by centaur: Arras 47, f. 211
astride with whip: Yale MS., f. 282v (*fig. 299*)
Knight and dog
astride horse/fish with spear and shied, charg-

- ing dog falling over backwards; Jacquemart 1, f. 39
- astride, with spear and shield: Melbourne 1254/3, f. 1v (*fig. 301*)

Knight and dragon (*see also* Quintain, tilting at)
- astride horse
  - fighting dragon breathing fire: Add. 10293, f. 1
  - fighting with spear: Y.T. 19, f. 31v
  - bitten by, two fighting with sword and ax: fr. 95, f. 100
  - confronted: Christ Church E.II, f. 2
  - fighting: Add. 49622, ff. 40v, 135, 138v; Christ Church E.II, f. 49v (with spear); fr. 95, f. 292v (also fighting lion, bitten by border dragon); G.K.S. 3384, f. 73v; Princeton 44-18, ff. 175v-176 (with sword and buckler); Rutland Ps., f. 91 (with sword and buckler)
  - killing with spear: G.K.S. 3384, f. 148
  - killing with sword: BBR 9391, f. 92 (at L., ape with fruit, hybrid man fighting snail); Douce 6, ff. 124v (below, stork with beak aimed at hindquarters of ape, holding pole on which knight stands; above, unicorn butting), 144v, 201 (dragon breathing fire, knight on horse; at L., castle; above, fox); latin 3893, f. 236 (at R., stork)

Knight and fox(?), fighting with pitchfork: Melbourne 1254/3, f. 9

Knight and giant, slaying with sword: Add. 24686, f. 17 (at L., lion with man in jaws) (*fig. 211*); Royal 10 E.IV, ff. 125-126v

Knight and goat, fighting with lance, ax, astride hybrid beasts: Royal 2 B.VII, f. 132v

Knight and griffin, killing with spear: Add. 24686, f. 18 (at L., large crow sitting on horse's saddle): Fitz. 47, f. 140

Knight and hare
- fighting with club: G.K.S. 3384, f. 144 (at R., man hunting hare, with club); W. 90, f. 148v (above, hedgehog)
- with sword and buckler: Add. 49622, f. 149v
- with sword and shield, hare with slingshot (David and Goliath parody?): Fitz. 298, f. 7
- frightened by: BBR 10607, f. 184; Douce 5, f. 82 (dropping sword) (*fig. 300*); Stowe 17, ff. 79v-80
- hunting with spear and shield, hounds, astride horse: BBR 9157, f. 1
- killed by, with spear: Verdun 107, f. 141v (*fig. 302*)
- seated beside: Christ Church E.II, f. 29v (2, one raising visor)

Knight and horse (*see also* Knight and dog; — and dragon; — and hare, hunting; — and hybrid man; — and lion; — and Saracen; — and snail; Knights fighting; — tilting; Swan pulling boat)
- astride: Douce 118, f. 26; Cambrai 87, f. 68 (shown from back); fr. 25526, f. 156v (approaching building); latin 16260, f. 561 (with spear, blue horse); St. Omer 5, f. 141 (red horse; Zechariah 1:8)
- astride, guided by man with staff: Trinity B.11.22, f. 31 (at R., woman with lap dog)
- astride seated horse, wielding sword (Futility? *cf.* King and horse): Chantilly 62, f. 182
- astride, with human head at knee height: Yale MS., f. 25
- climbing horse with aid of ladder, aided by boy (fabliau?): Jesus 40, f. 71 (at L., larger knight astride horse observing) (*fig. 314*)
- falling off, charged by woman astride horse with spear, hurling flowers: Add. 10294, f. 1
- falling off while tilting at quintain: Nancy 249, f. 196

Knight and hybrid man
- astride, charged by woman with spear and shield: Jacquemart 1, f. 82
- astride horse, charging with sword, hybrid man with mace and shield: Christ Church E.II, f. 35
- astride horse, fighting with spear, hybrid man with buckler: Cambrai 102, f. 339
- astride lion, fighting with lance, sword: Royal 2 B.VII, f. 135
- fleeing from, both with swords and bucklers: Stowe 17, f. 120
- kneeling before, shot by: Cambrai 102, f. 391
- tilting, unseated by: Cambrai 103, f. 410

Knight and hybrid woman
- astride collapsing horse backwards, fighting with sword, lance, and shield (*cf.* Knight and horse, astride seated horse): Royal 2 B.VII, f. 133v
- confronting with mace and buckler, hybrid woman with handbell and pipe: Cloisters 54.1.2, f. 103

Knight and lion (*cf.* Hybrid knight and)
- astride horse, charging with spear: Jacquemart 1, f. 13

K

confronting by tree, with shield and standard: Melbourne 1254/3, ff. 35v-36
confronting with sword, bitten in back by dragon: fr. 95, f. 292v (below, Samson rending lion) (*fig. 305*)
fighting with sword: BBR 10607, f. 94; Cambrai 102, ff. 6v, 342v (killing, aided by hybrid knight); latin 14284, f. 61v (issuing from border); Princeton 44-18, f. 17 (bitten by second lion); Royal 2 B.VII, f. 164v (astride horse); Stowe 17, f. 112 (*fig. 105*); W. 85, f. 69 (killing); Yale MS., f. 315 (killing) (*fig. 303*)
Guy of Warwick tale: Royal 10 E.IV, ff. 80v-88; Y.T. 13, ff. 14v-18
patting: Princeton 44-18, f. 145v (*fig. 304*)
Knight and man *see* Man and knight
Knight and minotaur, charging with spear: Cambrai 102, f. 387
Knight and monster (*see also* Knight with head of beast)
killing five-headed monster: Douce 366, f. 128 (with sword)
shooting: St. Omer 5, f. 281 (with crossbow; at side, man shooting stork)
tilting: Y.T. 19, f. 31v
Knight and nun *see* Knights fighting with swords
Knight and owl, beckoning to, holding basket of eggs: Cambridge Dd. 5.5, f. 55
Knight and saint, beheading with sword: latin 1076, f. 78
Knight and Saracen
astride horses, fighting with spears and shields: Hague 78.D.40, ff. 12, 34, 91v
pursued by half-nude Saracen astride horse with spear, knight with club: Jacquemart 1, f. 119v
pursuing: Fitz. 298, f. 127; Hague 78.D.40, ff. 107, 139v; Royal 2 B.VII, ff. 149v-150 (Saracen with abducted woman; *cf.* Knight and wild man); Stowe 17, ff. 212v-213; Y.T. 8, f. 193v
pursuing barefoot man in cloak (Sacracen?) astride horse with protesting woman: Christ Church E.II, f. 29
tilting, unseating: Add. 42130, f. 82
Knight and satyr(?), pursuing with spear: Cambrai 102, f. 387 (at L., horned animal seated, ?pleading) (*fig. 306*)
Knight and serpent, holding, aiming sword at: G.K.S. 3384, f. 54v
Knight and snail (*see also* Dog as knight: Hybrid knight and)
astride horse which rears at sight of snail: Yale MS., f. 169
confronting with bow and arrow, spear; woman pleading with him latin 14284, f. 15v (*fig. 311*)
confronting with spear and buckler: fr. 776, f. 176v (at L., centaur charging; lion between knight and snail) (*fig. 310*)
confronting with spear and buckler, woman pleading with him: Fitz. 298, f. 40v
fighting with club: Royal 10 E.IV, f. 107
fighting with falchion and shield: Add. 49622, f. 170
fighting with spear: Chantilly 64, f. 85; W. 90, f. 134; Y.T. 8, f. 321; Y.T. 19, f. 66
fighting with sword and shield: Add. 49622, f. 146; Arras 229, f. 706; Fitz. 298, ff. 6, 27v; G.K.S. 3384, f. 224v; W. 45, ff. 23 (at R., centaur with spear and shield), 82v (*fig. 309*); Y.T. 8, f. 191v; Y.T. 19, f. 88
frightened by (*cf.* Knight and hare): Chantilly 64, f. 85v
frightened by, dropping sword before: G.K.S. 3384, ff. 160v (*fig. 307*), 224v, 260v, 292v
kneeling before: Add. 49622, ff. 162v (*fig. 308*), 193v, 213v; W. 109, f. 134v (with lance, mace, sword; snail with four horns)
mocked by: Stowe 17, f. 22v (knight on horse; f. 223, man exposing hindquarters)
with mace, grasping horn of snail: Add. 49622, f. 185v
Knight and stag, astride, bearing banner with arms of Flanders, shield: latin 1076, f. 58v
Knight and stork *see* Knight and bird
Knight and swan *see* Swan pulling boat
Knight and unicorn, fighting with sword: Douce 6, f. 104v; Y.T. 8, f. 260
Knight and wild man, pursuing astride horse (fabliau)
charging, slaying: Douce 131, f. 81v (at L., queen in tent, man tied to tree)
wild man with abducted child: Princeton 44-18, ff. 41v-42 (child stolen from woman, handed to second wild man under tree)
wild man with abducted woman riding off on horse: Christ Church E.II, f. 29; Royal 10 E.IV, ff. 101-105
Knight and woman (*see also* Castle; Knight and horse, astride; — and hybrid man, astride; — and Saracen; — and snail, confronting; — and wild man)

charged by woman with distaff and spindle astride horse, knight defenseless, with raised hands: fr. 95, f. 226 (at R., ape holding out red fruit, probably apple) (*fig. 708*); Yale MS., f. 329 (*fig. 709*)
charged, upset by woman with spear astride goat, knight falling off ram: Y.T. 8, f. 224 (*fig. 710*)
confronting with raised sword and shield, woman with mirror: W. 85, ff. 115v-116
fighting with spear and shield, astride hybrid man: Jacquemart 1, f. 82
greeted by: W. 87, ff. 71v-72
holding mirror for, woman braiding her hair under flowering tree: BBR 9961-62, f. 74 (at R., dog pursuing hare)
killing two giants for: Royal 10 E.IV, ff. 125v-126v
killing with spear: Laud Lat. 84, f. 19
kneeling before: Yale MS., f. 187
with reel, woman with garland: Cambrai 87, f. 57v
woman holding helmet (*see also* Knights tilting): Nancy 249, f. 215v; Princeton 44-18, f. 79v (and spear); Trinity B.11.22, f. 12v (with lap dog)
woman holding sword and shield; Princeton 44-18, ff. 84v-85 (ff. 85v-86, knight kneeling before St. Catherine)
woman putting helmet on his head: Jacquemart 1, f. 28
tilting, unseated by: Princeton 44-18, f. 20; Y.T. 8, f. 224 (astride ram and goat) (*fig. 710*)
Knight balancing reel on pole: G.K.S. 3384, f. 118 (below, two men fighting with mace and sword)
Knight crippled, with crutch: Yale MS., f. 257v
Knight falling off horse *see* Knight and horse; — and woman, tilting
Knight, headless, with spear and shield: Melbourne 1254/3, f. 27v (below, lion with trumpet)
Knight in boat (*see also* Knights tilting, standing)
in initial, pulled by hybrid knight: Cloisters 54.1.2, f. 135v
rowing, confronting and shooting two knights in sailboat: Cambrai 102, f. 485 (in background, castle occupied by knights)
Knight kneeling (*see also* Knight and woman; Patron)
before St. Catherine: Princeton 44-18, ff. 85v-86
receiving shield from hand; Douce 118, f. 49v
Knight nude *see* Man nude and hare, hunting
Knight nude save for helmet: fr. 95, ff. 309 (killed with spear by devil), 340v
Knight performing feats for king (fabliau): Royal 10 E.IV, ff. 290v-314 (unidentified)
Knight praying (patron?): latin 1076, ff. 118, 156 (at L., St. Francis); Trinity B.11.22, f. 199v (*fig. 335*)
Knight receiving document from kneeling boy: Douce 5, f. 30v
Knight reclining on elbow, two retainers, page holding horse: Bodley 264, f. 139v
Knight shooting knight astride horse: fr. 95, f. 89v (2)
Knight spinning, woman with distaff and spindle dancing: Arras 47, f. 32 (winding reel) (*fig. 734*)
Knight tilting *see* Knight and bird; — and woman; Knights
Knight unsheathing sword: Add. 49622, f. 136
before pleading ape: Add. 49622, f. 137v
before seated knight with sword preparing to cut off his own leg: fr. 95, f. 291
Knight with ax and sword: Douce 118, f. 88v (issuing from border)
Knight with club and shield: BBR 10228, f. 6 (issuing from border; below, bandyball)
Knight with crossbow, loading: fr. 95, f. 203
Knight with ewer: W. 87, f. 73
Knight with head of
ass on spear: W. 90, f. 146
beast
brandishing sword: BBR 9427, f. 81v; Douce 24, f. 141v; G.K.S. 3384, ff. 62, 76 (above, man grasping sword); W. 82, f. 196 (above, hybrid man grasping sword)
dripping blood caught in basin by ape, brandishing sword (*cf.* Man and beast): Douce 5, ff. 57v, 167v
dripping blood caught in basin by man: Douce 6, f. 52a; G.K.S. 3384, f. 129 (below, line ending with cleric's head) (*fig. 312*); St. Omer 5, ff. 141 (issuing from border), 145v (bearded head)
woman, brandishing sword: Douai 193, f. 252v; latin 1076, f. 150v
Knight with pipe and tabor: Princeton 44-18, f. 119
Knight with pole, ball and chain suspended from end (*cf.* Hybrid woman with): W. 87, f. 53 (issuing from border)
Knight with reel *see* Knight and woman, kneeling before; Knight balancing; — spinning

K

Knight with scroll *see* Patron: Joffroy

Knight with shield bearing arms of Flanders: latin 10484, f. 109v

Knight with spear, pulling ?object out of hip, retainer holding horse: Trinity B.11.22, f. 33

Knight with stones, pelting hybrid knight below: Douce 6, f. 128v

Knight with sword (*see also* Knight and bird; — and dragon; — and hare; — and horse, astride seated; — and hybrid man; — and lion; — and monster; — and saint; — and serpent; — and snail; — and unicorn; — with ax)

  issuing from border: Add. 17444, f. 42v (fighting beast); BBR 9391, f. 4; Douce 5, f. 80 (fighting winged beast); Douce 118, ff. 88v, etc.; Trinity B.11.22, ff. 94v, etc.

  kneeling, preparing to cut off his leg(?): Arras 47, f. 246 (*fig. 313*)

  seated, preparing to cut off his leg(?): fr. 95, f. 291 (confronting knight unsheathing sword)

Knights approaching castle: Bodley 264, f. 95v (6, 2 on horseback)

Knights attacking castle *see* Castle

Knights confronted, one astride horse, the other (smaller) climbing ladder resting against his horse, propelled by boy with stick (fabliau?): Jesus 40, f. 71 (*fig. 314*)

Knights fighting

  in two boats (fabliau?): fr. 25526, f. 116v (4)

  melee of, trumpeter astride horse: Royal 2 B.VII, f. 186

  with sword and ax, bitten by dragons: fr. 95, f. 100

  with swords and shields, astride horses: Douce 131, f. 54 (at L., woman looking out of castle) (*fig. 136*); fr. 25526, ff. 10v, 89v; Verdun 107, f. 19v (*fig. 315*)

  with swords and shields, one killed: fr. 25526, f. 134 (at R., nun in brown habit, black veil, with basket on back, staff)

Knights shooting from battlement: Holkham 458, f. 44

Knights tilting: Ashmole 828, f. 1; C.B. 62, f. 194v; C.B. 64, f. 37v; Christ Church E.II, ff. 60v-62, 65v-66; Douce 5, f. 143 (at R., man with horn); Douce 6, f. 44 (at L., woman clasping hands); Douce 118, f. 60v; fr. 95, f. 297; fr. 25526, ff. 15v, 47v, 123v; Hague 78.D.40, ff. 99, 147v; Jesus 40, f. 8; latin 1029A, f. 10; M. 155, ff. 158v-159; M. 183, f. 105; M. 729, f. 286; M. 730, ff. 49v, 74, 80v, 155v, 243, 246v; M. 796, f. 75v; Melbourne 1254/3, ff. 7 (*fig. 318*), 29, 57; Royal 2 B.VII, f. 131v; Royal 14 E.III, f. 89; Stowe 17, ff. 95v-96; W. 82, f. 15 (at L., nude man with trumpet); W. 88, ff. 28v, 42, 146; W. 90, f. 155; W. 104, f. 81v; Y.T. 8, ff. 290v-291; Y.T. 19, f. 3

  flanked by two crowned hybrid women presenting helmets to kneeling knights; woman standing, holding crown, between tilting knights: Bodley 264, f. 67

  flanked by two women presenting helmets to kneeling knights: Bodley 264, f. 101v

  opening of tournament, knights riding toward each other with right hands extended; between them man with two standards; at sides bagpiper, man with pipe and tabor, trumpeters: Royal 14 E.III, f. 3

  queen and three female attendants looking on from tower (*cf.* Cockfight, hen): Royal 10 E.IV, ff. 65v-66 (*figs. 316-317*)

  woman in castle looking on (*cf.* Cockfight: hen): Douce 131, f. 54 (*fig. 136*)

  standing in two boats (*cf.* Knights fighting in): Royal 2 B.VII, f. 159 (f. 158v, three men and two women looking on)

  woman between them with two red staves in hands: Rylands lat. R.117, f. 9

Knowledge *see* Sacraments: Baptism

Knucklebones *see* Dice

Krummhorn *see* Hybrid man with; — with pipe and shawm

L

Ladder *see* Cleric nude, with; Hybrid man with; Jesus Christ, life of: Last Judgment: blessed; —: Last Judgment, Hell mouth, containing bell; Knight and horse, climbing; Man and bird, hunting bird; Nun and man, holding; Pig ascending; Snail ascending; Snail atop

Lady *see* Woman

Lamb *see* Joseph and; Man with greens; Sheep, references under

Lamb of God: Laud Lat. 84, f. 38; Trinity B. 11.22, f. 197v

Lamech *see* Cain and Abel, slain by

Lancaster, Thomas, Earl of, beheaded: Add. 42130, f. 56

Lantern *see* Ape with; Bird with; Man nude, straddling pole; Man with

Laocoön *see* Man and serpent, encircled by

Lap dog *see* Dog as pet; Hybrid man drinking with; Knight and woman, kneeling before, woman

Largesse *see* Lover in castle

Last Judgment *see* Jesus Christ, life of

Laundry *see* Ape and ape-child, approaching; Man washing; Woman washing

Lazarus *see* Dives and

Leapfrog: Bodley 264, f. 93 (variant? 3 boys); fr. 25526, f. 132 (4 boys); W. 88, f. 76v (2 boys)

Leatherworker (?) with hammer, casket (Minnekästchen?); at R., woman: Nancy 249, f. 27

Le Garçon et l'Aveugle (*cf.* Beggar, blind): Royal 10 E.IV, ff. 217v-220v

Lectern *see* Ape and ass, singing; Ape as cleric at; Ape at; Cleric at; Crow at; Fox and cock at; Fox as cleric at; Hare as cleric; Hybrid abbot; Hybrid bishop at; Hybrid cleric with book; Man at; Physician at; Pope; Ram as cleric

Leo, Pope *see* Virgin, miracles of: Pope Leo

Leopard (*see also* St. Mary the Egyptian, f. 278v); BBR 9961-62, f. 48v; Jacquemart 1, f. 41; Merton 0.1.3, f. 33; Munich c.g. 16, f. 30 (Bestiary representation, in cycle)

Leprosy *see* Moses, turning; Rattle, references under

Lessines, city gates of, man with mace (club?) standing before: BBR 1175, f. 105

Limbs detached from bodies *see* Detached limbs; Man nude, eating; Man nude, headless

Lion (*see also* Angel nude; Ape and; David, life of: David slaying; Epifagus fighting; Fox and; Hare and; Hybrid knight and; Hybrid man and; Knight and dragon, fighting; Knight and lion; Man and; Man nude, and; Mermaid and; Peacock and; Procession, funeral of fox; *Roman de Renart:* fox and; St. Mary the Egyptian, ff. 280, 284; Samson rending; Unicorn and; Wild man and; Woman and

Lion and bear
- confronted: Fitz. 242, f. 29 (bear?); Jacquemart 1, f. 96 (lion chained)
- with pipe and tabor, bear dancing: Hague 78.D.40, f. 39 (at R., man training horse)

L

Lion and bird (*see also* Lion with hare's ears)
- aiming ball at: Arras 47, f. 19v
- beside nest containing birds: Cambrai 102, f. 436v
- eating, stealing eggs from nest: Cambrai 102, f. 387 (*fig. 306*)
- ridden by, hybrid man charging with spear: Cambrai 102, f. 150
- standing on nest (basket?): W. 87, f. 84 (above, woman with shoe in either hand)

Lion and child
- devouring: Chartres 549, f. 252v
- stealing, running off with: Rylands lat R.117, f. 9 (pursued by woman with distaff and spindle) (*fig. 108*)

Lion and children, caring for (fabliau: Florent and Octavian): Royal 10 E.IV, ff. 119-125

Lion and cleric/snail, roaring at, frightening: Fitz. 298, f. 9v

Lion and cow, pursuing: Hague 78.D.40, f. 53

Lion and devil, tail bitten by: Rutland Ps., f. 32v

Lion and dog
- biting: Cloisters 54.1.2, f. 107v
- confronted: M. 88, ff. 151 (lion tied to post), 175v
- pursued by: Cambrai 102, f. 403v; W. 759, f. 44v (two)
- pursuing: Arras 1043, f. 114; Hague 78.D.40, f. 2v (dog pursuing hare)
- winged, lion with trumpet, dog with pipe and tabor: Hague 78.D.40, f. 17v

Lion and dragon
- devouring: Fitz. 242, f. 55v (Min.: Crucifixion) (*fig. 12*); Royal 2 B.VII, f. 148v
- grappling with: Christ Church E.II, f. 31v
- tail bitten by, hybrid man with hammer striking lion: Cloisters 54.1.2, f. 36

Lion and elephant with castle, unicorn: Y.T. 13, f. 188

Lion and fox *see* Lion as king; *Roman de Renart*

Lion and goat, pursuing: Yale MS., f. 137v

Lion and griffin
- confronted: Christ Church E.II, f. 14
- springing at: Royal 2 B.VII, f. 145v

Lion and horse, biting in back: Christ Church E.II, f. 43v (at R., oak tree)

Lion and lioness (panther?), fighting: Christ Church E.II, f. 53v

Lion and sheep, holding between paws (*see also* David, life of: D. tending sheep): Douce 5, f. 191v (at R., man brandishing mace); Royal 17 E.VII, f. 1 (plagued by four apes) (*figs. 18, 19*); Y.T. 19, f. 21v

L

Lion and snail, beside bird in nest: Cambrai 102, f. 436v
Lion and stag, pursuing: latin 16260, f. 4v (dog?)
Lion and unicorn, charging: Christ Church E.II, f. 46v
Lion and wolf *see* Lion as king
Lion approaching suspended gold nugget: Douce 118, f. 174
Lion as bishop: G.K.S. 3384, f. 301v; Glazier 24, f. 102v; W. 37, f. 17
Lion as king (*see also Roman de Renart*): Bodley 264, f. 189
  labeled "Ricardus rex": Lansdowne 451, f. 70v
  seated on column, holding scroll reading "jalusie, orgueil, envie"; flanked by fox as Franciscan, wolf as Dominican, both kneeling: Hague 78.D.40, f. 26 (*fig. 197*)
Lion as pilgrim (?), with tall cross and scrip: Melbourne 1254/3, f. 37
Lion, Bestiary representation: Fitz. 288, f. 154 (at R., pelican, phoenix; Min.: Crucifixion; Hours of the Holy Ghost); Maz. 34, f. 1 (at R., stag); Munich c.g. 16, f. 9 (in cycle); Royal 2 B.VII, ff. 85v-87 (in cycle); Stowe 17, f. 53 (Min.: Mocking of Christ)
Lion confronting lion: W. 88, f. 132
Lion chained or tied to post: Douce 118, f. 44 (f. 43v, cock) (*fig. 319*)
  confronting bear: Jacquemart 1, f. 96
  confronting seated dog: M. 88, f. 151
  hare with trumpet: Royal 3 D.VI, f. 234
  man with switch, dog on leash: Melbourne 1254/3, f. 123
  man with two switches, dog seated looking up at him: Douce 118, f. 124
Lion dancing
  ape with bagpipe: Tournai Ps., f. 216v
  ape with vielle: Add. 49622, f. 35
  dog with vielle, hare with hand bells: fr. 25526, f. 94v
Lion, Evangelist symbol *see* Evangelist symbols, St. Mark
Lion in cave, looking out: Fitz. 242, f. 55v (Min.: Crucifixion) (*fig. 12*)
Lion raising front paw: W. 37, ff. 102, 103
Lion seated on mound: Rutland Ps., f. 23
Lion under tree: Harley 6563, ff. 29, 29v
Lion with bagpipe: W. 45, f. 116v (above, fox running)
Lion with basket on head, confronting lion with pot on head: Hague 10 A.14, f. 27v (both with swords)
Lion with hand bells, dog with bagpipe, dog with pipe and tabor, hare dancing: fr. 25526, f. 30
Lion with hare's ears and tail, before nest containing two birds (*cf.* Bird with; Dragon with): W. 45, f. 197
Lion with harp: M. 796, f. 43v; Queens 117, f. 37v
Lion with horn and tabor: Auct.D.3.2, f. 89
Lion with pipe and tabor, hare dancing: Hague 78.D.40, f. 39 (at R., man training horse)
Lion with shawm: Cloisters 54.1.2, f. 103v
Lion with sword *see* Lion with basket
Lion with trumpet: Hague 78.D.40, f. 17v (winged, winged dog with pipe and tabor); Melbourne 1245/3, f. 27v (above, headless knight with spear and shield); W. 45, f. 166v (below, nude man with round red-orange object in hand; another man beating companion)
Lion with vielle: latin 14284, f. 30v (male siren dancing); Verdun 107, f. 26 (at R., falconer, man with hand bells) (*fig. 182*)
Literary references *see* Alexander; Arthurian references; Cycles; Fables; Fabliaux; Lover
Lizard (*see also* Falcon and; Jesus Christ, life of: Last Judgment: Pains of Hell, murderer): Add. 24686, f. 18v (sticking tongue out at dragon) (*fig. 378*); fr. 12400, ff. 20 (above, stork with ?rat in beak), 112
Lobster bitten by stork: C.B. 62, f. 199v (below, man beckoning to bird)
Lombards: BBR 1175, f. 14 (3)
London *see* St. Thomas of Canterbury
Longinus, delivered by St. Michael: Y.T. 13, f. 127
Loom
  man and woman seated at: M. 754, f. 22v (loom?)
  Naa-mah seated at: Munich c.g. 16, f. 20v (*fig. 724*)
  woman at: M. 754, f. 60v (loom?; at R., hybrid man)
Lot receiving angels, fire descending on Sodom, wife turned into pillar of salt: Munich c.g. 16, f. 25v
Louis VII *see* Virgin, miracles of
Love *see* Castle of; Man and woman, embracing; —, kissing; —, kneeling before
Lover, adventures of, in *Roman de la Rose:* Tournai CI, throughout
  Barons of Love: ff. 202, 232, 317
  beaten by Fair-Welcome and Danger: f. 68
  conversing with Friend: ff. 73, 142

conversing with Reason: f. 89
conversing with Reason before closed gate; ape handing bird's claw to parrot: f. 141
dreaming: f. 73
embracing woman
awaking from dream (in bed), man with pipe seated: f. 345
flanked by hare and dog; man with mandola, three couples dancing: f. 23
in castle of Jealousy with Love, Fair-Welcome, Largesse, Constraint, False-Seeming, and Courtesy: f. 232 (at L., with four Barons of Love)
kissing rosebud, denounced by Jealousy to Evil-Tongue: f. 78
kneeling before spring, drinking: f. 17
kneeling, swearing allegiance to Eros holding key: f. 49
led by Fair-Welcome: f. 78
Nature kneeling before Jesus Christ in aureole holding fish; in foreground, tree occupied by two doves; under tree, animals including ape, ram, fantastic beast; at R., Jesus Christ with globe, letters AEA in the three divisions: f. 280
planning with Love to besiege Jealousy's castle: f. 196
Pygmalion sculpting, five nude women before him; at R., kneeling man offering mandola to woman: f. 319 (*fig. 587*)
receiving rosebud from Fair-Welcome; at R., Shame, Fear, and Evil-Tongue seated: f. 66
with False-Seeming in clerical garb, with Barons of Love, Eros before castle of Jealousy: f. 202
with Venus wearing gold crown before tent; behind her, Eros; castle with Pygmalion's image in central tower; Shame, Fear, and Danger leaving castle: f. 341
Luttrell, arms of *see* Man with bellows, wearing on head
Luttrell, Sir Geoffrey *see* Banquet

M

Mace *see* Ape and bear, astride; Knight and snail, with; Man with
Magdalene *see* Jesus Christ, life of: Mary Magdalene; —: *Noli me tangere;* St. Mary Magdalene
Magi *see* Jesus Christ, life of: Adoration of
Magicians *see* St. Simon and St. Jude
Magpie (*see also* Fox running): Fitz. 2-1954, f. 47v
feeding three young in nest (*cf.* Bird flying): W. 45, f. 61
in tree, couple courting below: Stowe 17, f. 59
pecking eye of corpse: Trinity B.11.22, f. 159v (crow?)
with lion and ram: Add. 39810, f. 7 (*fig. 140*)
Mahaut de Brabant *see* Patroness
Malachi: Y.T. 13, f. 43v
Malachi and St. Thaddeus, Apostle (Old and New Law): latin 10483, f. 6; Y.T. 27, f. 11; Y.T. 75, f. 9
Mallard: Fitz. 2-1954, ff. 74v (teal?), 87
Man *see also* Hybrid man; Men; Obscaena
Man and ape (*see also* Ape and stag, astride; Ape as physician; Ape dancing; Elephant and castle, occupied by; Man nude, and; Man with bagpipe; — with pipe and tabor; Obscaena, bellows; —, finger; Physician and ape)
aiming at ball on pole with club, ape preparing to catch ball (*cf.* Club-ball): G.K.S. 3384, f. 120v
aiming trumpet at: W. 90, f. 144v
astride dragon led by ape with club: Tournai Ps., f. 20 (holding whip, goat's head)
astride, with sword and shield: Cambridge Dd. 5.5, f. 368 (hunting hare)
balancing in basin set on pole balanced on nose: Douce 5, f. 5v
balancing in basin set on pole held by man; ape with fruit: Trinity B.11.22, f. 211 (*fig. 323*)
beaten on head by, with club, man drawing sword: Douce 6, f. 131v (stork aiming beak at hindquarters of ape)
beheaded by, with sword: W. 85, f. 84v (man's head issuing from border)
conversing with ape in tree: Rutland Ps., f. 106v (*fig. 321*)
creeping toward ape with offspring in arms (Bestiary variant?): Douce 5, f. 115v (below, old man and woman conversing)
cutting hair of: G.K.S. 3384, f. 51
feeding: G.K.S. 3384, f. 37 (man with long animal legs) (*fig. 322*)
fighting with ax
ape pleading: Douce 6, f. 201v
ape with sword and buckler: Douce 6, f. 26v
fighting with club: G.K.S. 3384, f. 163v
fighting with spear and shield: Olschki 4, f. 175

M
fighting with swords and bucklers: Y.T. 8, f. 190v
given enema(?) by: M. 754, f. 27 (or ape inserting dagger, catching blood in cup; man nude, armless)
hunting with club, horn, hound, astride unicorn: W. 82, f. 62v (at L., ape reaching for unicorn's horn)
hunting with spear, ape climbing tree (*cf.* Ape, Bestiary): Royal 2 B.VII, f. 159v
led by: Cambridge Dd. 5.5, f. 307v
playing organ, ape pumping bellows: Add. 49622, f. 117
playing vielle, ape balancing two basins on two sticks, ape with bagpipe (*see also* Man with vielle): Add. 24686, f. 17v (*fig. 324*)
pulled by *see* Ape astride keg
pulling cart containing three apes: W. 109, f. 100
pursued by, half-nude: Jacquemart 1, f. 91
ridden by: Cambridge Dd. 5.5, f. 403; Glazier 24, f. 131v (man nude, saddled)
ridden by ape-bishop fighting ape with sword and shield: Add. 10292, f. 1
shooting
ape astride goat backwards: Stowe 17, ff. 213v-214
ape astride stag: G.K.S. 3384, f. 112v
ape with fruit: Cambridge Dd. 5.5, f. 359
ape with mandola: Add. 30029, f. 101v
at hindquarters of: Ashmole 828, f. 98v
shot by: Add. 10293, f. 1
struck with ax by: Douce 5, f. 74
threatened with battle-ax by: Add. 30029, f. 19v
trained by, with switch, man on rope doing handstand, flanked by two birds: Royal 20 D.IV, f. 260
training (*cf.* Man and ape, aiming; —, balancing)
ape doing handstand: Bodley 264, f. 119v; Cloisters 54.1.2, f. 76 (man with tabor)
ape on chain or leash: Add. 38114, f. 5 (bid farewell by woman); Cambrai 103, f. 350v; Chantilly 64, ff. 147, 147v; Fitz. 298, f. 8 (*fig. 326*); latin 14284, f. 64v; Laud Lat. 84, f. 227; M. 183, f. 183; Rutland Ps., f. 71 (second man with bagpipe); W. 104, ff. 28 (*fig. 11*), 45v (beside ape-physician, man playing ?board with rake); W. 760, f. 182
ape turning somersault: Add. 42130, f. 73; Y.T. 8, f. 297v (*fig. 325*)
holding out stick, ape jumping over: Stowe 17, f. 204
holding out stick for ape to jump over: Bodley 264, f. 119v
trapped in net by (*cf.* Man and woman, trapped by): Stowe 17, f. 240 (*fig. 327*)
trapping with tarred boots *see* Ape, Bestiary representation
upset by, falling over backwards, charged by ape with lance and shield astride beast: Royal 2 B.VII, f. 140v (with sword and shield)
with bagpipe: Add. 42130, f. 13 (below, tailed ape); Add. 49622, f. 57 (ape admonishing)
with book, ape pointing at book: Chantilly 64, ff. 109, 109v
with reliquary *see* Procession, man and ape
with vielle *see* Man and ape, playing
Man and ass (*see also* Windmill)
astride
bid farewell by woman: W. 104, f. 122
with bird and falchion (parody of falconer?): Stowe 17, f. 103v
with sack on shoulder: Hague 78.D.40, ff. 42, 143
carrying (fable or proverb; *cf.* Hybrid man and doe): G.K.S. 3384, f. 69v (toward stream); Glazier 24, f. 32 (horse?) (*fig. 328*)
driving: BBR 9391, f. 106v (horse? saddled, man covered with hair, bearing club; Min.: Nativity); Y.T. 8, f. 254 (ass loaded with sack)
with pipe and tabor, ass dancing: Chantilly 64, ff. 119, 119v
Man and basilisk, fighting with sword and buckler: Stowe 17, ff. 267v-268
Man and bear
aiming club at, bear eating head of second man: Rutland Ps., f. 51
astride, led on leash by man with club: Hague 78.D.40, f. 157v (at R., two men)
baiting with four dogs: Add. 42130, f. 161 (4)
bear chained, standing, man balancing basin on sticks: Bodley 264, f. 76 (*fig. 332*)
bear tied, man seated beside: Bodley 264, f. 89
beating: W. 85, f. 45 (bear?)
dancing with, second man with pipe and tabor, second ape tied to post (*cf.* below, — training, bear dancing): Bodley 264, f. 117v
fighting with sword and buckler: Add. 24686, f. 12v; Christ Church E.II, f. 36 (man nude)
piercing with spear, grappling with: BBR 9157, f. 45
pursued by, man in tree: Rutland Ps., f. 53

training, holding on chain or leash: Add. 30029, f. 93; Add. 49622, f. 59v; BBR 10607, f. 184v; Burney 275, f. 359v; Douce 5, f. 91 (above, falconer); Douce 48, f. 216v; Fitz. 288, f. 181; Fitz. 298, f. 92; fr. 25526, f. 108; latin 14284, f. 9v (at R., woman dancing); Nancy 249, f. 116; Royal 20 D.IV, f. 237v (at R., trained horse); Rutland Ps., f. 56; W. 85, f. 31v (hybrid man); W. 88, f. 36v; Y.T. 8, f. 175v

astride bear, led by man with club: Hague 78.D.40, f. 157v

bear dancing, man with pipe (*cf. above,* —, dancing): Trinity B.11.22, f. 8v

bear standing on head: fr. 95, f. 152 (man with pipe and tabor); Nancy 249, f. 158v (observed by three men, two women) (*fig. 330*)

bear standing upright *see above,* Man and bear, bear chained

bear straining on leash, growling at woman: Royal 2 B.VII, f. 131

woman holding child astride bear: Add. 38114, f. 5

wrestling: Fitz. 298, f. 23v; Y.T. 8, f. 297

Man and beast

bending crossbow at: Add. 42130, f. 54 (below, Moses with Tablets of the Law) (*fig. 504*)

fighting with club: G.K.S. 3384, ff. 50v, etc.

head devoured by beast: G.K.S. 3384, f. 28v

holding head of (*cf.* Knight with head of; Man —): Cambridge Dd. 5.5, f. 246 (with sword); Douce 6, f. 185; W. 85, f. 71 (bear ?man with polearm)

killing with sword, blood caught in bowl held by hand (*cf.* Knight with head of beast): G.K.S. 3384, f. 150

rending (Samson parody?): Chantilly 64, ff. 126 126v

shooting: Rylands fr. 1, f. 212; Tournai Ps., f. 156v; W. 85, f. 23

Man and bees, with sack, catching or releasing three bees (*see also* Beehive): Stowe 17, f. 148

Man and bird (*see also* Man and cock; — and falcon; Man balancing; Man nude, and; Man with gittern; Obscaena, beak; —, shooting)

attacked by, head seized in beak: Royal 10 E.IV, f. 77 (2, two; men on stilts; at R., woman on stilts; above, man; both also attacked by birds) (*fig. 331*)

beckoning to: C.B. 62, f. 199v (stork biting lobster) (*fig. 333*); fr. 25526, ff. 1v, 41 (pursuing?); M. 149, ff. 383v-384; Rutland Ps., f. 68v (conversing with? bird in tree)

clamping beak shut with pincers (*cf.* Man with pincers): G.K.S. 3384, f. 84

feeding bird in birdcage: Nancy 249, f. 119

fighting with sword, bird (hybrid) with club and buckler: G.K.S. 3384, f. 224 (2)

holding by neck: Add. 42130, f. 60 (hybrid bird)

holding in teeth string with bird attached (*cf.* Man and butterfly on string): Add. 42130, f. 159 (at R., man with lit taper)

hunting bird in nest, creeping toward: Douce 118, f. 36

hunting bird (or eggs) in nest in tree (cinomolgus? *cf.* Lion and bird; Man and stork, hunting): Douce 6, ff. 29 (3, one with ax chopping off branch), 135 (3, one on ladder, drawers pulled down by man behind whose leg is pulled by third man) (*fig. 336*); fr. 12400, f. 94v (2, climbing tree and cliff, pulled up on rope by companions) (*fig. 337*); Rutland Ps., f. 68v; Trinity B.11.22, f. 199v (with birdcage); W. 88, ff. 35, 115 (2), 167v (with ladder), 171 (with ladder)

hunting by swimming under water: fr. 12400, f. 115v (falcon; text illustration) (*fig. 472*)

hunting with bow and arrow (*see also* Man ringing bell): Add. 21926, f. 82 (Ps. 52); Add. 29253, f. 217v; Add. 30029, f. 103v; Add. 42130, f. 215 (parrot?); Add. 49622, ff. 13v, 190, 215; Arras 139, f. 8v; Arras 561, f. 112v; Arras 729, f. 151v (gold bird); BBR 9157, f. 1; BBR 9961-62, f. 96; BBR 10607, ff. 100, 169v; BBR 14682, f. 141; C.B. 62, f. 110; Cambrai 102, f. 232; Douce 5, ff. 77, 159v; Douce 6, f. 26v; Douce 118, ff. 10v, 71v, 95 (bird in nest); Fitz. 242, ff. 15, 153v (owl); Fitz. 298, ff. 18 (goldfinch), 51v (heron?), 96v (crossbill?), 101v, 113v, 133v; fr. 95, f. 327 (crippled monster sticking out tongue); fr. 25526, ff. 12, 67 (upper margin, hybrid dog with processional cross); G.K.S. 3384, ff. 5, 37v, 58v, 324v; Kraus 75/88, f. 138v; Lambeth 233, f. 81v; latin 3893, f. 142; latin 10483, f. 114; M. 183, f. 198 (crow?); M. 754, f. 69 (man in pot or vat, hybrid bird); M. 796, f. 118v (parrot?); Maz. 34, f. 24 (crossbow); Melbourne 1254/3, f. 25v; Montpellier H.196, f. 270; Princeton 44-18, ff. 34v-35, 77, 93v-94, 191; Royal 10 E.IV, f. 46 (observed by owl in tree); Rutland Ps., f. 67v; Rylands lat.

R.16, f. 154v; St. Omer 5, f. 1; Stowe 17, ff. 135, 241v; W. 37, ff. 28v-29, 67v (nude); W. 39, f. 96v; W. 45, ff. 79v (above, squirrel with nut), 232v; W. 87, f. 97; W. 88, ff. 82v, 87v (drawers lowered), 98; W. 90, f. 58v; W. 760, f. 122v; W. 761, f. 175; Y.T. 8, ff. 17v, 61 (crossbow), 195, 214, 222, 228v, 286v (crossbow), 302v, 304v, 339v, 356; Y.T. 15, f. 20 (man/bird); Y.T. 19, f. 3; Y.T. 27, f. 114v; Yale MS., ff. 1, 2v

hunting with club: BBR 9961-62, f. 14; Bodley 264, f. 29v (2); fr. 25526, f. 6; Trinity B.11.22, f. 199v (holding birdcage; bird in nest in tree) (*fig. 335*); W. 88, f. 21 (hybrid bird)

hunting with crossbow: Bodley 264, f. 95 (2, bird in tree); Maz. 34, f. 24; Royal 2 B.VII, f. 162v (2); Y.T. 8, ff. 61, 386v

hunting with lasso: Trinity B.11.22, f. 123v

hunting with lure: Add. 38114, f. 4v; W. 85, f. 6v

hunting with sling, bird in tree: Royal 14 B.V (cinomolgus?)

hunting with spear: fr. 2754, f. 1

hunting with stone, casting at bleeding bird: M. 183, ff. 14v, 38 (owl)

hunting with trap (hat?): M. 796, f. 1

killing with sword: fr. 25526, f. 80v

reading, bird looking over his shoulder (*cf.* Fox and hare): G.K.S. 3384, f. 172 (stork)

seated, listening to bird in tree, covering mouth with hand: Yale MS., f. 119 (*fig. 334*)

seated on hillock, bird hovering by his ear (St. Gregory reference?): Melbourne 1254/3, f. 10v

snaring with clapnet: BBR 9157, f. 1; Chantilly 64, f. 61v (hiding in bush); Y.T. 8, f. 273

snaring with decoy: Arundel 83, f. 14 (owl as decoy) (*fig. 338*); BBR 9411-26, f. 111; BBR 10607, ff. 174, 220; Chantilly 64, f. 61 (hood over face, with five sticks); fr. 95, f. 334v (2); Trinity B.11.22, f. 200; W. 37, ff. 161v-162 (2) (*fig. 339*); W. 88, f. 23; W. 761, f. 175v (2; erased)

snaring with decoy and birdcage: Bodley 264, f. 117; Douce 6, f. 51; M. 149, f. 1v; M. 729, f. 279; M. 754, f. 89v (three cages); W. 88, f. 9 (2; June; f. 8v, man with wheat sheaf on back); Y.T. 8, f. 31

snaring with net: Add. 42130, f. 63 (cleric); Bodley 264, f. 119 (owl as decoy); Douce 6, ff. 41v (with decoy), 134v; Royal 2 B.VII, ff. 111v-112 (partridge; Bestiary representation, in cycle); Stowe 17, f. 130; Y.T. 8, f. 273

training, with bird on right hand, stick in other: Douce 118, f. 148 (hooded)

with bird in basket on back: Rothschild MS., f. 165

Man and bishop, holding bowl containing small round objects; above, bishop blessing: Douce 5, f. 200

Man and boar

aiming ax at: Douce 5, f. 25

fighting with sword and buckler: Princeton 44-18, f. 169

hunting with bow and arrow: BBR 10607, f. 187; fr. 776, f. 167v; Hague 78.D.40, f. 47 (shooting); latin 3893, f. 157; W. 88, f. 139 (shooting)

hunting with club: Add. 38114, f. 5

hunting with horn, astride horse: fr. 25526, f. 21

hunting with spear: Add. 10293, f. 1; BBR 9157, f. 1; BBR 9961-62, f. 48v; BBR II 988, vol. I, f. 1; Cambrai 103, ff. 89v, 355v; Cambridge Dd. 5.5, f. 13; Douce 48, f. 235 (at R., angel with psaltery); fr. 776, f. 102 (boar pricked for transfer); fr. 6447, f. 10; G.K.S. 3384, f. 24v; Hague 78.D.40, ff. 35v, 151; Lambeth 233, f. 101; Lat. lit. f. 3, f. 5v; latin 14284, f. 19; M. 155, f. 82 (astride horse); M. 796, f. 92v; Melbourne 1254/3, ff. 79v-80 (hound chasing boar toward man); Princeton 44-18, ff. 69v-70, 132v-133 (2); Rothschild MS., f. 112; Royal 14 E.II, f. 3 (border); W. 82, f. 191v; W. 88, f. 139; Y.T. 8, ff. 234, 300v (and hounds)

hunting with sword: Princeton 44-18, ff. 24v-25 (and pole; 2); Y.T. 8, f. 180

Man and boy

killing, boy dropping cup and flagon: Nancy 249, f. 73

threatening with stick, boy in tree, eating cherries, his shoes on ground at base of tree: Add. 42130, f. 196v (*fig. 340*)

Man and bull, driving uphill with club, holding tail: Rutland Ps., f. 103

Man and butterfly

blowing shawm at: BBR 9157, f. 425

fighting with sword and buckler: Royal 10 E.IV, f. 91v

holding on string (*cf.* Man and bird, holding): G.K.S. 3384, ff. 23 (fly?), 88, 177; Royal 2 B.VII, f. 163v (2, another with bird on string)

- pursuing: Laud Lat. 84, f. 132
  - with club, turning around toward woman holding purse upside down (proverb?): Bodley 264, f. 44
  - with hood (proverb?): Bodley 264, f. 132v (5); Chantilly 64, ff. 105, 105v; G.K.S. 3384, f. 57v; latin 13260, f. 1 (two, on oak tree) (*fig. 342*); Trinity B.11.22, f. 137v; W. 88, ff. 119 (*fig. 343*), 133
- shooting: Cloisters 54.1.2, f. 76v (crowned hybrid man); Fitz. 2-1954, f. 1 (with crossbow; at L., woodcock; Ps. 1); latin 10483, f. 375v; latin 10484, f. 31v (with crossbow); Y.T. 8, f. 271v
- striking with ax: latin 3893, f. 216 (butterfly?)

Man and camel
- driving camel loaded with gold and red boxes: Chantilly 64, ff. 159, 159v
- holding on leash: Douce 48, f. 211v (Min.: Adoration of Magi)
- pursued into doorway by: Rothschild MS., f. 131 (nude)

Man and cat
- fishing, catch stolen by (*cf.* Ape and cat): Cracow 815, f. 11v
- holding: G.K.S. 3384, f. 166
- holding spindle, cat playing with: Cloisters 54.1.2, f. 51 (hooded, cleric?)
- holding stick, cat playing with: W. 759, f. 169
- kissing or whispering to: W. 88, f. 40
- leading on rope, another man leading lion on rope: W. 109, f. 277 (cat or tiger?)
- led by, on rope, in yoke: Jesus 40, f. 110
- pursued by (*cf.* Man and camel): Rothschild MS., f. 130 (nude)
- pursuing with distaff and spindle (Proverb?): Glazier 24, f. 66 (*fig. 341*)
- shooting: Stowe 17, ff. 258v-259 (cat climbing tree, bird at top)

Man and centaur *see* Centaur and man

Man and child (*see also* Beggar and child)
- holding in arms, wearing tall pointed hat, woman kneeling before him: Douce 118, f. 13v (child nude)
- holding infant in swaddling clothes: Cambridge Dd. 5.5, f. 388 (at L., two apes, one with mirror)
- killing with sword (*cf.* Jesus Christ, life of: Massacre of Innocents): Add. 42130, f. 169 (Ps. 93, v. 6)
- threatening with switch: Cambridge Dd. 5.5, f. 338v (bearded; Min.: Stigmatization of St. Francis)

Man and cleric *see* Cleric and man

Man and cock
- astride, fighting man: Douai 193, f. 143 (both nude)
- holding, balancing on pole held by two men, followed by man with banner: Bodley 264, f. 89 (*fig. 417*)
- holding, woman with hen: Trinity B.11.22, f. 161
- shooting: Hague 78.D.40, f. 1; W. 45, f. 232v
  - at cock and bird on stump: Royal 2 B.VII, f. 161 (2)
  - at cock on windmill: Royal 10 E.IV, f. 89 (weathervane? at L., giant) (*fig. 212*)
  - with crossbow from tower: Rothschild MS., f. 135
- with spindle and distaff, two cocks nibbling at spindle (*cf.* Man and cat): Douce 118, f. 7v

Man and corpse, shooting at *see* Solomon, judgment of

Man and cow (*cf.* Man and bull)
- accompanying: Cambridge Dd. 5.5, f. 392v
- aiming ax at head of, man with basin below (*cf.* Man and beast): Douce 6, f. 175
- ankles tied to rope around cow's neck, holding jug (proverb?): Add. 36684, f. 54v
- with head of cow on his back: BBR 10607, f. 125v

Man and crane (*cf.* Man and stork; Pygmy)
- fighting with club and shield: W. 85, f. 36; Yale MS., f. 1
- fighting with sword and buckler: Princeton 44-18, f. 98 (*fig. 344*); Rothschild MS., f. 114v (*fig. 345*)
- pulling feathers out of tail: Princeton 44-18, f. 82 (nude)
- shooting with crossbow: Arras 1043, f. 114; BBR 10228, f. 6

Man and crow, hunting with slingshot: Add. 42130, f. 171 (two; at R., man harrowing)

Man and devil *see* Devil; — and man

Man and doe, carrying on shoulders (fable or proverb?; *cf.* Man and ass; — and horse): Cloisters 54.1.2, f. 120 (hybrid) (*fig. 329*); Y.T. 27, f. 92

Man and dog (*see also* Dog as pet)
- astride, approaching man astride dog: Tournai Ps., f. 207 (at R., ape with fruit)
- astride backwards, pulling cart containing two couples: Stowe 17, f. 198v

M

astride, with trumpet: W. 88, f. 108v
balancing small dog on toe, astride man biting handle of rake: latin 10484, f. 2v
beating with club: Douce 118, f. 37v: G.K.S. 3384, f. 42; latin 14284, f. 33 (sheep?); M. 149, f. 505v
confronting with pipe and tabor: Bodley 264, f. 91
dancing with, woman with vielle: Stowe 17, f. 112
fighting with club and shield: W. 88, f. 62v
holding in hood: Cloisters 54.1.2, f. 173
holding nose to grindstone (proverb?): W. 109, f. 204 (*fig. 346*)
hunted by, with hare: W. 104, f. 168
in cart, pulled by: Royal 10 E.IV, f. 110v
playing like bagpipe: Cloisters 54.1.2, ff. 34v, 166
threatening with bone or club: Trinity B.11.22, f. 128v
to jump over stick: Bodley 264, f. 108 (at R., goat ?kissing same man)
to jump through hoop: Trinity B.11.22, f. 76 (two dogs) (*fig. 347*)
training: Douce 6, f. 108; Douce 118, f. 173v; G.K.S. 3384, f. 198v; W. 88, f. 101
lion tied to post: Douce 118, f. 124; Melbourne 1254/3, f. 123 (at L., hare)
man with horn, dog dancing: G.K.S. 3384, f. 130
man with pipe and tabor, dog dancing: Bodley 264, f. 91 (dog sitting up); Douce 118, f. 40v; G.K.S. 3384, f. 72v; latin 14284, f. 14; W. 90, f. 161v; W. 109, ff. 34, 301 (two)
man with triangle, dog dancing: G.K.S. 3384, f. 208 (below, man with hand organ, cow playing spoon with rake)
with ax, aiming at two-legged dog: fr. 95, f. 39
with bagpipe blown by dog carried across shoulder: Trinity B.11.22, f. 36v
with hand bells, dog sitting up opposite man in goat-costume: Bodley 264, f. 117v
with pet dog *see* Dog as pet
with psaltery, dog sitting up: Princeton 44-18, f. 31
with vielle: BBR 11040, f. 4 (standing on dog); Y.T. 19, f. 3 (dog dancing)
with wheelbarrow containing dog in basket: W. 88, f. 194v
Man and dragon (*see also* Man drinking; Man, head of: issuing;—: pierced; Man nude, and)
astride
backwards, with sword and buckler fighting knight astride horse with sword and buckler: Christ Church E.II, f. 33
grasping head of: Rutland Ps., f. 66
piercing with sword: W. 88, f. 107
rending: Jacquemart 1, f. 113v (at L., two angels with trumpets)
with ax raised: Glazier 24, f. 67
with bowl (nest?) containing bird: Tournai Ps., f. 211v
with club raised: Glazier 24, f. 95
with goat's(?) head, whip: Tournai Ps., ff. 20 (led by ape), 80v, 101v
with pipe and tabor, dog pursuing stag: Harley 616, f. 1
with spear and shield: Cloisters 54.1.2, f. 20
with sword, stabbing dragon in mouth: Jacquemart 1, f. 83
with trumpet: W. 88, f. 165
beseeching: Rutland Ps., ff. 9v-10
bitten by (*see also* Man headless, with head in hand; Man nude, and dragon): Cloisters 54.1.2, ff. 37, 73, 151v, 165 (tunic bitten, pulled), 187; fr. 95, ff. 1 (satyr? horned, bearded, unsheathing sword), 74; Lansdowne 451, f. 78; Rutland Ps., f. 14 (in foot); Vienna 1826 *, f. 11 (in foot)
devoured by, man with hands clasped: Christ Church E.II, f. 46v
fighting with club: BBR 9411-26, ff. 114, 116; Cloisters 54.1.2, f. 43v (half-nude); Jacquemart 1, ff. 76, 116v; Royal 14 B.V; Rutland Ps., f. 47v (and shield, nude save for cloak)
fighting with falchion: fr. 95, f. 326 (dragon with bat wings); G.K.S. 3384, f. 102 (and shield; above, frightened woman)
fighting with spear: BBR 10607, f. 184v; Christ Church E.II, f. 50v (standing on dragon); latin 10483, f. 99; M. 754, f. 63v (astride horse, dragon seated on ewer)
fighting with sword and buckler: Arras 1043, f. 160 (at R., ape gesturing); BBR 9391, f. 1v; BBR 9411-26, f. 4; BBR 10607, f. 24v; fr. 95, ff. 55 (2, two), 74 (two, one biting man); G.K.S. 3384, f. 84v; latin 1076, f. 122 (two, one biting man); M. 155, f. 85; M. 754, f. 15v; Princeton 44-18, f. 31v; Royal 2 B.VII, ff. 163, 186v-187; W. 39, f. 36; Yale MS., ff. 99, 110v
flanked by two dragons: Rutland Ps., f. 63v

frightened by: fr. 776, f. 183; latin 10483, f. 51v (throwing up hands, dragon breathing fire)
grappling with: BBR 10607, f. 58v
grasping head of, with sword: G.K.S. 3384, f. 179
holding in hands: Rutland Ps., f. 103v
holding in hands, dragon biting another man's head: G.K.S. 3384, f. 157
holding on string (*cf.* Man and bird; Wild man and lion): G.K.S. 3384, f. 83
saving woman from: G.K.S. 3384, f. 102
seated before: M. 754, f. 104v
shooting: Add. 42130, f. 54; fr. 95, f. 321; latin 14284, f. 12; W. 37, f. 43v; Y.T. 19, ff. 66, 88; Yale MS., f. 175
standing on
fighting with spear: Christ Church E.II, f. 50v
putting stone: latin 10483, f. 6
strangling: BBR 9411-26, f. 140 (*fig. 348*)
Man and duck (*see also* Bandyball)
beating with club, blood caught by man with basin (*cf.* Man and beast, killing): Douce 6, f. 57
hunting: Add. 24686, f. 14v (falconer); BBR 9961-62, f. 14 (seizing with crook) (*fig. 388*)
Man and eel
holding (proverb?): Douce 6, f. 74; G.K.S. 3384, ff. 14v, 156 (with basket; below, man with fish, ape with basket beckoning), 169, 173v
spearing with fork: G.K.S. 3384, f. 54 (above, cleric vomiting, bearded head) (*fig. 437*)
Man and elephant (*see also* Elephant and castle, occupied by man)
aiming ax at elephant's head: G.K.S. 3384, f. 55
astride horse, hunting with spear: Hague 78.D.40, f. 94v (at L., lion)
Man and falcon (*see also* Falconer): fr. 12400, throughout (text illustrations)
bathing: fr. 12400, ff. 158-160
breathing at: fr. 12400, f. 157
climbing tree and cliff, nest on top, pulled up by men with rope: fr. 12400, f. 94v (2) (*fig. 337*)
clipping with shears, blinding with taper before operation: fr. 12400, f. 136v (2)
feeding: fr. 12400, f. 99 (f. 99v, boiling two eggs for)
hunting with slingshot, falcon in nest (*cf.* Bird in nest): Add. 49622, f. 135v
mounting horse, riding with: fr. 21400, ff. 161-167
operating on wounded falcon: fr. 12400, ff. 103 (2), 104 (man with shears, knife), 104v (man with shears, leg operation), 113 (eye operation)
swimming under water: fr. 12400, f. 115v (falconer; at R., falcon striking duck) (*fig. 472*)
Man and fish (*see also* Man fishing; Man with lantern; *cf.* Man and eel)
chopping on board: Douce 6, f. 114 (blood from head caught in basin on ground); G.K.S. 3384, f. 49
confronting woman, offering fish in bowl to: latin 10483, f. 49v
eating: G.K.S. 3384, f. 72
holding: M. 754, f. 78; Trinity B.11.22, f. 79 (in basket)
issuing from (Jonah reference?): Cloisters 54.1.2, f. 171 (devoured by? above, hybrid bishop)
issuing from, with gittern, woman emerging from fish dancing: Y.T. 8, f. 256v
reaching in water for: G.K.S. 3384, f. 8
selling to woman and boy: W. 759, f. 108 (*fig. 185*)
stealing from basket on companion's back: W. 88, f. 153v
Man and fly (*cf.* Man and butterfly)
aiming slingshot at: G.K.S. 3384, f. 88
fighting with spear: Add. 49622, f. 7v (nude save for cape) (*fig. 353*)
pursuing: BBR 9411-26, ff. 126 (with sword), 131
sticking out tongue at: Add. 42130, f. 36v (hybrid) (*fig. 349*)
Man and fox (*see also* Man and serpent, asleep; *Roman de Renart:* fox and man)
carrying on his back upside down: Rutland Ps., f. 50v
hunting with bow and arrow: Add. 49622, ff. 55 (shooting), 103 (fox with goose); BBR 9961-62, f. 14 (*fig. 388*)
hunting with horns, hounds, digging out of burrow with spades: Royal 2 B.VII, ff. 174v-175 (2)
hunting with hounds: Add. 42130, f. 64v (preparing to unleash two hounds)
in basket on back of fox: Y.T. 8, f. 269 (4)
pursuing with ax and horn, fox stalking goose: Add. 42130, f. 66v
pursuing with club, fox with duck: Royal 2 B.VII, f. 160 (2)
pursuing with distaff and spindle, fox with cock: fr. 25526, f. 91
pursuing with flail, fox with goose: Harley 6563, ff. 60v-61

M

pursuing with paddle, fox with cock: W. 88, f. 58v (bald)
pursuing with pitchfork, woman with distaff and spindle, fox with cock: Fitz. 298, f. 1v (man half-nude)
with fox by tail (proverb?): Add. 10294, f. 1 (above, owl)
with pipe and tabor, ape-king with trumpet, fox dancing: Cambrai 103, f. 529
wrestling with: Y.T. 8, f. 179
Man and frog, fishing for: G.K.S. 3384, f. 15v
Man and geese
herding: Nancy 249, f. 189
waving hood and club at hawk circling above: Add. 42130, f. 169v
Man and giant (*cf.* Giant)
confronting with greens, giant with holes in knees of trousers fallen on his back (riddle? *cf.* Man with greens): Chantilly 64, ff. 27, 27v
with bagpipe, pulling head of giant on rope (David and Goliath reference?): BBR 9391, f. 4 (Ps. 1)
Man and goat (*see also* Exemplum [*figs. 351, 352*]; Man and dog, training, with hand bells; Man nude, and; Woman and lion, astride, with garland)
astride
goat with blue horns, labeled "Marculf": M. 812, f. 30
tilting with man astride goat: W. 104, f. 10v
with owl (*cf.* Ape as falconer, astride goat): Rothschild MS., f. 134 (two birds flying toward owl)
with sword and shield, charged by man with spear: Rothschild MS., f. 164
balancing basin on two sticks, goat on hind legs: Bodley 264, f. 130
dancing with: Rothschild MS., f. 184v
fighting: Yale MS., f. 56 (hybrid goat)
hunting with bow and arrow: W. 37, ff. 27v-28
warding off, holding horns (*cf.* Man and ram): Rothschild MS., f. 134v
with pipe and tabor, goat on hind legs: Bodley 264, f. 91v
Man and griffin, conversing(?) with: Cambrai 103, f. 100v (at L., men fighting with swords and bucklers)
Man and hare (*see also* Hare and man; Knight and hare; Tailor and hare)
beaten by, with club: Trinity B.11.22, f. 121v
beheaded by: Royal 10 E.IV, f. 61v
beheading: Trinity B.11.22, f. 90v
brought before ape-judge by: Royal 10 E.IV, f. 60v (ff. 60, tied; 61, dragged to gallows by hares)
carrying in basket on back: Y.T. 8, f. 268 (two, one blowing horn)
carrying on shoulders, hare blowing horn: Fitz. 298, f. 42
carrying, tied to stick across shoulder: Add. 49622, ff. 140, 145v (cleric; above, ?cleric warning fox to keep away from duck); BBR 10607, f. 13v (two hounds pursuing second hare) (*fig. 363*); Douce 6, f. 126; Fitz. 298, f. 77v; fr. 25526, f. 108v; Royal 2 B.VII, ff. 170v-171 (after hunting with bow and arrow); Trinity B.11.22, f. 209; W. 87, f. 59v; Y.T. 8, f. 261 (tied to spear)
confronting with sword and buckler: Princeton 44-18, ff. 129v-130 (*fig. 360*)
conversing with: Add. 49622, f. 56
defending castle against *see* Castle attacked by hares (*fig. 354*)
dragged by: Fitz. 298, f. 38 (clutching hood; tailor?); Royal 10 E.IV, f. 61 (to gallows; ff. 60-60v, tied, brought before ape-judge)
dropping sword before *see* Knight and hare, frightened by
feeding from dish
brandishing club: Cloisters 54.1.2, f. 16v
seizing by ears (*see also below,* —, seizing): G.K.S. 3384, f. 231 (below, man hunting hare with bow and arrow)
fighting with bow and arrow, hare with club and shield: Fitz. 298, ff. 11v, 85v
fighting with clubs and shields: Add. 17868, f. 155; Fitz. 298, f. 104v
fighting with rake, hare with spear: Trinity B.11.22, f. 99v
fighting with sword and buckler: M. 149, f. 346
fighting with sword and buckler, hare with club and shield: BBR 329-41, f. 47; Stowe 17, f. 240v
fighting with sword, seizing by ears (*see also below,* —, seizing): Fitz. 298, f. 134
flayed by: Fitz. 298, f. 74
frightened by: Stowe 17, f. 77v; Trinity B.11.22, f. 114v (*fig. 355*)
dropping sword: Add. 17868, ff. 35, 41, 159 (f. 158v, dog pursuing hare); latin 14284, f. 1v
turning to run from: Princeton 44-18, ff. 143v-144

holding hindquarters of hare running with purse around neck: Douce 6, f. 96v
hunted by: Add. 17868, f. 159; W. 109, f. 168 (man with horn and hound) (*fig. 358*)
  carried on stick across shoulder: BBR 10607, ff. 40v, 150 (another hare hunting man with horn and hound) (*fig. 357*); Bodley 264, f. 81v (at R., two hares, one with crossbow) (*fig. 356*); Chartres 549, f. 216v; Nancy 249, f. 1v; Trinity B.11.22, f. 28; Y.T. 8, f. 288 (tailor)
  with bow and horn: Harley 6563, ff. 97v-98
hunting, pursuing (*see also above,* — carrying): BBR 9411-26, f. 118; G.K.S. 3384, f. 275v (at R., man with hand organ); Stowe 17, f. 252v (astride horse)
hunting with basket, large black sack: G.K.S. 3384, f. 7v (above, man with harp)
hunting with bow and arrow: Add. 17868, ff. 32, 61; Add. 24681, ff. 41v-42; Add. 49622, ff. 18, 132v, 138, 156, 183, 216; Arras 1043, f. 128; Ashmole 828, ff. 5, 44v; BBR 9961-62, f. 47; Bodley 264, ff. 62v (two), 90 (and stag); Cambridge Dd. 5.5, f. 236; Christ Church E.II, f. 54v; Cracow 815, ff. 107, 213, 235; Douce 5, f. 162v (at. R., man with glove); Douce 6, f. 122v; Douce 118, f. 69 (half-figure); Fitz. 298, ff. 11v (hare with club and shield), 85v (the same); fr. 95, f. 297v; fr. 776, ff. 126 (hybrid), 165; fr. 6447, f. 10; G.K.S. 3384, ff. 49v, 59v, 194, 231 (at. R., man feeding hare); Kraus 75/88, f. 138v; Lambeth 75, f. 1 (at L., ape-falconer astride goat with owl on wrist) (*fig. 32*); latin 16260, f. 227v; M. 183, f. 38; Melbourne 1254/3, f. 30v (winged headdress); Princeton 44-18, ff. 155v-156 (with horn, astride horse), 197v-198 (2, astride horses, one with falcon), 202v-203; Rothschild MS., f. 145v; Royal 1 D.I, ff. 1 (*fig. 125*), 5; Rutland Ps., f. 57v (*fig. 362*); W. 37, f. 28; W. 82, f. 181v; W. 88, f. 128; W. 90, f. 90; W. 104, f. 16v; W. 109, f. 9; Y.T. 8, f. 24v; Y.T. 75, f. 148v; Yale MS., ff. 98, 174v, 267v, 286
hunting with club: C.B. 62, f. 181v (three-faced human head observing chase around margins) (*fig. 366*); Douce 6, ff. 12v (three hares in burrows, two disappearing, one emerging), 24v, 112; fr. 25526, f. 162 (upper margin, two hybrid men sticking out tongues at each other); G.K.S. 3384, ff. 71v, 144 (at L., knight with club fighting hare); W. 82, f. 210v
hunting with club, horn, hound: Add. 36684, f. 69 (two); Douce 5, f. 152; Douce 118, ff. 59, 86v; Fitz. 288, f. 159v; fr. 776, ff. 41 (astride horse), 154v, 205v; Glazier 24, f. 103v (*fig. 361*); Holkham 458, f. 41 (7, also with bow and ?trap); Melbourne 1254/3, f. 18v; Princeton 44-18, ff. 178v-179; Royal 2 B.VII, ff. 170v-171 (returning home with hare on stick across shoulder)
hunting with drum, horn, hound: fr. 25526, ff. 64-64v
hunting with horn: Glazier 24, ff. 46, 103v
hunting with horn and hound: Add. 10292, f. 76; BBR 9157, f. 1 (falconer, astride horse, also hunting stag); BBR 9961-62, f. 47; M. 183, f. 38; M. 754, ff. 1, 24; St. Omer 595, f. 1 (astride horse; at L., hound pursuing stag in opposite direction); Stowe 17, f. 239v; Verdun 107, f. 13 (*fig. 364*); Vienna 2542, f. 154; W. 82, f. 185; W. 88, ff. 4 (January), 157v
hunting with hound: BBR 10607, f. 13v (hare on stick across shoulder); Royal 2 B.VII, ff. 153v, 154; Trinity B.11.22, f. 75v
hunting with net: Add. 49622, f. 132v (before burrow)
hunting with sack: G.K.S. 3384, f. 7v (and basket); Trinity B.11.22, f. 180
hunting with spear: Add. 10293, f. 1; Add. 38114, f. 5; Ashmole 828, f. 16; G.K.S. 3384, f. 37 (*fig. 322*); Melbourne 1254/3, ff. 108v (with horn, hounds), 112v (the same); W. 90, ff. 163 (with horn), 216 (with horn, hounds)
hunting with sword: G.K.S. 3384, f. 209; Princeton 44-18, ff. 129v-130 (*fig. 360*), 155
imprisoned by, hands tied, holding hood: Fitz. 298, f. 48 (tailor, hair standing on end) (*fig. 365*)
killed by
  with crossbow (*cf.* Man and hare, hunted by): Bodley 264, f. 81v
  with spear or needle: Fitz. 298, ff. 34v, 47, 106 (tailor)
  with sword: Fitz. 298, f. 49v; Verdun 107, f. 96v; Y.T. 8, f. 327
killing with spear: G.K.S. 3384, f. 37
kissed by: Fitz. 298, f. 37 (kiss of death?)
leading on rope; Add. 49622, f. 209 (with whip); Fitz. 298, f. 72

ridden by: Metz 43, two photographs; Verdun 107, f. 105; Y.T. 8, f. 261v
seizing by ears: Fitz. 298, ff. 113 (tailed, hooded), 134 (fighting with sword); G.K.S. 3384, ff. 26 (at L., ape tilting at quintain), 65 (at L., man hunting stag), 231 (feeding hare from dish)
shot by
dropping bow and arrow, horn: Royal 10 E.IV, f. 59v
with crossbow, carried on stick across shoulder: Bodley 264, f. 81v
strangling: Trinity B.11.22, f. 38v
swinging on rope wound on pulley: Add. 36684, f. 144
threatened by
with club: Y.T. 8, ff. 192 (tailor kneeling, presenting his shears), 310 (holding rope tied around man's neck, hands also tied), 322 (pulling back garment of beseeching man, exposing fur lining)
with switch, beseeching, lying on ground; hare standing on his stomach: Y.T. 8, f. 304
threatening with stick: Add. 49622, f. 130
tied by: Royal 10 E.IV, f. 60 (ff. 60v-61, brought before ape-judge, dragged to gallows)
unsheathing sword before: latin 14284, f. 58v
with hand organ, hare standing on ears (headstand): Fitz. 298, f. 115
with horn and spear confronting hare with trumpet: Melbourne 1254/3, f. 121v
with pipe and tabor
hare running: Cambridge Dd. 5.5, f. 199
hare tilting at quintain: Trinity B.11.22, f. 214
with switch, dog on leash, lion chained to post, hare at side: Melbourne 1254/3, f. 124
with vielle, hare (squirrel?) dancing, ape doing handstand: Douce 118, f. 101
wrestling with Y.T. 8, f. 352
Man and horse (*cf.* King and horse; Knight and horse)
astride (*see also* Falconer astride horse; Man and hare, hunting with horn; Man and stag, hunting; Windmill): Chantilly 64, ff. 120 (twisting its tail), 120v (the same); Yale MS., f. 272v
astride collapsing horse (Futility? Pride? *cf.* King and horse): Princeton 44-18, f. 5
astride horse lying on ground: Chantilly 64, ff. 60, 60v
carrying, followed by man catching dung in raised hem of robe (proverb?): W. 82, f. 52
carrying through deep water (fable or proverb? *cf.* Hybrid man and doe; Man and ass): Douce 5, f. 147 (at R., goat on hind legs nibbling foliage; above, man with spear)
currying with comb: Jacquemart 1, f. 14v
driving: Add. 42130, f. 201 (water-carrier)
falling from (Pride? *see also* Man and woman, helped): Add. 42130, f. 53
killing with sword: Cambrai 87, f. 47
leading horse pulling cart: BBR 1175, ff. 8v (toward tavern) (*fig. 375*), 14, 85v, 98v, 116v
training
at L., lion with pipe and tabor, bear dancing: Hague 78.D.40, f. 39
to kick buckler: Add. 42130, f. 63v (holding sword); Bodley 264, ff. 73 (three children pointing at ape tied to post) (*fig. 374*), 96v; Douce 5, f. 98v (beside ape astride horse); W. 109, f. 141; Y.T. 8, f. 177v (holding club)
to stand on hind legs, with pipe and tabor; at L., bear tied to post: Royal 20 D.IV, f. 237v
Man and hybrid bird
astride: W. 88, f. 46v (cock? *cf.* Knight and cock)
confronting with slingshot: Arras 47, f. 224
confronting with sword and shield: Arras 47, f. 54
Man and hybrid bishop
astride with reel and spindle: W. 88, f. 124v
fighting with sword and buckler: W. 39, f. 13 (Hybrid bishop?)
Man and hybrid dragon, astride: Tournai Ps., ff. 20 (holding goat's head and whip, led by ape with club) (*fig. 369*), 80v (holding the same) (*fig. 370*), 101v (holding the same) (*fig. 371*), 211v (holding the same, ape offering bird in nest or bowl) (*fig. 372*)
Man and hybrid king, aiming ax at (or at border stalk; *cf.* Man pruning): latin 10483, f. 29v
Man and hybrid knight, charging with sword: fr. 776, f. 177v
Man and hybrid man (*see also* Hybrid man and man)
astride, with pipe and tabor: Cloisters 54.1.2, f. 16
balancing on shoulders of: Add. 42130, ff. 168, 188; W. 88, f. 89v
bending crossbow at: Cloisters 54.1.2, f. 153
charging with sword: BBR 10607, f. 150 (*fig. 357*); fr. 95, f. 199v (two swords; hybrid man nude with devil's head) (*fig. 367*)

confronted by, with sword and buckler: W. 88, f. 148v
confronting with club: W. 88, f. 27
fighting with club, hybrid man with shield: W. 88, f. 99
fighting with spears and shields: M. 729, f. 258v
fighting with sword and buckler: Cloisters 54.1.2, f. 21v; latin 10484, ff. 26v-27 (in center, dragon); latin 14284, throughout; Princeton 44-18, f. 108; W. 88, ff. 48v, 158v; W. 761, f. 253v; Yale MS., f. 39v (2)
fighting with swords and bucklers: Arras 1043, f. 114
kneeling before hybrid man with spear: M. 155, f. 149
pulling tail of: W. 88, f. 121 (basket on back containing two apes)
seated on
holding top of distaff held by hybrid man below: Cloisters 54.1.2, f. 168
shooting arrow up: Cloisters 54.1.2, f. 163
shooting: BBR 9427, f. 81v (hybrid man headless, holding head and sword); fr. 95, ff. 113v (hybrid man wearing doctor's cap), 311 (hybrid man horned; satyr?) (*fig. 368*); fr. 776, f. 167v; latin 10483, ff. 7v-8; W. 104, f. 12v (second hybrid man with pipe and tabor); W. 109, f. 9; Y.T. 15, f. 20
standing on, with spear piercing head of beast: W. 88, f. 172
threatening with ax, hybrid man protesting: latin 14284, f. 7 (at R., sheep)

Man and hybrid nun (praying), conversing with: W. 88, f. 60v

Man and hybrid woman
seated on, embracing: Cloisters 54.1.2, f. 52
shooting: latin 14284, f. 52v

Man and knight (*see also* Man and dragon, astride backwards)
bending crossbow at: Fitz. 298, f. 1 (winged headdress; knight astride horse; dog with trumpet)
charged by, knight with sword astride horse: Yale MS., f. 348 (man old, bearded)
charged by three knights with swords: Add. 42130, f. 162v (Ps. 88, v. 44)
fighting with ax, knight with sword: fr. 776, f. 126 (issuing from border)
fighting with spear and buckler: W. 45, f. 13v
fighting with sword and buckler, knight with spear: latin 14284, f. 60
fighting with sword and buckler, knight with sword: fr. 95, f. 268 (2; all issuing from border)
offering cup to, before inn: Bodley 264, f. 158v
shooting (fabliau? *cf.* Hybrid knight and man; Solomon, judgment of): Cambrai 102, f. 339v (2, knight tied to tree, praying) (*fig. 376*); fr. 95, f. 268 (knight with crocket); Princeton 44-18, ff. 46v-47 (knight lying under tree)

Man and lamb *see* Man and sheep; Man with greens

Man and lion (*see also* Man nude, and lion)
aiming sword at lion and whelp in initial: Cloisters 54.1.2, f. 47
astride, charging kneeling man with sword and shield: fr. 776, f. 246
astride with trumpet: Cambrai 87, f. 43v; W. 88, f. 96 (hybrid lion)
carried by (fabliau?): Add. 24686, f. 17 (at R., knight slaying giant) (*fig. 211*)
eating from plate set on table on lion's back: Nancy 249, f. 137 (at L., fighting with sword)
fighting with club and shield: Add. 17868, f. 156v; Douce 5, f. 180v; M. 754, f. 258 (no shield; at L., hedgehog, hare pursuing dog); W. 88, f. 104 (at L., head of bishop looking on); W. 109, f. 372
fighting with mace(?): Douce 5, f. 112
fighting with spear: Hague 78 D.40, ff. 35 (half-nude), 73 (half-nude); Princeton 44-18, ff. 23v-24; Rylands lat R.117, f. 236; Yale MS., f. 66
fighting with sword: Add. 24686, f. 18v (above, lizard, dragon; Ps. 7:1-2) (*figs. 377-378*); Add. 50000, f. 235; Christ Church E.II, f. 29 (unsheathing sword); Douce 5, f. 23; G.K.S. 3384, f. 279v; latin 16260, f. 592v (winged headdress); Nancy 249, f. 137 (at R., man eating from plate set on table on lion's back); Princeton 44-18, ff. 131v-132, 177 (f. 176v, hare); St. Omer 5, f. 220v (nude save for hood); W. 45, f. 116 (above, male siren with sword fighting dog); Yale MS., ff. 31, 357v
holding dog up to, brandishing whip: Royal 2 B.VII, f. 183
hunting with club and horn: Yale MS., f. 132v
in lionskin *see* Hercules
issuing from mouth of, praying (*cf.* Man and fish, emerging): latin 10484, f. 233

killing with hammer, dragon biting lion's tail: Cloisters 54.1.2, f. 36 (hybrid)
killing with sword: Add. 38114, f. 107v (in lion's jaws); C.B. 62, f. 48; Cambrai 87, f. 47 (astride white horse); fr. 95 f. 242; G.K.S. 3384, f. 152; latin 14284, f. 37v; M. 796, f. 1 (at R., half-nude man with spear); N.K.S. 41, f. 132
patting(?): W. 88, f. 188v (dog?)
rending *see* Samson
shooting: Cambrai 103, f. 105v; Christ Church E.II, f. 29v (with crossbow); M. 796, f. 21v; W. 109, f. 403 (confronting with bow and arrow)
standing on, brandishing club at border dragon: latin 14284, f. 60v (at R., woman with arms outstretched)
training, leading on leash: BBR 9157, f. 4v (two apes also on leash, man in drawers aiming bellows at hindquarters of ape); Douce 118, f. 124 (lion tied to post, dog standing on hind feet); G.K.S. 3384, f. 231v; Montpellier H. 196, f. 64 (with club and whip); Trinity B.11.22, f. 163 (with dog); W. 109, f. 277 (second man with cat or tiger on leash)
with bagpipe, barefoot, accompanied by lion: latin 16260, f. 5v
wrestling with: All Souls Lat. 6, f. 13

Man and man (nude, wearing small hat, face painted white and red like clown's), addressing: latin 14284, f. 61 (with staff)

Man and monster (*cf.* Man and beast; — and dragon)
astride, beating with club to which key is attached: Add. 42130, f. 166
astride with pipe: latin 10483, f. 62v
feeding with rolls from baker's tray: G.K.S. 3384, f. 168
fighting with sword: G.K.S. 3384, f. 61 (aimed at head); latin 10483, f. 49v (2; in center, owl)
head in jaws of: Douce 5, f. 166 (with sword, surprised; at L., stag running toward him)
offering ring to, falconer riding off with lady: latin 14284, f. 35
shooting: Douce 6, f. 117 (head of); Royal 10 E.IV, f. 128 (multiheaded); Spencer 2, f. 263v; St. Omer 5, ff. 268v (with crossbow), 273 (winged monster)
shot by: fr. 95, f. 321; St. Omer 5, f. 273v; W. 37, ff. 54v-55
with bowl, monster vomiting into (*cf.* Vomiting, references under): G.K.S. 3384, f. 62
with head of, in bowl: Douce 5, f. 176 (head of sheep?)
with head of, in hands: Douce 5, f. 112
with pincers and pointed cap; behind him monster with club and shield: Add. 42130, f. 58v
with sword, killing five-headed monster (*see also above,* —, fighting): Douce 366, f. 128

Man and mouse, holding stick, mouse walking along: G.K.S. 3384, f. 25v (squirrel?)

Man and nun *see* Nun and man; Obscaena, defecating: man

Man and owl
casting stones at: M. 183, f. 38
shooting: BBR 9961-62, f. 14 (*fig. 388*); Cambridge Dd. 5.5, f. 13; Fitz. 288, ff. 153v (Min.: Crucifixion), 170 (owl-type), 210 (Min.: Virgin, devil, and Theophilus); latin 3893, f. 206; latin 10483, f. 214 (at R., group of men pointing at Isaiah in initial); Liège 431, f. 56 (*fig. 379*); M. 796, f. 54v; Royal 1 B.XII, f. 153v
trapping birds with owl decoy: Arundel 83, f. 14 (hiding under bush; at L., stag and doe under tree; at R., hare); Bodley 264, f. 119 (*fig. 338*)
with owl on wrist (parody of falconer? *cf.* Ape as falconer holding): fr. 95, f. 199v (in gold robe); G.K.S. 3384, f. 31; Rothschild MS., f. 134 (two birds flying toward owl, ?mobbing, man astride goat)

Man and ox, astride, with forked stick across shoulder: Add. 42130, f. 62 (at L., two men wrestling pickaback)

Man and parrot
in drawers, reaching for: fr. 25526, f. 136 (parrot?)
shooting: Add. 42130, f. 215 (at R., man and woman conversing)

Man and pig
astride, playing jawbone with bundle of reeds: Trinity B.11.22, f. 38v
confronting with ax: Jacquemart 1, f. 26v; W. 88, f. 13v (f. 14, November; man feeding pig)
fighting with spear: Cambrai 103, f. 89v (boar?)
killing with ax: Cloisters 54.1.2, f. 12v (December); fr. 25526, f. 85v; G.K.S. 3384, f. 24v; M. 754, f. 39v; Schilling MS., December
shooting: W. 88, f. 139

Man and pigs, beating down acorns from tree for: Add. 42130, f. 59v (*fig. 380*); Add. 49622, ff. 21v-22, 79, 102 (man with ax), 142v, 154; Chantilly 64, ff. 41, 41v (no pigs); Cloisters 54.1.2, f. 11v (November); Schilling MS., November; W. 88, ff. 45, 140v; W. 90, f. 12v (December); Y.T. 27, f. 12 (December)

Man and pilgrim, giving alms to pilgrim with bowl: G.K.S. 3384, f. 78

Man and ram

- astride backwards with club, hunting stag: Stowe 17, ff. 158v-159
- astride, upset by woman astride goat with spear: Y.T. 8, f. 224
- baiting with basket (*cf.* Woman and ram): Douce 5, f. 205v (below, man with spear killing beast); G.K.S. 3384, ff. 194, 208v, 219v; Nancy 249, f. 267v; Rothschild MS., f. 58v
- baiting with buckler: latin 3893, f. 276v; W. 85, f. 16v
- baiting with cloth: BBR 10607, f. 42v (green, board?) (*fig. 381a*); Douce 5, f. 1a v (*fig. 471*); fr. 25526, f. 149v; at L., man with sling-shot, butting rams); Kraus 75/88, f. 77 (board?); Stowe 17, f. 142 (orange-red)
- kneeling, charged by: W. 88, f. 51v
- warding off: latin 14284, ff. 11 (with foot), 64v (with knee); Rutland Ps., f. 72v (with foot); Y.T. 75, f. 25 (shepherd with stool)

Man and Saracen, fighting with club and shield: G.K.S. 3384, f. 225 (at L., ?devil playing spoon with bow)

Man and serpent

- asleep on hill beside serpent; at L., fox or wolf approaching: Rutland Ps., f. 110 (*fig. 382*)
- climbing border stalk, followed by: M. 183, f. 242
- coiled around neck: W. 87, f. 54v (conical cap; below, nude man brandishing scourge)
- confronting with slingshot: Add. 42130, f. 36
- encircled by (Laocoön?): M. 729, f. 273 (above, double-headed eagle with bat wings) (*fig. 383*)
- with serpent in either hand: Rutland Ps., f. 79v
- with serpent in left hand
  - book in other: W. 87, f. 20v
  - sword in other: Cloisters 54.1.2, f. 153

Man and sheep (*see also* Hybrid man and; Man and ram; — and wolf, pursuing; Shepherd)

- milking in pen, two women walking off at R. with jugs on heads: Add. 42130, f. 163v (*fig. 381*)
- on shoulders (*cf.* Noah entering): Douce 6, f. 137 (below, crowned ?sheep's head looking up); G.K.S. 3384, f. 149 (*fig. 481*); W. 45, f. 91v (hybrid man); W. 85, f. 66
- shooting: BBR 9961-62, f. 26
- with head of, in hands (*cf.* Woman with head of sheep): Douce 5, f. 176 (head of monster?); G.K.S. 3384, ff. 25, 64v; W. 85, f. 91 (and pole)

Man and siren

- approaching with club: Rutland Ps., f. 107 (half-nude, siren with winged headdress)
- confronting with sword and buckler: W. 104, f. 21v
- shooting, male siren with club and shield: Y.T. 8, f. 292v

Man and snail (*see also* Knight and snail; Man nude, and —)

- astride, hunting stag: Fitz. 298, f. 46v
- astride with spear and shield, fighting hybrid bishop with sword and shield: Jacquemart 1, f. 122
- beseeching, armed with crossbow, spear, sword, and dagger: Y.T. 27, f. 31b
- beseeching with sword on his head: Bodley 264, f. 27v
- fighting with ax: Add. 49622, f. 180v; BBR 9411-26, f. 104; Chantilly 64, f. 33
- fighting with club: Harley 6563, ff. 61v-62
- fighting with slingshot: Douce 366, f. 38 (hybrid man); Royal 10 E.IV, f. 45
- fighting with spear: Cambrai 102, f. 354 (at R., hybrid knight with club and buckler fighting lion); Rothschild MS., f. 187 (attacking from behind); Rutland Ps., f. 48; W. 45, ff. 40v (and shield; below, falcon striking bird), 52v (and shield); W. 90, f. 151 (at L., hare; at R., dog, two men with bagpipe and psaltery)
- fighting with sword: G.K.S. 3384, ff. 63, 125, 219v, 278v, 324; Hague 78.D.40, f. 16v (at R., woman with distaff and spindle); Jesus 40, f. 71v (falchion; second small snail crawling along outstretched arm toward head of irate man); latin 3893, f. 169 (at R., hare); M. 88, f. 60v (snail on hillock from which hare emerges); N.K.S. 41, ff. 85v-86 (*fig. 384*)
- frightened by: BBR 9411-26, f. 105 (*fig. 385*);

Douce 366, f. 109; Stowe 17, f. 272 (woman/snail)
frightened by
dropping sword: Harley 6563, ff. 62v-63
riding away from (with sword): Cambrai 87, f. 50v
throwing up hands: latin 10483, f. 42
killing with spear: Chantilly 64, ff. 174, 174v
Man and snake *see* Man and serpent
Man and spider, striking with sword: BBR 9411-26, f. 126
Man and squirrel
as pet *see* Squirrel
balancing in basin atop pole: C.B. 61, f. 136
bending crossbow at: latin 14284, f. 66v
confronting with two candlesticks, squirrel ringing two bells on ropes: Douce 118, f. 124v (cleric?)
hunting with bow and sling: Royal 10 E.IV, f. 158 (2)
shooting: Y.T. 13, f. 187v
Man and stag
driving, leading on rope: Add. 49622, ff. 158 (with whip), 195v (the same); BBR 10607, f. 236v
hunting with arrow: Hague XX, f. 250
hunting with bow and arrow: Ashmole 828, f. 13 (below, ape with trumpet); BBR 9427, f. 214; BBR 9961-62, f. 14 (3; others with club and ax) (*fig. 388*); Bodley 264, f. 90 (and hare); Cambrai 103, f. 335v (shooting); Chantilly 62, f. 14v; Christ Church E.II, ff. 38, 50; Douce 5, f. 4v (May; above, man unsheathing sword, owl); Fitz. 242, f. 29; fr. 95, f. 39; fr. 776, f. 246; Hague 78.D.40, f. 177; latin 1076, f. 36; M. 796, f. 47 (winged headdress; dog pursuing hare); Melbourne 1254/3, ff. 87v-88; Princeton 44-18, ff. 127v-128; Royal 2 B.VII, ff. 151v-152 (and hounds); Royal 10 E.IV, f. 153v; W. 90, f. 100; Y.T. 8, ff. 45v (and hare), 197, 200
hunting with club: BBR 9433-34, f. 97 (partly erased); Douce 118, ff. 23v-24; fr. 776, f. 4; fr. 25526, f. 57 (3); Hague XX, f. 95v (and horn); Kraus 75/88, f. 19v (issuing from border); latin 14284, f. 64 (and horn); Laud Lat. 84, f. 153v; Melbourne 1254/3, ff. 28v, 32v; W. 82, f. 188 (and horn)
hunting with club, horn, and hounds: BBR 10607, f. 90; Cambrai 103, ff. 21, 39; Douce 118, ff. 108, 132v; Royal 2 B.VII, ff. 154v-155, 171v-172 (2, one with ax); W. 760, f. 152 (beaver? at L., elephant; all erased)
hunting with club, horn, hounds, astride stag backwards: W. 45, f. 70v (nude) (*fig. 386*)
hunting with crossbow: Princeton 44-18, ff. 69v-70
hunting with horn: Douce 118, ff. 47v-48; latin 14284, ff. 16v, 19v; latin 16260, f. 5v; Laud Lat. 84, f. 19; Montpellier H.196, ff. 246, 270 (astride horse); Royal 14 E.III, f. 3 (2, one astride horse; below, owl); Trinity B.11.22, f. 35v (2); Verdun 107, f. 12
hunting with horn and hounds: C.B. 62, ff. 15, 76; Fitz. 298, f. 46v (astride snail); fr. 95, f. 152; Hague 78.D.40, ff. 37v, 65; Melbourne 1254/3, f. 92v (astride horse); Royal 2 B.VII, f. 150v (astride horse); W. 104, ff. 19, 39v (astride horse); Yale MS., ff. 1, 66v, 209, 257v, 293
hunting with hound: G.K.S. 3384, ff. 65 (at R., man seizing hare's ears), 191, 235v
hunting with pipe and tabor, two hounds: Harley 616, f. 1
hunting with slingshot: Add. 49622, f. 74v
hunting with spear: Cambrai 102, f. 391 (and horn, hound) (*fig. 387*); fr. 25526, f. 42v (accompanied by woman); M. 155, f. 81v (2, one with sword, hounds); Princeton 44-18, f. 20v
threatening with switch: Douce 6, f. 104v (stag couchant)
Man and stork (*cf.* Man and crane; Obscaena; Pygmy)
eye pierced by: G.K.S. 3384, f. 238
feeding pellet from bowl (*cf.* Man feeding stork): G.K.S. 3384, f. 164
fighting man, with swords and bucklers, two storks seizing swords: Y.T. 8, f. 24v
fighting with ax: Cambridge Dd. 5.5, f. 217v; Corpus Christi E.II, f. 55v
fighting with club: BBR 10607, f. 91; G.K.S. 3384, ff. 107 (and buckler), 217v (and buckler, stork with frog in beak; below, knight with spear and buckler fighting bird)
fighting with sword: Fitz. 298, f. 56v (and buckler); Y.T. 8, f. 307 (stork wearing kerchief)
hand bitten by: Douce 5, f. 182; Douce 118, f. 38v (at L., ?goat with processional cross)
holding head of stork under arm while drinking: G.K.S. 3384, f. 112
hunting stork nesting (*cf.* Man and bird hunt-

  - ing): W. 82, f. 87v (2, on ladder; at L., dog pursuing stag)
  - offering chalice and wafer to: Jacquemart 1, f. 41v (seated)
  - reading, stork(?) looking over his shoulder (*cf.* Fox and hare): G.K.S. 3384, f. 172 (*fig. 389*)
  - shooting: Add: 30029, f. 47v (stork/cock); Add. 38115, f. 51; Egerton 1151, f. 95v; latin 3893, f. 151v (?pelican, web feet); latin 16260, f. 273 (hybrid; frog in stork's beak) (*fig. 390*); Melbourne 1254/3, ff. 28v, 94v-95; St. Omer 5, ff. 243, 281 (at side, knight shooting winged monster); W. 82, f. 195
- Man and swan *see* Man with harp before swan; Swan
- Man and thief
  - capturing cutpurse: Add. 49622, f. 153 (*fig. 409*)
  - capturing grape thief: Add. 49622, f. 155v (soldier)
  - threatening with club boy eating cherries in tree: Add. 42130, f. 196v
- Man and tiger *see* Man and lion, training
- Man and unicorn (*see also* Unicorn, Bestiary representation)
  - aiming switch at head of: G.K.S. 3384, f. 135
  - astride, beating with stick: Chantilly 64, ff. 100, 100v
  - fighting with club: Douce 6, ff. 143, 172
  - fighting with spear: Cloisters 54.1.2, f. 177
  - fighting with sword and shield: Y.T. 8, f. 324
  - holding wicker trap over, with spear: Cloisters 54.1.2, f. 177 (hybrid; below, hare)
  - hunting with club, horn, hound: W. 82, f. 62v (ape astride unicorn) (*fig. 391*)
  - hunting with horn, two hounds: Cambrai 103, f. 319
  - hunting with sword and shield: G.K.S. 3384, f. 203
  - killing with spear: Add. 39810, f. 7 (*fig. 140*)
  - seizing by horn: Douce 6, f. 151
  - warding off with basket (*cf.* Man and ram): G.K.S. 3384, f. 247v
- Man and wivern, shooting: Y.T. 15, f. 284
- Man and wolf (*see also* Man and serpent, asleep; Man with greens)
  - fighting with sword and buckler: Rutland Ps., f. 85v
  - killing pack of (part of unidentified fabliau sequence): Royal 10 E.IV, f. 296
  - killing with ax: BBR 10607, f. 158v (wolf?)
  - pursuing with hound, wolf with sheep in mouth: Douce 48, f. 209 (above, angel with trumpet; Min: Annunciation to shepherds)
- Man and woman (*cf.* Woman, references under)
  - approaching: BBR 9217, f. 205 (above, camel and dog)
  - asleep with head in her lap: Douce 6, f. 80 (above, Eros, couple embracing); Trinity B.11.22, f. 164v (below, man crowning woman with garland)
  - astride horses, hunting stag: fr. 25526, ff. 42, 42v (man with spear, woman riding sidesaddle)
  - at school *see* School
  - at well, woman brandishing distaff; at R., man brandishing huge ladle before woman: Hague 78.D.40, f. 40
  - baking, putting bread in oven: W. 88, f. 14v (December; f. 15, two women kneading dough)
  - bathing (*cf.* Man bathing; Man nude, bathing): Bodley 264, f. 75 (at L., bathhouse) (*fig. 392*); Chartres 549, f. 10 (man bringing two water buckets); Rothschild MS., f. 168; Tournai Ps., f. 233v; Trinity B.11.22, f. 215; W. 88, f. 75v
  - beaten by: Add. 42130, ff. 60 (with distaff), 169 (with *godendag;* Ps. 93, v. 6); Cambridge Dd. 5.5, f. 397 (*fig. 394*); Cloisters 54.1.2, f. 17 (with spoon); Princeton 44-18, f. 9 (with club); Royal 10 E.IV, ff. 142v-148 (*Wright's Chaste Wife* sequence)
  - before Eros, embracing: Douce 6, f. 80 (Eros with garland; below, man asleep with head in woman's lap)
    - in tree, embracing; woman with lapdog, hare between couple, bird at either side: Stowe 17, f. 273 (Eros flanked by two men with psaltery and vielle) (*fig. 397*)
    - in tree, kneeling, flanking; Eros aiming arrow at man: Trinity B.11.22, f. 30 (at R., two men with bagpipes, dragon with shawm) (*fig. 398*)
    - kneeling and praying, transfixed by arrows: Arras 139, f. 8 (*fig. 395*)
    - man approaching castle, greeted by woman in window: Douce 6, f. 126 (at L., Eros bending bow: man carrying hare on stick over shoulder, two dogs on leash)
    - man's head and hand grasped by Frau Minne: Douce 6, f. 159v (at R., man presenting bleeding heart transfixed by arrow to woman) (*fig. 402*)

M before Frau Minne *see* Cleric and woman, kneeling before; *below,* kneeling; *below,* standing before
bidden by woman to kill pig (*cf.* Man and pig): Trinity B.11.22, f. 25v
bombarded with flowers by: latin 10435, f. 61v
breaking up sod with mallets: Add. 42130, f. 171v (in agricultural cycle)
by fire, scolded by: Nancy 249, f. 271v
carrying pole: W. 88, f. 77
carrying poles across shoulder, basket or net attached to woman's pole: W. 109, f. 27v
confronted: BBR 9127, f. 205 (above, camel, dog); latin 10435, ff. 44v, 142 (under tree)
man reaching into purse, woman holding out her hands: Bodley 264, f. 61v
man with garland: Harley 6563, ff. 93v-94
man with hand on her breast: W. 88, f. 46
woman with falcon: Chantilly 62, f. 38v
confronting with basket, raised hand, under tree; woman holding up skirt containing small white round objects: BBR 9391, f. 110 (*fig. 399*)
confronting with club and bread(?), woman seated under tree: Princeton 44-18, f. 10v
confronting with garland: G.K.S. 3384, f. 232
confronting with garland, woman with vielle: M. 155, ff. 86v-87 (f. 87, hybrid knight bending crossbow at man)
conversing: Add. 42130, ff. 68, 215 (woman with three-lobed plant); Douce 5, f. 115v (old man; above, man creeping toward ape with offspring in arms, ?Bestiary variant) (*fig. 39*)
man astride horse: Nancy 249, f. 165v
seated: Auct. D.3.2, f. 238 (barefoot); Douce 5, f. 61 (above, butterfly); Royal 2 B.VII, ff. 200v and 201v (two couples on bench), f. 202 (three cupbearers)
cooking sequence: Royal 10 E.IV, ff. 108-109v
crowning with garland: Trinity B.11.22, f. 164v (below, man asleep in woman's lap)
dancing in pairs or groups (*see also* Man with bagpipe; — with vielle; Woman dancing): G.K.S. 3384, f. 117 (below, fox); Y.T. 8, ff. 7, 53 (3 women, man and woman with vielle and tabor)
hands joined by ribbons, man with mandola: Royal 2 B.VII, ff. 173v-174 (another with vielle, two couples), 189 (four men)
hands joined by ribbons, man with cymbals, two trumpeters: Royal 2 B.VII, ff. 178v-179 (two couples)
hands joined by ribbons, two women with tambourines: Royal 2 B.VII, ff. 181v-182 (two couples)
man with gittern; at R., woman and falconer: Bodley 264, f. 138 (two couples)
man with kettledrums on back, played by companion: Bodley 264, f. 58 (two men, three women holding hands)
men in costume as apes (or four apes), four women, two men with hand bells and tabor: Bodley 264, f. 110
men with kettledrums on back played by companion, vielle, hand organ: Bodley 264, f. 172v (three men, two women)
men with pipe and tabor, cymbals, hand bells: Bodley 264, f. 175 (two groups of dancers: seven men facing six women; six women and one man in circle)
men with pipe and tabor, vielle: Spencer 2, f. 161v
with ape, man beating drum with hands, three apes dancing with wild man: Bodley 264, f. 106 (two couples, second girl holding hand of ape who offers trilobed branch to bird)
directed by, two men bearing chest toward building: Douce 6, f. 100v (woman with purse) (*fig. 737*)
donors *see* Patrons
drinking under tree, attendant bringing silver flagon: Trinity B.11.22, f. 102
drinking, woman remonstrating: Harley 6563, ff. 66v-67
embracing: fr. 25526, ff. 5 (below, man and woman playing chess or checkers), 110 (at R., mermaid and merman embracing); Princeton 44-18, ff. 112 (at L., woman seated with lap dog), 127; Rylands fr. 2, f. 212 (*fig. 523*)
lying on grass: latin 3893, f. 234
man crowned, woman holding gold heart(?), lap dog: Stowe 17, f. 29v
man (half-nude) in fox costume, blowing trumpet: Chantilly 62, f. 201
man with mirror: Douce 6, f. 121 (above, ape)
observed by dog and lion: latin 10435, f. 108
under tree full of birds, woman with falcon, accompanied by pet dog: Y.T. 19, f. 18v

M

woman in bed: Douce 6, f. 160v (in building; at R., man and woman approaching; above, hare) (*fig. 404*)
woman with falcon: Chantilly 62, f. 38v; Y.T. 19, f. 18v (under tree full of birds, with pet dog)
emptying purse before young girl (*cf.* Cleric and woman): Add. 49622, f. 95 (*fig. 113*)
fighting (*see also* Proverbs: fight)
man astride ram upset by woman astride goat with spear: Y.T. 8, f. 224
man with basket and stick, woman with stool basket and tongs: Cloisters 54.1.2, f. 123v (another man grasping stick of male combatant)
with swords and bucklers: Add. 36684, f. 26v
following devil astride woman walking on all fours, pointing: Rutland Ps., f. 62
given enema by: W. 88, f. 81v
giving cloak to: G.K.S. 3384, f. 12v (two men?)
hawking *see* Falconer and woman
heads under hood (proverb? *cf.* Hood): Cloisters 54.1.2, f. 200
helped by, to climb on horse, then falling off into her arms: Jesus 40, f. 110
helping her remove her shoe (*Wright's Chaste Wife* sequence): Royal 10 E.IV, f. 146v
holding garland before (*cf. below,* —, kneeling; —, receiving): G.K.S. 3384, f. 232
holding in lap: Stowe 17, f. 143
hunting stag with spear: fr. 25526, f. 42v
in bed: fr. 25526, f. 63 (nude; at R., woman with large paddle, nude man approaching building; upper margin, hybrid physician)
intercourse: Merton 0.1.3, ff. 65v (at R., woman with child by fire; above, two hares) (*fig. 405*), 69v
kissing (*cf.* Hybrid man and hybrid woman; king and queen): BBR 9961-62, f. 72v (attendant holding horse); Bodley 264, ff. 20v (old man, young girl), 58, 69v, 76v; Cloisters 54.1.2, f. 31; Douce 5, f. 177 (at R., man brandishing club) (*fig. 216*); Douce 6, ff. 84v, 138; fr. 95, f. 13v; latin 10435, f. 78; Rylands fr. 2, f. 212; W. 82, f. 100 (heads issuing from border); Yale MS., ff. 29, 66v, 203 (heads only)
kneeling (*see also* Proverbs: gameboard; *cf. above,* —, before Frau Minne, references under): Douce 6, f. 89 (at L., woman receiving garland from hand)
in line ending, basket of flowers at her side; above, man holding architectural canopy); latin 10435, ff. 17v, 21v, 45, 46, 46v, 60v, 80, 107, 137, 147, 155, 158v, 163v, 166, 170; Tournai Ps., f. 102 (before man seated with hands raised)
kneeling before
beseeching, woman aiming arrow (Frau Minne? *cf. above,* —, before Frau Minne, references under): Princeton 44-18, f. 15 (*fig. 400*)
crowned with garland by: BBR 10607, f. 126; Kraus 75/88, f. 116; Yale MS., f. 110v
receiving garland from: Cambridge Dd. 5.5, ff. 199, 302; fr. 95, f. 249v; Jacquemart 1, f. 59; latin 10435, ff. 44v, 85v, 117, 146v, 168v; latin 10483, f. 135v; Nancy 249, f. 152; W. 85, f. 45v
woman aiming arrow, (Frau Minne?): fr. 95, f. 24v (with lap dog; at L., man with wheelbarrow containing woman) (*fig. 403*)
woman aiming spear, crowning him with garland and accompanied by child: Douce 118, f. 68v
woman piercing him with spear (Frau Minne?): Hague 78.D.40, f. 75 (both wearing chaplets)
woman with arrow and heart (Frau Minne?): Princeton 44-18, ff. 75v-76 (cleric)
woman with switch: Princeton 44-18, f. 79
woman with sword and buckler: Harley 6563, ff. 63v-64
kneeling with, before seated man with hands raised: Tournai Ps., f. 102
offered heart by, offering purse to: Bodley 264, f. 59 (*figs. 407, 408*)
offering cup to: BBR 9157, f. 428v (man winged; both issuing from border)
offering fish in bowl to: latin 10483, f. 49v
offering ring to (*cf.* Falconer and woman, riding): Add. 49622, f. 199v; Douce 366, f. 131; latin 10435, f. 73v (man nude, woman holding two leaves)
on horseback, both with chaplets, woman with lap dog: Stowe 17, f. 106 (at R., ape tied to tree) (*fig. 406*)
parting, man riding off behind man with spear: Douce 5, f. 3v (April; above, man with trumpet)
playing games *see* specific game
presenting cup to woman in doorway of building (fabliau? *cf.* Man and woman, offering): fr. 25526, f. 109

presenting with sword, shield, ring (fabliau?): Bodley 264, f. 83
pulled by, in boat, bleeding from neck (fabliau?): Nancy 249, f. 236
pursued by, with distaff: Cambridge Dd.5.5, ff. 207, 397 (at R., woman with large full basin held high over head; at L., man before structure gesturing to fleeing man)
pursuing fox *see* Man and fox
pursuing with distaff: latin 10484, f. 29v (hybrid woman)
pushing in wheelbarrow: fr. 95, ff. 24v (at R., woman with lap dog aiming arrow at kneeling man), 209v
reaping *see* Man reaping
receiving garland from (*cf. above,* —, kneeling before): latin 10483, f. 259v; latin 10484, f. 223 (with hands clasped); M. 729, f. 293 (man astride goat riding toward woman with garland astride lion)
saving from dragon: G.K.S. 3384, f. 102
sawing border stalk with: Bodley 264, f. 63v
scolded by *see* Man with mallet
scything *see* Man scything
seated at loom with: M. 754, f. 22v (loom?)
seated on bed or pillows with: Douce 6, f. 106v (at R., falcon)
standing before; woman with garland, aiming spear (Frau Minne? *cf.* Man and woman kneeling before): Douce 118, f. 130 (defending himself with shield (*fig. 401*)
stealing purse from, arrested by soldier: Add. 49622, f. 153 (*fig. 409*)
supporting woman balancing or dancing on his shoulders: Add. 42130, f. 68
swinging hood at *see* Man with hood, waving
threatening with club, woman beseeching: latin 14284, f. 62 (issuing from border; at R., bald man observing)
throwing fruit (cherries?) down to, from tree: BBR 9961-62, f. 39v (at L., ape with belled collar sitting in another tree picking fruit while bear stands with front paws against tree trunk)
tilting astride horses: Hague 78.D.40, f. 88v
trapped by, in net (*cf.* Man and ape, trapped by): Douce 6, f. 83v (*fig. 711*)
weeding: Add. 42130, f. 172 (in agricultural cycle)
with basket (winnowing?), woman with stool basket, both with tongs (*cf.* Man and woman fighting, man): Y.T. 27, f. 110
with mirror (huge), holding up to (*cf.* Knight and woman holding): G.K.S. 3384, ff. 116v, 320
with top *see* Top-whipping

Man approaching brothel(?): Bodley 264, f. 91v (2)

Man asleep (*cf.* Hybrid man asleep): Douce 6, f. 80 (in woman's lap); Jacquemart 1, f. 14v; latin 16260, f. 591v (or resting on his elbow); Rutland Ps., f. 24; Trinity B.11.22, f. 164v (in woman's lap)

Man astride *see* Ape and dog, astride, approaching; Ape astride keg; Coach; Falconer subentries; Hybrid man; Jew, with book; Knight, references under; Man and goat; — and hare, hunting with club, horn, hounds; — and horse; — and hybrid bird; — and pig; — and snail; — and stag, hunting with horn; — and unicorn; — and woman, on horseback; Man nude, astride; Man with tabor; Men fighting, one; — tilting; Windmill

Man astride man crawling on all fours (Phyllis and Aristotle parody?): Arras 729, f. 131 (youth following; at R., man with trumpet)

Man at lectern: Cloisters 54.1.2, f. 65v (physician with urinal); latin 16260, f. 562v (listening attentively; Min.: Epistles to Timothy)

Man at table (top split by ax blade), hands clasped (butcher? *see also* Banquet; Man and lion, eating): W. 45, f. 91v (above, hybrid man carrying sheep on shoulders) (*fig. 242*)

Man baking bread *see* Baker

Man balancing (*cf.* Contortionist; Man juggling; Quintain, balancing)
ape sitting in gold basin atop pole: Trinity B.11.22, f. 211
ball on cone before group of men, one exposing hindquarters: Bodley 264, f. 90v
ball on hat: W. 88, f. 70
basin on chin, spear on left heel: Yale MS., f. 175
basin on pole across shoulder, man beating on it with two poles: G.K.S. 3384, f. 211
basins (two, gold) on poles: Add. 29253, f. 410v (at R., ape defecating gold ?coins into bowl); Add. 30029, f. 166; Arras 47, f. 255v; Arras 729, f. 31; Ashmole 828, f. 43v; Bodley 264, ff. 76 (one; chained bear standing on hind legs), 90 (one; another man with tabor, tumbler), 130 (one; goat standing on hind legs); C.B. 61, f. 136 (one, containing squirrel); Cambrai 87, ff. 20v (three); 37v (three); Cambrai 102, f. 375v (fire in basins); Clois-

ters 54.1.2, ff. 45 (one; hybrid tumbler), 150v, 174; Douce 5, f. 88 (below, beast with psaltery, man with sword; at L., owl; above, hare and squirrel); Douce 6, ff. 59 (below, man with pipe and tabor), 93a; fr. 95, f. 214; G.K.S. 3384, ff. 71, 172 (one) (*fig. 389*), 202 (one), 260, 299; latin 10483, f. 6v (one); Nancy 249, ff. 14, 129; St. Omer 5, f. 125 (*fig. 411*); Stowe 17, ff. 28v (one), 183 (one, balanced on rope); Trinity B.11.22, ff. 6v, 13v, 114; W. 45, ff. 21v, 74; W. 90, ff. 132v (ape tied to post), 137v (ape seated; falconer, dog pursuing stag), 177 (at L., dog running); W. 104, ff. 5v, 28 (one) (*fig. 11*); Y.T. 19, f. 40 (one, very large)

basket on pole balanced on nose, holding shorter pole in right hand: latin 10483, f. 6v

bird on string held in mouth, another man with lighted candle: Add. 42130, f. 159

board (tray?) on nose or chin: BBR 10607, f. 47 (above, hybrid couple kissing) (*fig. 410*); C.B. 61, f. 116 (*fig. 412*); G.K.S. 3384, f. 45 (below, man with pipe and tabor)

cup on pole: BBR 10607, f. 89 (balanced on nose); Kraus 75/88, f. 82 (balanced on nose) (*fig. 413*); latin 10483, f. 292v (large ?glass); Yale MS., f. 175 (spear on heel) (*fig. 414*)

funnel in mouth, lying on back; another man pouring liquid from pitcher into funnel: Add. 42130, f. 157v (*fig. 415*)

on board held by two men, beside him three swords balanced on board: Bodley 264, f. 104v

on border stalk, clinging to, from below: latin 14284, f. 22v (at R., man with ball taking aim)

on hands, man with pipe and tabor: W. 88, f. 176v

on hands of man: Cloisters 54.1.2, f. 54 (shepherd) (*fig. 511*)

on hands on border stalk: latin 14284, f. 15 (at R., two storks)

on head of hybrid man playing dog like bagpipe, with ball in mouth: Cloisters 54.1.2, f. 166 (*fig. 516*)

on one foot

conversing with ape wearing hood: latin 14284, f. 42

flanked by two men: latin 14284, f. 9 (frog-in-the-middle?)

steadying himself with spear: W. 85, f. 36v

on pole, hanging upside down by knees: Bodley 264, f. 108v

on pole held and pushed by man trying to unbalance him: Rutland Ps., f. 65v (*fig. 416*)

on pole held by two men: Add. 42130, f. 69v (nude, with bladder); Bodley 264, f. 89 (holding cock, followed by man with banner) (*fig. 417*); Rutland Ps., f. 71v

on pole on ground, kneeling, trying to pick up object with teeth(?): Add. 42130, f. 158v

on pole, seated cross-legged with taper and torch over tub of water: Bodley 264, f. 98

on shoulders of hybrid man: Add. 42130, ff. 168, 188

on shoulders of man: W. 88, f. 110v

on shoulders of man with bagpipe: Y.T. 19, f. 3

on shoulders of woman with trumpet: Lambeth 233, f. 44 (*fig. 422*)

on table, bending down to bowl on ground filled with water, trying to pick up apple(?): Bodley 264, f. 86 (at L., man giving coins to another, man with cymbals)

on tightrope: Chartres 549, f. 11; Rylands lat. R. 117, f. 193 (large hoop balanced beside him)

rope with basin set on top: G.K.S. 3384, f. 94 (basin on short pole); Stowe 17, f. 183

shield(?) on pole: Rothschild MS., f. 120

spear on heel, cup on chin: Yale MS., f. 175 (*fig. 414*)

spear on nose: Burney 345, f. 53 (*fig. 418*); W. 85, ff. 1, 49

squirrel in basin atop pole: C.B. 61, f. 136

sword on chin: BBR 9411-26, f. 139v; Bodley 264, f. 40; Chantilly 62, f. 140v (sword as tall as man); G.K.S. 3384, f. 164; Kraus 75/88, f. 62; Trinity B.11.22, f. 10v

sword on hand: Douce 5, f. 99 (two) (*fig. 420*); Douce 6, f. 93b

sword on hand, another man balancing wheel on shoulder: Bodley 264, f. 78v

sword on nose: BBR 10607, f. 23v (*fig. 419*); Cambrai 87, f. 34v; latin 10483, f. 53 (steadying it with pole, standing on hybrid man); W. 88, f. 1; Yale MS., f. 25

sword on shoulder: Laud Lat. 84, f. 77v

tapers (lit) on wooden stand held in mouth, running, playing triangle (*cf.* Beast balancing): Trinity B.11.22, f. 148 (*fig. 421*)

wheel *see above,* — sword on hand

Man bathing (*see also* Man and woman; Man nude): W. 87, ff. 36v, 85; W. 88, f. 75v (2, each in wooden tub, leaning on wooden supports; treading grapes?)

Man bathing feet: Trinity B.11.22, f. 179v (at L., man with pitcher, hare) (*fig. 423*)

Man bathing hand in tub set on two sawhorses: G.K.S. 3384, f. 45v (above, head of woman in line ending) (*fig. 424*)

Man beaten *see* Lover beaten; Man and woman, beaten by

Man beating down acorns *see* Man and pigs

Man beating man (*cf.* Men fighting, beating): G.K.S. 3384, f. 132 (on head with club); W. 45, f. 166v (second man baring buttocks over vessel); W. 88, f. 163 (second man baring buttocks)

Man before oven *see* Baker; Proverbs: man yawning

Man begging *see* Beggar

Man beheaded: BBR 9391, f. 99v

Man bending down to touch toes, preparing to jump over stick on ground: Add. 42130, f. 56v

Man biting boot (proverb?): Harley 6563, f. 65v (second boot on ground beside him)

Man biting border stalk: Cloisters 54.1.2, f. 160

Man biting column *see* Proverbs: man

Man biting tip of hood: Douce 5, f. 118v

Man biting knife (bone? stick?): Cloisters 54.1.2, f. 27

Man biting stone (?): Y.T. 27, f. 122

Man biting sword: Cambridge Dd.5.5, f. 28v (Ps. 52)

Man blind *see* Beggar and dog; Beggar blind (*figs. 425-429*)

Man blindfolded *see* Blindman's buff; Man with hood over face

Man blowing bellows like trumpet *see* Man with bellows

Man blowing pipe with pinwheel attached to end (*cf.* Windmill, toy) G.K.S. 3384, f. 36v (*fig. 322*)

Man blowing spoon: latin 10483, ff. 111v, 139

Man blowing toasting fork, prongs embedded in gold disk, another fork over shoulder (proverb?) Cambridge Dd.5.5, f. 253 (*fig. 595*)

Man bowling *see* Bowls

Man building church, tower, wall (*see also* St. Dunstan, f. 246; St. Mary the Egyptian, f. 289v): Douce 6, ff. 95 (3, with hammers, chisels) (*fig. 430*), 129 (building wall, with trowel and hod); G.K.S. 3384, ff. 36 (building tower; below, man with hod), 114 (below, ape at table); St. Omer 5, f. 140 (3, one mixing mortar, one with hod, one on scaffold with trowel; another man hammering stone, supporting man holding initial; text: Haggai)

Man by fire, seated (*cf.* Hybrid man by; Man nude by): Add. 49622, f. 138v (hybrid man with bellows); Bodley 264, f. 83; Cambridge Dd. 5.5, f. 264 (holding boot; reference to February?); Cloisters 54.1.2, f. 2v (February); Nancy 249, f. 271v (scolded by woman); Rutland Ps., f. 109; W. 90, f. 3v (February; barefoot, holding boot)

Man carrying ass *see* Man and ass

Man carving image *see* Sculptor

Man carving (painting? repairing?) roof tiles of structure occupied by woman and pet dog: Douce 6, f. 84v

Man chopping stone with hatchet: Holkham 458, f. 46 (Text: How to use stones in warfare)

Man chopping wood: Add. 39810, f. 7 (2); Add. 49622, ff. 92v, 137, 155; M. 183, f. 252v (Offices of the Dead); Nancy 249, f. 190 (2, splitting wood with ax, wedge); Royal 10 E.IV, f. 100v (2); W. 88, ff. 6 (March; chopping trees with ax; f. 5v, man pruning tree), 69v, 75 (holding rope and hook to pull down tree, hybrid man with ax); W. 90, f. 7v (June; bearing faggots, ax in tree)

Man climbing border stalk (*cf.* Ape; Man nude): Add. 42130, f. 55v; Add. 50000, f. 84 (shot by nude man); M. 183, f. 242 (followed by serpent)

Man combing hair *see* Man with comb; *cf.* Man cutting hair

Man cooking

blowing through pipe at fire under pot: G.K.S. 3384, f. 18v

boiling two eggs in pot over fire for falcon: fr. 12400, f. 99v

chopping pig, boiling, preparing, and serving food to Sir Geoffrey Luttrell and company: Add. 42130, ff. 207v-208

roasting meat on spit: Add. 42130, f. 206v (2); Bodley 264, ff. 83v, 170v, 204 (before inn); Douce 5, f. 1a (January); Douce 6, f. 91; G.K.S. 3384, f. 17; Melbourne 1254/3, f. 4v (with winged headdress, holding knife; woman with mortar and pestle) (*fig. 432*); Trinity B.11.22, f. 159 (2) (*fig. 431*); W. 87,

f. 75v (winged, with shield; f. 76, holding fork, full dish); Y.T. 27, f. 108a (hybrid, drinking)
sampling with spoon, pot over fire: Douce 6, f. 139v
stirring pot over fire with spoon: Add. 42130, f. 207 (two men chopping food, pounding mortar); Chantilly 64, ff. 148, 148v (wearing apron); Douce 6, f. 155v (bid by companion to stir); G.K.S. 3384, f. 163; W. 88, ff. 4v-5 (February; another man with bellows), 94v
Man counting money (?): Stowe 17, f. 269
Man crawling in and out of oven (proverb?): M. 754, f. 3v
Man crippled (*cf.* Beggar): Add. 36684, f. 56; Arras 47, f. 222v; Cambridge Dd.5.5, f. 368 (at R., ape with fruit); Chantilly 64, ff. 97, 97v; Cloisters 54.1.2, f. 97; fr. 95, f. 295v; fr. 25526, f. 118v (2); Princeton 44-18, ff. 162v-163 (confronting woman); Rutland Ps., f. 64 (2); Trinity B.11.22, ff. 9, 90v, 102v, 213 (*fig. 553*); W. 102, f. 60v
fighting with crutch, hand trestles: Bodley 264, f. 109 (3)
given alms by man: Add. 42130, f. 186v (seated in wheelbarrow pushed by second man); W. 82, f. 193v (with bowl in mouth, hand trestles)
given bread: Douce 118, f. 50 (by woman); W. 82, f. 193v (by man)
greeted by woman: W. 88, f. 186v
holding out bowl to woman with churn: W. 88, f. 97v
observing woman dancing on shoulders of man with bagpipe: Yale MS., f. 180
with keg on back: Cloisters 54.1.2, f. 123 (hybrid)
Man cutting cloth (leather?), approached by man with staff: W. 109, f. 204 (*fig. 346*)
Man cutting hair (head?) of man, with sword (*cf.* Barber; Man with sickle): Cloisters 54.1.2, f. 85
Man dancing *see* Hybrid man playing bellows; Hybrid man with pipe and tabor; — with vielle; Hybrid woman with vielle; Man and woman; Man with bagpipe; — with gittern; — with harp, end; — with tabor; — with trumpet; — with vielle; Men dancing; Woman with vielle
Man defecating *see* Obscaena, defecating
Man digging grave: Add. 49622, f. 89v; M. 88, f. 189 (Text: Offices of the Dead; at L., hare emerging from burrow); W. 82, f. 164v (Text: Offices of the Dead; at L., two women seated with books; at R., man mourning)
Man diving off border: latin 14284, f. 56
Man drawing water out of well: Chantilly 64, ff. 14, 14v; Douce 6, f. 125v (second man with two water buckets on pole across back approaching long flight of steps leading to house)
Man dreaming *see* Lover dreaming; — embracing
Man drinking (*see also* Hybrid man; King; Man nude; Man reaping; — treading; — with bellows, blowing): Add. 21114, f. 24v; Add. 29253, f. 325v; Add. 39810, f. 7 (*fig. 140*); Cambridge Dd. 5.5, f. 106; Douce 6, ff. 11, 60 (3), 62, 83v (*fig. 711*), 100 (below, unicorn drinking), 114, 154 (holding spoon); fr. 95, f. 190v; G.K.S. 3384, ff. 35, 40, 51v, 63, 95 (holding spoon), 112 (holding stick), 150v, 177v, 178 (second man pruning border with sword); latin 10483, f. 174; latin 14284, ff. 1 (at L., keg; nude woman seated), 43v; latin 16260, f. 592v; Y.T. 27, f. 9 (September)
fed by man with covered tankard: Douce 6, f. 155 (above, man with vielle)
kneeling before keg, man dancing: W. 760, f. 163 (erased)
man with pipe and tabor: Spencer 2, f. 185v
pouring liquid into bowl from pitcher, drinking: latin 10483, f. 92v; latin 10484, f. 266v
pouring liquid into bowl from pitcher, man dancing expectantly before him: Bodley 264, f. 51
sipping through pipe from keg on man's shoulders: Douce 6, f. 157
tapping keg: Douce 6, f. 114
with cup and pitcher: W. 87, f. 103v (below, dog/snail)
with two pitchers, filling cup of wild-haired nude man: fr. 95, f. 173
woman remonstrating: Harley 6563, ff. 66v-67 (*figs. 434-435*)
Man eating (*see also* Banquet): Douce 6, f. 161 (below, stork aiming beak at dish in man's hand; *cf.* Fables: fox and stork, Part I, variant) (*fig. 404*); G.K.S. 3384, ff. 72, 136 (at L., apes fighting); Nancy 249, f. 137 (from plate set on table on lion's back)
Man entering church *see* Church
Man exposing himself *see* Man balancing ball; Man beating; Obscaena, exposing
Man extracting tooth of man: Cloisters 54.1.2, f. 80v
Man, Fall of *see* Adam and Eve; Vices: apostasy

M

Man feeding (*cf.* Ape feeding; Hybrid man —; Man and falcon, —)
animal head: Douce 6, ff. 164, 178
animal with rolls (eggs?) from basket: G.K.S. 3384, f. 137
bird in birdcage: Nancy 249, f. 119
bird's head (*cf.* Fables: fox and stork, Part I, variant): W. 85, f. 28 (possibly physician with urinal before bird), 86, 88v
grotesque with spoon from dish: G.K.S. 3384, f. 210
man's head: Douce 6, f. 160 (line endings; pouring liquid down from bowl) (*fig. 402*)
monster with two rolls from baker's tray: G.K.S. 3384, f. 168
stork from bowl (*cf.* Fables: fox and stork, Part I, variant): G.K.S. 3384, f. 164; W. 82, f. 179v (hybrid man); W. 88, f. 79v
woman: G.K.S. 3384, f. 294

Man fetching water for wife (*Wright's Chaste Wife* sequence): Royal 10 E.IV, ff. 140v-141v

Man fighting *see* Man and ape; — and bear; — and crane; — dragon; — and fly; — and goat; — and hybrid man; — and knight; — and lion; — and monster; — and snail; — and woman; Man nude and snail; Men

Man fishing (*cf.* Man and eel; Man and fish): Busch 293, pl. XLVII; Cambridge Dd. 5.5, f. 358; Cracow 815, f. 11v (catch stolen by cat); Douce 6, f. 115v (catching fish in hands); G.K.S. 3384, ff. 15v (for frog), 129v, 189; latin 10483, f. 170; Melbourne 1254/3, f. 12 (ringing bell with other hand); Nancy 249, f. 168v (*fig. 438*); Royal 10 E.IV, f. 59 (net on pole); W. 87, f. 106v (*fig. 436*); W. 88, f. 180

Man giving alms to pilgrim (*see also* Man crippled given): G.K.S. 3384, f. 78 (*fig. 439*)

Man giving food to seated children: Harley 6563, ff. 88-88v

Man grinding corn (*Wright's Chaste Wife* sequence): Royal 10 E.IV, f. 144

Man hanged from border, in drawers (*cf.* Vices: despair; Virgin, miracles of: Ebbo): latin 3893, f. 94v

Man hanging from tree limb: W. 88, f. 76

Man hanging from bar, upside down: M. 730, ff. 233v, etc.

Man hanging from border stalk, by hands: Exeter 47, f. 32

Man harrowing: Add. 42130, f. 171 (another man aiming sling at two crows; in agricultural cycle)

Man hawking *see* Falconer

Man headless (*see also* Man nude, headless): Verdun 107, f. 98
fighting headless man, both in drawers with swords, holding large head between them: M. 730, f. 107; W. 88, f. 44v
hybrid, with sword, holding bleeding human head: Stowe 17, f. 73 (2) (*fig. 443*)
raising head off head with left hand as if in greeting: Cloisters 54.1.2, f. 120 (*fig. 329*); Y.T. 27, f. 93v
with head in hand: Verdun 107, f. 99 (2, confronted) (*fig. 440*)
with head in hand, confronting headless man, both with swords: Glazier 24, f. 70v (*fig. 442*)
with head in hand, lower leg in other: Glazier 24, ff. 52v (nude; below, dragon) (*fig. 441*), 158v
with sword, bitten in buttocks by dragon (*cf.* Man and dragon, bitten by): fr. 95, f. 4v (nude)
with sword in one hand, his head in the other: M. 183, f. 69v (Ps. 51); Melbourne 1254/3, f. 73; W. 90, f. 208v

Man, head of (*cf.* Detached limbs, head; Man with head of)
bleeding, held by man brandishing bloody sword: W. 90, f. 208v (*fig. 489*)
devoured by beast: G.K.S. 3384, f. 28v
held by man brandishing club: Bodley 264, f. 39
hooded, bearded, on lower border stalk: Melbourne 1254/3, f. 75
impaled on spear held by man: latin 10483, f. 142v (at R., man with ?stone)
in basin held by man: Cambridge Dd. 5.5, f. 325
issuing from dragon's mouth (*cf.* Man and dragon, devoured by; Man and fish, issuing): Glazier 24, f. 50v
looking out of oven (proverb? *cf.* Man crawling; Oven): Add. 36684, f. 66v; Glazier 24, f. 52v; Harley 6563, f. 28 (five grimacing heads)
Negroid: Rutland Ps., f. 26
pierced by border spike, ears bitten by dragons: Rutland Ps., f. 12v
three-faced, balanced on back of crane: Rutland Ps., f. 15 (above, king's head)

three-faced, observing man with club and hounds hunting hare around margins: C.B. 62, f. 181v
Man hiding eyes (unidentified game): Bodley 264, f. 125v (3)
Man hoarding(?), holding sock, putting sack in chest (*cf.* Man counting): Princeton 44-18, f. 7v (f. 7, woman doing the same)
Man horned, with shawm (*cf.* Hybrid man, horned): latin 16260, f. 569v (satyr?)
Man hunchbacked: Jesus 40, f. 88v
Man hunting *see* Man and ape; — and bird; — and boar; — and butterfly; — and crane; — and crow; — and dog; — and hare; — and stag; Woman and dragon
Man imprisoned by soldier (*cf.* Man and hare, imprisoned by): fr. 25526, f. 83v (at L., king)
Man in basket on back of fox: Y.T. 8, f. 269 (4)
Man in bed (*cf.* Man and woman): Harley 6563, f. 37 (Age of man? Old age; f. 37v, tomb; f. 36v, youth combing hair, with mirror)
Man in boat (*cf.* Knight in boat): Add. 42130, f. 161v (warship occupied by large group of men); Douce 118, f. 36v (2)
directing another man swimming in water: Royal 2 B.VII, ff. 169v-170
rowing, pulled by man with rope: W. 88, f. 153
rowing, pulled by two men with rope: Add. 42130, f. 160 (4; below, snail) (*fig. 468*)
with bleeding neck (corpse?), pulled by woman with rope around her neck (fabliau?): Nancy 249, f. 236
Man in cart
drawn by ass, approaching three cripples fighting with hand trestles and crutch: Bodley 264, f. 109
drawn by dogs (three), with horn: Royal 10 E.IV, f. 110v (man pushing cart)
drawn by horse, approaching tower (church?), holding bowl (beggar?): W. 82, f. 208v
drawn by horse, conversing with man: Verdun 107, f. 157 (*fig. 444*)
Man in costume as (mummer)
ape, confronting six women, accompanied by men in costume as ass, bird, bull, goat, wivern: Bodley 264, f. 181v
ass, with pipe and tabor astride ram charging man in costume as stag astride fox: Hague 78.D.40, f. 160
ass, with scythe: latin 14284, f. 31v
boar, accompanied by men in costume as hare, stag: Bodley 264, f. 21v (at L., man with gittern; at R., nun and hybrid cleric brandishing switch) (*fig. 445*)
boar, dancing with ape: Chantilly 64, ff. 69, 69v
dog, held on leash by seated man: Bodley 264, f. 71v (3, one with scroll inscribed "je sui cre . . . ," one with ?stone)
fox (half-nude) with trumpet, man and woman embracing: Chantilly 62, f. 201
goat, confronting dog sitting up, second man with hand bells: Bodley 264, f. 117v
hare: Tournai Ps., f. 45 (confronting siren with horn)
lion, with trumpet: C.B. 64, f. 89
ram, confronting manticora: Arundel 83, f. 47 (Ps. 68)
stag (*cf. above,* boar; Stag horns, references under); Add. 30029, ff. 61v, 99 (doe), 132 (variant); Cloisters 54.1.2, f. 193v; M. 754, f. 42v; Rothschild MS., f. 175
man with bagpipe: fr. 95, f. 261 (*fig. 446*)
man with pipe and tabor: Bodley 264, f. 70 (at R., woman and two children); G.K.S. 3384, f. 11v; W. 88, ff. 115v (2), 156v
with trumpet: Cambrai 87, f. 69
Man in oven *see* Oven
Man in tree *see* Ape as king, with asperge; Man and bear, pursued by; — and thief; — and woman, presenting; Man nude, balancing
Man in tub *see* Man bathing; —, treading grapes
Man in water, upside down (*cf.* Man swimming): Vienna 1826*, f. 58 (Ps. 68)
Man in wheelbarrow *see* Man with wheelbarrow, containing
Man juggling
balls: BBR 9411-26, f. 138v (at L., beaver?); latin 10483, f. 54v; Trinity B.11.22, f. 143 (two, red)
knives: Douce 6, f. 93b v (three, over pot) (*fig. 448*); fr. 95, f. 318 (three) (*fig. 447*)
swords (*cf.* Man balancing): fr. 95, f. 237
Man jumping, one hand on his heart: Jacquemart 1, f. 66
Man killing man (*cf.* Man and hare; — and lion)
shooting: Add. 50000, f. 84; latin 10483, f. 94 (shooting male head in eye)
with sword: Cambridge Dd. 5.5, f. 386; Chantilly 64, ff. 129, 129v
Man kneeling *see* Cleric at altar; Man and woman, before; —, kneeling; Patron
Man kneeling before Crucifixion figure on altar, another man pointing at him: Princeton 44-18, f. 114v

M

Man leading horse *see* Man and horse
Man looking out of oven *see* Man, head of
Man making bed: W. 88, f. 177v (2) (*fig. 450*)
Man mourning (*cf.* Man digging grave): Add. 49622, f. 73; Harley 6563, f. 90 (before tomb)
Man nude and ape
conversing, ape kneeling, holding out small round object (*cf.* Ape with fruit): Jacquemart 1, f. 14
conversing with ape in tree: Rutland Ps., f. 106v (nude save for short cape)
defecating, hands tied, ape swinging sickle at him: Glazier 24, f. 57 (Templar's hat?)
ridden by, ape with shield: Glazier 24, f. 131v
Man nude and bear
astride, wrestling with nude man astride lion: Douce 366, f. 147v
fighting with sword: Christ Church E.II, f. 36 (*fig. 452*)
pursued into tree by: Rutland Ps., f. 53 (f. 52v, bear with pipe)
Man nude and beast
confronting with falchion: W. 87, ff. 86v-87
cringing before: W. 102, f. 73v
Man nude and bird
conversing (*cf.* Man and bird, seated): Arsenal 6329, f. 42 (woman?)
holding in hand: M. 754, f. 11v
hunting with bow and arrow: W. 37, f. 67v; W. 88, f. 192; W. 102, f. 73v
hunting with net: Douai 193, f. 213v; W. 88, f. 177
Man nude and bishop (?) with pipe and tabor, dancing before: W. 102, f. 76
Man nude and boar
astride with club and shield, charging nude man astride goat with spoon and basket: Hague 10.A.14, f. 7
pursuing with ax: Add. 36684, f. 31
Man nude and butterfly, pursuing with cloth (*cf.* Man and butterfly): M. 729, f. 346
Man nude and camel, pursued by: Rothschild MS., f. 131
Man nude and cat, pursued by: Rothschild MS., f. 130 (above, spider spinning web) (*fig. 453*)
Man nude and centaur (*see also* Centaur as knight)
fighting with club, centaur with sword and buckler: fr. 95, f. 13v
kneeling, killed by: fr. 95, ff. 309, 380
Man nude and cleric, reprimanding him for defecating: Add. 49622, f. 82
Man nude and cock
astride backwards (*cf.* Knight and cock): St. Omer 5, f. 14
astride, fighting nude man: Douai 193, f. 143
Man nude and cow, leading (*see also* Man nude, with Saracen headdress): Douce 5, f. 86 (at R., man with spear)
Man nude and crane *see* Man and crane; Pygmy
Man nude and devil with scourge, ridden by: fr. 95, ff. 61v, 209v
Man nude and dog
astride backwards, with trumpet: Arras 47, f. 38v (wolf?)
astride, fighting snail with distaff: Melbourne 1254/3, f. 12
astride, with trumpet: W. 90, f. 90 (hunting hare)
hunting with horn, hounds: Glazier 24, f. 61v (dog?)
Man nude and dragon (*cf.* Man and dragon; Man two-torsoed; Monster, with fourteen legs)
astride: Rutland Ps., f. 106
astride backwards, with club: Rutland Ps., f. 83 (at R., in foliage of tail, nude man with hands raised)
astride, pulling tail of: Rutland Ps., f. 75v
astride tail, confronting amphisboena: Rutland Ps., f. 82
astride, with branch: Rutland Ps., ff. 15v (gold branch), 99v (*fig. 451*)
astride, with club: Rutland Ps., f. 64
astride, with horn: Cloisters 54.1.2, f. 120 (dragon with human head)
bitten by (*cf.* Hybrid man and dragon; Knight and —; Man and —): fr. 95, f. 4v (headless, with sword); Rutland Ps., f. 13v (two, biting feet)
confronting, leaning on spear: W. 85, f. 39
confronting with scourge, wearing ailettes, dragon breathing fire: M. 754, f. 45
fighting with club: Rutland Ps., f. 111v
fighting with dagger: Rutland Ps., f. 102v
fighting with sword: Christ Church E.II, f. 38v; fr. 95, f. 82v; Stowe 17, f. 42v
grasping neck of: Cloisters 54.1.2, f. 37
headless, bitten in back by, with sword: fr. 95, f. 4v
holding in hands: Rutland Ps., f. 49 (nude save for cloak)
kneeling on, holding shield emblazoned with monster: Jacquemart 1, f. 49v
pulling tail of: Rutland Ps., f. 41v

putting hand in mouth of: Glazier 24, f. 42v
shooting in mouth: Glazier 24, f. 154

Man nude and eagle, confronted: Christ Church E.II, f. 55 (one-legged)

Man nude and elephant, astride backwards with trumpet: fr. 95, f. 82v

Man nude and fox, pursuing with spear fox with gold bird in mouth (*cf.* Man and fox, pursuing): Cambrai 103, f. 500 (in center, gold nest in tree, three gold birds in nest)

Man nude and goat
astride, mitered, tilting at quintain: Douce 118, f. 33
astride, with spoon and basket, fighting nude man astride boar with club and shield; Hague 10.A.14, f. 7 (*fig. 461*)

Man nude and hare (*see also* Hare and man, astride)
blowing hare out of trumpet, cock pecking buttocks: Royal 14 E.III, f. 89
embraced by: Glazier 24, f. 65
fighting with club: W. 37, ff. 57-57v (hunting?)
fighting with pole: Add. 36684, f. 44
flanked by two hares: Yale MS., f. 295
hunting, astride dog, with trumpet: W. 90, f. 90
hunting with horn and hounds: Glazier 24, f. 61v
hunting with spear, wearing helmet, ailettes: W. 90, f. 145v
shooting: W. 88, f. 125v

Man nude and hybrid man
arguing with: W. 88, f. 69
astride, with ax and whip (Phyllis and Aristotle parody?): Arras 47, f. 235v
fighting with bow and club: W. 88, ff. 183v-184
fighting with lance and bellows, pot on head; hybrid man with club and basket, pot on head: W. 88, f. 175
fighting with spear and club and buckler: W. 88, f. 72v
holding on string (or pulled by): Bodley 264, f. 55
shooting, hybrid man with vielle: Auct. D.3.2, f. 193
shot by, seated on hillock, hands clasped on chest, wearing hat with low tripartite dome: W. 37, ff. 54v-55
tailed, with claw foot, hoof, fighting with spear hybrid man with sword and shield: W. 102, f. 52
with winged headdress, aiming club at: Rutland Ps., f. 107

Man nude and ibex, astride: Add. 38115, f. 50v

Man nude and lion (*cf.* Hybrid man and; Knight and; Man and)
astride, brandishing sword, putting hand in lion's mouth (rending? Samson?): Christ Church E.II, f. 35v (nude save for cape)
astride, lion held by man, accompanying woman astride lion: Fitz. 242, f. 3
astride, rending (Samson?): Y.T. 8, f. 221
astride, with trumpet, confronting woman astride goat with trumpet: Yale MS., f. 119
astride, wrestling with nude man astride bear: Douce 366, f. 147v
between two lions (Daniel?): Add. 50000, f. 14v (below, cock at lectern, fox stalking cock; Ps. 97)
fighting with dagger (man wearing short hooded cape): Rutland Ps., ff. 46v, 97
fighting with spear and buckler: Hague 78.D.40, f. 40 (winged headdress)
killing with sword: Christ Church E.II, f. 52v; Rutland Ps., f. 70 (*fig. 454*)
kneeling on lion/horse: Arras 47, f. 199v
shooting: fr. 95, f. 347v
turning back on, walking away from hybrid woman dancing, hybrid man with gittern: M. 729, f. 40

Man nude and man with falchion and spear aimed at his head: Add. 49622, f. 179v (nude man old, bearded, beseeching) (*fig. 455*)

Man nude and merman with sword and shield, crawling before, on all fours: Jacquemart 1, f. 72 (merman/knight)

Man nude and monster
astride backwards, wearing chain-mail coif: St. Omer 5, f. 247
beaten with whip by: Princeton 44-18, f. 70v
kneeling before, monster charging: fr. 95, f. 309
putting hand in mouth of: Glazier 24, f. 42v (hybrid man balancing sword on nose)

Man nude and ostrich (?), shooting: latin 3893, f. 154v

Man nude and ram
astride: Add. 38115, f. 50v
confronting, crouching before butting ram: Douai 193, f. 53v

Man nude and snail
astride dog, fighting with distaff: Melbourne 1254/3, f. 12
fighting with ax: W. 90, f. 39 (at L., hare)
kneeling before: Add. 49622, f. 184v

M

Man nude and stag
astride backwards, pursued by man with horn and hounds: W. 45, f. 70v (nude save for cape)
astride backwards, with trumpet, wild hair: fr. 95, f. 311
astride, confronting seated ape with spear: W. 90, f. 38
astride, followed by dog(?) attached by rope: Rothschild MS., f. 133
hunting with club and horn: Douce 6, f. 200 (nude save for cape)
shooting: Arras 561, f. 46v (winged headdress), 103 (tailed, with three hounds) (*fig. 456*)
Man nude and stork, shooting: latin 3893, f. 98
Man nude and unicorn (hybrid), astride: G.K.S. 3384, f. 253v (at L., hybrid peacock)
Man nude and wolf (*see also* Man nude and dog, astride)
admonishing(?): Rutland Ps., f. 109v
asleep on hill, guarded(?) by serpent, approached by wolf (fox?): Rutland Ps., f. 110
Man nude and woman
embracing woman nude save for headdress: Add. 49622, f. 17
offering ring to (*cf.* Man and woman, offering): latin 10435, f. 73v
with spear, woman dancing: M. 108, f. 1
with staff, blessing kneeling woman: W. 88, f. 180v
Man nude, armless (*see also* Man and ape, given)
ape seated on his head: M. 754, f. 50v
as bishop: M. 796, f. 79
hand issuing from hindquarters, holding gold chalice: M. 754, f. 19
seated in silver bowl: M. 754, f. 64v
two, one with bow on head, arrow pointing up: M. 754, f. 60
walking on sword (*cf.* Ape with sword, straddling): M. 754, f. 67 (behind him, red and white ?ball; hybrid)
with shawm, man with trumpet: M. 754, f. 99
Man nude as bishop: W. 88, f. 86v (partly inked over)
astride goat, tilting at quintain: Douce 118, f. 33
holding crosier like broom: Glazier 24, f. 122v
Man nude as devil (devil's head), attacking man with two swords: fr. 95, f. 199v
Man nude as falconer, crowned, tailed: Yale MS., f. 363
Man nude as fox, with trumpet, confronting man and woman embracing: Chantilly 62, f. 201
Man nude, astride *see* Man nude and bear; — and boar; — and cock; — and dog; — and dragon; — and elephant; — and goat; — and hybrid man; — and lion; — and monster; — and ram; — and stag; — and unicorn; Man nude, straddling; — with Saracen headdress; Men nude, fighting; Men tilting
Man nude, balancing
on hands, man with pipe and tabor; Rothschild MS., f. 167
on pole borne by two men, with bladder: Add. 42130, f. 69v
on pole borne by two men, with pipe and tabor: Royal 10 E.IV, f. 93 (at L., man in tree shooting nude man hiding in tree at R.)
Man nude, bathing
entering door of bathhouse held open by woman: W. 82, f. 100 (at L., nude man approaching; at R., woman with two water buckets) (*fig. 393*)
in tub, hands raised (bathing?): Add. 36684, f. 7v; W. 87, f. 85
Man nude, beaten by monster with whip: Princeton 44-18, f. 70v
Man nude, before tree, talking: Rutland Ps., f. 101 (loincloth)
Man nude, bending bow: M. 754, f. 51
Man nude, blessing *see* Man nude and woman, with staff
Man nude, bowling *see* Bowls
Man nude, by fire
drinking: Rutland Ps., f. 109 (seated in chair)
raising left leg over flames: M. 754, f. 92
seated, arms folded across chest: W. 87, f. 49
Man nude, climbing border stalk (*cf.* Ape climbing; Man —): Douce 5, f. 18; M. 754, f. 45v; W. 87, f. 6; W. 90, f. 154
Man nude, cripple
with crutch, four legs, confronting nude man with one leg: Rutland Ps., f. 64
with crutches (three): W. 102, f. 61
with hand trestles (two), jumping: W. 88, f. 52v (hooded)
Man nude, dancing: BBR 10607, f. 203; W. 37, ff. 165v-166 (ape with vielle)
Man nude, defecating *see* Obscaena, defecating
Man nude, digging grave (*cf.* Man digging): Add. 36684, f. 141 (at L., skeleton lying on ground)

Man nude, drinking
  by fire: Rutland Ps., f. 109 (seated in chair) (*fig. 458*)
  holding cup in either hand: Tournai Ps., f. 7
  hybrid man filling bowl for: fr. 95, f. 173 (with two pitchers; recipient tailed, with wild hair) (*fig. 459*); Yale MS., f. 311
Man nude, eating his amputated leg (*cf.* Man headless, with head): Glazier 24, f. 50v (without legs) (*fig. 449*)
Man nude, exposing hindquarters *see* Obscaena, exposing
Man nude, fighting *see* Man nude and bear; — and centaur; — and dragon; — and hybrid man; — and lion; — and snail; Men nude, fighting
Man nude, grasping his buttocks: BBR 9411-26, f. 134v (above, man with churn)
Man nude, hanging from pole by feet: Rothschild MS., f. 145
Man nude, headless (*cf.* Detached limbs, head; man headless)
  raising club to beat head set on beak of grotesque: Glazier 24, f. 51
  stooping to pick up head of ass: Glazier 24, f. 109v
  with head in either hand: Glazier 24, f. 61
  with head in left hand, amputated leg in right hand (*cf.* Man nude, eating): Glazier 24, f. 52v (at R., head looking out of oven; proverb?) (*fig. 441*)
  with sword, bitten in back by dragon: fr. 95, f. 4v
Man nude, holding heads of man and woman (wearing hairnet) below: fr. 95, f. 158v
Man nude, holding mitered head (bishop's?): Glazier 24, f. 53v (below, hybrid abbot with spindle)
Man nude, in cave, conversing with man/monster: Rutland Ps., f. 84
Man nude, in tree *see* Man nude, balancing
Man nude, in tub *see* Man nude, bathing
Man nude, putting stone *see* Putting
Man nude, reclining on elbow (*cf.* Moses reclining)
  pointing to text (Ps. 119, v. 97): M. 102, f. 129
  seen from back: Burney 275, f. 449 (four red dots near right shoulder-blade)
Man nude, ringing bell on rope: M. 754, f. 16
Man nude, seated: Cloisters 54.1.2, f. 160v; M. 102, f. 167v (line ending)
  head buried in arms: Add. 42130, f. 54 (tonsured?); BBR 8469, f. 7v (legs crossed)
  legs crossed: latin 14284, f. 25
  on grass under tree; at R., man with club and buckler fighting hybrid knight with club: Cambrai 102, f. 386
  on shoulders of man in drawers: Glazier 24, f. 110v (*fig. 179*)
  with horn and spear: W. 87, f. 81
  with polearm across shoulder (*cf.* Man nude, tailed): W. 87, f. 30 (conical cap)
  with round orange-red object in hand (*cf.* Man with fruit): W. 45, f. 166v (above, lion with trumpet)
Man nude, skeleton-thin: Add. 49622, f. 123v
Man nude, standing on his head in caldron: M. 754, f. 93 (beside bird in same position)
Man nude, standing on human head: Rutland Ps., f. 16
Man nude, sticking out tongue (*cf.* Sticking out tongue, references under): Cambrai 102, f. 162 (shot by knight); Rutland Ps., f. 110v (at nude man seizing his foot; both wearing capes)
Man nude, straddling pole to which are attached rondels (mirrors?), lantern on head, another rondel on ground (*cf.* Ape with sword, straddling): M. 754, f. 72 (without arms)
Man nude, swimming *see* Man swimming
Man nude, swinging from border stalk by one hand (*cf.* Ape swinging): Jacquemart 1, f. 73
Man nude, tailed (*see also* Man nude as falconer; Man nude, drinking; Man tailed): M. 102, ff. 90 (line ending), 153 (line ending, pointing at text), 162v (line ending, one arm, one leg; pointing at text); W. 102, f. 84
  kneeling: BBR 10607, f. 188
  pleading with nun: Add. 49622, f. 90v
  shooting stag: Arras 561, f. 103 (with three hounds)
  with claw foot, hoof, fighting with spear hybrid man with sword and shield: W. 102, f. 52
  with foot in beak of stork(?) issuing from border: W. 102, f. 49
  with gittern, man dancing: BBR 10607, f. 71 (tall pointed hat)
  with polearm (*cf.* Man nude, seated): W. 87, f. 43
Man nude, tearing hair (Despair?; *cf.* Hybrid woman tearing hair): fr. 95, f. 350 (*fig. 460*)
Man nude, tilting at keg: Bodley 264, f. 56 (3)
Man nude, tumbling (doing handstand): BBR II 988, vol. II, f. 214v; M. 754, f. 45v
Man nude, unsheathing sword: latin 1076, f. 42 (stork aiming beak at hindquarters)

M

Man nude, urinating into jug: Glazier 24, ff. 27v (simultaneously defecating into jug), 103v (domed cap) (*fig. 361*); W. 88, f. 109 (hooded)
Man nude, wearing pot on head *see* Pot, references under
Man nude, with
ax *see* Man nude and boar
bagpipe: Glazier 24, ff. 31v (*fig. 462*), 88
ball and chain attached to pole: Melbourne 1254/3, f. 13 (at L., dog lying on ground)
blanket, seen from back: Y.T. 8, f. 308v
claw feet, one hairy leg, conical cap (*cf.* Hybrid man with; Man nude, tailed, with; Man with): W. 102, f. 50
club: Add. 42130, f. 157 (Ps. 86, v. 4); W. 37, f. 57v
crosier *see* Man nude as bishop
cup *see* Man nude drinking
gittern, man dancing: BBR 10607, f. 71 (tailed, tall pointed cap)
hand bell and horn: W. 87, f. 5
head of devil: fr. 95, f. 199v
head of man on spear: Rothschild MS., f. 131v (two men carrying basket on pole) (*fig. 38*)
heads of man and woman *see* Man nude, holding
hooves instead of feet, aiming club at seven balls on ground (club-ball variant?): M. 754, f. 40v
horn and spear, seated: W. 87, f. 81
knife, hybrid man with knife, confronting dragon: M. 754, f. 23v
one leg, confronting eagle (*cf.* Man nude, cripple): Christ Church E.II, f. 55
pipe: W. 85, f. 90 (below, stork's head)
pipe and tabor: Add. 49622, ff. 192v, 204
rope tied to stone: W. 88, f. 88 (below, nude bishop with book)
sack of greens on back, hybrid man with sack(?) on back: M. 754, f. 62
Saracen headdress, spear, coffin under arm, astride cow pursuing man astride horse: Hague 78.D.40, f. 154v
scourge: M. 754, ff. 6 (with hybrid man with scythe), 45 (wearing ailettes; below, dragon breathing fire); W. 87, f. 54v (above, man with serpent coiled around neck)
shawm: Cloisters 54.1.2, f. 120 (*fig. 329*)
spear, nude woman dancing: M. 108, f. 1
staff: W. 85, f. 78
sun in hand, leaf issuing from head: M. 102, f. 140v (Ps. 136, v. 8)
switch: W. 87, f. 35
sword (*cf.* Hybrid man with sword; Man nude and dragon, fighting with; Man nude, unsheathing; Men nude, fighting with): Princeton 44-18, f. 73 (stabbing himself in head); W. 102, f. 83v (stabbing himself in upper thigh; wearing right shoe only); Y.T. 15, f. 117 (and buckler)
trumpet: Arras 47, f. 36; Douce 366, f. 71v (hooded); W. 41, f. 65v; W. 82, f. 190 (wearing ?veil); W. 90, f. 193v (nude save for cape)
astride dog (wolf?) backwards: Arras 47, f. 38v
astride dog pursuing hare: W. 90, f. 90
astride elephant, backwards: fr. 95, f. 82v
astride lion, confronting woman astride goat: Yale MS., f. 119
astride stag, backwards, wild hair: fr. 95, f. 311
held to hindquarters (*cf.* Obscaena, trumpet): Glazier 24, f. 25; Rothschild MS., f. 134 (above, man with trumpet); W. 88, f. 157 (also blowing trumpet)
man with ape on back before him: Rothschild MS., f. 183v
tilting knights at R.: W. 82, f. 15 (with fluttering head veil)
woman with bowl and sword: W. 87, f. 87v
vielle
nude cleric dancing: W. 759, f. 99
nude man with shawm: Fitz. 242, f. 3
war hammer and shield: W. 87, f. 71
wheelbarrow: W. 88, f. 67v (wearing belt, tall cap)
wheelbarrow containing nuns and clerics, approaching church: Bodley 264, f. 22 (at R., three nuns and three clerics playing club-ball) (*fig. 128*)
Man nude, wrestling *see* Wrestling, men
Man old, with staff (*cf.* Man in bed): latin 1076, f. 159
Man on ladder set against tree (*cf.* Man and bird, hunting bird): Rothschild MS., f. 174 (basket hanging from ladder); W. 88, f. 45v (with club; at R., ?lion seated)
Man on litter, seated
carried by two boys through wheatfield: Hague 78.D.40, f. 15v
drawn by horse led by man, large stone(?) on string around neck: Royal 10 E.IV, f. 94
Man on stilts *see* Stilts
Man painting *see* Illuminator; Painter
Man picking cherries *see* Man and thief

Man picking flowers (*cf.* Hare picking): Stowe 17, f. 203 (hybrid); W. 82, ff. 87v, 181v (into basket, with curved stick)

Man picking fruit from tree (*cf.* Man and woman, throwing)
- man wearing hood below; at R., fruit tree, man below removing(?) hood: Bodley 264, f. 96
- with basket and club: G.K.S. 3384, ff. 15, 61

Man picking grapes: Add. 49622, f. 107; BBR 10607, f. 134v (off border, basket on back) (*fig. 463*); Cloisters 54.1.2, f. 9v (2, one in vat treading grapes; another taking basket from woman eating off vine; September) (*fig. 464*); Nancy 249, f. 161 (2, another bringing basket to vat); Schilling MS., October; W. 90, f. 10v (into basket; September)

Man picking leaves off border into basket: Douce 6, f. 3; latin 10483, f. 31

Man playing (*cf.* Hybrid man playing; Man with bellows)
- arm(?) with bow: G.K.S. 3384, f. 229
- bellows like bagpipe: Douce 6, f. 130
- bellows with broom: W. 88, f. 191v
- bellows with grill: Cambridge Dd.5.5, f. 46
- bellows with rake: BBR 10607, f. 74; Chantilly 62, f. 53; Stowe 17, ff. 92v, 145v; W. 104, f. 14v (bellows?)
- bellows with tongs: Cambridge Dd.5.5, ff. 253 (*fig. 595*), 295; Stowe 17, f. 178v (f. 179, hybrid woman dancing); Trinity B.11.22, f. 20 (cleric) (*fig. 508*)
- cock with tongs, hare with harp: Stowe 17, f. 92v
- dog like bagpipe: Cloisters 54.1.2, ff. 34v, 166 (*fig. 516*)
- games *see* specific game
- grill with distaff, another man playing broom with spoon: Trinity B.11.22, f. 91v
- grill with rod (scourge?): Douce 6, f. 188; latin 10483, f. 118v
- grill with tongs, wearing pot on head; another man playing spoon with stick; man with trumpet: Douce 5, f. 164v (*fig. 518*)
- jawbone with bundle of reeds: Trinity B.11.22, f. 38v (astride pig)
- jawbone with plectrum, crowned, dog dancing: Cloisters 54.1.2, f. 54 (hybrid) (*fig. 511*)
- jawbone with rake: Douce 6, f. 52; G.K.S. 3384, f. 23
- jawbone with rod (scourge?): G.K.S. 3384, f. 31
- jawbone with spoon: Cloisters 54.1.2, f. 158v
- jawbone with tongs: Princeton 44-18, ff. 107v, 153
- organ (*cf.* Cleric playing): Douce 6, f. 1; M. 754, f. 13v (at L., man gesturing) (*frontispiece*)
- organ, angel with timbrel: Stowe 17, f. 129
- organ, man working bellows: Add. 42130, f. 55; Add. 49622, ff. 122v, 126
- spoon, blowing like trumpet: Douce 6, f. 134
- spoon with bow: G.K.S. 3384, f. 285v
- spoon with bow, hybrid man with bat wings playing psaltery: BBR 329-41, f. 162
- spoon with rake: G.K.S. 3384, f. 221
- spoon with stick, another man playing grill with tongs (wearing pot on head): Douce 5, f. 164v (*fig. 518*)
- vielle with rake: BBR 9411-26, f. 116; Chantilly 62, f. 117 (woman dancing) (*fig. 517*); Douce 6, f. 52; G.K.S. 3384, f. 281v (dog raising paw)
- vielle with tongs: latin 10483, f. 24

Man plowing: Add. 36684, f. 33v (two horses) (*fig. 466*); Add. 42130, f. 170 (2, four oxen; in agricultural cycle); Add. 49622, f. 153v (two oxen; butterfly in air); BBR 1175, f. 156v (*fig. 465*); Bodley 264, f. 44 (horse); Douce 6, f. 129 (horse; harrowing?); Munich c.g. 16, f. 14v (horse); Rothschild MS., f. 147v (another man sowing)

Man pointing to eye: latin 14284, f. 52v (above, in line ending, human-headed peacock/serpent)

Man pointing up (text: "Levavi oculos meos in montes"): latin 14284, f. 57

Man pouring water from basin into man's mouth below: Douce 6, f. 160

Man pouring water from spouted three-legged vessel into basin held by man below: Douce 6, f. 139

Man praying: *see* Patron (*fig. 467*); Pilgrim, beggar

Man pruning border foliage with ax: BBR 9961-62, f. 74; Bodley 264, f. 61; Douce 5, ff. 178 (owl on branch), 180v (below, owl); fr. 25526, ff. 5v, 49v, 71 (hybrid); Jacquemart 1, ff. 38, 131 (lower half nude); Jesus 40, f. 88v; latin 3893, f. 202v; latin 10483, ff. 6 (November; behind man, fire), 261v (hybrid); W. 85, f. 42v; Y.T. 27, f. 3 (March)

Man pruning border foliage with knife: Add. 50000, f. 101 (second man with horn, ax); W. 85, f. 51 (in drawers)

Man pruning border foliage with stick: G.K.S. 3384, f. 198

M

Man pruning border foliage with sword: Add. 42130, f. 54; Douce 6, f. 146v; G.K.S. 3384, ff. 37 (*fig. 322*), 178 (another man drinking); latin 10483, ff. 39v (holding basket full of small round objects in left hand), 258v; W. 110, f. 127v

Man pruning tree: Cloisters 54.1.2, f. 3v (March; another man with manure basket); Lambeth 233, ff. 3v (March), 134; Schilling MS., March; W. 88, f. 5v (March), 6 (man with ax chopping down tree); W. 90, f. 4v (March)

Man pulling (*see also* Man with rope; Quintain, balancing: men seated)
- boat containing four men rowing: Add. 42130, f. 160 (2; below, snail) (*fig. 468*)
- border stalk: latin 10484, f. 32 (2)
- down tree with rope and hook, hybrid man with ax: W. 88, f. 75
- hood over face: Cloisters 54.1.2, ff. 25v (hybrid), 50v; Y.T. 27, f. 61
- tail of hybrid man, with basket on back containing two apes: W. 88, f. 121

Man raking: Cloisters 54.1.2, f. 6v (June; another scything); W. 88, f. 150v (another carrying wheat sheaves)

Man reaching for border foliage (*cf.* Man pulling): latin 10484, f. 101v

Man reading
- ape pointing at book: Chantilly 64, ff. 109, 109v
- bird (stork?) reading over his shoulder (*cf.* Fox and hare, reading): G.K.S. 3384, f. 172
- kneeling before cleric, with book: Douce 6, f. 139v

Man reaping with sickle: Add. 36684, f. 139; Add. 42130, ff. 172v (three women reaping), 173 (five men stacking), 173v (4, driving and pushing haywain pulled by three horses; all scenes in agricultural cycle); BBR 9391, f. 95v; Bodley 264, f. 62 (another man scything); Cloisters 54.1.2, f. 7v (July); fr. 25526, f. 131 (another man threshing); G.K.S. 3384, f. 17v; latin 10483, f. 217v (hybrid, cutting border leaf); Schilling MS., August; W. 88, ff. 8v (June; man with wheat sheaf on back), 10v (August; f. 11, man drinking from jug, flanked by stacks of wheat), 150 (f. 150v, two harvesters, one drinking from jug, the other carrying two wheat sheaves on pole across shoulder) (*fig. 469*); W. 90, f. 9v (August); Y.T. 27, f. 8 (August; tying bundle of wheat)

Man reclining (*cf.* Man asleep)
- on elbow: Cloisters 54.1.2, f. 175
- on mat, holding sword; at L., man with shawm kneeling: W. 88, f. 164v
- on stool, head in arms, legs raised: Glazier 24, f. 166 (at L., butterfly)

Man ringing bell on bell rope: Add. 10292, f. 1 (two); Fitz. 288, f. 189 (two; issuing from border; above, man shooting bird; at R., cock crowing; Offices of the Dead); latin 14284, f. 17; M. 754, f. 16 (nude); Nancy 249, f. 42 (hare with hand bell); Stowe 17, f. 151v (issuing from border)

Man ringing bell with stick (*cf.* Man with hand bell): Douce 6, f. 153 (bell attached to hood of beggar with basket on back containing ape) (*fig. 52*)

Man rowing *see* Man in boat

Man sawing wood (*cf.* Man and woman, sawing; Man chopping): Royal 2 B.VII, f. 99v (2); Royal 10 E.IV, f. 99v (2); W. 88, f. 43 (2)

Man sculpting *see* Sculptor

Man scything: Arras 47, f. 248v; BBR 1175, ff. 116, 177; BBR 9391, f. 95; Bodley 264, ff. 35v, 62 (another man reaping); Cambridge Dd. 5.5, f. 325 (at R., man sowing) (*fig. 470*); Chantilly 64, ff. 27v, 158; Cloisters 54.1.2, f. 6v (July; another man raking); Douce 118, f. 114; Lambeth 233, f. 6v (June; carrying scythe over shoulder); latin 3893, f. 216v; Rothschild MS., f. 165; Schilling MS., July; W. 88, ff. 9v (July; at R., jug and whetstone hanging on pole; f. 10, woman with rake, man with pitchfork, right hand on her breast), 123v; W. 90, f. 8v (July); Y.T. 27, f. 7 (July)

Man seated *see* Man at lectern; Man nude

Man serving food and drink *see* Banquet

Man shoeing goose *see* Proverbs: goose

Man shooting arrow at border: Douce 118, ff. 155v, 161v, 168

Man shooting male head in eye: latin 10483, f. 94

Man singing from book: Douce 6, f. 191 (crowned cock's head below)

Man singing from scroll with two clerics: G.K.S. 3384, f. 138

Man sitting in basket *see* Fox with basket; Proverbs: eggs

M

Man sleeping *see* Man asleep

Man sliding, propelling himself with two sticks, another man skating: Douce 5, f. lav (February) (*fig. 471*)

Man sowing: Add. 42130, f. 170v (at R., dog chasing away crows; in agricultural cycle); BBR 329-41, f. 123v; Cambridge Dd. 5.5, ff. 274 (at L., man with pipe and tabor), 325 (at L., man scything) (*fig. 470*); Cloisters 54.1.2, f. 10v (October); Munich c.g. 16, f. 14v; Rothschild MS., f. 147v (another man plowing); Schilling MS., September (*fig. 126*); W. 88, ff. 11v (September; f. 12, woman leading horse pulling harrow), 147; W. 90, f. 11v (October); Y.T. 13, f. 96 (at R., fall of idols); Y.T. 75, f. 61 (approached by Herod's men)

Man spading (*cf.* Adam delving; Hybrid man shoveling; Man digging grave): Add. 49622, f. 158v; BBR II 988, vol. II, f. 186v; Harley 6563, f. 89; latin 14284, f. 53v

Man spinning: G.K.S. 3384, f. 35v (at R., man with spear looking through telescope); Royal 10 E.IV, f. 147v (*Wright's Chaste Wife* sequence)

Man spitting *see* Man vomiting

Man stabbing himself *see* Man nude with sword; Man with —

Man standing on broken fence: Add. 42130, f. 162v (Ps. 88, v. 41)

Man standing on hands *see* Man balancing

Man standing on table *see* Woman nude, straddling

Man stealing fish out of basket on man's back (*cf.* Man fishing): W. 88, f. 153v

Man sticking out tongue (*cf.* Hybrid man; Man nude): Add. 42130, f. 53 (game? kneeling, gesturing, flanked by two seated men, one holding chin, the other pulling his mouth to sides with both hands)

Man stringing up hammock: Add. 42130, f. 200 (2)

Man supporting initial *see* Initial

Man swimming: fr. 12400, f. 115v (nude; falconer; garments heaped on bank; at R., falcon striking duck) (*fig. 472*); G.K.S. 3384, f. 57 (at R., man removing garment, another man holding garment) (*fig. 473*); Royal 2 B.VII, f. 170 (f. 169v, man in boat directing); Trinity B.11.22, f. 121 (2)

Man tailed, dragging hare by ears (*cf.* Man nude, tailed): Fitz. 298, f. 113

Man tearing hair (Despair? *Cf.* Man nude; Woman tearing): G.K.S. 3384, f. 82 (another man vomiting gold coins into man's lap)

Man threatening unarmed man, with sword and buckler: Add. 42130, f. 169 (Ps. 93, v.6)

Man three-faced, at table, eating and drinking (*cf.* Cleric; Janus; Man, head of): latin 3893, f. 216 (wearing cap)

Man threshing: Add. 42130, f. 74v (2); Add. 49622, f. 121 (2); BBR 9411-26, f. 129; Chantilly 64, f. 39v; Cloisters 54.1.2, f. 8v (August); fr. 25526, f. 131 (another man reaping); G.K.S. 3384, ff. 161, 301; latin 10483, f. 284; Royal 2 B.VII, f. 165v; W. 88, ff. 12v (October; f. 13, man winnowing), 118v (*fig. 476*), 145v; W. 760, f. 185 (another man winnowing; erased)

Man tied to tree *see* Wild man and knight, slain

Man tilting *see* Men tilting; Quintain, tilting at

Man training *see* Man and ape; — and bear; — and dog

Man treading grapes (*cf.* Man picking): Bodley 264, f. 133 (7, also sampling); Cloisters 54.1.2, f. 9v (September; another taking basket from woman eating off vine, two others picking grapes); fr. 25526, f. 36v (at L., two men with baskets on back); W. 88, f. 75v (2, bathing?)

Man tumbling *see* Contortionist; Man balancing; Tumbler, references under

Man turning grindstone, man sharpening knife: Add. 42130, f. 78v (2)

Man turning winch(?): Douce 6, f. 192 (2) (*fig. 474*)

Man two-faced
  drinking from two cups (*cf.* Hybrid man, two-faced; Janus; Man three-faced): latin 10483, f. 48v (wearing cap)
  with two trumpets (*cf.* Hybrid man, two-faced): Douce 118, f. 159; M. 754, f. 11 (hybrid man with pipe and tabor, four apes dancing)

Man two-torsoed (nude), fighting crowned dragon in tree, with sword and shield: Rutland Ps., f. 72

Man tying faggots, another carrying faggots (*cf.* Man chopping): latin 14284, f. 56

Man unsheathing sword *see* Man with sword, unsheathing

Man vomiting (or spitting): Douce 5, f. 154 (wind, blowing?); Lambeth 233, f. 2 (January)
  attended by ape with basin: Add. 49622, f. 62 (*fig. 477*)

M attended by hybrid man with basin: Add. 49622, f. 48v
attended by man holding his head: W. 88, f. 63 (into basin)
attended by woman with basin: Add. 49622, f. 124v
coins (gold) into man's lap, tearing hair (Gluttony and Despair? *Cf.* Man nude, tearing hair): G.K.S. 3384, f. 82 (*fig. 475*)
liquid: Douce 6, f. 77 (green liquid into basin, tearing hair); G.K.S. 3384, f. 54 (cleric?)
spoons (four): Douce 6, f. 176
Man washing (*cf.* Man bathing)
dishes: Royal 10 E.IV, f. 143v (*Wright's Chaste Wife* sequence)
laundry: G.K.S. 3384, f. 45v (hands? above, woman looking on); Royal 10 E.IV, f. 144v (*Wright's Chaste Wife* sequence)
Man wearing animal costume *see* Man in costume as
Man wearing pot on head *see* Pot, references under
Man weeding with woman, breaking up clods with mallets: Add. 42130, ff. 171v-172 (in agricultural cycle)
Man whipping top *see* Top-whipping
Man whipped(?) by two men with whips to which gloves are attached; in center, man holding rope tied to stake: Douce 6, f. 94v
Man winding wool *see* Man with reel
Man winding wool on spit, bishop supervising: Cloisters 54.1.2, f. 167v (2, hybrids)
Man winged *see* Man with wings
Man winnowing *see* Man threshing
Man with abacus: Christ Church E.II, f. 44v (Min.: King, man with two moneybags; text: "On the removal of avaricious men from the court")
Man with asperge and situla (cleric?): G.K.S. 3384, f. 220 (above, bishop)
Man with ax (*see also* Man and boar, aiming; — and cow, aiming; — and dog, with; — and dragon, astride, with; — and fox, pursuing; — and hybrid king; and hybrid man, threatening; — and knight, fighting; — and pig, confronting; — and snail, fighting; — and wolf, killing; — at table; — chopping wood; — nude and snail, fighting; — pruning; — with column): fr. 95, f. 30; Lambeth 233, ff. 167, 175v
aiming at head of bald man: latin 10483, f. 100v
brandishing: BBR 10607, f. 207v
confronting three men issuing from border: Add. 49622, f. 139v
striking at green mound: Add. 49622, f. 211v
Man with bagpipe (*see also* Men dancing; Queen accompanied): Add. 42130, ff. 13 (below, tailed ape), 176; Add. 49622, f. 107v; Bodley 264, ff. 26, 36v, 44, 58; Cambridge Dd. 5.5, f. 253 (*fig. 595*); Cloisters 54.1.2, ff. 25, 49, 63v, 143, 155; G.K.S. 3384, ff. 160v (*fig. 307*), 182; Glazier 24, f. 31v; Lambeth 233, f. 69v; latin 10483, ff. 43v, 167v; M. 754, f. 65v; Stowe 12, f. 257; W. 37, ff. 127v, 129; W. 88, ff. 19, 25v, 31, 54; W. 110, f. 18v (issuing from border); Yale MS., f. 308
Annunciation to shepherds below: Add. 24681, f. 44
ape making admonishing gesture: Add. 49622, f. 57
balancing on man's shoulders: Y.T. 19, f. 3
barefoot, accompanied by lion: latin 16260, f. 5v
blown by dog across shoulder: Trinity B.11.22, f. 36v
cleric playing organ: BBR 9961-62, f. 66 (above, woman with birdcage) (*fig. 118*)
crippled, confronting ape with basket on back containing three apes: fr. 95, f. 64v
dog dancing: G.K.S. 3384, f. 209; W. 88, f. 113v
dragging helmeted head of giant (David and Goliath?): BBR 9391, f. 4
followed by tall man in stag costume: fr. 95, f. 261
fox dancing: BBR 9411-26, f. 103v (dog?)
half-nude, hybrid man dancing: Arras 1043, f. 126v
half-nude, woman with vielle, half-nude man in blue hood dancing: St. Omer 5, f. 1
hybrid bird with eel: Jacquemart 1, f. 16
man and woman kneeling before Eros: Douce 6, f. 159v (*fig. 402*)
man dancing: Cloisters 54.1.2, f. 166 (on bagpiper's head) (*fig. 516*); Fitz. 298, f. 90v; fr. 776, f. 291v; W. 90, f. 60v
man playing dog like bagpipe: Cloisters 54.1.2, ff. 34v, 166 (*fig. 516*)
man training ape: Rutland Ps., f. 71
man with mortar and pestle: Arras 1043, f. 149v
man with pipe and tabor: Add. 36684, f. 46v (apes dancing); W. 88, f. 119v
man with psaltery, man fighting snail with spear: W. 90, f. 151 (at L., hare)
man with tabor: Bodley 264, f. 104v

men fighting with swords and bucklers: Royal 14 E.III, f. 140
men with gittern, hand organ, harp, trumpet, vielle: W. 104, f. 61
men with hurdy-gurdy (blind, with dog), flageolet, hand organ, kettledrums on back, gittern, harp, psaltery, vielle (*cf.* Man with cymbals): Bodley 264, f. 180v
men with trumpets, kettledrums on back, harp, cornet, vielle: Bodley 264, f. 157v
one-legged, confronting ape with basket on back containing apes: fr. 95, f. 64v
wearing garland on head: W. 45, f. 282v (above, Franciscan seated)
woman dancing: BBR 9391, f. 108v (Min.: Annunciation to shepherds); BBR 10607, f. 97; D.P. 35, f. 40 (two); Douce 5, ff. 119, 153v, 216; fr. 95, f. 262; Hague 78.D.40, f. 74; M. 754, f. 59v (at R., two men dancing; above, man with vielle); W. 104, f. 3; W. 109, ff. 310v, 353; Yale MS., ff. 75, 175 (cripple looking on), 202v, 277
man standing on her shoulders: BBR 9961-62, f. 66 (*fig. 118*)
on shoulders of man with bagpipe: Add. 10293, f. 1; Add. 29253, f. 36; BBR 10607, f. 133 (woman dancing with hybrid man); Burney 345, f. 127v; C.B. 62, f. 208v; Cloisters 54.1.2, f. 39; Douce 5, f. 125; Douce 6, f. 129v; G.K.S. 3384, ff. 58, 196 (above, man with vielle); N.K.S. 41, f. 132 (supporting initial on her back); Royal 14 E.III, f. 3; Stowe 17, f. 31 (ape with pipe and tabor); Y.T. 27, f. 82v; Yale MS., f. 180
with three men: fr. 25526, f. 107
with two men: fr. 25526, f. 43
woman doing handstand: Douce 5, f. 18; fr. 95, ff. 205, 262
woman with garland in hands: G.K.S. 3384, f. 34
woman with vielle *see* Man with bagpipe, half-nude
Man with ball (*cf.* Club-ball; Handball; *see also* Man balancing, on head)
aiming at second ball placed on mound; at R., man gesturing (form of *boccie?*): fr. 776, f. 154
gesturing, back turned to bald man with club: latin 10484, f. 14
issuing from mouth of monster, grasping its tail (*cf.* Man and fish emerging): latin 14284, f. 27
juggling, playing with: latin 10483, f. 54v
Man with basin (*see also* Knight with head of beast; Man and beast, killing; Man vomiting): Cambridge Dd. 5.5, f. 302
catching liquid flowing from large vessel tipped by man and woman with long pole: Douce 6, f. 98
human head in basin: Cambridge Dd. 5.5, f. 325
Man with basket *see* Man and eel; — and woman, fighting; Man and woman, with; Man picking
Man with basket on back (*cf.* Beggar)
approaching hybrid woman(?), gesturing: latin 3893, f. 197v
containing ape: BBR 10607, f. 34v; Cambrai 87, f. 25 (two apes); Chantilly 62, f. 141v (two apes); Laud Lat. 84, f. 227 (two apes) (*fig. 478*); Rothschild MS., f. 135v (falling forward); W. 88, f. 121 (two apes; man pulling tail of hybrid man); Yale MS., f. 66v
containing belts(?): Douce 6, f. 128 (basket tied with strap across chest)
containing birds(?): Rothschild MS., f. 165
containing bread(?); at L., man striking stone(?) with hammer: Cambridge Dd. 5.5, f. 392v
containing bread, woman spinning (*Wright's Chaste Wife* sequence): Royal 10 E.IV, f. 116
containing child(?): Rothschild MS., f. 136
containing child, approaching woman wringing her hands: W. 109, f. 74v
containing fish: Douce 6, f. 134; W. 88, f. 153v (another man stealing fish)
containing fruit(?): Cambridge Dd. 5.5, f. 386
containing grapes, picking grapes off border: BBR 10607, f. 134v
containing hares: Y.T. 8, f. 263 (two, one with horn)
physician(?): G.K.S. 3384, f. 39 (low domed cap; above, bishop's head)
with club and staff: W. 90, f. 89
with staff, wearing gold robe: fr. 95, f. 33v
Man with bat wings
putting stone: Arras 1043, f. 7
with hand organ: Arras 139, f. 89
with trumpet: Arras 47, f. 31
Man with beakers (silver), peddling to man: Douce 118, f. 55
Man with bell *see* Man ringing; Man with hand bells
Man with bellows (*see also* Man playing; — play-

ing organ; Men fighting with spoon; Obscaena, bellows)
blowing into like trumpet (drinking from? *Cf.* Hybrid man with): Cloisters 54.1.2, ff. 21 (below, hybrid man with pot), 203 (with mock crosier); latin 10483, ff. 37, 184; latin 10484, f. 2v; Y.T. 27, f. 72v (with triangle)
blowing into mouth of head issuing from border: W. 88, f. 99v
wearing on head
carrying helmet, confronting man with Luttrell arms on banner: Add. 42130, f. 157
with crosier, blessing: Cloisters 54.1.2, f. 37
working under fire: BBR 10607, f. 103v (Min.: St. Lawrence martyred; Ps. 68); Burney 345, f. 69 (on his head, devil with scourge; Min.: St. Lawrence martyred; Ps. 51); Royal 10 E.IV, f. 142 (pot cooking over fire; *Wright's Chaste Wife* sequence)
Man with birdcage *see* Man and bird, hunting bird
Man with birdcages (two), selling(?): Bodley 264, f. 126v (at L., woman snaring birds with dummy fox)
Man with bladder on stick, man with horn (*cf.* Man nude, balancing on pole): W. 88, f. 29
Man with blankets(?) on head, leaving house: Douce 6, f. 108v (three: orange, white, blue)
Man with bone (club?), threatening dog: Trinity B.11.22, f. 128v
Man with book (*cf.* Man reading)
and serpent, issuing from border: W. 87, f. 20v (hooded)
beside him on ground, small open box: Exeter 47, f. 37v
half-nude: W. 45, f. 161 (above, ape-falconer seated on hillock)
showing book to hybrid man: G.K.S. 3384, f. 301
Man with boot, holding (*cf.* Man with shoe): Douce 6, ff. 67 (also coin), 165
Man with boots, holding, with black (iron?) hoop on pole across shoulder: Cambridge Dd.5.5, f. 191v
Man with bow and arrow *see* Archer; Archery; references under Man and (name of prey), hunting with; Man and (name of prey), shooting; Man with pipe and tabor, man bending bow
Man with bowl (*cf.* Man with basin)
containing fish(?): Y.T. 27, f. 2 (February)
containing stork pecking man's eye (*cf.* Fables: fox and stork, Part I, variant): G.K.S. 3384, f. 44v
pouring greenish liquid into, from pitcher (*cf.* Man drinking, pouring): Auct. D.3.2, f. 193
wearing on head, with staff: Fitz. 2-1954, f. 159
Man with branch: Cloisters 54.1.2, f. 4v (April; standing between two young trees); Schilling MS., April (two)
Man with bucket (*see also* Man and woman, bathing)
filling at well: fr. 25526, f. 8 (2, two)
holding, jug on head: Y.T. 27, f. 1 (January)
on pole across back: Cloisters 54.1.2, f. 19v (two); fr. 25526, ff. 110v (two), 84 (two); latin 10483, f. 164 (two, gesturing)
Man with buzines *see* Man with double pipe
Man with calipers, measuring column: G.K.S. 3384, f. 111 (*fig. 479*)
Man with censer: W. 760, f. 182
Man with chalice (*cf.* Man with cup)
and wafer, presenting to stork (fable reference?): Jacquemart 1, f. 41v
presenting to woman in doorway of building (fabliau?): fr. 25526, f. 109
raising two fingers: latin 1076, f. 7 (Ps. 1)
Man with chest on back: Douce 6, f. 101; G.K.S. 3384, f. 149 (followed by man hammering nail into lid) (*fig. 481*)
Man with churn: BBR 9411-26, f. 134v (below, nude man grasping buttocks); Chantilly 64, ff. 29, 29v; Douce 5, f. 24 (pot? mortar?); W. 88, ff. 16, 17v (at R., dog climbing into jug)
Man with claw feet (*cf.* Hybrid man with; Man nude, tailed; Man nude, with)
carrying rake across shoulder: W. 90, f. 161 (at L., rider)
confronting man/bird with ax: Christ Church E.II, f. 53
fighting with sword and buckler man issuing from border: W. 761, f. 11v
supporting initial, falcon perched on one of his feet (*cf.* Hybrid man as falconer): W. 85, f. 66 (above, man carrying sheep on his back)
Man with cloak(?), holding: G.K.S. 3384, ff. 127v, 266v
Man with club *see* Hercules; Man and woman, confronting with; Man nude with

Man with coin (*cf.* Man counting; — hoarding; — vomiting): latin 10483, f. 128v (wafer?)
aiming at gameboard: Douce 6, f. 195v
and stool basket, before physician: W. 82, f. 75v
Man with column, biting *see* Proverbs: man
Man with column, carrying: Royal 10 E.IV, ff. 17v, 90 (log? another man with ax between two trees)
Man with comb
and mirror, combing hair: fr. 95, f. 295v; G.K.S. 3384, f. 288; Harley 6563, f. 36v (f. 37, old man in bed; Ages of man?)
combing hair of man (*cf.* Barber; Man cutting): G.K.S. 3384, f. 73
Man with cornet *see* Man with horn
Man with crocket (*cf.* Hare balancing; Sheep —): Yale MS., f. 248
Man with crook, beast balancing tapers at either end of rod held in mouth: Douce 5, f. 39 (*fig. 480*)
Man with crosier *see* Bishop; Man with bellows
Man with crossbow (*see also* Man and [name of prey], bending)
aiming at beast: Add. 42130, f. 54
bending: St. Omer 5, f. 245
loading: Yale MS., ff. 85v, 132v
Man with cup and pitcher (*cf.* Man drinking; Man with chalice)
another man bearing serving dish, pointing to right (*cf.* Banquet): fr. 776, f. 67
offering cup to woman: Douce 6, f. 96
Man with cups tied to himself, astride horse, followed by man with spear and jug: Douce 6, f. 129v (greeting bagpiper, woman dancing on his shoulders; at R., trees)
Man with cymbals: Bodley 264, f. 86
contortionist: Rutland Ps., f. 73 (*fig. 433*)
hybrid man with triangle: latin 10484, f. 29
men with hand bells, bagpipe, kettledrums on back, tabor, hand organ, vielle, mandola, harp (*cf.* Man with bagpipe, men): Bodley 264, f. 173
men with hand bells, double trumpet, gittern, hand organ, psaltery, vielle, hybrid man with bagpipe: Bodley 264, f. 188v
men with hand bells, tabor: Bodley 264, f. 120v
men with trumpets; Royal 2 B.VII, f. 178v (2)
Man with distaff and spindle: Douce 5, f. 159; G.K.S. 3384, f. 170
approaching steaming tankard: M. 754, f. 94 (distaff?)
followed by dog and woman brandishing stick: Douce 5, f. 129
pursuing cat (proverb? *cf.* Man nude and cat): Glazier 24, f. 66
pursuing fox with cock: fr. 25526, f. 91
two cocks nibbling at spindle (*cf.* Cocks, confronted): Douce 118, f. 7v (hooded woman?) (*fig. 133*)
woman spinning (*cf.* Man with reel): Arras 47, f. 208v
Man with double pipe (*see also* Man with harp, end): Cloisters 54.1.2, f. 58; Douce 6, f. 123; Harley 6563, ff. 34, 38; Royal 10 E.IV, f. 58 (woman with pipe and tabor, another balancing on two sword points)
Man with double trumpet (*cf.* Centaur with shawms): Bodley 264, f. 35; Douce 118, f. 159 (two-faced); latin 10483, ff. 50, 258v; M. 754, f. 11 (two-faced; hybrid man with pipe and tabor, four apes dancing)
Man with drill (?)
drilling border stalk: latin 14284, f. 34v
drilling human head on ground: W. 88, f. 80v
Man with eel *see* Man and eel
Man with egg (*see also* Proverbs: eggs)
aiming at egg on mound: fr. 776, f. 154 (stone?)
beating with stick (proverb?): Cloisters 54.1.2, f. 170 (stone?)
buying from woman with basket of eggs: Trinity B.11.22, f. 160v
feeding beast from basket (*cf.* Man feeding animal): G.K.S. 3384, f. 137 (rolls?)
holding up, examining: latin 14284, f. 58v
holding up, flanked by two apes (one robed) stealing and sampling eggs; above, sun: Douce 6, f. 93av
holding up board on which are placed four eggs (rolls?): Douce 6, f. 58 (above, stork aiming beak at man's eye)
preparing as food for falcon, boiling in pot over fire: fr. 12400, f. 99v
Man with faggots (*cf.* Man chopping wood): latin 14284, f. 56 (2, tying, carrying); W. 90, f. 7v (June); Y.T. 27, f. 54 (carrying on back)
Man with falcon *see* Falconer; Man and falcon
Man with ferret (rat?) on shoulder, kneeling; two birds flying nearby: Jesus 40, f. 71v
Man with flail *see* Man threshing
Man with fork *see* Man blowing toasting fork
Man with fruit (apple?), aiming at devil with branches (*cf.* Ape with fruit; Man picking):

Rutland Ps., ff. 24-23v (f. 24, man asleep)
Man with garland *see* Man and woman, kneeling; Man with vielle, garland
Man with gittern (*see also* Man and woman, dancing; Man in costume as boar; Man with cymbals, men with hand bells): Bodley 264, ff. 23v, 58; Cambrai 87, f. 29; Fitz. 298, f. 1; G.K.S. 3384, f. 43; Laud Lat. 84, ff. 79v, 197 (at L., St. Margaret); M. 729, f. 342 (above, bird flying); St. Omer 5, f. 125; Trinity B.11.22, f. 199v
  man dancing: Christ Church E.II, f. 31v; fr. 776, f. 10v; W. 88, f. 80
  mermaid/siren dancing: Y.T. 8, f. 276v
  woman dancing: BBR 10607, f. 65; G.K.S. 3384, f. 184; Laud Lat. 84, ff. 272v-273; Stowe 17, f. 128
  woman playing organ, man with shawm: M. 88, f. 23 (ape pointing at woman)
  woman with vielle, woman dancing: Fitz. 298, f. 1 (*fig. 566*)
Man with greens
  confronting giant with holes in knees of trousers, fallen over backwards (fabliau or riddle?): Chantilly 64, ff. 27, 27v
  with wolf and lamb preparing to cross river in boat (riddle): Douce 366, f. 89 (*fig. 482*)
Man with grill *see* Man playing
Man with grindstone, holding dog's nose to (proverb?): W. 109, f. 204 (*fig. 346*)
Man with hammer (*see also* St. Dunstan)
  coinmaker(?): Cambridge Dd.5.5, f. 217v; Trinity B.11.22, f. 192v (*fig. 483*)
  hammering nail into border of initial (*cf.* Man with drill): Douce 5, f. 205v
  hammering nail into lid of chest on man's back: G.K.S. 3384, f. 149
  hammering peg into head of bearded man (*cf.* Man with drill): Douce 6, f. 197
  hammering pot, holding chisel (punch?): Douce 6, f. 136
  hammering round object on stand: Cambridge Dd.5.5, f. 392v
  hammering tall object on anvil: latin 10484, f. 26
  kneeling, hands raised, three stones(?) in background: Christ Church E.II, f. 27
  leatherworker(?) with Minnekaestchen(?); at R., woman: Nancy 249, f. 27 (*fig. 484*)
  supporting miniature of Christ bearing the cross: Cloisters 54.1.2, f. 61v
Man with hammock, stringing: Add. 42130, f. 200 (2)
Man with hand on heart, jumping: Jacquemart 1, f. 66
Man with hand bells (*see also* Man and dog with; Man and woman, dancing; Man ringing bell; Man with cymbals; Men dancing): BBR II 988, vol. II, f. 287; Cloisters 54.1.2, ff. 22 (below, goat playing jawbone with rake) (*fig. 510*), 69v (three on strings, also with pipe), 92 (striking with stick; below, wild-haired hybrid man praying); Douce 6, ff. 10, 145 (another man with ?lantern; below, man praying), 157v (two); latin 3893, ff. 220 (two), 234 (two); latin 10483, ff. 36v (at R., dragon), 107 (three on strings); latin 14284, f. 15v (and pipe, woman dancing) (*fig. 311*); Princeton 44-18, f. 175 (woman dancing); Verdun 107, f. 26 (two; at L., falconer, lion with vielle) (*fig. 182*); W. 88, ff. 146v, 168; Y.T. 27, f. 130 (three on strings)
Man with hand organ (*see also* Men dancing; Queen accompanied): Add. 10293, f. 1; Add. 42130, f. 176; Add. 49622, ff. 99, 119, 139; Arras 47, f. 52 (crowned) (*fig. 485*); Arras 139, f. 89 (with bat wings); Arras 729, f. 8; Cambrai 87, f. 19; Cambrai 102, f. 283v; Christ Church E.II, f. 29 (another man with vielle); Douce 6, f. 162; Fitz. 298, f. 115 (hare standing on his ears before him); fr. 95, f. 273; G.K.S. 3384, ff. 116, 122, 208, 232v, 241v, 275v, 280v, 286, 303v, 348v; latin 1076, f. 7 (Ps. 1); latin 14284, f. 63 (Ps. 1); Laud Lat. 84, f. 230v; St. Omer 5, ff. 41, 89 (*fig. 486*); W. 88, f. 131; W. 90, f. 135 (another man with vielle), 192v; Yale MS., f. 62v (another man with vielle)
Man with harmonica(?): Cloisters 54.1.2, f. 166 (whistle?) (*fig. 516*)
Man with harp (*see also* Banquet, men; Man with vielle, men): Add. 49622, f. 153v; BBR 10607, f. 116; Bodley 264, f. 17v (above, butterfly); Fitz. 298, f. 39v (peaked hood); Lambeth 233, f. 34v; M. 761, f. 95v (adjacent text: "coment lon doit harpe temprer"); Melbourne 1254/3, f. 89; Rutland Ps., f. 50; W. 82, f. 211v (tall peaked cap, bell at tip); W. 88, f. 83 (bald); Yale MS., f. 209 (winged headdress) (*fig. 487*)
  before swan (Bestiary representation): Cambrai

102, f. 361; Douce 118, f. 65; Stowe 17, f. 46 (crowned, standing on swan's neck); Trinity B.11.22, f. 79v; W. 85, f. 98v
dog dancing: W. 88, f. 169
end of harp resting in carrying case, man with double pipe, man dancing: Christ Church E.II, f. 31
man and woman seated at gameboard under tree, dog leaping over stream, hybrid abbot: M. 754, f. 33v
man with sword and buckler, hybrid man as physician: W. 104, f. 32v
man with trumpet: Add. 42130, f. 174v (Ps. 97: 5, 6)
men with bagpipe, psaltery, vielle: Vienna 1826,* f. 85v (Ps. 97)
men with pipe and tabor, psaltery, trumpet: Spencer 2, f. 137v
men (2) with vielles, two men with pipes standing on heads of men beating tabors: Exeter 47, f. 33v
woman dancing: BBR 10607, f. 144v

Man with harrow (?) (*cf.* Man harrowing)
carrying, hybrid man with psaltery: W. 88, f. 100v
carrying on back, with trumpet, woman dancing: fr. 95, f. 325v

Man with head of (*cf.* Man and beast, holding; Man, head of)
cow (bull?) on back: BBR 10607, f. 125v
devil, praying: W. 87, f. 108v
leaves: Add. 38114, f. 67v (*fig. 488*)
sheep in hands (*cf.* Man and sheep): G.K.S. 3384, f. 25
stag on spear, barefoot: W. 90, f. 167v (at R., deer running toward him)

Man with hood (*cf.* Blindman's buff; Hood; Merman with; Strike-the-pot)
clutching, dragged by hare: Fitz. 298, f. 38 (tailor?)
containing dog: Cloisters 54.1.2, f. 173
holding, pointing at man (woman?) with red hood over face bending down toward gray hood on ground: fr. 25526, f. 153v (2, with orange, blue hoods)
over face, with club, approaching wheat sheaf, man looking on: W. 88, f. 74v
scraping with knife, pierced with spear or long needle by hare: Fitz. 298, f. 47 (tailor)
throwing in air: Douce 5, f. 95 (gold)
waving hood at hybrid creature with two heads (male and female): W. 88, f. 33
waving hood at woman conversing with man with back turned: fr. 25526, f. 157

Man with hoop: Douce 5, f. 127v; Nancy 249, f. 156v; Trinity B.11.22, f. 147v
carrying two hoops suspended from rod and stick across shoulder: Cambridge Dd. 5.5, f. 46
holding, another man doing somersault: Trinity B.11.22, f. 201v
holding, another man preparing to jump through: Bodley 264, f. 64v
sitting on tightrope on which large hoop is balanced: Rylands lat. R.117, f. 193
training two dogs to jump through: Trinity B.11.22, f. 76

Man with horn (*see also* Man and [name of prey], hunting with, references under): Add. 42130, f. 164v (cornet); Add. 49622, f. 43v; Douce 366, f. 71v; Lambeth 233, ff. 100v, 137, 154, 163, 166v; W. 82, ff. 28, 205v; W. 88, ff. 27v, 38, 42v, 83v (and spear); W. 104, f. 34 (at R., hare); W. 111, f. 108v
cleric at altar: W. 88, f. 77v
cleric with psaltery, two hybrid men with bagpipe and horn: W. 104, f. 39v (3)
dog dancing: G.K.S. 3384, f. 130
dog following: W. 82, f. 42 (hunter)
woman dancing: Add. 38114, f. 1
woman dancing on his shoulders: Nancy 249, f. 62

Man with hurdy-gurdy (*cf.* Man with symphony)
hare with hand bells: fr. 25526, f. 8v
woman dancing: Christ Church E.II, f. 36 (*fig. 452*)

Man with jug (or pitcher; *cf.* Jug, references under; Man balancing funnel; — drinking; Man with bowl; Men fighting, with spoon): Fitz. 2-1954, f. 176v; G.K.S. 3384, f. 133; W. 87, f. 60 (and bowl)
and gold cup, man with serving dish: fr. 776, f. 67
and paddle across shoulder: Exeter 47, f. 91
carrying on shoulder: Douce 5, ff. 94, 218 (below, cleric with book)
emptying: W. 87, f. 49v (hybrid, leaves issuing from cap)
on half-nude man kneeling below: Cloisters 54.1.2, f. 178v
on hybrid woman below threatening dog with switch: Douce 5, f. 54
on head: Cloisters 54.1.2, f. 173; Exeter 47, f. 87 (border plant growing out of jug)

on head, water bucket in hand: Y.T. 27, f. 1 (January)
Man with keg *see* Man drinking
Man with keg on back: Cloisters 54.1.2, f. 123 (hybrid, crippled); G.K.S. 3384, ff. 33 (below, man with ?coin), 124 (another man holding out cup)
Man with kettledrums, playing (*see also* Man and woman, dancing; Man with bagpipe, men; Man with trumpet, men): Add. 42130, ff. 59, 176
Man with knife *see* Man biting; — juggling; Man with hood, scraping
Man with lantern, pointing at fish wearing cape (*see also* Man with hand bells): Cloisters 54.1.2, f. 56
Man with leaves growing out of head, barefoot, with staff (*cf.* Man with jug, emptying): Add. 38114, f. 67v
Man with log *see* Man with column; — with faggots
Man with lure (*cf.* Falconer): Add. 38114, f. 4v (hunting bird); W. 85, f. 6v (swinging before bird)
Man with mace, before city gate of Lessines: BBR 1175, f. 105
Man with mallet, raised to strike ladder on top of which sits woman with distaff and spindle (scold?): Rutland Ps., f. 66
Man with mandola (*see also* Banquet, men; Man and woman, dancing, hands; Men dancing, hands joined by ribbons): Bodley 264, f. 105; Chantilly 62, f. 131; Cloisters 54.1.2, f. 16; Trinity B.11.22, f. 199v (*fig. 335*); W. 87, f. 65v
Man with message: Chantilly 64, ff. 130, 130v (for woman praying at *prie-dieu*); Douce 5, f. 30v (for knight with spear and shield)
Man with mirror (*see also* Man with comb): Douce 6, f. 124; G.K.S. 3384, f. 13v (above, abbot's head); M. 754, f. 32
  confronting hare with single gold horn (unicorn variant?): Trinity B.11.22, f. 18
  holding huge mirror up to woman (*cf.* Knight and woman, holding): G.K.S. 3384, ff. 116v, 321
  looking into, hand to face, bearded: Cloisters 54.1.2, f. 197
Man with mortar and pestle: Cambridge Dd. 5.5, f. 388
  ape drinking, woman at table on which are three rolls(?): M. 754, f. 43
  ape roasting fowl on spit: Stowe 17, f. 176
  man with bagpipe: Arras 1043, f. 149v
Man with ointment jar *see* Jesus Christ, life of: Deposition
Man with oven, carrying burning oven on back, ape pulling out tray containing two rolls (proverb? *cf.* Baker): G.K.S. 3384, f. 67
Man with pickax (*cf.* Man with ax): Add. 49622, f. 211v
Man with pincers (*cf.* Ape vomiting; Proverbs: goose; St. Dunstan)
  approaching hybrid man: Add. 42130, f. 34
  clamping bird's beak shut: G.K.S. 3384, f. 84
  wearing pointed cap; behind him at R., monster with club and shield: Add. 42130, f. 58v
Man with pipe: G.K.S. 3384, f. 173
  and bell, woman dancing: G.K.S. 3384, f. 15v
  dog dancing: G.K.S. 3384, f. 130
  woman dancing: G.K.S. 3384, f. 100
Man with pipe and tabor: Add. 39810, f. 7 (*fig. 140*); Lambeth 233, f. 175; latin 10483, f. 79v; W. 88, ff. 26, 119v
  ape crawling to catch bird: G.K.S. 3384, f. 102v
  ape dancing, wearing coif: W. 87, f. 29v
  ape on hobbyhorse: G.K.S. 3384, f. 86v (*fig. 49*)
  ass dancing: Chantilly 64, ff. 119, 119v
  astride hybrid man: Cloisters 54.1.2, f. 16
  bear doing headstand: fr. 95, f. 152
  bird/hybrid aiming beak at hindquarters: fr. 95, f. 254
  confronting quadruped: W. 88, f. 176v
  dog dancing: Bodley 264, f. 91 (sitting up); Douce 118, f. 40v; G.K.S. 3384, f. 72v; latin 14284, f. 14; W. 90, f. 161v; W. 109, ff. 34, 301 (two)
  fox dancing, ape as king with trumpet: Cambrai 103, f. 529
  goat standing on hind legs: Bodley 264, f. 91v
  hare running: Cambridge Dd.5.5, f. 199
  hare tilting at quintain: Trinity B.11.22, f. 214 (*fig. 592*)
  hybrid couple kissing: BBR 10607, f. 33v
  hybrid man with staff, pointing: latin 14284, f. 68v
  hybrid man with trumpet: Maz. 34, f. 123
  man balancing board on nose: G.K.S. 3384, f. 45
  man bending bow at: Princeton 44-18, ff. 36v-37
  man drinking: Spencer 2, f. 185v
  man in costume as stag: Bodley 264, f. 70; G.K.S. 3384, f. 11v; W. 88, ff. 115v (2, as stags?), 156v

man nude, with sword and buckler: Y.T. 15, f. 117
man standing on hands: Rothschild MS., f. 167 (nude); W. 88, f. 176v
man with shawm: W. 104, f. 32v
man with vielle, men and women dancing: Spencer 2, f. 161v
men processing out of gate of city labeled "Constantinople," with cornet, trumpets: Add. 42130, f. 164v
men with harp, psaltery, trumpet: Spencer 2, f. 137v
woman balancing sword on chin: Cambridge Dd.5.5, f. 55 (*fig. 720*)
woman dancing: Douce 6, f. 64; Hague 78.D.40, f. 13; latin 3893, f. 204v; Rylands lat. R.117, f. 236; W. 104, f. 9v; Y.T. 8, f. 345v (*fig. 490*)
woman with vielle: Yale MS., f. 14
Man with pitcher *see* Man with jug
Man with pitchfork *see* Man and fox, pursuing; Man scything
Man with plow *see* Man plowing
Man with pole across shoulder, followed by woman with pole across shoulder, net or basket suspended from it: W. 109, f. 27v
Man with psaltery (*see also* Hare running out of sack; Man and woman before Eros in tree; Man with harp, men; Man with pipe and tabor, men; Man with vielle, men; Men tilting): Add. 39810, f. 7 (*fig. 140*); Add. 49622, f. 88v; Cloisters 54.1.2, f. 147; latin 10483, f. 163v; M. 754, f. 15v; Rutland Ps., f. 73v; Stowe 17, f. 144v; W. 37, f. 23 (cleric?); W. 88, ff. 100v, 133v; W. 90, f. 35 (at L., bird); Yale MS., f. 347
ape dancing: Douce 6, f. 143
astride hybrid man: Stowe 17, f. 86v (f. 87, hybrid man dancing)
dog sitting up: Princeton 44-18, f. 31
woman dancing: G.K.S. 3384, f. 174; Yale MS., f. 137v
woman playing psaltery with rake (*cf.* Man playing bellows; — jawbone; — spoon; — vielle): M. 754, f. 86
woman with gittern: Bodley 264, f. 109v
Man with purse (*see also* Man and thief; Man and woman, offered)
and tablet: Douce 6, f. 168
emptying before young girl: Add. 49622, f. 95
holding up coin(?) to man with blanket: Douce 6, f. 66
picking up coin: BBR 9961-62, f. 74
Man with quoit, pulling: Rutland Ps., f. 69v (2, seated, tug-of-war) (*fig. 663*)
Man with rake (*see also* Man playing bellows; — jawbone; — spoon; — vielle; Man raking; Man with claw feet): Cloisters 54.1.2, f. 32
Man with rattle *see* Rattle, references under
Man with rebec (*cf.* Man with vielle): Rutland Ps., f. 48v
in carrying case (*cf.* Man with harp, end): Rutland Ps., f. 52
woman dancing: C.B. 62, f. 162v
Man with reel: M. 754, f. 67v (woman reclining on elbow); W. 82, f. 192v (and spindle; woman with bird's head, distaff) (*fig. 90*)
Man with ring *see* Man and monster, offering; Man and woman offering
Man with roast animal impaled on pole: Douce 6, f. 169
Man with rope
coiled noose, held over woman's head: G.K.S. 3384, f. 153
coiled lasso on ground: latin 14284, f. 27
pulling omitted verse into place: W. 102, ff. 33v (*fig. 491*), 39v
pulling sack out of windmill: G.K.S. 3384, f. 192
Man with sack and basket, hunting hare: G.K.S. 3384, f. 7v
Man with sack on back *see* Windmill
Man with sack over shoulder (*see also* Man hoarding): Douce 6, f. 101v (below, woman shearing sheep); G.K.S. 3384, ff. 21 (below, man raising tunic), 66, 77, 121
Man with scourge: Cloisters 54.1.2, f. 53 (Min.: Flagellation); Y.T. 75, f. 55v (winged headdress, beside horses of three Magi; Min.: Adoration of Magi)
Man with scroll (*cf.* Patron, unidentified; Prophet): Add. 39810, f. 7 (*fig. 140*); W. 104, ff. 51 (6), 81v (2, shown with man and nun kneeling and two other men)
bearded, hybrid man pulling cap over ears: Cloisters 54.1.2, f. 33v
kneeling: Douce 118, f. 103v
observed by hybrid man: W. 759, f. 108
singing from, with two clerics: G.K.S. 3384, f. 138
young, pointing: Cloisters 54.1.2, f. 158
Man with scythe *see* Man scything
Man with shawm (*see also* Man horned; Man reclining): Add. 42130, f. 40; BBR 9961-62, f. 14 (*fig. 388*); Chantilly 62, f. 137v; Cloisters 54.1.2, ff. 34v (bell attached), 86, 96v,

158; Trinity B.11.22, f. 191v; W. 41, f. 153v; W. 85, f. 29; W. 104, f. 28 (*fig. 11*)
blowing at butterfly: BBR 9157, f. 425
issuing from dragon's tail (*cf.* Obscaena, defecating, ape): Glazier 24, f. 47v
man shooting hare: W. 104, f. 16v
man with pipe and tabor: W. 104, f. 32v
man with vielle: W. 104, f. 16
playing from book held open by hybrid man: W. 88, f. 38
woman balancing on shoulders: Cloisters 54.1.2, f. 150; W. 90, f. 61v (dancing)
Man with shield (coat of arms), supporting on back: Fitz. 298, f. 1 (*fig. 566*)
Man with shoe (*cf.* Man with boot; Stilts, man): Cloisters 54.1.2, f. 70 (putting on or removing)
Man with sickle, leaves sprouting from sickle (*see also* Man reaping): Cloisters 54.1.2, f. 75 (hooded)
Man with sickle (or sword), seizing hair with other hand (*cf.* Man cutting hair): Cloisters 54.1.2, f. 127
Man with slingshot (*see also* Man and bird, hunting with; Man harrowing; Rams butting): Cloisters 54.1.2, f. 41; fr. 25526, f. 149v (at R., two rams butting, man waving cloth); Stowe 17, f. 153 (with winged beast on chain); W. 109, f. 24
Man with snare drum: Cloisters 54.1.2, ff. 46 (and pipe), 94
Man with sock *see* Man hoarding
Man with sores (unidentified fabliau): Royal 10 E.IV, ff. 297v-314
Man with spade *see* Man spading
Man with spear (*see also* Man and boar, hunting with; — and dragon, fighting with spear; — and hare; — and snail; Man nude with; Man with head)
and man with bow and arrow: Add. 42130, f. 45
astride horse: W. 90, f. 86 (Min.: Flight into Egypt)
fighting hybrid man with club, wearing pot on head: W. 88, f. 175
stabbing beseeching nude bearded man in mouth: Add. 49622, f. 179v
Man with spoon *see* Man blowing; — cooking, sampling; — cooking, stirring; — playing; Men fighting
Man with staff (*cf.* Beggar): Douce 5, f. 39 (crook; above, beast balancing two tapers on bar in mouth); Fitz. 2-1954, ff. 58v (old), 60v (old); latin 14284, f. 39v (beckoning to man with ?bone)
Man with stag horns (*cf.* Hybrid man with): Kraus 75/88, f. 9 (with bagpipe; at L., dog barking at hare sitting between antlers; issuing from tree-like border, Marsyas reference?); W. 87, f. 109v (blue horns)
Man with stilts *see* Stilts
Man with stone (*see also* Man with egg; Putting)
picking up: Stowe 17, f. 88
throwing at man issuing from border above: latin 14284, f. 48v (at R., man with spear, point tied to pole)
Man with stool basket *see* Physician and man, ministering to
Man with stream of water under each arm, standing in large basin: Add. 36684, f. 154 (above, cloud)
Man with sword (*see also* Man and [name of creature], fighting; — hunting; —, killing; Man balancing; Man headless, with; Man juggling; Man nude with; Men fighting with; Pilgrim, beggar; Pot worn on head by man with)
and buckler, attacked by three men-at-arms, two with swords, one with falchion: Add. 42130, f. 162v (Ps. 88, v. 44)
cleaving head and walking away from man with sword through stomach: fr. 25526, f. 148
conversing with man: M. 761, f. 38
holding left leg, wielding sword: W. 90, f. 140 (in drawers)
in drawers: M. 730, f. 108
stabbing himself (*cf.* Hybrid man with sword; Man nude, with sword): BBR 9391, f. 31v (Ps. 52; issuing from border)
unsheathing (*cf.* Knight with sword, seated): fr. 95, f. 48v
before dragon: fr. 95, f. 1 (horned, bearded, bitten by)
before lion: Cloisters 54.1.2, f. 79 (hybrid Saracen)
before man above seated on hybrid man: Cloisters 54.1.2, f. 19
standing on dragon, beside initial containing lion: Cloisters 54.1.2, f. 82
Man with swords and bucklers, three of each, selling(?) to man unsheathing sword: Bodley 264, f. 114v

Man with symphony (*cf.* Man with hurdy-gurdy): Add. 42130, ff. 81v, 176

Man with tablet (inscribed; *cf.* Scribe): Trinity B.11.22, ff. 11, 20v

Man with tabor (see also Man with pipe and tabor; Queen): Bodley 264, f. 31v
- ape doing handstand: Cloisters 54.1.2, f. 76
- astride dog backwards pulling cart containing two couples: Stowe 17, f. 198v
- man with bagpipe: Bodley 264, f. 104v
- men with timbrel, trumpet, dancing: BBR 9961-62, f. 26
- sow suckling three young, standing upright: Bodley 264, f. 124v
- woman juggling three knives: Rutland Ps., f. 51v

Man with taper (*see also* Man and falcon, clipping; Man balancing; Proverbs: man biting): Cambridge Dd.5.5., f. 106 (lit; butterfly above); Douce 5, f. 124 (lit); G.K.S. 3384, ff. 139v (2, holding long lit taper), 147
- before man holding rope in teeth, bird attached to rope: Add. 42130, f. 159
- woman above (saying such as "carrying a torch"?): G.K.S. 3384, f. 147

Man with telescope *see* Astronomer; Man spinning; Man with trumpet, looking through

Man with timbrel *see* Man with tabor, men

Man with tongs *see* Man playing; Men fighting, with spoon

Man with tool for weeding (?; *cf.* Man weeding): Y.T. 27, f. 5 (May)

Man with top *see* Top-whipping

Man with toy windmill *see* Windmill: toy, man with

Man with trap (wicker), holding over hare and unicorn, with spear: Cloisters 54.1.2, f. 177

Man with triangle: Cambridge Dd.5.5, f. 368; Chantilly 64, ff. 14v, 78, 78v; Cloisters 54.1.2, f. 60; Douce 6, f. 63; G.K.S. 3384, f. 155 (above, woman)
- ape rending beast: G.K.S. 3384, f. 235
- dog dancing: G.K.S. 3384, f. 241
- holding triangular instrument (triangle?) on stand over gameboard, five dice at side: Douce 6, f. 158
- man with trumpet: G.K.S. 3384, f. 241
- running, balancing two lit tapers on wooden stand in mouth (*cf.* Beast balancing): Trinity B.11.22, f. 148
- woman dancing: G.K.S. 3384, f. 52; Trinity B.11.22, f. 20 (*fig. 508*)

Man with trumpet (*see also* Cleric at altar; Elephant and castle, occupied by; Man and woman, dancing, hands; Man nude with; Man playing grill; Man with bellows, blowing; — with double trumpet; — with pipe and tabor, men; — with tabor, men; — with vielle, men; Men dancing): Arras 729, ff. 131, 156; Chantilly 62, f. 137v (banner of Flanders as standard); Douce 5, f. 164v (*fig. 518*); Douce 366, f. 72; Exeter 47, f. 124v (Min.: St. Matthew writing); Lambeth 233, ff. 22v (hybrid), 45, 50, 66v, 99, 107v, 123v, 176v, 214v; latin 10483, f. 169; M. 754, f. 19v; W. 82, ff. 28, 205v; W. 104, f. 28 (*fig. 11*); Yale MS., ff. 14 (2), 56 (2)
- aiming at seated ape: W. 90, f. 144v
- and quiver: M. 183, f. 107v
- astride dog: W. 88, f. 108v
- astride dragon: W. 88, f. 165
- astride goat: latin 1029A, f. 36
- astride horse: Douce 118, f. 89v
- astride lion: Cambrai 87, f. 43v; W. 88, f. 96 (hybrid lion)
- beggar with vielle, child in sling on back: D.P. 12, f. 76
- bird looking in wide end: G.K.S. 3384, f. 106
- hare running: Trinity B.11.22, f. 73
- looking through (like telescope): Douce 5, f. 182; G.K.S. 3384, f. 126; Melbourne 1254/3, f. 60v (holding staff); N.K.S. 41, f. 44v; Schilling MS., November; W. 87, f. 107 (nude); Y.T. 42, f. 40
- man dancing: G.K.S. 3384, f. 93; W. 761, f. 268
- man nude, armless, with shawm: M. 754, f. 99
- man with harp: Add. 42130, f. 174v (Ps. 97:5, 6)
- man with triangle: G.K.S. 3384, f. 241
- man with vielle: G.K.S. 3384, f. 22
- men tilting, two trumpeters astride horses at R.: fr. 776, f. 230v
- men with harp, tabor, hand organ, kettledrums on back, woman with hand organ: Bodley 264, f. 182
- one-legged: M. 102, f. 24v
- standing on woman's shoulders: Lambeth 233, f. 44 (*fig. 422*)
- wearing stag costume (*cf.* Man in costume as stag): Cambrai 87, f. 69
- with bat wings: Arras 47, f. 31
- woman dancing: Add. 29253, f. 90; fr. 95, f. 325v (trumpeter carrying ?harrow on back); latin 14284, f. 4v; Nancy 249, f. 62 (on his shoul-

ders); Princeton 44-18, ff. 186v-187; W. 90, f. 22
woman with pipe and tabor, astride ape: Add. 42130, f. 215
woman with psaltery: Bodley 264, f. 34v
Man with vielle (*see also* Banquet, king; —, men (3); Man and woman, before Eros in tree; —, dancing, men; Man playing; Queen; Woman as falconer): Add. 10293, f. 1; Add. 10294, f. 1; Add. 49622, ff. 100, 137v, 211v; Arras 47, f. 7v; Arras 729, f. 164v (at L., cat and mouse, hybrid bishop); Bodley 264, f. 29; Cambrai 87, f. 49; Chantilly 62, f. 154; Glazier 24, f. 56; Lambeth 233, ff. 64, 85v, 98v, 145v, 174v; latin 10483, f. 24; M. 754, ff. 1, 13v (*frontispiece*); Melbourne 1254/3, f. 109v (double-peaked belled hood); Royal 14 E.III, f. 89; Spencer 2, f. 259v; St. Omer 5, f. 134; Stowe 17, f. 134 (2); W. 45, ff. 49 (*fig. 572*), 277v; W. 87, f. 65v; W. 88, f. 113; W. 104, f. 33 (at R., dog); W. 760, f. 220; Yale MS., f. 31
ape balancing two basins on sticks, ape with bagpipe: Add. 24686, f. 17V (*fig. 324*)
ape dancing: G.K.S. 3384, f. 228 (another ape with bagpipe); Laud Lat. 84, f. 40v
ape doing handstand, hare (squirrel?) dancing: Douce 118, f. 101
ape with psaltery: M. 754, f. 40v
astride hybrid man backwards: Cloisters 54.1.2, f. 103
beggar with child in sling on back, man with trumpet: D.P. 12, f. 76
centaur dancing: Arras 1043, f. 126v
crowned, man with bagpipe, nude child with ball(?) beckoning to woman: Stowe 17, ff. 233v-234
dog dancing: Y.T. 19, f. 3
garland on head: M. 155, f. 150
man dancing: W. 109, f. 43 (two men)
man doing handstand: W. 88, f. 60
man with gittern: All Souls lat. 7, f. 7
man with hand organ: W. 90, f. 135; Yale MS., f. 62v
man with pipe and tabor, men and women dancing: Spencer 2, f. 161v
man with shawm: W. 104, f. 16
man with triangle: Yale MS., f. 194v
man with trumpet: G.K.S. 3384, f. 22
men with harp, psaltery, trumpet, two men tilting on horseback: W. 104, f. 19
standing on dog: BBR 11040, f. 4
woman and two men dancing, man with bagpipe: M. 754, f. 59v
woman dancing: Arras 729, f. 164v; BBR 9157, f. 1 (at L., embracing couples, man crowning woman with garland, falconer and woman); Douce 6, f. 1; latin 14284, ff. 63 (Ps. 1), 69v; M. 729, f. 389; Princeton 44-18, f. 158 (contortionist); Stowe 17, f. 104v; W. 37, ff. 21-20v (man with garland on head); W. 85, f. 87v (woman with distaff and spindle); W. 109, ff. 330, 358v; Y.T. 8, f. 189
on shoulders: W. 37, f. 5
on shoulders of man with bagpipe: G.K.S. 3384, f. 58
Man with wheat sheaf *see* Man reaping
Man with wheel, holding: M. 754, f. 96 (on end of stick); W. 87, f. 99v
Man with wheelbarrow, containing (proverb? *cf.* Ape with; Cleric with; Hybrid knight with)
ape with bird's head: W. 88, f. 105v
cleric and nuns, approaching church: Bodley 264, f. 22 (nude; at R., three clerics and three nuns playing club-ball) (*figs. 127-128*)
cripple, approaching man opening purse (*cf.* Alms, references under): Add. 42130, f. 186v
devil: Rothschild MS., f. 169v
dog in basket: W. 88, f. 194v
four humans, approaching ape: BBR 9391, f. 130v (*fig. 494*)
man: BBR 9427, f. 124; Bodley 264, f. 158v (at R., man offering knight cup before inn)
woman: Douai 193, f. 10; fr. 95, ff. 24v (at R., ?Frau Minne with lap dog aiming arrow or spear at kneeling man) (*fig. 403*), 209v (beside devil with scourge astride nude man)
Man with whip *see* Man with scourge
Man with windmill (toy) *see* Windmill, toy
Man with winged headdress *see* Winged headdress
Man with wings like flames, nude save for hood and cloak: Add. 42130, f. 169
Man wrestling *see* Wrestling
Man writing *see* Scribe
Man yawning *see* Proverbs: man
Manasseh (*see also* Isaiah; Joseph [Old Testament]: Jacob's journey): Y.T. 13, f. 50v
Mandola *see* Ape with; Hybrid man with; Lover; Man with, references under; Woman with
Mandrake, Bestiary representation: Royal 2 B.VII, ff. 119v-120 (in cycle) (*fig. 495*)

Manoah and wife, entreating Lord: Munich c.g. 16, f. 88v (at R., angel)
Manticora
and hare, pursuing: Arras 1043, f. 155 (manticora?)
Bestiary representation: Munich c.g. 16, f. 35 (in cycle) (*fig. 496*)
greeting man in costume as ram: Arundel 83, f. 47 (Ps. 68)
Manure basket *see* Man pruning tree
March *see* Ape spinning; Man pruning border foliage with ax; Man pruning tree
Marcolf *see* Man and goat, astride
Mark *see* Evangelist symbols; St. Mark
Marriage *see* Bride; David, life of: D. and Abigail; —: D. and Bathsheba; Proverbs: fight; Sacraments; St. Thomas of Canterbury; Samson; *Wright's Chaste Wife*
Marriage at Cana *see* Jesus Christ, life of
Marsh titmouse(?): Fitz. 2-1954, f. 82v
Marsyas(?) *see* Man with stag horns
Martyrdom *see* St. —
Marvels of the East *see* Centaur; Epifagus; Panatios; Pygmy; Sciapode
Mary Magdalene *see* Jesus Christ, life of: Mary Magdalene; —: *Noli me tangere;* —: Resurrection; St. Mary Magdalene
Mary the Virgin *see* Virgin
Mason *see* Man building church
Mass *see* Ape as bishop, before altar; Bishop; Cleric; Cleric and angel; Dog and fox, singing; Dog and hare beside
Massacre of Innocents *see* Jesus Christ, life of
Maxentius *see* St. Catherine
May *see* Falconer; Man and stag, hunting with bow; Owl with fish
Medicine *see* Dentist; Enema; Operation; Physician; Virgin, miracles of
Men bowling *see* Bowls
Men conversing, ape with sword: M. 761, f. 38
Men dancing, hands joined (*cf.* Man and woman, dancing; Man dancing, references under): Royal 2 B.VII, f. 204 (4; f. 203v, banquet, man with harp seated)
by ribbons: Bodley 264, f. 51v (5; at R., man drinking); Royal 2 B.VII, f. 189 (4; man with mandola)
men with bagpipe, hand organ: Bodley 264, f. 84v (5, wearing hoods, two belled)
men with bagpipe, tabor: Royal 2 B.VII, ff. 196v-197 (3, one singing or directing)
men with hand bell (dancing), tabor: Bodley 264, f. 129 (5, with long tailed hoods; at R., man in similar hood stretched out on litter borne by two men, man with hand bell; reference to Exemplum of dancers condemned to dance forever?)
men with trumpets: Bodley 264, f. 78 (5, with pointed hoods, two belled, three trumpeters); Royal 2 B.VII, f. 201 (4, two)
Men fighting (*cf.* Hybrid men fighting)
one astride cock: Douai 193, f. 143 (both nude)
one beating the other over the head with rock or jug (*cf.* Hybrid man with jug; Man beating man): W. 88, f. 181v
one half-nude, with rock, protesting as the other puts his foot through bloody hole in his side (foot coming out the back): Y.T. 8, f. 182v
one with club (proverb?): W. 88, f. 53v (at L., bowl and pitcher; at R., gameboard; *cf.* Proverbs: gameboard)
over gameboard *see* Checkers; Chess; Dice
slapping each other, seated on stools: Bodley 264, f. 3
with arrows and shields: St. Omer 5, f. 144v (short spears?)
with bow and arrow, battleax: latin 14284, f. 66v
with bow and arrow, sword and buckler: fr. 776, f. 9v; latin 14284, f. 62
with club and bow: Christ Church E.II, f. 21v
with clubs and bucklers: Bodley 264, f. 61v
with clubs and shields: Arsenal 6329, f. 55 (one in drawers); Jacquemart 1, f. 120; W. 88, f. 97
with daggers: Rutland Ps., f. 79
with falchion and spear: Douce 5, f. 147 (man at R. prodded with pole by man in line ending) (*fig. 373*)
with hammers (war hammers) and shields: Add. 38114, f. 136 (square shields); Douce 6, f. 168; W. 85, f. 72v
with hand trestles, crutch (cripples): Bodley 264, f. 109 (3)
with mace and sword: G.K.S. 3384, f. 118 (above, knight balancing reel on pole)
with scourge and box (gold?), pole and basket: W. 88, f. 134v (man with scourge nude)
with spear and buckler, club and buckler: Fitz. 298, f. 1 (*fig. 566*)
with spear and dagger: Rutland Ps., f. 69

with spear and polearm: Yale MS., f. 143v (issuing from border)

with spear and sword: Christ Church E.II, f. 33v; Douce 5, f. 147 (at R., man with pole prodding rear of man with sword; *cf. above, —,* with falchion)

with spoon and bellows, tongs and pitcher: fr. 25526, f. 107

with sticks: Bodley 264, f. 108v (and shields); W. 88, f. 137v (one nude)

with stilts: Bodley 264, f. 123

with sword and buckler, bow and arrow: fr. 776, f. 9v; latin 14284, f. 62

with sword and buckler, club: W. 90, f. 66v

with sword and buckler, polearm: latin 14284, f. 27v (hybrids)

with sword and shield, astride goat, charged by man with spear: Rothschild MS., f. 164

with sword and shield, sword and pot as shield: W. 88, f. 42

with sword, seizing opponent (unarmed): latin 10483, f. 160v

with sword, seizing opponent (with bow and arrows): Fitz. 2-1954, f. 100v

with swords and bellows: fr. 25526, f. 1v

with swords and bucklers (*cf.* Man with sword and buckler; Ram on column): Add. 17868, f. 32; Add. 38115, f. 51; Add. 49622, ff. 7v (*fig. 353*), 69, 126v; BBR 9391, f. 93v; BBR 10607, ff. 12v, 19 (one hybrid); Bodley 264, f. 61v; C.B. 62, f. 195 (above, bishop's head); Cambrai 87, f. 60; Cambrai 103, f. 100v (man gesturing before griffin); Douce 6, f. 4; Douce 118, f. 92; Douce 131, f. 20; Fitz. 298, f. 63; fr. 95, f. 42; fr. 776, f. 271v; fr. 25526, ff. 79v, 116, 127 (one man killed); G.K.S. 3384, ff. 28, 200; Hague 78.D.40, ff. 27v (women?), 130v; latin 3893, ff. 166v, 262v; latin 13260, f. 12; latin 14284, ff. 43v (issuing from border), 49, 49v, 60, 64v; M. 155, f. 87v (both with scalp and face wounds); M. 183, f. 123; Marseilles 111, f. 3; Montpellier H. 196, f. 63v; Princeton 44-18, ff. 102v-103; Royal 2 B.VII, ff. 146v-147; Royal 14 E.III, f. 140 (at R., man with bagpipe); Royal 20 D.IV, f. 1; Rutland Ps., f. 62v; Seligman 11, p. 22; Spencer 2, f. 111; St. Omer 5, f. 237; Stowe 17, ff. 44v-45, 224v-225; Troyes 89, f. 216; W. 85, f. 15v; W. 88, ff. 146, 191; W. 104, f. 104; W. 109, f. 47v; W. 759, f. 176v (one knight); W. 760, f. 97 (barefoot; erased); Y.T. 8, ff. 24v (storks seizing swords from behind), 190; Y.T. 75, f. 29v; Yale MS., ff. 2v, 27v, 209, 262, 333

with whip and bow: Douce 24, f. 138v (issuing from border)

Men in boat *see* Man in boat

Men making bed: W. 88, f. 177v (2)

Men nude

astride horse and stag (or horse with antlers), charging each other: Bodley 264, f. 55

fighting: M. 754, f. 16v (grappling)

astride monster/bird and lion: Rutland Ps., f. 107v (nude save for short capes)

boxing: W. 88, f. 171v (one barefoot)

with swords and bucklers: W. 102, ff. 81v-82

Men, school of *see* School

Men tilting (*see also* Knights; Man with vielle, men)

astride goats: W. 104, f. 10v (beside hybrid man as physician)

astride horse and dog: Bodley 264, f. 50 (at R., cockfight)

astride horses: Cambrai 87, f. 53v; fr. 776, ff. 230v (at R., two men astride horses, with trumpets), 271v (at R., centaur with trumpet); W. 104, f. 19 (men with harp, psaltery, trumpet, vielle, woman dancing)

at keg on pole (*cf.* Quintain, tilting at, man nude): Cloisters 54.1.2, f. 15v

Men wrestling *see* Wrestling

Mephibosheth see David, life of: D. and; —: D. and Ziba

Merab *see* David, life of: D. and Saul

Merlin presenting book to king: Lansdowne 451, f. 76

Mermaid (*cf.* Sciapode, variant; Siren; *see also* Ape and; Centaur as knight, with sword and shield): Add. 42130, f. 70v; BBR 10607, f. 179; Cambrai 103, f. 365v (2, one with vielle); Fitz. 47, f. 85 (line ending); Kraus 75/88, f. 164; M. 754, f. 31v (beside bird with bell hung around neck, fish, hybrid man); Vienna 1826*, f. 58; W. 87, f. 93v; Y.T. 27, f. 52v

Mermaid and hybrid beast with tall domed hat (Templar's?), holding by tail, brandishing sword: Glazier 24, f. 101v

Mermaid and hybrid man on stilts, conversing: Christ Church E.II, f. 55v

Mermaid and lion, astride with trumpet: Bodley 264, f. 43v

Mermaid and merman, embracing: fr. 25526, f. 110 (at L., man and woman, possibly nun embracing)
Mermaid and offspring: Add. 24686, f. 13 (suckling, ape doing handstand on her tail) (*fig. 498*); BBR 10607, f. 179v
Mermaid dancing
  hybrid men with cymbals, psaltery: fr. 25526, f. 38
  hybrid men with shawm, hand bells, harp: Add. 38114, f. 1
  merman with pipe and tabor: BBR 10607, f. 35v (below, centaur bending bow)
  merman with trumpet: Y.T. 8, f. 17v
  merman with vielle: Cambrai 103, f. 365v
Mermaid in position of sciapode, approached by nude man astride monster, with club: Rutland Ps., f. 108v
Mermaid playing jawbone with tongs (proverb? *Cf.* Man playing): Glazier 24, f. 40 (*fig. 520*)
Mermaid swimming in water: Rutland Ps., f. 96
Mermaid tearing hair (*cf.* Hair, references under): M. 183, f. 252v (Offices of the Dead)
Mermaid with
  bagpipe: BBR 10607, f. 48v (dragon seizing hair); Kraus 75/88, f. 174
  bird: Douce 6, f. 6
  club and buckler: Add. 17868, f. 166v
  distaff and spindle, another with mirror and comb: fr. 25526, f. 62v
  fish: BBR 10607, f. 42v (and trumpet); Fitz. 298, ff. 4v (two; at R., sciapode), 74v (and mirror); Holkham 438, f. 16v (two); Lambeth 233, f. 3 (February); latin 3893, f. 272v; Y.T. 8, f. 178; Yale MS., f. 29 (*fig. 499*)
  gittern, another with vielle: Yale MS., f. 99v
  hand bells: Princeton 44-18, ff. 60, 107, 124v, 152v-153 (and merman), 192v, 205
  harp: Rothschild MS., f. 175v (winged); Royal 2 B.VII, f. 191 (another with trumpet and mirror); W. 85, f. 73v
  mirror: Arsenal 5218, f. 20 (another with vielle); Burney 275, f. 404; Chantilly 64, ff. 147 (two), 147v (two); Cloisters 54.1.2, f. 103v; Christ Church E.II, f. 66v; Fitz. 298, f. 74v (and fish); G.K.S. 3384, f. 41; Royal 2 B.VII, f. 191 (and trumpet, another with harp); W. 82, f. 191v; W. 87, f. 98
  mirror and comb: Add. 42130, f. 70v; Chantilly 64, ff. 122v, 150, 150v; Cloisters 54.1.2, f. 98; Douce 6, f. 83; Douce 118, f. 8v; fr. 25526, ff. 62v (another with distaff and spindle), 126 (with merman as knight); Jacquemart 1, f. 127v; M. 494, f. 298v; W. 87, f. 93v; Y.T. 27, f. 52v
  pipe: Kraus 75/88, f. 69v
  trumpet (*see also* Mermaid with fish; — with harp): Hague 78.D.40, ff. 48 (2), 129 (2) (*fig. 497*)
  vielle: Arsenal 5218, f. 20 (another with mirror); BBR 10607, f. 98v; Tournai Ps., f. 104 (male siren dancing) (*fig. 500*); W. 45, ff. 45 (garland on head), 236v (fish dancing); Yale MS., f. 99v (another with gittern)
Merman and ape, crowned, tail stepped on by: W. 85, f. 81v
Merman and beast, shooting: Queens 17, f. 1
Merman and bird, shooting: Corpus Christi 53, f. 189
Merman and fish, beside crowned and mitered fish at R.: M. 754, f. 59 (below, fish swimming out of oven)
Merman and hybrid bird, fighting with falchion: G.K.S. 3384, f. 195v
Merman and hybrid man
  in water, aiming spear at hybrid man with shawm: Cambrai 102, f. 470v (as knight)
  shooting: Jacquemart 1, f. 34v
  shot by: Y.T. 8, f. 350 (with sword and shield)
Merman and hybrid woman with distaff and spindle, confronting: Cloisters 54.1.2, f. 106
Merman(?) and man (nude, with monstrous face), shot by: Rutland Ps., f. 87v (*fig. 502*)
Merman as bishop
  conversing with hybrid cardinal(?): fr. 25526, f. 148v
  with pipe: Christ Church E.II, f. 52
Merman as falconer: W. 39, f. 24 (above, stork)
Merman as king
  ape stepping on his tail: W. 85, f. 81v
  with fish: BBR 5163-64, f. 103v
  with vielle: Fitz. 288, f. 170v
Merman as knight: W. 37, f. 35v
  confronting hare with trumpet: Add. 30029, f. 106
  hybrid, three dragons' heads issuing from tail: Cambrai 103, f. 272
  in water, aiming spear at hybrid man with shawm: Cambrai 103, f. 519
  mermaid with mirror and comb: fr. 22526, f. 126
  tilting with knight/merman: Yale MS., f. 100v
  with spear and round object (*cf.* Merman with stone): Melbourne 1254/3, f. 15v

M

with spear and shield, confronting hybrid man using animal leg as club: latin 3893, f. 300
with standard, arms of Hainaut: Kraus 75/88, f. 190v
with sword and buckler, fighting beast: Cambrai 102, f. 470v
with sword and buckler, fighting dragon breathing fire: Cambrai 102, f. 9
with sword and shield, challenging man (nude) crawling on all fours: Jacquemart 1, f. 72
with sword and shield, confronting hybrid knight with bellows and scimitar: Princeton 44-18, ff. 191v-192
with sword, fighting hybrid knight with sword: latin 14284, f. 1

Merman balancing spear on chin (*cf.* Man balancing): Kraus 75/88, f. 34 (*fig. 503*)

Merman dancing
hare with harp: Fitz. 298, f. 14
hybrid man with vielle: W. 88, f. 50
mermaid with vielle: Tournai Ps., f. 104 (male siren) (*fig. 500*)
merman with trumpet: Hague XX, f. 49v

Merman embracing mermaid: fr. 25526, f. 110 (at L., man and woman, possibly nun, embracing)

Merman fishing, ass playing bellows with jawbone: M. 729, f. 268

Merman tilting *see* Merman as knight, tilting

Merman with
bagpipe: Yale MS., f. 127
book *see* Procession, funeral, coffin borne by dog
double pipe: Y.T. 8, f. 187v (double tail)
double trumpet: Hague 78.D.40, f. 31v
fish: Rutland Ps., f. 76 (2)
harp, mermaid dancing: Kraus 75/88, ff. 163v-164
hood (gold), waving at man below with hands raised (*cf.* Man with hood): Douce 5, f. 38v
pectoral cross: Cloisters 54.1.2, f. 67v
pipe: fr. 25526, f. 148v (as bishop); Glazier 24, f. 137v (ape dancing)
pipe and tabor: BBR 10607, f. 35v (mermaid dancing; below, centaur bending bow); Jacquemart 1, f. 133v (winged headdress; centaur dancing)
reel and distaff: Stowe 17, f. 166
stone (egg?): Cloisters 54.1.2, f. 56v (below, hybrid man with club and shield); Melbourne 1254/3, f. 15v (and spear; stone?)
sword: Glazier 24, f. 89v
trumpet: Hague 78.D.40, f. 31v (two); Hague XX, ff. 12, 49v (merman dancing); Melbourne 1254/3, f. 85v; W. 45, f. 81; Y.T. 8, f. 17v (mermaid dancing)
vielle: Cambrai 103, f. 365v (mermaid dancing) (*fig. 501*); Fitz. 288, f. 170v (crowned); W. 39, f. 125

Mermen
confronted: Christ Church E.II, f. 66 (2)
fighting with spears and shields, in water: Royal 2 B.VII, f. 143v

Messenger *see* Document, references under; St. Thomas of Canterbury; Woman kneeling

Micah *see* David, life of: D. and

Micah and Bartholomew, Apostle (Old and New Law): Y.T. 27, f. 7; Y.T. 75, f. 7

Michal *see* David, life of: D. and Ish-bosheth

Mice, two, in tall, three-legged caldron (Proverb? *see also* Castle; Cat and mouse; *cf.* Sheep in caldron): Glazier 24, f. 142

Midianites *see* Moses, revenge on

Mill *see* Watermill; Windmill

Miller (*see also* Windmill; Virgin, miracles of: hermit): BBR 1175, f. 15v

Miniature supported by (*cf.* Border; Initial)
angel: Cloisters 54.1.2, f. 16 (Min.: Annunciation)
beggars: Cloisters 54.1.2, f. 142v (2, Min.: St. Louis ministering to sick)
hare: Cloisters 54.1.2, f. 34
hybrid man: Cloisters 54.1.2, ff. 48v, 81, 82v (2; Min.: Entombment), 98v, 173v (2; Min.: Procession at Saint-Denis)
man: Bodley 264, ff. 42v, 51v (2); Cloisters 54.1.2, ff. 53v (2, one with flail; Min.: Flagellation), 54 (Min.: Nativity), 61v (2, one with hammer; Min.: Christ bearing the cross), 76 (2; Min.: Deposition), 95v (2, soldiers; Min.: Resurrection), 123v (Min.: St. Louis feeding a leprous monk), 148v (2, barefoot, with swords; Min.: St. Louis washing feet of the poor), 154v (2, one barefoot, with Saracen headdress; the other with ?turban, spear and buckler; Min.: Miracle of the Breviary), 159v (2; Min.: St. Louis burning the bones of the crusaders), 165v (2, hooded, mourning; Min.: death of St. Louis), 182v (2; Min.: Christ enthroned)
man and woman: Cloisters 54.1.2, f. 102v (Min.: a miracle of St. Louis)

M

Minne *see* Cleric and woman, kneeling; Man and woman, kneeling before; —, standing before
Minnekästchen *see* Leatherworker; Painter
Minotaur, charged by knight with spear: Cambrai 102, f. 387
Miracles *see* Jesus Christ; St. Denis; St. Dominic; St. Dunstan; St. Helena; St. John the Evangelist; St. Louis; St. Nicholas; Virgin
Mirror *see* Ape with; Centaur with; Cleric nude, on stairway; Hybrid ape with; Hybrid man with; Hybrid woman with; Man with; Mermaid with; Siren with; Skeleton with; Woman with
Miser *see* Avarice, references under; Dives and Lazarus; Jesus Christ, life of: Last Judgment: Pains of Hell; Man hoarding; Woman hoarding
Moab *see* David, life of: D. and; Moses: Israelites
Mocking of Christ *see* Jesus Christ, life of
Mole: Trinity B.11.22, f. 31v
Monde renversé see specific entries, e.g., Cat and mouse; Dog and hare
Money *see* Coin, references under; Miser; Purse
Money-changers *see* Jesus Christ, life of: expulsion
Moneylender *see* Ape as
Monk *see* Cleric
Monogram, AEA *see* Lover, Nature
Monster *see also* Centaur and; Knight and; Man and; Man nude and
Monster and hybrid man, shot by: Add. 21114, f. 121 (monster/man); Hague 10.B.21, f. 20v
Monster as bishop: Y.T. 75, f. 55v
Monster crippled, sticking tongue out at man shooting bird: fr. 95, f. 327
Monster dancing, hybrid man with pipe: Rutland Ps., f. 86v
Monster spitting liquid (*cf.* Spout): Add. 36684, f. 96v; Cloisters 54.1.2, f. 89 (through tube, flanked by hooded hybrid men)
Monster vomiting: G.K.S. 3384, f. 62 (into bowl held by man); M. 754, f. 6v
Monster with
five heads (*cf.* St. John the Evangelist, vision of): Cambrai 103, f. 511 (bird, beast, three human heads, charged by knight/centaur) (*fig.* 77); Douce 366, f. 128 (slain by knight with sword); Stowe 17, f. 101v (beast, four human heads; hand wielding sword as tail) (*fig.* 76)
four heads, charged by man with spear and buckler: W. 45, f. 13v (ape, dog, two human heads)
fourteen legs, ridden by nude man with club seated backwards: Rutland Ps., f. 83
gittern, beggar with child in sling on back: fr. 95, f. 106v
seven-headed tail, winged, confronted by hybrid man with sword and shield: W. 45, f. 256v
stag horns: G.K.S. 3384, f. 100v (head only)
three heads: Rutland Ps., ff. 85 (ridden by man with Phrygian cap), 101v (fighting unicorn/dragon); W. 45, f. 14v (dog, two dragon heads)
transverse flute: latin 10484, f. 264
winged headdress, with bellows: Add. 49622, f. 138v
woman seated on: Jacquemart 1, f. 70 (winged, headless)
Mont-Saint-Michel *see* Virgin, miracles of: woman
Monument *see* Eleanor cross
Moon(?): W. 41, f. 318v (female head suspended in sickle)
Moon and sun (*see also* Creation): Add. 36684, f. 100
Morris board, man and woman sitting at: Bodley 264, ff. 60, 76v, 112
Mortar and pestle *see* Ape with; Ass with; Hybrid knight with; Hybrid man with; Man with; Woman with
Moses (*see also* Hybrid man, horned)
and Aaron
Hebrews witnessing earthquake in Egypt: Munich c.g. 16, f. 56v
leading Israelites, pursuers drowning in Red Sea: Munich c.g. 16, f. 57v; Y.T. 8, f. 220
pursuers drowning in Red Sea: Add. 39810, f. 57v; M. 88, f. 137 (at R., peacock) (*fig.* 505)
and brazen serpent: Add. 39810, f. 57v; Munich c.g. 16, f. 62v
as infant in basket on river, discovered by three women: Y.T. 8, f. 213v (*fig.* 506)
before burning bush: Add. 39810, f. 57v; Y.T. 8, f. 214v (*fig.* 507)
before Pharaoh, throwing crown on ground: Add. 39810, f. 57v; Munich c.g. 16, f. 46v; Y.T. 8, f. 218v
before Pharaoh, with Aaron and elders of Israel: Munich c.g. 16, f. 52v
breaking Tablets of the Law, Israelites worship-

M ing golden calf: Add. 39810, f. 57v; Munich c.g. 16, f. 61v
building of tabernacle: Add. 39810, f. 57v
commanding children of Israel: Munich c.g. 16, f. 67v
Israelites embracing daughters of Moab: Munich c.g. 16, f. 63v
marrying Tarbis, giving her ring of forgetfulness: Munich c.g. 16, ff. 47v, 48v
receiving Tablets of the Law: Add. 39810, f. 57v; Munich c.g. 16, f. 59v
reclining on elbow, pointing at four men: M. 102, f. 158v (Deut. 32)
revenge on Midianites: Munich c.g. 16, f. 66v
smiting rock at Horeb: Munich c.g. 16, f. 58v
turning leprous, water poured on land turning to blood: Munich c.g. 16, f. 50v
with Tablets of the Law: Add. 42130, f. 54 (*fig. 504*)
with two Hebrews: Munich c.g. 16, f. 49v
with Zipporah (crowned) and son at table before angel of the Lord: Munich c.g. 16, f. 51v
Mother and child *see* Ape and ape-child; Hare and offspring; Mermaid and —; Sow suckling; Virgin and Child; Woman and child
Mount Carmel *see* Carmel
Mount Sinai *see* St. Catherine
Mountains, birds of prey resting on: fr. 12400, ff. 80-83v (text illustration)
Mourner *see* Bier; Man mourning; Procession, funeral; Woman with book
Mouse *see* Cat and hare; Cat and; Hybrid woman with pyx; Man and; Mice; Owl with
Mulbarton, Elisabeth of *see* St. Omer, William de
Mummer *see* Man in costume
Murderer *see* Jesus Christ, life of: Last Judgment: Pains of Hell
Musical instruments *see* specific instruments
Musical chairs, variant(?): Bodley 264, f. 98 (three boys rising from stools, one covering eyes)
Musical instruments, parody *see* Ape playing; Ass playing; Bagpipe, references under; Centaur playing; Cleric playing; Cow playing; Devil playing; Dog and hare, blowing; —, playing; Dominican playing; Franciscan playing; Goat playing; Hare with hand bells; Hybrid king playing; Hybrid man playing; Man and pig, astride; Man blowing; — playing; Mermaid playing; *also* references under names of animals (e.g., Ape with bagpipe; Ape with double pipe)
Musicians *see* David and; *also* references under specific musical instruments

N

Naa-mah weaving: Munich c.g. 16, f. 20v (*fig. 724*)
Naasson: Y.T. 13, f. 33 (genealogy of Christ)
Nathan *see* David, life of: D. and; —: D. and Solomon
Nativity *see* Jesus Christ, life of
Nature *see* Lover
Navarre, Jeanne II of *see* Patroness
Nebuchadnezzar and Daniel: St. Omer 5, f. 115v (at R., vision in dream) (*fig. 521*)
Negro, head of: latin 10484, f. 120v (Saracen? gold turban, white veil); Rutland Ps., f. 26
Negroid head attached to dragon's body: Jacquemart 1, f. 3v
Nero *see* St. Paul
Nest *see* Ape and bird, stealing; Bird in; Man and bird, hunting; Proverbs: eggs
Net *see* Cleric and bird; Man and ape, trapped; — and bird, snaring; — and hare, hunting; — and woman, trapped; Man nude and bird; Partridge
New Testament *see* Cycles, pertinent subentries; Jesus Christ; Virgin; *also* specific subjects
Nicholas *see* Illuminator; St. Nicholas
Nicodemus *see* Jesus Christ, life of: Deposition
Ninepins *see* Clubkayles
Noah (*see also* Goat standing on hind legs)
ark: Add. 39810, f. 7 (construction of; pulled by two men) (*fig. 140*); Munich c.g. 16, f. 21v (construction of, afloat) (*fig. 522*); Spencer 26, f. 21v (at L., God); Y.T. 13, f. 26v
drunkenness of: Add. 39810, f. 7 (*fig. 140*); Munich c.g. 16, f. 22v
entering ark with man with sheep on back (*cf.* Man and sheep): Add. 39810, f. 7 (corpses in water, raven feeding on carrion) (*fig. 140*)
in ark, welcoming dove: Add. 49622, f. 165 (below, raven feeding on carrion); Y.T. 13, f. 27 (the same)
Nob, priests of *see* David, life of: D. and Saul, flight
Noli me tangere see Jesus Christ, life of
November *see* Man and pig(s); Man pruning border foliage with ax; Man with trumpet, looking through

N

Nun *see* Abbess; Bishop and; Cleric and; Hybrid nun; Man in costume as boar; Obscaena, exposing; Virgin, miracles of: drowning nun; —: nun

Nun and ape
- before ape-physician, with stool basket: Stowe 17, f. 51
- suckling (*cf.* Mermaid and offspring; Woman and child): Rylands fr. 2, f. 212 (at L., woman seated under stool basket; at R., physician) (*fig. 523*)
- with book, ape-cleric with book: latin 14284, f. 8

Nun and cleric *see* Nun with book

Nun and Dominican, confessing before: Stowe 17, f. 191

Nun and hybrid man, fighting with spears: Jacquemart 1, f. 78 (nun with shield)

Nun and man
- blessing man seated on three-legged pot: W. 87, f. 36v
- conversing: latin 14284, f. 58 (below nun, bishop's head issuing from border)
- embracing: fr. 25526, ff. 106v (fabliau?; at L., nun with basket by Phallisbaum), 132v (at R., before church: man, aroused, with staff, offering purse; possibly cleric); Stowe 17, f. 145 (man crowned, Dominican nun)
- holding by string tied to his organ; at R., same man climbing ladder to tower in which stands nun: fr. 25526, f. 106 (cleric?)
- intercourse: fr. 25526, ff. 111 (at L., man kneeling, beseeching nun), 111v
- receiving male organ from (fabliau?): fr. 25526, f. 160 (2, in gray habit with black veils, holding male organs, flanking Phallisbaum; man bearded, in dark brown robe, ?cleric)
- receiving purse from, in front of church (fabliau? *cf.* Cleric and nun, offering; Nun and man, embracing): fr. 25526, f. 132v (in white habit with black veil; man, possibly cleric, in brown robe, with staff, aroused)

Nun, Cistercian *see* Patroness: Marie of Viane

Nun, Dominican
- embracing king: Stowe 17, f. 145
- emptying jug (urinal?), one hand raised to chest: W. 87, f. 37v
- with book: Stowe 17, f. 156v (f. 157, hybrid Franciscan with crosier)
- with crosier: Stowe 17, f. 162
- with distaff, cat playing with spindle (*cf.* Cleric with distaff): Stowe 17, f. 34 (Dominican?) (*fig. 524*)

Nun, Franciscan (*cf.* Franciscan)
- before ape-physician, with stool basket: Stowe 17, f. 51
- dancing, Franciscan playing bellows with staff: Stowe 17, f. 38
- disputing over gameboard with Franciscan reaching for her breast: Heidelberg Cod. Sal. 9,51, f. 272v (*fig. 151*)
- kneeling before St. Clare: W. 45, f. 89v
- with book: Stowe 17, ff. 29v, 116v

Nun kneeling, praying: Trinity B.11.22, ff. 145v, 146; W. 761, f. 196v (Cistercian)
- at altar: Douce 118, f. 85 (above, angel blessing; at side woman in deep lavender robe, black headdress)
- at *prie-dieu:* Douce 118, ff. 129, 136v (with book, before altar containing gold cross and chalice)
- before angel with scroll: latin 1076, f. 148
- before man defecating: Bodley 264, f. 56
- before St. Christopher: Stowe 17, f. 113v
- before St. Stephen: W. 761, f. 125 (blessed by)

Nun with asperge and book: Melbourne 1254/3, f. 9 (observed by beast)

Nun with basket on back, staff: fr. 25526, f. 134 (in brown habit, black veil; at L., knights fighting with swords and shields, one killed)

Nun with bellows: W. 87, f. 110v

Nun with book (*see also* Nun, Dominican; Nun kneeling at *prie-dieu;* Nun with asperge; Procession, funeral: coffin borne by ape and man): G.K.S. 3384, f. 207; M. 754, f. 81v
- ape-cleric with book: latin 14284, f. 8
- cleric/bird below: W. 87, f. 16v
- clerics (6) and two hybrid nuns, each with book: W. 104, f. 74 (*fig. 123*)
- kneeling, reading: latin 1076, ff. 66v, 76
- making love with cleric: Add. 10293, f. 1
- raising stick: W. 87, f. 91 (f. 90v, woman with antlers as wings)

Nun with club *see* Hare running out of sack

Nun with distaff, cat playing with spindle (*cf.* Cleric with distaff): Stowe 17, f. 34 (Dominican?) (*fig. 524*)

Nun with horn: W. 87, f. 98v

Nun with psaltery: Chantilly 62, f. 64; Royal 2 B.VII, f. 177 (cleric with mandola)

Nut *see* Man and pigs; Squirrel with

O

- Obadiah (Abdias): Y.T. 13, f. 45v
- Obscaena (*cf.* Ape and fish; Hybrid man and woman; Nun and man)
  - bagpipe issuing from hindquarters attached to crowned head: Glazier 24, f. 42v
  - beak aimed at genitals, dragon–hybrid ape: Add. 50000, f. 240
  - beak aimed at hindquarters
    - bird–ape: Add. 36684, f. 24 (ape with churn); Douce 6, f. 102v (ape with book, kneeling before bishop); Douce 118, f. 122 (ape with censer); lat. lit. f.3, throughout: Y.T. 15, ff. 144 (at R., goat), 307v
    - bird–man (*see also* Illuminator): latin 3893, f. 98 (at L., ape shooting crane)
    - bird–man half-nude, with pipe and tabor: fr. 95, f. 254 (hybrid)
    - bird–man nude: M. 754, f. 16v
    - cock–man nude, blowing hare out of trumpet: Royal 14 E.III, f. 89
    - stork–ape: Douce 6, ff. 51 (ape with gold basin), 124v, 131v, 149; Tournai Ps., ff. 184v (another ape cheering), 209v (the same) (*fig. 526*); W. 82, f. 196 (at L., hare)
    - stork–hybrid man: Royal 1 D.I, f. 350v
    - stork-man holding dog: W. 88, f. 90v
    - stork–man nude, unsheathing sword: latin 1076, f. 42
    - stork–man nude, with conical cap: W. 88, f. 187
    - stork–stag: Melbourne 1254/3, f. 23
  - bellows aimed at hindquarters, hybrid woman – ape: M. 88, f. 173 (at R., man bending bow at wild man with gold pot on head, holding ?stone)
  - crossbow aimed at hindquarters *see below*, —, shooting
  - defecating
    - ape: BBR II 988, vol. II, f. 239 (at R., ape with ax approaching); Melbourne 1254/3, f. 14v; Tournai Ps., f. 125v (at L., hare eating; at R., hybrid goat) (*fig. 527*)
    - ape, into bowl: Schilling MS., August
    - ape, into mouth of dragon: Glazier 24, f. 47v (man with shawm issuing from dragon's tail) (*fig. 529*)
    - ape, producing gold coins(?): Add. 29253, f. 410v (man balancing two gold basins on sticks)
    - ape with bagpipe, confronting man with trumpet issuing from border: Add. 29253, f. 328v
    - ape with basin held up to stag's mouth, another ape catching droppings in pitcher, aiming stick at him: Douce 6, f. 149 (at R., stork aiming beak at second ape)
    - ape with pitcher, confronting dog with battle-ax: Glazier 24, f. 155v
    - cleric, reprimanded by nude man: Add. 49622, f. 82
    - devil, approached by ape with asperge and situla: Douce 6, f. 181v
    - hybrid man, producing gold coins(?) caught by ape in bowl: Add. 29253, f. 41v
    - king (Saul?): Add. 10294, f. 1
    - man: fr. 25526, f. 35 (at L., strike-the-pot); W. 45, f. 166v (baring hindquarters over vessel; at L., man raising club)
    - man, before kneeling nun: Bodley 264, f. 56 (*fig. 528*)
    - man, into gold bowl, another man with gold bowl approaching woman with bowl: Trinity B.11.22, f. 73 (*fig. 530*)
    - man, into jar, urinating into another jar: Glazier 24, f. 27v (nude save for cape) (*fig. 532*)
    - man, looking up at sun(?): BBR II 988, vol. II, f. 224
    - man nude: fr. 25526, ff. 4v, 148 (shot by hybrid man)
    - man nude, distorted, above woman with mirror: Add. 36684, f. 51v
    - man nude (Templar?), into bowl, hands tied, ape threatening him with sickle, grasping his right hand: Glazier 24, f. 57 (*fig. 531*)
  - eating feces, hare; ape defecating (*see also* Enema): Tournai Ps., f. 124v
  - exposing genitals
    - ape with shawm: Add. 49622, f. 120v
    - bishop: W. 88, f. 86v (partly overpainted)
    - contortionist: Add. 49622, f. 62v
    - man nude, tailed–nun pointing: Add. 49622, f. 90v (*fig. 525*)
  - exposing hindquarters
    - ape–ape: Tournai Ps., ff. 30v (hybrid couple embracing), 54v (*fig. 533*)
    - ape–hare with bagpipe: Arsenal 5218, f. 15 (with staff)

O

ape–hybrid bishop: Glazier 24, f. 95v (observed by owl)
ape–man: Add. 49622, ff. 102v (astride horse), 124
bird/man–hybrid man: Add. 49622, f. 104
cleric–nun: Tournai Ps., f. 56
cleric–Templar: Glazier 24, f. 93 (without torso)
hybrid beast–bishop blessing: W. 88, f. 106
hybrid man–bishop with censer: M. 754, f. 81v (nude, armless, hooved)
man (*see also* Man balancing ball; Man beating): Add. 49622, f. 61; Stowe 17, f. 223
man–archer: BBR 9391, f. 93; BBR 10607, f. 17
man–bishop, seated, pointing: W. 88, f. 47
man–hybrid woman with mirror: W. 88, f. 149 (holding large ?apple)
man–man: W. 109, f. 197v
man–man, seated: Bodley 264, f. 79 (another man with ?sack)
man nude–sun: M. 754, f. 73v (above, hybrid man as physician)
man nude, probing: BBR 9411-26, f. 134v; Glazier 24, f. 49v (before hybrid bishop); W. 102, ff. 89v (f. 90, centaur bending bow), 92v
man, shooting bird: W. 88, f. 87v

finger aimed at hindquarters, ape–man, half-nude: fr. 25526, f. 135

handling genitals
man–man: W. 88, f. 80
man nude: W. 102, f. 53 (upside down)

intercourse *see* Intercourse, references under

kissing or peering at hindquarters (proverb?)
beast–ape: Glazier 24, f. 102 (*fig. 534*)
human face–ape: latin 3893, f. 96 (in border)
hybrid bishop–ape with bow: Glazier 24, f. 95v (observed by owl) (*fig. 535*)
hybrid man–hybrid man: Add. 49622, ff. 158, 206v
hybrid man–man nude: M. 754, f. 49v
Templar–cleric nude: Glazier 24, f. 93 (*fig. 536*)

phallis (gold) aimed at head of hybrid man: M. 754, f. 26v

pole aimed at hindquarters
ape–ape: Douce 6, f. 123v
ape–hindquarters in oven: M. 754, f. 48v (above, ape as baker)
bird–man: latin 3893, f. 98
centaur–ram: Arras 47, f. 127v
dog–ape: Tournai Ps., f. 204
knight–self: W. 88, f. 189 (nude save for helmet, shoes)

revering hindquarters: Glazier 24, ff. 41 (ass-cleric) (*fig. 538*), 78 (ape) (*fig. 537*)

shooting hindquarters
ape–ape: Douce 6, f. 120 (crossbow); Hague 10 A.14, f. 151; Hague 78.D.40, f. 36; Tournai Ps., f. 248v
centaur–ape: Add. 49622, f. 78; Cambrai 102, f. 179v
centaur–man nude, with pointed ears, horn (satyr?): fr. 95, f. 190v (bird stabbing man in eye with beak)
hybrid man–ape: BBR II 988, vol. I, f. 187v
knight–man: Yale MS., f. 40v (crossbow)
knight–man nude, sticking out tongue: Cambrai 102, f. 462
knight–wild man: M. 88, f. 173 (at L., hybrid woman aiming bellows at hindquarters of ape; wild man with pot on head, holding ?stone)
man–ape: Ashmole 828, f. 98v
man–knight half-nude: Yale MS., f. 220
man–man: Bodley 264, f. 3; BBR 9391, f. 93 (upper half nude) (*fig. 539*); BBR 10607, f. 17v (*fig. 540*); Hague 78.D.40, f. 158v (crossbow); Liège 431, f. 44; M. 88, f. 176v
man–man nude: fr. 25526, f. 155 (at L., building, face looking out of window)
man-merman *see* Merman(?) and man

spear aimed at hindquarters
ape astride crane–man, nude: Rutland Ps., ff. 66v-67 (crane?)
hybrid man (winged)–ape catching fish: Melbourne 1254/3, f. 16 (*fig. 541*)
knight–ape: W. 90, ff. 67v, 78v (astride horse)
knight–man: Olschki 4, f. 191v (fowl impaled on spear)

sword aimed at hindquarters, ape–hybrid bishop, half-nude: fr. 95, f. 214

trumpet aimed at hindquarters
ape–ape: Yale MS., f. 147 (*fig. 542*)
man nude–horse: Stowe 17, f. 153v (horse walking on ?eggs)
man nude–self: Glazier 24, f. 25; Rothschild MS., f. 134 (above, man with trumpet) (*fig. 543*); W. 88, f. 157 (also blowing trumpet)

tube blown at hindquarters, ape–ape: Stowe 17, f. 61v; Yale MS., f. 147

O

urinating, man: Glazier 24, ff. 27v (into jar, defecating into another jar), 103v (*fig. 361*)
Occupations *see* specific subjects
Octavian *see* Florent and
October *see* Man picking grapes; — sowing; — threshing
Ointment jar *see* Hybrid woman with; Jesus Christ, life of; Deposition; St. Mary Magdalene; Sacraments: Extreme Unction
Old Law destroyed for New Law *see* Cycles
Old Testament *see* Cycles; *also* names of individuals and specific subjects
Olybrius *see* St. Margaret
Onocentaur *see* Centaur
Operation
on men: Trinity 0.1.20, ff. 239-296v (surgical; text illustrations)
on wounded falcons: fr. 12400, ff. 104v, 113 (text illustrations)
on head of seated man, observed by two men and woman: Hague 78.D.40, f. 11v (operation?)
Order *see* Sacraments
Organ *see* Cleric playing; Dog and hare, playing; Jubal; Man and ape, playing; Man playing; Man with gittern, woman; *cf. also* Hand organ, references under
Ostrich (*see also* Ape and crane, astride)
Bestiary representation (in cycle): Munich c.g. 16, f. 28 (*fig. 544*); Royal 2 B.VII, ff. 113v-114
eating snail: Rutland Ps., f. 81v (above, falcon striking duck)
shot by nude man: latin 3893, f. 154v (ostrich?)
with horseshoe in beak: latin 1076, f. 16v (ostrich?) (*fig. 545*); Merton 0.1.3, f. 33; Rothschild MS., f. 113
Oven (*see also* Ape as baker; Ape drinking; Baker; Fish swimming; Man crawling; Man, head of, looking; Man with; Proverbs: man yawning)
containing hindquarters: Add. 36684, f. 94v; M. 754, f. 48v (ape aiming pole at; above, ape-baker)
containing hindquarters of hybrid beast with trumpet: Add. 36684, f. 82
containing man: Add. 36684, f. 110
Owl (*see also* Ape and; Ape as physician, ministering to; Fox and cock, stealing; Hare with pipe; Hybrid man and; Hybrid man with gittern, owl; — with psaltery; Man and bird, snaring; Man and fox, with fox; Man and goat, astride; Man and; Obscaena, exposing hindquarters, ape; —, kissing; *Roman de Renart,* fox and lion; Siren with pipe, Skeletons): Arras 790, throughout (horned); C.B. 61, f. 76 (Ps. 51); Fitz. 2-1954, ff. 21v, 57v; fr. 12400, ff. 16 (2, one horned), 18 (on tree, three birds in nest); Queens 17, f. 10v; Rutland Ps., ff. 22v, 27, 94
Owl and birds, mobbed by: All Souls lat. 6, f. 13; Rothschild MS., f. 134 (owl held by man astride goat, two birds flying toward owl)
Owl and cock: Glazier 24, f. 33
Owl and goat: Rutland Ps., f. 63
Owl and hare, striking: M. 796, f. 69v
Owl, Bestiary representation: Royal 2 B.VII, ff. 128v-129 (in cycle)
Owl flying: fr. 12400, f. 66
Owl in tree (*see also* Dogs fighting; Hybrid knight and hare, under tree; Rabbit burrow): fr. 12400, f. 18 (three birds in nest); Rothschild MS., f. 125
Owl with fish in beak: Stowe 17, f. 7 (May)
Owl with mouse in talons: Add. 42130, f. 37
Owl with wheelbarrow containing three apes: Trinity B.11.22, f. 206v
Ox *see* Man and; Man plowing
Ox with club and horn, pursuing dog, with sheep (hunting parody): Trinity B.11.22, f. 37

P

Pains of Hell *see* Jesus Christ, life of: Last Judgment
Painter (*see also* Illuminator; Virgin, miracles of)
decorating lid of small casket (Minnekästchen?): G.K.S. 3384, f. 113 (*fig. 546*)
painting eye of head issuing from line ending: Douce 5, f. 185 (wearing gold robe, hood)
Palmer *see* Jesus Christ, life of: Last Judgment, Pains of Hell, false palmer; *cf.* Pardoner, references under
Panatios: Rutland Ps., f. 88v (at L., monster) (*fig. 547*); W. 37, f. 192v (possibly)
Panther, Bestiary representation: Munich c.g. 16, f. 21 (in cycle) (*fig. 548*); Royal 2 B.VII, ff. 108v-109 (in cycle); Trinity B.11.22, f. 28v (*fig. 549*)
Pants, fight over *see* Proverbs: fight

Papal tiara *see* Ape with; Hybrid ape with; Hybrid man with; Pope
Paradise *see* Adam and Eve, Expulsion; St. Peter; Virgin, miracles of: poor man; Virgin with pennant
Parandros, Bestiary representation: Munich c.g. 16, f. 37 (in cycle)
Pardoner *see* Ape as; Fox as tradesman; Hare as; Palmer, reference under
Parrot: Add. 42130, f. 51 (with ?crow, jay, robin); C.B. 61, f. 78 (Ps. 52); Fitz. 2-1954, f. 155v; Fitz. 242, f. 49v; M. 796, throughout; Rutland Ps., f. 10v
 on hand of hybrid woman: Bodley 264, f. 58
 shot by centaur: fr. 95, f. 319
 shot by hybrid man: W. 88, f. 174v (parrot?)
 shot by man: Add. 42130, f. 215; M. 796, f. 118v (parrot?)
Partridge
 Bestiary representation: Royal 2 B.VII, ff. 111v-112 (in cycle)
 entering decoy net: Rothschild MS., f. 185 (5)
Paschasius *see* St. Lucy
Passion, instruments of *see* Jesus Christ, life of: Passion
Pastimes *see* Games, references under; *also* specific activities
Patroculus *see* St. Paul praying
Patron (and presumed patron) *see also* Patrons
 Joffroy d'Aspremont (knight), kneeling: Douce 118, ff. 49v (receiving shield from hand), 67 (above, in cloud, Godhead), 73, 74v, 77, 104 (with scroll: "je suis cortois je suis d'artois"), 109, 110v (with scroll "domine exaudi orationem meam"), 127, 132 (blessed by hand), 141v, 169v, 172; Melbourne 1254/3, ff. 53v (flanked by dog and hare raising paw to mouth), 70 (man and cleric), 119 (above, in cloud, Godhead)
 Richard of Canterbury (Benedictine monk), kneeling: Glazier 53, f. 115v
 unidentified, kneeling: latin 1076, ff. 102, 149; M. 754, f. 47v; Princeton 44-18, ff. 85v (knight; f. 86, St. Catherine), 114v (before Crucifixion figure on altar) (*fig. 467*); Stowe 17, ff. 232v (before saint), 255v, 266, 271, 271v (before Virgin and Child, receiving scroll); W. 37, ff. 37v (knight), 116 (knight)
Patroness (and presumed patroness) *see also* Patrons
 Isabelle de Kievraing, kneeling: Douce 118, ff. 38 (at altar, before cleric), 40 (before cross), 57 (before Crucifixion figure), 61v (the same), 76v (before cross, with book), 77 (in chapel; above, head of angel; below, knight), 91v (before cross), 96 (crowned), 99v (above, in cloud, hand blessing), 104v (at altar), 106v (the same), 116v (at *prie-dieu,* before cross), 122v (at *p.-d.*, before seraphim), 127 (at *p.-d.*), 137 (at *p.-d.*, before nimbed figure, ?angel, with harp), 138 (at *p.-d.*; above, in cloud, nimbed hand), 139v (with book, before head of angel in initial), 153 (at *p.-d.*, with book), 154v (the same), 160 (same as f. 139v), 167 (at *p.-d.*), 169 (open book on *p.-d.*), 170 (same as f. 153); Melbourne 1254/3, ff. 30 (dog lying under tree), 41v, 50, 54v (at L., tall cross; at R., dragon), 57v, 64v, 68 (with woman, both with books), 74v, 78v, 83, 90v, 96, 107, 110, 123v, 124v, 132 (same as f. 68), 137
 Jeanne II of Navarre, kneeling with book: Y.T. 75, ff. 55v, 65v (with pet dog), 183, 186
 Jeanne of Savoy, kneeling: Jacquemart 1, f. 24v
 Joan Fitzpayn, kneeling with pet dog: Fitz. 242, f. 3
 Mahaut of Brabant, kneeling: Cambrai 87, ff. 63v, 65, 90v (with female companion), 91 (the same), 92v-107, 110 (before Virgin and Child), 200v, 201, 202v, 207, 210, 231v, 232v, 233v, 235v, 237v
 Margaret of Flanders and Hainaut, kneeling: Kraus 75/88, f. 80v (with pet dog)
 Marguerite de Beaujeu, kneeling (*frontispiece*): Add. 36684, ff. 39, 43, 46v, 49, 56, 60; M. 754, ff. 1 (under canopy), 5, 5v, 9, 11, 13v, 15v, 17v (with male companion), 19v, 25 (under canopy), 33v, 38 (with pet dog), 40v, 43, 45v (with book), 47v (the same), 50v (with pet dog), 55v (under canopy), 63v (with pet dog), 65v, 67v, 69v (with book), 71v (the same, with male companion), 74v (with book), 78 (the same, and pet dog), 80, 114 (with pet dog)
 Marie of Viane and her daughter (or niece) Clementia, kneeling: W. 759, f. 3v (both Cistercian nuns, names inscribed)
 Mary de Bohun, kneeling: Thott 547, f. 1
 unidentified, kneeling: Add. 24681, ff. 32, 70, 77; BBR 9961-62, f. 74; Chantilly 62, ff. 145v, 165v (with book), 202 (before Virgin and Child);

Fitz. 2-1954, f. 119; Fitz. 288, f. 210 (nun); fr. 6447, f. 10 (with pet dog); G.K.S. 3384, ff. 5, 53 (with book), 193 (the same), 349v; latin 1076, ff. 21, 69; Laud Lat. 84, ff. 327, 335; Marseilles 111, ff. 8, etc.; Nancy 249, f. 49v (at altar, before angel with trumpet); Princeton 44-18, ff. 25v (?man, in gold robe), 28, 44v; Stowe 17, ff. 147, 271; Trinity B.11.22, f. 53v (with scroll; below, St. Agnes); W. 82, f. 171; W. 85, f. 32; W. 88, f. 100v; W. 90, f. 135; W. 104, f. 32v; W. 110, ff. 132v, 136v

Yolande of Flanders, kneeling: Y.T. 27, f. 44v

Patrons (couple)

Joffroy d'Aspremont (knight) and Isabelle de Kievraing, kneeling: Melbourne 1245/3, ff. 5v (behind them, unicorn couchant; at R., ape with fruit, stag), 11 (*fig. 550*), 31v (retainer with sword holding horse), 32v, 33v, 50v, 120 (dog lying beside them)

Mahaut de Brabant and husband, kneeling: Cambrai 87, ff. 30 (with cleric, before David harping in clouds), 202

Marguerite and Renaud de Bar, kneeling before Christ in Majesty: Y.T. 8, f. 31

Sir Geoffrey Luttrell and wife *see* Banquet

Sir Richard Grey and Joan Fitzpayn, kneeling: Fitz. 242, ff. 2v, 28v, 29, 55v (patron only) (*fig. 12*)

unidentified, kneeling: Auct. D.4.2, f. 15v; Fitz. 2-1954, f. 119; M. 155, f. 114v; M. 754, ff. 17v, 71v (with pet dog); Marseilles 111, f. 141v; Stowe 17, ff. 270v, Death of Virgin) (*fig. 677*), 271 (before Assumption of Virgin); Trinity B.11.22, f. 37v (above, Christ with orb); W. 104, f. 81v (man and nun; four men, two with scrolls); Y.T. 13, ff. 88, 118v (crowned)

William of St. Omer (or Thomas, his son) and Elisabeth of Mulbarton, kneeling: Add. 39810, f. 7 (*fig. 140*)

Peacock: Add. 17868, f. 43v; Add. 21926, f. 26 (Ps. 1); Add. 24686, f. 16v (and peahen, cock, hybrid angel with trumpet); Add. 39810, f. 7 (Ps. 1) (*fig. 140*); Add. 42130, f. 35; Add. 48985, f. 2 (Ps. 1); Add. 50000, f. 56v; All Souls lat. 6, f. 13; BBR 5163-64, ff. 27, 81v; BBR 9157, f. 316; BBR 10607, ff. 36v, 85v; Bodley 264, f. 128; C.B. 61, f. 139; Cambrai 87, f. 66; Cambrai 103, f. 57; Chantilly 62, f. 29v; Christ Church E.II, f. 53; D.P. 12, f. 76; D.P. 35, f. 56v; Douce 5, variant throughout; Douce 6, f. 4 (man picking feather?); Egerton 1151, f. 7; Fitz. 47, f. 170v; Fitz. 288, f. 2v; fr. 776, ff. 10v, 270v; fr. 12400, ff. 6v, 15, 15v, 41, 51v; Glazier 24, f. 34v; Hague 78.D.40, ff. 1, 37v-38 (2, one with open, one with closed, tail); Lambeth 75. f. 1 (*fig. 32*); Lambeth 209, f. 1; Lambeth 233, f. 232v (hybrid); latin 1076, ff. 33v (Ps. 26), 63v (Ps. 51); latin 3893, ff. 113v (pecking border leaf), 154, 282; latin 10483, f. 17v; latin 14284, ff. 35, 37 (variants); Laud Lat. 84, ff. 173v, 234; M. 88, ff. 109, 137 (at L., pursuers of Moses drowning in Red Sea) (*fig. 505*); M. 102, f. 2; M. 729, f. 333v; M. 754, ff. 19v, 51, 79v (with hare, swan, lion, dog); Maz. 34, f. 5; Melbourne 1254/3, ff. 15, 42v; Princeton 44-18, f. 64v; Royal 1 D.I, ff. 1 (*fig. 125*), 5; Royal 3 D.VI, f. 234; Rutland Ps., f. 104v; Stowe 17, ff. 33v (confronting cock), 71, 251 (hybrid man with peacock's tail, with mirror), 255; Vienna 1826*, f. 58; W. 87, ff. 2v-3 (hybrid peacock; hybrid bishop aiming crook at), 3 (ape kneeling), 25

Peacock and ape

charged by, with club and buckler: Douce 118, f. 31v

ridden by: BBR 10607, f. 177 (at L., Jonah issuing from whale) (*fig. 290*)

Peacock and hybrid bishop, aiming crook at: W. 87, ff. 2v-3 (hybrid peacock; f. 3, ape kneeling)

Peacock and hybrid man, shot by: Melbourne 1254/3, ff. 37v-38

Peacock and lion, confronted: latin 13260, f. 46v

Peacock and stork, confronted: Cambrai 102, f. 249

Peacock, Bestiary representation, two confronted: Munich c.g. 16, f. 54 (in cycle); Royal 2 B.VII, ff. 124v-125 (in cycle)

Peacocks, two, confronted (Bestiary representation?): Add. 28784B, f. 14; Add. 50000, f. 56v

Peacocks under tree with Queen Teminie (*cf.* Alexander for other adventures in series): Bodley 264, f. 97

Pea pods and blossoms on plant: Add. 42130, f. 79v; Arras 790, f. 195v; latin 10483, f. 28v (butterfly and snail on plant); M. 729, f. 16

Pectoral cross *see* Merman with

Pedlar, with silver beakers (*cf.* Ape and; Ape as): Douce 118, f. 55 (*fig. 551*)

Pelican and bat: Chantilly 64, ff. 113, 113v

P

Pelican in piety (*cf.* Bird pecking): Add. 38114, f. 121; Add. 42130, ff. 44, 178 (Ps. 101: 7); BBR II 988, vol. I, ff. 83, 194v; Cambrai 87, f. 30v; Cambrai 102, f. 345 (*Te igitur*); Cambrai 103, f. 168; Chantilly 62, f. 58; Christ Church E.II, f. 69; D.P. 35, f. 68v; Douce 118, ff. 66, 142v; Douce 366, ff. 71v, 109; Fitz. 288, f. 154 (on top of Crucifixion cross in miniature, flanked by lion with whelps and phoenix; Hours of the Holy Ghost); fr. 25526, f. 124; lation 1076, f. 146; latin 10435, f. 6 (at R., phoenix) (*fig. 552*); latin 13260, f. 74v; Melbourne 1254/3, f. 55; Merton 0.1.3, f. 52v (at R., beehive); Princeton 44-18, f. 190; Stowe 17, f. 228v (no nest); Trinity B.11.22, f. 213 (*fig. 553*); W. 45, f. 174v; W. 85, f. 33v; W. 87, ff. 65, 103; W. 102, f. 83

Pelican in piety, Bestiary representation (in cycle): Munich c.g. 16, f. 59; Royal 2 B.VII, ff. 90v-91

Penda *see* St. Oswald

Penitence *see* Sacraments

Pentecost *see* Jesus Christ, life of

Peridexion, Bestiary representation: Munich c.g. 16, f. 63 (in cycle; four doves in tree)

Pet *see* Dog as; Squirrel as

Phallis *see* Obscaena

Phallisbaum *see* Nun and man, embracing

Pharaoh *see* Joseph (Old Testament) brought before; Moses before

Pheasant: Add. 42130, f. 84v (at L., tiger looking into mirror, Bestiary theme)

Philistines *see* Israelites and; Samson

Philosopher *see* Phyllis and Aristotle

Phoenix, Bestiary representation: Fitz. 288, f. 153 (at L., lion with whelps, pelican in piety on Crucifixion cross in miniature; Hours of the Holy Ghost); latin 10435, f. 6 (at L., pelican in piety) (*fig. 552*); Munich c.g. 16, f. 60 (in cycle); Royal 2 B.VII, ff. 93v-94 (in cycle)

Phyllis and Aristotle (*cf.* possible parodies under Hare and man, astride; Man astride man; Man nude and hybrid man, astride; Woman and beast):

- seated on back of: Arras 47, f. 74 (*fig. 554*); C.B. 62, f. 206v; fr. 95, f. 61v (in gold robe) (*fig. 557*); Y.T. 8, f. 187 (*fig. 555*)
- standing before, philosopher seated, reading: fr. 95, f. 254 (in gold robe; above, hare pouncing on cringing dog) (*fig. 556*)

Physician (all with urinal) *cf.* Ape as; Centaur as; Fox as; Hybrid man as; Woman with jug

Physician and ape

- holding urinal up to sun, ape with coin and stool basket: Douce 6, f. 82
- ministering to: W. 104, f. 28 (*fig. 11*)

Physician and bird-headed man (cleric?) with purse, ministering to: Melbourne 1254/3, f. 11v (*fig. 558*)

Physician and bird's head, ministering to (feeding?): W. 85, f. 28

Physician and crane, feeling pulse of: Fitz. 298, f. 81

Physician and dragon

- bitten by two dragons: fr. 95, f. 68v
- ministering to: latin 10483, f. 102v

Physician and hybrid man, confronting: W. 37, ff. 185v-186

Physician and man

- accompanied by man with mortar and pestle, man with trefoil rod, two women with stool basket and jar: Fitz. 288, f. 6v (above, rondels of the twelve months)
- bleeding: Add. 42130, f. 61 (at R., kingfisher) (*fig. 559*)
- ministering to: G.K.S. 3384, f. 104 (man with stool basket, handle held in teeth); W. 82, f. 75v (man with coin and stool basket); W. 88, f. 122 (?cleric with man confessing?)
- seated before man exposing hindquarters: Bodley 264, f. 79 (physician?) (*fig. 560*)
- with two men putting shroud on corpse, another man holding nose, two angels with soul: Trinity B.11.22, f. 55v (*fig. 137*)

Physician and woman, ministering to: BBR 10607, f. 17; Cloisters 54.1.2, f. 143; G.K.S. 3384, f. 289 (woman with stool basket) (*fig. 562*); Yale M.S., f. 154v (*fig. 561*)

Physician at lectern: Cloisters 54.1.2, f. 65v; Y.T. 27, f. 116v (book on lectern)

Physician practicing surgery: Trinity 0.1.20, 239-236v

Physician with stool basket: G.K.S. 3384, f. 12

Physician with urinal, alone: Chantilly 64, f. 33v (fur-lined garment); Douce 5, f. 45; G.K.S. 3384, f. 86 (above, in line ending, male head); Lambeth 233, f. 43v; latin 10483, f. 411v

Physiologus *see* Bestiary, references under

Pied wagtail(?): Fitz. 2-1954, f. 84v

Piety *see* Sacraments: Eucharist

Pig (*see also* Ape and; Man and; School)

- and unicorn, stag grazing: Cambrai 102, f. 207v (Min.: Resurrection)
- ascending ladder (*cf.* Snail): Add. 36684, f. 142v

intercourse: Merton 0.1.3, f. 137v (at L., dogs having intercourse)
with bagpipe: BBR 10607, f. 182; Rothschild MS., f. 177v
with distaff and spindle, hare with reel: fr. 25526, f. 102v
Pigeon, Bestiary representation: Royal 2 B.VII, ff. 117v-118 (in cycle)
Pigs: Add. 39810, f. 7 (*fig. 140*)
Pilate (*see also* Jesus Christ, life of: before; —: Pilate): Add. 48985, f. 32v (washing hands; Min.: Christ before Pilate)
Pilgrim (*see also* Alms; Ape as; Fox as; Hybrid man as; Lion as; Palmer, references under): Douce 5, f. 190v (on ?stilts); Douce 6, f. 77v; latin 14284, f. 31v; Melbourne 1254/3, f. 81v
astride ass, accompanied by two dogs: Bodley 264, f. 57v
beggar(?), with staff, pointing at angel with censer and incense boat flanked by man praying and man with raised sword: latin 10483, ff. 40v-41
blind(?), led by dog: Royal 10 E.IV, f. 110
crippled, blessed by bishop: Yale MS., f. 311
hooded, with staff, confronting monster/dragon: Rutland Ps., f. 104
Pilgrimage *see* Virgin, miracles of: Woman in childbirth
Pincers *see* Man with Proverb: goose; St. Dunstan
Pipe (and tabor) *see* Ape with; Ass with; Bear with; Centaur with; Devil with; Dog; Double pipe, references under; Goat with; Hare with; Hybrid ape with; Hybrid beast with; Hybrid man with; Jesus Christ, life of: Last Judgment: Pains of Hell: devil roasting man; King and horse, astride; Knight with; Man in costume as ass; — as stag; Man nude with; Man with; Mermaid with; Merman with; Procession, funeral of fox; Siren with; Stag with
Pisa *see* Virgin, miracles of: cleric of
Pitcher *see* Ape with; Detached limbs, hand with tankard; Hybrid man drinking; Jug, references under; Woman with jug
Pitchfork *see* Hybrid man with; Knight and fox; Man and fox, pursuing with; Man scything
Pitch-in-the-hole: Add. 42130, f. 193v (2 men)
Platform shoes: W. 88, ff. 106v (worn by hybrid beast), 159v (worn by hybrid woman)
Plautilla *see* St. Paul
Plowing *see* Ape; Cain; Man
Pond
containing fish: fr. 12400, f. 54
containing waterfowl: fr. 12400, ff. 6, 10v, 12v, 13, 13v, 14, 20, 23, 51, 52v, 68v
Pontigny *see* St. Thomas of Canterbury
Pope (*see also* Hybrid cleric praying; Jesus Christ, life of: Last Judgment: Pains of Hell; Papal tiara, references under; St. Dominic; St. Thomas of Canterbury; Virgin, miracles of: Pope Leo; —: sinning)
admonishing crowned hybrid man: latin 10483, f. 163; latin 10484, f. 136 (with book, cross)
at lectern: Add. 49622, f. 68
cleric kneeling, presenting book: fr. 25526, f. 12v (at L., two cardinals)
seated, with crosier: Add. 42130, f. 60
with bishop: Add. 49622, f. 207
with key, two clerics in black habits kneeling: Stowe 17, f. 180
Porcupine *see* Hedgehog
Pot *see also* Ape with; Hybrid man playing; Man cooking; Men fighting, with sword and shield; Strike-the-pot; Woman cooking
Pot on fire, boiling: M. 754, ff. 19 (bellows blowing fire), 92 (filled with water issuing from pump)
Pot worn on head by
bird (goose?): M. 729, f. 268
centaur with bellows and tongs fighting centauress with distaff and broom: Hague 78.D.40, f. 10v
centaur with club: W. 88, f. 183
dog: BBR 9217, f. 169
hybrid creature: Exeter 47, f. 89
hybrid man (*see also* Man nude and hybrid man): Add. 42130, f. 182v; Cloisters 54.1.2, ff. 117, 194; M. 754, f. 72; M. 796, f. 49v (falconer, with owl); Y.T. 27, f. 69v (with ax)
knight: latin 10483, ff. 33 (with club and shield), 49
lion: Hague 10 A.14, f. 27v (another wearing basket on head; both with swords)
man: Cloisters 54.1.2., f. 173 (jug)
bearded, with basket and flabellum(?): Douce 6, f. 103 (below, man throwing up hands)
nude, issuing from tail of hybrid man with bagpipe: W. 88, f. 189v
playing grill with tongs: Douce 5, f. 164v (above, man playing spoon with bow or stick; man with trumpet) (*fig. 518*)

with spear fighting hybrid man with club, also with pot on head: W. 88, f. 175

with sword and buckler, threatening pleading man: latin 10483, f. 105v

monster: Add. 42130, f. 182v

Saracen with falchion and shield: Cloisters 54.1.2, f. 45 (bucket?)

wild man holding stone(?), looking over shoulder at man bending bow: M. 88, f. 173 (hybrid woman aiming bellows at hindquarters of ape)

Preaching *see* Bishop; Cleric; Doctor; Dominican; Fox as Franciscan; Franciscan; Jesus Christ, life of; St. Barnabas; St. Denis; St. Dominic; St. Francis; St. James the Greater; St. John the Baptist; St. John the Evangelist; St. Paul; St. Stephen

Presentation in the Temple *see* Jesus Christ, life of

Pride *see* Jesus Christ, life of: Last Judgment: Pains of Hell, proud man; Man and horse, astride

Prie-dieu see Man with message; Patroness, kneeling

Priest (*see also* Bride; Cleric; St. Paul; Samson, marrying; Virgin, miracles of): BBR 1175, f. 82

Prison *see* Man and hare, imprisoned by; St. Catherine; St. Margaret; St. Paul; St. Peter

Prisoner *see* Man and thief; Man with sword and buckler; St. —, esp. those in preceding entry

Procession

angels with censer, two candlesticks, book: Add. 42130, f. 102v (4; f. 103, Christ in Majesty seated on rainbow, showing wounds, feet on globe; four Evangelist symbols in corners of panel)

angels with censer, (two) with tapers, gold incense boat and spoon, moving toward church or shrine on mound: Add. 42130, f. 103v (5)

ape-bishop with asperge, ape-cleric with book and situla (filled by man issuing from border with ewer), moving toward church: Douce 6, f. 95v (*fig. 564*)

ape-cleric with asperge and situla, ass with processional cross, three apes (one mitered): Glazier 24, f. 75 (*fig. 565*)

boar on litter borne by two apes, ape with processional cross, another ape with hand bells: Arsenal 5218, f. 81 (at R., squirrel running up pole to its house) (*fig. 563*)

butterfly with taper, followed by two clerics with cross, hand bells, three clerics praying, two clerics with bagpipe, raised vielle: M. 754, f. 25 (in outer margins, hybrid cleric, hybrid man, hybrid woman, bird, angel, ape, all with lit tapers)

clerics with asperge and situla, processional cross, with bishop moving toward church: Fitz. 298, f. 1 (*fig. 566*)

clerics with reliquary, processional cross: Nancy 249, f. 157v

Dominicans with reliquary: latin 10483, f. 184 (in foreground, two cripples); latin 10484, f. 218v (the same, preceded by three clerics with tapers and processional cross, followed by four Dominicans, one with book) (*fig. 567*)

fox-cleric with book, hare with processional cross, approaching cleric ringing two bells suspended from frames above: Melbourne 1254/3, f. 29v (*fig. 571*)

funeral *see also* Virgin, life of: Death of

coffin borne by ape and man (both issuing from border), man with hand bells, nun with book, ape with processional cross: G.K.S. 3384, f. 292 (*fig. 573*)

coffin borne by dog and hybrid abbot, followed by merman with book: W. 45 f. 49 (at R., man with vielle) (*fig. 572*)

coffin borne by hybrid men (2); hybrid bishop with two sets of three hand bells: Jacquemart 1, f. 116

coffin borne by men: Nancy 249, f. 267 (Offices of the Dead) (*fig. 574*)

coffin borne by men (4), preceded by two men each with two tapers; man with processional cross, all moving toward church: BBR 9391, f. 116 (above, at L., cleric with book issuing from border; Min.: funeral service, four clerics, three mourners; Offices of the Dead) (*fig. 568*)

funeral of dog; hares with hand bells, tapers, processional cross; hare-clerics with asperge and censer; two hares carrying bier, hare with trumpet seated on coffin: Add. 49622, f. 133 (*fig. 569*)

funeral of fox, *Roman de Renart* episode: ape with asperge and situla, two lions with processional cross and tapers, horse and dog carrying bier from which fox escapes with cock in mouth: Bodley 264, f. 79v (*fig. 599*)

funeral of fox, *Roman de Renart* episode: camel with hand bells, elephant-pilgrim, bull with horn, horse with pipe and tabor, ass with pipe and bell, dog with bagpipe, ape-mother and three young, stag and cat bearing bier, cock with censer, wolf as bishop, cat with tabor, ram with processional cross, beast with horn, ram with asperge and situla, boar with mattock, hare ringing bells in church tower: W. 102, ff. 73-80 (*fig. 131:* f. 77v)

funeral of fox, *Roman de Renart* episode: fox supported by two nuns(?), drawn by six geese; led by cock with mace, followed by hare with asperge: Royal 10 E.IV, f. 49 (f. 48v, fox hung by geese, cock, hens, ducks; in *Roman de Renart* sequence)

hares with book, processional cross, ringing bell (*cf.* Hare, funeral of): Add. 36684, f. 24v (9) (*fig. 570*)

men with trumpets, cornet, pipe and tabor, processing out of city labeled "Constantinople": Add. 42130, f. 164v

Processional cross (*see also* Ape as bishop with; Procession)

goat(?) with: Douce 118, f. 38v (at R., stork biting man's hand)

goat with, fox-cleric with book: BBR 9157, f. 1

hybrid dog with: fr. 25526, f. 67 (below, man shooting bird)

Professions *see* specific subjects

Prophet (*see also* Cycles, Old and New Law; —, Prophets; names of individuals): Add. 28784B, throughout (with scrolls); Arundel 83, f. 14; BBR 9391, f. 156 (2, one with scroll; Min.: Last Supper); Cambridge Dd.5.5, f. 13; Cloisters 54.1.2, ff. 33v, 113, 138, 158 (all hybrids, with scrolls; prophets?); Douce 118, ff. 39, 90v, 130v (with scroll "vere languores nostros ipse tulit"); Harley 6563, ff. 1, 1v (both with scrolls); Kraus 75/88, f. 199; M. 155, f. 97v (with scroll); Melbourne 1254/3, ff. 43, 101 (with scroll "vere deus et homo est"), 111; Stowe 17, ff. 71v, 89 (2), 131 (2), 149v, 235v; Trinity B.11.22, f. 20 (*fig. 508*); Y.T. 75, f. 55v (with scroll)

Proverbs (for other possible proverbs, *see* Ape with pitcher; Bull and man, rope; — and woman; Dolphin; Fish swimming; Hare with purse; Hood, two heads; Hybrid man, shoveling; Hybrid man with jug, breaking; Man and ass, carrying; — and butterfly, pursuing; — and dog, holding; — and eel, holding; — and fox, with; — and horse, carrying; — and woman, heads; — blowing toasting fork; — crawling; Man, head of, looking; Man playing, subentries under; Man with distaff and spindle, pursuing cat; — with oven; — with taper; Men fighting, one with club; Obscaena, kissing; Pot worn on head, subentries under; Sheep in caldron; Spider; Wheelbarrow, references under; Woman as falconer; Woman with tray

ape as falconer, owl on glove, astride ass (*cf.* entries under Ape as falconer): M. 812, f. 34 (labeled "Neyhther no less than an ape and an owl and an ass")

ass, bleeding, leaning over sharp fence post around small enclosure: M. 88, f. 71 (labeled "qui plus connoitre que doit, la connoitise le defoit") (*fig. 575*)

eggs in nest or basket, hatched by (*cf.* Ape with egg, sitting; Hybrid man with egg; Man with egg; this motif has various proverbial meanings, among them "Hier is een narr op eijer geset." See Bibliography, III, Randall, "A Mediaeval Slander")

ape: Glazier 24, f. 105v

ass/bird: W. 45, f. 44v (or bird with hare's ears)

man: BBR 10607, f. 130; Cambrai 103, ff. 324, 340; Douce 6, f. 93v (at L., horned owl) (*fig. 584*); fr. 95, f. 343 (*fig. 582*); latin 10435, f. 125v; Trinity B.11.22, f. 216v; W. 82, f. 179v (*fig. 581*); Yale MS., f. 31 (*fig. 583*)

fight over pants, between man and woman: Cloisters 54.1.2, f. 202 (woman holding pants); Glazier 24, f. 30v (*fig. 576*)

gameboard and pitcher hung on trees: BBR 9217, f. 116 ("zijn lier an de wilgen hangen," i.e., to give up sinful pleasures) (*fig. 577*)

gameboard held by man kneeling before woman with basket: BBR 9217, f. 123 ("Hij kriegt den korf," i.e., jilting a suitor) (*fig. 578*)

goose being shoed (needless meddling; *cf.* Man with pincers): Add. 10292, f. 1; Bodley 264, f. 124v (2 men, one with pincers clamping goose's beak shut); G.K.S. 3384, f. 110 (man) (*fig. 580*); Melbourne 1254/3, f. 7v (man and hare) (*fig. 579*); Stowe 17, f. 112v (2 women)

man biting column, hands tied behind his back, companion with lit taper (*cf.* Man biting): Add. 42130, f. 158 (possibly a "Pilaerbijter," i.e., a hypocritical churchgoer) man yawning before oven: BBR 9427, f. 14 ("Hij gaapt tegen den oven" — a braggard)

woman with basket on head (*cf.* Fables: woman with jug; proverb such as "Don't count your chickens before they are hatched"?): Cambridge Dd. 5.5, f. 264 (another with jug on head; at L., man with finger held to nose, holding ?sack); Douce 6, f. 118v (containing eggs; above, hare; below, ape with distaff and spindle); Stowe 17, f. 67 (with second basket containing hare over arm; at L., monstrous hybrid pointing); Y.T. 8, f. 186v (wild woman, basket containing three birds); Y.T. 27, f. 85v (with distaff)

Prudence *see* Virtues

Pruning *see* Ape; Cleric with sword; Hare with ax; Hybrid bird; Hybrid man; Man

Psaltery *see* Ape with; Cat with; Centaur with; Hybrid man with; Man with; Nun with; Woman with

Pulpit *see* Doctor; Dominican preaching

Pump, water issuing: M. 754, ff. 91v, 92 (into caldron over fire)

Puppet show before audience: Bodley 264, ff. 54v (children seated) (*fig. 585*), 76 (four men standing) (*fig. 586*)

Purse *see* Ape and hare, standing; Ape as physician, ministering to ape; Ape with; Cleric and nun, offering; Cleric and woman, emptying; Hare with; Hybrid woman with; Man and butterfly, pursuing with club; Man and woman, offered; Nun and man, receiving; Physician and bird-headed man; Scribe, man; Woman as falconer; Woman with

Putting stone, man (*cf.* Hybrid man with stone; Man with egg, aiming): Add. 17868, f. 33v; Add. 30029, f. 92v; Add. 42130, ff. 40, 198 (another man disrobing); Add. 49622, f. 74; Arras 47, f. 31 (*fig. 493*); Arras 1043, f. 7 (with bat wings); BBR 9961-62, f. 74; BBR 10607, f. 186 (above, owl); Bodley 264, ff. 30, 50; Cambridge Dd. 5.5, f. 246; Cloisters 54.1.2, ff. 54 (*fig. 511*), 73, 137v, 156v, 187 (all hybrids); Douce 5, f. 105v (huge rock; hybrid man aiming pole, prodding man putting); Douce 6, f. 17; Douce 118, f. 118 (nude); fr. 95, ff. 108, 195v (2, one holding stone to ear, the other carrying stone on back; in center, lion devouring ?bone); fr. 776, f. 154v (egg?); latin 3893, f. 234; latin 10483, ff. 6 (standing on dragon), 56 (hybrid), 173; latin 14284, ff. 9 (2, one picking up stone), 22v, 42v; M. 183, f. 248v; Royal 10 E.IV, f. 96 (3); Rutland Ps., f. 41; St. Omer 5, ff. 62 (*fig. 492*), 170, 272v; Trinity B.11.22, f. 4 (*fig. 29*); W. 88, ff. 22v, 86; W. 90, f. 45; W. 761, f. 28 (issuing from border, head erased); Y.T. 27, f. 17v

Pygmalion, sculpting image (for other episodes in sequence, *see* Lover; *cf.* Sculptor): Tournai CI, f. 319 (*fig. 587*)

Pygmy

and centaur, fighting with spear and sword: fr. 95, f. 230v (2, nude)

and crane, astride, with bell: Rothschild MS., f. 141

and crane, fighting: Rothschild MS., ff. 114v (2) (*fig. 345*), 171v (astride ape)

and crane, swinging by neck, another pygmy with dog: Rothschild MS., f. 145v

and goat with pipe, listening(?) to: Rutland Ps., f. 49v

Pyx *see* Hybrid woman with

P

Q

Queen (*see also* Alexander; Ape and hare, as king; Coach; Edward III confronting; Hen crowned; Hybrid queen; King and; Wild man and knight, astride horse, slain by)

accompanied by six ladies, two men, musicians with bagpipe, hand organ, tabor, vielle: Bodley 264, f. 172

praying (*cf.* Patroness: Jeanne II of Navarre; —: Jeanne of Savoy; —: Yolande of Flanders): Melbourne 1254/3, f. 36v

with bird (falcon?), lure: Douce 118, f. 164v

with vielle: Douce 118, f. 160v; Melbourne 1254/3, f. 33 (issuing from border)

Quintain, balancing ("human quintain")

ape seated on trestle with shield, ape charging with pole: Arsenal 5218, f. 40

ape seated on woodpile, ape approaching: Schilling MS., April (*fig. 588*)

apes, one seated on barrel, touching soles: Douce 6, f. 117 (2)

apes seated back to back: M. 754, f. 30

man and woman, seated, soles touching, holding rope: Nancy 249, f. 37

Q

man nude, seated on stool, nude man with leg extended: Add. 42130, f. 152v
man seated opposite standing man: Bodley 264, f. 90; fr. 25526, f. 79 (two)
man seated on back of man: latin 14284, f. 51 (two men preparing to charge); M. 88, f. 178 (three men gesturing); Princeton 44-18, f. 183 (man charging) (*fig. 589*); W. 109, f. 58 (man standing)
man seated on stool
  leg extended: fr. 25526, ff. 11v (opposite three men), 20 (two apes approaching), 41v (opposite three men)
  man on swing pushed toward him by third man: Bodley 264, f. 78v (*fig. 590*)
  opposite man: Royal 2 B.VII, f. 162; Royal 10 E.IV, f. 95v (two men conversing, gesturing); Rutland Ps., f. 43v
  with shield and helmet, opposite man with lance: Bodley 264, f. 100
men seated, soles touching: Bodley 264, f. 100; Cambridge Dd. 5.5, f. 221; Chantilly 64, f. 25 (pulling stick); Nancy 249, f. 35v (pulling stick); Rutland Ps., f. 69v (pulling quoit; tug-of-war) (*fig. 663*)

Quintain, tilting at
  ape: Douce 5, f. 36 (at R., hare in gold tunic); Douce 118, ff. 83v (ape/horse), 94v (hybrid ape); Nancy 249, f. 159v; Tournai Ps., f. 205
  ape astride dog and horse: Add. 29253, f. 47 (2)
  ape astride dog, ape with buckler as target: Princeton 44-18, ff. 49v-50
  ape astride dog, with basket: N.K.S. 41 f. 181
  ape astride goat(?): Melbourne 1254/3, f. 61
  ape astride horse: Douce 6, f. 71v (2, one on foot)
  ape astride pig: G.K.S. 3384, ff. 279 (hare?), 294v
  ape astride ram: G.K.S. 3384, f. 222 (above, ape with trumpet)
  ape astride stag: Douce 118, f. 133
  ape astride stork: G.K.S. 3384, f. 26 (above, man seizing hare by ears)
  hare: Melbourne 1254/3, f. 5 (astride cock); Trinity B.11.22, f. 214 (at R., man with pipe and tabor) (*fig. 592*)
  hybrid knight: Jacquemart 1, f. 19
    with basket on head: W. 88, f. 173v
    with bird's body, aiming long fork at egg(?) balanced on pole: Jacquemart 1, f. 3v
  knight: Douce 6, f. 113 (above, Christ head between stag horns, ape with bowl kissing head in line ending, tub on ground) (*fig. 594*); fr. 25526, ff. 2, 23; Nancy 249, f. 29
  knight astride horse: Douce 118, f. 102 (target: bird's head); Melbourne 1254/3, ff. 116, 126v-127; (target: dragon balancing coat of arms in mouth); Nancy 249, ff. 29, 196 (falling from horse)
  knight/centaur: Hague 78.D.40, f. 30v; Melbourne 1254/3, f. 40v
  man: BBR 9391, f. 98v; Clumber 938, f. 107v
    astride horse: Hague 78.D.40, f. 16 (2); Nancy 249, f. 193 (*fig. 593*)
    in boat: Bodley 264, f. 89
    in cart: Bodley 264, f. 82v (at L., two men tilting at another target)
    nude: Bodley 264, f. 56 (3, keg on pole as target); Douce 118, f. 33 (astride goat, mitered)

Quoit
  held by two hybrid men with winged headdresses: Hague 10 A.14, f. 26
  held by two men seated, soles touching, pulling on (quintain, balancing): Rutland Ps., f. 69v (tug-of-war) (*fig. 663*)

R

Rabbah *see* David, life of: D. and Nathan
Rabbit burrow (*see also* Hare disappearing; Woman and fox, trapping; — and lion, fighting): Add. 39810, f. 7 (*fig. 140*); Add. 49622, ff. 8, 153, 172v, 178v and line endings throughout; Hague 10 A.14, ff. 106v, 144; M. 102, f. 127 (line ending); Princeton 44-18, ff. 19, 136 (owl in tree); Rylands lat R.117, f. 9
  ape with ax approaching: Trinity B.11.22, f. 137v
  ferret entering: Add. 42130, f. 176v
  hybrid king hunting hare with horn and hound; at L., five hares running in and out of burrow: Add. 49622, f. 107v
  hybrid man building fence before, hare observing: Add. 49622, f. 150
  man with net before: Add. 49622, f. 132v
  supported by man issuing from border: Cambrai 87, f. 61 (three men entering church, cock as weathervane; sun in cloud, rain pouring down)
Rahab *see* Joshua, marriage

Rake *see* Ape playing vielle; Ape with; Hybrid man playing bellows; — playing jawbone; — raking; — reaping; Man playing bellows; — playing jawbone; — raking; Ram playing
Ram (*see also* Ape and; Dog and; Goat with astrolabe; Hare and; Hybrid man and; Man and; Man nude and; Obscaena, pole: ram; Procession, funeral of fox; Woman and)
and snail, butting: Douai 193, f. 213v
and stag, butting: Royal 2 B.VII, f. 142
and unicorn, butting: Cambrai 102, f. 273
as bishop *see* Bishop, parodied
as cleric, at lectern with fox-cleric: Hague 78.D.40, f. 25 (at R., archer; at L., hybrid man with trumpet) (*fig. 196*)
butting border foliage: W. 82, f. 62v; W. 87, ff. 9 (above, cleric with asperge), 68, 99v
butting ram *see* Rams butting
on column before two men flanking two wrestlers: Hague 78.D.40, f. 130v (at L., two men fighting with swords and bucklers)
on column, flanked by three gesturing clerics and two wrestlers (in drawers): Hague 78.D.40, f. 34v (at R., two men fighting with war hammers and shields)
playing jawbone with rake, hooded: Cloisters 54.1.2, f. 22
with bell between horns: Add. 42130, f. 59
with four horns: Add. 42130, f. 169; fr. 12400, f. 57v (text illustration)
with trumpet: Arsenal 6329, f. 211
Rams butting (2): Add. 29253, f. 60; Add. 30029, f. 103v; Add. 36684, f. 116v; Add. 38114, f. 309; Add 39810, f. 7 (*fig. 140*); Arsenal 5218, f. 50; C.B. 62, f. 9; Cambrai 103, f. 107; Chartres 549, f. 244; Douce 24, f. 7v; Fitz. 47, f. 75 (line ending); Fitz. 288, f. 162 (Min.: Annunciation); fr. 95, f. 108v; fr. 25526, ff. 78 (at L., St. Christopher), 145v, 149v (flanked by man with cloth and man with slingshot; *cf.* Man and ram, baiting); Hague 78.D.40, ff. 69v, 103 (at L., two lions extending right paws to each other), 127 (at R., fox); Hague XX, f. 3v (observed by ape with basket; *cf.* Ape and ram, warding); Jacquemart 1, f. 27v; latin 14284, f. 43v; Nancy 249, f. 61; Royal 2 B.VII, f. 141v; W. 37, ff. 174v-175; Y.T. 8, f. 179v; Y.T. 13, ff. 89v, 183; Y.T. 15, f. 292v; Yale MS., f. 325
Rams butting, Bestiary representation: Munich c.g. 16, f. 39 (in cycle)
Rattle *see* Beggar woman; Hybrid man as beggar; Hybrid woman with; *cf.* Windmill, toy
Raven *see* Fables: fox, raven; Noah
Reaping *see* Hybrid man; Man
Reason *see* Lover, conversing with
Rebec *see* Man with
Reel *see* Ape spinning; Ape with; Bird with; Boar with distaff; Hare winding; Hare with; Hybrid bishop and hybrid woman; Hybrid man with distaff and spindle; — with reel; Hybrid woman with, references under; Knight and woman, kneeling before; Knight balancing; Man and hybrid bishop, astride; Woman with distaff and spindle and; — with spindle
Reliquary borne by bishop and king (*see also* Procession: clerics; —: Dominicans): latin 14284, f. 25
Renaud de Bar *see* Patrons: Marguerite and Renaud de Bar
Resurrection *see* Jesus Christ, life of
Reynard the Fox *see Roman de Renart*
Richard, King *see* Lion as king
Richard of Canterbury *see* Patron: Richard of Canterbury
Riddle *see* Man with greens
Ring *see* Hybrid man with; Man and woman, offering; St. Edward the Confessor; St. Thomas of Canterbury; Samson presenting; Siren with
Ringtoss, two apes playing: Cambridge Dd.5.5, f. 253 (man blowing toasting fork; man playing bellows with tongs; man with bagpipe) (*fig. 595*)
Robber *see* Jesus Christ, life of: Last Judgment: Pains of Hell; Man and thief
Robin *see* Parrot
Roman de Renart (*cf.* Fox, subentries under)
ape and pedlar: Royal 10 E.IV, ff. 149-151 (*figs. 20-24*)
fox and geese, hung by, assisted by cock and two hens; two ducks looking on: Royal 10 E.IV, ff. 48v, 49 (dragged to gallows) (*fig. 191*)
fox and goose, stealing (*cf.* Fox and cock, stealing): Royal 10 E.IV, ff. 49v (at L., fox-bishop preaching to fowl), 175 (pursued by women with distaff or stick)
fox and hare, running with hare in jaws: Royal 10 E.IV, f. 48 (at L., man with horn)

R

fox and lion
as physician (with urinal), ministering to: All Souls lat. 6, f. 13; Royal 10 E.IV, ff. 54 (feeling pulse of lion, which has bandaged head), 54v (leaving lion asleep)
bringing letter to: Trinity B.11.22, f. 205 (owl behind lion)
covering with wolf's skin: Royal 10 E.IV, f. 57 (2) (*fig. 597*)
presenting pouch to: Royal 10 E.IV, f. 56
presenting purse and dead goose to lion/pilgrim: Royal 10 E.IV, f. 55 (at R., fox turning his back on dead geese and hares) (*fig. 596*)
fox and man, pursued by; another man kneeling and holding net over exit to fox's hole (*cf.* Man and fox, pursuing): Royal 10 E.IV, f. 53
fox and wolf
as physician (with urinal), approaching wolf seated by tree: Royal 10 E.IV, f. 158v
leading wolf (hare?) on rope before lion: Royal 10 E.IV, f. 55v
leaving in well, man pulling wolf up in bucket: Fitz. 298, f. 138v (*fig. 598*)
receiving message from hare with spear: Royal 10 E.IV, f. 53v
skinning: Royal 10 E.IV, f. 56v (2)
fox as bishop, preaching to nine birds (including duck, goose, goslings, hens, stork; *cf.* Fox and fowl, preaching to): Royal 10 E.IV, f. 49v (at R., woman with distaff or stick pursuing fox with goose in jaws)
fox as pilgrim: Royal 10 E.IV, ff. 55, 57v (confronting hare aiming arrow at him)
fox, funeral of *see* Procession, funeral of fox
Romans *see* St. Paul
Romulus and Remus, suckled by she-wolf: W. 102, f. 29v (line ending)
Rooster *see* Cock
Rosary *see* Beggar and child on back
Rowing *see* Ape; Man in boat; Sailboat

S

Sack *see* Ape as moneylender; Hybrid man with; Man and hare, hunting with; Man hoarding; Man with; Windmill; Woman and ass
Sacraments (*cf.* juxtaposed themes listed under Vices; Virtues)
Baptism; youth kneeling in door of house, cleric with bowl leaning down from roof; gift of Holy Ghost — Knowledge: latin 1052, f. 207; latin 10483, f. 7
Confirmation; youth with scroll in door of church, bishop leaning down from roof; gift of Holy Ghost — Fortitude: latin 1052, f. 238; latin 10483, f. 37; latin 10484, f. 32
Eucharist; cleric in door of church, with wafer; gift of Holy Ghost — Piety: latin 1052, f. 226; latin 10483, f. 24v
Extreme Unction; old man in bed in house, cleric with ointment jar leaning down from window; gift of Holy Ghost — Wisdom: latin 1052, f. 217; latin 10483, f. 17v; latin 10484, f. 12v
Marriage; couple in door of church, cleric pointing from roof; gift of Holy Ghost — Fear of God: latin 1052, f. 245v; latin 10483, f. 45v; latin 10484, f. 40
Order; youth kneeling in door of church, with chalice, bishop leaning down from roof; gift of Holy Ghost — Intelligence: latin 1052, f. 232 (*fig. 669*); latin 10483, f. 31; latin 10484, f. 25v (*fig. 668*)
Penitence; youth in door of church, cleric leaning down from roof; gift of Holy Ghost — Council: latin 1052, f. 252v (*fig. 670*); latin 10483, f. 53
Sacristan *see* Virgin, miracles of: drowned; —: sacristan
Sadoc: Y.T. 13, f. 47
Sailboat (*cf.* Boat, references under): Add. 36684, f. 144
apes in: Add. 36684, f. 151 (2); Stowe 17, f. 76v (3; at L., another ape)
man (woman?) in, on red sea: Douce 118, f. 76
men in: fr. 12400, ff. 10 (3, two rowing), 25 (3, one rowing)
St. Agatha: Add. 36684, f. 72 (Litany); Royal 2 B.VII, ff. 214v (before king), 242 (martyred); Y.T. 8, ff. 294v (martyred), 295 (healed by St. Peter)
St. Agnes: Douce 118, f. 63; latin 10483, f. 135v (in Heaven, surrounded by virgins; below, group of virgins kneeling); Royal 2 B.VII, ff. 238v (before judge), 239 (martyred)
St. Alban: Royal 2 B.VII, ff. 251v (before king), 252 (martyred)
St. Amalberga: Add. 29253, f. 409 (*fig. 618*); Douce 6, f. 196

St. Anastasia: Y.T. 13, ff. 88v (warning Mary and Joseph arriving at house of Jurdan), 89 (beheaded)
St. Andrew: Add. 42130, f. 40 (martyred); Add. 49622, ff. 11, 75 (martyred); Douce 6, f. 193v; Royal 2 B.VII, ff. 285v (before king), 286 (martyred); W. 104, f. 71; Y.T. 13, ff. 36, 84v; Y.T. 27, f. 4 (and Daniel; Old and New Law); Y.T. 75, f. 5v (the same)
St. Anne *see* Virgin, life of: birth
St. Anthony: Royal 10 E.IV, f. 282v
St. Apollonia: Add. 42130, f. 59v (*fig. 380*); Trinity B.11.22, f. 171 (martyred)
St. Augustine: Add. 42130, f. 58
St. Barbara: M. 155, ff. 14 (with three sheep), 14v-15 (before man with cudgel), 15v-16 (man with cudgel, same man before seated man gesturing), 17v-18 (man with cudgel conducting St. B. toward seated man, man with club), 18v-19 (seated man and man with club looking at St. B. in tower), 20v-21 (same as 17v-18), 158 (with palm, tower), 164 (with palm, sheep)
St. Barnabas: latin 10483, f. 188v (martyred); Royal 2 B.VII, ff. 250v (preaching), 251 (martyred)
St. Bartholomew: Add. 36684, f. 71v (Litany) (*fig. 630*); Add. 42130, ff. 107v (martyred), 108 (beheaded, angel with soul); Add. 49622, ff. 11v, 183; Royal 2 B.VII, ff. 263v (before king), 264 (martyred); Y.T. 13, f. 42; Y.T. 27, f. 7 (and Micah; Old and New Law); Y.T. 75, f. 7 (the same)
St. Benedict (Dominic?): Y.T. 27, f. 107v
St. Bon, bishop of Clermont *see* Virgin, miracles of
St. Catherine: Add. 36684, f. 73v (Litany); Add. 42130, ff. 30v, 39; Cambrai 103, f. 479v; Christ Church E.II, f. 35v; Douce 6, f. 196; Douce 118, ff. 27v, 98; fr. 25526, f. 9v (before king, martyred); Princeton 44-18, f. 86 (f. 85v, knight [patron?] kneeling (*fig. 601*); Royal 2 B.VII, ff. 280v (before Emperor Maxentius), 281 (scourged), 281v (imprisoned), 282 (in prison, ministered to by angels, visited by empress), 282v-283 (martyred), 283v (entombed by angels on Mt. Sinai); Y.T. 13, f. 86; Y.T. 27, f. 58v
St. Cecilia: Royal 2 B.VII, ff. 277v (before king), 278 (martyred)
St. Christina: Royal 2 B.VII, ff. 256v (rescued from sea by two angels), 257 (martyred)
St. Christopher: Add. 42130, f. 45v; Christ Church E.II, f. 2v; fr. 25526, f. 78 (at R., two rams butting); Stowe 17, f. 113v (at R., nun praying) (*fig. 600*); Y.T. 13, f. 194v (beckoning to Christ child); Y.T. 27, f. 107v
St. Chrysogonus: Royal 2 B.VII, ff. 279v (before king), 280 (martyred)
St. Clare: latin 1076, f. 160; W. 45, ff. 89v, 90v, 112, 139v, 191 (with St. Elizabeth of Hungary, St. Francis) (*fig. 611*)
St. Clement: Royal 2 B.VII, ff. 278v (before king), 279 (martyred)
St. Cosmas and St. Damian: Royal 2 B.VII, ff. 268v (before king), 269 (martyred)
St. Cyprian: Royal 2 B.VII, f. 267v (martyred)
St. Damian *see* St. Cosmas
St. Denis: Royal 2 B.VII, ff. 270v (expostulating), 271 (martyred); Y.T. 13, f. 192v (preaching), 193 (martyred), 193v (stooping to pick up head, flanked by two angels)
St. Dominic: BBR 10607, f. 190 (preaching); latin 1076, f. 168; latin 10484, f. 272 (before Pope, receiving document; receiving staff and book from two saints); Melbourne 1254/3, f. 21 (receiving staff from saint) (*fig. 602*); Princeton 44-18, f. 68 (praying); Y.T. 13, ff. 182v (preaching), 189v-190 (man falling off horse, breaking neck, revived) (*figs. 603-604*); Y.T. 27, f. 107v (St. Benedict?)
St. Donatus: Royal 2 B.VII, ff. 259v (restoring broken chalice), 260 (martyred)
St. Dorothy(?): Princeton 44-18, f. 8
St. Dunstan (*see also* Virgin, miracles) of: Add. 42130, f. 54v (pinching devil's nose with gold pincers; at R., two wrestlers in drawers); Royal 10 E.IV, ff. 197 (cripples healed at his tomb) (*fig. 605*), 197v (in Canterbury), 198-198v (miracle of Virgin), 198v-208 (visions of), 241 (mitered, asleep in bed, bed lifted at posts by four angels), 241v (as bishop at altar, holding up stone or board; behind him, cleric at lectern), 242 (consecrating church; behind him acolyte with situla; devil escaping from roof of church), 242v (turning from altar, two clerics at lectern containing book), 243 (king with sword conversing with St. D. seated at desk containing open book, angel with scroll descending), 243v (as bishop before church, receiving book from angel descending from cloud; behind him, two clerics), 244 (woman with candlestick,

S

group of kneeling women with candlesticks, before church or palace), 244v (seated, cleric kneeling, five clerics following), 245 (before king with sword, seated, accused by man at L.), 245v (king seated before castle, arguing with St. D.), 246 (as cleric astride horse, attacked by beast; angel descending from sky; at R., palace), 246v (as abbot, observing construction of church by man winding up stone, man with hammer in doorway), 247 (as cleric, fighting devil and hounds, with club), 247v (as abbot, with staff and sack, before Paul and Peter, two other disciples), 248 (as cleric seated at desk, painting butterfly; at R., youth kneeling, showing bleeding leg from which foot is missing; *cf.* Virgin, miracles of: woodcutter): 248v (as cleric, at desk; three clerics pointing at youth with bleeding stump), 249 (as abbot, approaching cleric in cell, writing; youth with restored foot following), 249v (as abbot, with two clerics, in doorway; at R., devil without foot), 250 (as cleric, seated before wheel, working with goldsmith's hammer; at R., altar, angel with harp), 250v (as cleric, putting glowing iron stick in beast's mouth; behind him, youth tending fire with bellows)

St. Edmund, king and martyr: Add. 42130, f. 46; Royal 2 B.VII, ff. 276v (before king), 277 (martyred); Y.T. 13, f. 192 (martyred)

St. Edward, king and martyr: Royal 2 B.VII, ff. 244v (riding to hunt), 245 (stabbed by cupbearer)

St. Edward the Confessor: Y.T. 13, f. 190v (with ring; f. 191, St. John the Evangelist) (*figs. 606-607*)

St. Egide: Add. 36684, f. 73 (Litany)

St. Eligius: Add. 42130, f. 52

St. Elisabeth and the Virgin: Y.T. 75, f. 186 (Min.: Birth of St. John the Baptist)

St. Elisabeth of Hungary: latin 1076, ff. 130, 164v; W. 45, ff. 90v, 191 (with St. Clare, St. Francis) (*fig. 611*)

St. Ethelreda (?): Add. 42130, f. 51v

St. Eustace *see* St. Hubert

St. Fabian: Royal 2 B.VII, ff. 237v (before emperor), 238 (martyred)

St. Faith: Royal 2 B.VII, ff. 269v (before mitered judge), 270 (martyred)

St. Felix: Royal 2 B.VII, ff. 265v (before mitered judge), 266 (martyred)

St. Francis: Add. 36684, f. 51; latin 1076, ff. 59, 71, 75v, 81v, 87v, 125v, 141, 145v, 153v, 156v, 158, 159v, 161v, 163, 165

covering face with hands: latin 1076, f. 104v (Ps. 82:18) (*fig. 608*)

cutting habit: Y.T. 13, f. 180v (f. 181, six friars in towers, about to go out into the world) (*fig. 610*)

kneeling, praying: latin 1076, ff. 75v, 87v, 105v (above, stag), 116, 135v, 145v, 159v (above, nun with book)

kneeling, praying, before seraphim: Stowe 17, f. 175 (*fig. 612*)

preaching to birds: Add. 42130, f. 60v (at R., lion seated; hooded cleric, Brother Leo?, at L.); Auct. D.3.2, f. 122 (*fig. 609*); Kraus 75/88, f. 72v; Princeton 44-18, f. 120; W. 45, f. 191 (at R., St. Clare, St. Elisabeth of Hungary) (*fig. 611*); Y.T. 13, f. 181v

preaching to birds and animals: Marseilles 111, f. 139 (ape with fruit, birds, lion); W. 45, f. 139v (bird, dog, sheep)

showing stigmata: Add. 42130, f. 60v (preaching to birds); latin 1076, ff. 153v, 155, 161, 170, 173, 181; Y.T. 13, f. 182

with book: latin 1076, ff. 108v, 113v, 163 (kneeling)

with staff and book: latin 1076, ff. 112v, 156 (and scrip), 172

with staff, confronting saint with book greeting him: latin 1076, f. 151

St. Fronton *see* St. Martha

St. Gabriel the Archangel *see* St. Michael

St. George (*see also* Virgin, miracles of): Add. 42130, f. 39v; Cambrai 102, f. 447 (fighting centaur with sword and buckler); Douce 118, ff. 28, 29v, 45, 109v, 119v, 139, 149v; Y.T. 27, f. 70v

astride white horse: Stowe 17, ff. 86, 154v (f. 155, dragon) (*fig. 613*)

fighting centaur with sword and buckler: Cambrai 102, f. 447

slaying dragon: fr. 25526, f. 131v (at L., two men kneeling); M. 155, ff. 52v-53

St. Giles: Add. 42130, f. 55; Liège 431, f. 140v; Stowe 17, ff. 93v-94; Y.T. 27, f. 107v

St. Gregory (?) *see* Man and bird, seated

St. Gudwald: Add. 29253, f. 342

St. Helena: Add. 42130, f. 53; latin 10483, f. 178; Y.T. 75, f. 183 (at R., man reviving female corpse)

St. Hippolytus: Royal 2 B.VII, ff. 262v (scourged), 263 (martyred)

St. Hubert (*cf.* Stag with bagpipe): Hague 78.D.40, f. 66v (*fig. 614*); Royal 10 E.IV, ff. 229-230v

St. James the Greater: Add. 42130, ff. 32, 75 (in hair tunic, opposite grotesque); Royal 2 B.VII, ff. 257v (preaching), 258 (martyred); St. Omer 5, f. 267 (martyred; text: General Epistle of St. James); Y.T. 13, f. 40; Y.T. 27, f. 3 (and Isaiah, Old and New Law); Y.T. 75, f. 5 (the same)

St. James the Less: latin 1076, f. 111v; Royal 2 B.VII, ff. 248v (praying), 249 (martyred); Y.T. 13, f. 37; Y.T. 27, ff. 9 (and Haggai; Old and New Law), 86v; Y.T. 75, f. 8 (the same)

St. Jerome, writing: Y.T. 13, f. 7

St. John the Baptist (*see also* Detached limbs, head of man in bowl): Add. 42130, ff. 40v, 53v (beheaded); Hague 78.D.40, f. 108 (feast of Herod, Salome dancing) (*fig. 617*); latin 1076, f. 143; latin 10484, f. 318v (beheaded, bones burned; at L., Salome with salver) (*fig. 616*); Princeton 44-18, f. 56; Royal 2 B.VII, ff. 264v (dance of Salome), 265 (martyred); Stowe 17, ff. 137v-138 (beheaded, feast of Herod) (*fig. 615*); W. 104, f. 71; Y.T. 13, ff. 53v 54 (birth announced), 54v 55 (birth of), 104 (baptizing Christ), 104v (preaching), 105-106 (before Herod, imprisoned, again before Herod), 106v (dance of Salome), 107 (beheaded), 107v (Salome with head), 108 (head buried), 108v (entombment), 109 (skeleton in tomb, two men with bones), 109v-110 (bones burned, ashes scattered); Y.T. 27, f. 80v

St. John the Evangelist (*see also* Evangelist symbols; Jesus Christ, life of: Last Judgment; —: Resurrection): Add. 36684, f. 71 (Litany); Add. 42130, f. 39; BBR 1175, f. 170; C.B. 61, f. 1 (writing); Cambrai 87, f. 230 (writing; at L., Trinity); Fitz. 2-1954, f. 156 (and Virgin); Lambeth 209, ff. 2, 3, 6, 8v, 27; latin 10483, f. 111v (writing; at R., church); latin 10484, f. 2v (and David, Old and New Law); Royal 2 B.VII, ff. 234v (preaching), 235 (martyred); St. Omer 5, f. 208v (martyred); Trinity B.11.22, f. 200v (writing); Y.T. 13, ff. 38, 137 (interceding with Virgin in Last Judgment cycle, two angels with crown of thorns and three nails), 191 (f. 191v, St. Edward the Confessor with ring); Y.T. 27, ff. 2 (and David, Old and New Law), 80v; Y.T. 75, ff. 4v (and David, Old and New Law), 187 (Drusiana raised from coffin)

St. John the Evangelist, vision of: fr. 25526, f. 125 (lion with antlers surmounted by crowns, mane composed of six beast heads)

St. Jude (*see also* St. Simon): Add. 42130, f. 52v

St. Juliana: Royal 2 B.VII, ff. 243v (before judge), 244 (martyred)

St. Justina: Royal 2 B.VII, f. 268 (martyred)

St. Kenelm: Royal 2 B.VII, ff. 254v (hunting), 255 (martyred)

St. Landrada: Add. 29253, f. 361

St. Lawrence: Add. 29253, f. 374v (martyred); Add. 36684, f. 72 (Litany) (*fig. 630*), Add. 42130, f. 48; BBR 1175, f. 81v; BBR 10607, f. 103v (man working bellows; Min.: St. Lawrence martyred); Burney 345, f. 69 (man working bellows, devil with scourge standing on his head; Min.: St. Lawrence martyred) (*fig. 619*); fr. 25526, f. 9 (martyred); Princeton 44-18, f. 45 (martyred); Royal 2 B.VII, ff. 260v (before emperor), 261 (martyred); Y.T. 13, f. 85 (martyred)

St. Leodegare: Add. 36684, f. 72 (Litany)

St. Leonard of Brittany (?): Y.T. 75, f. 190

St. Louis of Marseilles: Y.T. 75, f. 191 (saving five drowning children)

St. Lucy: Royal 2 B.VII, ff. 286v (before king), 287 (martyred); Y.T. 8, ff. 263v (with Paschasius before gold idol on column), 265 (dragged and pushed by four men)

St. Luke (*see also* Evangelist symbols): Add. 36684, f. 71v (Litany); latin 16260, f. 510 (writing); Melbourne 1254/3, f. 24v (before him, woman kneeling)

St. Margaret: Add. 42130, f. 37 (standing on dragon); Douce 118, ff. 23, 127; fr. 25526, ff. 44 (with distaff and spindle, seated on hillock amidst sheep; man with spear, king astride horse), 51v (in prison, praying; beheaded), 54 (beheaded, soul borne to heaven by angel), 56, 95 (with distaff and spindle, feet on ram with gold horns; at R., rider departing), 161v (issuing from dragon, crowned by Holy Spirit); Kraus 75/88, f. 196 (*fig. 620*); Laud Lat. 84, f. 197; M. 754, ff. 114v (baptized), 15 (with four sheep), 116v (rejecting suitor), 117v (kneeling before king), 120v (in basket, lowered from tower),

121 (nude, nimbed, before tower), 122 (tormented by devil), 122v (and dragon), 123v (three men in caldron over fire), 124 (issuing from dragon), 125 (praying), 126 (praying in tower), 127 (beheaded, angel with censer), 128v (praying), 129v (soul borne to Heaven, Holy Ghost descending); Princeton 44-18, f. 118; Royal 2 B.VII, ff. 255v, 256, 307v (spinning among sheep, approached by prefect Olybrius), 308v (tortured), 309 (imprisoned), 310 (scourging two devils), 310v (before prefect), 311 (in caldron over fire), 311v (before prefect), 312 (led to execution), 312v (praying before mocking executioners), 313 (beheaded, two men struck prostrate by lightning), 313v (entombed, blessed by hand of God), 314 (kneeling before Christ, supported by two angels); Stowe 17, f. 156; Valenciennes 838, ff. 55v (*fig. 621*), 97v; W. 102, f. 30v (Jonah?); Y.T. 13, f. 86v (imprisoned, issuing from dragon)

St. Mark (*see also* Evangelist symbols): Royal 2 B.VII, f. 246v (mocked); Y.T. 27, f. 58v

St. Martha: latin 10484, f. 262 (Christ appearing to St. Fronton, together entombing St. M.)

St. Martin of Tours and beggar: Add. 42130, f. 56v; BBR 1175, f. 92 (*fig. 622*); Douai 171, f. 83v; Laud Lat. 84, f. 269; M. 754, f. 55; Stowe 17, f. 98; Y.T. 27, f. 70v; Y.T. 75, f. 147v (two beggars, one lying under tree)

St. Mary Magdalene: Add. 36684, f. 73 (Litany); Add. 42130, f. 48v (with ointment jar); Add. 49622, f. 208 (*Noli me tangere*); fr. 25526, f. 76v (*Noli me tangere;* at L., Doubting Thomas); latin 10484, f. 255v (*Noli me tangere*); M. 183, f. 180 (*Noli me tangere;* at R., journey to Emmaus); Princeton 44-18, f. 92 (*Noli me tangere*); Royal 2 B.VII, ff. 299v (conversing with three youths), 300 (anointing feet of Christ), 300v (*Noli me tangere*), 301 (announcing Resurrection to Apostles), 301v (borne to Heaven by angels), 302 (entombed, blessed by hand of God); Verdun 107, f. 90v (*Noli me tangere*); Y.T. 13, ff. 87 (borne to Heaven by angels), 128v (announcing Resurrection to Apostles)

St. Mary the Egyptian: Royal 10 E.IV, ff. 268v (rebuked by priest), 269 (praying between two devils), 269v (praying before Virgin and Child figure on altar), 270 (the same, Christ child descended, standing with open arms to receive St. M.), 270v (kneeling, imploring monk Zosimus; at R., boy stirring boiling caldron), 271 (imploring woman in door of house, boy coming out of house), 271v (receiving three loaves of bread from woman holding loaf; boy in door of house), 272 (with loaves, walking toward river Jordan), 272v (with loaves in boat, nude, praying, crossing river), 273 (on other shore of river), 273v (two youths confronted, with ?slings), 274 (holding garment to throw into river, body covered with hair from here on), 274v (standing with three loaves between trees), 275 (feeding ape in tree, another ape also in tree), 275v (with three loaves, reclining by tree, birds, and boar), 276 (standing, flanked by lions licking her feet), 276v (asleep, angel appearing), 277 (feeding bird in tree; below, bear and unicorn), 277v (asleep, angels dancing in circle around her), 278 (seated in grass, with three loaves, flanked by bear and lion), 278v (standing, with three loaves; at R., lion followed by stag, ?leopard, boar), 279 (asleep, protected by birds in trees), 279v (asleep, angel with harp), 280 (standing, warding off lion and stag jumping at her), 280v (feeding lion; behind him, bear and stag) (*fig. 623*), 281 (asleep, protected by lion who fights devil), 281v (three clerics outside chapel, two conversing, third praying), 282 (three clerics, one touching a tree, another bending to the ground, third one praying), 282v (turning away from cleric), 283 (following cleric toward chapel), 283v (standing on mound with hands raised, cleric with hands raised approaching), 284 (cleric prostrate before her; at R., lion; at L., lioness, both turning away), 284v (blessed by Zosimus, both kneeling), 285 (kneeling before cleric with wafer; behind her, the three loaves), 285v (cleric welcomed by cleric in door of chapel), 286 (kneeling before cleric with chalice and wafer), 286v (kneeling, receiving wafer from cleric with chalice), 287 (lying dead, protected by two roaring lions), 288 (entombed by cleric and lion), 289 (same as f. 285v), 289v (two clerics bearing coffin to church to which chapel is being added; mason with shovel, two others winding up stone), 290 (clerics singing at lectern before octagonal funerary chapel)

St. Matthew (*see also* Evangelist symbols): latin 16260, f. 485v (writing in structure elaborated with two gargoyles; above, in cloud, Godhead); Y.T. 27, f. 8 (and Joel, Old and New Law); Y.T. 75, f. 7v (the same)

St. Matthias and Zechariah (Old and New Law): latin 10483, f. 6v; Y.T. 27, f. 12; Y.T. 75, f. 9v

St. Maurice: Royal 2 B.VII, ff. 266v (before king), 267 (martyred)

St. Mercurius *see* Virgin, miracles of: St. George

St. Michael: Add. 39810, f. 7 (archangel, spearing prostrate figure) (*fig. 140*); Add. 42130, f. 101 (archangel with two angels fighting many-headed devil; at R., St. Gabriel, archangel); Stowe 17, f. 144 (slaying dragon); Y.T. 13, f. 127 (delivering Longinus); Y.T. 27, f. 107v (slaying dragon); Y.T. 75, f. 184 (on Mount Gargano)

St. Nicasius: Add. 36684, f. 72v (Litany); Royal 2 B.VII, ff. 271v (before judge), 272 (martyred); Y.T. 75, f. 146v (holding head, supported by two angels)

St. Nicholas: Add. 29253, f. 430v; Add. 36684, f. 72v (Litany; miracle of three boys); Fitz. 288, f. 79 (miracle of rescue at sea); fr. 25526, ff. 75 (miracle of three daughters), 78v (miracle of three boys); Royal 2 B.VII, ff. 314v (birth of), 315 (refusing mother's breast), 316v-317 (consecrated), 315v-317 (miracle of three daughters), 317v (miracle of three boys), 318 (miracle of rescue at sea); Y.T. 8, f. 259 (miracle of three daughters) (*fig. 624*); Y.T. 13, f. 86 (miracle of three daughters); Y.T. 27, f. 86v; Y.T. 75, f. 192 (miracle of three daughters)

St. Omer, William de (or Thomas, his son) and wife Elisabeth of Mulbarton, kneeling (patrons): Add. 39810, f. (*fig. 140*)

St. Oswald: Royal 2 B.VII, ff. 258v (riding to battle against Penda), 259 (killed in battle)

St. Pancras: Royal 2 B.VII, ff. 249v (before emperor), 250 (martyred)

St. Paul (*see also* St. Dunstan, f. 247v; St. Peter and): Add. 36684, f. 71 (Litany); Add. 49622, f. 159; Kraus 75/88, f. 79 (possibly); latin 10483, ff. 6 (and Philemon), 6v (and four Hebrews); latin 10484, ff. 2 (conversion), 2v (preaching to Romans), 242 (bitten by viper, destroying viper in fire); Laud Lat. 84, f. 234v; Royal 2 B.VII, ff. 240v (receiving letters from high priest), 253v (before emperor), 254 (martyred), 302v (same as f. 240v), 303v (led by Ananias), 304 (at table, addressed by Ananias), 304v (baptized), 305 (preaching, nimbed), 305v (praying, Nero enthroned, Patroculus falling, flanked by devils), 306 (before Nero, borrowing Plautilla's veil), 306v (martyred), 307 (before Nero and empress); St. Omer 5, f. 220v (imprisoned; at R., man fighting lion); Stowe 17, f. 97 (conversion); Trinity B.11.22, f. 86v; Valenciennes 838, f. 61v (conversion) (*fig. 625*); Y.T. 8, ff. 285 (conversion), 285v (baptism); Y.T. 27, f. 1 (conversion), 2-8 (preaching to Romans, Corinthians, Galatians, Ephesians, Philippians, Colossians, Thessalonians, respectively), 9-12 (with Timothy, Titus, Philemon, four Hebrews, respectively); Y.T. 75, f. 4 (conversion), ff. 4v-7v (same as Y.T. 27, ff. 2-8), 8-9v (same as Y.T. 27, ff. 9-12)

St. Peter (*see also* St. Dunstan, f. 247v; Jesus Christ, life of: Resurrection; Virgin, life of: Death of): Add. 49622, ff. 16, 166v; BBR 10607, f. 129 (confronting cock); Douce 6, f. 110v (revered by cripple, two men); latin 1076, f. 155; latin 10484, f. 2 (and Jeremiah, Old and New Law); Laud Lat. 84, f. 239; Royal 2 B.VII, ff. 252v (before emperor), 253 (martyred); St. Omer 5, f. 270 (imprisoned, aided by angel; text: First Epistle General of St. Peter); Y.T. 8, f. 295 (healing St. Agatha); Y.T. 13, ff. 35, 84 (martyred), 138v (receiving blessed in Paradise); Y.T. 27, f. 1 (and Jeremiah, Old and New Law); Y.T. 75, ff. 4 (the same), 188 (martyred)

St. Peter and St. Paul: Cambrai 87, f. 93v (with other disciples); Laud Lat. 84, f. 234v; W. 104, f. 71; Y.T. 27, f. 96v

St. Peter of Verona: Y.T. 13, f. 191v (martyred)

St. Philip: Add. 42130, f. 57 (probably); latin 10483, f. 176 (martyred); Y.T. 13, f. 41; Y.T. 27, f. 5 (and Hosea, Old and New Law); Y.T. 75, f. 6 (the same)

St. Quintin: Royal 2 B.VII, ff. 274v (before judge), 275 (martyred)

St. Remy: BBR 1175, f. 171

St. Saturninus and St. Sisinnius: Royal 2 B.VII, ff. 284v (before judge), 285 (martyred)

Saint Simon: Add. 36684, f. 71v (Litany) (*fig. 630*); Royal 2 B.VII, ff. 273v (and St. Jude, with three magicians), 274 (and St. Jude, mar-

tyred); Y.T. 13, f. 44; Y.T. 27, f. 10 (and Ezekiel, Old and New Law); Y.T. 75, f. 8v (the same)
St. Sisinnius *see* St. Saturninus
St. Stephen: Add. 36684, f. 72 (Litany) (*fig. 630*); Add. 42130, f. 37v (St. S.? two men stoning cleric); Douce 6, f. 194; Douce 118, f. 66v (martyred) (*fig. 626*); fr. 25526, f. 65 (martyred); Royal 2 B.VII, ff. 233v (preaching), 234 (martyred); W. 761, f. 125 (blessing kneeling nun); Y.T. 13, f. 84 (martyred)
St. Thaddeus and Malachi, Old and New Law: latin 10483, f. 6; Y.T. 13, f. 45 (St. T., alone); Y.T. 27, f. 11; Y.T. 75, f. 9
St. Theodore: Royal 2 B.VII, f. 276 (martyred)
St. Thomas, Apostle (*see also* Jesus Christ, life of: Doubting Thomas): Add. 42130, f. 57v (probably); latin 10483, f. 105v (martyred); Royal 2 B.VII, ff. 287v (before king), 288 (martyred); Y.T. 13, f. 39; Y.T. 27, f. 6 (and Zephaniah, Old and New Law); Y.T. 75, f. 6v (the same)
St. Thomas of Canterbury: Add. 42130, f. 57v (martyred); latin 10483, f. 118 (martyred); Royal 2 B.VII, ff. 236v (at table, receiving messengers), 237 (martyred), 288v (arrival of mother in London), 289 (baptism of mother), 289v (marriage of parents), 290 (birth of), 290v (appointed archbishop), 291 (consecrated), 291v (before king), 292 (exiled), 292v (kindred banished), 293 (kindred crossing Channel), 293v (kindred journeying on foot), 294 (kindred welcomed and blessed by), 294v (resigning ring and cross to Pope Alexander III at Sens), 295 (at table with Pope Alexander III), 295v (welcomed by abbot at Pontigny), 296 (praying, vision of Christ), 296v (reconciliation with king), 297 (return to England), 297v (at table, messenger reporting arrival of four knights), 298 (martyred), 298v (entombed), 299 (kneeling before Christ enthroned, supported by two angels); Y.T. 13, f. 85v
St. Tiburtinus: Royal 2 B.VII, ff. 245v (before judge), 246 (martyred), 261v (before king), 262 (martyred)
St. Ursula, eleven thousand virgins of (*see also* Saints, unidentified, female, with bow): Exeter 47, f. 124; Royal 2 B.VII, ff. 272v (in ship), 273 (landing, two martyred by swordsmen in armor) (*fig. 627*)
St. Valentine: Royal 2 B.VII, ff. 242v (before judge), 243 (martyred)
St. Veronica with sudarium: Y.T. 27, f. 44v (Min.: Annunciation)
St. Vincent: Royal 2 B.VII, ff. 239v (before judge), 240 (martyred); Y.T. 8, f. 280 (martyred)
St. Vitalis: Royal 2 B.VII, ff. 247v (before judge), 248 (martyred) (*fig. 628*)
St. Wandregisilus: Add. 29253, f. 366
St. Wulfram (?): Add. 29253, f. 325v
Saints, unidentified, female: Cambrai 87, f. 95; fr. 25526, f. 90v
bathing, assisted by the Virgin: Add. 42130, f. 97v (error for Virgin bathing? *see* Virgin, life of: Death of)
before female saint tied to tree: Cambrai 103, f. 479v (at L., hare with bagpipe)
beheaded: Douce 118, f. 105v
beheaded, soul borne to Heaven by two angels: fr. 25526, f. 20
blessing patroness kneeling before her: Melbourne 1254/3, ff. 82v-83
seated at desk, writing; scroll on desk "qui com u usu": Douce 118, f. 176
with book: Add. 42130, f. 59 (behind her, ram with bell between horns); latin 1076, f. 153 (and crosier); Melbourne 1254/3, f. 129 (and palm)
with bow and arrows: latin 1076, ff. 51v, 55 (St. Ursula?)
Saints, unidentified, male: Add. 42130, ff. 105-107, 108v; Douce 5, f. 138v; Douce 6, ff. 193-196 (Litany); Laud Lat. 84, f. 142; Stowe 17, f. 232v
at altar: Valenciennes 838, f. 55v (at L., angel with censer and same saint flanking tomb, archer) (*fig. 629*)
beheaded: Add. 29253, f. 356; fr. 25526, ff. 17v (mitered), 20v (crowned), 90v (mitered); latin 1076, f. 78; Y.T. 8, ff. 330 (2, before king), 344v
borne on litter by two men: Nancy 249, f. 129
crowned: fr. 25526, f. 20v (beheaded); Princeton 44-18, f. 181
crowned, Godhead in clouds: Douce 118, f. 53
leading nude couple toward tower: Cambrai 87, f. 51 (angel?)
mitered: fr. 25526, ff. 17v (beheaded), 37 (2), 90v (mitered)
seated at desk, scroll on desk: Melbourne 1254/3, f. 41

with arms of Flanders on robe: Kraus 75/88, f. 63
with censer: Douce 118, f. 140v; Melbourne 1254/3, ff. 39v (and candlestick), 61v (and incense boat), 87 (and spear; f. 86v, hybrid man bending bow)
with harp, seated: Douce 118, f. 137
with king, two bishops: Y.T. 13, f. 87v
with pastoral staff: Melbourne 1254/3, f. 88v
with scroll "Benedictum sit nomen domini nostri" and spear: Melbourne 1254/3, f. 68v
with scroll, confronting three men seated on ground: BBR 9391, f. 57
Saints, unidentified, male and female, conversing with child with staff (Christ child?): Princeton 44-18, f. 63 (1, 2)
Salamander, Bestiary representation: Add. 24686, ff. 12, 18v; Cambrai 103, f. 393 (at L., tiger, Bestiary representation): Munich c.g. 16, f. 63 (in cycle); Royal 2 B.VII, ff. 116v-117 (in cycle); Trinity B.11.22, f. 92v
Salmon *see* Joshua, marriage of
Salome *see* St. John the Baptist
Samson (for possible parodies, *see* Ape and dragon, astride; Ape and lion, rending; Man and beast, rending)
birth of: Munich c.g. 16, f. 89v
blind
mocked: Royal 10 E.IV, f. 36
with horn: Royal 10 E.IV, f. 37v (f. 38, wall collapsing on group at table)
working at stone wheel: Royal 10 E.IV, f. 36v
blinded by Philistines: Munich c.g. 16, f. 93v; Royal 10 E.IV, f. 35v
confronting woman: Royal 10 E.IV, ff. 29 (S. with ring), 29v (woman with ring), 30v (the same; Samson conversing with youth coming out of house)
gates of Gaza on his back: Add. 39810, f. 57v; Munich c.g. 16, f. 92v; Royal 10 E.IV, ff. 32-32v
finding honey, giving it to woman of Timnath: Munich c.g. 16, f. 90v
marrying Philistine woman before priest: Royal 10 E.IV, f. 31
presenting ring to Delilah: Royal 10 E.IV, f. 33
rending lion (*cf.* Man nude and lion, astride): Add. 29253, f. 309v (below, David with sling); Add. 39810, f. 57v; Add. 42130, f. 56; BBR 9961-62, f. 41; Douce 5, f. 223v; Fitz. 298, f. 83v; fr. 95, f. 292v (above, knight killing lion) (*fig. 631*); Munich c.g. 16, f. 90v; Royal 10 E.IV, f. 30 (two woman looking on in amazement); W. 88, f. 164; Y.T. 8, f. 221 (nude); Y.T. 13, f. 7v (labeled) (*fig. 632*); Yale MS., f. 300v
shorn by Delilah (*see also* Vices: Fear): Royal 10 E.IV, f. 34
tearing down house of Philistines: Add. 39810, f. 57v; Munich c.g. 16, f. 94v; Stowe 17, f. 122v (*fig. 633*)
with jawbone of ass: Stowe 17, f. 80v
Samuel, life of (*see also* David, life of: D. and; —: D. and Saul)
ark drawn by kine, sacrifice of kine, ark kept by Eleazar: Munich c.g. 16, ff. 105v-106v, 107v, 108v
birth of: Munich c.g. 16, f. 95v
coming before Eli: Munich c.g. 16, f. 97v
Eli commanding sons not to return without ark: Munich c.g. 16, f. 99v
Eli, death of: Munich c.g. 16, f. 101v
going to Shiloh with Hannah and Elkanah: Munich c.g. 16, f. 96v
Israelites battling with Philistines: Munich c.g. 16, ff. 98v, 100v (slaying sons of Eli), 109v
Jonathan smiting Philistines, eating honey, told he must die: Munich c.g. 16, ff. 111v, 112v, 113v
Philistines finding Dagon fallen: Munich c.g. 16, ff. 103v, 104v
Saul anointed by: Munich c.g. 16, f. 110v
Saul falling on sword, head cut off and borne by Philistines: Munich c.g. 16, ff. 118v, 119v
Saul's crown, bracelet brought to David, messenger slain: Munich c.g. 16, f. 120v
Saul's sons slain: Spencer 26, f. 47
Saul taking Agag, destroying Amalekites: Munich c.g. 16, f. 115v
Saracen (*see also* Ape as; Hybrid man and insect; Knight and; Man nude, with; Miniature supported by man; Unicorn butting): Y.T. 27, f. 53v
astride horse, fighting dragon with spear: Add. 42130, f. 83v; Hague 78.D.40, f. 52v
confronting lion, unsheathing sword: Cloisters 54.1.2, f. 79 (hybrid)
with falchion and shield, bucket (?) on head: Cloisters 54.1.2, f. 45
Satyr (*cf.* Hybrid man horned; Man horned)
and woman dancing: Royal 2 B.VII, f. 166
bitten by dragon: fr. 95, f. 281v

S

Saul *see* David, life of: D. and Amalekites; —: D. and Goliath, with head of, before; —: D. and Jonathan; —: D. and Samuel; —: D., famine; —: D., harping; King defecating; Samuel, life of: Saul

Sawing *see* Hybrid ape; Hybrid man; Man and woman; Man sawing; Woman sawing

Scales *see* Virtues: Justice; Woman with

School, attended by

- apes, ape-master with switch (*cf.* Ape with book, seated): Bodley 264, f. 94v (3, with books); Cracow 815, f. 109 (2); Douce 5, f. 146 (5; one reciting, two with books, two fighting; at R., ape astride horse; Ps. 52); Fitz. 298, f. 76v (book on desk, five apes seated on ground) (*fig. 635*); fr. 95, f. 355 (4; one beaten, two reading, one writing on slate, master tonsured) (*fig. 636*); G.K.S. 3384, f. 131v (3, with slate, books; f. 132v, school of clerics); Glazier 24, f. 30 (3; one beaten); Hague 78.D.40, f. 29 (ape kneeling before ape with switch); latin 14284, f. 69v (3; one with book; at L., bishop blessing; at R., nun with book before cleric) (*fig. 639*); Nancy 249, f. 41 (6; one with asperge and flabellum) (*fig. 637*); Princeton 44-18, ff. 116v-117 (3; two with books), 148 (2; one with book); Royal 20 D.IV, f. 1 (4 with books, one kneeling before master); Stowe 17, ff. 108v-109 (chained bear observing two groups of apes; in one group, ape beaten, another drinking; in the other, three apes listening attentively; reference to verse above(?): "Declaratio sermonum tuorum illuminat: et intellectum dat parvulis"; Sunday, Nones) (*fig. 634*); W. 104, f. 28 (*fig. 11*); Y.T. 8, f. 175 (1, seated, with book, on red ball); Yale MS., f. 325 (2; one beaten, one with book, reading)
- boys with open books: Bodley 264, f. 123v (4)
- clerics: G.K.S. 3384, f. 132v (f. 131v, school of apes)
- fowl, ass as master: Chantilly 64, ff. 89, 89v
- hares: fr. 25526, f. 113v (4; one with book)
- men and woman: Stowe 17, f. 181 (sermon?) (*fig. 638*)
- men, ape as master: Nancy 249, f. 214v
- pigs: Glazier 24, f. 31 (6; below, cock and three hens feeding) (*fig. 641*)

Schoolmaster

- ape, beast reciting or singing before him: Glazier 24, f. 76 (book on ground) (*fig. 640*)
- ape, woman with book before him: Melbourne 1254/3, f. 12v (*fig. 642*)
- ass, fowl before him: Chantilly 64, ff. 89, 89v

Sciapode: Add. 36684, ff. 81v (female), 105 (possibly), 146v (above, sun), 147v (possibly); Cambrai 103, f. 482; Christ Church E.II, f. 44v (and ape); Douai 193, f. 220 (balancing red ball); Fitz. 298, ff. 4v (at L., merman with fish), 24v (bishop blessing), 40 (grotesque man with foliate cap); M. 102, f. 136 (line ending); W. 45, f. 92 (female) (*fig. 643*); Y.T. 8, f. 250v

Sciapode, variant

- large foot: G.K.S. 3384, ff. 104v (*fig. 738*), 185
- man with huge foot growing out of left ear(?): G.K.S. 3384, f. 108v (*fig. 644*)
- man with webfoot, nude, monstrous man shooting hindquarters: Rutland Ps., f. 87v (merman?) (*fig. 502*)
- mermaid, approached by man (nude save for cloak) with club astride monster: Rutland Ps., f. 108v

Scimitar *see* Merman as knight, with sword and shield

Scourge *see* Devil and man with; Devil with; Man nude with; Man with bellows, working; St. Catherine; St. Hippolytus; St. Margaret

Scribe (*see also* St. Dunstan; St. John the Evangelist)

- ape as: G.K.S. 3384, f. 293 (writing on tablet); Hague 78.D.40, f. 124 (3, with cleric writing)
- cleric: Cambridge Dd. 5.5, f. 13 (seated on beast); Cloisters 54.1.2, f. 42; Douce 6, f. 61; G.K.S. 3384, ff. 16, 38v; Seligmann 11, p. 21; W. 761, f. 1 (Cistercian, with scroll "Ego Iohannes scripsi hunc librum") (*fig. 645*)
- hybrid man: Cloisters 54.1.2, f. 55v
- man: BBR 9427, f. 81v (at R., man approaching with scroll and spear); Douce 6, f. 105v (at R., woman with hand in gold purse); fr. 12400, f. 1; fr. 25526, f. 77 (2; candle in stand, inkwell, quill), 77v (two finished sheets hung across pole behind him; at R., illuminator seated, sheet hung across pole behind him); G.K.S. 3384, f. 99v (at R., ape pursuing hare)
- omission by, pulled in place by man *see* Man with rope

prophet (Jubal) writing on column: Munich c.g. 16, f. 17v (shown twice, beside organ and ?harp)
saint, female, scroll on desk "qui com u usu": Douce 118, f. 176
woman: Trinity B.11.22, f. 100
Scroll *see* Angel with; Hybrid man with; Isaiah with; Lion as king; Man with; Patron: Joffroy; Prophet; Sacraments: Confirmation; Scribe; Stork with; Zechariah
Sculptor working on
statue of man: Douce 6, f. 94 (tomb figure? below, man with lit taper)
statue of woman (Pygmalion; *see* Lover for other subjects in sequence): Tournai CI, f. 319 (five nude women before him) (*fig. 587*)
tomb figure: G.K.S. 3384, f. 120
Scything *see* Hybrid man with scythe; Man scything
Sea battle (*cf.* Boat): fr. 25526, f. 116v (knights); Royal 10 E.IV, f. 19 (men and ?giants)
Seesaw: Rothschild MS., ff. 131v (apes on), 155 (man with owl's head on)
Sens *see* St. Thomas of Canterbury
September *see* Man drinking; Man picking grapes; Man sowing
Seraphim: Douce 118, f. 122v (woman praying before); Stowe 17, f. 175 (St. Francis before); W. 104, f. 70v (angels with harp, vielle, two others praying)
Serpent (*see also* Hybrid man with head of bull; Man and; Moses and brazen serpent)
and cock, fighting: Royal 2 B.VII, f. 187v
Bestiary representation: Royal 2 B.VII, ff. 127v-128 (in cycle)
coiled around border stalk (*see also* Bird as bishop): W. 87, ff. 82v, 88
crawling on hill: Add. 42130, f. 185 (7; in foreground, ferret)
hybrid man holding: Douce 118, f. 73 (nude, with trumpet); latin 14284, f. 57 (on wrist, like falcon)
knight holding, aiming sword at: G.K.S. 3384, f. 54v
rebuked by God (in Creation cycle; *cf.* Adam and Eve, subentries): Y.T. 13, f. 22
wolf as bishop, holding: G.K.S. 393, f. 301v
woman holding: G.K.S. 3384, f. 87
Serra(?): M. 729, ff. 258v, 286 (2, confronted)
Serra, Bestiary representation: Royal 2 B.VII, ff. 88v-89 (in cycle)
Sextant *see* Goat with astrolabe
Shame *see* Lover with Venus
Shawm *see* Ape with; Centaur with; Hybrid man with; Lion with; Man horned with; Man nude, armless, with; Man with
Shearing *see* Sheep shorn
Shears *see* Cleric with; Tailor and hare, kneeling; Tailor, ape as; — cutting
Shechem and Shechemites *see* Jacob
Sheep (*see also* Ape and; Fables; Fox and; Lamp, references under; Lion and; Man and; Ox with club; St. Barbara; St. Margaret; *cf.* Ram)
as cleric, with trumpet: Douce 118, f. 84 (rising out of ground)
balancing church on tall ears (hare's? *cf.* Hare balancing; Man with crocket): Yale MS., f. 75
in caldron (proverb?): Glazier 24, f. 142 (3)
intercourse: Merton 0.1.3, f. 111v
pursuing dog: Trinity B.11.22, f. 37
separated from goats: Munich c.g. 16, f. 16v (in Old Testament cycle)
shorn by woman: Douce 6, f. 101v (above, man with large sack over shoulder)
Shepherd (*see also* David, life of: D. tending; Jacob approaching; Jesus Christ, life of: Annunciation to shepherds; —: Nativity; Man and sheep)
and fox, pursuing: Bodley 264, f. 52
bitten by dragon: Cloisters 54.1.2, f. 88v
tending flock: BBR 9961-62, f. 26 (with shawm; woman picking flowers, two women winding garland); Cambrai 103, f. 332; Douce 118, ff. 61 (with bagpipe), 114v (with pipe); Melbourne 1254/3, f. 100 (with bagpipe); W. 82, ff. 62v, 188; W. 109, f. 222v
Shimei *see* David, life of: D. and
Ship *see* Boat; Sailboat; Sea battle; St. Ursula
Shoe *see* Boot, references under; Hybrid beast with platform shoes; Woman with
Shoeing the goose *see* Proverbs: goose
Sidonia *see* Jesus Christ, miracles of: Joseph
Singing *see* Ape and hybrid beast; Ape as bishop, with book; —as cleric at lectern; Ass and apes; Cleric; —and man; Dog and fox
Sins *see* Vices
Siren (*cf.* Mermaid)
Bestiary representation (in cycle): Munich c.g. 16, f. 18 (2, one bearded); Royal 2 B.VII, ff. 96v-97

S

bitten in face by small winged dragon, shot by hybrid man: Cambrai 102, f. 195v (male)
confronting ape with double pipe: Tournai Ps., f. 1
confronting knight/siren with sword: fr. 776, f. 1
confronting man (half-nude) with club: Rutland Ps., f. 107 (winged headdress)
confronting man with sword and buckler: W. 104, f. 21v
conversing with king/siren: fr. 776, f. 18
dancing, mermaid with vielle: Tournai Ps., f. 104 (male) (*fig. 500*)
fighting dog, with sword: W. 45, f. 116 (male; below, man fighting lion)
fighting siren, both with swords and bucklers: Cambrai 102, f. 13v (males)
holding breast: Chantilly 64, f. 192
holding two apples to breast (Eve parody?): Chantilly 64, f. 192v
playing vielle with rake, hybrid man dancing: latin 14284, f. 5
shooting boar: W. 45, f. 108v (male)
shot by man, with club and shield: Y.T. 8, f. 292v
with censer and incense boat: Douce 118, f. 43 (male)
with fish: BBR 5163-64, f. 103v
with horn, man in costume as hare dancing: Tournai Ps., f. 45 (male)
with mirror: fr. 776, f. 24v (before male siren); W. 87, f. 93v (and comb)
with pipe: latin 16260, f. 536 (below, owl)
with pipe and tabor, siren dancing: Rutland Ps., ff. 44v-45 (male)
with ring: Add. 49622, f. 20 (in border)
with vielle: Stowe 17, ff. 9 (male, with Jewish cap; July), 103 (crowned, hybrid man dancing)

Sisera *see* Jael and
Situla *see* Asperge, references under
Skating and sliding, two men: Douce 5, f. 1a v (February) (*fig. 470*)
Skeleton (*see also* Centaur as; Man nude, digging; —, skeleton-thin; St. John the Baptist; Wild man with skull)
and skulls: Add. 36684, ff. 83-91v (throughout margins of Offices of the Dead; f. 90, five skulls stacked in tent)
astride cow, with spear, coffin under arm, approached by woman falconer astride lion: Hague 78.D.40, f. 91
confronting falconer: latin 3893, f. 169v
drinking: Add. 36684, f. 100
with mirror(?): M. 796, f. 91v (f. 91, woman dancing)
Skeletons, three
beckoning to three men, the dead rising to witness the death of Jesus: Y.T. 13, f. 123 (in cycle of life of Jesus)
confronting three kings, Three Living and Three Dead: Royal 10 E.IV, ff. 258v-259 (ff. 259v-268, series of hunting scenes, one king going to Heaven, two others to Hell); Stowe 17, ff. 199v-200 (at R., owl in tree) (*figs. 657-658*); Y.T. 13, ff. 179v-180
Skull (*see also* Skeleton and skulls): Add. 42130, f. 213 (on winged, tailed body); Cloisters 54.1.2, f. 196 (above, hybrid man with distaff and spindle); M. 754, f. 83 (on larva-like body)
Sleeping *see* Man asleep; St. Mary the Egyptian
Sliding *see* Skating
Slingshot *see* Ape as bishop, astride pig; David, life of: D. and Goliath, combat; Hybrid man and bird, hunting with; Hybrid man with; Knight and hare, with sword; Man and crow; — and falcon, hunting with; — and hybrid bird; — and snail, fighting with; — and stag, hunting with; Man with
Smith *see* Blacksmith
Snail (*see also* Ape and; Centaur and; Cleric and; Crane and; Dog and; Dragon and; Fox and; Hare and; Hybrid bishop and; Hybrid knight and; Hybrid man and; Knight and; Man and; Man nude and; Pea pods; Ram and; Woman and): Add. 42130, ff. 159, 160; Cloisters 54.1.2, ff. 81v, 83v, 130
ascending ladder: Add. 36684, f. 61v; Add. 42130, f. 160 (3)
atop ladder: M. 754, f. 70v (beside beast with lit taper)
atop stairs: Add. 36684, f. 64v (2, with monstrous heads)
balancing on crossbar: M. 754, f. 22v
beside bird's nest, lion: Cambrai 102, f. 436v
confronting snail: BBR 10607, f. 240v
labeled "limasconn": BBR 329-41, f. 198v
labeled "Lymasoun": M. 812, f. 27
on stilts: Add. 36684, f. 55v
preceding boat *see* Man in boat
pulling wine keg on cart: M. 88, f. 177v (at R., stork)
sitting on wall: M. 754, f. 44 (3; at L., pond)

Snake *see* Serpent, references under
Snare drum *see* Man with
Sodom *see* Lot
Soldier (*cf.* Knight, references under; Man with sword and buckler; Miniature supported by man): Chantilly 62, f. 145v (Min.: Crucifixion)
Solomon (*see also* David, life of: D. and; Jesus Christ, life of: Last Judgment: blessed ascending): Y.T. 13, f. 33v (in cycle of genealogy of Christ)
and Jacob: Y.T. 13, f. 30v
judgment of, two women and child: fr. 25526, f. 117; Hague 78.D.40, f. 50; Stowe 17, f. 125; Y.T. 13, ff. 47v-48
judgment of, three youths, shooting at father's corpse (*cf.* Man and knight, shooting): Douai 171, f. 83v; M. 183, f. 70; Nancy 249, f. 94 (*fig. 647*); Stowe 17, ff. 117v-118 (*fig. 646*); Trinity B.11.22, f. 99
kneeling, hands joined in prayer: Y.T. 8, f. 316 (at R., altar; both motifs in separate structures under trefoil arches)
life of, in cycle (*cf.* David, life of: D. and Solomon):
Joab slain, buried: Spencer 26, ff. 111-112
receiving request of Adonijah, death of A.: Spencer 26, ff. 109v-110
replacing Abiathar with Zadok: Spencer 26, f. 110v
with scroll, David harping: Corpus Christi 53, f. 1
Soul *see* Jesus Christ, life of: Last Judgment: Pains of Hell
Sow
before ape-physician: Bodley 264, f. 168
standing over tub containing six young: Glazier 24, f. 81a (below, ape with fruit)
suckling three young, standing upright before man with tabor: Bodley 264, f. 124v (at R., proverb: goose shoed)
Sowing *see* Man
Spade *see* Ape astride bird; Hybrid man with; Woman with
Spading *see* Man spading
Sparrow hawk: Fitz. 2-1954, f. 128v
Spear *see* Ape with; Apes fighting; Cat and mouse, killed; Hybrid knight with; Hybrid man and dragon, fighting with; — and hybrid woman, confronted; — and lion; — and man; — and nun; — and snail; — and stag; — and unicorn; — with; Hybrid men fighting; Knight and dog; — and dragon; — and hare; — and hybrid man; — and Saracen; — and snail; — and woman; Man and ape; — and bear, piercing; — and bird, hunting; — and boar; — and dragon; — and hare, hunting; — and hare, killed by; — and hybrid man, fighting; — and knight, fighting; — and lion, fighting; — and pig; — and snail, astride; — and snail, fighting; — and stag, hunting; Man balancing; — nude with; — with; Men fighting; Merman balancing; Pygmy and centaur; St. Michael
Spider
in web (proverb?): Trinity B.11.22, f. 155 (*fig. 648*)
spinning web (proverb?): Rothschild MS., f. 130 (below, nude man pursued by cat) (*fig. 453*)
struck by man with sword: BBR 9411-26, f. 126
Spindle *see* Distaff and, references under
Spinning *see* Ape; Eve; Knight; Man; St. Margaret; Woman
Spit *see* Ape cooking, roasting; Man cooking, roasting
Spitting *see* Man vomiting
Spoon *see* Ape as philosopher; Ape playing ram's head; Cleric and hybrid woman; Cleric playing; Hybrid beast with; Hybrid man and dog, threatening; Hybrid man with; Man and woman, beaten; Man blowing; — vomiting; Stork and hybrid man; Woman and ape, observing; Woman playing tongs
Spoonbill: Christ Church E.II, f. 38
Sports *see* name of specific sport
Spout (*see also* Monster spitting): Douce 6, f. 180 (in monster's head); Douce 118, f. 129v (in stag's mouth, water issuing; attached to spired edifice)
Squirrel (*see also* Cleric and; Man and)
as pet of cleric: Christ Church E.II, f. 43v (cleric gesturing, squirrel with back turned); Nancy 249, f. 221 (also with pet dog)
as pet of man: Cloisters 54.1.2, f. 53; Douce 118, f. 29; latin 10483, f. 97 (man beckoning to)
as pet of woman: Add. 42130, ff. 33, 181v (queen in coach); BBR 10607, ff. 86, 88; Christ Church E.II, f. 29v; latin 10483, f. 260 (hybrid woman); Nancy 249, f. 212v (fed by); Royal 2 B.VII, f. 200v
ascending border stalk: M. 108, f. 1 (with nut); W. 45, f. 30v

S

ascending pole: Arsenal 5218, f. 81 (house on top of pole) (*fig. 563*); Douce 5, f. 80; Trinity B.11.22, f. 35
astride goat, tilting with ape astride unicorn: Y.T. 19, f. 3
balancing in basin on pole balanced by man: C.B. 61, f. 136
chained, perched on tall house: Arsenal 5218, f. 55 (*fig. 26*)
entering its house: Add. 30029, ff. 99, 131v
reaching for red berry or nut growing in border: W. 85, f. 34v
running after gold nut: Douce 118, ff. 68v, 155v
seated on back of dragon: Vienna 2542, f. 341
with distaff and spindle: M. 149, f. 410
with horn: Arsenal 5218, f. 75; Douce 118, ff. 137v, 141
with nut (*cf.* Ape with fruit): Add. 29253, f. 90v; Add. 30029, throughout; Ashmole 828, ff. 1 (tied to border stalk), 63; BBR 9157, f. 1; BBR 9433-34, f. 60; BBR 9961-62, f. 14; BBR 10607, f. 12v (with stork, dog, lion; Ps. 1); Cloisters 54.1.2, f. 183; Douce 5, throughout; Douce 118, ff. 82, 117v, 119, 136v, 147; Douce 366, ff. 38 (*fig. 239*), 71v; fr. 776, ff. 18, 24v, 165, etc.; fr. 25526, f. 6v; lat. lit. f. 3, f. 74 (chained to its house); latin 16260, ff. 2, 234v, 306; Laud Lat. 84, ff. 170v, etc.; M. 108, f. 1 (ascending border stalk); M. 796, f. 89; M. 812, f. 33; Melbourne 1254/3, f. 32; Nancy 249, f. 211; Royal 3 D.VI, f. 234; Royal 14 E.III, f. 89; Stowe 17, ff. 47v, 120v; Vienna 1826*, f. 100; W. 37, f. 19; W. 45, ff. 29 (above, hare), 79v (below, man shooting bird); W. 85, f. 42 (Min.: Entombment); W. 104, f. 8v; Y.T. 8, throughout; Y.T. 15, throughout
with nut, at base of own tall house: Arsenal 5218, f. 70v (at L., ape hunting hare, with spear)
with trumpet: Melbourne 1254/3, ff. 5v (?cock confronting beast), 75v, 78, 111v, 115v

Stag (*see also* Ape and; Ass and; Centaur and; Dog and; Fables: fox and stork, Part I, variant: stork drinking; Fox with basket; Hybrid centaur and; Hybrid man and; Knight and; Lion and; Man and; Man nude and; Procession: funeral of fox; St. Mary and Egyptian, ff. 278v, 280; Wild man and; Woman and)
and doe: Arundel 83, f. 14 (Ps. 1) (*fig. 338*)
and unicorn, grazing: Cambrai 102, f. 207v (Min.: Resurrection)
and unicorn, pursuing: Y.T. 8, f. 233v
Bestiary representation: Add. 24686, f. 12; Fitz. 298, f. 130v; Munich c.g. 16, f. 37 (Parandrus, in cycle): Royal 2 B.VII, ff. 115v-116 (in cycle); Rutland Ps., f. 87
couchant: Add. 42130, f. 13; Bodley 264, f. 57v; Cloisters 54.1.2, f. 192v; Harley 6563, ff. 27, 27v, 45, 45v; Holkham 458, f. 17v; Princeton 44-18, f. 32v; W. 82, f. 87v (held at bay by two dogs)
diving into water: Add. 36684, f. 68v
drinking: latin 14284, f. 50 (Bestiary representation? at L., small doe; at R., small serpent); Melbourne 1254/3, ff. 40 (grazing?), 110v (the same); Princeton 44-18, f. 33
grazing: Cambrai 102, f. 207v (Min.: Pentecost; with pig and unicorn); Douce 118, f. 115 (two ?magpies on antlers); Melbourne 1254/3, ff. 40 (drinking?), 110v (the same)
head lowered as though drinking: Douce 118, f. 78v
issuing from mountain: M. 754, f. 17
on hind legs: M. 754, f. 78 (man holding fish; cleric, ape-bishop)
pursued by dog *see* Dog and stag
pursuing dog and hare: Melbourne 1254/3, f. 78v
running at tree: Douce 118, f. 170v
scratching ear with hind leg: Cloisters 54.1.2, f. 41v; Fitz. 2-1954, f. 119 (at L., wolf; below, patrons; Ps. 109); fr. 12400, f. 97v; Maz. 34, f. 5; Rylands lat. R.117, f. 9
seated: Cloisters 54.1.2, f. 172v; W. 85, f. 30 (left front hoof raised)
tail bitten by bird: Cambrai 102, f. 416
with bagpipe: Douce 6, f. 202
with bagpipe, head of Christ between antlers (reference to St. Hubert? *cf.* Hybrid man with bagpipe; Hybrid stag): Douce 6, f. 113; W. 82, f. 31 (*fig. 649*)
with gold horns: Add. 29253, throughout
with harp: Y.T. 8, f. 176v
with head of Christ between antlers *see above,* — with bagpipe
with pipe: Kraus 75/88, f. 68v
with sword and shield, wearing cape: Douce 6, f. 129 (or, lion vair rampant)
with trumpet: Douce 118, f. 96v; Melbourne

1254/3, f. 98v; Y.T. 8, f. 252 (hare with pipe and tabor)
with vielle, man dancing: Y.T. 8, f. 249
Stag costume *see* Man in costume
Stag horns *see* Cleric with book; Hybrid ass; Hybrid man with; Hybrid woman with; Man with; Monster with
Stairs *see* Snail atop
Statue *see* Patron kneeling; Patroness: Isabelle de Kievraing; St. Mary the Egyptian, ff. 269v-270; Sculptor; Virgin, miracles of: Jew
Stephen, King *see* Boar as king
Sticking out tongue *see* Ape as bishop, confronting; Ape playing jawbone; Hybrid man; King; Man; Man nude; Monster, crippled
Stilts, worn by
ape: Arsenal 5218, f. 20; Bodley 264, f. 43v (2); Cambrai 102, f. 266v (at R., stork with fish, hybrid woman gesturing); Douce 6, f. 158v (observed by ape); latin 14284, f. 18v; W. 82, f. 175 (wearing tall pointed hood held by man issuing from border)
bird: M. 754, f. 30
bishop (nude), two devils reaching for him with scourges: W. 90, f. 153 (*fig. 84*)
cock: Bodley 264, f. 91
hybrid man conversing with mermaid: Christ Church E.II, f. 55v
hybrid man with sword, aiming at head issuing from tail: W. 102, f. 56
man: Add. 42130, f. 70v; BBR 9961-62, f. 14 (*fig. 388*); Bodley 264, ff. 65 (2), 123 (2, arguing, then removing stilts and beating one another); Fitz. 298, f. 116; fr. 95, f. 319; Glazier 24, f. 64 (one shoe off, one shoe on) (*fig. 651*); latin 14284, f. 62v (standing on one, the other across shoulder); M. 754, ff. 63v, 71v (seated, putting on stilts); Nancy 249, f. 108v; Rothschild MS., f. 166; W. 88, ff. 36 (f. 35v, ape astride ape, pointing), 103v (at R., man wielding stick)
man and woman, bitten by huge birds: Royal 10 E.IV, f. 77
snail: Add. 36684, f. 55v
woman with child in arms, jug on head (*cf.* Fables: woman with jug): Royal 10 E.IV, f. 29v
Stone *see* Hybrid man with; Man and bird, hunting with; Man with egg; Man with hammer, kneeling; Pot worn on head by wild man; Putting
Stool basket *see* Ape and hybrid man, astride; Ape as bishop, before; — Ape as physician, ministering to nun; — to owl; Cleric with; Hare running out of sack; Hybrid man with; Physician and ape; — and man; — and woman; Physician with; Woman with
Stork (*see also* Ape and; Centaur and; Cleric preaching; Fables: fox and; —: wolf and; Fox and; Hare and; Hybrid stork; Knight and bird; Man and; Obscaena, beak)
and bullfinch: Fitz. 2-1954, ff. 65v, 83v
and butterfly, pecking at: M. 796, f. 106
and eel, in beak: BBR 10607, f. 26v; Douce 6, f. 137; fr. 12400, throughout; Glazier 24, f. 89; Stowe 17, ff. 82v-83 (shot by hybrid man); W. 87, f. 4v
and fish, in beak: Cambrai 102, f. 266v; Douce 6, f. 121v; fr. 12400, throughout; lat. lit. f. 3, throughout; latin 13260, f. 1; W. 88, ff. 16, 34
and frog
fishing for, in water: fr. 12400, throughout; G.K.S. 3384, f. 98
in beak: Burney 345, f. 86v; Cambrai 102, ff. 4v (2, pulling frog between them), 7; Douce 6, f. 88v; fr. 12400, throughout; G.K.S. 3384, f. 217v (confronting man with club and buckler; below, knight with spear and buckler confronting bird); Kraus 75/88, f. 19v; latin 13260, f. 113; latin 16260, f. 273 (shot by hybrid man) (*fig. 390*); Melbourne 1254/3, f. 128v; Rothschild MS., f. 186v (2, one frog); W. 88, f. 88v (2, one frog)
in beak, Bestiary representation: Munich c.g. 16, f. 48 (in cycle)
and hybrid man
eating from flat dish held by (*cf.* Fables: fox and stork, Part I, variant): G.K.S. 3384, f. 173v
fed by, with spoon: W. 82, f. 179v
inserting beak in throat of (parody of fable of wolf and stork?): Royal 1 D.I, f. 353v
observing hybrid man with club and buckler: Add. 17868, ff. 81, 162 (attacking same)
shot by: latin 16260, f. 273 (frog in beak)
and lobster, impaled on beak: C.B. 62, f. 199v (below, man beckoning to bird)
and peacock, confronted: Cambrai 102, f. 252v
and rat (ferret?), in beak: fr. 12400, f. 20 (below, lizard)
and snail, eating: fr. 12400, f. 19v

S

as woman, with distaff and spindle: G.K.S. 3384, f. 79
flying: fr. 12400, ff. 11 (4), 12v (3), 13 (3), 25 (4), 25v (5), 26v (6), 27 (3), 27v (4), 28 (12), 35v (2), 66 (over pond)
in nest (*see also* Falconer and companions): Chantilly 62, f. 32; fr. 12400, f. 20v (atop church tower); latin 13260, f. 65 (flanked by two storks); latin 14284, f. 12
with pellets in beak: M. 796, f. 132v (three, gold)
with scroll in beak: Chantilly 64, ff. 88v ("A lauci tule va tout"?), 114 and 114v ("Bonne pensée a lui . . ."), 122 ("A Dieu toute la . . . paign . . . A laventure va va gau . . . am"?)
Strike-the-pot (*cf.* Man with hood): Bodley 264, f. 125v (4 boys); Cambridge Dd. 5.5, f. 91 (4 boys); Douce 6, f. 82v (6 boys); fr. 25526, ff. 35 (3 boys; at R., man defecating), 129v (3 boys); G.K.S. 3384, f. 27v (man); M. 754, f. 65 (nude man); Nancy 249, f. 97 (three boys)
Styx *see* Jesus Christ, life of: Last Judgment, Pains of Hell: soul
Sudarium, Veronica with: Y.T. 27, f. 44v (Min.: Annunciation)
Suicide *see* Hybrid man with sword; Man with sword, stabbing
Sun *see* Creation; Hybrid man as physician, confronting; Man nude with; Obscaena, exposing hindquarters: man nude; Proverbs; eggs
Sun and moon (*see also* Alexander, journey): Add. 36684, f. 100
Sundial *see* Goat with astrolabe
Swallow: Munich c.g. 16, f. 53 (Bestiary representation, in cycle); Rothschild MS., f. 157 (and fly)
Swan: Fitz. 2-1954, ff. 30v, 86; fr. 12400, throughout, with other birds; W. 37, f. 94v (raising one foot, in position of Bestiary representation of crane depicted on f. 95v)
Bestiary representation (confronted by man with harp; *cf.* Woman with harp): Cambrai 102, f. 361 (*fig. 654*); Munich c.g. 16, f. 46 (fish in beak; in cycle); Trinity B.11.22, f. 79v (*fig. 653*); W. 85, f. 98v
in water: M. 88, f. 156v (3, with two mallards); W. 87, f. 100
king with harp standing on its neck (Bestiary reference?): Stowe 17, f. 46
pulling boat containing knight and horse (Swan-knight?): Cambrai 103, f. 314 (*fig. 652*)
pulling boat containing men (four): Nancy 249, f. 140v
shot by man: Cloisters 54.1.2, f. 106v (above, falconer)
with dog, hare, lion, peacock: M. 754, f. 79v
with three cygnets on back: Christ Church E.II, f. 37
woman with harp, two men dancing (Bestiary reference?): W. 109, f. 197v
Swan-knight *see* Swan pulling boat
Swimming
ape: Douce 6, f. 153 (2; at R., beggar with ape in basket on back)
falconer: fr. 12400, f. 115v (garments heaped on bank; at R., falcon striking duck) (*fig. 472*)
man: G.K.S. 3384, f. 57 (at R., man disrobing; above, man holding garment); Royal 2 B.VII, f. 170 (f. 169v, man in boat, directing); Trinity B.11.22, f. 121 (2)
mermaid: Rutland Ps., f. 96
Swinging *see* Ape; Man nude
Switch *see* Ape with; Man in costume as boar; Man nude with
Sword *see* Ape with *godendag;* Ape with sword; Bird with bell; Hybrid knight with; Hybrid man and dragon; — and hare; — and lion; — and man; — and snail; — and stag; — nude with; — walking on; — with; Hybrid woman and hare, pursuing; King with; Knight and bird; — and dragon; — and giant; — and hare; — and horse, astride seated; — and hybrid man; — and hybrid woman; — and lion; — and monster; — and saint; — and serpent; — and snail; — and woman; Knight balancing; Knight with head of beast; — with sword; Lion with basket; Man and bird; — and boar; — and butterfly; — and child; — and dragon; — and hare; — and horse; — and knight; — and lion; — and monster; — and siren; — and snail; — and stork; — and unicorn; — and wolf; — and woman, fighting; Man balancing; — headless; — juggling; — nude and dragon; — and lion; — and merman; — with; Merman as knight; Merman with; Wild man with; Woman balancing
Sword tied to tree, three men approaching (fabliau?): fr. 25526, ff. 22v (one nude, two in drawers), 40 (one in drawers)

Swordplay *see* Apes fighting; Hybrid knights fighting; Hybrid men fighting; Knights fighting; Man and hybrid man fighting; Men fighting

Swordsmith (*see also* Blacksmith; Tubal-cain): Royal 10 E.IV, f. 92 (possibly)

Symphony, man with: Add. 42130, f. 81v

Synagogue
- and Ecclesia: Princeton 44-18, ff. 115v-116 (*figs. 655-656*)
- destruction of, construction of Ecclesia (cycle throughout calendar pages; *cf.* Cycles, Old and New Law): latin 10483, ff. 6, 6v; latin 10484, ff. 2, 2v; Y.T. 27, ff. 1-12; Y.T. 75, ff. 4-9v

T

Tabor *see* Ape with; Boar with; Cat with; Dog with; Hare with; Hybrid man with; Man and ape, training; — and woman, dancing; Men dancing; Pipe and tabor, references under

Tail bitten *see* Ape and boar; Ape and dog; Cat and dog, biting; Devil and lion; Dog and dragon; Fox and cock, stealing; Hare disappearing; Lion and dragon; Stag, tail

Tail pulled *see* Centaur and dog; Man and hybrid man, pulling; Man nude and dragon, astride

Tail stepped on *see* Merman and ape

Tailor
- and hare (*cf.* Man and hare)
  - approaching hare with two young hares in swaddling clothes: Fitz. 298, f. 79
  - borne on shoulders of: Y.T. 8, f. 288
  - dragged on ground by, hands and feet tied: Fitz. 298, f. 120
  - grappling with: Fitz. 298, f. 93v
  - imprisoned by: Fitz. 298, f. 48 (*fig. 365*)
  - kneeling before hare with club, presenting shears to: Y.T. 8, f. 192
  - pierced by, with spear or long needle: Fitz. 298, ff. 34v, 47 (scraping hood with knife), 100 (hare astride horse), 106
- ape as(?), cutting cloth with shears: Hague 78.D.40, f. 119v
- cutting out robe with shears (*cf.* St. Francis, cutting): Harley 6563, f. 65

Tambourine *see* Apes fighting with swords and shields; Hybrid man with; Man and woman, dancing, hands; Woman with

Taper *see* Beast balancing; Man balancing bird; — balancing on pole, seated; — balancing tapers; Man with; Procession

Tarbis *see* Moses marrying

Tavern *see* Inn

Teal (mallard?); Fitz. 2-1954, f. 74v

Tearing hair *see* Hair, references under

Telescope *see* Astronomer; Hybrid man with trumpet, looking; Man with trumpet, looking

Teminie, Queen *see* Alexander

Temperance *see* Virtues

Templar *see* Ape as; Cleric and; Mermaid and hybrid beast; Obscaena, defecating: man nude; —, kissing; Wild man as; Wolf, as; Wrestling, men

Temple *see* Jesus Christ, life of: expulsion; : Presentation in; Virgin, life of: Presentation in

Temptation *see* Jesus Christ, life of

Tent *see* Ape and hare, as king; Vices: Cruelty; Wild man and knight, slain

Terrobuli, Bestiary representation: Munich c.g. 16, f. 25 (in cycle)

Theater *see* Apes performing; Man in costume; Puppet show

Theft *see* Ape and bird, stealing; Ape and child; — and pedlar; Ape fishing, catch; Fox and bird; — and child; — and cock; — and duck; — and goat; — and goose; — and sheep; Jesus Christ, life of: Last Judgment: Pains of Hell: robber; Lion and bird; Man and bird, hunting bird; — and thief; Man stealing; Virgin, miracles of: Ebbo; Wild man and child; — and knight; Woman and lion

Theophilus *see* Virgin, miracles of

Thessalonians *see* St. Paul

Thomas, Doubting *see* Jesus Christ, life of

Thomas, Earl of Lancaster, beheaded: Add. 42130, f. 56

Thomas of St. Omer *see* Patrons (couple): William

Three-faced *see* Hybrid bishop; Man, head of; Man

Three Living and Three Dead (*cf.* Skeleton): Royal 10 E.IV, ff. 258v-259 (ff. 259v-268, series of hunting scenes, one king going to Heaven, two others to Hell); Stowe 17, ff. 199v-200 (at R., owl in tree) (*figs. 657-658*); Y.T. 13, ff. 179v-180

T

Three Maries at tomb *see* Jesus Christ, life of
Threshing *see* Ape; Hare; Hybrid man; Man
Thrush: Fitz. 2-1954, f. 85
Tiger, Bestiary representation: Add. 42130, f. 84v (at R., pheasant); BBR II 988, vol. I, f. 201v; Cambrai 102, f. 282v; Cambrai 103, f. 393 (at R., salamander); M. 183, f. 198 (looking out of cave into mirror, hunter escaping); Munich c.g. 16, f. 29 (in cycle) (*fig. 662*); Rothschild MS., f. 182v; Royal 2 B.VII, ff. 122v-123 (in cycle); W. 85, f. 53v (tiger before mirror)
Tightrope *see* Man balancing on; Man with hoop, sitting
Tilting *see* Ape tilting, references under; Beast astride cat; Centaur with trumpet; Dog and ram; Hare tilting, references under; Hybrid knights; Knight and hybrid man; — and monster; — and woman; Knights; Man and goat, astride; Men; Merman as knight; Quintain, tilting at; Squirrel astride; Woman and Dominican; Woman nude and goat, astride; Woman tilting
Timbrel *see* Angel with; Ass with pipe; Hare with
Timnath *see* Samson, finding
Tinker with bellows on back, dog (biting his leg?): Add. 42130, f. 70v
Tomb *see* Bishop and cleric; Jesus Christ, life of: Last Judgment, corpses; Man mourning; Saints, unidentified, male, at altar; Sculptor; Virtues: Faith
Tongs *see* Ape playing bellows; — jawbone; Centaur playing; Dominican playing; Hybrid man playing; Man playing; Mermaid playing; Woman playing
Tongue, sticking out *see* Sticking out tongue, references under
Tooth, extraction of: Cloisters 54.1.2, f. 80v (two men, line endings)
Top-whipping
- ape: G.K.S. 3384, f. 185v (*fig. 660*)
- man: Bodley 264, f. 64 (2); Cloisters 54.1.2, f. 183 (*fig. 661*); Royal 2 B.VII, f. 164 (2); Royal 10 E.IV, f. 97; Trinity B.11.22, f. 170v; W. 88, f. 93; W. 104, f. 45v (2, possibly)

Tortoise: M. 729, f. 258v (at R., ?serra); W. 102, f. 57
Tournament (*see also* Tilting, references under): Bodley 264, f. 102 (preparations for, horsemen bringing helmet, lances, carts with equipment; f. 101v, knights tilting)
Tower of Babel, construction (*cf.* Man building): Munich c.g. 16, f. 24v (in Old Testament cycle)
Tradesman *see* Fox as
Training of animals *see* Ape and bear; — and hare; Hare and bear; Hybrid man and bear; Man and ape; — and bear; — and horse; — and lion; Man with bagpipe; — with hoop, training
Transverse flute *see* Hybrid man with
Trap, trapping *see* Hybrid man and unicorn; Man and ape, trapped; —, trapping; Man and bird, hunting with; — and woman, trapped by; Watermill; Wild man and bird
Treasure chest
- woman directing two men bearing chest toward church: Douce 6, f. 100v (*fig. 737*)
- woman pouring coins into, three others drinking, tearing hair, holding mirror (Vices?): fr. 95, f. 134 (*fig. 671*)
- woman with, opening, holding distaff and spindle: Trinity B.11.22, f. 213 (below, cripple; at R., dog running toward)

Tree *see* Alexander, journey; Ape and bear, pursued by; —, training; Ape holding; Ass and stag; Bear; Bird in nest; Goat standing; Jesse; Man and bird, hunting; — and woman, before Eros; Man chopping; Man in, references under; Man pulling; Nun and man, embracing; Owl; Peridexion
Trestles *see* Cripple, references under
Triangle *see* Hybrid man with; Man with
Trinity *see* Jesus Christ, life of
Trumpet *see* Angel with; Ape with; Ass with; Cat with; Centaur with; Dog with; Fox with; Goat with; Hare with; Hybrid ape with; Hybrid man with; Man and woman, dancing, hands; —, embracing, man (half-nude); Man in costume as lion; Man nude and lion, astride with; Man nude with; Man two-faced; Man with double trumpet; — with; Men dancing; Mermaid with mirror; — with trumpet; Merman with; Procession, men; Stag with
Trumpet, military, gigantic, worked by six men blowing bellows: Holkham 458, f. 42v
Tubal-cain, forging sword, carving plates of metal: Munich c.g. 16, f. 19v (in Old Testament cycle)
Tug-of-war
- apes with long rope: G.K.S. 3384, f. 47 (2)

men with quoit, seated: Rutland Ps., f. 69v (2) (*fig. 663*)
Tumbler *see* Ape as; Bear tumbling; Cleric and nun, turning somersaults; Contortionist; Man balancing; Man nude, tumbling; Man with hoop; — with pipe and tabor; — with vielle
Turtledove, Bestiary representation (in cycle; *cf.* Peridexion): Munich c.g. 16, f. 50; Royal 2 B.VII, ff. 114v-115
Two-faced *see* Ape; Eagle double-headed; Hybrid man two-faced; Janus; Man
Two-torsoed *see* Hybrid man two-torsoed; Man two-torsoed

U

Ulcer *see* Virgin, miracles of: cleric cured
Unicorn (*see also* Hybrid man and; Hybrid unicorn; Jesus Christ, life of: Last Judgment: Hell mouth containing devil; Man and; Monster with three heads; Patrons: Joffroy d'Aspremont; St. Mary the Egyptian, f. 277)
and ape, charging from behind: Add. 29253, f. 255v
and bear, charged by: Royal 10 E.IV, f. 157
and dog, pursued by: Cambrai 102, f. 337v; Cambrai 103, f. 218; Douce 118, f. 75v; Glazier 24, f. 33; W. 82, ff. 31 (two) (*fig. 649*), 62v (ridden by ape, pursued by man), 211v (two)
and dragon, bitten by: W. 85, f. 15
and griffin, charging: C.B. 64, f. 98v
and lion, charging: Christ Church E.II, f. 46v (piercing with horn); Douce 48, f. 221v (the same); Hague 78.D.40, f. 49v; Royal 2 B.VII, f. 190v
and lion, pursued by: Hague 78.D.40, f. 128v
and lion, pursuing: Hague 78.D.40, f. 41 (below, capture of unicorn, Bestiary representation)
and lions (two), elephant with castle: Y.T. 13, f. 188v
and ram, butting: Cambrai 102, f. 273
and stag, grazing: Cambrai 102, f. 207v (Min.: Resurrection)
and stag, pursuing: Y.T. 8, f. 233v
Bestiary representation, captured by hunters: Add. 39810, f. 7; Cambridge Dd. 5.5, f. 106; Christ Church E.II, f. 39v; Douce 5, f. 74; Douce 6, f. 39; Douce 118, ff. 32v, 45v; Douce 366, f. 55v (*fig. 667*); Fitz. 298, ff. 81v (*fig. 664*), 131v (*fig. 665*); Hague 78.D.40, ff. 9, 41 (above, unicorn pursuing lion), 149v; latin 10484, f. 4v; M. 729, f. 263; Marseilles 111, f. 61v; Munich c.g. 16, f. 14 (in cycle); Nancy 249, f. 39; Royal 2 B.VII, ff. 100v-101 (in cycle); Royal 10 E.IV, f. 156v; Royal 20 D.VI, f. 168v; Stowe 17, ff. 90v-91; Verdun 107, ff. 5v (*fig. 666*), 47v; Y.T. 13, f. 8
butting: Add. 29253, throughout; Add. 42130, f. 15; Ashmole 828, f. 17v; BBR 11040, f. 4 (at L., hybrid couple kissing); BBR II 988, vol. II, f. 274; C.B. 62, f. 170; Cloisters 54.1.2, ff. 99v, 133v (parodied); Douce 5, throughout line endings; Douce 6 (the same) (f. 3, beside Saracen with spear and buckler); fr. 95, f. 52v; G.K.S. 3384, ff. 114, 145v; latin 14284, f. 35; M. 149, throughout; Melbourne 1254/3, f. 69; N.K.S. 41, f. 85v (*fig. 384*); Schilling MS., July; W. 82, ff. 31 (*fig. 649*), 191v, 205v; W. 87, f. 108 (f. 107v, hybrid man brandishing club); W. 110, f. 43v; Yale MS., ff. 250, 320v
Universe *see* Creation
Uriah *see* David, life of: D. and Bathsheba; —: D. and Joab
Urinal *see* Ape as physician; Ass as —; Detached limbs, hand with; Hybrid cleric as physician; Hybrid man as —; Nun, Dominican, emptying; Physician, references under; Physician with
Urinating *see* Ape; Man nude
Usurer *see* Jesus Christ, life of: Last Judgment: Pains of Hell; Virgin, miracles of

V

Vanity *see* Mirror, references under
Vaux *see* Bardolf-Vaux
Venus *see* Lover with
Veronica, with sudarium: Y.T. 27, f. 44v (Min.: Annunciation)
Viane *see* Patroness: Marie de
Vices (*cf.* juxtaposed themes cited under Sacraments; Virtues; *see also* Avarice, references under; Despair, references under; Hybrid man drinking, hybrid women; Ire, reference

V

under; Jesus Christ, life of: Last Judgment: Pains of Hell; Pride, references under
Apostasy—Fall of Man (*see also* Adam): latin 1052, f. 207; latin 10483, f. 7
Cruelty—death of Holofernes, killed in tent by Judith: latin 1052, f. 245v; latin 10483, f. 45v; latin 10484, f. 40
Despair—Judas hanged: latin 1052, f. 217; latin 10483, f. 17v; latin 10484, f. 12v
Despair, Vanity, Gluttony, Avarice: fr. 95, f. 134 (*fig. 671*)
Fear, Weakness—Samson shorn by Delilah (*see also* Samson): latin 1052, f. 238; latin 10483, f. 37; latin 10484, f. 32
Hate—Cain slaying Abel (*see also* Cain): latin 1052, f. 226; latin 10483, f. 24v
Imprudence—king dethroned: latin 1052, f. 232 (*fig. 669*); latin 10483, f. 24v; latin 10484, f. 25v (*fig. 668*)
Injustice committed—condemned man going to gallows: latin 1052, f. 252v (*fig. 670*); latin 10483, f. 53
Vielle *see* Angel with; Ape dancing; Ape with; Ass with; Boar with; Cat with; Centaur with; Dog and hare, with; Fool with; Hare with; Horse with; Hybrid cleric with; Hybrid king with; Hybrid man with; Hybrid woman with; Lion with; Man and woman, dancing; Man nude with; Man playing; Man with; Mermaid with; Woman with
Viper, Bestiary representation (*see also* St. Paul; Serpent, references under): Royal 2 B.VII, ff. 126v-127 (in cycle)
Virgin: Add. 36684, f. 70v (Litany)
Virgin and Apostles: Add. 49622, f. 218 (heads only) (*fig. 672*)
Virgin and blessed (Virgin of Mercy): Vienna 1826*, f. 141 (below, Hell-mouth; Min.: Last Judgment)
Virgin and Child (*see also* St. Mary the Egyptian, f. 269v; Virgin, miracles of: Christ child; Woman and Christ child)
before kneeling cleric, with scepter: Spencer 2, f. 252
before kneeling patron, presenting scroll: Stowe 17, f. 271v
before kneeling patroness: Cambrai 87, f. 110 (with red three-flowered sprig; Mahaut de Brabant); Chantilly 62, f. 202; Melbourne 1254/3, f. 46v (figure on altar; Isabelle de Kievraing; at R., dragon)
beside Christ with orb, blessing; with Jesse, David, Solomon: Corpus Christi 53, f. 1 (Ps. 1)
emblem of Notre Dame of Cambrai: BBR 1175, ff. 158, 160v, 161
feeding from breast: Add. 42130, f. 13
leading, Christ child with basket: Add. 28784B, f. 4v
man fetching water from spring at R.: BBR 9391, f. 103 (Min.: Annunciation, Visitation; beginning of Hours of the Virgin) (*fig. 673*)
seated: M. 761, f. 87v (inscription: "ke notre dame est notre esperance")
seated on Mount Carmel, both with apples: Y.T. 13, f. 194 (clerics' heads issuing from six holes, stream from a seventh) (*fig. 674*)
Virgin and saint (female) in tub, assisting at bath: Add. 42130, f. 97v
Virgin and St. John the Evangelist (*see also* Jesus Christ, life of: Last Judgment: intercession): Fitz. 2-1954, f. 156
Virgin, life of (*see also* pertinent episodes under Jesus Christ, life of)
Annunciation: Add. 42130, ff. 44v, 86 (*fig. 675*); BBR 9391, f. 134v; fr. 25526, ff. 43v, 104v, 137; Stowe 17, ff. 220v-221; Y.T. 8, f. 311
arrival at house of Jurdan with Joseph, St. Anastasia warning them from window: Y.T. 13, f. 88v (f. 89, St. Anastasia beheaded)
Assumption of: Add. 42130, f. 100; Stowe 17, f. 271 (f. 270, death); Y.T. 13, f. 135
at table, with Jesus and ten apostles: Y.T. 13, f. 131
birth of: Y.T. 13, ff. 55v-56 (angel before Joachim), 56v-57 (angel before St. Anne), 57v (meeting at the Golden Gate), 58 (birth of Virgin)
bringing garment to Apostles in church: latin 10483, f. 376 (Virgin? one haloed figure in church)
Coronation of: Add. 42130, f. 100v; Stowe 17, f. 139 (f. 138v, Harrowing of Hell) (*fig. 267*); Y.T. 13, ff. 59v (in miniature; in margin, angel with ewer), 135v
Death of: Add. 29253, f. 379; Add. 42130, ff. 97 (annunciation of death), 97v (bathing or assisting female saint bathing in tub), 98 (deathbed of, giving palm to St. John), 98v (death of), 99 (funeral of, Jew hanging from bier by hands), 99v (burial of); Stowe 17, f. 270v (f. 271, Assumption) (*figs. 676, 677*);

Y.T. 13, ff. 132v (annunciation of death), 133 (death of), 133v (funeral of, Jew hanging by hands from bier), 134 (Jews baptized by Peter), 134v (burial of)
Presentation in temple: Y.T. 13, f. 139
presenting crowned woman to Christ: Y.T. 13, f. 139
Visitation: fr. 25526, ff. 43v, 97; Y.T. 75, f. 186 (Min.: Birth of St. John the Baptist)
Virgin, miracles of
abbess unchaste, hermit receiving child: Add. 42130, f. 104 (*fig. 678*); Fitz. 48, ff. 166-167; Royal 2 B.VII, ff. 208v-209; Royal 10 E.IV, f. 266; Thott 547, f. 1; Y.T. 13, ff. 156v-158
addressing group of worshipers: Royal 2 B.VII, f. 216
Amoras, selling his wife: Fitz. 48, ff. 172v-175v; Royal 2 B.VII, ff. 216v-217; Y.T. 13, ff. 162-164
Anselm and wine stain: Royal 2 B.VII, f. 215v
bishop saved in shipwreck: Royal 2 B.VII, ff. 224v-225
captive son restored to mother: Royal 2 B.VII, ff. 229v-230
Christ child as hostage: Thott 547, f. 18
cleric
and matron: Fitz. 48, ff. 167v-171v; Royal 2 B.VII, ff. 217v-218; Y.T. 13, ff. 167v-170v
and roses: Thott 547, f. 20
assailed by devil in guise of lion: Royal 2 B.VII, f. 207
cured of leprosy: Y.T. 13, f. 153
cured of lip cancer: Royal 2 B.VII, f. 221
cured of ulcer with Virgin's milk: Royal 2 B.VII, ff. 230v-231
ill, offered bowl by Virgin: Royal 10 E.IV, f. 227v; Y.T. 13, f. 179
leaving bride: Royal 2 B.VII, ff. 227v-228
of Cambrai: Royal 2 B.VII, ff. 231v-232
of Cologne dies unconfessed: Royal 2 B.VII, f. 214v
of Pisa, leaving bride for monastery: Royal 2 B.VII, ff. 223v-224
on deathbed: Royal 2 B.VII, f. 210v
restored to life: Fitz. 48, ff. 154v-155
taught Ave Maria: Fitz. 48, f. 158v
who daily said five Psalms: Royal 2 B.VII, f. 220v
who stole treasure: Fitz. 48, ff. 160v-165v; Royal 10 E.IV, ff. 221-225v; Y.T. 13, ff. 171v-174
clerk of Chartres: Fitz. 48, f. 159; Royal 2 B.VII, ff. 209v-210; Royal 10 E.IV, ff. 228-228v; Y.T. 13, ff. 161-161v
dead child revived: Fitz. 48, ff. 154v-155
drowned sacristan: Fitz. 48, ff. 159v-160; Royal 2 B.VII, ff. 205v, 213v; Royal 10 E.IV, ff. 226-227; Thott 547, f. 24v; Y.T. 13, ff. 151v-152
drowning nun saved: Royal 2 B.VII, f. 220; Royal 10 E.IV, ff. 192-192v; Y.T. 13, f. 152v
Ebbo, thief, on gallows: Royal 2 B.VII, f. 206
hermit and miller's wife saved from devil: Y.T. 13, ff. 176-178v
hermit saved from devil: Y.T. 13, f. 167
Jew and merchant, statue of Virgin arriving safely despite storm: Thott 547, f. 28v
Jew of Bourges: Fitz. 48, ff. 188v-189; Royal 2 B.VII, ff. 207v-208; Royal 10 E.IV, ff. 210v-213v; Thott 547, f. 14v
king's soul saved from devil: Royal 10 E.IV, ff. 265v-268 (*fig. 679*)
knight converted: Royal 2 B.VII, ff. 221v-222
Louis VII led to believe in miracles: Royal 2 B.VII, f. 215
nun, Eulalia, reprimanded for saying Ave Marias too fast: Royal 2 B.VII, ff. 225v-226
nun, sinner, replaced in abbey: Royal 2 B.VII, ff. 218v-219
painter of the Virgin: Fitz. 48, ff. 182-183; Royal 2 B.VII, f. 211 (*fig. 680*); Royal 10 E.IV, ff. 209-210
poor man called to Paradise: Royal 2 B.VII, f. 212
Pope Leo, cut-off hand restored: Fitz. 48, ff. 157-158; Royal 10 E.IV, ff. 193-195v; Y.T. 13, f. 164v
priest
repenting incontinence: Royal 2 B.VII, f. 206v
saved after debauching nun: Royal 2 B.VII, f. 219v
who knew only Virgin's Mass: Royal 2 B.VII, ff. 212v-213
sacristan and knight's lady: Royal 10 E.IV, ff. 185-191v (*fig. 114*)
St. Bon, bishop of Clermont, given vestment: Royal 2 B.VII, ff. 226v-227
St. Dunstan, visions of: Royal 2 B.VII, ff. 228v-229; Royal 10 E.IV, ff. 198-198v
St. George revived and armed: Fitz. 48, ff. 152v-154; Royal 2 B.VII, ff. 222v-223 (St. Mercurius?); Royal 10 E.IV, ff. 214-216v; Y.T. 13, ff. 153v-154
St. Mercurius revived *see above*, —, St. George

sinning pope forgiven (*see also above,* —, Pope): Fitz. 48, ff. 155v-156v
strangled couple restored to life: Y.T. 13, ff. 165-166
Theophilus: Fitz. 48, ff. 176-181v; M. 183, f. 286v; Royal 2 B.VII, ff. 204v-205 (*fig. 681*); Royal 10 E.IV, ff. 161-172v; Thott 547, f. 6v; Y.T. 13, ff. 158v-160v
usurer(?) pardoned: Thott 547, f. 22v
woman
and Host: Fitz. 48, ff. 187-188
in childbirth on pilgrimage to Mont-Saint-Michel: Add. 42130, f. 104v; Royal 2 B.VII, f. 214
rid of evil spirit: Y.T. 13, ff. 154v-155, 175
saved from falling off horse frightened by devil: Y.T. 13, f. 166v
selling garments to Jews: Fitz. 48, ff. 183v-186v
sinner, enters convent, soul saved: Royal 10 E.IV, ff. 177-184v
woodcutter, with cut-off leg (or foot): Fitz. 48, f. 172; Royal 2 B.VII, f. 211v; Royal 10 E.IV, ff. 196-196v (*cf.* St. Dunstan, ff. 248 on); Y.T. 13, f. 156
Virgin (*see also* Saints, unidentified, female)
saint(?), with book, three prophets(?) before her, one with scroll: fr. 25526, ff. 16v, 114v (two prophets, man)
with pennant on gate of Paradise (*cf.* juxtaposed themes cited under Cycles, Old and New Law and under St. Paul): latin 10483, ff. 6, 6v; latin 10484, ff. 2, 2v; Y.T. 27, ff. 1-12; Y.T. 75, ff. 4-9v
Virgins *see* St. Agnes; St. Ursula
Virgins, wise and foolish (one of each): Y.T. 8, f. 354v (*fig. 682*)
Virtues (*cf.* juxtaposed themes listed under Sacraments; Vices)
Charity—woman crowned and haloed, approached by beggar with bowl; Hand of God emerging from clouds: latin 1052, f. 226; latin 10483, f. 24v
Faith—woman crowned and haloed, against circular frame with representations of angels, dead rising from tombs, saints, Crucifixion, Resurrection and Ascension: latin 1052, f. 207; latin 10483, f. 7
Fortitude—woman crowned and haloed, standing on lion: latin 1052, f. 238; latin 10483, f. 37; latin 10484, f. 12v
Hope—woman crowned and haloed; below, angels bearing crowns descending from clouds: latin 1052, f. 217; latin 10483, f. 17v; latin 10484, f. 12v
Justice—woman crowned and haloed, with scales, flanked by two men: latin 1052, f. 252v (*fig. 670*); latin 10483, f. 53
Prudence—woman crowned and haloed, before two men: latin 1052, f. 232 (*fig. 669*); latin 10483, f. 24v; latin 10484, f. 25v (*fig. 668*)
Temperance—woman crowned and haloed, seated at banquet table with woman: latin 1052, f. 245v; latin 10483, f. 45v; latin 10484, f. 40
Vomiting *see* Cleric; Hybrid man; Man; Monster; Woman
Vultures: fr. 12400, ff. 18v (surrounding dog biting stag), 19
devouring ass: fr. 12400, ff. 16, 19v
devouring stag: fr. 12400, f. 8

Wafering iron *see* Woman with
Walker *see* Woman and child, child in; Woman crippled
War hammer *see* Apes fighting; Hybrid bishop and man; Hybrid men fighting with; Man nude with; Men fighting with hammers
Warwick *see* Guy of
Washing *see* Bathing, references under; Jesus Christ, life of; Man; Woman
Watermill: Add. 42130, f. 181 (2; basketwork eel traps in river); BBR 1175, ff. 13v, 15, 24v, 47v, 98v, 116v; M. 754, f. 63 (beast emptying jar into stream)
Waterspout *see* Spout
Weapons *see* specific weapons
Weasel, Bestiary representation (in cycle): Royal 2 B.VII, ff. 112v-113
Weathervane *see* Cock as
Weaving *see* Ape; Loom
Wedding *see* Marriage, references under
Weeding *see* Man and woman
Well *see* Joseph (Old Testament) in; Man drawing water; *Roman de Renart,* fox and wolf; Woman and ape, lowering; Woman drawing

W

Whale, Bestiary representation (in cycle; *see also* Jonah): Munich c.g. 16, f. 64 (*fig. 683*); Royal 2 B.VII, ff. 110v-111

Wheat *see* Hybrid man playing; Jesus Christ, miracles of; Reaping, references under; Woman with

Wheel *see* Ape crawling; Man balancing sword on hand

Wheel of Fortune: BBR 14682, f. 3 (occupied by humans) (*fig. 685*); Hague 78.D.40, f. 33 (2, occupied by humans and animals) (*fig. 684*); M. 730, f. 20v (occupied by humans)

Wheelbarrow *see* Ape with; Beggar crippled; Cleric with; Fox with; Hybrid knight with; Jesus Christ, life of: Last Judgment: Pains of Hell: devil with; —: Hell-mouth: devil with; Man nude with; Man with; Owl with

Whetstone *see* Man scything

Whistle(?), hybrid man with: Cloisters 54.1.2, f. 166

Wife *see Wright's Chaste Wife*

Wildcat and dragon, springing at: Royal 2 B.VII, f. 188

Wildman (*see also* Man and woman, dancing, with ape; Obscaena, shooting hindquarters: knight); Add. 39810, f. 7 (*fig. 140*); Add. 42130, f. 70; L.M. 13, f. 35; Glazier 24, f. 78v; Y.T. 8, f. 171

Wild man and bird: Glazier 24, ff. 45 (astride; cock?), 148 (snaring)

Wild man and centaur *see* Centaur and

Wild man and child (fabliau)
- holding swaddled infant and club: fr. 25526, f. 101
- stealing from woman, pursued by knight astride horse, handing child to second wild man: Princeton 44-18, ff. 41v-42v

Wild man and dog
- catching hold of: Glazier 24, f. 104 (fox?) (*fig. 686*)
- dragged by, holding by tail: Glazier 24, f. 74v
- pursuing: Y.T. 8, f. 270

Wild man and Enyas, abducting woman, killed by (fabliau): Y.T. 13, ff. 60v-63 (ff. 63v-67v, woman going off with youth, E. slaying youth, leaving woman) (*fig. 687*)

Wild man and fox, with club, holding fox on chain: fr. 25526, f. 86

Wild man and king astride stag, pursued by: Bodley 264, f. 69v (abducting woman) (*fig. 688*)

Wild man and knight, astride horse (fabliau)
- charged by, wielding club: Douce 131, f. 68v (wild man? at L., youth in door of tent; at R., woman riding off) (*fig. 690*)
- pursued by, escaping with child, handing child to second wild man: Princeton 44-18, ff. 41v-42v
- pursued by, escaping with woman (*cf.* King and wild man): Christ Church E.II, f. 29 (*fig. 689*); Royal 10 E.IV, ff. 69v, 72-74v (slain by, with spear), 101-106
- slain by, with spear, wielding club: Douce 131, f. 81v (wild man? at L., queen seated on bed in tent; in center, man tied to tree) (*fig. 691*)

Wild man and lion
- holding rope, other end in lion's mouth: Glazier 24, f. 40v
- looking back at: Bodley 264, f. 82 (flying head scarf)

Wild man and stag
- astride, pursued by ape with club astride lion: Bodley 264, f. 95
- astride, pursued by two dogs, killing one with sword: Y.T. 8, f. 270

Wild man and stork, hand bitten by: Douce 6, f. 38 (at L., lion)

Wild man and wild woman: Christ Church E.II, ff. 44v, 64v (*fig. 694*)

Wild man and woman *see* Wild man and knight

Wild man as Templar: Glazier 24, f. 136v

Wild man crawling toward cave, accompanied by stag, boar, sheep: Royal 10 E.IV, ff. 117v-118

Wild man with
- ax, shot by wild man: Glazier 24, f. 143v
- bellows: Glazier 24, f. 139
- club, swaddled infant: fr. 25526, f. 101
- ferret(?) in mouth, one hand raised: Glazier 24, f. 151v
- hands raised, crossed over his head: Glazier 24, f. 75
- pot on head, holding stone(?): M. 88, f. 173 (looking back at man bending bow; at L., hybrid woman aiming bellows at hindquarters of ape)
- skull and bone: Cloisters 54.1.2, f. 50v (above, man pulling hood over his face) (*fig. 693*); Y.T. 27, f. 56
- sword, reclining: Glazier 24, f. 50 (below, dragon)

Wild man/merman with club, holding female head (*cf.* Knight with head): Cloisters 54.1.2, f. 86v

W

Wild woman
and wild man: Christ Church E.II, ff. 44v, 64v (*fig. 694*)
crawling on all fours: Jacquemart 1, f. 15v
with basket containing birds on head, staff (proverb? *cf.* Proverbs: woman): Y.T. 8, f. 186v (wild man?) (*fig. 695*)
Winch *see* Man turning
Wind, blowing: BBR 15001, f. 143v (human head; Min.: Christ calming waters); Douce 5, f. 154 (human head with wild hair, ?vomiting)
Windmill (*see also* Giant): BBR 1175, ff. 15v (and miller), 18v, 26v
hare running up steps to: M. 754, f. 62
horse with sack leaving: fr. 25526, f. 18
man ascending steps: Bodley 264, f. 49 (at L., woman seated; at R., horse grazing)
man pulling sack out of, with rope: G.K.S. 3384, f. 192
man with sack, astride horse, approaching: Nancy 249, f. 148v
man with sack on back, approaching: Bodley 264, f. 81 (at R., man with whip astride horse); fr. 25526, f. 13v (at R., man with stick driving horse to mill); Valenciennes 838, f. 55 (at R., man with stick driving ass loaded with sack) (*fig. 699*)
man with sack on head, astride ass, approaching: Stowe 17, f. 89v (*fig. 696*)
man with whip, astride sack on horse; at R., miller receiving sack from woman: Add. 42130, f. 158 (at L., dog seated) (*fig. 697*)
toy, ape with: W. 82, f. 207 (rattle? at R., two beggars) (*fig. 82*)
toy, man with (rattle?): Douce 6, f. 85; G.K.S. 3384, ff. 27 (*fig. 28*), 192 (propelling it with stick)
toy, woman with (*cf.* Beggarwoman): Y.T. 27, f. 97a (rattle?)
woman with sack on head, approaching, setting on fire (fabliau?): Royal 10 E.IV, ff. 70v-71 (*fig. 698*)
Wine keg, on cart pulled by snail: M. 88, f. 177v
Wine kegs (2), one flowing: M. 754, f. 28 (at R., cup, nude man)
Winged headdress worn by
centaur
fighting centaur: Hague 78.D.40, ff. 47v (with spears and shields), 58 (with bow and arrow, spear and shield)
shooting boar: Hague 78.D.40, f. 134
shooting centaur with pot on head and sword and shield: Hague 78.D.40, f. 38v
shooting dragon: Hague 78.D.40, f. 86v
shooting hindquarters of ape: Hague 78.D.40, f. 133v
shooting stork: Hague 78.D.40, f. 23
with pipe and tabor: Hague 78.D.40, f. 29v
with spear, pursuing ape: Hague 78.D.40, f. 143
falconer: fr. 12400, f. 143v
hybrid beast with vielle, ape dancing: Douce 118, f. 17
hybrid man: Cloisters 54.1.2, f. 145v; Hague 10 A.14, f. 26 (2, holding quoit); Jacquemart 1, throughout; Lambeth 233, f. 164v; latin 3893, f. 273; St. Omer 5, f. 22v; Yale MS., f. 74
with cymbals: latin 10484, f. 30 (below, hybrid man with tabor)
with double pipe: Royal 2 B.VII, f. 193v (hybrid man with hand organ)
with gittern: W. 45, f. 85v (at R., hybrid dog with trumpet)
with trumpet: Royal 2 B.VII, f. 196 (hybrid man with vielle)
with vielle: St. Omer 5, f. 132v
hybrid woman: Jacquemart 1, throughout
man
fighting lion with sword and buckler: latin 16260, f. 592v
gesticulating wildly: latin 10483, f. 62
head of: Douce 5, f. 215 (line ending; below, man holding up bowl containing round green objects)
nude, fighting lion with spear and buckler: Hague 78.D.40, f. 40
roasting meat on spit, with knife: Melbourne 1254/3, f. 4v (*fig. 432*)
shooting hare: Melbourne 1254/3, f. 30v
shooting knight astride horse: Melbourne 1254/3, f. 1
shooting stag: M. 796, f. 47
supporting border, arms akimbo: Rutland Ps., f. 11 (at R., two wrestlers)
with coiled rope and basin: Bodley 264, f. 74 (at R., king with two pages holding mantle; two men approaching with pole across shoulders and seat attached in middle; man with nude man across shoulder; fabliau?)
with crown of thorns containing three nails, grasping hands of Christ bearing the cross,

W

followed by man, St. John, and the Virgin: Add. 42130, f. 93
with harp: Yale MS, f. 209
with scourge, beside horses of three Magi: Y.T. 75, f. 55v (Min.: Adoration of Magi)
men fighting with swords and bucklers, flanked by two lions: Hague 78.D.40, f. 61
merman
shooting hybrid man: Jacquemart 1, f. 34v
with pipe and tabor, centaur dancing: Jacquemart 1, f. 133v
monster with bellows: Add. 49622, f. 138v
siren confronting nude man (wearing cape) with club: Rutland Ps., f. 107

Winnowing *see* Hybrid man threshing; Hybrid man with flail; Man and woman, with basket; Man threshing

Wisdom *see* Sacraments: Extreme Unction

Wise and foolish virgins: Y.T. 8, f. 354v (one of each) (*fig. 682*)

Witch of Endor *see* David, life of: D. and Saul

Wivern
and bird, attacking: All Souls lat. 6, f. 13
and man, shot by: Y.T. 15, f. 284

Wodehouse *see* Wild man

Wolf (*see also* Dog and dragon; Dog and fox, pursuing; Fables; Man and; Man nude and; Procession, funeral of fox; *Roman de Renart;* Romulus and Remus)
and fox, wrestling: W. 109, f. 227v (wolf?)
and stag, observing stag scratching its ear: Fitz. 2-1954, f. 119 (below, patrons)
as bishop, with serpent: G.K.S. 393, f. 301v (flanking text with mitered ass, two mitered rams, mitered ?lion, mitered ape) (*fig. 238*)
as cleric, with ram-cleric: Hague 78.D.40, f. 25v
as Dominican *see* Lion as King
as Templar, with whip: Glazier 24, f. 93v
Bestiary representation: Fitz. 47, f. 163 (line ending); Harley 6563, ff. 19-19v; M. 183, f. 222 (man with club and nude man in pursuit); Munich c.g. 16, f. 23 (in cycle); Royal 2 B.VII, ff. 120v-122 (in cycle); Rutland Ps., ff. 109v-110
biting right front paw: W. 85, ff. 52v, 86
drinking: Glazier 24, f. 126v (wolf?)

Woman *see also* entries under Abbess; Beggar-woman; Bishop and; Hybrid woman; Nun; Patroness; Physician and; Queen; Virgin, miracles of: woman

Woman and ape (*see also* Ape as physician)
aiming bellows at hindquarters: M. 88, f. 173 (at R., man bending crossbow at wild man with pot on head, holding ?stone)
astride, with pipe and tabor; man with trumpet: Add. 42130, f. 215
confronting ape-cleric with horn, gesture of disgust: Douce 118, f. 87 (chaplet on head)
lowering jug on rope down to well, ape prodding jug with pole: Douce 5, f. 39v (at same time kissing man, both in line endings)
observing ape eating with spoon: Douce 5, f. 29 (*fig. 700*)
offering flowers to ape-falconer, both seated on bench: Stowe 17, f. 62
patting bird, imitated by ape: Nancy 249, f. 150 (*fig. 8*)
with distaff and spindle, ape with reel: Douce 6, f. 48

Woman and ass
accompanied by, with child: Yale MS., f. 85v
astride, with distaff and spindle, sack across shoulder; two apes on stilts: Arsenal 5218, f. 20

Woman and bear (*see also* Man and bear, training)
eaten by: Royal 10 E.IV, f. 106v (two)
hunting with two goats: M. 88, f. 109

Woman and beast with head of man, astride (Phyllis and Aristotle reference?): Y.T. 27, f. 21v (holding bowl and ?)

Woman and bird (*see also* Woman as falconer)
grappling with, holding by throat: C.B. 62, f. 207v
holding, with whip: Douce 118, f. 123
snaring with basket, dummy fox as decoy (Bestiary motif, variant): Bodley 264, f. 126v (at R., man with two huge birdcages)
snaring with net; behind her couple embracing and another man: Bodley 264, f. 21v (at L., hybrid man with infant)
with birdcage containing parrot (?hawk) and magpie(?): BBR 9961-62, f. 66 (chaplet on head) (*fig. 118*)

Woman and boar, hunting with spear: Royal 10 E.IV, f. 45v; Y.T. 13, ff. 76-78 (part of *Jeu des Dames* cycle)

Woman and bull, milked by (proverb?): Trinity B.11.22, f. 118v

Woman and butterfly, pursuing with hood: Bodley 264, f. 135 (8, blue hoods)

Woman and cat, striking with distaff cat feeding from bowl: Rothschild MS., f. 156v

W

Woman and chickens, feeding: Add. 42130, f. 166v (with distaff, pan) (*fig. 701*)
Woman and child (*see also* Jesus Christ, life of: Massacre; Man and bear, training; Woman with basket): Chantilly 64, ff. 128, 128v (below, white horse with gold saddle); G.K.S. 3384, f. 91; Y.T. 27, f. 23
  bathing (*cf.* Woman and Christ child): Melbourne 1254/3, f. 10 (at L., winged, crowned hybrid man with taper) (*fig. 704*)
  by fire: Merton 0.1.3, f. 65v (at L. and in miniature: intercourse) (*fig. 405*)
  by fire, cooking: Douce 6, f. 22 (at R., bald man with bellows; above, woman with basket of firewood) (*fig. 702*)
  child in cradle on back: Glazier 24, f. 34 (raising skirt with left hand) (*fig. 703*)
  child in walker: G.K.S. 3384, f. 104v
  children (2) lying on ground, Florent and Octavian: Royal 10 E.IV, f. 119 (ff. 120-125, carried off by lioness, suckled, baptized)
  holding by hand: Bodley 264, f. 70 (two; at L., man in stag costume, man with pipe and tabor)
  holding in arms, wearing stilts, jug on head (*cf.* Fables: woman with jug): Royal 10 E.IV, f. 29v
  man kneeling before, woman holding spear, offering garland (*cf.* Man and woman, before Frau Minne, references under; Man and woman, kneeling): Douce 118, f. 68v
  suckling, bending over cradle (*cf.* Mermaid and offspring; Nun and ape): Royal 10 E.IV, f. 127v; Y.T. 75, f. 50 (at L., old man/monster hugging infant)
  with bat wings: Douce 118, f. 18v
Woman and Christ child, bathing (*cf.* Woman and child, bathing): Douce 118, f. 135 (above, angel with taper in cloud) (*fig. 705*)
Woman and cleric *see* Cleric and woman
Woman and cripple: Douce 118, f. 50 (giving bread to); Princeton 44-18, ff. 162v-163
Woman and devil *see* Devil and woman; Woman balancing on hands
Woman and dog *see* Dog as pet
Woman and Dominican, tilting astride horses: Yale MS., f. 100v (*fig. 706*)
Woman and dragon (*see also* Dragon coiled)
  disgorging: Add. 42130, f. 43v (above, man with horn astride horse)
  standing on head of: C.B. 62, f. 188v
Woman and ducks, hunting *see* Woman as falconer
Woman and falconer *see* Falconer and woman
Woman and fly(?), turning toward: BBR 9391, f. 113v (frightened by?)
Woman and fox (*see also* Hybrid woman and fox)
  beseeching fox-bishop: Y.T. 8, f. 185
  beseeching fox in cloak holding cock: Y.T. 8, f. 312
  hunting with dog: Royal 10 E.IV, f. 67
  pursuing fox with cock (or goose) in mouth (*cf.* Fox and cock): Add. 49622, f. 157v (wringing hands); All Souls lat. 6, f. 13 (with distaff and spindle); BBR 10607, f. 132 bis (with distaff); Chantilly 64, ff. 172 (with distaff and spindle), 172v (the same); Douce 366, f. 71v (with distaff and spindle); Fitz. 298, f. 1v (with distaff and spindle, man with pitchfork); Hague 78.D.40, ff. 31 (*fig. 190*), 59v, 103v, 156 (all with distaff and spindle); Harley 6563, ff. 59v-60 (with distaff, fox disappearing in hole in hill); Jacquemart 1, f. 31v (half-nude, with distaff and spindle); latin 1029A, f. 45v (with distaff and spindle); M. 183, f. 238 (with distaff and spindle); Princeton 44-18, ff. 134v-135 (with distaff and spindle); Royal 2 B.VII, f. 158 (with distaff, fox with duck); Royal 10 E.IV, ff. 40 (same as Harley 6563, ff. 59v-60; two foxes, urged on by two men), 49v (with distaff, fox with goose; at L., fox-bishop preaching to fowl; in *Roman de Renart* sequence), 175 (the same; at R., ape holding owl); Stowe 17, ff. 64v-65 (with distaff), 209v-210 (woman driving chickens, ducks, geese; fox escaping with cock); Verdun 107, f. 57 (with distaff and spindle); W. 85, f. 91v (with distaff and spindle); W. 88, f. 155 (confronting with paddle) (*fig. 189*); Y.T. 27, f. 41 (beating with distaff); Yale MS., f. 199 (with distaff and spindle)
  trapping: Royal 10 E.IV, f. 53 (2; fox disappearing in burrow, hind legs held by woman; the other holding meshed frame over hole; at R., man and woman with garland in enclosure; in background, rabbit burrows)
Woman and goat *see* Exemplum; Knight and woman, tilting; Man and ram, astride; Man nude and lion, astride; Woman and bear; — and ram; Woman nude and goat
Woman and hare, hunting: Royal 10 E.IV, ff. 41 (2, with bow and arrow, club), 48 (fox es-

caping with hare in mouth), 160v (with lapdog, three hares in burrow, fourth outside); Y.T. 13, ff. 68-72 (as falconer; part of *Jeu des Dames* cycle)
with club, astride bird/horse: BBR 329-41, f. 162 (above, owl and two hybrid men with psaltery and vielle) (*fig.* 707)
with ferret, net placed over hole in burrow, beating hares with clubs (*cf.* Woman and fox, trapping): Royal 2 B.VII, ff. 155v-156 (2)
Woman and hen *see* Man and cock; Woman and chickens
Woman and hermit *see* Hermit
Woman and horse *see* Knight and woman; Woman and Dominican
Woman and hybrid man *see* Beggarwoman
Woman and king, playing backgammon(?): Add. 42130, f. 76v
Woman and knight *see* Knight and woman
Woman and lion (*see also* Virtues: Fortitude)
astride
accompanied by nude boy astride lion held by man: Fitz. 242, f. 3
as falconer, riding toward skeleton astride cow with spear and coffin under arm: Hague 78.D.40, f. 91
with garland, riding toward man astride goat(?): M. 729, f. 293
with scourge: Douce 6, f. 154v (at R., ape with crosier kneeling before ape with book crouching in initial)
with trumpet: M. 729, f. 16 (at L., ape with trumpet; at R., man with club leading lion)
fighting with sword: Rylands lat R.117, f. 9 (dog by rabbit burrow)
pursuing with distaff and spindle, lion with child in mouth: Rylands lat. R.117, f. 9
Woman and man *see* Man and woman
Woman and manticora(?), astride backwards: Douce 118, f. 107 (biting tail)
Woman and monster, seated on winged headless monster, dancing: Jacquemart 1, f. 70
Woman and ram, baiting with basket: (*cf.* Woman and unicorn; *see also* Woman nude and goat): Bodley 264, f. 20v (*fig.* 712); G.K.S. 3384, ff. 161 (goat?) (*fig.* 307), 348; Nancy 249, f. 65
Woman and satyr, dancing: Royal 2 B.VII, f. 166
Woman and serpent, holding (*cf.* Knight and serpent; Man and —): G.K.S. 3384, f. 87
Woman and sheep
accompanied by ape: G.K.S. 3384, f. 141v
leaving sheep pen with jugs on head, man in pen milking sheep: Add. 42130, f. 163v (2) (*fig.* 381)
shearing: Douce 6, f. 101v (above, man with large sack over shoulder)
Woman and snail, charging with broom (*see also* Knight and snail, confronting): Chantilly 62, ff. 32, 32v
Woman and squirrel *cf.* Squirrel as pet
Woman and stag, hunting: Add. 24686, f. 13v (with hounds; young suckling) (*fig.* 714); Bodley 264, ff. 77 (2, with spear, hounds), 122v (*fig.* 715); fr. 25526, f. 42v (with man, both astride horses); Nancy 249, f. 184 (carrying stag with gold antlers across shoulder); Royal 2 B.VII, ff. 152v-153 (with horn, hound); Royal 10 E.IV, ff. 44 (with hounds), 160 (with hounds); Y.T. 13, ff. 78v-83v (part of *Jeu des Dames* cycle)
Woman and unicorn, baiting with basket (*cf.* Woman and ram): Nancy 249, f. 206v (*fig.* 713)
Woman and wild man *see* Wild man and knight
Woman as falconer (*see also* Ape and bird, patting; Man and woman, embracing; Woman crowned): Bodley 264, ff. 77 (2), 80v (3); Burney 275, f. 184; Chantilly 62, f. 43; Christ Church E.II, f. 50v; Fitz. 298, f. 1 (?dancing; woman with vielle); Hague 78.D.40, f. 49 (2); M. 796, f. 106 (with falconer, both astride horses); Royal 2 B.VII, ff. 177v-178 (2); Royal 10 E.IV, ff. 77v-79; Verdun 107, f. 12 (at R., falconer with garland on head; at L., man with vielle; in center, purse hung on tree, glove on ground (*fig.* 716); *cf.* Proverbs, gameboard); Y.T. 13, ff. 72v-75v (part of *Jeu des Dames* cycle); Y.T. 15, f. 53v (accompanied by dog and lion); Y.T. 19, f. 18v (seated beside youth with dog under tree filled with birds)
Woman as tumbler *see* Contortionist; Woman balancing
Woman ascending steps of water-drawing machine: Rothschild MS., f. 168 (*fig.* 730)
Woman at altar, kneeling before angel with trumpet (patroness?): Nancy 249, f. 49v
Woman at table
set with cup, knife, pitcher: Chantilly 64, f. 154
three rolls(?) on table; man with mortar and pestle, ape drinking: M. 754, f. 43

W

Woman at loom *see* Weaving, references under
Woman baking *see* Man and woman, baking; Woman cooking
Woman balancing
  on hands: Y.T. 19, f. 10
    devil applauding: Rutland Ps., f. 65 (*fig. 718*)
    hybrid man standing on her calves: C.B. 62, f. 23
  on shoulders of hybrid man with shawm: Cloisters 54.1.2, f. 160
  on two swordpoints, accompanied by woman with pipe and tabor, man with double pipe: Royal 10 E.IV, f. 58
  sword on chin: Cambridge Dd. 5.5, f. 55 (steadying it with stick; at L., man with pipe and tabor, another reaching for one of two swords on table) (*fig. 720*)
Woman bathing (*see also* Man and woman, bathing; Woman and child, bathing): M. 730, f. 72 (2)
Woman beating laundry with broad paddle on bank of stream: Y.T. 27, f. 109v
Woman beating man *see* Man and woman, beaten by
Woman before Eros *see* Man and woman, before; Woman kneeling
Woman by fountain (?) filling cups: latin 10435, f. 38v (2) (*fig. 717*)
Woman carding wool: Add. 42130, f. 193 (another spinning); Douce 6, f. 73 (below, pet dog); Royal 10 E.IV, ff. 138, 138v (*Wright's Chaste Wife* sequence)
Woman cooking (*see also* Woman with wafering iron)
  kneading dough(?) in bowl: latin 14284, f. 11v
  stirring pot over fire: Chantilly 64, ff. 76, 76v; Douce 6, f. 22 (nude baby in lap; at R., bald man with bellows; above, woman with basket of firewood); G.K.S. 3384, ff. 106v, 298; Melbourne 1254/3, f. 4v (at L., man with winged headdress, knife, roasting meat on spit); Trinity B.11.22, f. 37v
Woman crippled, old, with three-wheeled walker: Chantilly 64, ff. 191, 191v
Woman crowned (*see also* Queen; Virgin, life of: presenting; Virtues): Douce 118, ff. 81v (with bird, ?falcon), 96 (praying), 160v (with vielle)
Woman crowning man kneeling before her: Yale MS., f. 110v
Woman dancing (*see also* Cleric with gittern; Hybrid cleric playing bellows; Hybrid man with bagpipe; — with hand bells; — with mandola; — with trumpet; Hybrid woman with vielle; Knight spinning; Man and bear, training; Man and woman, dancing; Man playing vielle; Man with bagpipe; — with gittern; — with hand bells; — with harp; — with pipe and tabor; — with psaltery; — with triangle; — with trumpet; — with vielle; Woman nude; Woman with vielle): Add. 39810, f. 7 (*fig. 140*); BBR 9391, f. 108v; BBR 10607, f. 97; Cambrai 87, f. 40 (issuing from border); Laud Lat. 84, f. 298v; M. 796, f. 91 (f. 91v, skeleton with ?mirror); W. 110, f. 91v
  on man's shoulders: Add. 42130, f. 68; Cambridge Dd. 5.5, f. 295; Cloisters 54.1.2, f. 49; G.K.S. 3384, f. 349v (at R., patroness); Nancy 249, f. 62
  seated on winged headless monster: Jacquemart 1, f. 70
Woman drawing water out of well (*cf.* Man): G.K.S. 3384, f. 49v
Woman drinking, three others, one pouring coins into coffer, one tearing hair, one with mirror (Vices?; *see also* Woman nude and man): fr. 95, f. 134 (*fig. 671*)
Woman eating grapes *see* Man picking grapes
Woman fighting *see* Knight and woman; Man and woman; Woman and snail, charging; Woman nude and snail; Women
Woman hawking *see* Woman as falconer
Woman hoarding(?), holding sock, putting sack in chest: Princeton 44-18, f. 7 (f. 7v, man doing the same)
Woman hunting *see* Woman and bear; — and bird; — and boar; — and butterfly; — and stag; Woman as falconer
Woman in bed, man seated on stool beside her (*cf.* Man and woman, in bed): Douce 6, f. 160v (at R., man and woman approaching house)
Woman in sailboat, in red sea: Douce 118, f. 76 (man?)
Woman in wheelbarrow *see* Man with wheelbarrow
Woman in tower *see* Knights tilting, queen
Woman juggling three knives; at L., man with tabor: Rutland Ps., f. 51v
Woman kidnaped *see* Knight and Saracen; — and wild man

Woman kneeling (*see also* Man and woman, before Eros; —, kneeling; Patroness; Woman praying)
at altar, before angel with trumpet: Nancy 249, f. 94v
at *prie-dieu,* before her messenger with standard and letter, kneeling: Chantilly 64, ff. 130, 130v
before Eros with mandola, in golden robe (*cf.* Man and woman, before): Princeton 44-18, ff. 27v-28
Woman mourning *see* Woman with book
Woman nude (*see also* Devil and woman)
and beast, astride, holding gold branch: Douce 118, f. 116 (beside ram rearing)
and cleric, playing dice(?), kneeling: Add. 36684, f. 53
and dragon, bitten in thigh by, with shawm: Y.T. 27, f. 42
and goat, astride with distaff and spindle, charging woman astride ram, also with distaff and spindle (parody of tournament?): Arsenal 5218, f. 10 (flanked by two apes with bagpipe and trumpet) (*fig. 719*)
and hybrid fox(?), riding sideways: W. 88, f. 102v
and man drinking: latin 14284, f. 43v
and man nude, lying on backs, hands raised: Add. 36684, f. 56 (bird drinking from tall chalice; Min.: Flight into Egypt)
and snail, fighting with spear and buckler: Harley 6563, ff. 86v-87 (*fig. 721*)
and unicorn, astride, charging grotesque beast: Y.T. 19, f. 10
dancing, nude man with spear: M. 108, f. 1
straddling border; man in drawers, bearded, with sword, standing on stool or table (*cf.* Man nude, straddling): M. 754, f. 76
tearing hair, on monster's shoulders (Despair? *cf.* Woman drinking): fr. 95, f. 230v
with spear and buckler: Harley 6563, f. 86 (f. 85v, missing)
Woman on stilts, holding child, wearing jug on head (*cf.* Fables: woman with jug): Royal 10 E.IV, f. 29v
Woman picking flowers (*cf.* Man): Add. 49622, f. 20 (winding wreath); BBR 9961-62, f. 26 (two others winding wreath; shepherd and dog, sheep, with shawm)
Woman picking leaf off border: latin 10484, f. 133
Woman playing
games *see* name of game
organ, two men with gittern and shawm, ape pointing at woman: M. 88, f. 23
psaltery with rake, man with psaltery: M. 754, f. 86
tongs with spoon: Trinity B.11.22, f. 191v (*fig. 519*)
Woman pouring out coins *see* Woman drinking
Woman praying (*see also* Patroness)
at altar, before angel(?) with book in clouds: Douce 118, ff. 24v, 70v
at altar, before angel with trumpet: Nancy 249, f. 94v
at *prie-dieu,* before her kneeling messenger with standard and letter: Chantilly 64, ff. 130, 130v
before statue of mitered saint: Douce 118, f. 27
Woman pulling boat containing man (corpse?) with bleeding neck (fabliau?); Nancy 249, f. 236 (*fig. 722*)
Woman pulling lips sideways (*cf.* Hybrid man, hooded): Christ Church E.II, f. 35v (confronting hooded hybrid man)
Woman reaping: Add. 42130, f. 172v (3; man with sickle stacking sheaf; in cycle)
Woman reclining on elbow, man with reel: M. 754, f. 67v
Woman sawing border stalk with man: Bodley 264, f. 63v
Woman setting fire to mill *see* Windmill
Woman shearing sheep: Douce 6, f. 101v (above, man with large sack over shoulder)
Woman spinning (*cf.* Bird with reel; St. Margaret; Woman with distaff and spindle): Royal 10 E.IV, ff. 137, 139 (large spinning wheel on table), 142, 146, 147 (*Wright's Chaste Wife* sequence)
winding reel, man with distaff and spindle: Arras 47, f. 208v (*fig. 735*)
woman carding wool: Add. 42130, f. 193
Woman suckling child *see* Woman and child
Woman tearing hair (Despair? *see also* Woman drinking; Woman nude): fr. 95, ff. 134 (*fig. 671*), 267v
Woman tilting
with Dominican, astride horses: Yale MS., f. 100v
with woman, astride horses: Royal 2 B.VII, f. 197v (f. 198, two woman with trumpets)
Woman vomiting (spitting) into basin below (*cf.* Vomiting, references under): Douce 6, f. 77 (below, man with spoon and pot); Y.T. 27, f. 81v (possibly; partially effaced)

W

Woman washing, beating laundry with paddle on bank of stream: Y.T. 27, f. 109v

Woman washing hair: Cloisters 54.1.2, ff. 45 (hybrid; below, woman with large basin) (*fig. 723*), 87 (hybrid; below, Saracen with ?bucket on head); Y.T. 27, f. 50v (hybrid; over basin)

Woman weaving (*see also* Loom): Cambridge Dd. 5.5, f. 379v; Munich c.g. 16, f. 21 (Naa-mah) (*fig. 724*)

Woman with arrow *see* Man and woman, kneeling before

Woman with bagpipe, on shoulders of hybrid man with staff: Y.T. 19, f. 1

Woman with basket (*see also* Proverbs: game-board; —: woman with basket; Wild woman with —; Woman and bird; — and ram; Woman cooking)

containing child bedecked with red flowers: Douce 6, f. 122v (2; at R., ape on roof of ?church)

containing eggs: BBR 1175, f. 59 (2; two women considering wares) (*fig. 727*); Trinity B.11.22, f. 160v (man with purse, purchasing) (*fig. 725*)

Woman with birdcage (*see also* Woman and bird): BBR 9961-62, f. 66 (*figs. 118, 729*)

Woman with book (*see also* Patroness): Add. 49622, f. 64v; Arras 1043, f. 190v; BBR 9391, f. 123v (Min.: man digging grave, three clerics, one with asperge; Offices of the Dead); G.K.S. 3384, f. 38 (below, woman with distaff and spindle): Melbourne 1254/3, f. 12v (before ape with switch); W. 82, f. 164v (seated, man digging grave; at R., man mourning; Offices of the dead); W. 104, f. 74 (2; in remaining margins, six clerics: two Dominicans, two Franciscans, two ?Cistercians; Offices of the Dead)

Woman with bowl (*cf.* Beggarwoman): Rothschild MS., f. 168 (three, pointing at) (*fig. 730*); W. 87, ff. 56v (and horn; holding up bowl), 87v (and sword; below, nude man with trumpet)

Woman with buckets *see* Man nude, bathing

Woman with bundle on head, carrying jar and bread(?) *cf.* Fables: woman with jug): Fitz. 2-1954, f. 131v (*fig. 728*)

Woman with chalice and jar: Y.T. 27, f. 83

Woman with churn: Add. 10294, f. 1 (approached by beggar); Bodley 264, f. 3 (boy kneeling with bowl); Cambrai 87, f. 29v; Douce 6, f. 65; G.K.S. 3384, f. 304; Nancy 249, ff. 58v (dog eating out of bowl), 211v (the same); Princeton 44-18, ff. 26v (f. 27, white dog looking on), 194v; W. 88, ff. 97v (cripple holding out bowl), 188; Yale MS., f. 300v

Woman with coin (*see also* Proverbs: woman with jug): Rutland Ps., f. 39 (holding two ?coins)

Woman with comb, seated, maid with mirror dressing her hair (*cf.* Woman with mirror and comb): Add. 42130, f. 63 (at R., dragon) (*fig. 732*)

Woman with distaff and spindle (*see also* Woman and fox; — nude and goat; — with spindle): BBR 10607, f. 234; Chantilly 62, f. 124; Chantilly 64, ff. 42, 42v, 84, 84v; Douce 5, ff. 50, 185; G.K.S. 3384, ff. 38 (above, woman with book), 103 (2); Glazier 24, f. 145v (skirt raised); latin 16260, f. 292v (above, hybrid bishop); Laud Lat. 84, ff. 176v, 204v; Trinity B.11.22, f. 199v (*fig. 335*); W. 85, f. 87v (above, crowned man with vielle); W. 87, f. 94v; W. 90, f. 59; Yale MS., f. 169 (Eve; at R., Adam delving)

and reel: fr. 95, ff. 101v (2), 339v (2)

ape with reel: Douce 6, f. 48

astride ass: Arsenal 5218, f. 20

atop shell, dolphin in margin below: Glazier 24, f. 107 (*fig. 733*)

beating man (*cf.* Man and woman, beaten by) Add. 42130, f. 60

child in three-wheeled walker: G.K.S. 3384, f. 104v (*fig. 738*)

dancing, knight spinning: Arras 47, f. 32 (*fig. 734*)

dancing, man with vielle: W. 85, f. 87v

dog running off with spindle: Cambrai 102, f. 229 (at R., bird flying)

feeding chickens: Add. 42130, f. 166v (*fig. 701*)

knight with head of ass on spear: W. 90, f. 146

merman observing: Cloisters 54.1.2, f. 106

observing knight fighting hybrid woman: Royal 14 E.III, f. 3

on ducking stool: Rutland Ps., f. 86 (below, man wielding mallet) (*fig. 731*)

opening treasure chest: Trinity B.11.22, f. 213 (at R., dog comes running; below, cripple) (*fig. 553*)

pointing at butterfly(?), following woman with distaff and spindle: BBR 9391, f. 96 (skirts

raised; at R., man with spear approaching tower)
pursuing fox *see* Woman and fox
pursuing lion *see* Woman and lion
running toward two dogs fighting: Princeton 44-18, ff. 29v-30 (owl in tree)
seated, seen from back: fr. 95, f. 141
striking cat eating out of bowl: Rothschild MS., f. 156v

Woman with ewer and basin, dragon bending down (*cf.* Fables: fox and stork, Part I, variant): C.B. 62, f. 76

Woman with falcon *see* Woman as falconer

Woman with garland (*see also* King with branches; Knight and woman, kneeling before; Man and woman, kneeling; —, kneeling before, Man with bagpipe; Woman picking flowers): Douce 6, f. 67 (and flowering branch); Kraus 75/88, f. 70v (garland made from hole in parchment)

Woman with gittern: Bodley 264, ff. 102, 109v (man with psaltery); W. 85, f. 16

Woman with hand organ: Kraus 75/88, f. 105 (in gold robe, chaplet on head)
hybrid man with bagpipe: M. 754, f. 5v
woman dancing: M. 754, f. 34

Woman with harp: Vienna 1826*, f. 141 (beside her, woman and dog); W. 39, f. 118; W. 109, f. 197v (two men dancing; swan; *cf.* Swan, Bestiary representation)

Woman with harrow *see* Man sowing

Woman with head
of child: Chantilly 64, f. 81v (Min.: Massacre of Innocents)
of sheep (*cf.* Man with head of): G.K.S. 3384, f. 107v

Woman with horn, holding up bowl: W. 87, f. 56v

Woman with jug (*cf.* Jug, references under)
emptying (urinal?): W. 87, f. 37v (below, ape with flabellum and rod, doctor's cap, seated; f. 38, ape-bishop with bagpipe, beckoning)
holding up urinal (?): W. 87, f. 60v
on head, kneeling, holding bowl and spoon: Exeter 47, f. 73v

Woman with lapdog *see* Dog as pet; Man and woman, embracing; Man with wheelbarrow, containing woman

Woman with mandola: Add. 30029, f. 101 (male head attached to instrument)

Woman with mirror (*cf.* Hybrid woman with; Knight and woman, confronting; —, holding; Man with; Woman drinking)
and comb: Cloisters 54.1.2, ff. 33 (hag, combing hair), 123 (hybrid, combing hair); Cambridge Dd. 5.5, f. 358 (at L., ape observing); Douce 5, f. 42 (above, man with bagpipe); G.K.S. 3384, f. 162v; latin 10483, f. 253 (combing hair)
arranging hair: Ashmole 828, f. 37 (wearing hairnet); Exeter 47, f. 37v; G.K.S. 3384, f. 110; Stowe 17, f. 202v (below, ape exposing hindquarters)
arranging veil: St. Omer 5, f. 193 (at R., falconer with mirror, stork)
confronting knight brandishing sword and shield: W. 85, ff. 115v-116
holding up to man: G.K.S. 3384, ff. 268, 321
holding up to woman with comb, seated, arranging hair: Add. 42130, f. 63 (at R., dragon) (*fig. 732*)
looking into: Bodley 264, f. 119 (at R., owl-decoy, man snaring birds); C.B. 62, f. 133 (large gold disk, mirror?); Chartres 549, f. 242; Douce 6, f. 97v (above, large male head looking down; at R., dragon in line ending) (*fig. 210*); latin 10483, f. 118v; Nancy 249, ff. 196v, 203v; W. 85, f. 115
hand at face: Cloisters 54.1.2, f. 149 (hybrid); Kraus 75/88, f. 124 (half-figure)
seeing reflection: Bodley 264, f. 28 (or holding man's head?); Harley 6563, f. 2
man defecating on: Add. 36684, f. 51v
unicorn running toward: Royal 10 E.IV, f. 153

Woman with mortar and pestle: Melbourne 1254/3, f. 4v (man with winged headdress, knife, roasting meat on spit) (*fig. 432*); Nancy 249, ff. 32 (seated), 40 (seated)

Woman with pitcher *see* Woman with jug

Woman with psaltery
ape dancing: BBR 10607, f. 23
man dancing: W. 109, f. 67
man directing: Princeton 44-18, f. 122
man with trumpet: Bodley 264, f. 34v

Woman with purse, putting hand in (*see also* Man and butterfly, pursuing with club; Treasure chest): Douce 6, f. 105v (at L., pet dog; below, scribe seated)

Woman with rakes (2), by fire (*see also* Man scything): St. Omer 5, f. 134 (at L., centaur-knight pulling dog's tail)

W

Woman with reel (*see* Hybrid man with distaff): Arras 47, f. 208v (man with distaff) (*fig. 735*)
Woman with scales (*cf.* Virtues: Justice): Princeton 44-18, f. 113v (2)
Woman with shoe in either hand: W. 87, f. 84 (below, lion standing on basket or nest)
Woman with sock *see* Woman hoarding
Woman with spade and shield: W. 87, f. 17v (below, goat seated)
Woman with spear *see* Man and woman, kneeling before
Woman with spindle
and reel: G.K.S. 3384, f. 33
holding between two fighting cocks: Douce 118, f.7v (*fig. 133*); Y.T.8, f. 335
Woman with stool basket, seated under (*see also* Man and woman, with basket; Physician and woman): Rylands fr. 2, f. 212 (*fig. 523*)
Woman with sword
fighting lion: Rylands lat. R.117, f.9
kneeling under tree, sword on ground, hands raised: Princeton 44-18, f. 13
Woman with tabor
before hybrid man: Douce 118, f. 100v
standing on head of crowned hybrid man: Royal 10 E.IV, f. 29
Woman with tambourine (*see also* Man and woman dancing, hands): Add. 42130, f. 61; Harley 6563, f. 14; Y.T. 27, f. 17
Woman with taper: Douce 6, ff. 30, 173 (two; below, veiled head—mourner?); Schilling MS. (February)
Woman with toy windmill *see* Windmill, toy
Woman with tray on head containing three gold balls (*cf.* Proverbs: woman with basket): Chantilly 64, ff. 43, 43v
Woman with treasure chest (open; *see also* Treasure chest; Woman drinking; — hoarding; Woman with distaff and spindle, opening): Harley 6563, f. 4 (f. 3v, Jew pointing at her)
Woman with vielle: Douce 118, f. 160v (crowned); Lambeth 233, f. 85v; St. Omer 5, f. 1
dog dancing: Jacquemart 1, f. 72v
man and hooded dog dancing: Stowe 17, f. 112 (*fig. 105*)
man dancing: latin 13260, f. 116v (doubled over backwards); Laud Lat. 84, f. 366v; W. 88, f. 41
man with garland: M. 155, ff. 86v-87 (f. 87, above man, hybrid knight bending crossbow)
man with gittern, woman dancing: Fitz. 298, f. 1 (*fig. 566*)
man with pipe and tabor: Y.T. 8, f. 53 (at R., three woman dancing); Yale MS., f. 14
woman dancing: Christ Church E.II, f. 51v
Woman with wafering iron, by fire, making wafer: Douce 6, f. 119 (above, man with fish in basin, bishop, man with trumpet)
Woman with walker: Chantilly 64, ff. 191, 191v (old)
Woman with wheat sheaf: Add. 49622, f. 136v (2)
Woman with wreath *see* Woman with garland, references under
Woman writing *see* Scribe
Women (men?) fighting with swords and bucklers: Hague 78.D.40, f. 27v
Woodchopping *see* Ape chopping; Man chopping; Man with ax
Woodcock: Fitz. 2-1954, f. 1 (at R., man shooting butterfly)
Woodcutter *see* Virgin, miracles of
Woodpecker: Fitz. 2-1954, ff. 9, 83v
Worm *see* Bird with
Wrestling
apes (2): C.B. 64, f. 63v (on shoulders of men); fr. 95, f. 269; fr. 25526, f. 58v (at R., hare bearing offspring to hare in bed); Glazier 24, f. 36v; M. 754, f. 17v (on shoulders of apes; at L., king pointing); Royal 14 E.III, f. 3; W. 45, f. 68v (above, fox with book, stork); W. 88, ff. 136 (dancing?), 158
ape with bear: C.B. 62, f. 196v
ape with fox: Y.T. 8, f. 179
bears (2), pierced with spear by soldier: BBR 9157, f. 4v
cats (2): latin 16260, f. 4v
fox with wolf(?): W. 109, f. 227v
hybrid men: Cloisters 54.1.2, f. 94; Jacquemart 1, f. 38v
Jacob with angel: Munich c.g. 16, f. 33v (in Old Testament cycle)
lion and man: All Souls lat. 6, f. 13
lions (2): Hague 78.D.40, f. 83
man with bear: Fitz. 298, f. 23v; Y.T. 8, f. 297
man with fox: Y.T. 8, f. 179
man with hare: fr. 12400, f. 1; Glazier 24, f. 65 (huge hare with lion's tail); Y.T. 8, f. 352

men (2; *see also* Ram on column): Add. 39810, f. 120; Add. 42130, f. 54v (in drawers); Add. 49622, ff. 101, 212; C.B. 62, f. 128v; Chantilly 64, ff. 119, 119v, 125, 125v; Douce 366, f. 109; Glazier 24, f. 110v (one in drawers, the other nude with ?Templar's hat); latin 3893, f. 97; M. 729, f. 259v (in drawers); M. 730, f. 24; Melbourne 1254/3, f. 47v; Princeton 44-18, ff. 154, 182; Royal 2 B.VII, ff. 160v (flanked by spectators; at L., man holding prize, cock on pole), 168 (nude); Royal 10 E.IV, f. 58v (in drawers); Rutland Ps., ff. 11 (at L., man with winged headdress) (*fig. 739*), 58; Stowe 17, f. 121 (f. 120v, bird with worm in beak observing, squirrel with nut) (*fig. 736*); W. 88, ff. 16v, 50v, 109v, 171v; W. 102, f. 83 (f. 82v, centaur shooting at them); W. 109, f. 231; Yale MS., f. 333
nude, astride bear and lion: Douce 366, f. 147v (2)
on shoulders of hybrids: Yale MS., f. 290v (2)
pickaback: Add. 39810, f. 7 (*fig. 140*); Add. 42130, f. 62; Bodley 264, ff. 3, 91; fr. 95, f. 326 (one nude); Jesus 40, f. 150 (corpses rising from tombs) (*fig. 272*); Princeton 44-18, ff. 22, 121; Royal 2 B.VII, f. 161v; Rutland Ps., f. 70v; Stowe 17, f. 100v (one with bleeding head); Y.T. 8, f. 92
Wright's Chaste Wife, sequence based on version of?: Royal 10 E.IV, ff. 137-148 (man performing various tasks such as fetching water, washing dishes, grinding corn, washing laundry, baking bread, spinning; beaten by his wife after each task)
Writing *see* Scribe

Y

Yale, Bestiary representation: Munich c.g. 16, f. 38 (in cycle)
Yawning *see* Proverbs: man yawning

Z

Zadok *see* David, life of: D. and Solomon
Zechariah: Y.T. 13, f. 44v
and St. Matthias (Old and New Law): latin 10483, f. 6v; Y.T. 27, f. 12; Y.T. 75, f. 9v
annunciation to: Y.T. 13, ff. 53v-54
with scroll: Douce 118, f. 173 ("Zacharias propheta"); Y.T. 13, f. 55 ("Iohannes est nomen")
Zephaniah: Y.T. 13, f. 42v
Zephaniah and St. Thomas, Apostle (Old and New Law): Y.T. 27, f. 6; Y.T. 75, f. 6v
Ziba *see* David, life of: D. and
Ziklag *see* David, life of: D. and Abigail
Zipporah *see* Moses with
Zodiac, signs of: Cloisters 54.1.2, ff. 2-13 (calendar)
Capricorn: Cloisters 54.1.2, f. 13 (December); Jacquemart 1, f. 77v (below, hybrid knight with spear and shield); W. 37, f. 159 (f. 158v, bee stinging hare), 179 (possibly); W. 87, f. 89v
Janus: Cloisters 54.1.2, f. 1v (January); W. 88, f. 3v (January); W. 90, f. 2v (January)
possible derivations from *see* Centaur; Rams butting; Woman with scales
Zosimus *see* St. Mary the Egyptian, f. 270v

Plates

When several subjects appear in the margins of a page, they are listed in sequence proceeding from the first subject of the caption counterclockwise around the page.

Parentheses are used to designate themes such as birds or grotesques not listed in the index. They are also used for groups of themes cited separately in the index, as in the section "Musical instruments, parody" in figures 508 to 520.

nobis do
mus os

1

ue maria gra plena do

2

3

I 1. Abbot and clerics: Hague 78.D.40, f. 109 2. Adam and Eve, Expulsion: Stowe 17, f. 29 3. Angel with hand organ: Rylands fr. 1, f. 82

dist li contes du saint Graal

4

coleurs sans

5

6

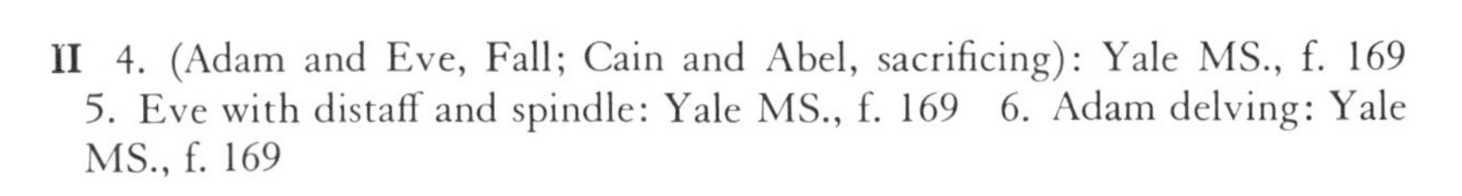

II 4. (Adam and Eve, Fall; Cain and Abel, sacrificing): Yale MS., f. 169 5. Eve with distaff and spindle: Yale MS., f. 169 6. Adam delving: Yale MS., f. 169

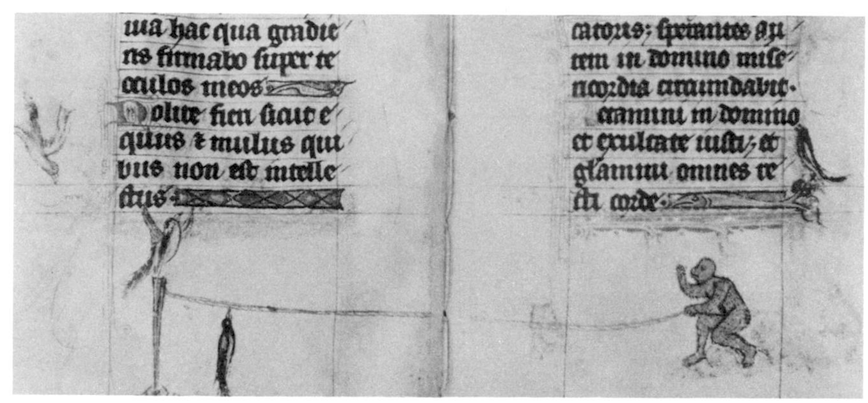
uia hac qua gradie
ris firmabo super te
oculos meos
olite fieri sicut e
quus ⁊ mulus qui
bus non est intelle
ctus
catoris: sperantes au
tem in domino mise
ricordia circumdabit.
etamini in domino
et exultate iusti; et
gloriamini omnes re
cti corde

7

do eum: et ostendam illi salu
tare meum
Bonum est confiteri dño: et
psallere nomini tuo al
tissime

8

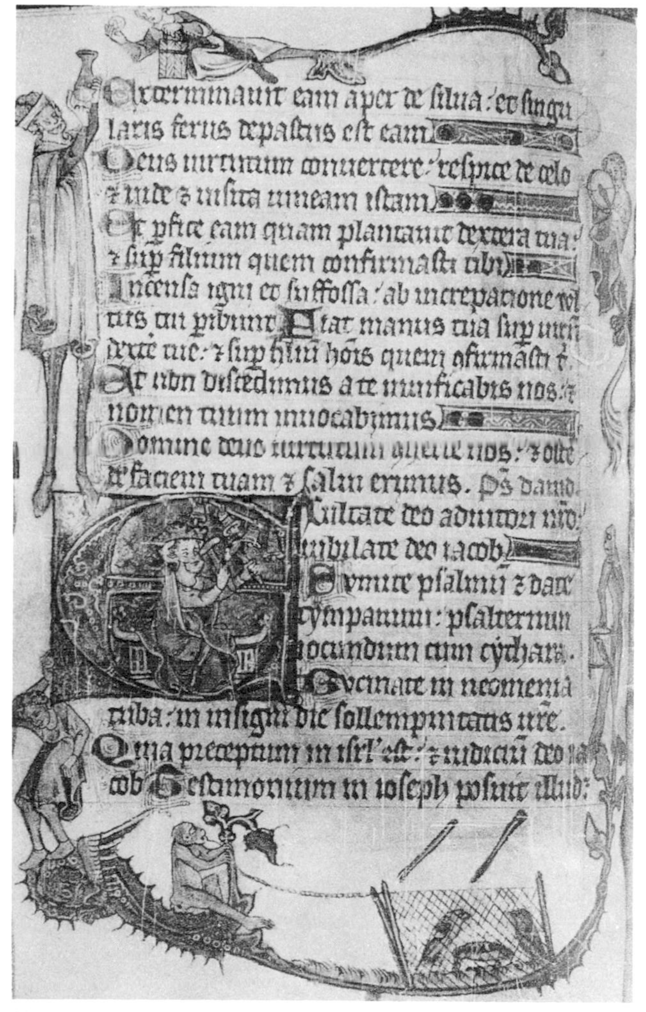
Exterminauit eam aper de silua: et singu
laris ferus depastus est eam
Deus uirtutum conuertere: respice de celo
⁊ uide ⁊ uisita uineam istam
Et perfice eam quam plantauit dextera tua:
⁊ sup filium quem confirmasti tibi
Incensa igni et suffossa: ab increpatione vul
tus tui peribunt. Fiat manus tua sup uirum
dextere tue: ⁊ sup filium hominis quem confirmasti t.
Et non discedimus a te uiuificabis nos: ⁊
nomen tuum inuocabimus
Domine deus uirtutum conuerte nos: ⁊ oste
de faciem tuam ⁊ salui erimus. Ps. Dauid.
Exultate deo adiutori nostro:
iubilate deo iacob
Sumite psalmum ⁊ date
tympanum: psalterium
iocundum cum cythara.
Buccinate in neomenia
tuba: in insigni die sollempnitatis uestre.
Quia preceptum in israel est: ⁊ iudicium deo ia
cob. Testimonium in ioseph posuit illud:

10

9

III 7. Ape and bird, snaring: Princeton 44-18, ff. 201v-202 8. Ape and bird, patting, imitating woman: Nancy 249, f. 150 9. Ape and bear, pursued by: Royal 10 E.IV, f. 151v 10. Ape and bird, snaring with clapnet; Ape with birdcage; Hybrid man with tabor; Physician and man; Initial supported by man: W. 82, f. 75v

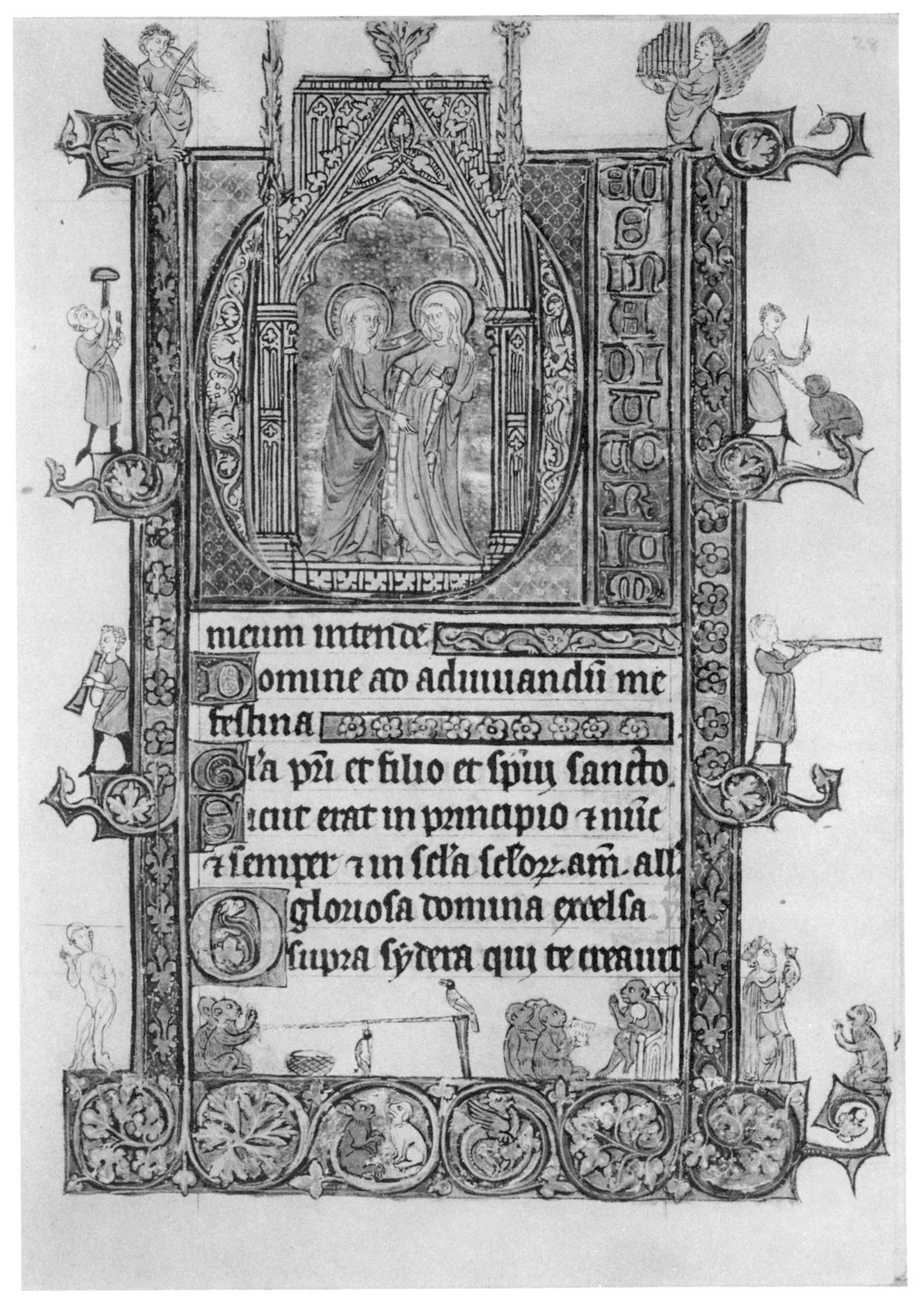
meum intende
Domine ad adiuuandū me
festina
Sicut erat in principio et nunc
O gloriosa domina excelsa
supra sydera qui te creauit

11

IV 11. Ape and bird, snaring with decoy; Hare and dog, confronted; School of apes; Physician and ape; Man with trumpet; Man and ape, training; Hybrid angel with hand organ; Hybrid angel with vielle; Man balancing basin; Man with shawm; Cleric nude: W. 104, f. 28

Septem Psalmi Penitentiales.
Our Saviour on the Cross.

12

13

14

15

V 12. Ape and fox, astride; Lion and dragon; (Grotesques); Patrons: Sir Richard Grey and Joan Fitzpayn; Hedgehog; Bear; Doe; Lion in cave; (Bird): Fitz. 242, f. 55v 13. Ape and crane: Kraus 75/88, f. 19v 14. Ape and knight: Stowe 17, ff. 79v-80 15. Ape and knight; Cock and hen: Stowe 17, f. 94v

16

17

18

19

20

VI 16. Ape and hare: Nancy 249, f. 4v 17. Ape and lion, rending: Y.T. 8, f. 197v 18, 19. Ape and lion; Lion and sheep: Royal 17 E.VII, f. 1 20. Ape and pedlar, robbing (*Roman de Renart* episode): Royal 10 E.IV, f. 149

21

22

23

24

VII 21-24. Ape and pedlar, robbing (*Roman de Renart* episode): Royal 10 E.IV, ff. 149v-151

25

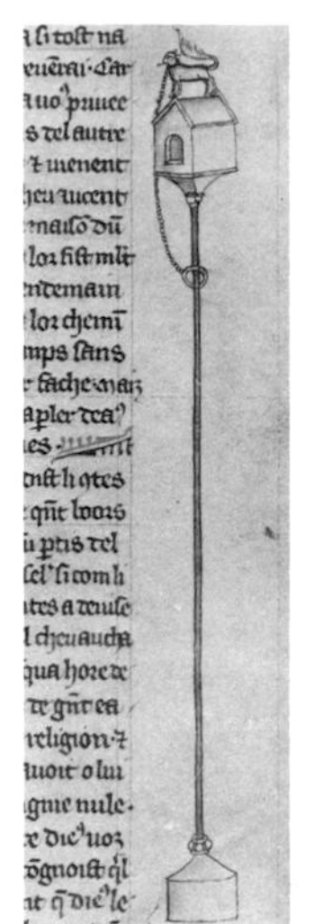

26

27

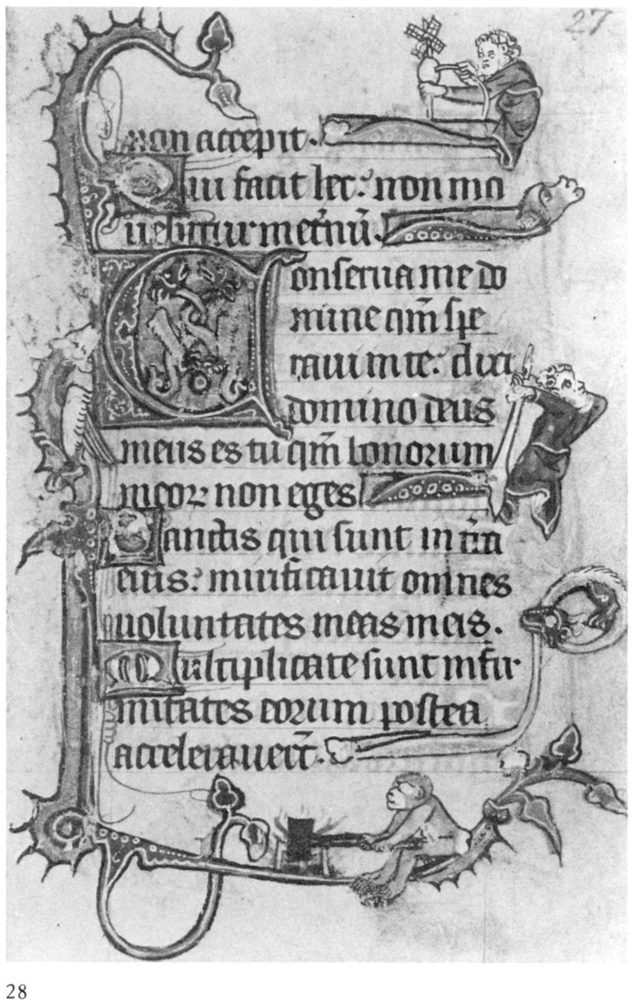

28

29

30

VIII 25. Ape and ram: Arsenal 5218, f. 55 26. Squirrel, chained: Arsenal 5218, f. 55 27. Ape and snail, fighting: BBR 9391, f. 94 28. Ape as blacksmith; Man and dragon, fighting; Windmill, toy, man with: G.K.S. 3384, f. 27 29. Ape as bishop, before altar; Putting stone, man: Trinity B.11.22, f. 4 30. Ape as cleric, patting bird, fox-cleric: Cambrai 103, f. 384

31

32

33

34

35

36

37

IX 31. Ape as falconer: Cambrai 103, f. 421 32. Ape as falconer; Man and hare, hunting: Lambeth 75, f. 1 33. Ape as king, borne by two hares: Y.T. 8, f. 295v 34. Ape as queen, in tent: Y.T. 8, f. 296 35. Ape as pedlar: Harley 6563, f. 100 36. Ape as physician, ministering to owl: Chantilly 62, f. 36v 37. Ape balancing basins; Hybrid man drinking; (Crucifixion): N.K.S. 41.8, ff. 105v-106

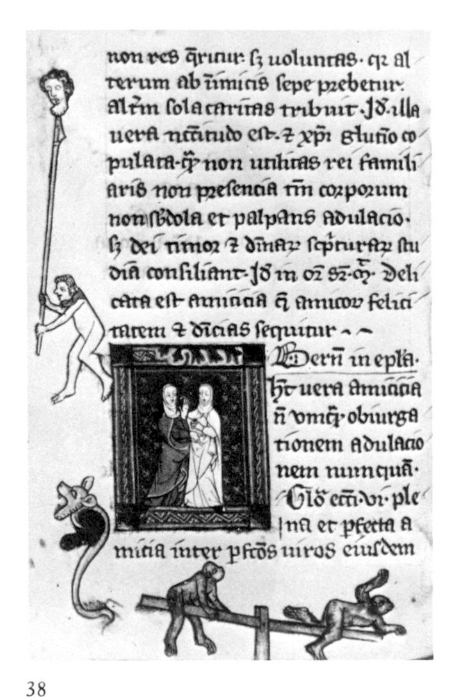

non res qriuur: s; uoluntas · cu al
terum ab inimicis sepe prebetur.
altm sola caritas tribuit · Jd · illa
uera necitudo est · & xpi glutino co
pulata · q non utilitas rei famili
aris non presencia tm corporum
non subdola et palpans adulacio ·
s; dei timor & diuinar scripturar stu
dia consiliant · Jd in or sr · cy · Deli
cata est amicicia q amicor felici
tatem & dicias sequitur ~ ~
Bern in epla ·
hr uera amicicia
n vmq · obiurga
tionem adulacio
nem nunquam ·
Glo enim · vi · ple
na et pfecta a
micitia inter pfcos uiros eiusdem

38

Ego autem mendi
cus sum et pauper dns
solicitus es mei
Adiutor meus et pro
tector meus tues ne tar
daueris.
Beatus qui intel
ligit super ege
num et pauperem
in die mala liberauit eu
dominus.
Dominus conseruet
eum et uiuificet eum: &

39

m te.

40

41

enuence delqz en siecle.
Li ciel recuntent la glorie deu: e les oures de ses mains
annuncet le firmament.
Li iorn fousmet parole: e nuit a nuit demustret science.
paroles ne sermuns: des quels ne oies les uoiz de ls.

42

tue: sanctum est templum tuu
mirabile in equitate

43

X 38. Ape balancing on seesaw; Man nude, with head of man on spear: Rothschild MS., f. 131v 39. Ape, Bestiary; Man and woman, conversing: Douce 5, f. 115v 40. Ape, Bestiary: Rutland Ps., f. 88 41. Ape, Bestiary: Yale MS., f. 203 42. Ape, Bestiary: Munich c.g. 16, f. 20 43. Apes fighting: Tournai Ps., f. 105

44

45

46

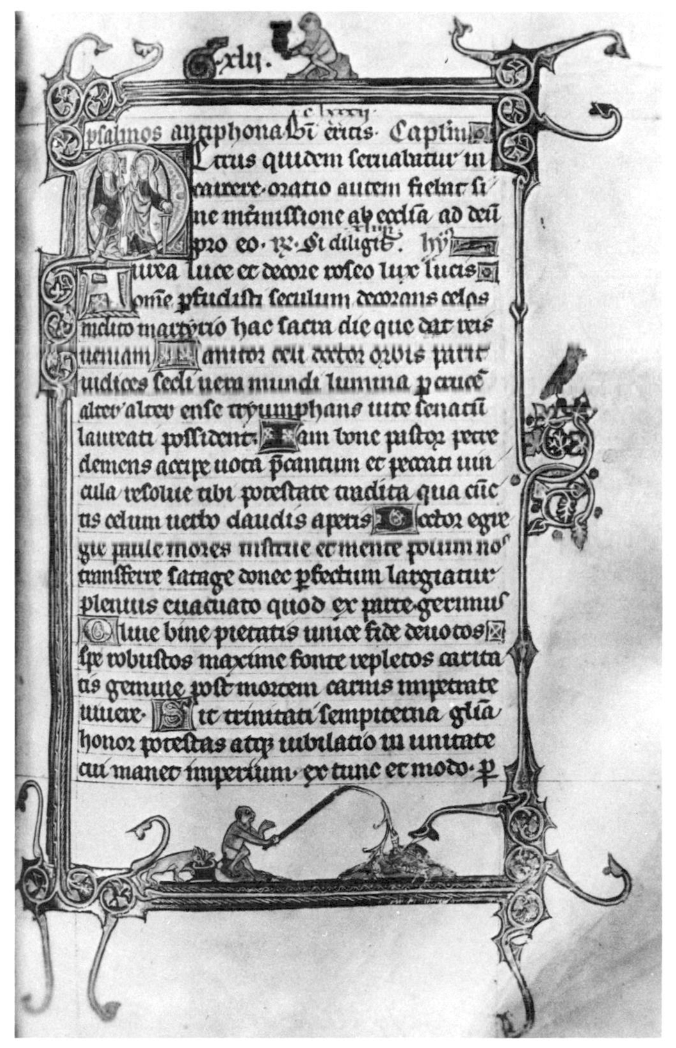

47

48

XI 44. Ape fishing, catch stolen by cat: Hague 78.D.40, f. 44 45. Ape fishing, catch stolen by fox: Arras 229, f. 655 46. Ape fishing: Melbourne 1254/3, f. 70v 47. Ape fishing, catch stolen by fox; Ape as physician, ministering to snail: Cambrai 103, f. 313 48. Ape juggling; Ass with vielle: W. 109, f. 20

49

50

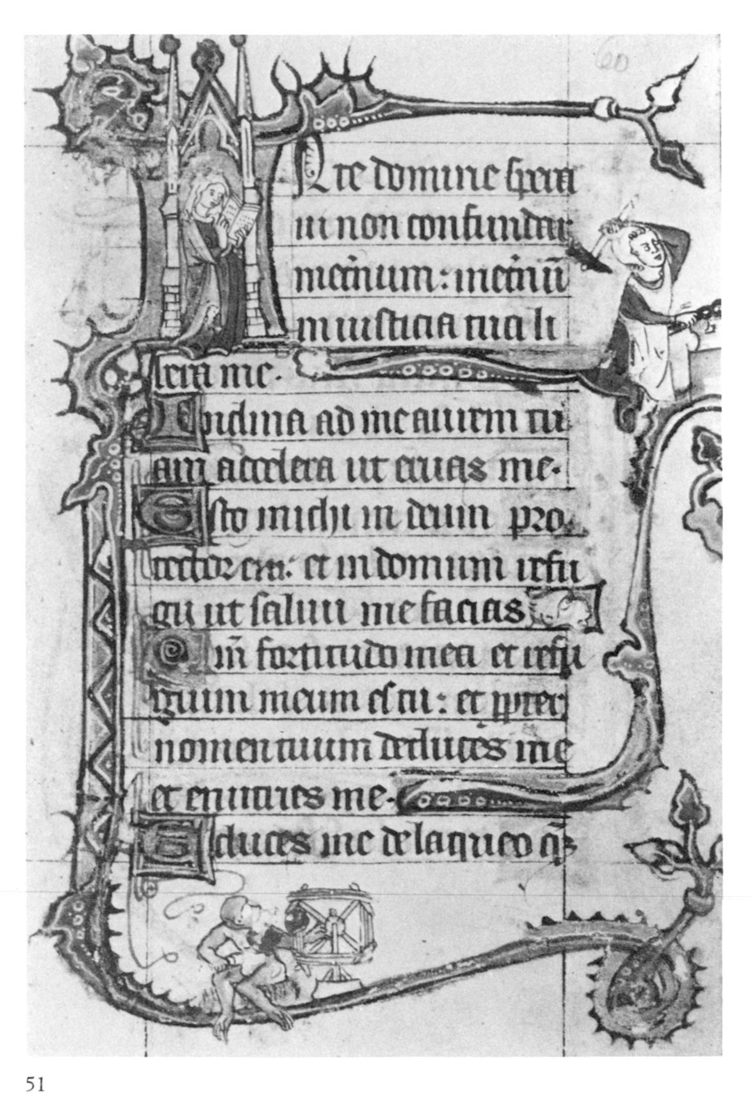

51

52

53

XII 49. Ape on hobbyhorse, man with pipe and tabor: G.K.S. 3384, f. 86v 50. Ape plowing: Add 49622, f. 15v 51. Ape spinning; Blacksmith: G.K.S. 3384, f. 60 52. Ape swimming; Beggar with basket on back; Man ringing bell; Ape winding rope: Douce 6, f. 153 53. Ape swinging: Glazier 24, f. 126v

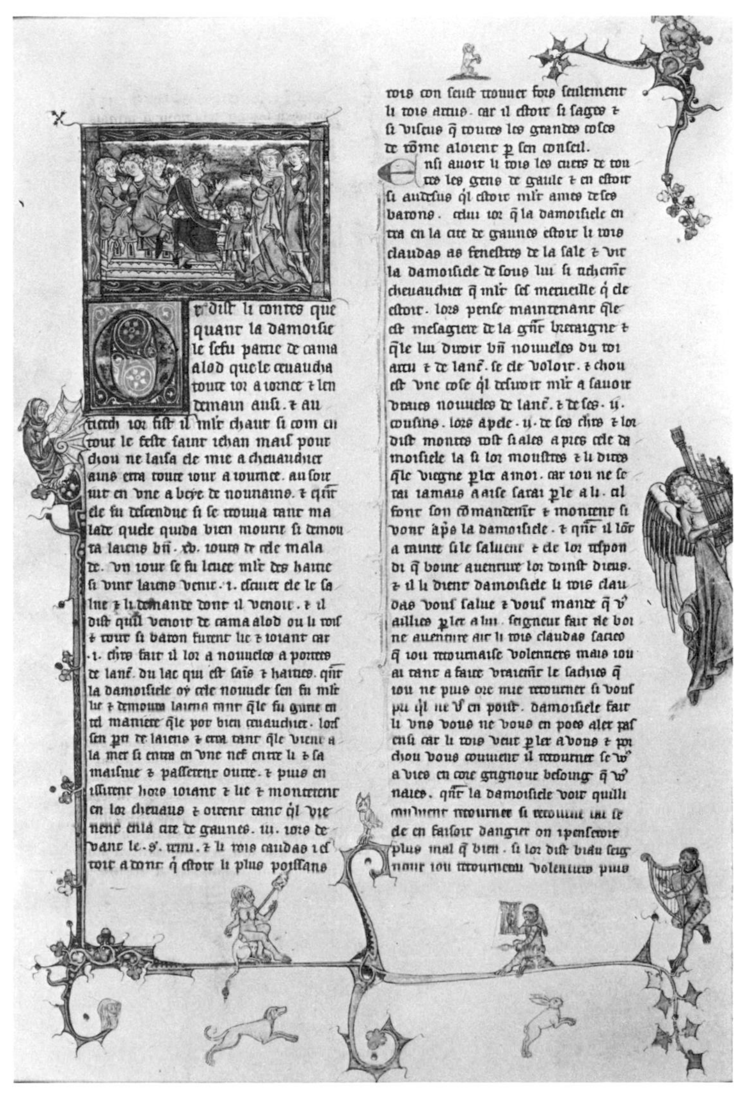

54

55

56

57

58

58a

XIII 54. Ape with distaff and spindle, ape winding wool; Dog and hare, pursuing; Ape with harp; Angel with hand organ; Hybrid man with vielle, dog dancing; Hybrid cleric with book: Rylands fr. 1, f. 82 55. Ape with hood: Tournai Ps., f. 115 56. Ape with hood, ape with bagpipe: Tournai Ps., f. 236 57. Ape with mortar and pestle, stork: Tournai Ps., f. 73 58. Ape with wheelbarrow containing ape: G.K.S. 3384, f. 145v 58a. Ape with wheelbarrow containing apes, drawn by owl: Trinity B.11.22, f. 206

59

60

61

62

63

64

65

XIV 59. Apothecary: Cracow 816, f. 101v 60. Ape with mirror: Fitz. 2-1954, f. 152v 61. Apes tilting astride birds: W. 45, f. 166 62. Ass and apes, singing at lectern: Glazier 24, f. 48 63. Ass as physician: Glazier 24, f. 76v 64. Astronomer: G.K.S. 3384, f. 126 65. Astronomer: Stowe 17, f. 205v

66

67

69

70

68

XV 66. Backgammon, men disputing: Stowe 17, f. 268v 67. Baker; Hot cockles: Cambridge Dd. 5.5, f. 280 68. Baker carrying tray on back, grotesque balancing oven: Add. 36684, f. 48 69. Baker carrying oven (flaming) on back, ape retrieving rolls: G.K.S. 3384, f. 67 70. Bandyball, apes: W. 82, f. 209v

autre si est li cors de cest liure q
piles de sapience. Si come celui
qui est estrais de tous les mem
bres de philosophie en une somme
briement. Et la premiere par
tie de cest tresor est autresi come
de deniers contans por despendre
tous iors es coses besoignables:
cest adire que le traite dou co
mencement dou siecle & de la
ancienete des vieles istores & des
establissement dou monde & de
la nature de toutes coses en
somme & ce apertient a la pre
miere science de philosophie.

qui donent a home de lit & ver
tu. Cest adire quels choses on doit
fere & quels non non & monstre
la raison por coi & ce apertient
a la segonde partie. Et la tierce
partie de philosophie cest a pratica
que & logique. La tierce partie
dou tresor est de fin or. Cest a
dire que le enseigne a home par
ler selonc la doctrine de recto
rique & coment li sires doit go
uerner ses gens qui sont sous soi
ajeisinement selonc les us as
ytaliens & tout ce apertient
a la segde science de philosophie

71

Et lors seruirent merlins
au roi artu: se li dist: Sire
la dieu merchi: vous aues
la terre deliuree de la mauuaise
gent a ceste fois: si entendes que

72

dedit filiis hominum

73

nomen domini inuocaui

74

XVI 71 Bandyball, men: BBR 10228, f. 6 72. Bandyball, men: fr. 95, f. 321 73. Banquet, Sir Geoffrey Luttrell, preparations: Add. 42130, f. 207v 74. Banquet, Sir Geoffrey Luttrell, served: Add. 42130, f. 208

75

76

77

78

79

XVII 75. Barber: G.K.S. 3384, f. 51 76. (Beast) Monster with five heads: Stowe 17, f. 101v 77. (Beast) Monster with five heads, charged by knight/centaur: Cambrai 103, f. 511 78. Beaver: Lambeth 209, f. 7v 79. Beaver, Bestiary representation: Munich c.g. 16, f. 15

80

81

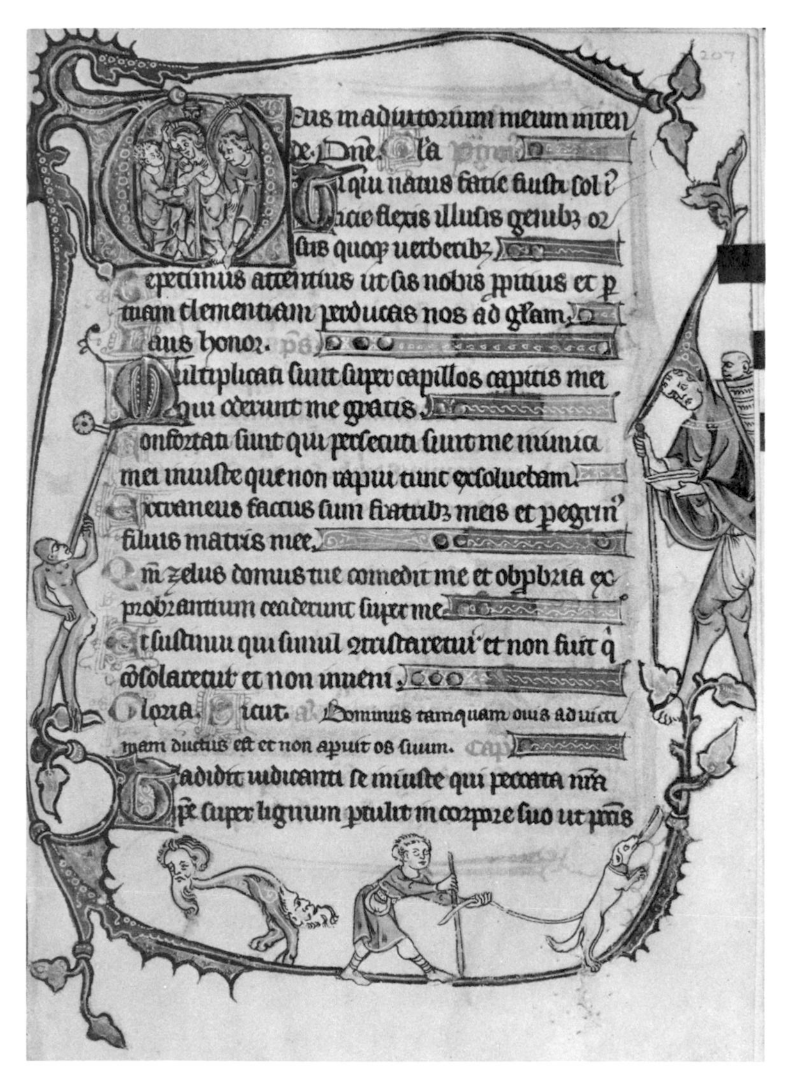

82

83

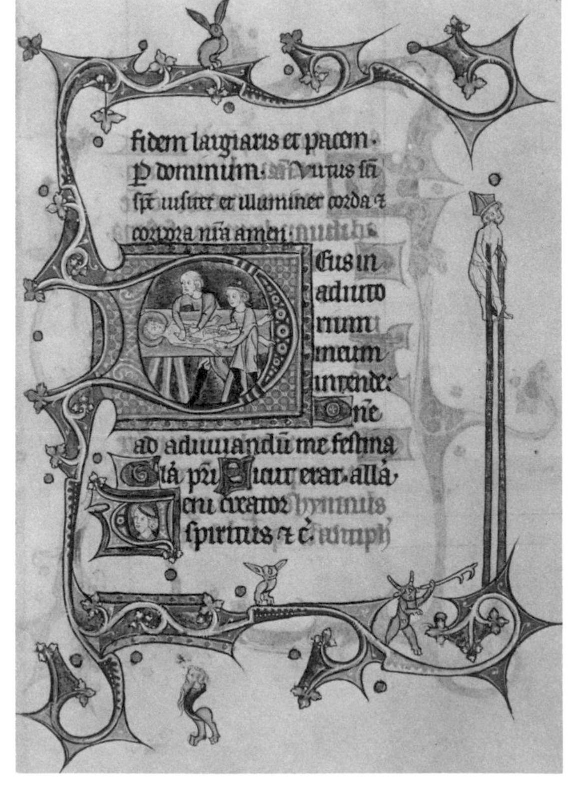

84

XVIII 80. Bee and dog, stinging: Stowe 17, f. 48 81. Bee and hare, stinging; Capricorn: W. 37, ff. 158v-159 82. Beggar with basket on back containing ape; Ape with pinwheel: W. 82, f. 207 83. Beehive, Bestiary representation: Munich c.g. 16, f. 57 84. Bishop on stilts: W. 90, f. 153

85

86

87

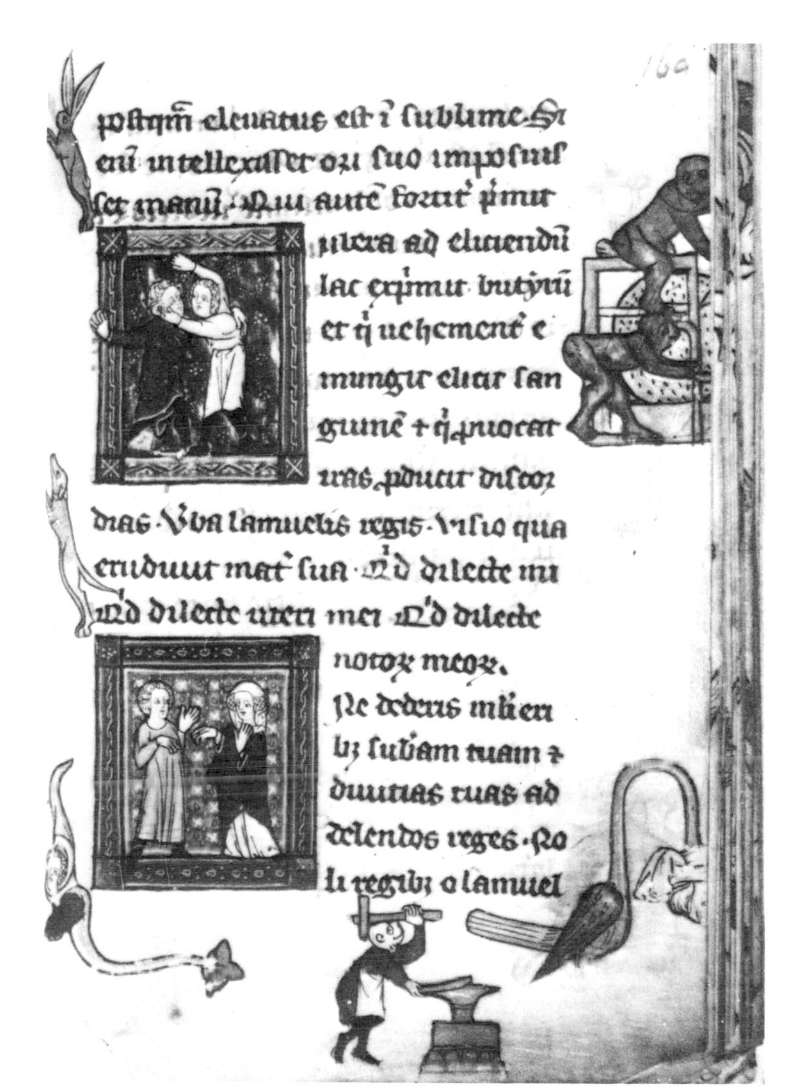

88

89

XIX 85. Bishop: Kraus 75/88, f. 200 86. Bishop (or abbot) and nun: Add. 49622, f. 117 87. Bishop and ass, astride: Yale MS., f. 104v 88. Blacksmith; Ape turning grindstone; Dog and hare, pursuing: Rothschild MS., f. 169 89. Bowls, men: Troyes 1905, f. 171

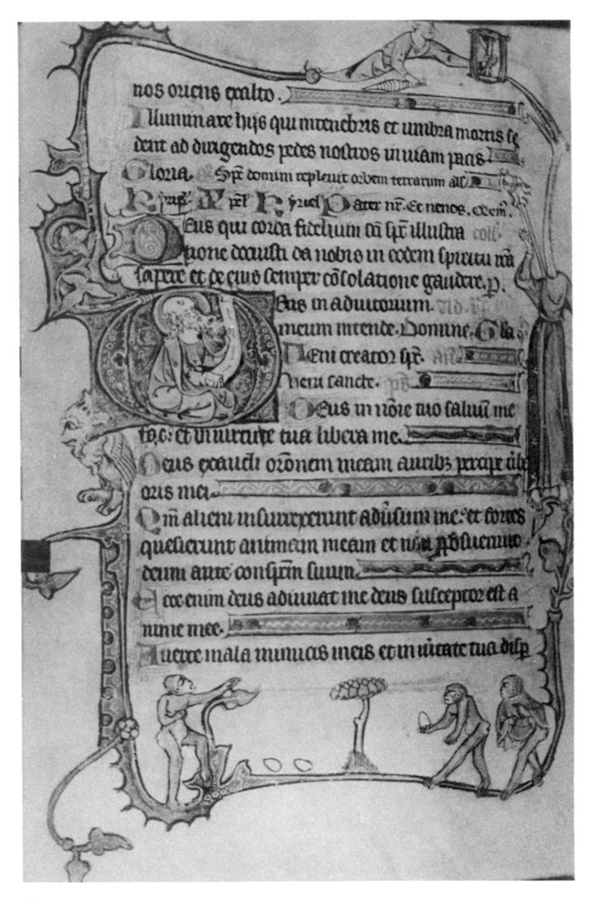

90

92

93

91

94

95

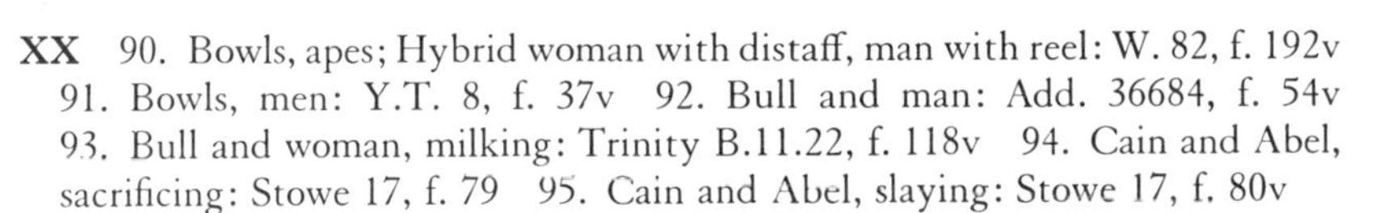

XX 90. Bowls, apes; Hybrid woman with distaff, man with reel: W. 82, f. 192v 91. Bowls, men: Y.T. 8, f. 37v 92. Bull and man: Add. 36684, f. 54v 93. Bull and woman, milking: Trinity B.11.22, f. 118v 94. Cain and Abel, sacrificing: Stowe 17, f. 79 95. Cain and Abel, slaying: Stowe 17, f. 80v

96

98

97

99

100

101

XXI 96. Castle of Love attacked by knights: Add. 42130, f. 75v 97. Castle occupied by women: Yale MS., f. 18 98, 99. Castle attacked by mice, defended by cat: Harley 6563, ff. 71v-72. 100. Cat and mouse, baited by hare: Nancy 249, f. 234v 101. Cat and mouse, hanged by: Rutland Ps., f. 61

102

104

103

105

106

107

XXII 102. Checkers or chess, man (monseigneur Jehan de Lens) and woman: latin 10435, f. 61 103. Chess, men: Rutland Ps., f. 78v 104. Chess, man and woman; Ape playing jawbone with plectrum: Bodley 264, f. 112 105. Chess, men (loser beset by devil); Hybrid men fighting: Stowe 17, f. 111v; Woman with vielle, dog and man dancing; Knight and lion, fighting: Stowe 17, f. 112; 106. Child stolen by ape, replaced by ape in cradle: Add. 10292, f. 76 107. Child stolen by dog(?): W. 87, f. 34

108

109

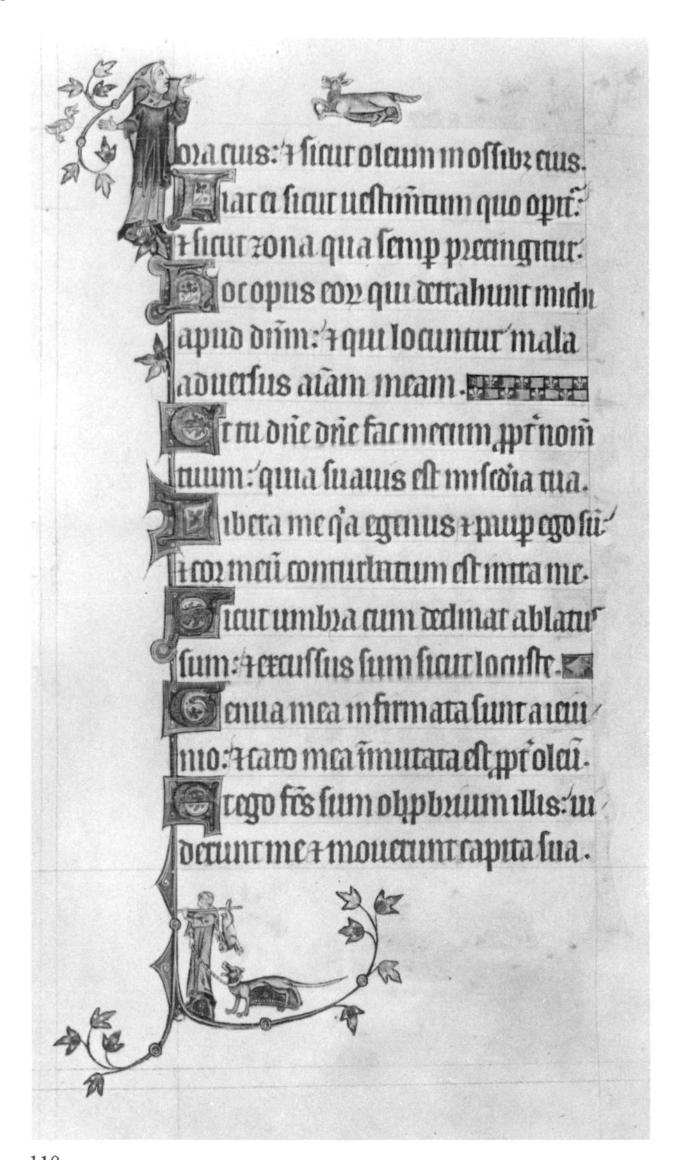

110

111

112

XXIII 108. Child stolen by lion; Knights tilting; Knight with helmet before knight with spear and shield: Rylands lat. R.117, f. 9 109. Cleric at lectern: Add. 49622, f. 68 110. Cleric and hare; Cleric and fox, duck at left: Add. 49622, f. 145v 111. Cleric(?) and man, slashing shoulder of: Add. 49622, f. 40 112. Cleric and nun, hearing confession of, two men pointing: Stowe 17, ff. 190v-191

113

114

115

116

117

XXIV 113. Cleric and woman, emptying purse before: Add 49622, f. 95 114. Cleric and woman in stocks (Virgin, miracles of: sacristan and knight's lady): Royal 10 E.IV, f. 187 115. Cleric and woman (fabliau?): W. 109, f. 39 116. Cleric and woman; Cleric with book: latin 13260, f. 130 117. Cleric playing organ: BBR 9961-62, f. 66

XXV (opposite page) 118. Cleric playing organ; Woman with birdcage; Man with bagpipe balancing on woman's shoulders: BBR 9961-62, f. 66 119. Cleric preaching: G.K.S. 3384, f. 132v 120. Cleric with distaff, cat playing with spindle: Cloisters 54.1.2, f. 51 121. Cleric with distaff and spindle; (Squirrel): Stowe 17, f. 113 122. Cleric(s) at lectern: Hague 78.D.40, f. 41v

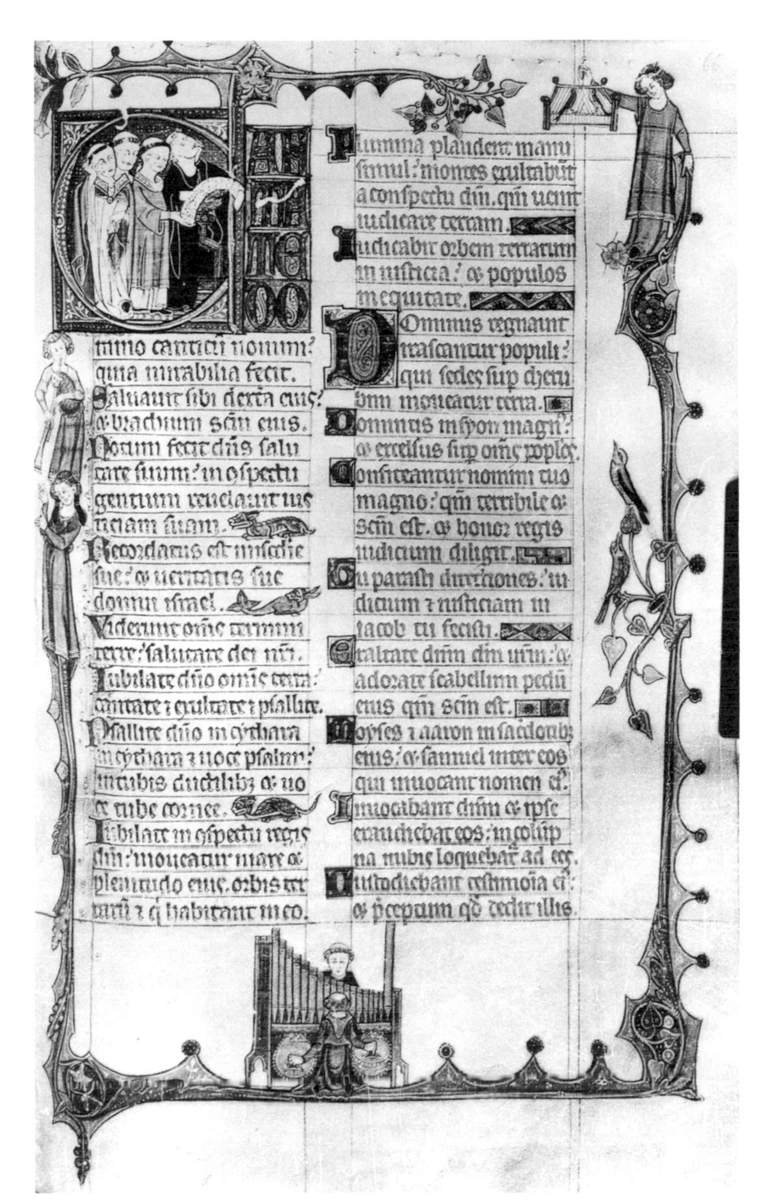

118

119

120

121

122

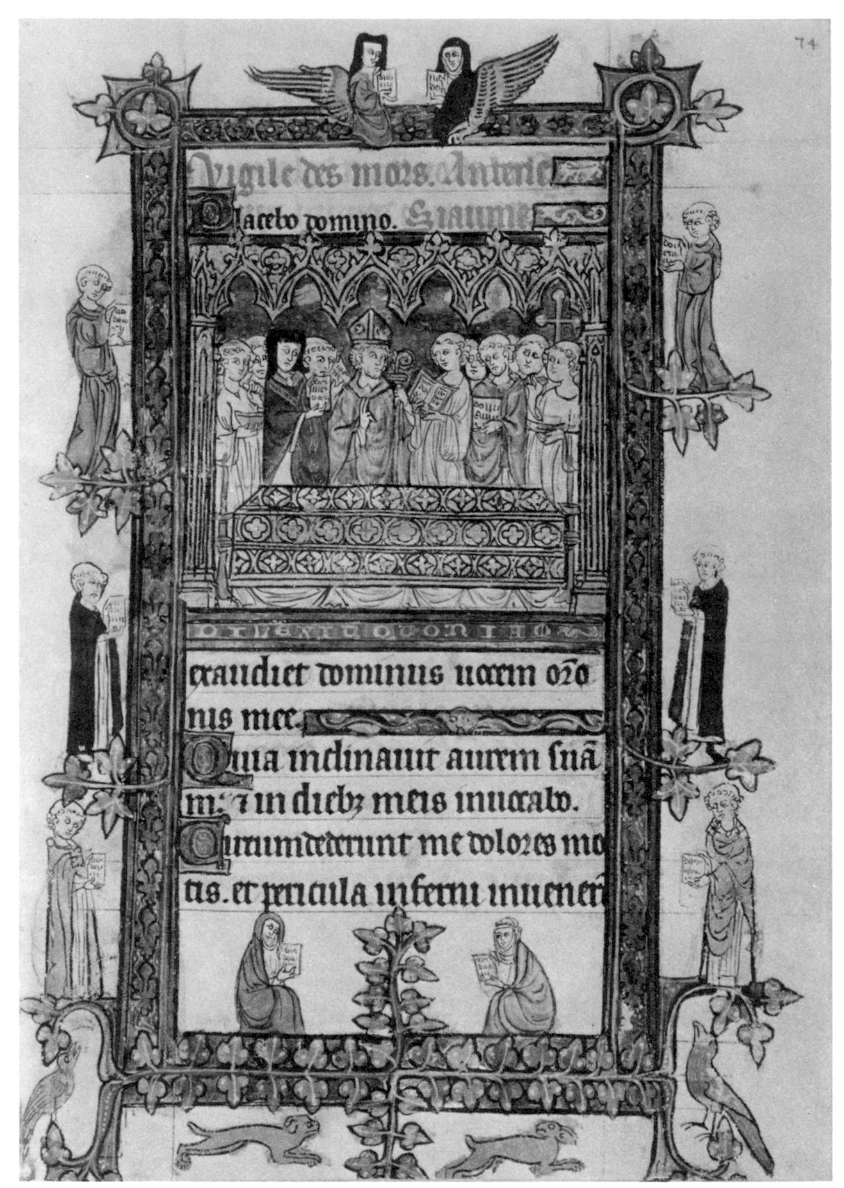

123

124

XXVI 123. Cleric(s) with book(s); Nun(s) with book(s); Hybrid nun(s) with book(s): W. 104, f. 74 124. Clubkayles, ape: Tournai Ps., f. 28v

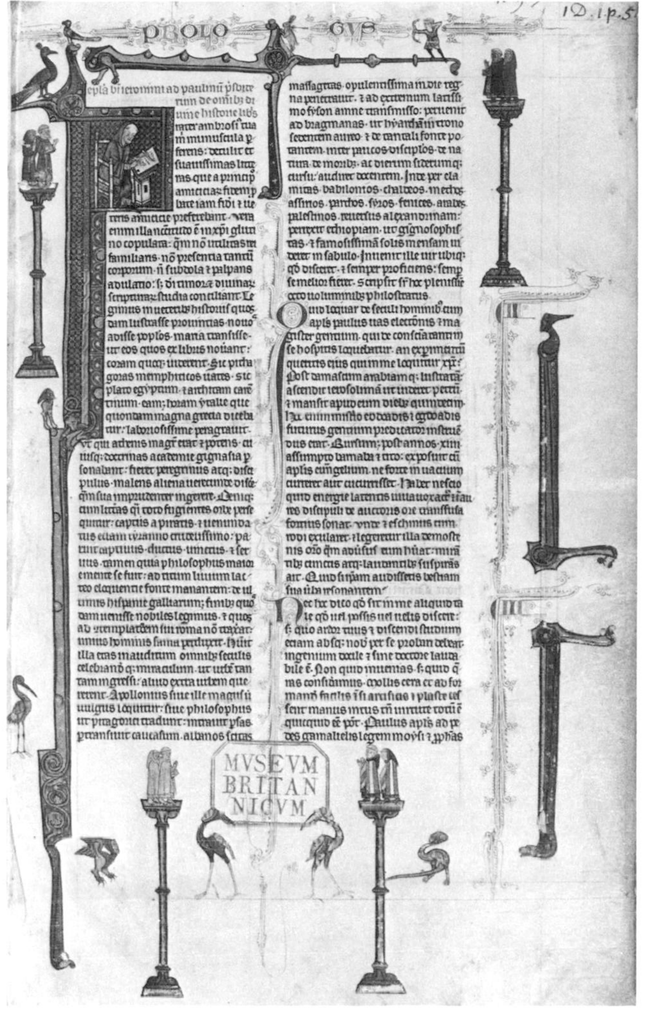
MVSEVM
BRITAN
NICVM

125

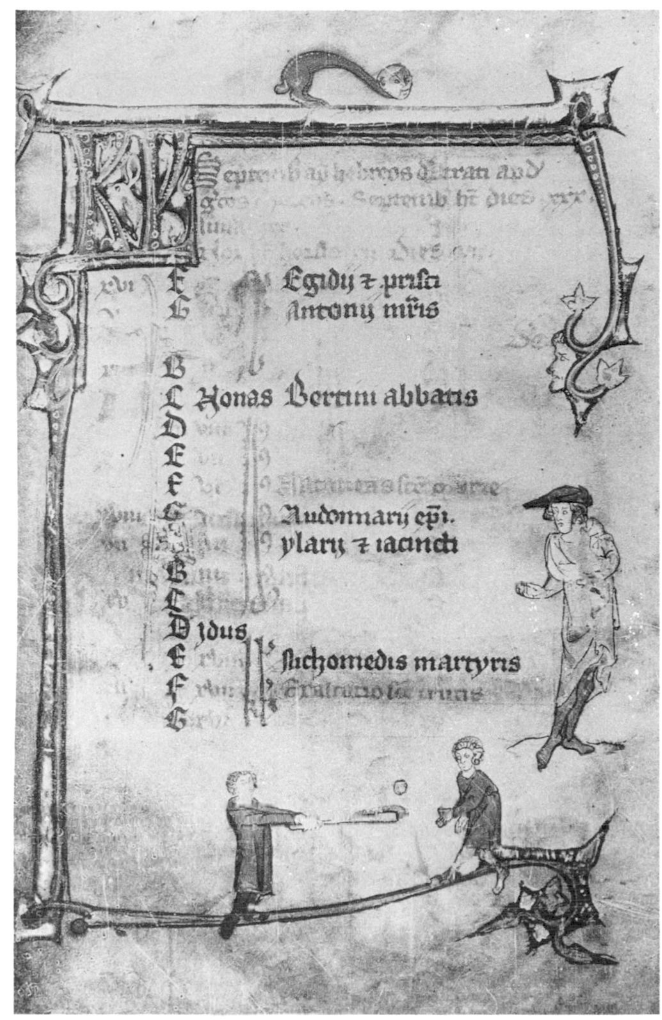
Egidy ⁊ prisci
Antony mris
Jonas Bertini abbatis
Audomari epi.
ylari ⁊ iacinchi
Idus
Nichomedis martyris

126

euant porter les armes ⁊ mener les del

127

fiert laciano; que lescu li fait fendre
e plus hardi des lo; ⁊ si estoit le mendre
ies ert othelerie el champ le fist estendre
i la mort abatu lame li estuet rendre
ses vaches garder ne porta mes entendre

128

XXVII 125. Cleric(s) on column(s); Man and hare, hunting with bow and arrow; Peacock: Royal 1 D.I, f. 1 126. Club-ball, men; Man sowing: Schilling MS., September 127, 128. Man nude with wheelbarrow containing nuns; Club-ball, clerics and nuns: Bodley 264, f. 22

129

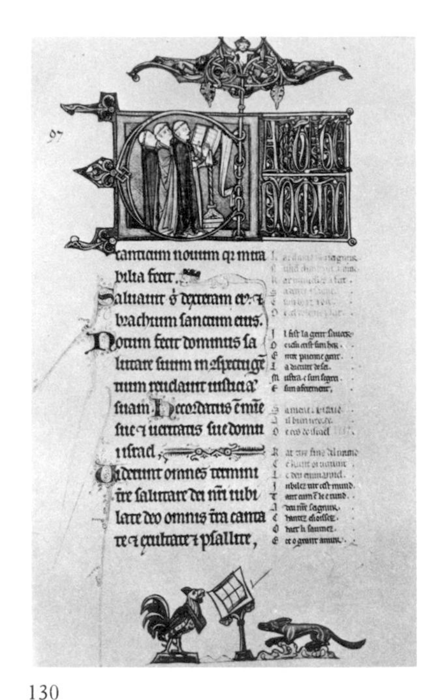

130

131

132

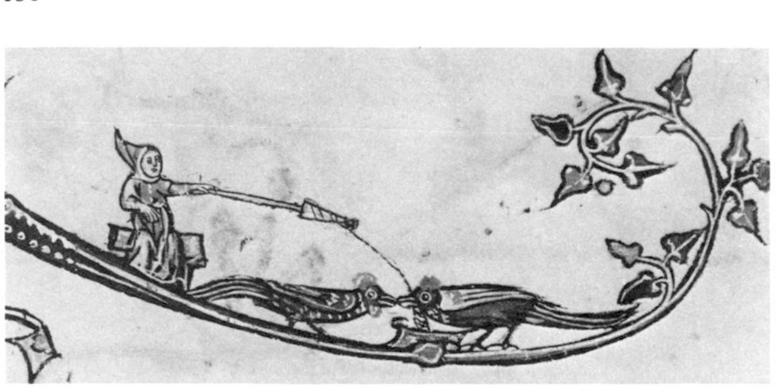

133

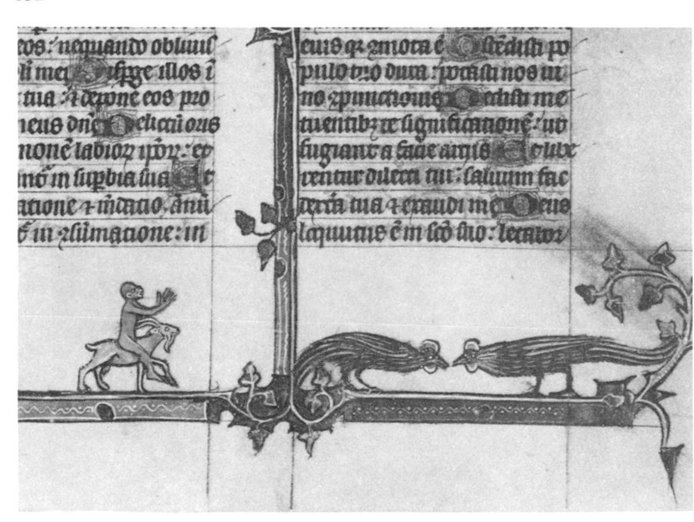

134

XXVIII 129. Coach containing two female apes: Douce 6, f. 200v 130. Cock at lectern: Add. 50000, f. 146v 131. Cock with censer; Raven, Bestiary representation; Ape with fruit: W. 102, f. 77v 132. Cockfight: Y. T. 8, f. 335 133. Cockfight: Douce 118, f. 7v 134. Cockfight, ape astride goat applauding: latin 1029A, f. 27

135

136

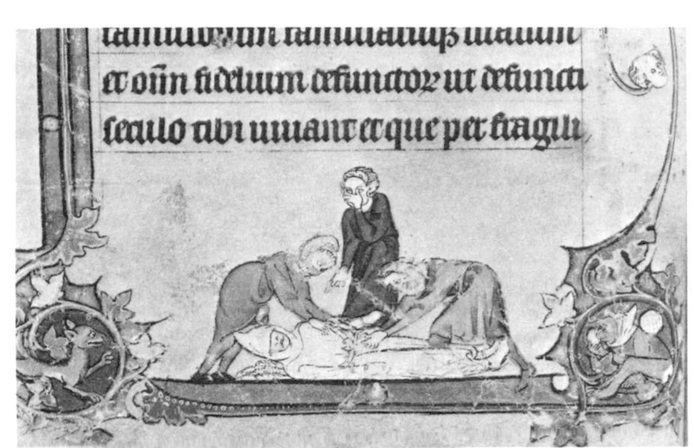

137

138

139

XXIX 135. Cockfight, hen (crowned) looking on; Hybrid woman with bagpipe; Hybrid man with mandola: Douce 131, f. 42v 136. (Cockfight comparison) Knights tilting, woman in castle looking on: Douce 131, f. 54 137. Corpse laid out: Trinity B.11.22, f. 55v 138. Crane, Bestiary representation: W. 88, f. 154v 139. Creation of animals: Stowe 17, f. 24

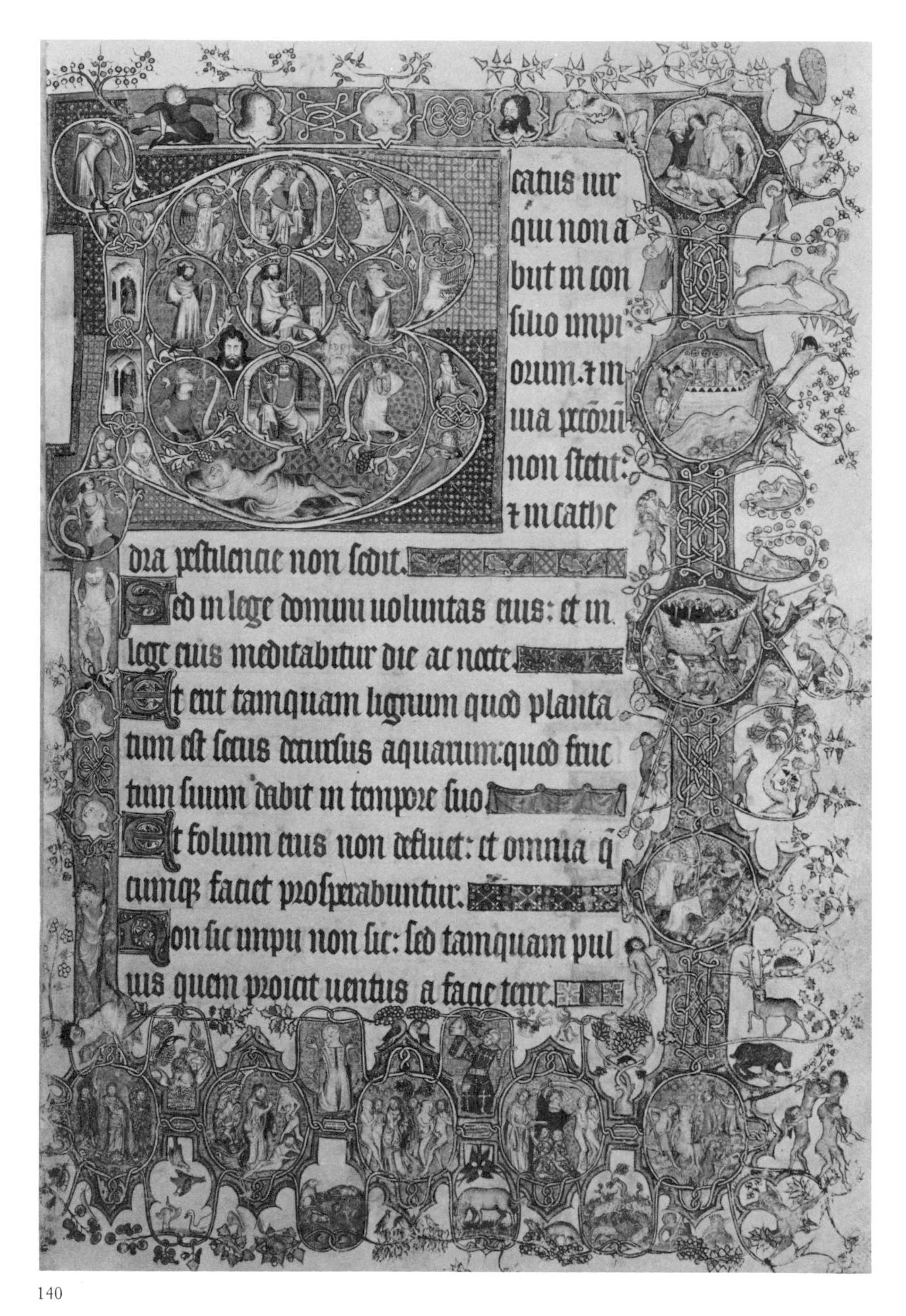
eatus uir
qui non a
biit in con
silio impi
orum. & in
uia peccatorum
non stetit:
& in cathe
dra pestilencie non sedit.
Sed in lege domini uoluntas eius: et in
lege eius meditabitur die ac nocte.
Et erit tamquam lignum quod planta
tum est secus decursus aquarum: quod fruc
tum suum dabit in tempore suo.
Et folium eius non defluet: et omnia que
cumque faciet prosperabuntur.
Non sic impii non sic: sed tamquam pul
uis quem proicit uentus a facie terre.

140

XXX 140. Creation of animals; Magpie, lion, ram; Crane, swan, falcon, duck; Adam and Eve, creation of Eve; Patrons: William de St. Omer (or Thomas, his son) and Elisabeth of Mulbarton; Rabbit burrow; Adam and Eve, temptation; Horse grazing; Adam and Eve kneeling before Creator; Adam and Eve, expulsion; Pigs; Rams butting; Adam delving, Eve spinning; Cain and Abel sacrificing; Wrestling, men pickaback; Cain and Abel, slaying; Bear; Stag; Hedgehog; Cain slain by Lamech; Noah, construction of ark; Noah entering ark; Noah, drunkenness of; Man and unicorn, killing; Peacock; Man drinking; St. Michael; Initial supported by man: Add. 39810, f. 7

141

142

143

144

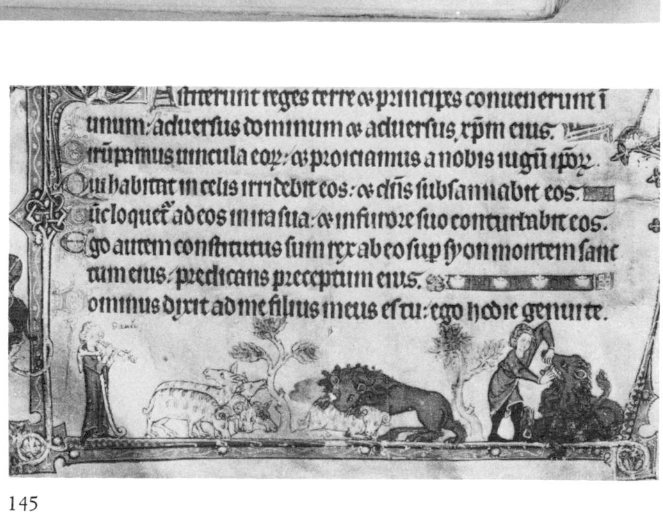

145

XXXI 141. David, life of: harping: Cambrai 87, f. 30 142. David, life of: David and Goliath: Verdun 107, f. 149v 143. David, life of: David and Goliath: W. 45, f. 16 144. David, life of: David and Bathsheba: BBR 15001, f. 63 145. David, life of: David tending sheep, rending lion: Munich c.g. 16, f. 7v

146

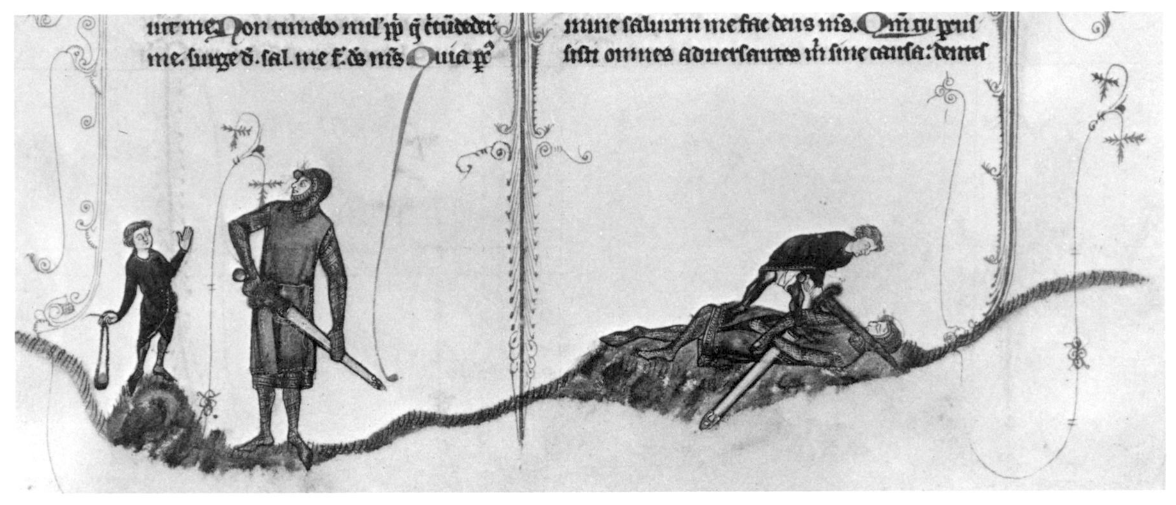

147

148

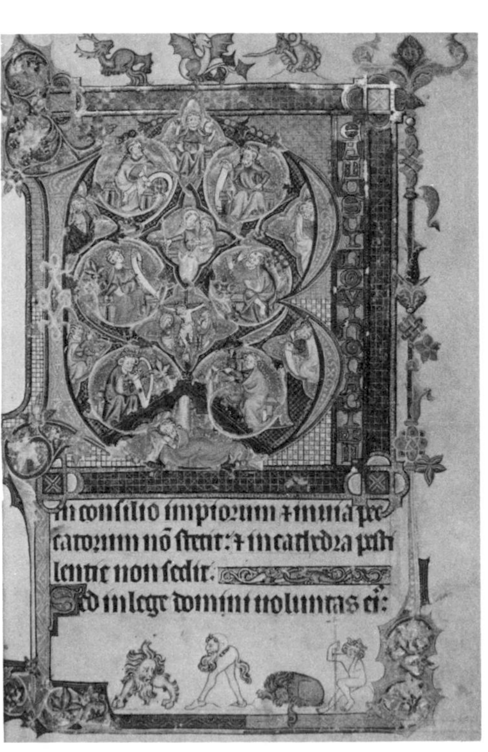

149

XXXII 146. David, life of: David and Goliath, with head of G., coming before Saul: Spencer 26, f. 17 147. David, life of: David and Goliath: Auct. D.3.2, f. 195 148. David, life of: David and Goliath: BBR 9427, f. 14 149. David, life of: David nude, lion at feet; (Grotesques): Lambeth 233, f. 15

150

151

153

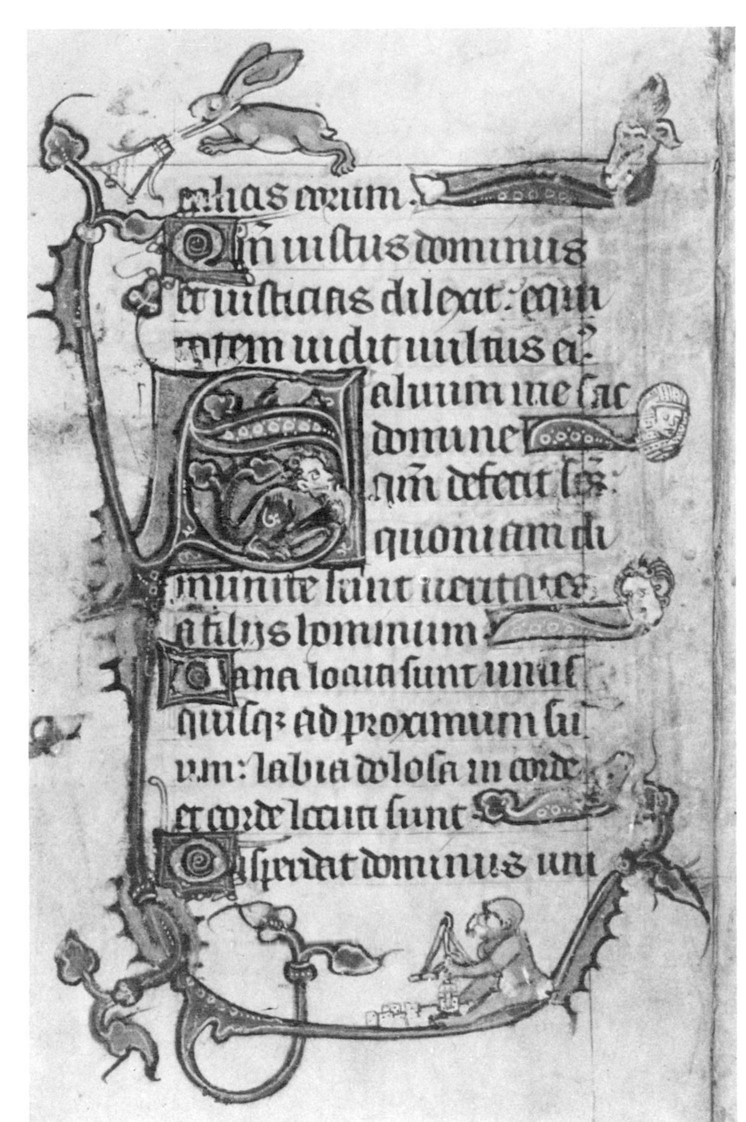

152

154

XXXIII 150. Dice, apes; Saint; Hybrid bishop: Douce 5, f. 138v 151. Dice, cleric and nun: Heidelberg Cod. Sal. 9, 51, f. 272v 152. Dice, ape weighing(?); Hare with purse: G.K.S. 3384, f. 22v 153. Dives and Lazarus: W. 759, f. 60 154. Dives (and Lazarus): death of Dives: W. 759, f. 90

155

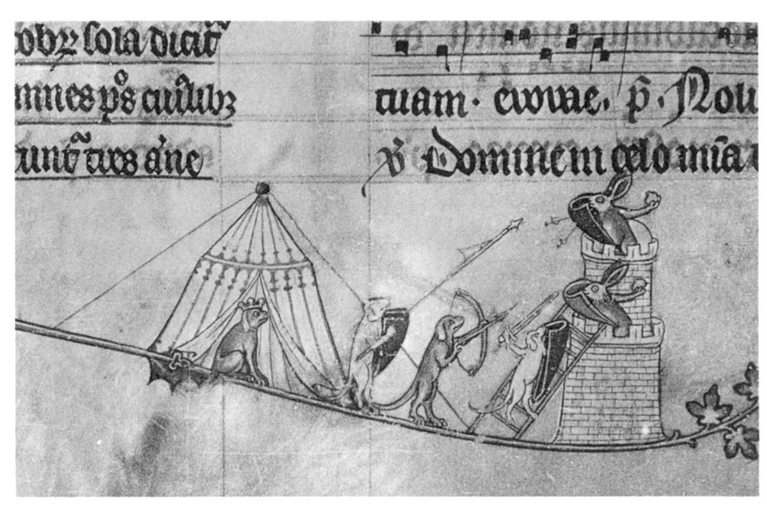

156

droit chemin

157

s uirginis.

158

159

160

XXXIV 155. Dog and hare, working bellows, hare playing organ: Add. 49622, f. 116v 156. Dog and hare, crowned, in tent, commanding attack of castle: Verdun 107, f. 137v 157. Dog and hare, pursuing hare: Yale MS., f. 286 158. Dog and hare, tilting: Y. T. 8, f. 294 159. Dog with book, hare with censer: BBR 9157, f. 419v 160. Dog with pipe and tabor: Add. 49622, f. 82

161

162

163

164

165

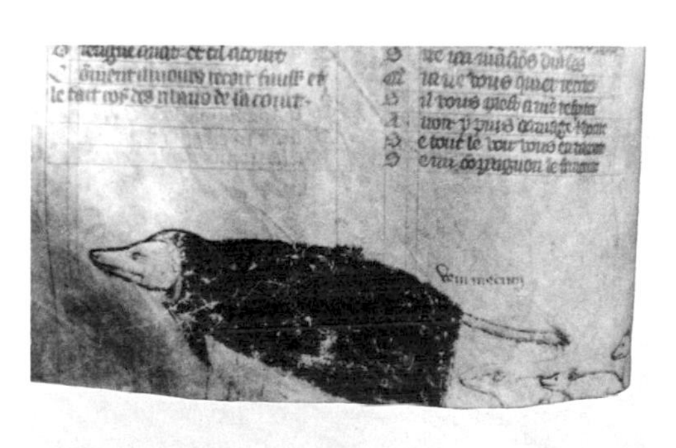

166

XXXV 161, 162. Dog with bone; Fox with ax and dagger: Harley 6563, ff. 53v-54 163. Dog with stone (ape?): Royal 10 E.IV, f. 159 164. Dominican(?) preaching: Bodley 264, f. 79 165. Dominican(?) parodied: Christ Church E.II, f. 69v 166. Dominican parodied: W. 143, f. 72v

167

168

169

170

171

172

XXXVI 167. Elephant and castle: latin 14284, f. 18 168. Elephant and castle, parodied(?): Fitz. 2-1954, f. 25v 169. Elephant and castle: Fitz. 298, f. 26 170. Elephant and castle (in Bestiary cycle): Munich c.g. 16, f. 22 171. Epifagus, fighting: Add. 17868, f. 156 172. Fables: fox, raven, and cheese: Yale MS., f. 238

173

enedictus domi
ri custodiam m

174

175

176

er uero letabitur in de
buntur omnes qui i
eo: quia obstructum
ouentium iniqua.
raudi deus oratio
am cum deprecor

177

Si se vit se
ne pucele.
ne. & auoit
la feme ou
tost cele ch

178

XXXVII 173. Fables: fox, raven, and cheese: Rothschild MS., f. 116 174. Fables: fox and stork, Parts I and II: BBR 9427, f. 62v 175. Fables: fox and stork, Part I: Add. 24681, f. 87 176. Fables: Fox and stork, Part II; Fox as tradesman: W. 109, f. 82 177. Fables: fox and stork, Part II: W. 45, f. 104 178. Fables: fox and stork, Part II: Yale MS., f. 27v

179

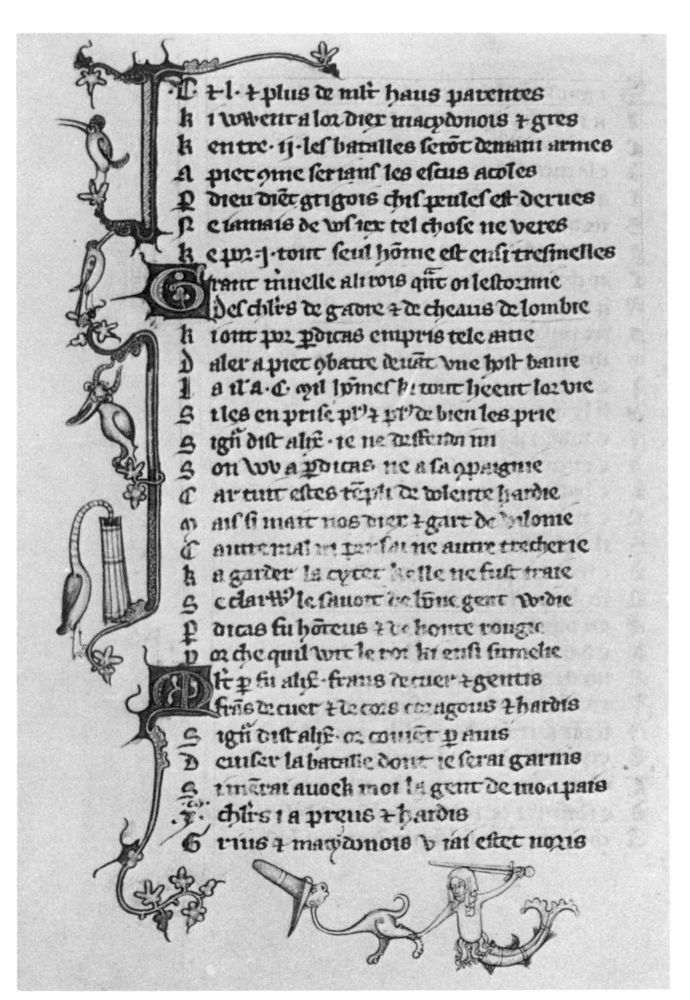

180

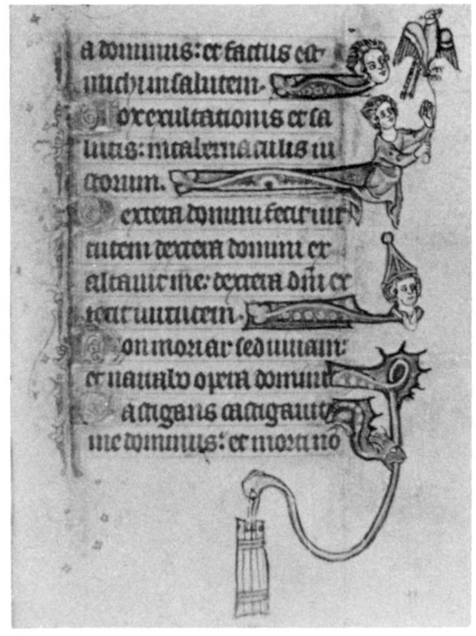

181

182

XXXVIII 179. Fables: fox and stork, Part II; Man, nude, seated on shoulders of man: Glazier 24, f. 110v 180. Fables: fox and stork, Part II; Mermaid and hybrid beast: Glazier 24, f. 101v 181. Fables: fox and stork, Part II: Douce 6, f. 92 182. Falconer, seated; Lion with vielle; Angel with hand bells: Verdun 107, f. 26

183

184

185

186

187

188

XXXIX 183. Falconer, crowned, nude, tailed: Yale MS., f. 363 184. Fishmonger: G.K.S. 3384, f. 49 185. Fishmonger: W. 759, f. 108 186. Fool before David: BBR 9391, f. 31v 187. Fool with belled hood and bauble: Add. 42130, f. 167 188. Fool: Burney 345, f. 70

189

bi hostiam laudis

190

191

192

193

194

195

XL 189. Fox and cock: W. 88, f. 155 190. Fox and cock: Hague 78.D.40, f. 31 191. Fox and geese, hanged by (*Roman de Renart* episode): Royal 10 E.IV, f. 49 192. Fox and hare, confronted: BBR 9961-62, f. 94 193. Fox and hare: C.B. 61, f. 61 194. Fox and hare: BBR 10607, f. 86 195. Fox and hare: Yale MS., f. 133v

196

197

198

199

200

201

XLI 196. Fox and ram as clerics: Hague 78.D.40, f. 25 197. Fox as Franciscan, wolf as Dominican, kneeling before crowned lion seated on column holding scroll: "jalusie, orgueul, envie": Hague 78.D.40, f. 26 198. Fox as knight (crusader?): W. 90, f. 26 199. Fox and fowl, preaching to: Stowe 17, f. 84 200, 201. Fox, Bestiary representation: Royal 2 B.VII, ff. 99v-100

202

203

204

205

206

207

208

XLII 202. Fox and fowl, preaching to: Rutland Ps., f. 98v 203. Fox and fowl, preaching to: Royal 2 B.VII, f. 157v 204. Fox with harp: Fitz. 2-1954, f. 158 205. Franciscans: Y.T. 13, f. 181 206. Frog-in-the-middle: W. 109, f. 53 207. Frog-in-the-middle: Princeton 44-18, f. 181 208. Frog-in-the-middle: Montpellier H.196, f. 88

209

210

211

212

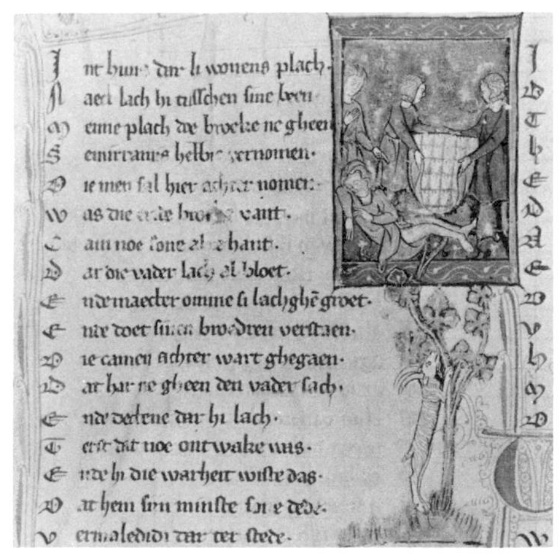

213

XLIII 209. Frog-in-the-middle: latin 14284, f. 63 210. Frog-in-the-middle; Woman with mirror: Douce 6, f. 97v 211. Giant and knight; Man and lion, carried by: Add. 24686, f. 17 212. Giant before castle; Man and cock: Royal 10 E.IV, f. 89 213. Goat standing on hind legs, feeding: BBR 15001, f. 9

214

215

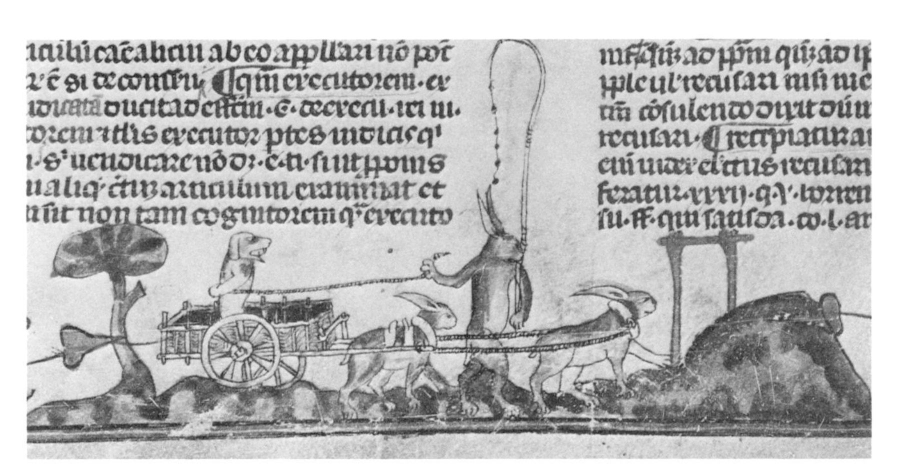

217

218

216

XLIV 214. Goat with astrolabe, fox with celestial globe, ape with pillar sundial, bear and ram with sextant: Burney 275, f. 390v 215. Handball, man and woman: Douce 5, f. 123 216. Hare and dog; Ape and unicorn; Man with club; Man and woman kissing: Douce 5, f. 177 217. Hare and dog, capturing, driving to gallows: Royal 10 E.IV, f. 63v 218. Hare and bear, training: Add. 49622, f. 71v

219

220

221

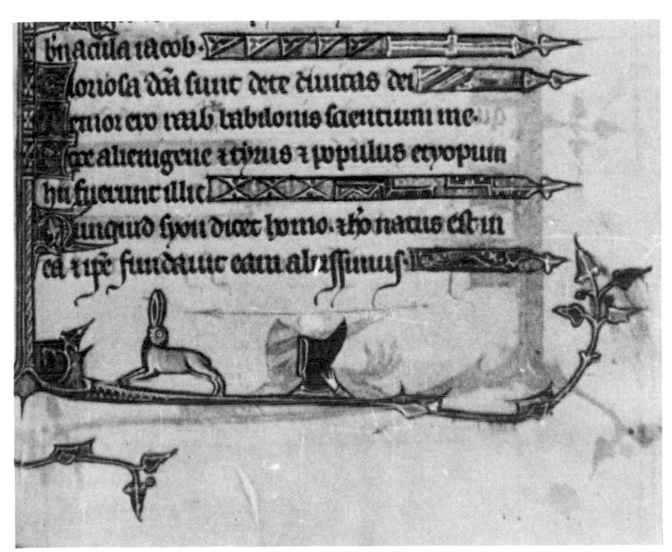

222

223

224

XLV 219. Hare and dog, pursued by: Melbourne 1254/3, f. 94 220. Hare and dog, pursued by: Add. 49622, f. 202v 221. Dog running into hood: Melbourne 1254/3, f. 42 222. Hare running out of or away from hood: Douce 118, f. 97 223. Hare and lion, devoured by: Trinity B.11.22, f. 155v 224. Hare and lion, hunting with spear: Y.T. 8, f. 283

225

226

227

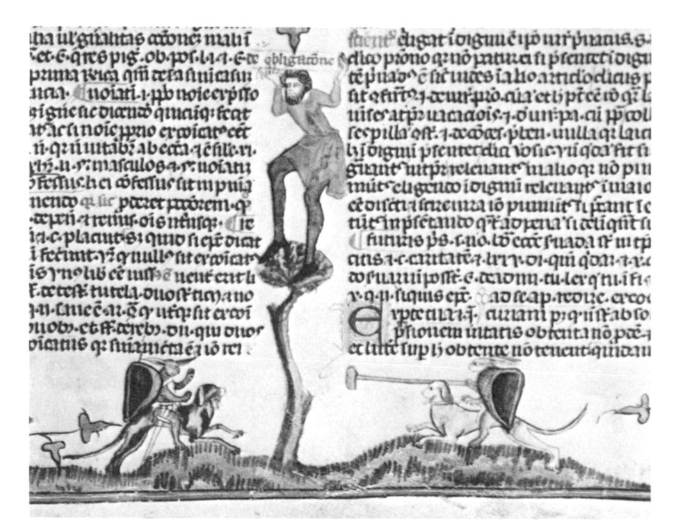

228

229

XLVI 225. Hare and lion, astride, fighting man/snail: Verdun 107, f. 89 226. Hare as cleric, with book at lectern flanked by hybrid king and hybrid bishop: BBR 329-41, f. 54 227. Hare and offspring: Y.T. 8, f. 264 228. Hares tilting (man in tree): Royal 10 E.IV, f. 70 229. Hare as fool(?): Tournai Ps., f. 92

Quoniam tu dominus altissimus
super omnem terram: nimis exalta
tus es super omnes deos.

230

231

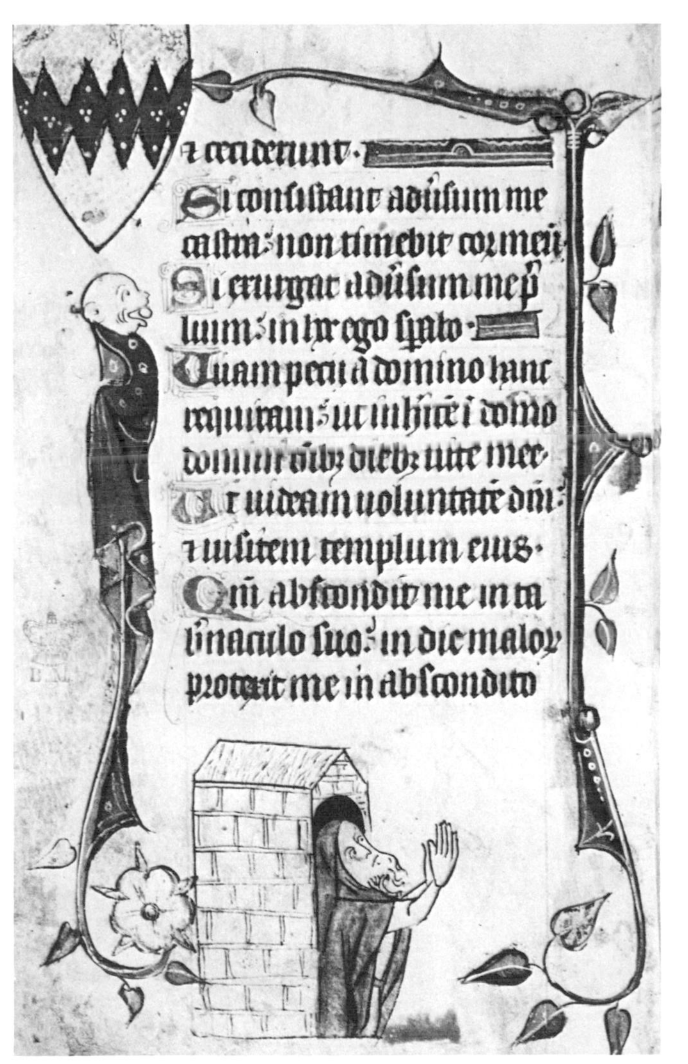

232

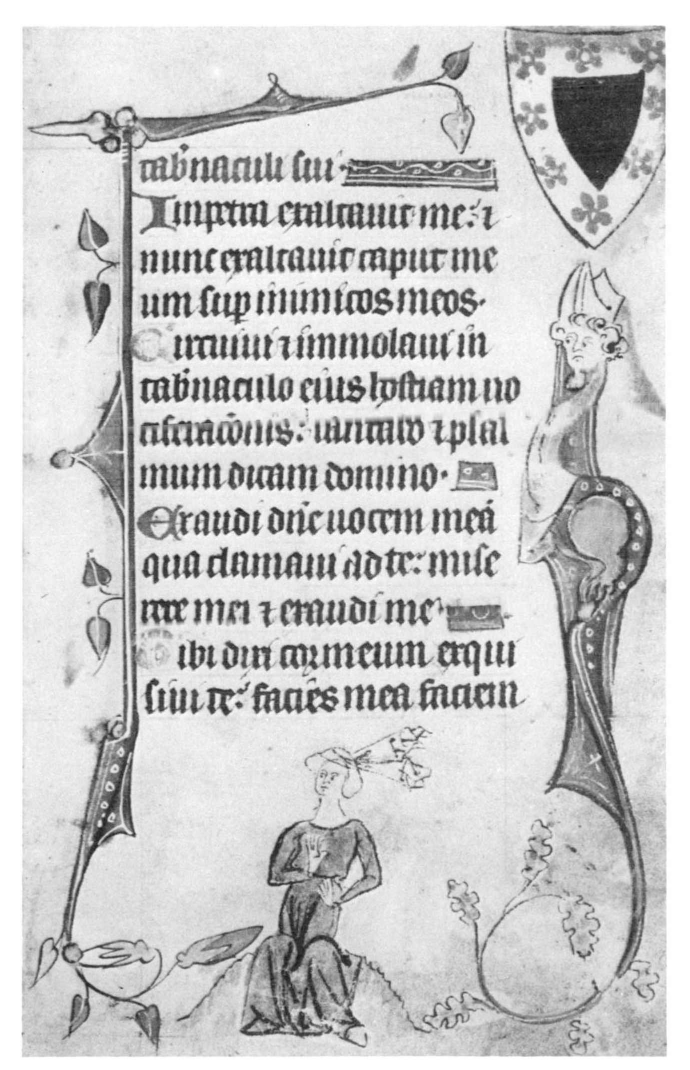

233

XLVII 230. Haywain: Add. 42130, f. 173v 231. Hedgehog: L.M. 13, f. 41v 232, 233. Hermit pleading with woman; (Hybrid beast and hybrid bishop): Harley 6563, ff. 67v-68

agnificata est
celos mia tua
nubes ueritas
re sup celos de
omnē terram
ueit utiq;
iustitiam lo
quimini recta
iudicate filii

234

longues durees afin que par semblables guises
ils puissent les leur terres deffendre a gouuner:
que il conquistrent la rondesce du monde
Et que pour ce aleurs fais merueilleus

235

seullent entrer

236

dibz: & nobiles eor in
manicis ferreis

237

238

XLVIII 234. Hercules(?): G.K.S. 3384, f. 106 235. Hercules and Cacus: Ste. Gen. 777, f. 7 236. Hybrid bishop(s) investing bishop: Yale MS., f. 133v 237. Hybrid cleric with book: W. 88, f. 173 238. Hybrid clerics: G.K.S. 393, f. 301v.

239

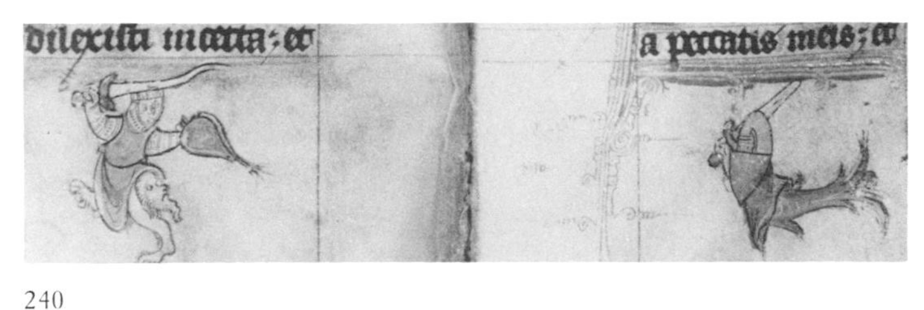

240

241

XLIX 239. Hybrid man as falconer; Squirrel with nut; Hybrid man and butterfly; Hybrid man and snail: Douce 366, f. 38 240. Hybrid knight and merman/knight: Princeton 44-18, ff. 191v-192 241. Hybrid knight and snail; David, life of: David issuing from water: BBR 9391, f. 39

243

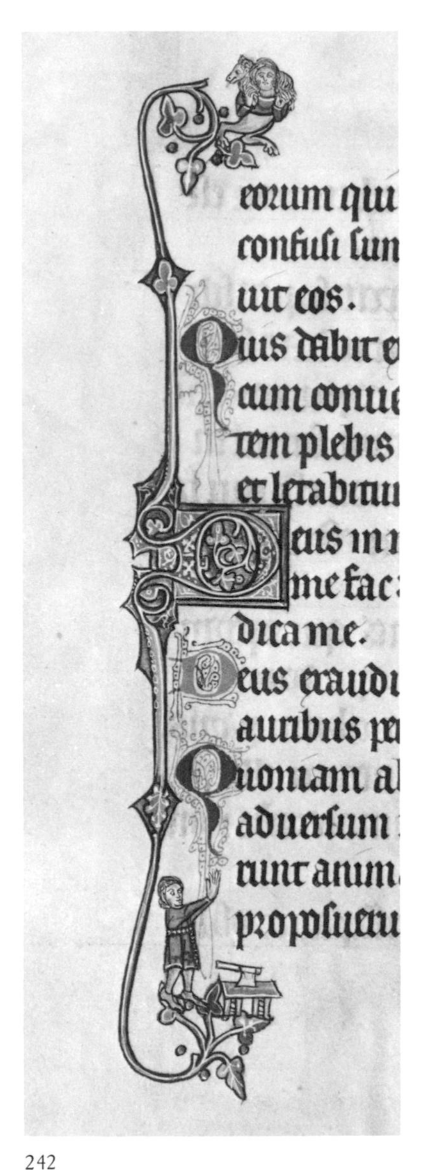

242

244

245

246

L 242. Hybrid man and sheep; Man at table: W. 45, f. 91v 243. Hybrid man as falconer: M. 796, f. 49v 244. Hybrid man and man nude (physician?): W. 37, ff. 54v-55 245. Hybrid man with sword: Yale MS., f. 223 246. Hybrid man with mirror and comb: fr. 95, f. 295v

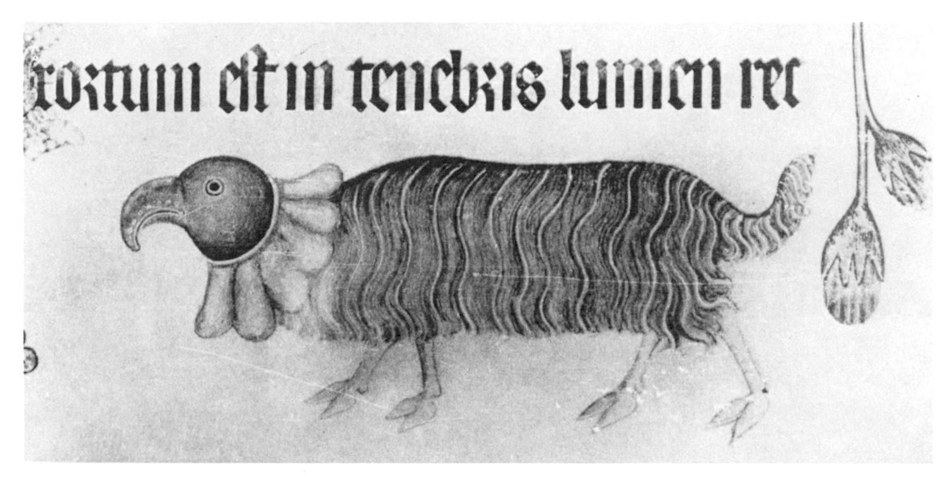
rortum est in tenebris lumen rec

247

enedicite omnia opera d
domino: laudate et sup

248

249

251

LI 247. Hybrid sheep: Add. 42130, f. 204v 248. Hybrid woman and dragon: W. 45, f. 256v 249. Hybrid woman with mirror and comb: Douce 366, f. 29 250. Hybrid woman with pyx; (Man with sword and buckler); Man with sack(?): Cloisters 54.1.2, f. 20v 251. Ibex, Bestiary representation: Munich c.g. 16, f. 19

250

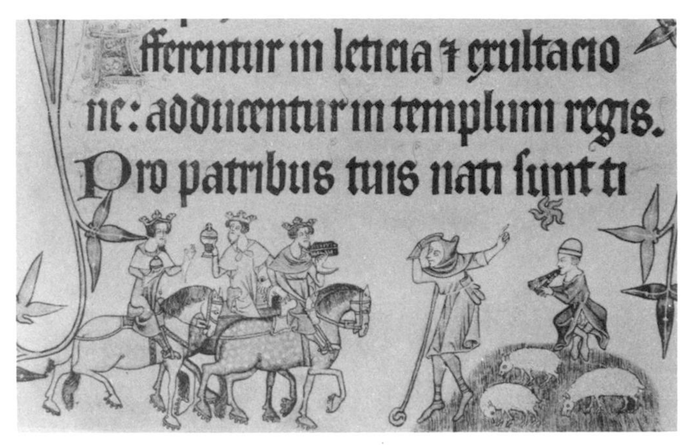
Afferentur in leticia ⁊ exultacio
ne: adducentur in templum regis.
Pro patribus tuis nati sunt ti

252

253

254

255

LII 252. Jesus Christ, life of: Adoration of Magi, journey of Magi: Add. 42130, f. 87v 253. Jesus Christ, life of: Adoration of Magi, man kneeling, holding camel: Douce 48, f. 211v 254. Jesus Christ, life of: Annunciation to shepherds: Cloisters 54.1.2, f. 62 255. Jesus Christ, life of: Annunciation to shepherds: Add. 28784B, f. 6v

tingat extremum digiti sui

256

mum patris tui.

257

258

260

259

LIII 256. Jacob approaching shepherds: Y.T. 8, f. 204v 257. Jesus Christ, life of: Annunciation to shepherds: Add. 42130, f. 87 258. Jesus Christ, life of: bearing cross: BBR 9391, f. 161 259. Jesus Christ, life of: bearing cross: latin 1076, f. 28 260. Jesus Christ, life of: Crucifixion: Add. 49622, f. 199

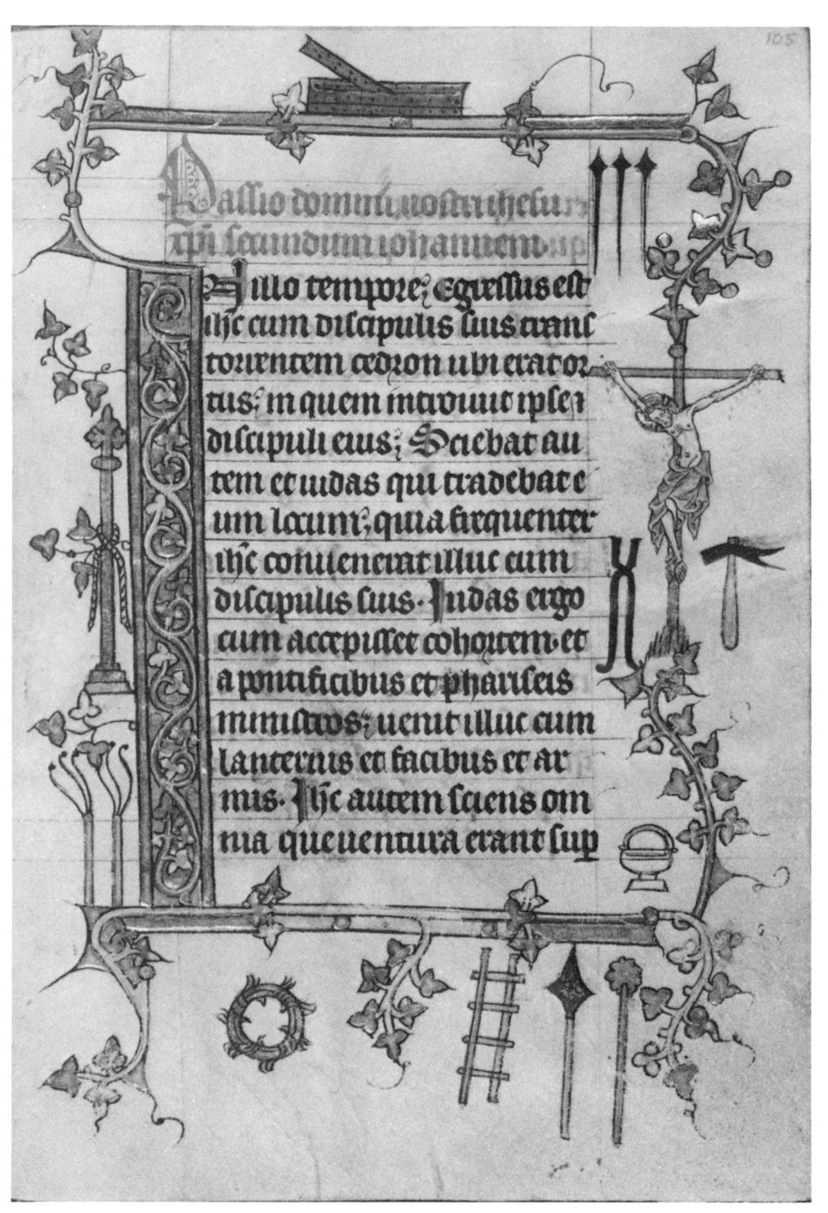

261

262

263

LIV 261. Jesus Christ, life of: Crucifixion;—: Passion, instruments of: M. 754, f. 105 262. Jesus Christ, life of: Crucifixion parody(?): W. 102, f. 56v 263. Jesus Christ, life of: Deposition: Add. 42130, f. 94v

264

265

266

267

268

LV 264. Jesus Christ, life of: Deposition, Nicodemus: BBR 9391, f. 100v 265. Jesus Christ, life of: Entombment: Add. 42130, f. 95 266. Jesus Christ, head of: Add. 41751, f. 162 267. Jesus Christ, life of: Harrowing of Hell; Virgin, life of: Coronation: Stowe 17, ff. 138v-139 268. Jesus Christ, life of: in aureole: latin 10483, f. 213

269

270

271

272

LVI 269. Jesus Christ, life of: Last Judgment; Dives and Lazarus: BBR 15001, f. 309 270. Jesus Christ, life of: Last Judgment: Hell mouth: Add. 42130, f. 157v 271. Jesus Christ, life of: Last Judgment, Pains of Hell: Devil with scourge: BBR 9411-26, f. 133v 272. Jesus Christ, life of: Last Judgment: Corpses rising: Jesus. 40, f. 150

273

274

275

276

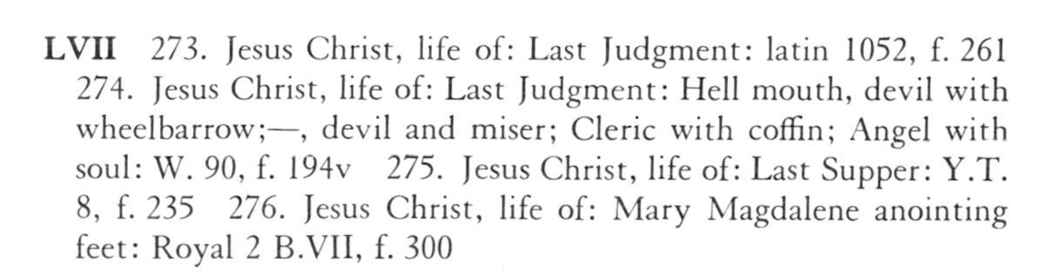

LVII 273. Jesus Christ, life of: Last Judgment: latin 1052, f. 261 274. Jesus Christ, life of: Last Judgment: Hell mouth, devil with wheelbarrow;—, devil and miser; Cleric with coffin; Angel with soul: W. 90, f. 194v 275. Jesus Christ, life of: Last Supper: Y.T. 8, f. 235 276. Jesus Christ, life of: Mary Magdalene anointing feet: Royal 2 B.VII, f. 300

277

278

280

279

281

LVIII 277. Jesus Christ, life of: Massacre of Innocents: Cloisters 54.1.2, f. 69 278. Jesus Christ, miracles of: Draught of fishes: Y. T. 8, f. 249v 279. Jesus Christ, life of: Flight into Egypt, fall of Idols: Cloisters 54.1.2, f. 83 280. Jesus Christ, miracles of: healing the blind: Stowe 17, f. 135 281. Jesus Christ, life of: mocking of: BBR 9391, f. 158v

282

283

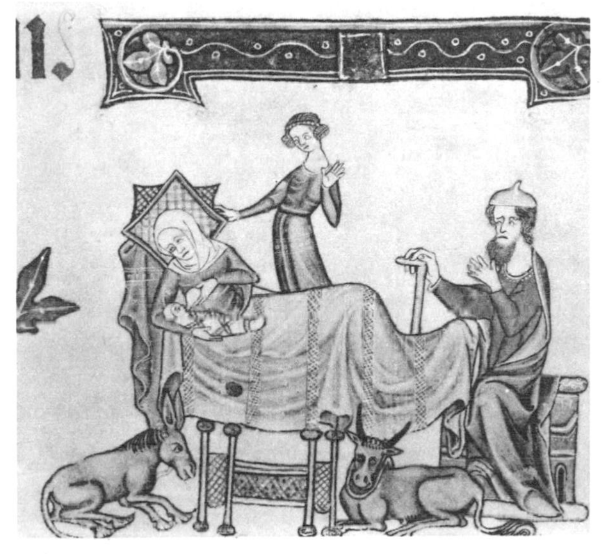

284

285

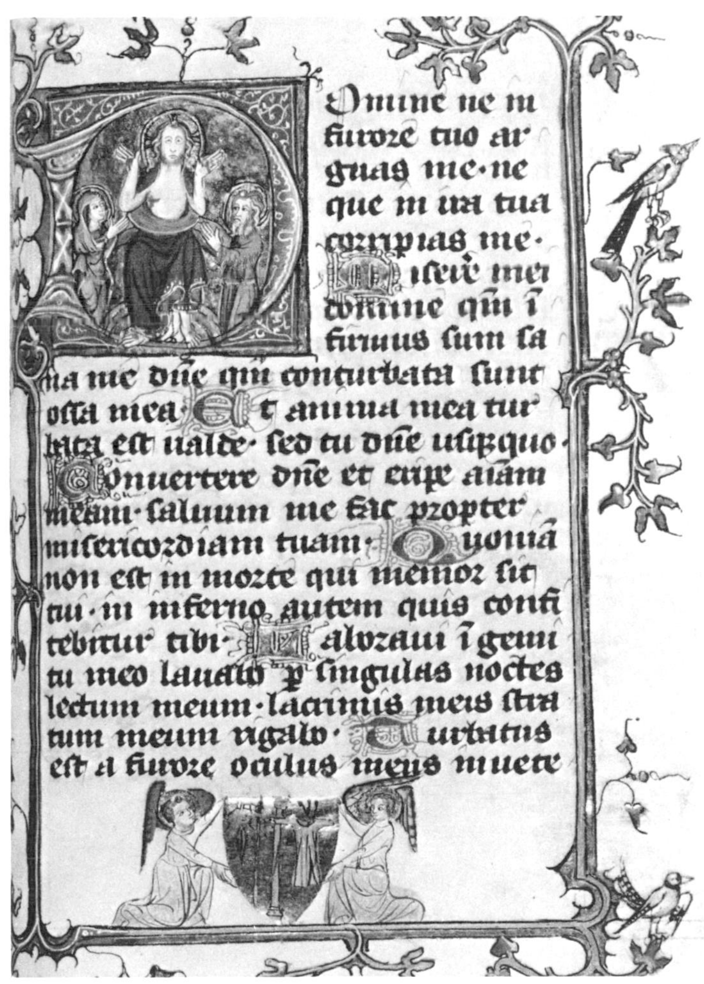

286

LIX 282. Jesus Christ, life of: mocking of: Princeton 44-18, f. 57 283. Jesus Christ, life of: mocking of: Troyes 1905, f. 19 284. Jesus Christ, life of: Nativity: Add. 42130, f. 86v 285. Jesus Christ, life of: *Noli me tangere;*—: Doubting Thomas: Verdun 107, f. 90v 286. Jesus Christ, life of: Passion, instruments of: M. 88, f. 179

287

290

288

289

LX 287. Jesus Christ, life of: Resurrection: Chantilly 62, f. 155 288. Jesus Christ, life of: Supper at Emmaus: Princeton 44-18, f. 88v 289. Jesus Christ, life of: Washing of feet: Y.T. 8, f. 236v 290. Jonah; Ape and peacock, astride: BBR 10607, f. 177

291

292

293

295

294

296

LXI 291. Jonah; Beggar: St. Omer 5, f. 133 292. Joseph and lamb, cloak shown to Jacob: Munich c.g. 16, f. 36v 293. Joseph in well: Y. T. 8, f. 207 294. Jubal: Munich c.g. 16, f. 17v 295. Judith and servant: BBR 15001, f. 106v 296. King and horse, astride: Add. 49622, f. 125

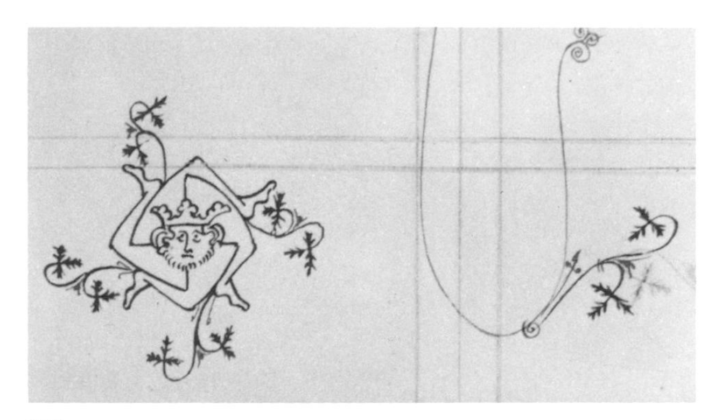

297

298

300

299

301

LXII 297. King, geometric configuration: Auct. D.3.2, f. 136 298. Knight and ape, charging: W. 90, f. 78v 299. Knight and cock, astride: Yale MS., f. 282v 300. Knight and hare, frightened by: Douce 5, f. 82 301. Knight and dog, astride (knight/snail): Melbourne 1254/3, f. 1v

302

hastel · & retorne

303

in deo & laudabunt

304

305

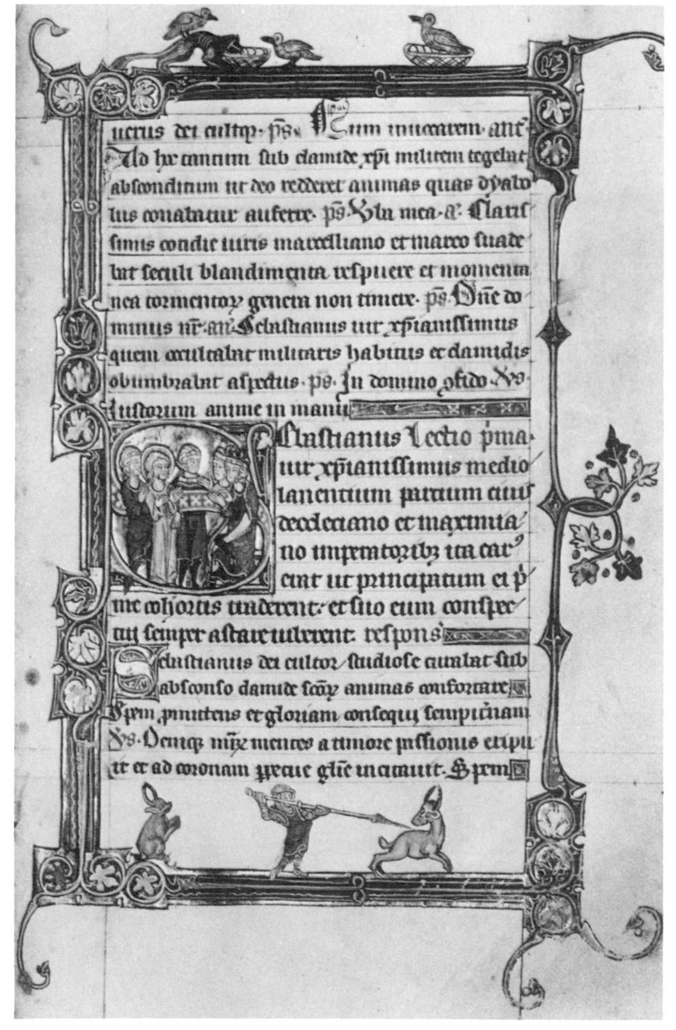

306

LXIII 302. Knight and hare, killed by: Verdun 107, f. 141v 303. Knight and lion, fighting: Yale MS., f. 315 304. Knight and lion, patting: Princeton 44-18, f. 145v 305. Knight and lion, confronting with sword: fr. 95, f. 292v 306. Knight and satyr; Bird in nest; Lion and bird: Cambrai 102, f. 387

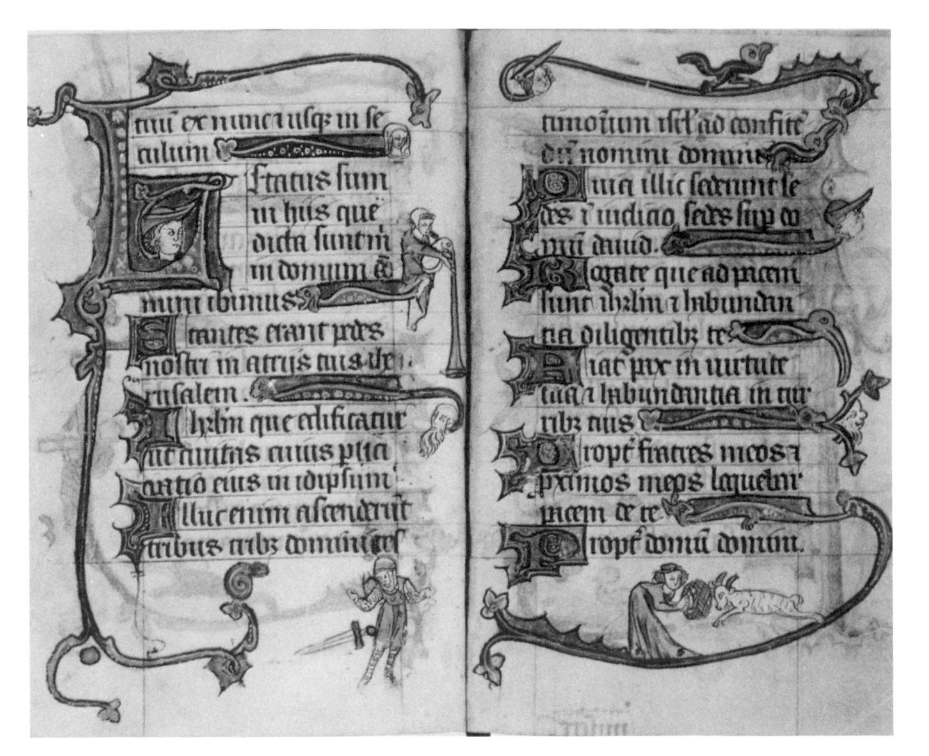

307

308

309

310

LXIV 307. Knight and snail, frightened by; Man with bagpipe; Woman and ram: G.K.S. 3384, ff. 160v-161 308. Knight and snail, kneeling before: Add. 49622, f. 162v 309. Knight and snail, confronting: W. 45, f. 82v 310. Knight and snail, fighting: fr. 776, f. 176v 311. Knight and snail, confronting; Man with hand bell and pipe, woman dancing: latin 14284, f. 15v

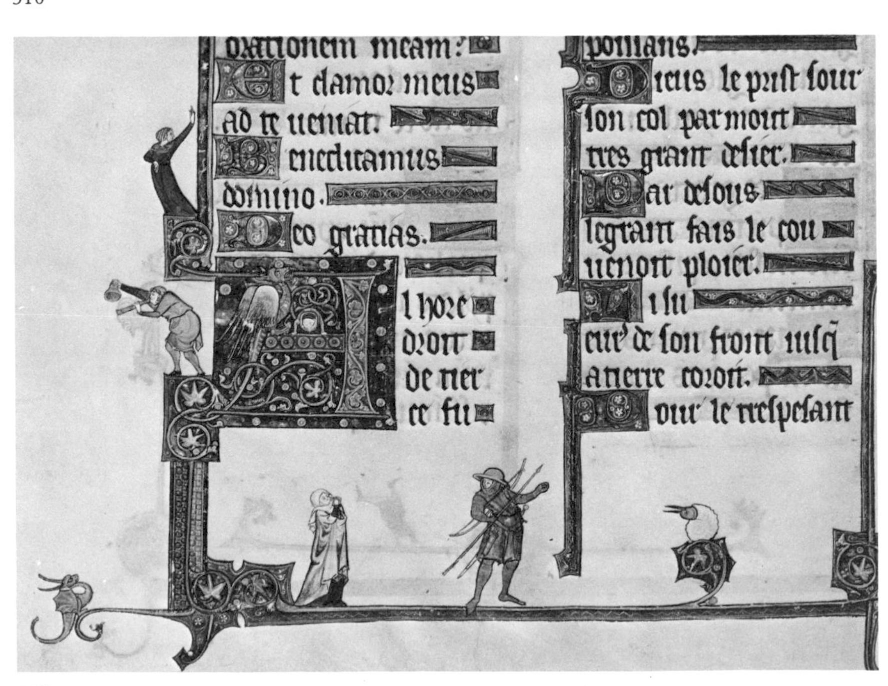

311

figar· libi me ab hijs
o derunt me & de pfūdis
aquarum
on me demergat te
s aque neq3 absor
mepfundum ne
rgeat sup me puteꝰ
uum
audi me domine
benigna est misedia
secundū multitudi
misatiōnū tuarū.
e i me.
neauertas faciē
a puero tuo qm t

312

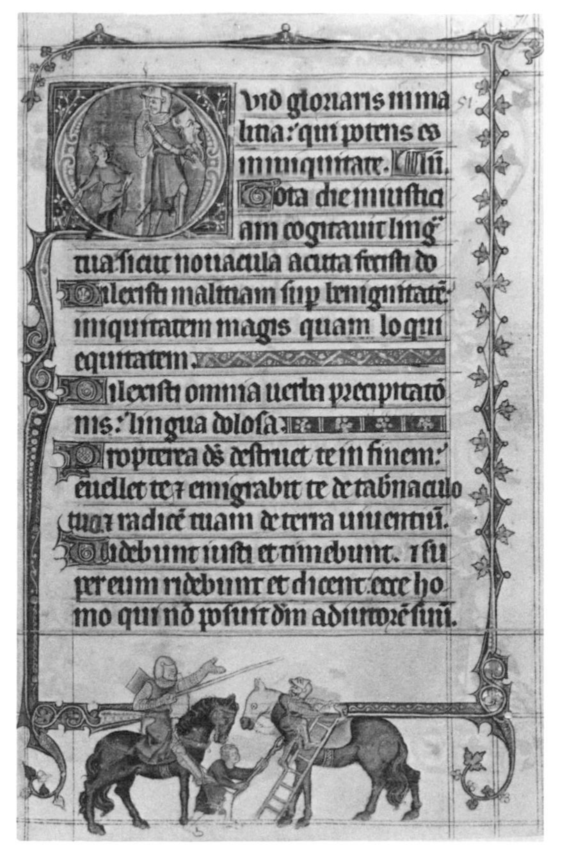
vid gloriaris in ma
litia: qui potens es
in iniquitate.
Tota die iniusti
ciam cogitauit ling
ua sicut nouacula acuta fecisti do
Dilexisti maliciam sup benignitatē:
iniquitatem magis quam loqui
equitatem.
Dilexisti omnia uerba precipitatō
nis: lingua dolosa.
Propterea ds destruet te in finem:
euellet te & emigrabit te de tabnaculo
tuo: & radicē tuam de terra uiuentiū.
Videbunt iusti et timebunt. & su
per eum ridebunt et dicent: ecce ho
mo qui nō posuit dm adiutorē sum.

314

313

dies meos: et substantia mia
tanquam nichilum ante te.
as·
ne sileas qm aduena su ego

315

316

317

LXV 312. Knight with head of beast: G.K.S. 3384, f. 129 313. Knight with sword, kneeling: Arras 47, f. 246 314. Knights, confronted (fabliau?): Jesus 40, f. 71 315. Knights fighting with swords and shields: Verdun 107, f. 19v 316, 317. Knights tilting, queen looking on: Royal 10 E.IV, ff. 65v-66

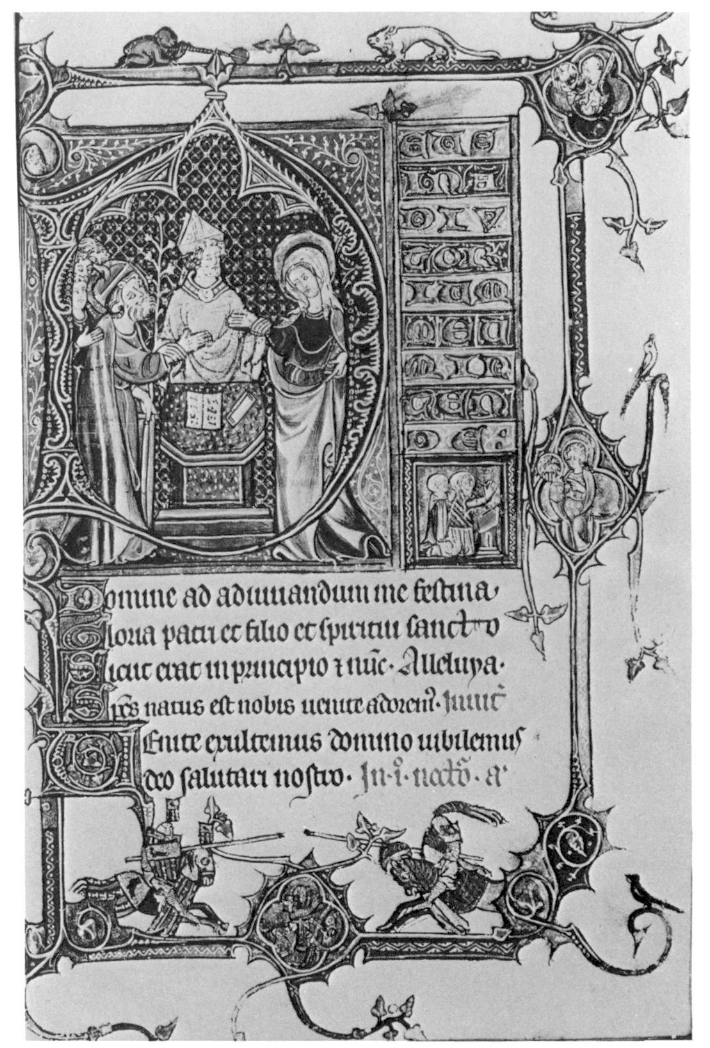

318

319

320

321

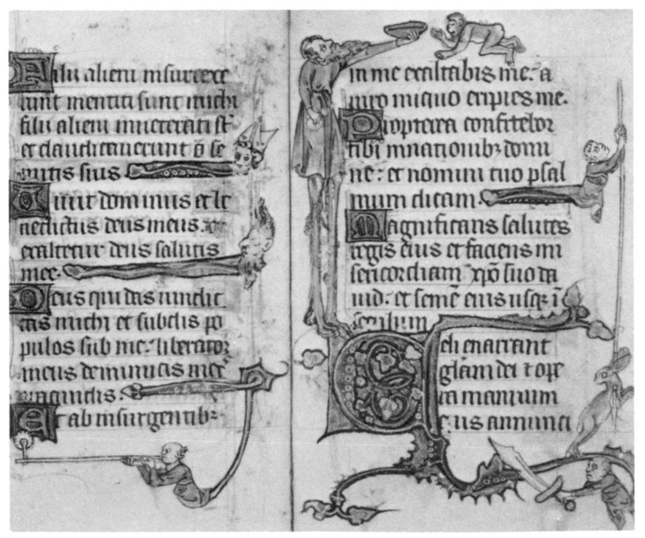

322

LXVI 318. Knights tilting; Ape, chained, confronting lion: Melbourne 1254/3, f. 7 319. Lion, chained to post: Douce 118, f. 44 320. Lion and unicorn, charging: Christ Church E.II, f. 46v 321. Man and ape, conversing: Rutland Ps., f. 106v 322. Man and ape, feeding; Man and hare, hunting with spear; Man pruning with sword; Man with pinwheel: G.K.S. 3384, ff 36v-37

323

324

325

326

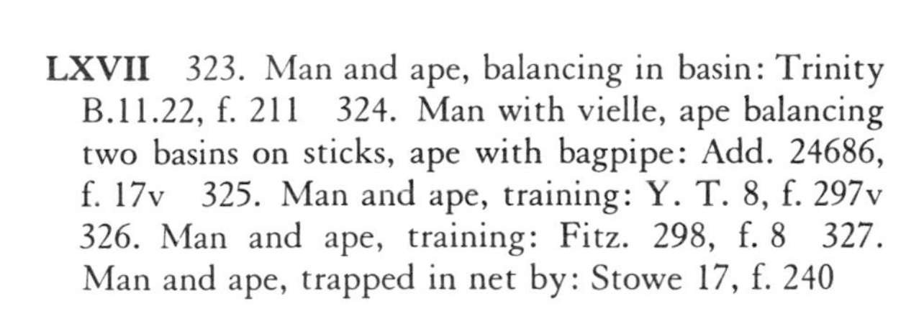

LXVII 323. Man and ape, balancing in basin: Trinity B.11.22, f. 211 324. Man with vielle, ape balancing two basins on sticks, ape with bagpipe: Add. 24686, f. 17v 325. Man and ape, training: Y. T. 8, f. 297v 326. Man and ape, training: Fitz. 298, f. 8 327. Man and ape, trapped in net by: Stowe 17, f. 240

327

328

329

330

331

332

LXVIII 328. Man and ass, carrying (fable or proverb): Glazier 24, f. 32 329. Man and doe(?), carrying (fable or proverb) Man, headless: Man nude with shawm: Cloisters 54.1.2, f. 120 330. Man and bear, training: Nancy 249, f. 158v 331. Man and bird, attacked by: Royal 10 E.IV, f. 77 332. Man and bear: Bodley 264, f. 76

333

334

335

336

LXIX 333. Man and bird, beckoning to; Lobster bitten by stork: C.B. 62, f. 199v 334. Man and bird, seated, listening to: Yale MS., f. 119 335. Man and bird, hunting with club; Woman with distaff and spindle; (Falcon); Ape with sword; Knight praying; Man with gittern: Trinity B.11.22, f. 199v 336. Man and bird, hunting; Handball, men: Douce 6, f. 135

a meniere daler au
nis pour ce quil sot
trait dan qui est diuerse se
lonc ce que li nis sont en
diuers leus car ce li niz est
sus aubres li hom doit mō
a me il sont norri
niere par quoi li oisel
sont trait dou nis est dite
ce est a dire cōmant li leus
doit estre apparilliez on quel
il sont norri et cōmant il

337

Et folium eius nō deflu
gentes hereditatē tuā: et

338

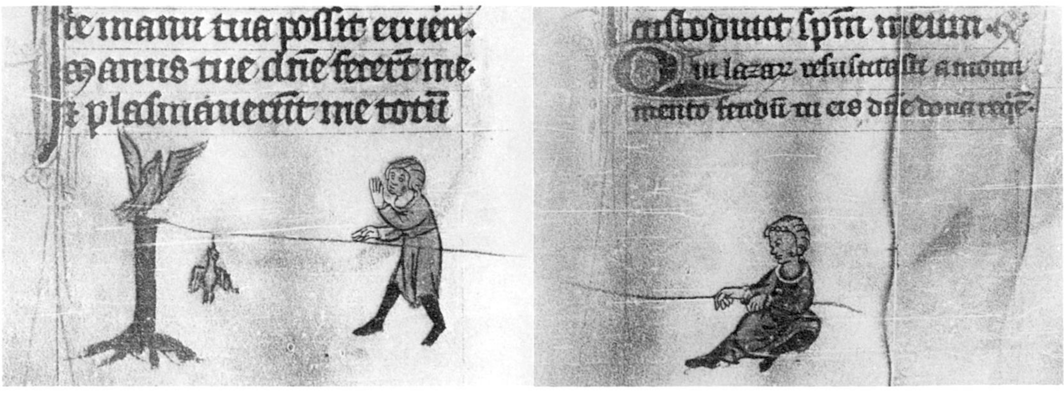
te manu tua possit eruere
Manus tue dn̄e fecerūt me
plasmauerunt me totū

339

LXX 337. Man and bird, hunting: fr. 12400, f. 94v 338. Man and bird, snaring with decoy (owl); Stag and doe: Arundel 83, f. 14 339. Man and bird, snaring with decoy: W. 37, ff. 161v-162

omnis sapiencia eorū
ta est

340

341

342

343

protectio tua

344

345

LXXI 340. Man and boy, threatening with stick, boy in tree eating cherries: Add. 42130, f. 196v 341. Man and cat, pursuing with distaff and spindle: Glazier 24, f. 66 342. Man and butterfly, pursuing with hood: latin 13260, f. 1 343. Man and butterfly, pursuing with hood: W. 88, f. 119 344. Man and crane, fighting: Princeton 44-18, f. 98 345. Man (pygmy?) and crane, fighting; Man nude (pygmy?) and crane: Rothschild MS., f. 114v

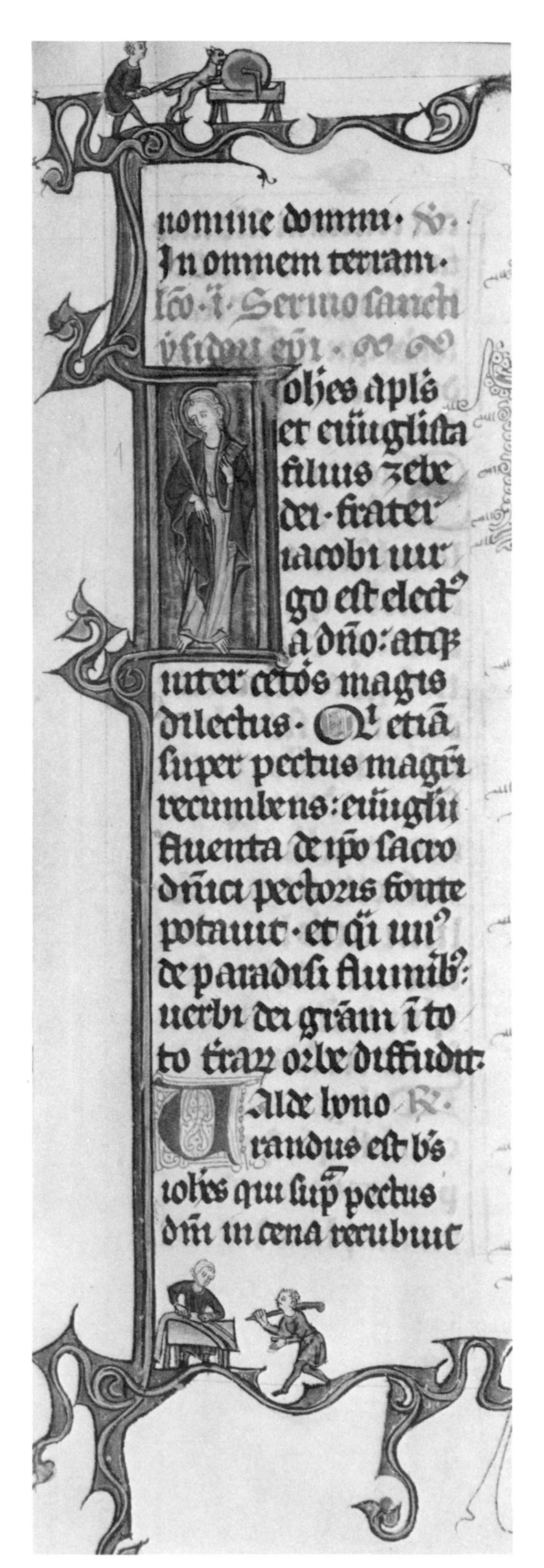

346

347

ue visces par diestre

348

t disciplina tua correxit me

349

LXXII 346. Man and dog, holding nose to grindstone (proverb?); Man cutting cloth (leather?): W. 109, f. 204 347. Man and dog, training: Trinity B.11.22, f. 76 348. Man and dragon, strangling: BBR 9411-26, f. 140 349. Man (hybrid) and dragonfly, sticking out tongue at: Add. 42130, f. 36v

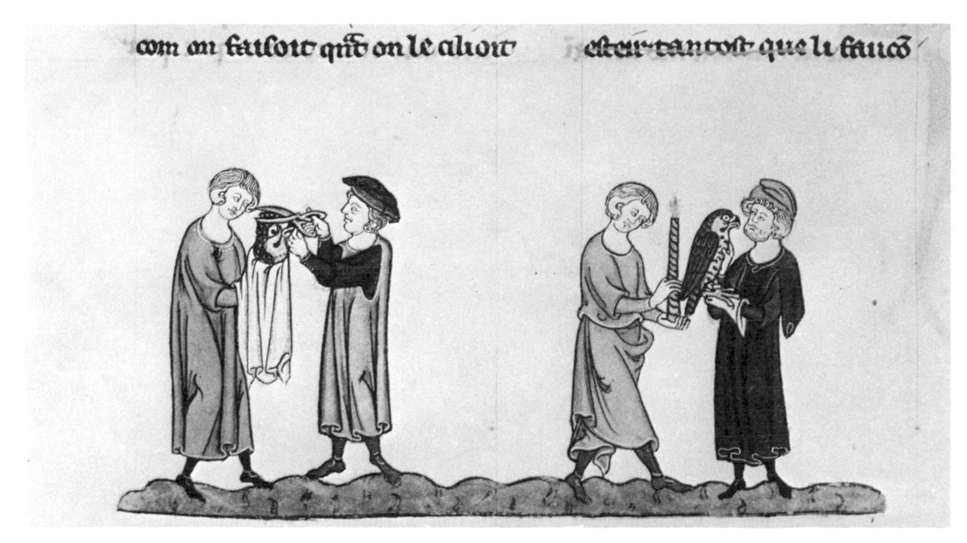

350

351

352

353

LXXIII 350. Man and falcon, clipping;—, operation: fr. 12400, f. 136v 351. Man and goat, astride (exemplum): Royal 10 E.IV, f. 156 352. Man and goat, astride (exemplum): Douce 366, f. 72 353. Man and fly, fighting with spear; Men fighting: Add. 49622, f. 7v

354

355

357

356

358

LXXIV 354. Man and hare, defending castle against: Fitz. 298, f. 41 355. Man and hare, frightened by: Trinity B.11.22, f. 114v 356. Man and hare, hunted by: Bodley 264, f. 81v 357. Man and hare, hunted by; Man and hybrid man, fighting with sword: BBR 10607, f. 150 358. Man and hare, hunted by: W. 109, f. 168

359

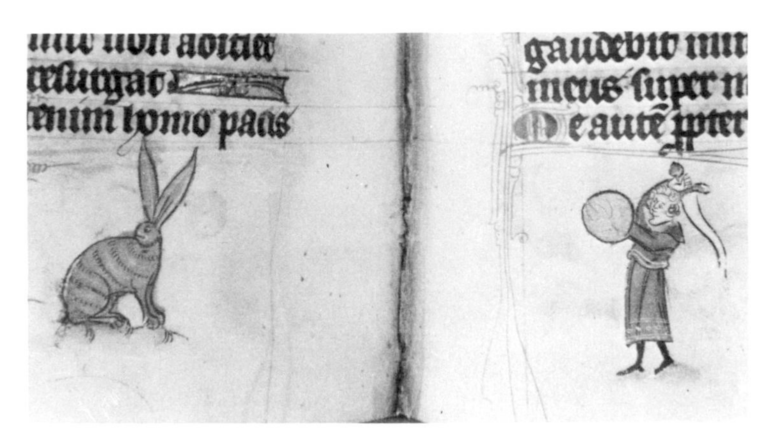

360

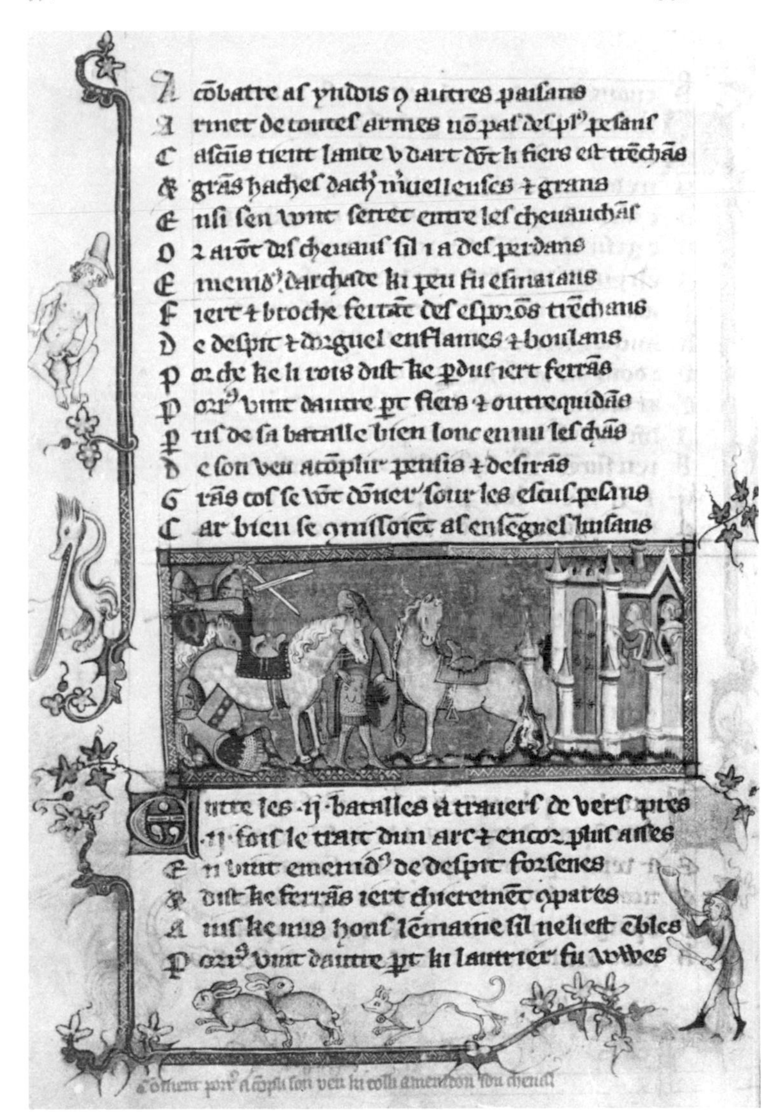

361

362

363

LXXV 359. Man and hare, hunting with sword: Princeton 44-18, f. 155 360. Man and hare, confronting with sword: Princeton 44-18, ff. 129v-130 361. Man and hare, hunting with club; Man nude, urinating: Glazier 24, f. 103v 362. Man and hare, hunting with bow and arrow: Rutland Ps., f. 57v 363. Man and hare, carrying tied to stick across shoulder: BBR 10607, f. 13v

364

365

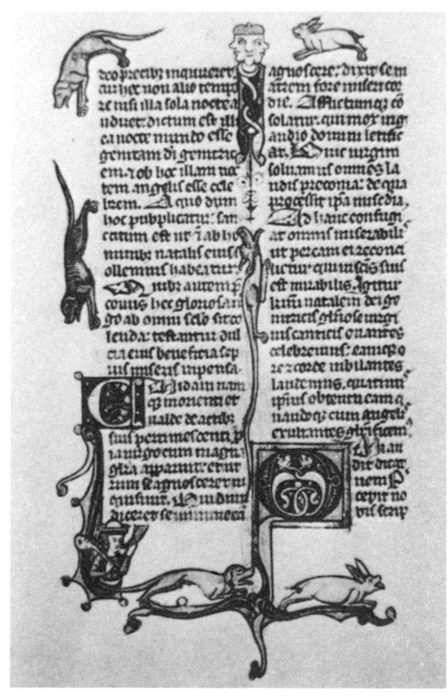

366

367

368

LXXVI 364. Man and hare, hunting with horn and hound: Verdun 107, f. 13 365. Man (tailor) and hare, imprisoned by: Fitz. 298, f. 48 366. Man and hare, hunting with club: C.B. 62, f. 181v 367. Man and hybrid man, charging: fr. 95, f. 199v 368. Man and hybrid man, shooting: fr. 95, f. 311

369

370

371

LXXVII 369-372. Man and dragon, astride (variations on a theme): Tournai Ps., ff. 21, 80v, 101v, 211v

372

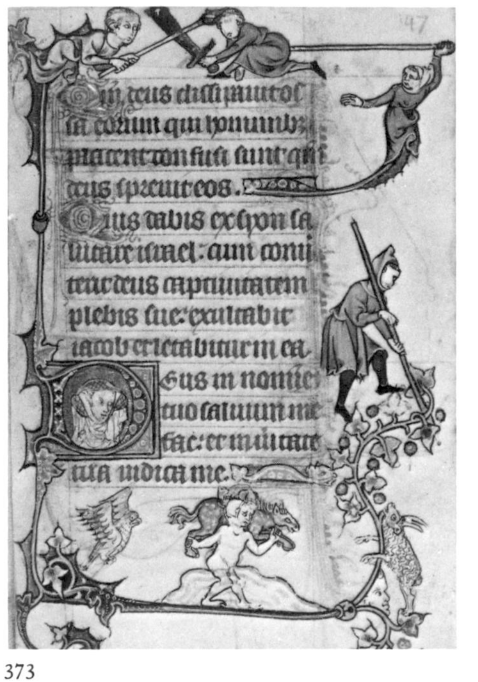

373

375

374

376

378

377

LXXVIII 373. Man and horse, carrying (fable or proverb); Goat standing on hind legs; (Man with pole); Men fighting with falchion and spear: Douce 5, f. 147 374. Man and horse, training; Ape chained: Bodley 264, f. 73 375. Man and horse, leading toward tavern: BBR 1175, f. 8v 376. Man and knight, shooting: Cambrai 102, f. 339v 377, 378. Man and lion, fighting; Lizard: Add. 24686, f. 18v

379

uam dies hesterna que

381

domine.

381a

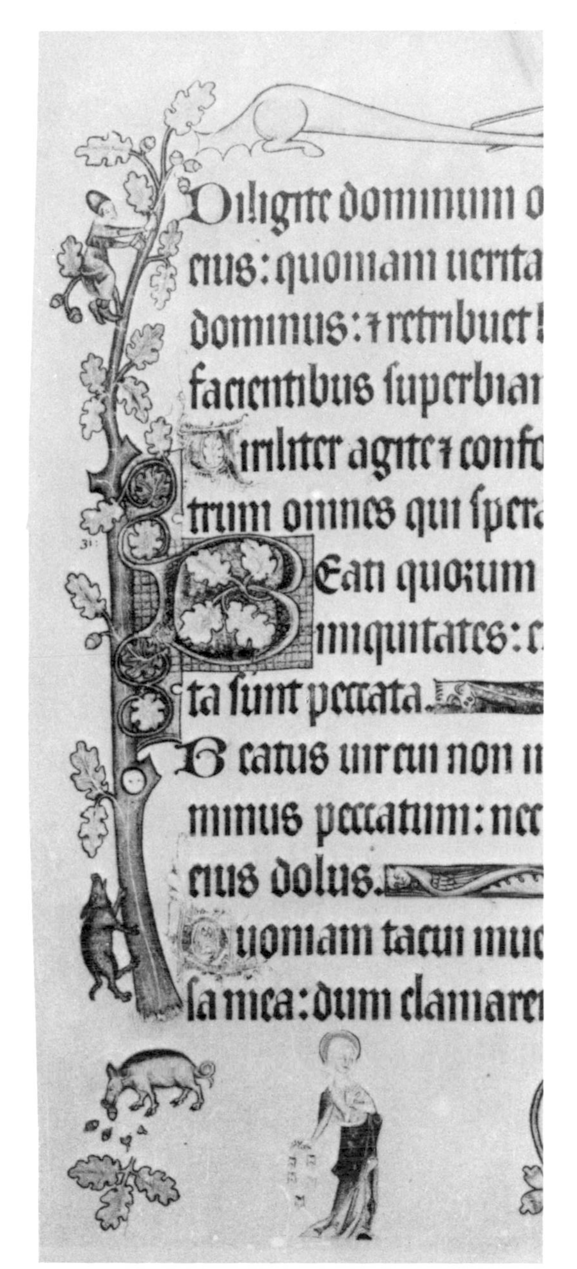

380

382

LXXIX 379. Man and owl, shooting: Liège 431, f. 56 380. Man and pigs, beating down acorns; St. Apollonia: Add. 42130, f. 59v 381. Man and sheep, milking: Add. 42130, f. 163v 381a. Man and ram, baiting: BBR 10607, f. 42v 382. Man and serpent: Rutland Ps., f. 110

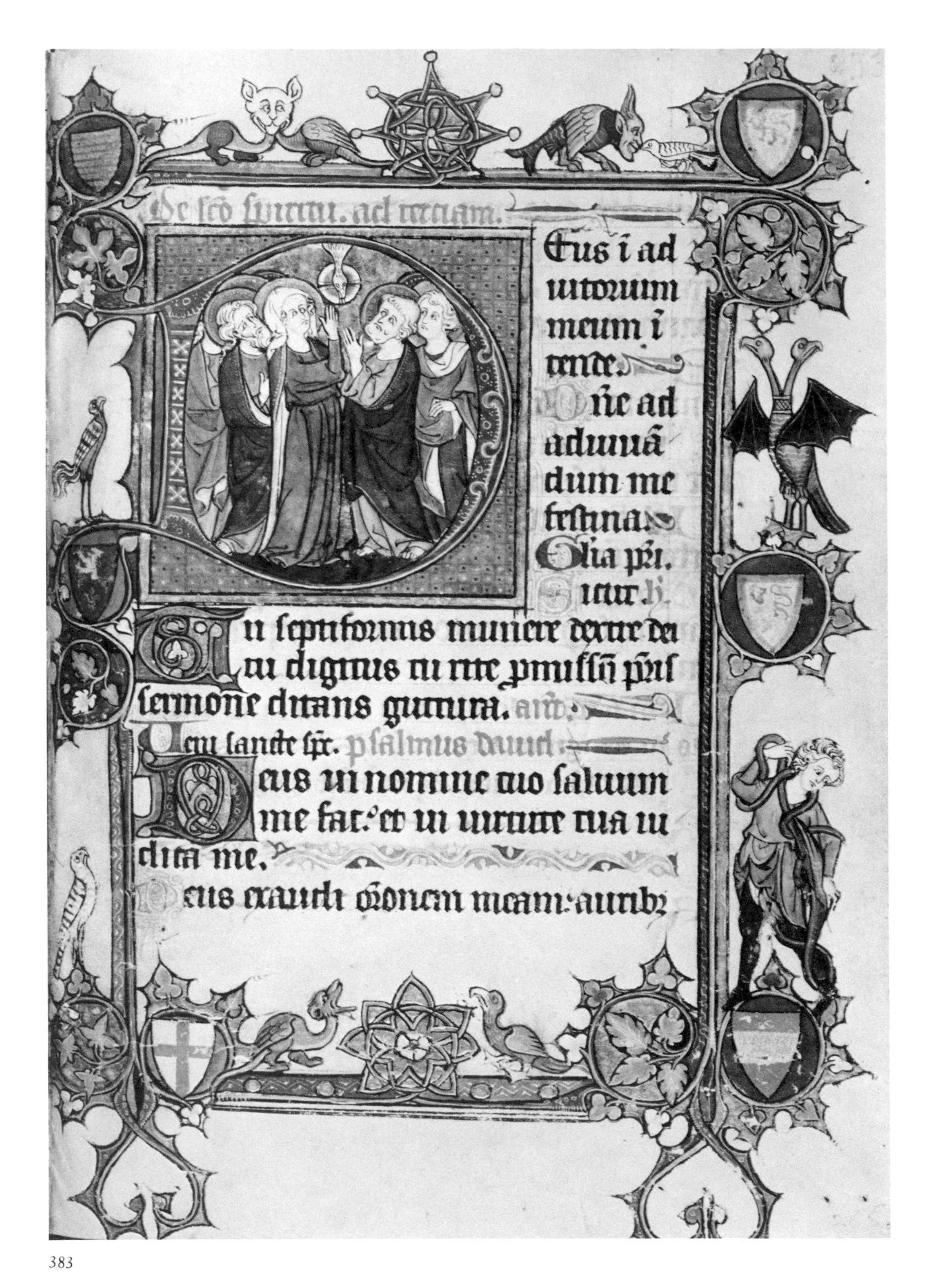

383

LXXX 383. Man and serpent (Laocoön?); Eagle, double-headed; (Grotesques; Birds): M. 729, f. 273

LXXXI (opposite page) 384. Man and snail, fighting with sword; Unicorn butting; (Christ bearing cross): N.K.S. 41, ff. 85v-86 385. Man and snail, frightened by: BBR 9411-26, f. 105 386. Man and stag, hunting with club: W. 45, f. 70v 387. Man and stag, hunting with spear; Centaur and knight, shooting: Cambrai 102, f. 391

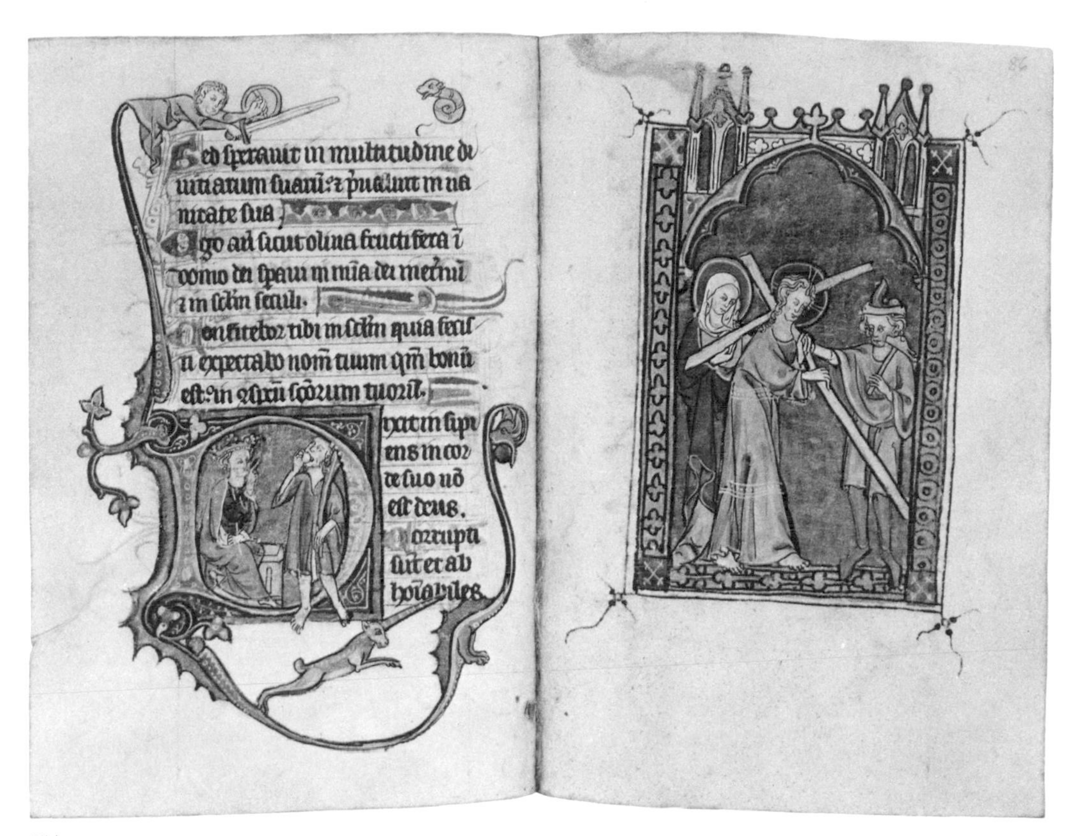

384

385

nouatus est

386

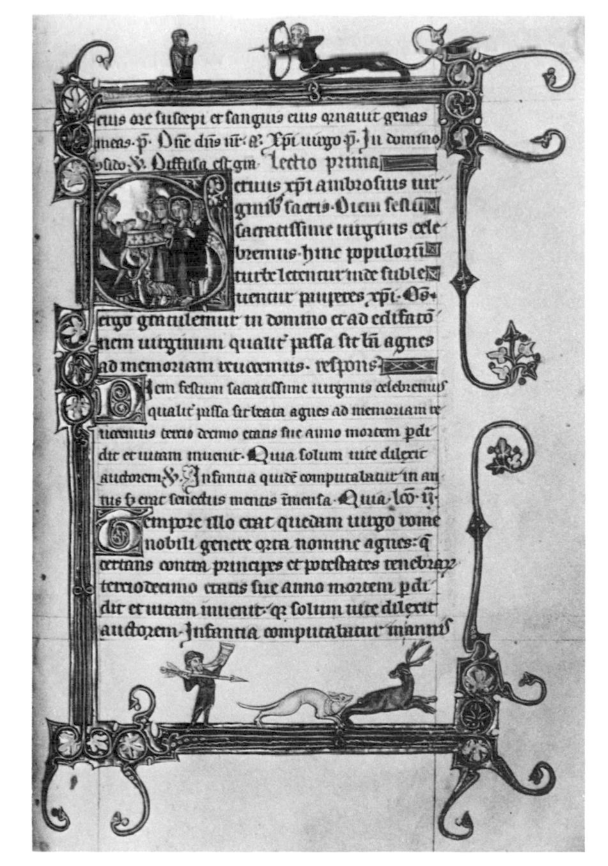

387

388

389

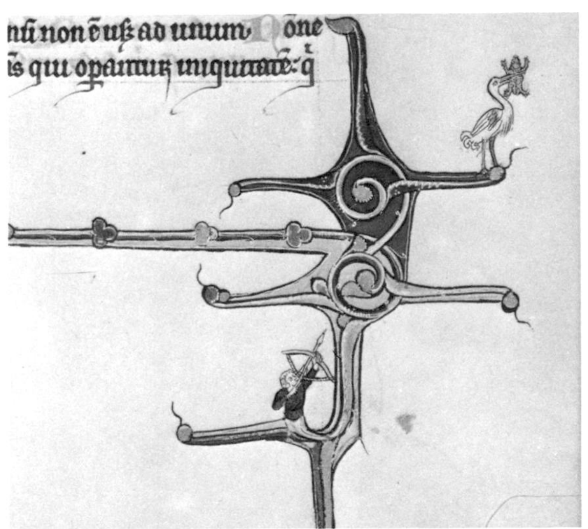

390

391

LXXXII 388. Man and stag, hunting; (Man with club); Fables: sheep and crow; Man with shawm; (Birds; Falcon); Ape and goat, astride backwards; Fox and cock; Man and owl, shooting; David, life of: David and Goliath; Man and duck, hunting; Stilts, worn by man: BBR 9961-62, f. 14 389. Man and stork, reading; Man balancing basin: G.K.S. 3384, f. 172 390. Man and stork, shooting: latin 16260, f. 273 391. Man and unicorn, hunting; Ape and unicorn, astride: W. 82, f. 62v

392

393

394

395

396

397

LXXXIII 392. Man and woman, bathing: Bodley 264, f. 75 393. Man nude, bathing: W. 82, f. 100 394. Man and woman, beaten by: Cambridge Dd.5.5, f. 397 395. Man and woman, before Eros, kneeling: Arras 139, f. 8 396. (Man and woman, before Eros in tree): BBR 9543, f. 12 397. Man and woman, before Eros in tree: Stowe 17, f. 273

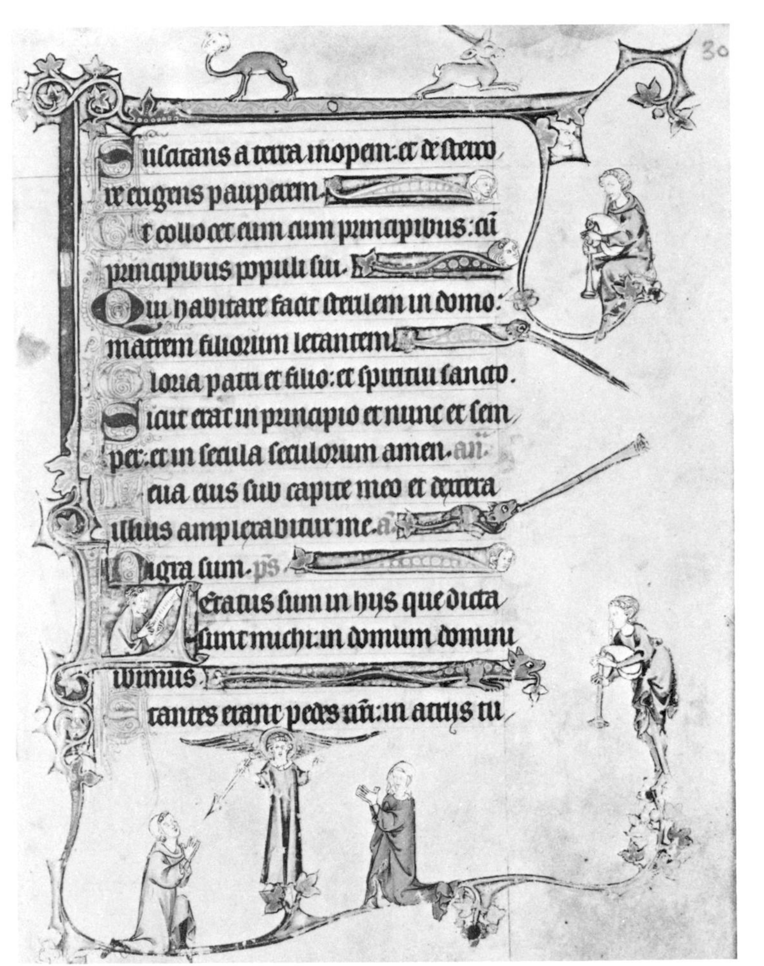

398

399

400

401

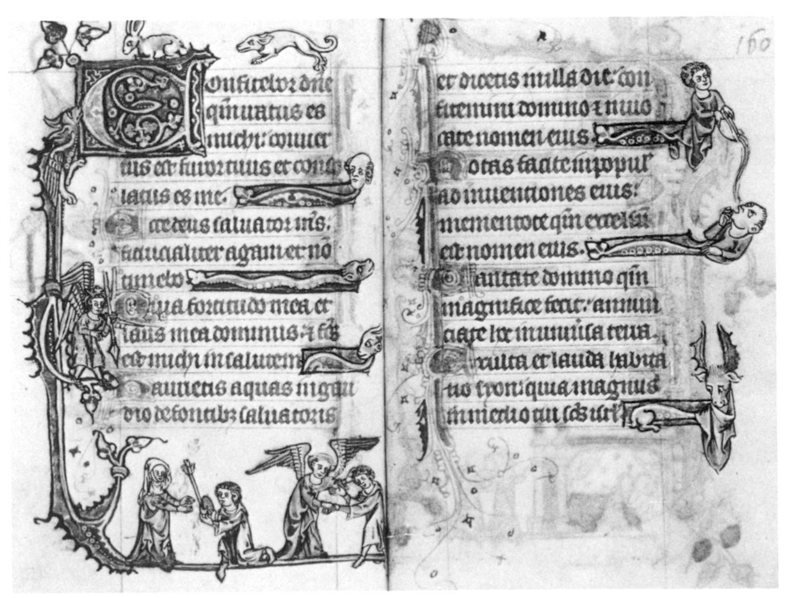

402

LXXXIV 398. Man and woman, before Eros; Man with bagpipe; Dragon with trumpet: Trinity B.11.22, f. 30 399. Man and woman, confronting with basket: BBR 9391, f. 110 400. Man kneeling before (Frau Minne?): Princeton 44-18, f. 15 401. Man standing before (Frau Minne?) Douce 118, f. 130 402. Man and woman before Eros: Man presenting heart to woman; Man feeding man's head: Douce 6, ff. 159v-160

403

405

404

406

407

408

LXXXV 403. Man and woman, kneeling before (Frau Minne?); Man with wheelbarrow: fr. 95, f. 24v 404. Man and woman, embracing; Man eating: Douce 6, ff. 160v-161 405. Man and woman, intercourse; Woman and child by fire: Merton 0.1.3, f. 65v 406. Man and woman on horseback; Ape tied to tree: Stowe 17, f. 106 407, 408. Man and woman, offered heart by, offering purse to: Bodley 264, f. 59

409

410

411

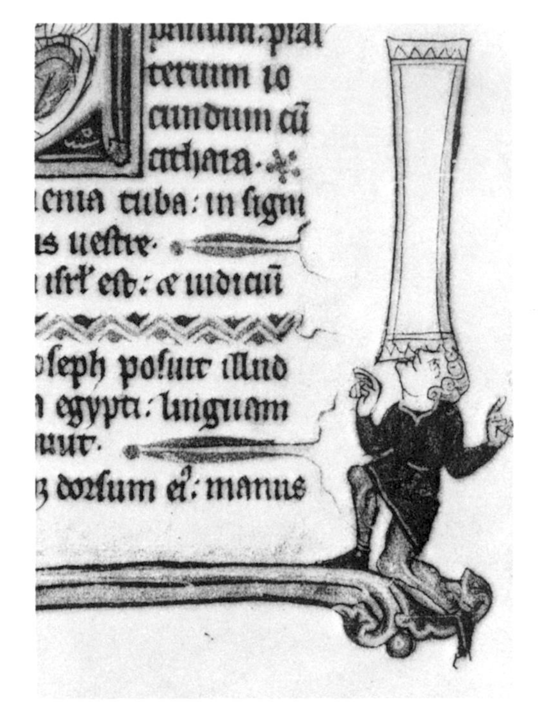

412

413

414

LXXXVI 409. Man and woman, stealing purse from, arrested: Add. 49622, f. 153 410. Man balancing board: BBR 10607, f. 47 411. Man balancing basin: St. Omer 5, f. 125 412. Man balancing board: C.B. 61, f. 116 413. Man balancing cup: Kraus 75/88, f. 82 414. Man balancing cup: Yale MS., f. 175

415

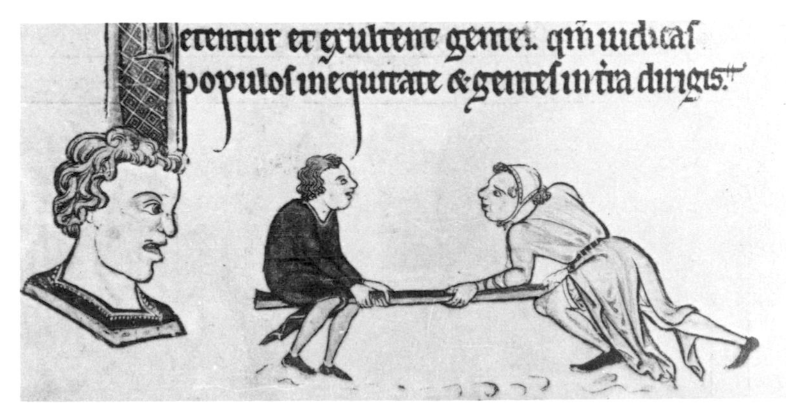

416

417

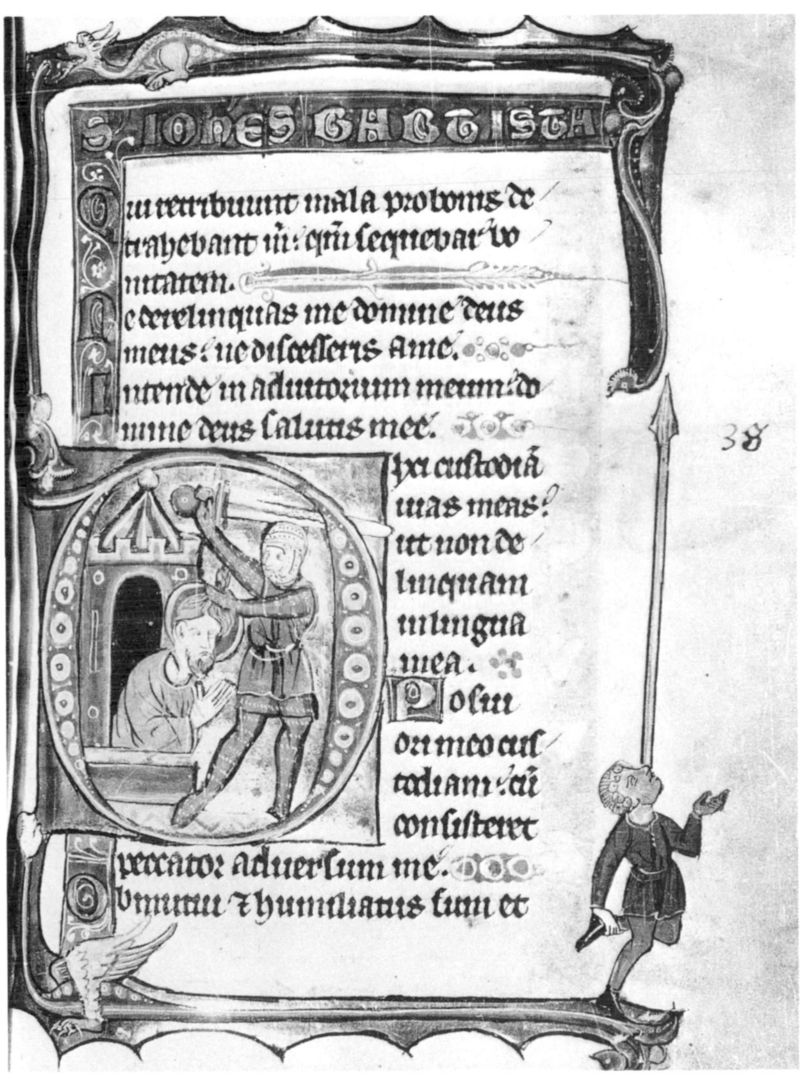

418

419

LXXXVII 415. Man balancing funnel: Add. 42130, f. 157v 416. Man balancing on pole: Rutland Ps., f. 65v 417. Man balancing on pole: Bodley 264, f. 98 418. Man balancing spear: Burney 345, f. 53 419. Man balancing sword: BBR 10607, f. 23v

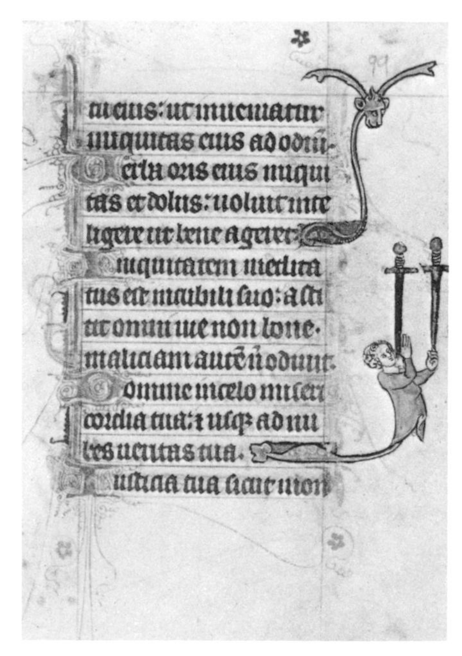

420

421

422

423

424

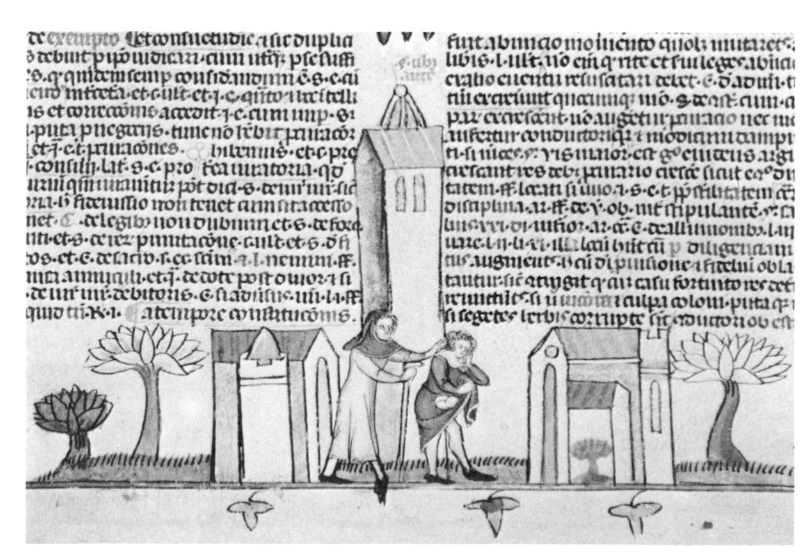

425

LXXXVIII 420. Man balancing sword(s): Douce 5, f. 99 421. Man balancing tapers, playing triangle: Trinity B.11.22, f. 148 422. Man balancing, with trumpet, woman dancing: Lambeth 233, f. 44 423. Man bathing feet: Trinity B.11.22, f. 179v 424. Man bathing hands (washing laundry?): G.K.S. 3384, f. 45v 425. Man, blind, led by boy (fabliau): Royal 10 E.IV, f. 218

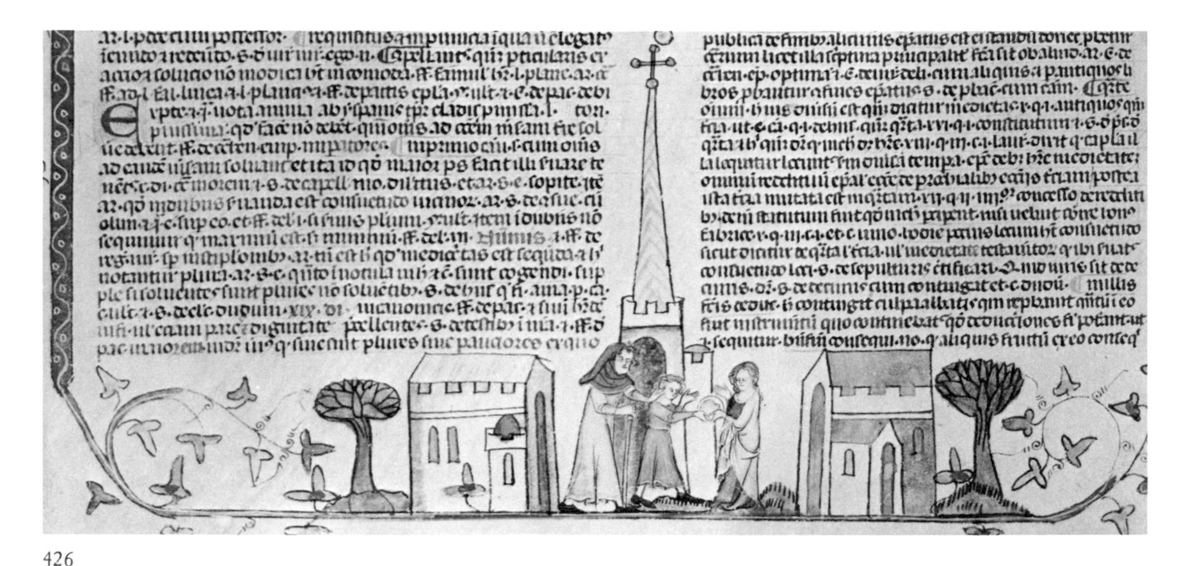

426

427

428

429

LXXXIX 426-429. Man, blind, led by boy (fabliau): Royal 10 E.IV, ff. 218v, 219, 219v, 220

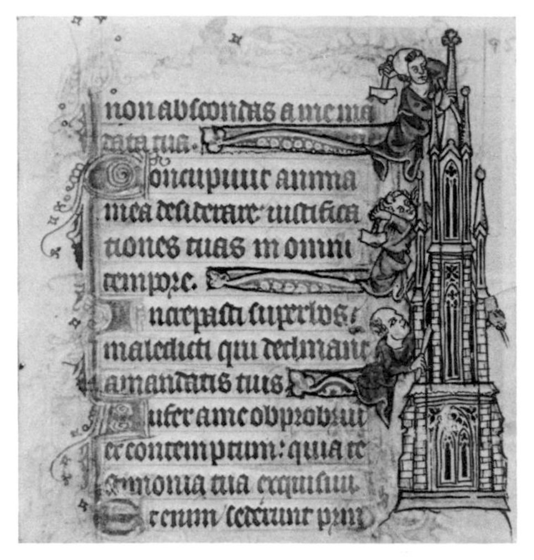

430

431

432

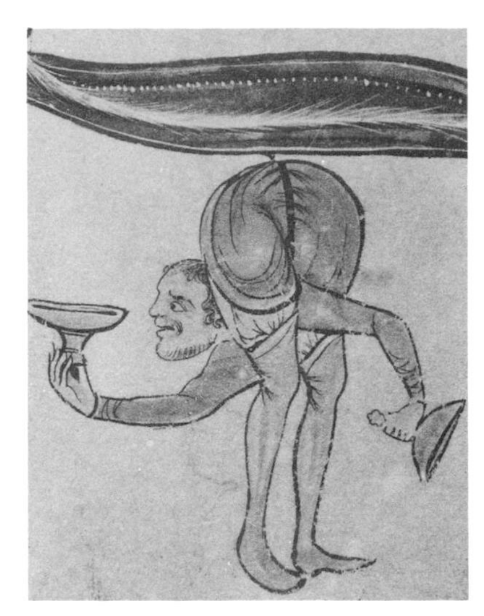

433

434

435

XC 430. Man building church: Douce 6, f. 95 431. Man cooking, roasting meat on spit: Trinity B.11.22, f. 159 432. Man cooking, roasting meat on spit; Woman with mortar and pestle: Melbourne 1254/3, f. 4v 433. Man (contortionist) with cymbals: Rutland Ps., f. 73 434, 435. Man drinking, woman remonstrating: Harley 6563, ff. 66v-67

436

437

438

439

440

XCI 436. Man fishing: W. 87, f. 106v 437. Man and eel, spearing: G.K.S. 3384, f. 54 438. Man fishing: Nancy 249, f. 168v 439. Man giving alms to pilgrim: G.K.S. 3384, f. 78 440. Man, headless, with head in hand, fighting: Verdun 107, f. 99v

441

si premiers iouster
or ke doie couster
ices fors est a conquester
uska lostel mener
or · l · fois peser
caschuns le regarda

442

deus adiuuat me

443

444

afaille et coment cil de tyr le deffendirent
rent ki nonciet le uosist a alixandre.

445

us avant senciaust li contes
ndroit de aus aparler et si
s dirons de merlin et de ses
ures coment il ouura main
merueille.

446

XCII 441. Man, headless, with head in hand: Glazier 24, f. 52v 442. Man, headless, with sword: Glazier 24, f. 70v 443. Man, headless, hybrid, with sword: Stowe 17, f. 73 444. Man in cart: Verdun 107, f. 157 445. Man in costume as stag, hare, boar (mummers), man with gittern, woman, nun, and hybrid cleric with switch: Bodley 264, f. 21v 446. Man in costume as stag (mummer), man with bagpipe: fr. 95, f. 261

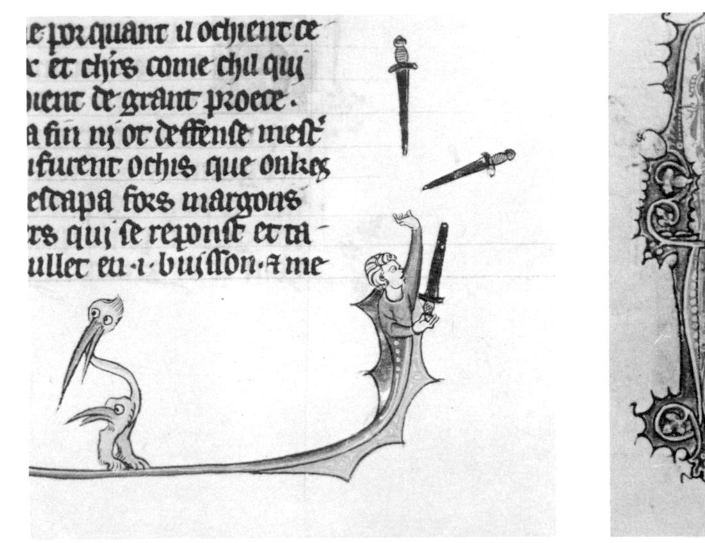

447

448

449

450

451

XCIII 447. Man juggling knives: fr. 95, f. 318 448. Man juggling knives: Douce 6, f. 93bv 449. Man nude, eating his leg: Glazier 24, f. 50v 450. Man making bed; Hybrid man and hare, hunting: W. 88, ff. 177v-178 451. Man nude and dragon, astride: Rutland Ps., f. 99v

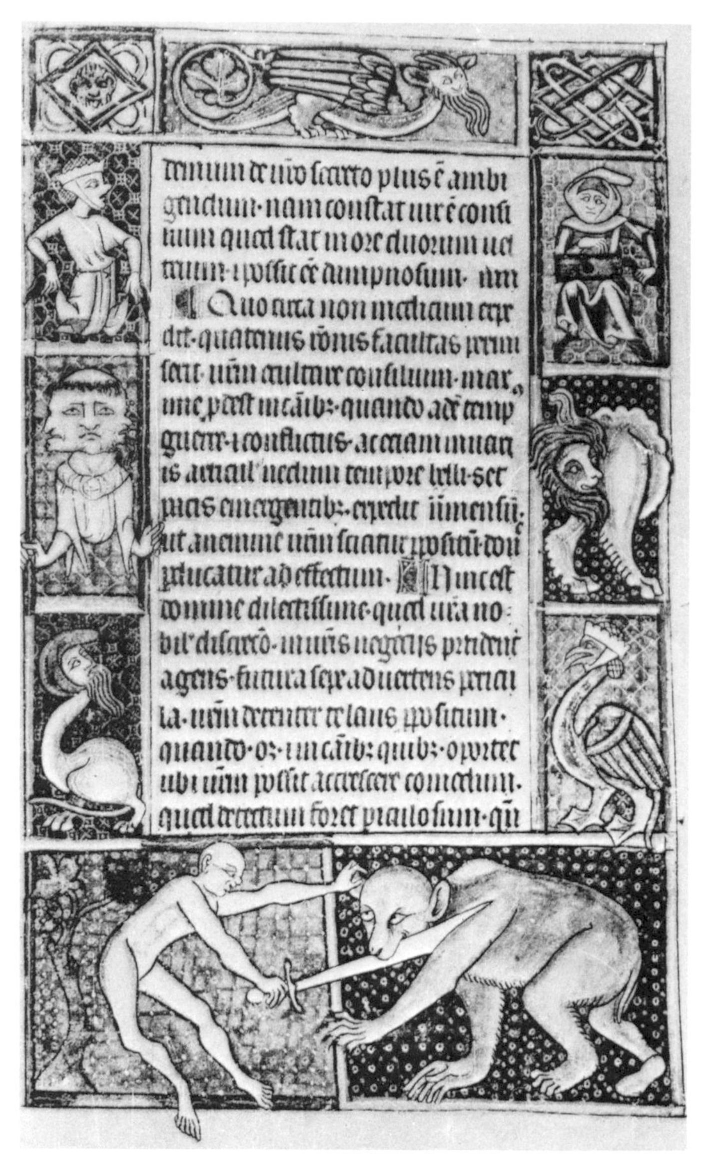

452

453

455

454

456

XCIV 452. Man nude and bear, fighting with sword; Man with hurdy-gurdy, woman dancing; Cleric, three-faced; (Grotesques): Christ Church E.II, f. 36 453. Man nude and cat; Spider: Rothschild MS., f. 130 454. Man nude and lion, killing: Rutland Ps., f. 70 455. Man nude and man aiming falchion and spear: Add. 49622, f. 179v 456. Man nude and stag, hunting: Arras 561, f. 103

457

458

459

460

461

XCV 457. Man nude drinking: Yale MS., f. 311 458. Man nude drinking: Rutland Ps., f. 109 459. Man nude drinking: fr. 95, f. 173 460. Man nude tearing hair: fr. 95, f. 350 461. Man nude and goat, astride, charging nude man astride boar: Hague 10 A.14, f. 7

462

463

464

465

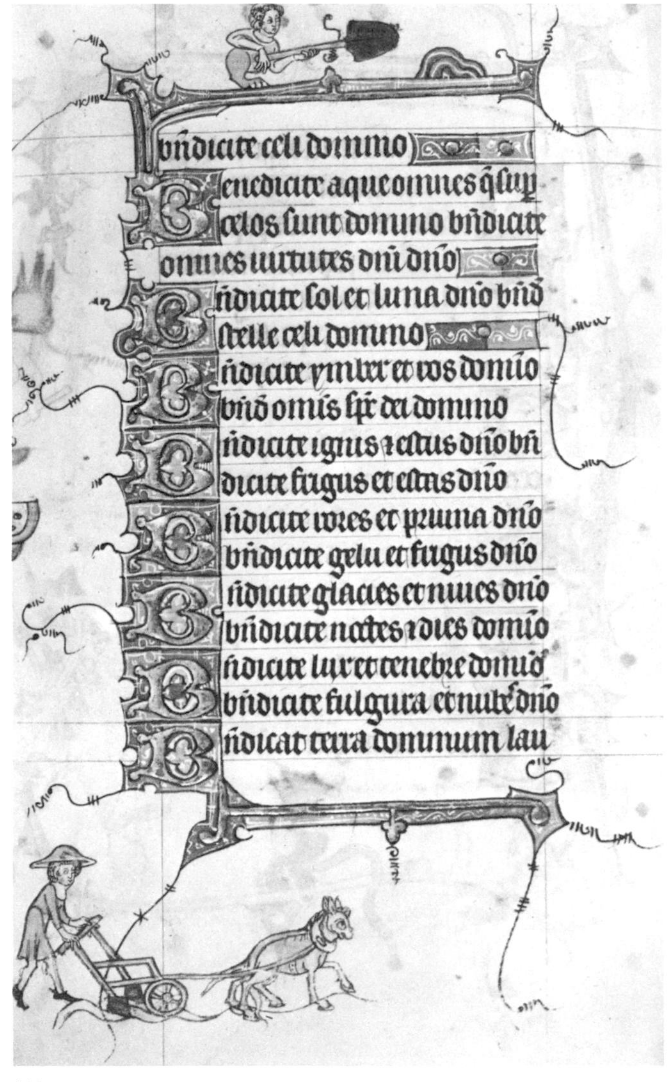

466

XCVI 462. Man nude with bagpipe: Glazier 24, f. 31v 463. Man picking grapes: BBR 10607, f. 134v 464. Man picking grapes, woman picking grapes, man treading grapes (September): Cloisters 54.1.2, f. 9v 465. Man plowing: BBR 1175, f. 156v 466. Man plowing; Hybrid man shoveling water (proverb?): Add. 36684, f. 33v

467

469

470

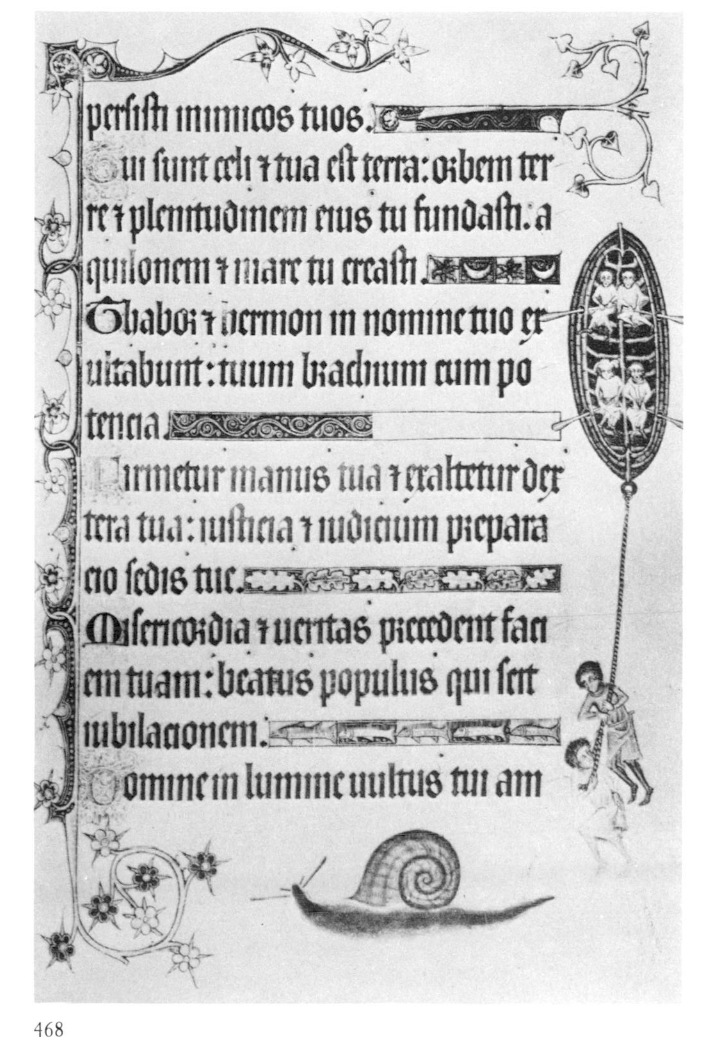
persisti inimicos tuos.
ui sunt celi ꝛ tua est terra: orbem ter
re ꝛ plenitudinem eius tu fundasti: a
quilonem ꝛ mare tu creasti.
Thabor ꝛ hermon in nomine tuo ex
ultabunt: tuum brachium cum po
tencia.
irmetur manus tua ꝛ exaltetur dex
tera tua: iusticia ꝛ iudicium prepara
cio sedis tue.
Misericordia ꝛ veritas precedent faci
em tuam: beatus populus qui scit
iubilacionem.
omine in lumine vultus tui am

468

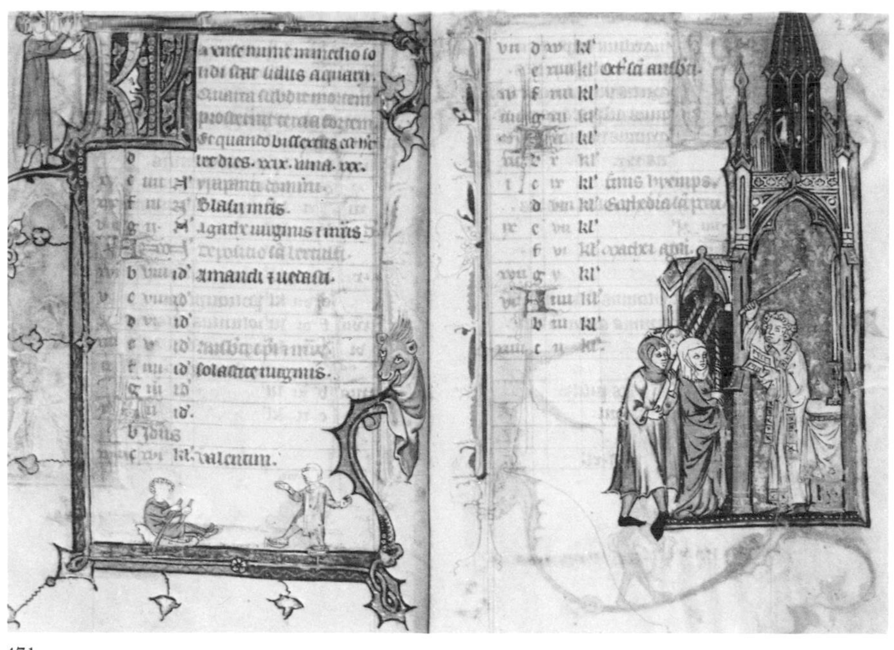

471

XCVII 467. Man praying (patron): Princeton 44-18, f. 114v 468. Man pulling boat; (Snail): Add. 42130, f. 160 469. Man reaping (harvesters): W. 88, f. 150 470. Man scything; Man sowing: Cambridge Dd.5.5, f. 325 471. Man sliding; Man skating; Man and ram, baiting (Candlemas; February): Douce 5, ff. lav-2

472

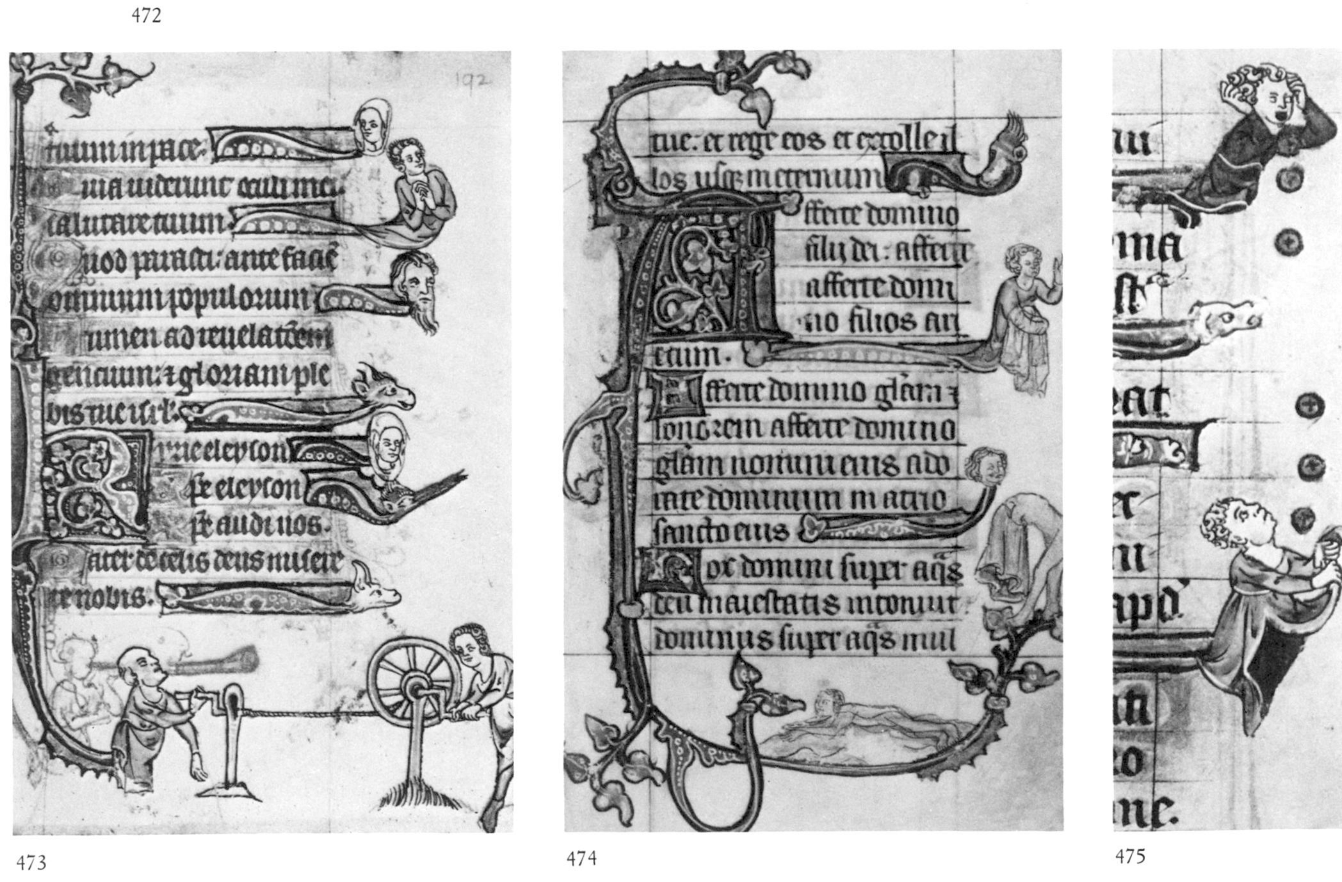

473 474 475

XCVIII 472. Man swimming (falconer); Falcon and duck, striking: fr. 12400, f. 115v 473. Man turning winch: Douce 6, f. 192 474. Man swimming; (Man disrobing, another holding garment): G.K.S. 3384, f. 57 475. Man vomiting coins: G.K.S. 3384, f. 82

476

477

gloriam eius in omnibus

478

479

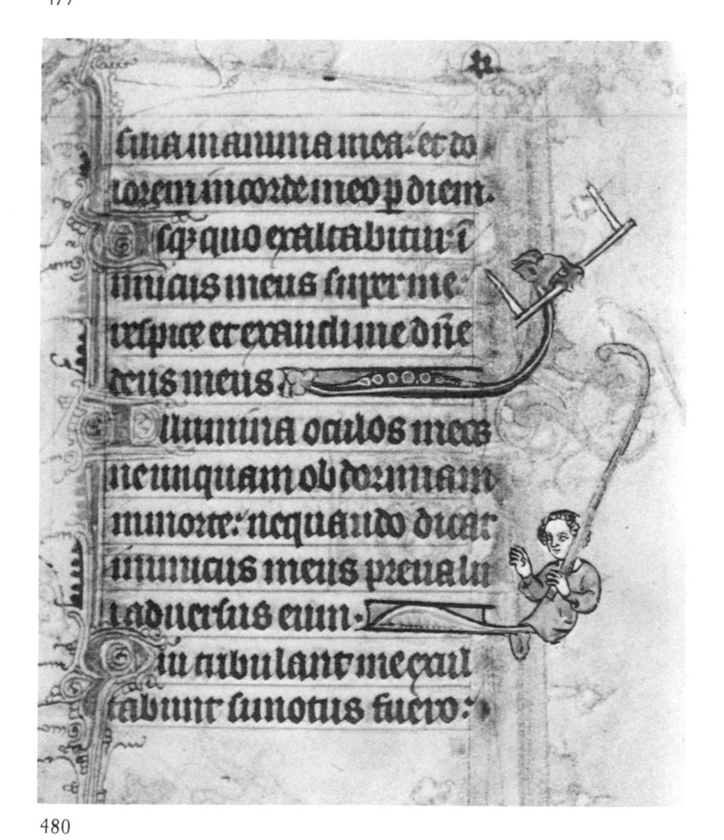

480

XCIX 476. Man threshing: W. 88, f. 118v 477. Man vomiting: Add. 49622, f. 62 478. Man with basket on back containing ape(s): Laud. Lat. 84, f. 227 479. Man with calipers, measuring column; Hybrid elephant; G.K.S. 3384, f. 111 480. Man with crook, beast balancing tapers: Douce 5, f. 39

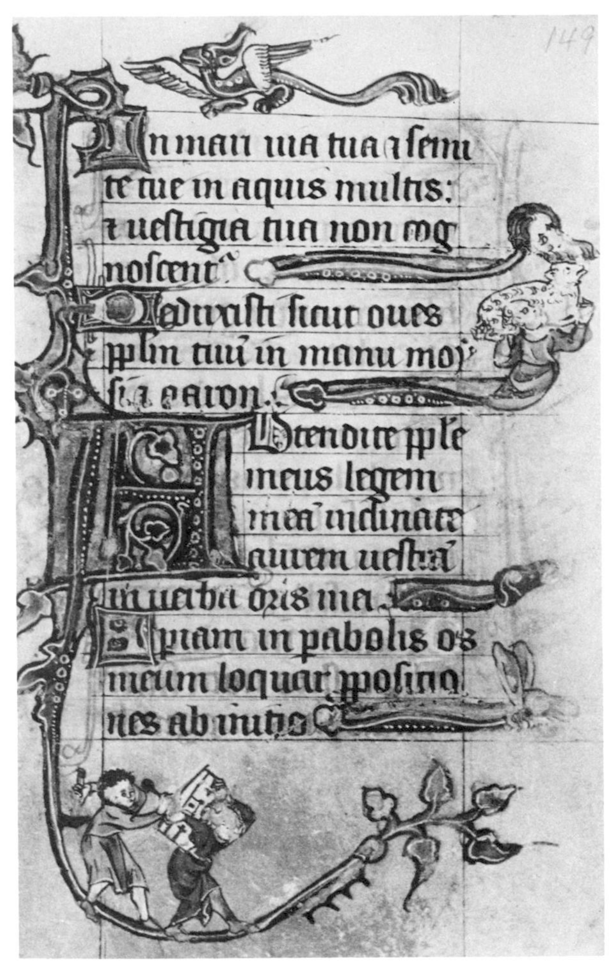

481

483

484

482

485

486

487

488

489

C (opposite page) 481. Man with chest on back; Man and sheep, carrying: G.K.S. 3384, f. 149 482. Man with greens (riddle): Douce 366, f. 89 483. Man with hammer and punch: Trinity B.11.22, f. 192v 484. Man with hammer and punch: Nancy 249, f. 27

CI 485. Man with hand organ: Arras 47, f. 52 486. Man with hand organ: St. Omer 5, f. 89 487. Man with harp: Yale MS., f. 209 488. Man with head of leaves: Add. 38114, f. 67v 489. Man, head of: W. 90, f. 208v

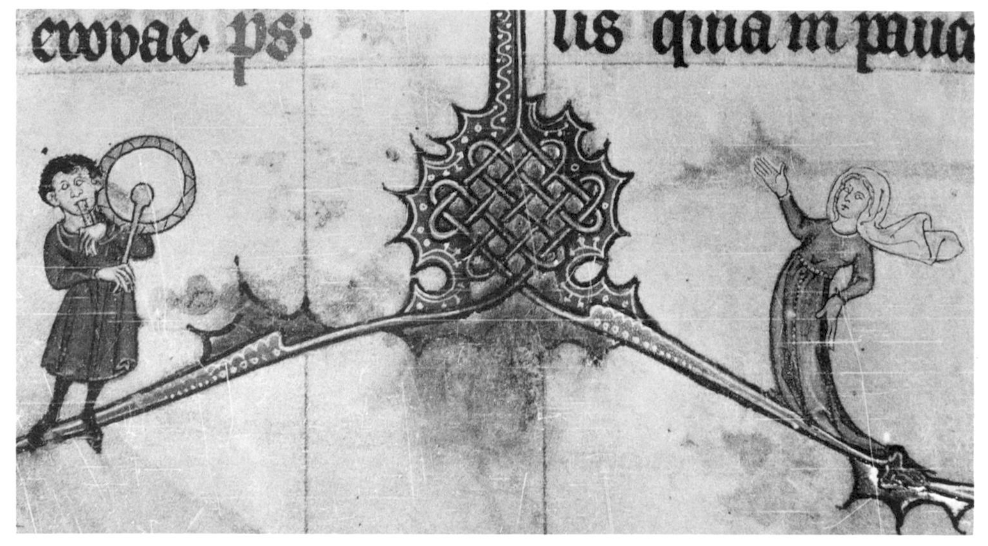
evovae. ps.
lis quia in pauc

490

492

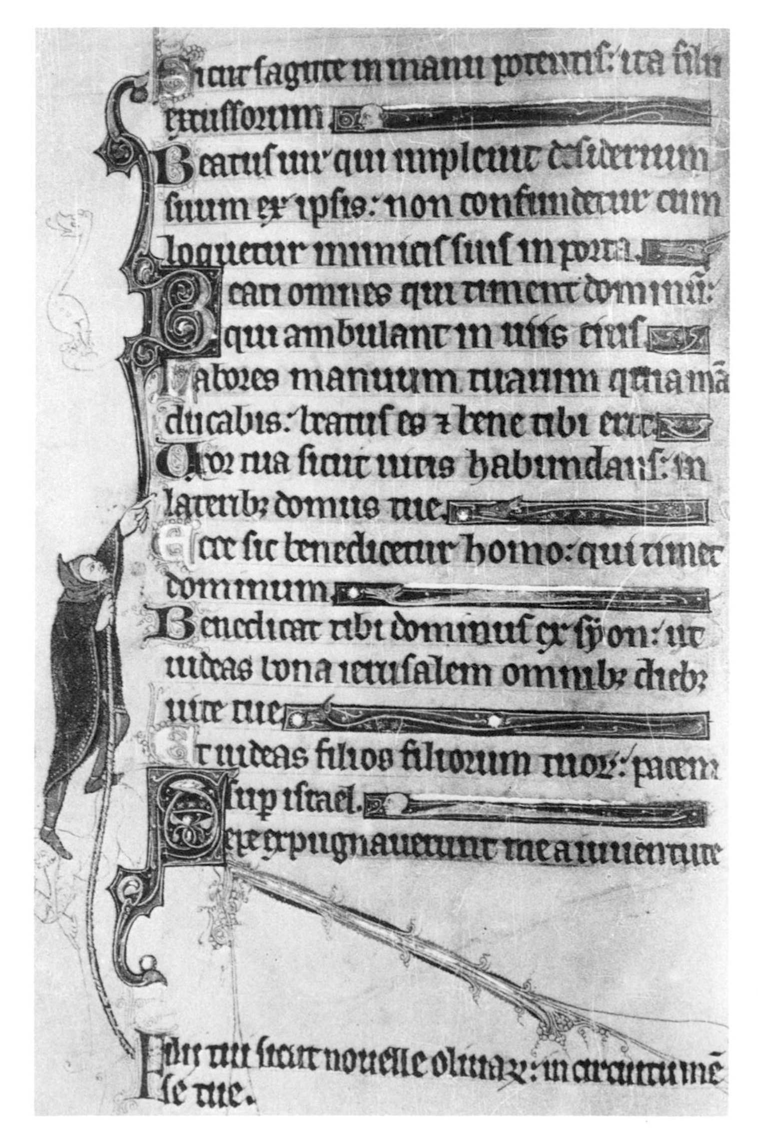

Sicut sagitte in manu potentis: ita filii
excussorum.
Beatus vir qui implevit desiderium
suum ex ipsis: non confundetur cum
loquetur inimicis suis in porta.
Beati omnes qui timent dominum:
qui ambulant in viis eius.
Labores manuum tuarum quia mā
ducabis: beatus es et bene tibi erit.
Uxor tua sicut vitis habundans: in
lateribus domus tue.
Ecce sic benedicetur homo: qui timet
dominum.
Benedicat tibi dominus ex syon: ut
videas bona ierusalem omnibus diebus
vite tue.
Et videas filios filiorum tuorum: pacem
super israel.
Sepe expugnaverunt me a iuventute
Filii tui sicut novelle olivarum: in circuitu mē
se tue.

491

493

CII 490. Man with pipe and tabor, woman dancing: Y. T. 8, f. 345v 491. Man with rope, pulling omitted verse into place: W. 102, f. 33v 492. (Man with stone) Putting: St. Omer 5, f. 62 493. (Man with stone) Putting: Arras 47, f. 31

494

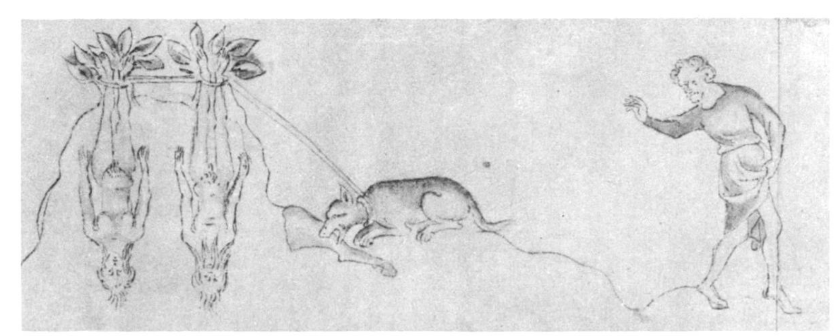

495

496

497

Conuertere domine et eripe animam meam:
saluum me fac propter misericordiam tuam.

498

CIII 494. Man with wheelbarrow containing four humans: BBR 9391, f. 130v 495. Mandrake, Bestiary representation: Royal 2 B.VII, f. 119v 496. Manticora, Bestiary representation: Munich c.g. 16, f. 35 497. Mermaid(s) with trumpet(s): Hague 78.D.40, f. 129 498. Mermaid and offspring, suckling: Add. 24686, f. 13

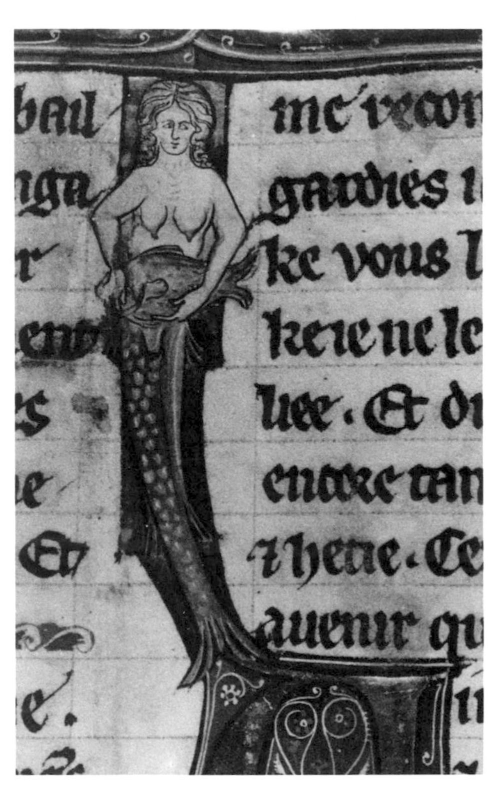

499

uia exacuerunt ut gladium

500

501

posuerunt te in conspectu suo.

502

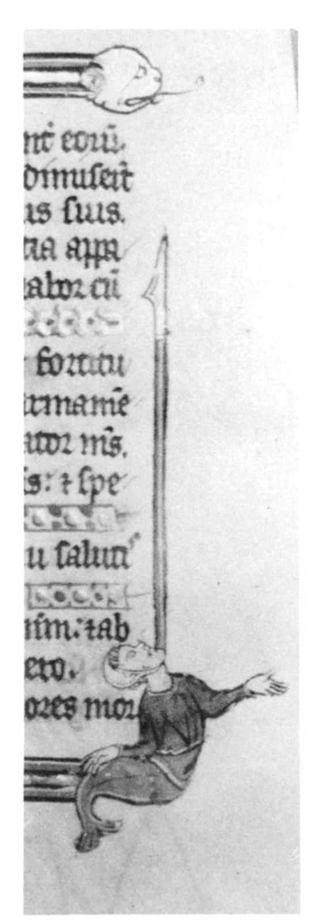

503

CIV 499. Mermaid with fish: Yale MS., f. 29 500. Mermaid with vielle (siren dancing): Tournai Ps., f. 104 501. Merman with vielle (mermaid dancing): Cambrai 103, f. 365v 502. Merman and man, shot by: Rutland Ps., f. 87v 503. Merman balancing spear: Kraus 75/88, f. 34

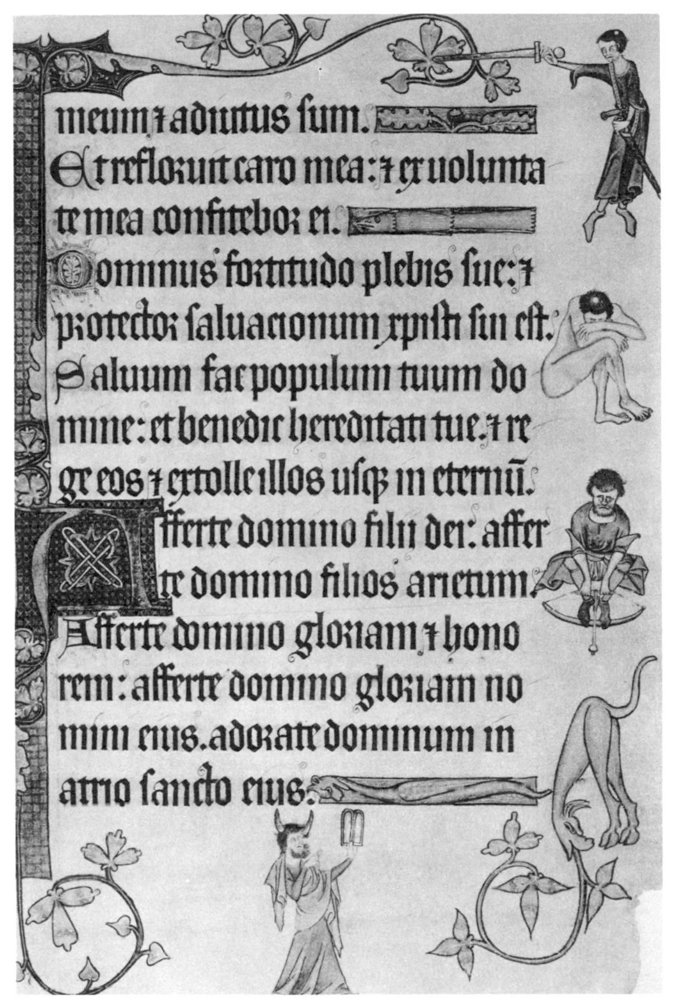

504

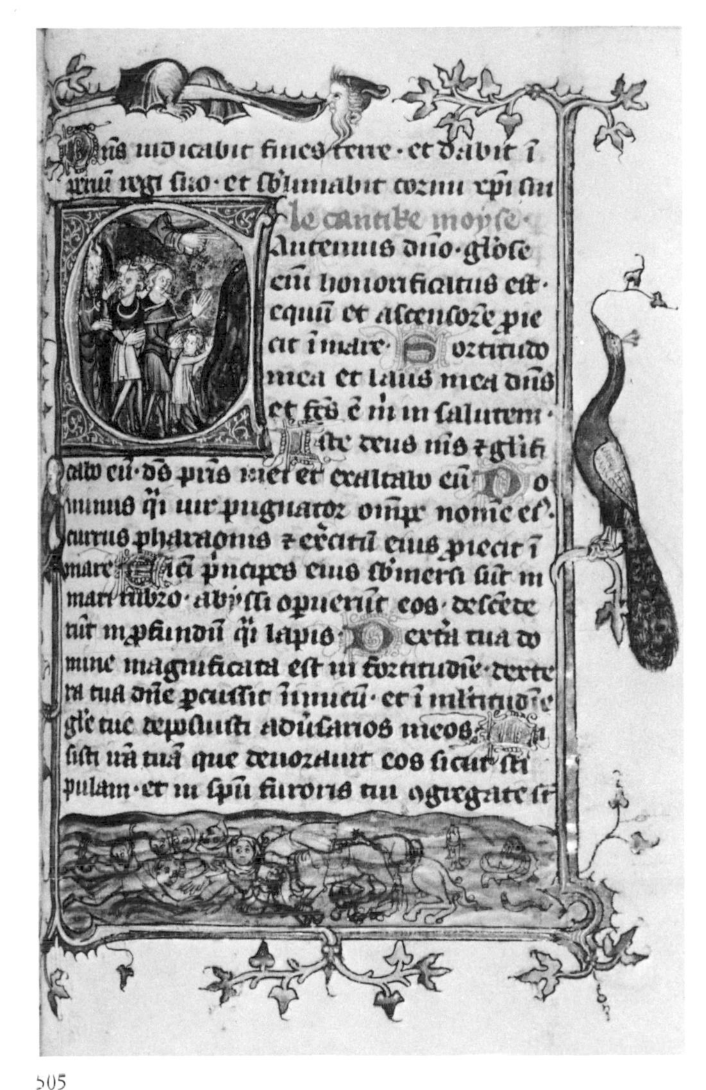

505

506

507

CV 504. Moses with Tablets; Man and beast, bending crossbow at; Cleric nude, seated; Cleric with sword: Add. 42130, f. 54 505. Moses and Aaron, pursuers drowning; Peacock: M. 88, f. 137 506. Moses as infant: Y.T. 8, f. 213v 507. Moses before burning bush: Y.T. 8, f. 214v

508

509

510

511

512

CVI 508. (Musical instruments, parody) Cleric playing bellows with tongs; Hybrid man with triangle; Cleric with trumpet, woman dancing; Ape and dog, seated; Prophet; Dog and stag, pursuing: Trinity B.11.22, f. 20 509. (Musical instruments, parody) Cleric playing bellows with distaff, woman dancing: Stowe 17, f. 38 510. (Musical instruments, parody) Goat playing jawbone with rake; Dog with bone; Hybrid man with hand bells: Cloisters 54.1.2, f. 22 511. (Musical instruments, parody) Hybrid king playing jawbone with plectrum, dog dancing; Putting; Man balancing on hands of man: Cloisters 54.1.2, f. 54 512. (Musical instruments, parody) Hybrid man playing bellows with tongs: Arras 229, f. 187v

513

514

515

516

517

CVII 513. (Musical instruments, parody) Hybrid man playing bellows with tongs: Douce 366, f. 24 514. (Musical instruments, parody) Hybrid man playing cock with tongs; Hare with harp: Stowe 17, f. 92v 515. (Musical instruments, parody) Hybrid man playing wheat sheaf with rake: BBR 9391, f. 113v 516. (Musical instruments, parody) Hybrid man playing dog like bagpipe, man balancing on his head, dancing; Man with harmonica (whistle?); Hybrid cleric with harp; Hybrid man with mandola; Soldier: Cloisters 54.1.2, f. 166 517. (Musical instruments, parody) Man playing vielle with rake, woman dancing: Chantilly 62, f. 117

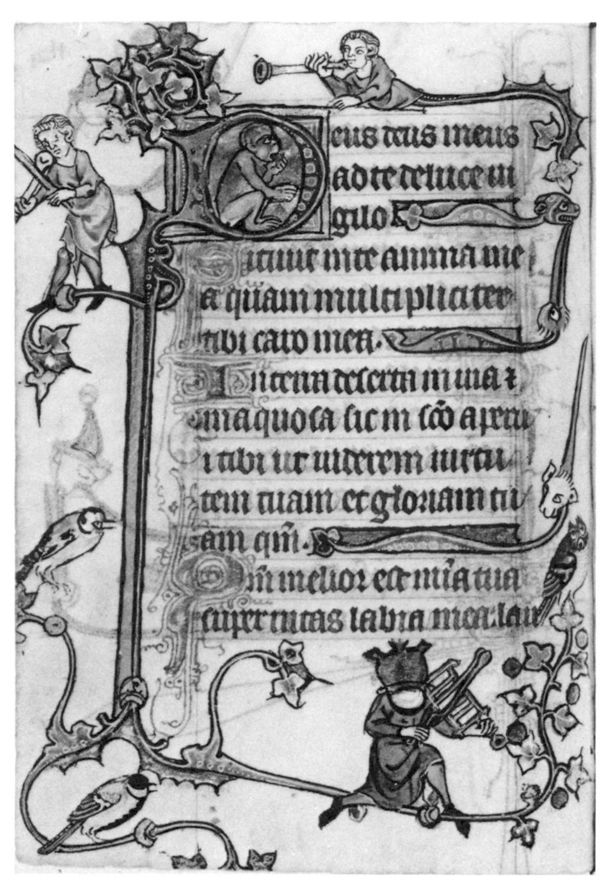

518

519

520

521

522

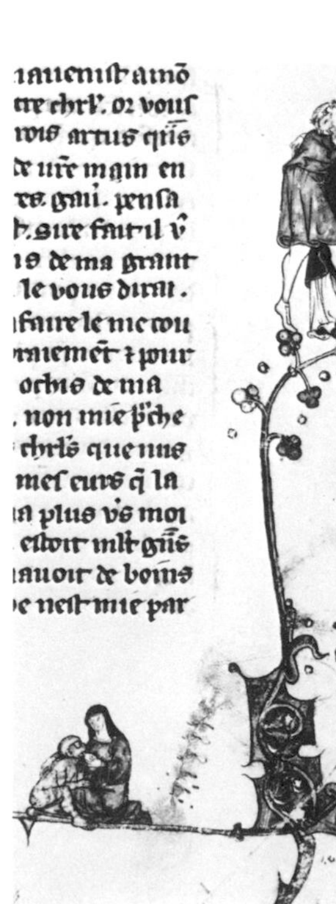

523

CVIII 518. (Musical instruments, parody) Man playing grill with tongs (pot on head); Man with trumpet; Man playing spoon with stick: Douce 5, f. 164v 519. (Musical instruments, parody) Woman playing tongs with spoon: Trinity B.11.22, f. 191v 520. (Musical instruments, parody) Mermaid playing jawbone with tongs: Glazier 24, f. 40 521. Nebuchadnezzar and Daniel: St. Omer 5, f. 115v 522. Noah: Munich c.g. 16, f. 21v 523. Nun and ape, suckling; Man and woman embracing: Rylands fr. 2, f. 212

524

526

525

527

me alixand li donent cops

528

CIX 524. Nun with distaff, cat playing with spindle: Stowe 17, f. 34 525. Obscaena: exposing genitals, man (nude, tailed) before nun: Add. 49622, f. 90v 526. Obscaena: beak aimed, stork at ape: Tournai Ps., f. 209v 527. Obscaena: defecating, ape: Tournai Ps., f. 125v 528. Obscaena: defecating, man before kneeling nun: Bodley 264, f. 56

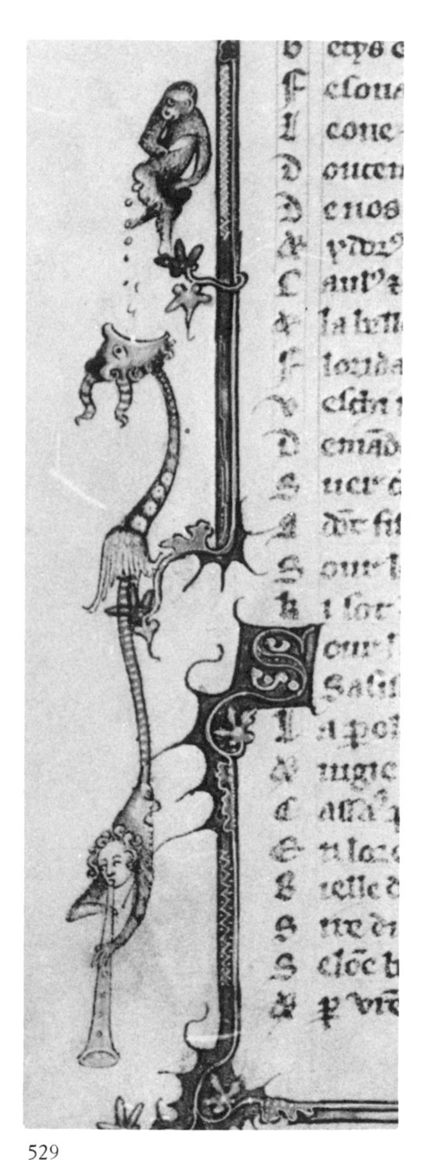

529

530

531

532

533

CX 529. Obscaena: defecating, ape; (Hybrid man with trumpet): Glazier 24, f. 47v 530. Obscaena: defecating, man: Trinity B.11.22, f. 73 531. Obscaena: defecating, man nude (Templar?) before ape: Glazier 24, f. 57 532. Obscaena: defecating, man: Glazier 24, f. 27v 533. Obscaena: exposing hindquarters, ape: Tournai Ps., f. 54v

534

535

536

537

CXI 534. Obscaena: kissing hindquarters, beast and ape: Glazier 24, f. 102 535. Obscaena: kissing hindquarters, hybrid bishop and ape: Glazier 24, f. 95v 536. Obscaena: kissing hindquarters, Templar and cleric: Glazier 24, f. 93 537. Obscaena: revering hindquarters, ape: Glazier 24, f. 78

538

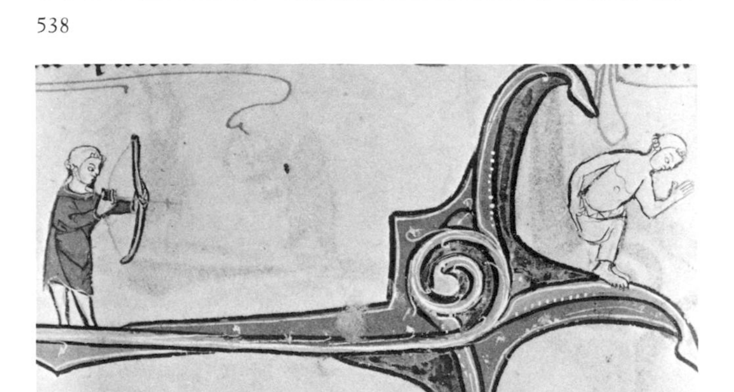

539

540

541

542

CXII 538. Obscaena: revering hindquarters, ass: Glazier 24, f. 41 539. Obscaena: shooting hindquarters: BBR 9391, f. 93 540. Obscaena: shooting hindquarters: BBR 10607, f. 17v 541. Obscaena: spear aimed at hindquarters: Melbourne 1254/3, f. 16 542. Obscaena: trumpet aimed at hindquarters: Yale MS., f. 147

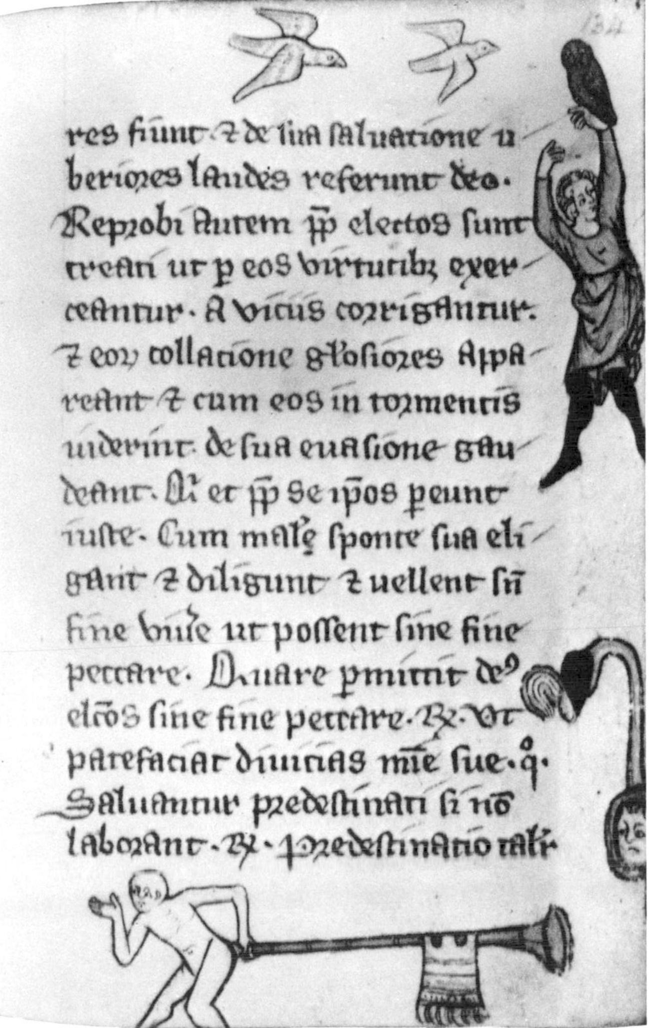

543

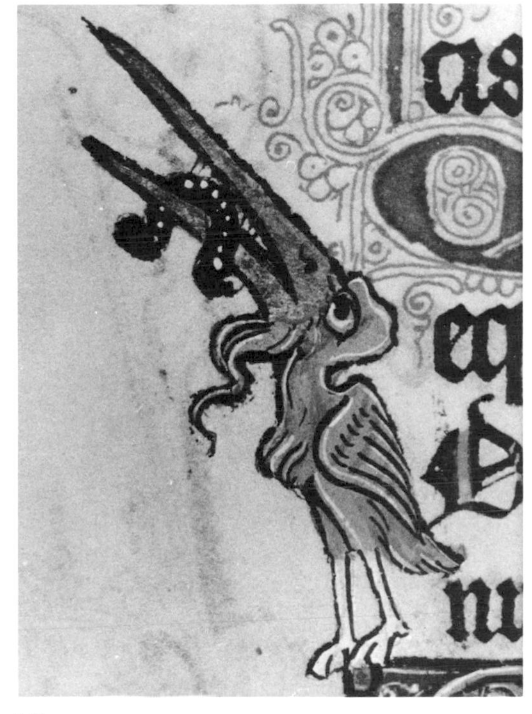

545

544

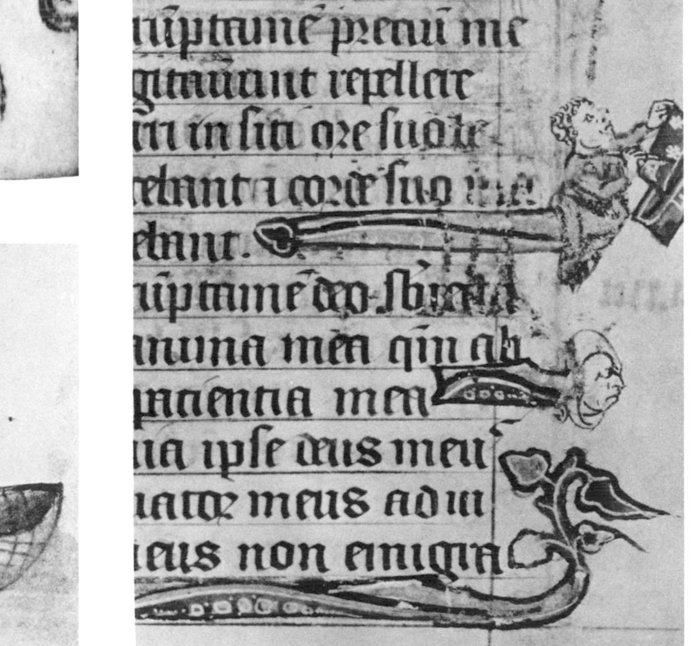

546

CXIII 543. Obscaena: trumpet aimed at hindquarters; Falconer: Rothschild MS., f. 134 544. Ostrich, Bestiary representation: Munich c.g. 16, f. 28 545. Ostrich with horseshoe: latin 1076, f. 16v 546. Painter: G.K.S. 3384, f. 113

547

548

549

550

CXIV 547. Panatios: Rutland Ps., f. 88v 548. Panther, Bestiary representation: Munich c.g. 16, f. 21 549. Panther, Bestiary representation: Trinity B.11.22, f. 28v 550. Patrons (couple); Ape with sword, climbing border stalk; Centaur as cleric: Melbourne 1254/3, f. 11

551

552

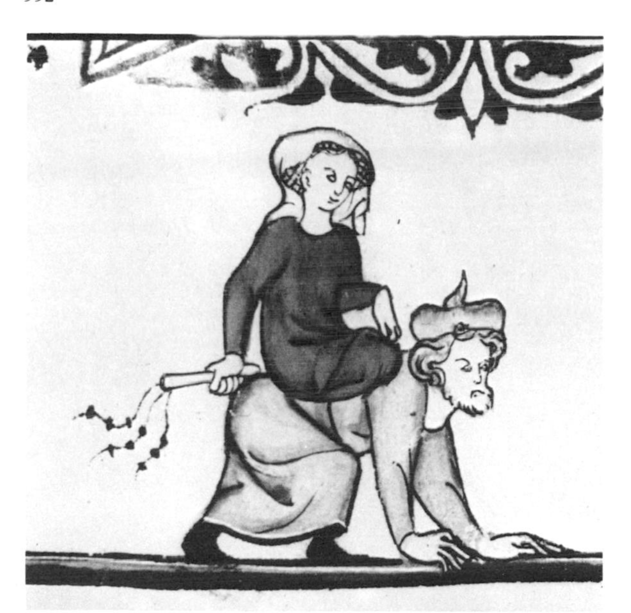

554

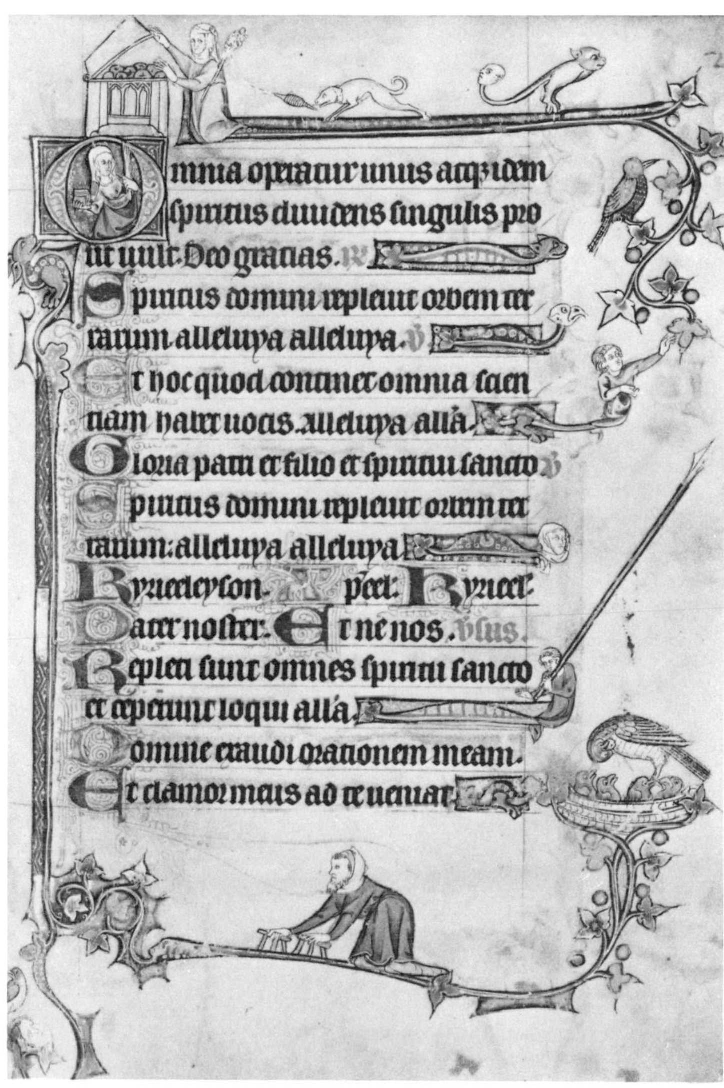

553

8·Ecce ascendimus ihero

555

CXV 551. Pedlar with silver beakers: Douce 118, f. 55 552. Pelican in piety; Phoenix: latin 10435, f. 6 553. Pelican in piety; Woman with distaff and spindle, opening treasure chest; Man, crippled: Trinity B.11.22, f. 213 554. Phyllis and Aristotle: Arras 47, f. 74 555. Phyllis and Aristotle: Y.T. 8, f. 187

556

558

559

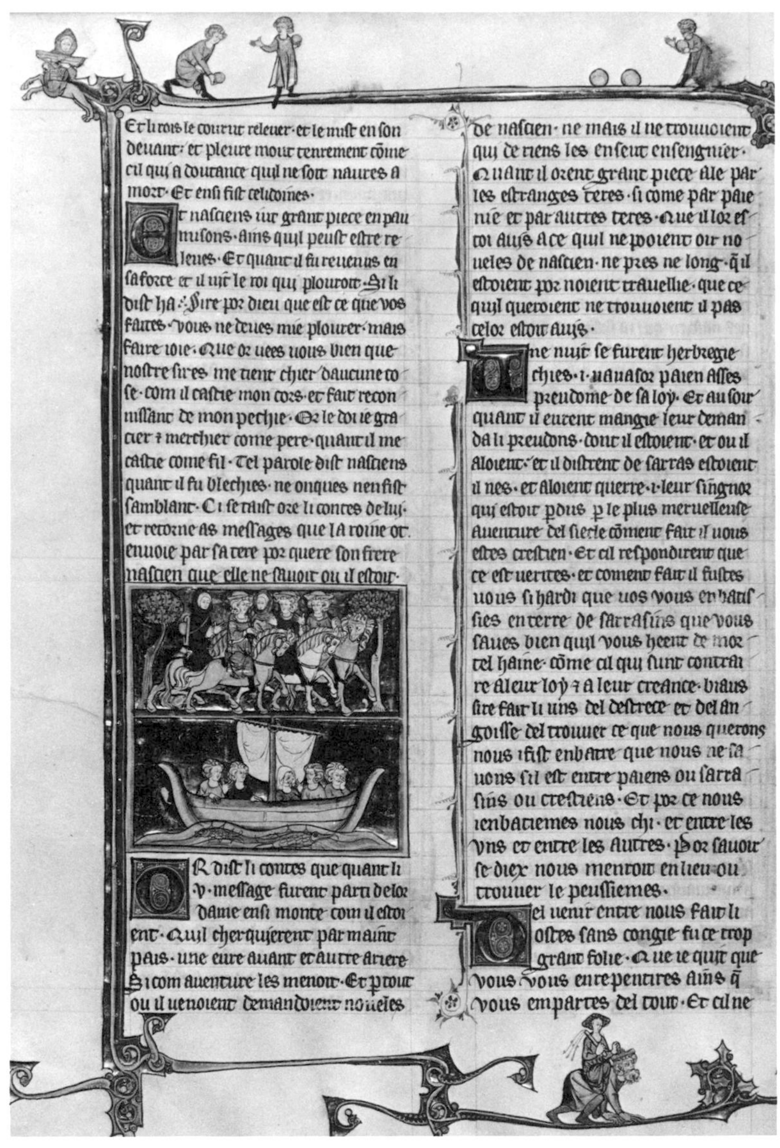

557

CXVI 556. Phyllis and Aristotle: fr. 95, f. 254 557. Phyllis and Aristotle: Bowls, men; Centaur with psaltery: fr. 95, f. 61v 558. Physician and bird-headed man (cleric?) with purse: Melbourne 1254/3, f. 11v 559. Physician and man, bleeding: Add. 42130, f. 61 560. Physician(?) and man, seated before: Bodley 264, f. 79

560

561

562

564

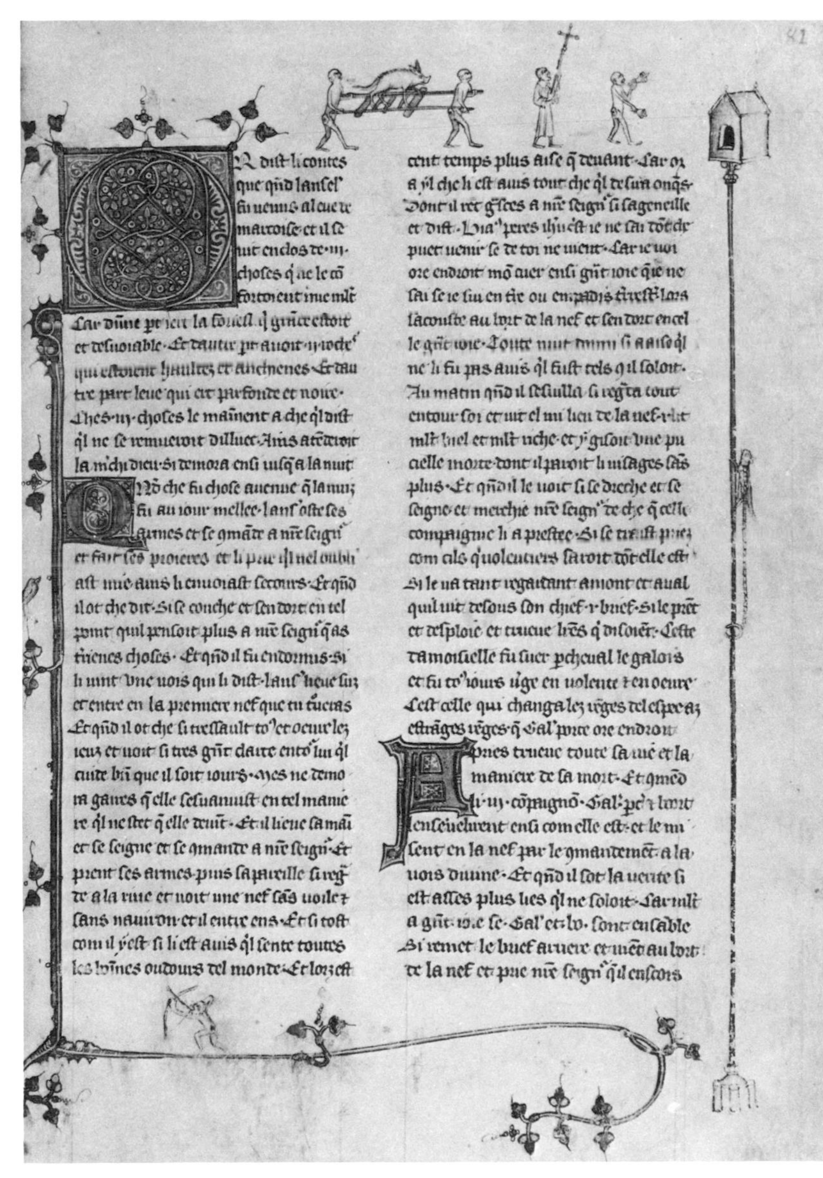

563

565

CXVII 561. Physician and woman: Yale MS., f. 154v 562. Physician and woman: G.K.S. 3384, f. 289 563. Procession: boar on litter borne by apes; Squirrel ascending pole; Ape and bird, hunting: Arsenal 5218, f. 81 564. Procession: ape-bishop: Douce 6, f. 95v 565. Procession: ape-cleric(s), ass-cleric: Glazier 24, f. 75

rdo in dedicatione ecclesie. Pridie an
tequam ecclia consecretur. asferant
reliquie in loco honesto extra ecclesiã sub
tentorio. fiantq ibi uigilie p totam noc
tem. In preparando se ad diuinũ officiũ
in bñdictõe ecclie. dicat eps in ipa domo
in q preparat se hanc oronem sine. Dns
uobiscũ. Et sine. Oremus. oratio.
irtutum celestium deus de cuius

566

CXVIII 566. Procession: clerics; Woman with vielle, woman dancing; Man with shield; Man with gittern; Hybrid men fighting: Fitz. 298, f. 1

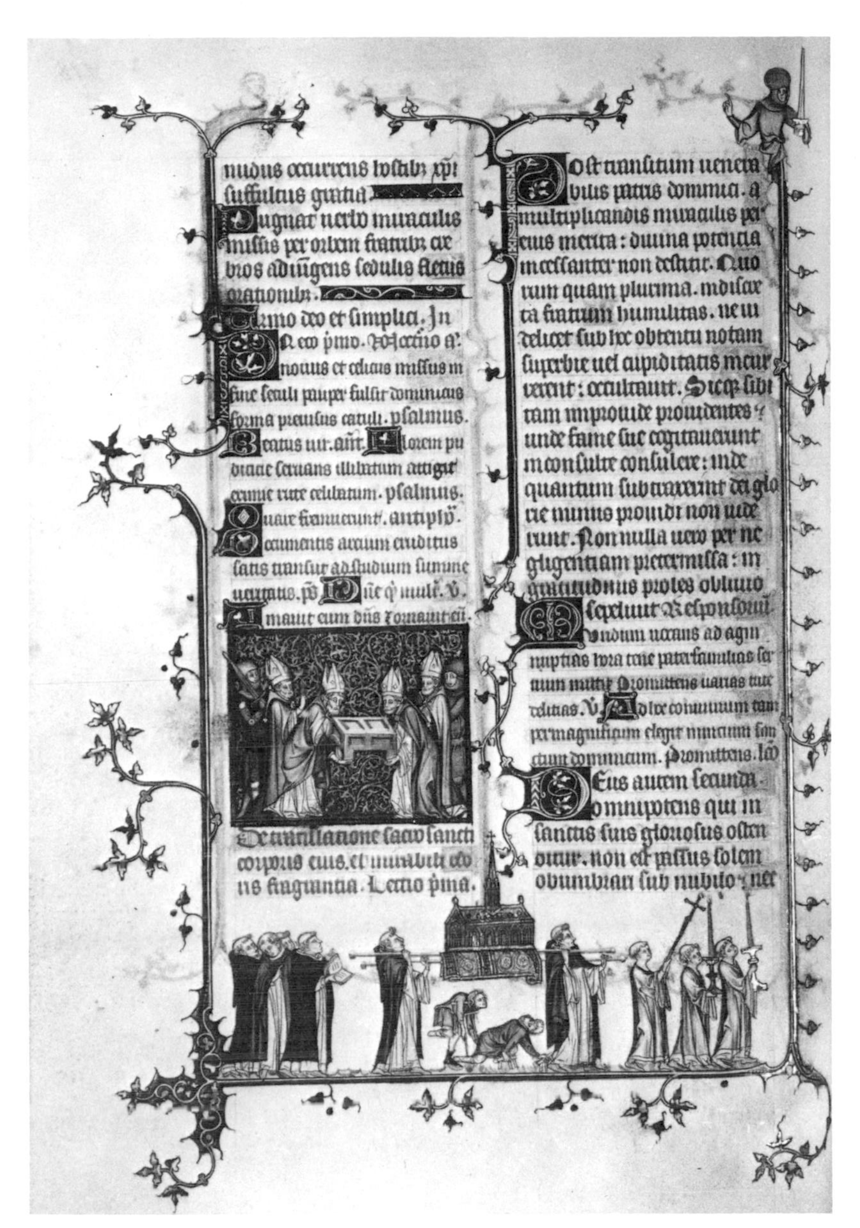

567

568

CXIX 567. Procession: Dominicans: latin 10484, f. 218v 568. Procession: funeral: BBR 9391, f. 116

569

570

571

572

CXX 569. Procession: funeral of dog: Add. 49622, f. 133 570. Procession: hares: Add. 36684, f. 24v 571. Procession: hare-cleric, ram-cleric: Melbourne 1254/3, f. 29v 572. Procession: funeral; Man with vielle: W. 45, f. 49

domino deo ipsius qui
fecit celū ꝛ terrā mare
ꝛ omnia que in eis sūt.
Qui custodit ueritatē
ī seculū facit iudicium
iniuriam paciētibz dat
escam esurientibz
Dominꝰ soluit compedi
tos dominꝰ illuminat
cecos.
Dominus erigit elisos
dns diligit iustos.
Dominus custodit ad
uenas pupillū ꝛ uidu
am suscipiet ꝛ uiam pec

573

267
Placebo dño
in regione
uiuorum
ps Dilexi
qm ꝛ Heu
m quia in
colatus me
us prolongatus est ps Ad do
minum ꝛ Dominus custodit
te ab omni malo custodiat a
nimam tuam dominus ps
Leuaui ꝛ Si iniquitates obs
eruaueris domine domine quis
sustinebit ps De pfundis ꝛ
Opera manuum tuarum do
mine ne despicias ps Confite
C.lxxxvii
.cc.vii.
cc.vii.
.cc.xii.
.cc xix.

574

575

576

CXXI 573. Procession: funeral; Hybrid nun with book; Hybrid man with hand bells: G.K.S. 3384, f. 292 574. Procession: funeral: clerics and mourners: Nancy 249, f. 267 575. Proverbs: ass bleeding, leaning over fence: M. 88, f. 71 576. Proverbs: fight over pants: Glazier 24, f. 30v

577

579

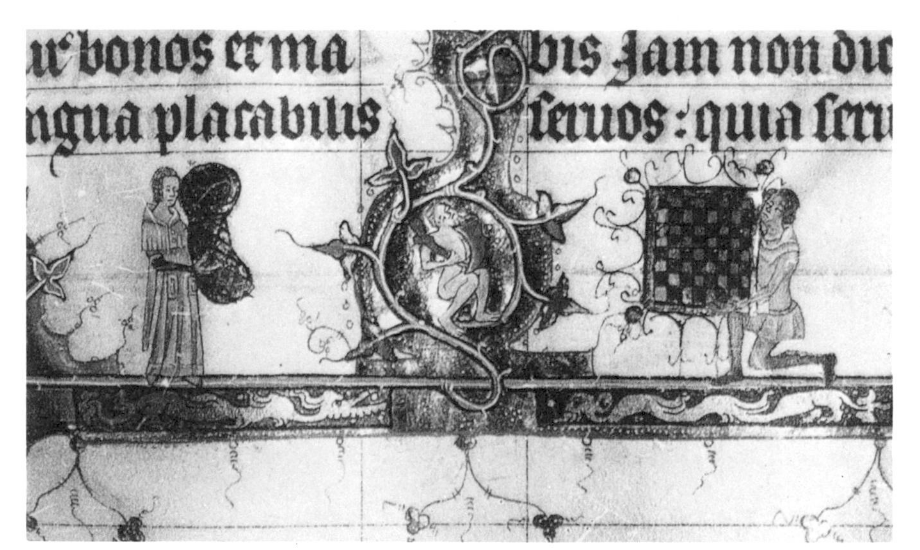

578

580

581

582

CXXII 577. Proverbs: gameboard and pitcher on trees: BBR 9217, f. 116 578. Proverbs: gameboard held by kneeling man before woman with basket: BBR 9217, f. 123 579. Proverbs: goose shoed: Melbourne 1254/3, f. 7v 580. Proverbs: goose shoed: G.K.S. 3384, f. 110 581. Proverbs: eggs in nest: W. 82, f. 179v 582. Proverbs: eggs in nest; Centaur with shawms: fr. 95, f. 343

583

585

584

586

587

CXXIII 583. Proverbs: eggs in nest: Yale MS., f. 31 584. Proverbs: eggs in nest: Douce 6, f. 93v 585. Puppet show: Bodley 264, f. 54v 586. Puppet show: Bodley 264, f. 76 587. Pygmalion: Tournai CI, f. 319

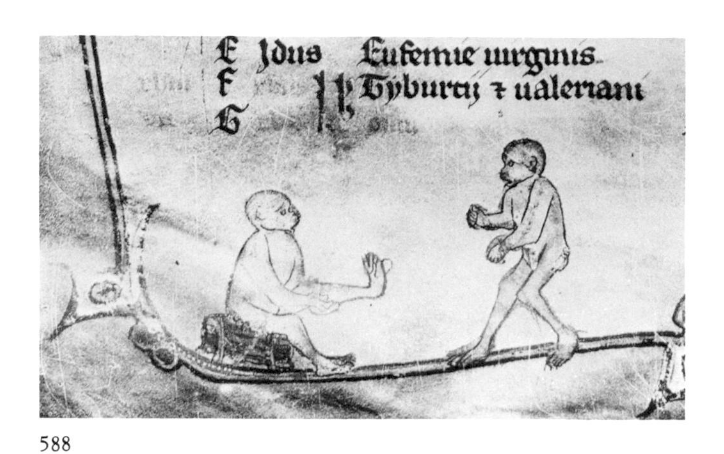
Jdus Eufemie uirginis
Tyburtij + ualeriani

588

589

ustice + droit du duc qui la robe
cans respont de toute sa cite

590

antate domino canticum psalm
nouu quia mirabilia fecit

591

592

593

CXXIV 588. Quintain, balancing: ape: Schilling MS., April 589. Quintain, balancing: man: Princeton 44-18, f. 183 590. Quintain, balancing: man: Bodley 264, f. 78v 591. Quintain, tilting at: ape: Melbourne 1254/3, f. 61 592. Quintain, tilting at: hare; Man with pipe and tabor: Trinity B.11.22, f. 214 593. Quintain, tilting at: man: Nancy 249, f. 193

594

595

596

597

CXXV 594. Quintain, tilting at: knight; Ape and beast kissing; Jesus Christ, head of, between stag antlers: Douce 6, f. 113 595. Ringtoss: apes; Man blowing toasting fork; Man playing bellows with tongs; Man with bagpipe: Cambridge Dd. 5.5, f. 253 596. *Roman de Renart:* fox and lion: Royal 10 E.IV, f. 55 597. *Roman de Renart:* fox and lion: Royal 10 E.IV, f. 57

e placatus accipias

598

Quil na si bele dame iusquas bonnes artus
La roine respont tais par pute aventure

599

600

601

CXXVI 598. *Roman de Renart:* fox and wolf: Fitz. 298, f. 138v 599. (*Roman de Renart*) Procession: funeral of fox: Bodley 264, f. 79v 600. St. Christopher: Stowe 17, f. 113v 601. St. Catherine: Princeton 44-18, f. 86

mea non custodierint

602

nes & omnes abyssi
Ignis grando nix glacies spi
ritus procellarum: que faciunt
verbum eius
Montes & omnes colles: ligna
fructifera & omnes cedri
Cy un home debrusa sun col.

603

exaltavit cornu populi sui
Ympnus omnibus sanctis eius: fi
lius israel populo appropinquanti sibi.
Cantate domino canticum
novum: laus eius in ec
clesia sanctorum

604

605

CXXVII 602. St. Dominic: Melbourne 1254/3, f. 21 603, 604. St. Dominic: miracle of man with broken neck: Y.T. 13, ff. 189v-190 605. St. Dunstan: Royal 10 E.IV, f. 197

606 607

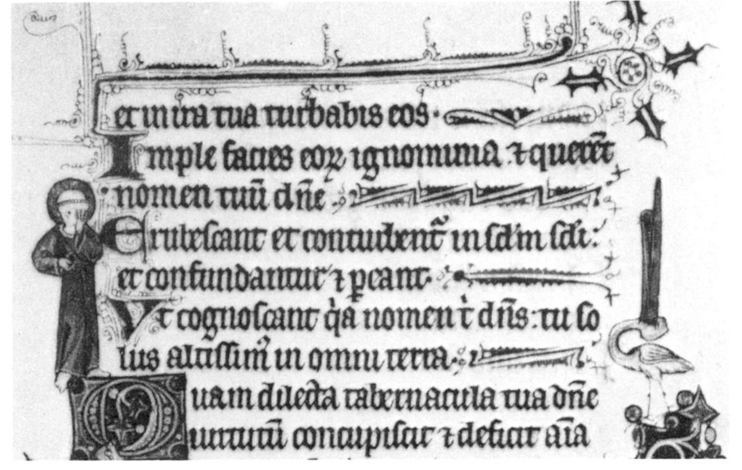

608

609

610

CXXVIII 606, 607. St. Edward the Confessor and St. John the Evangelist: Y. T. 13, ff. 190v-191 608. St. Francis covering face: latin 1076, f. 104v 609. St. Francis preaching to birds: Auct. D.3.2, f. 122 610. St. Francis cutting habit: Y.T. 13, f. 180v

611

613

614

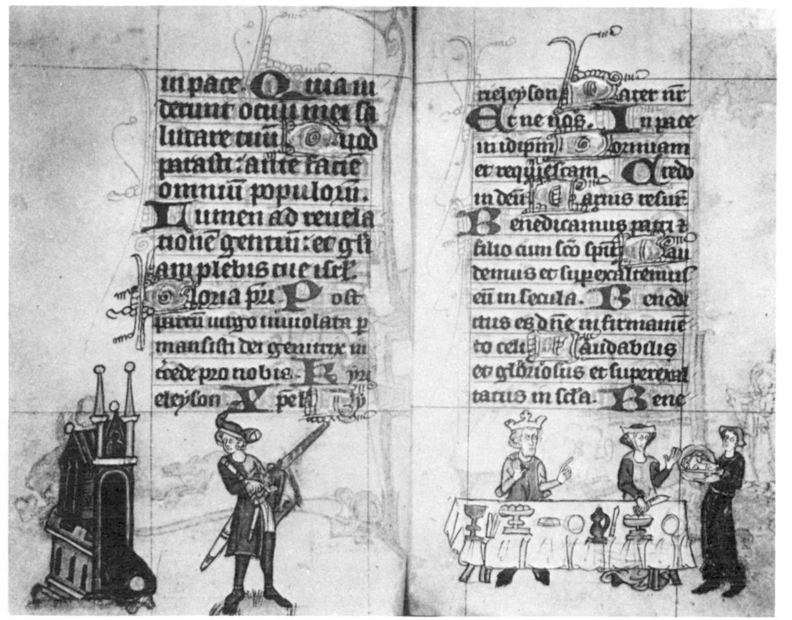

615

612

CXXIX 611. St. Francis preaching to birds; St. Clare and St. Elisabeth of Hungary: W. 45, f. 191 612. St. Francis kneeling: Stowe 17, f. 175 613. St. George: Stowe 17, ff. 154v-155 614. St. Hubert: Hague 78.D.40, f. 66v 615. St. John the Baptist; (Salome): Stowe 17, ff. 137v-138

616

618

617

619

620

621

CXXX 616. St. John the Baptist (burning of saint's bones): latin 10484, f. 318v 617. St. John the Baptist; (Salome): Hague 78.D.40, f. 108 618. St. Amalberga: Add. 29253, f. 409 619. St. Lawrence: Burney 345, f. 69 620. St. Margaret: Kraus 75/88, f. 196 621. St. Margaret: Valenciennes 838, f. 55v

moitie au noel 7 moitie apasque dentour

622

623

ationus discipulus effectus est

624

625

CXXXI 622. St. Martin (and the beggar): BBR 1175, f. 92 623. St. Mary the Egyptian: Royal 10 E.IV, f. 280v 624. St. Nicholas (miracle of three daughters): Y. T. 8, f. 259 625. St. Paul (conversion of): Valenciennes 838, f. 61v

626

627

628

629

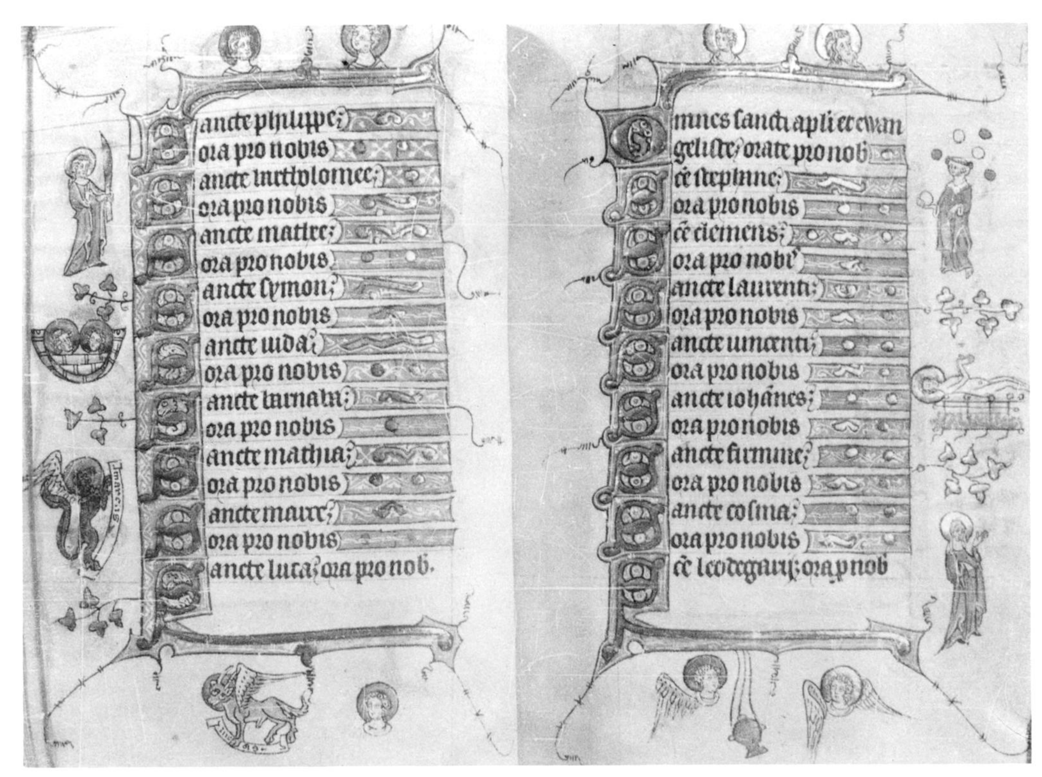

630

CXXXII 626. St. Stephen: Douce 118, f. 66v 627. St. Ursula: Royal 2 B.VII, f. 273 628. St. Vitalis: Royal 2 B.VII, f. 248 629. Saint, unidentified, male; Angel with censer: Valenciennes 838, f. 55v 630. St. Bartholomew; St. Simon; St. Jude; Evangelist symbols; St. Lawrence; St. Stephen: Add. 36684, ff. 71v-72

631

632

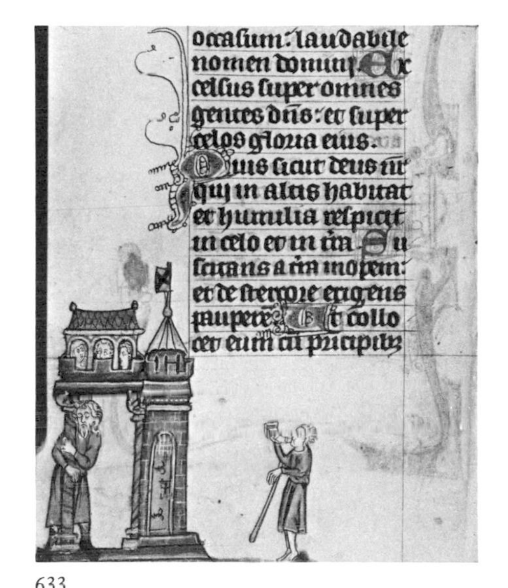

633

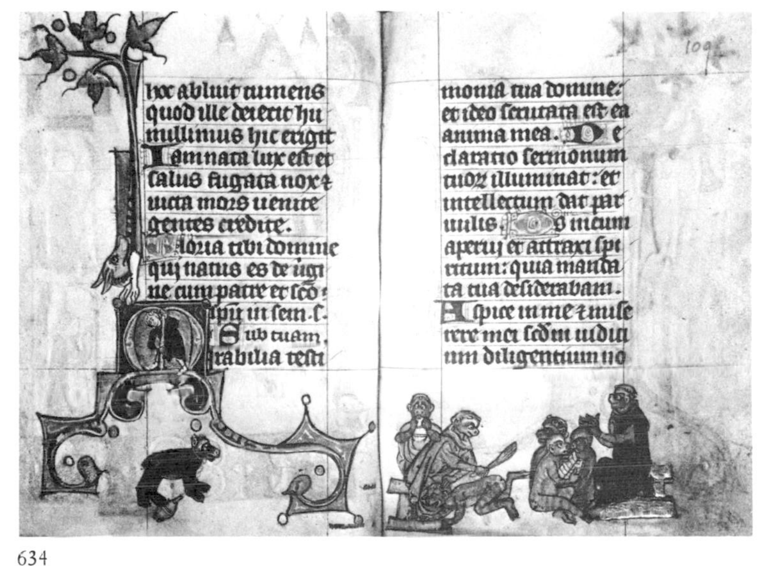

634

635

636

CXXXIII 631. Samson and lion, rending: fr. 95, f. 292v 632. Samson and lion, rending: Y. T. 13, f. 7v 633. Samson tearing down house of Philistines: Stowe 17, f. 122v 634. School attended by apes; Bear chained: Stowe 17, ff. 108v-109 635. School attended by apes: Fitz. 298, f. 76v 636. School attended by apes: fr. 95, f. 355

o dabit: dominus benedicet
populo suo in pace
Exaltabo te domine quo
niam suscepisti me: nec
delectasti inimicos meos super
me
Domine ds mis clamaui ad
te et sanasti me.
Domine eduxisti ab inferno a
nimam meam: saluasti me
a descendentibus in lacum.
Psallite domino sci eius: et

637

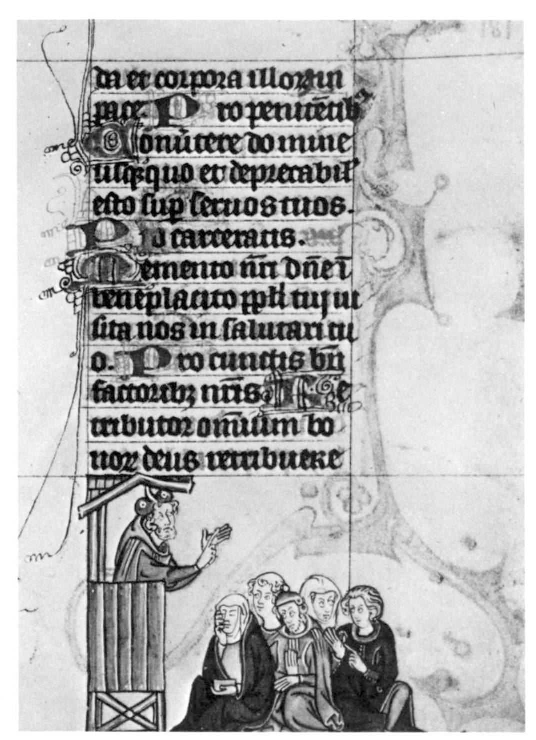

da et corpora illorum
pace. Pro penitentib
Conuertere domine
usquequo et deprecabil
esto sup seruos tuos.
Pro carceratis.
Memento nri dñe i
beneplacito ppli tui ui
sita nos in salutari tu
o. Pro cunctis be
nefactoribz nris. Re
tributor omnium bo
norum deus retribuere

638

Illumina oculos
Dominus de celo pro

639

estoit grans t lons
nus nos en irons
les paullons
puis si nos armerons
ki estoit biaus t lons
ulant vers de candhol
saili es archons

640

D ot on proit son cuer engrant par me ieter
K i pense sens deour il lessiet desirer
S i fort kil est menes pres iusq a la famer
C ar de son desirier le couient osirer
S il gist en son lit il ne puet reposer
A ins le couient souent fremir t tressuer
D e lun costet sur lautre tourner t retourner

641

CXXXIV 637. School attended by apes: Nancy 249, f. 41 638. School attended by men and women (sermon?): Stowe 17, f. 181 639. School attended by apes; Bishop; Cleric and woman: latin 14284, f. 69v 640. Schoolmaster: ape, beast reciting or singing: Glazier 24, f. 76 641. School attended by pigs; Cock and hens: Glazier 24, f. 31

642

643

644

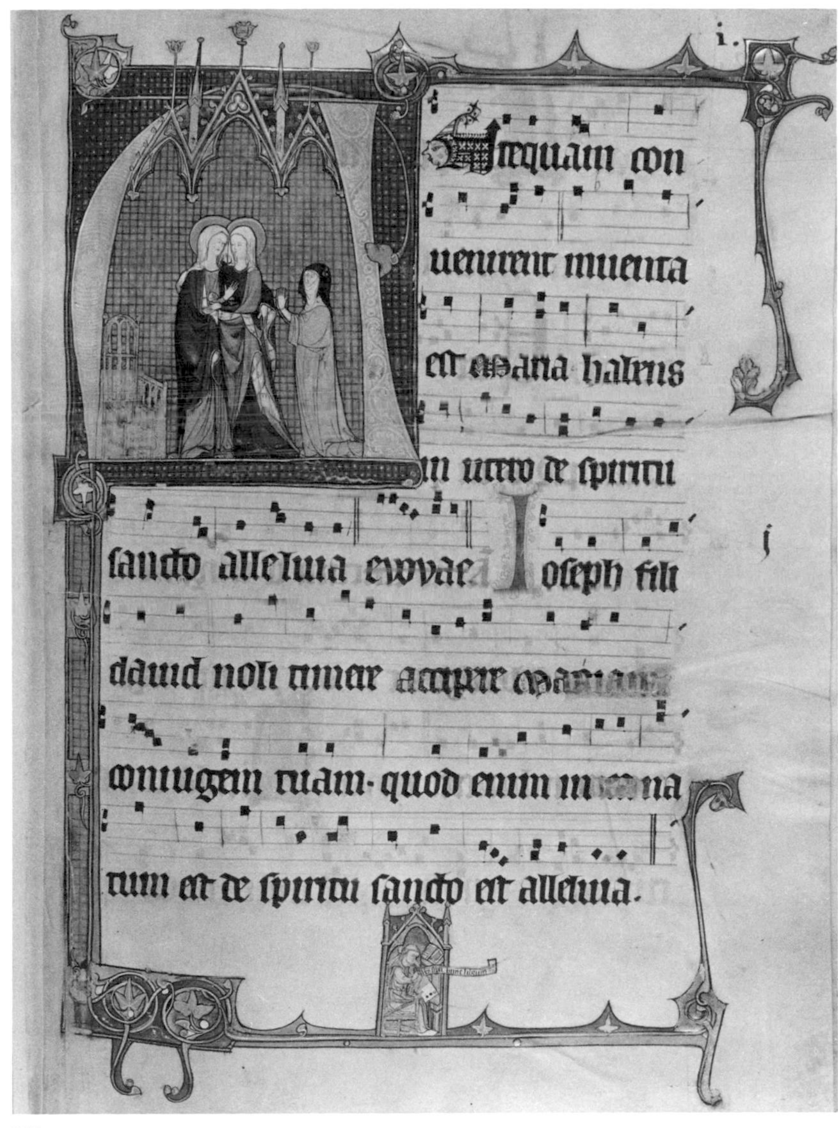

con
uenirent inuenta
est maria habens
in utero de spiritu
sancto alleluia
oseph fili
dauid noli timere
coniugem tuam quod enim
tum est de spiritu sancto est alleluia.

645

CXXXV 642. Schoolmaster: ape, woman with book: Melbourne 1254/3, f. 12v 643. Sciapode: W. 45, f. 92 644. Sciapode, variant: G.K.S. 3384, f. 108v 645. Scribe (cleric): "ego Iohannes scripsi hunc librum": W. 761, f. 1

646

647

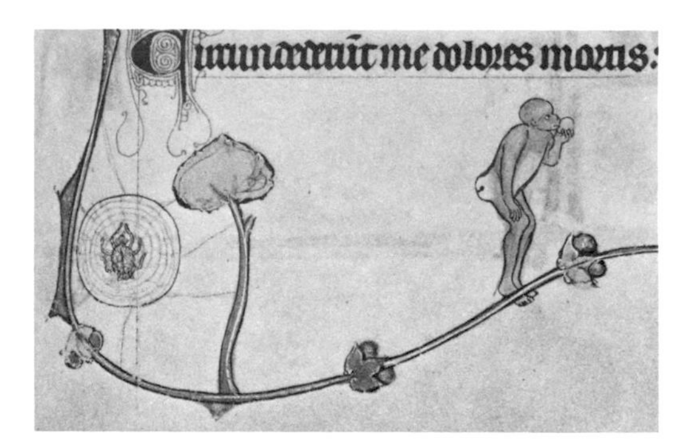

648

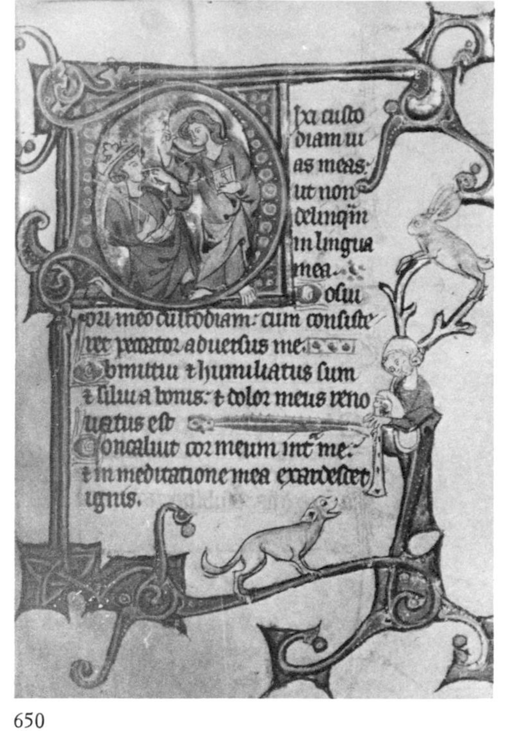

650

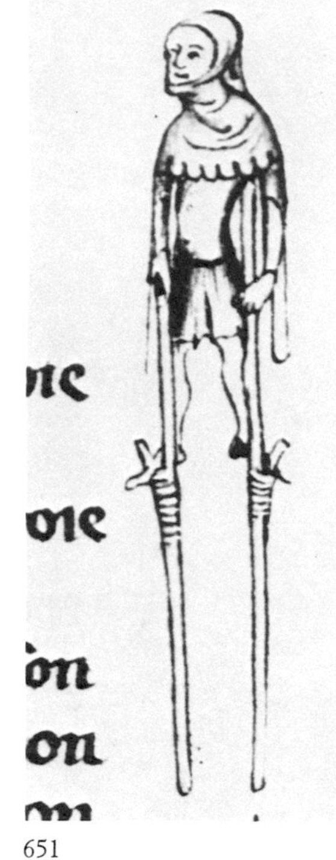

651

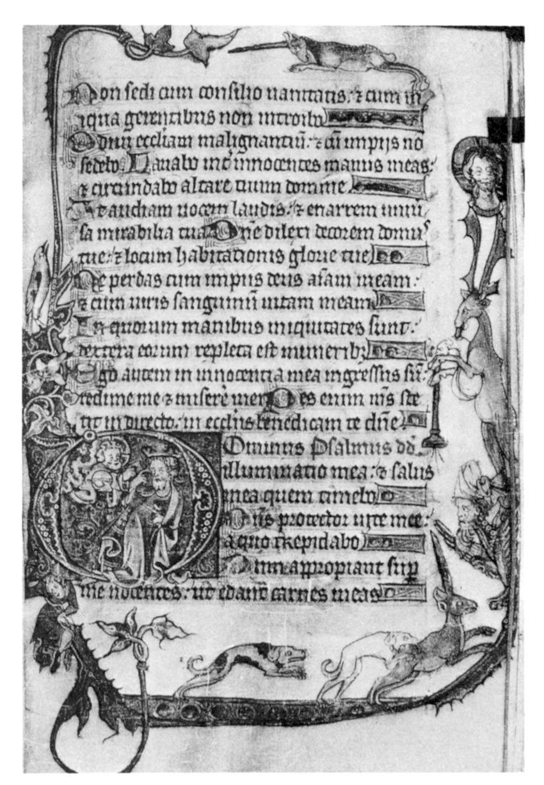

649

CXXXVI 646. Solomon, judgment of: Stowe 17, f. 117v 647. Solomon, judgment of: Nancy 249, f. 94 648. Spider; Ape with fruit: Trinity B.11.22, f. 155 649. Stag with bagpipe, Christ head between antlers, standing on hybrid bishop; Unicorn and dog, pursued by; Unicorn butting; (Bird); Initial supported by man: W. 82, f. 31. *Cf.* Fig. 650. Hybrid man with bagpipe, hare between antlers, dog barking: Kraus 75/88, f. 9 651. Stilts, worn by man: Glazier 24, f. 64

652

653

654

655

656

CXXXVII 652. Swan pulling boat containing knight (fabliau): Cambrai 103, f. 314 653. Swan, Bestiary representation: Trinity B.11.22, f. 79v 654. Swan, Bestiary representation: Cambrai 102, f. 361 655, 656. Synagogue, Ecclesia: Princeton 44-18, ff. 115v-116

si reddidi retribuen
tibus michi mala: de
cidam merito ab ini
micis meis inanis.
Persequatur inimi
cus meus animā me
am: et cōprehendat et
conculcet in terra ui
tam meā: et gloriam
meā in puluerem dedu
cat. Exurge dñe i
ra tua: et exaltare in
finibz inimicoꝝ meoꝝ.

657

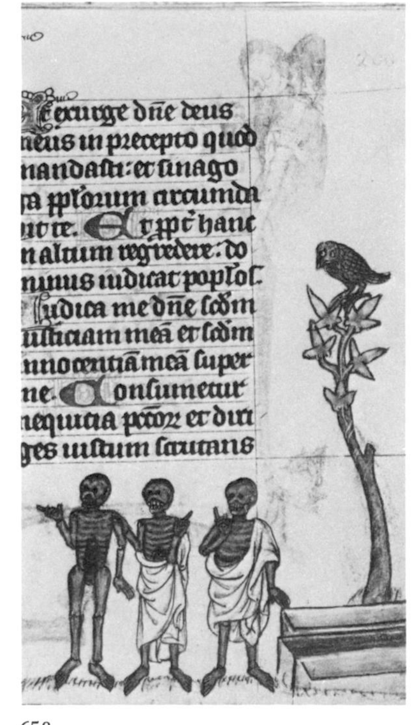
Exurge dñe deus
meus in precepto quod
mandasti: et sinago
ga ppłorum circumda
bit te. Et ꝓpt̄ hanc
in altum regredere: do
minus iudicat popłos.
Iudica me dñe scdm
iusticiam meā et scdm
innocentiā meā super
me. Consumetur
nequicia pctoꝝ et diri
ges iustum scrutans

658

inier
ier
sbrier
ngier
er

659

exultare qui

660

ucied ta langue te mal: e tes levres qne parolent tricherie
siue te te de mal e fai bien: enquier la pais e par sui la.

662

Incipiunt septem psal
mi penite
nciales.
Domine
ne in furo
re tuo arguas me neqꝫ
in ira tua corripias me.
Miserere mei domine
quoniam infirmus sū
sana me domine quoni
am conturbata sunt os

661

ur in escam meam fel & in sitim

663

664

665

666

CXXXVIII (opposite page) 657, 658. Three living and three dead: Stowe 17, ff. 199v-200 659. Templar and cleric: Glazier 24, f. 90 660. Top-whipping, ape: G.K.S. 3384, f. 185v 661. Top-whipping, man; Hybrid man with pyx: Cloisters 54.1.2, f. 183 662. Tiger, Bestiary representation: Munich c.g. 16, f. 29 663. Tug-of-war: Rutland Ps., f. 69v

CXXXIX 664. Unicorn, Bestiary representation: Fitz. 298, f. 81v 665. Unicorn, Bestiary representation: Fitz. 298, f. 131v 666. Unicorn, Bestiary representation: Verdun 107, f. 5v

667

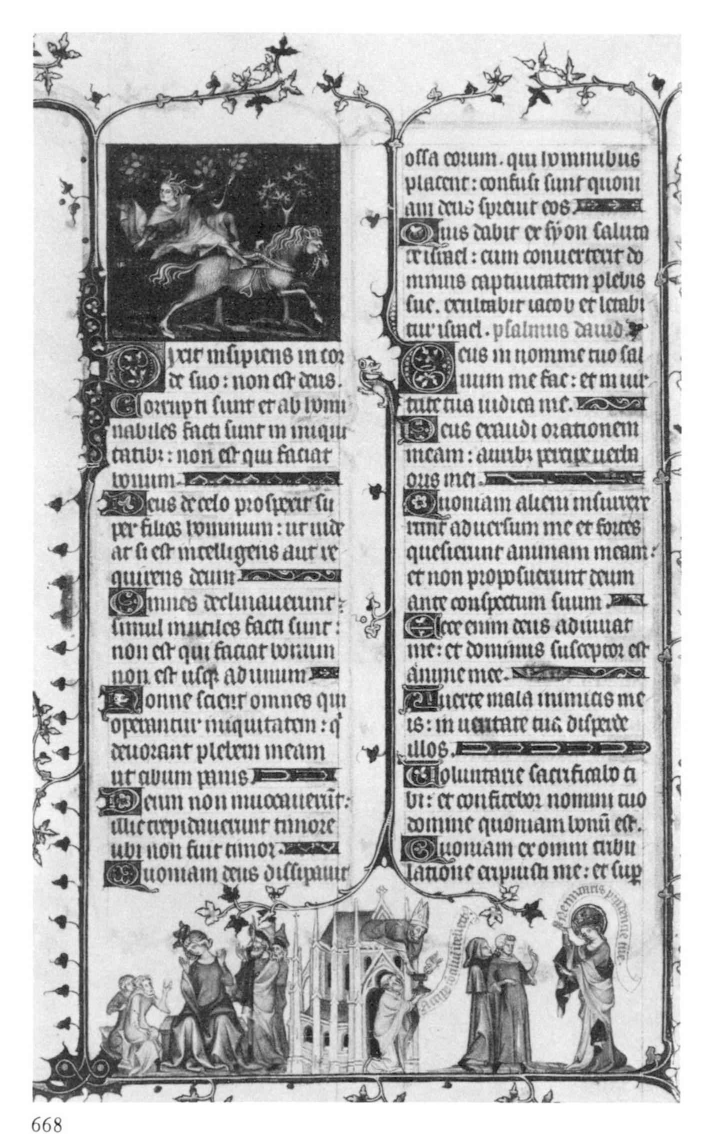

668

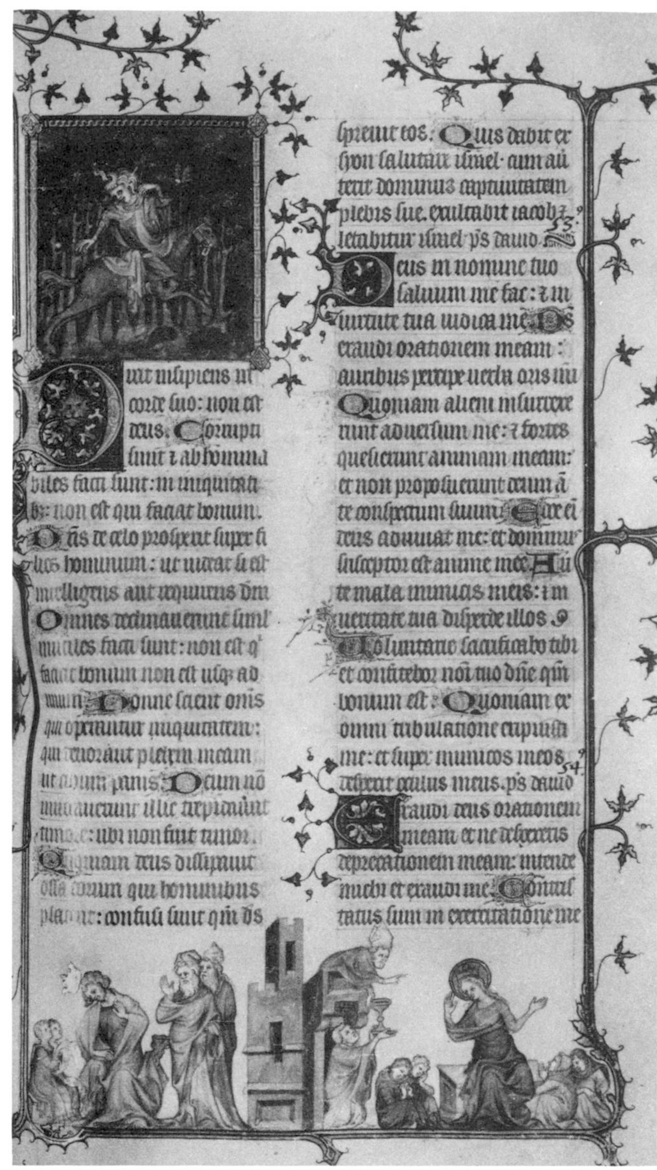

669

670

CXL 667. Unicorn, Bestiary representation: Douce 366, f. 55v 668. Vices: Imprudence; Sacraments: Order; Virtues: Prudence: latin 10484, f. 25v 669. Vices: Imprudence; Sacraments: Order; Virtues: Prudence: latin 1052, f. 232 670. Vices: Injustice; Sacraments: Penitence; Virtues: Justice: latin 1052, f. 252v

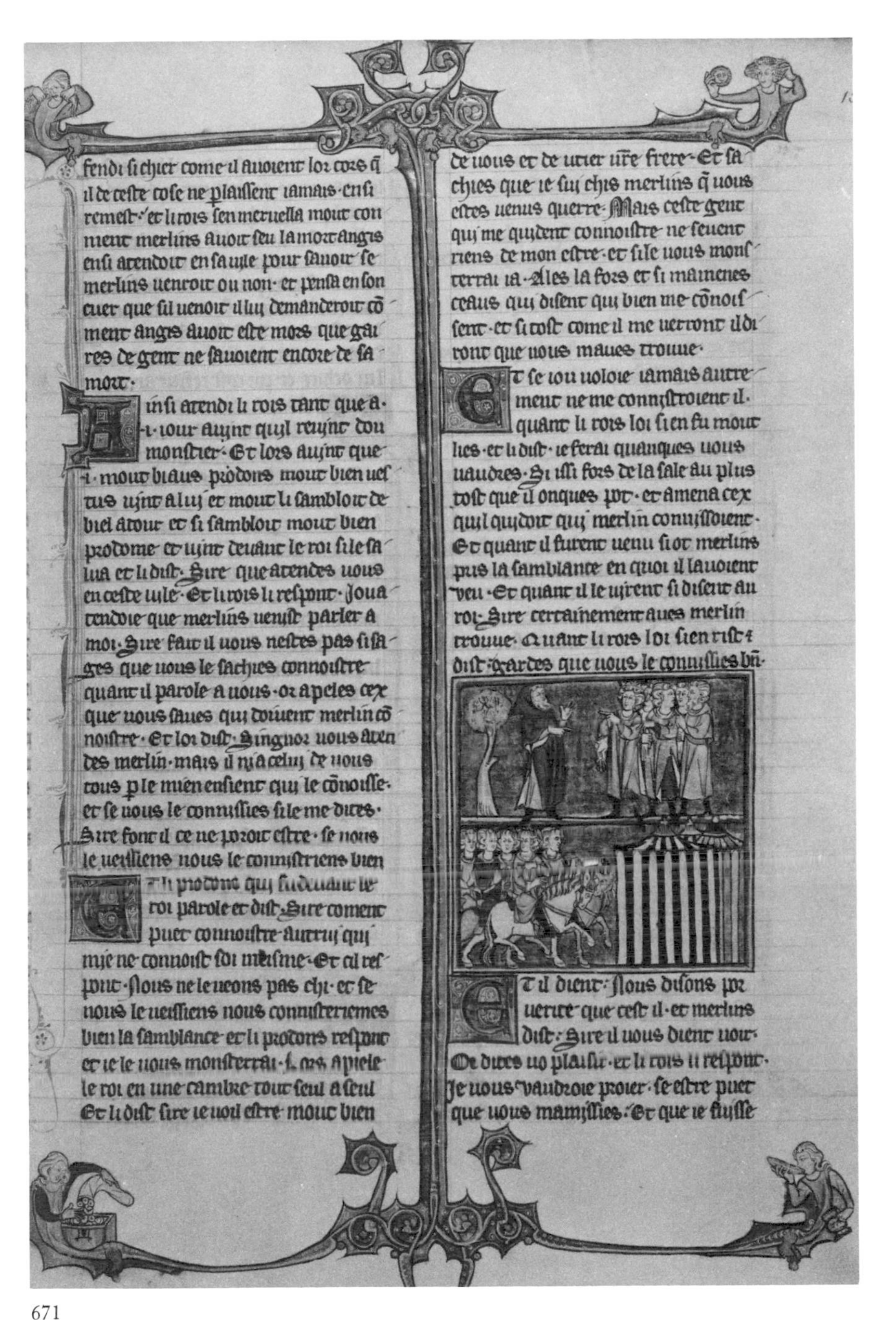

671

672

CXLI 671. Vices: Avarice, Gluttony, Vanity, Despair: fr. 95, f. 134 672. Virgin and Apostles: Add. 49622, f. 218 673. Virgin and Child, man fetching water: BBR 9391, f. 103 674. Virgin and Child, seated on Mount Carmel: Y. T. 13, f. 194

673

674

675

676

677

678

CXLII 675. Virgin, life of: Annunciation: Add. 42130, f. 86 676, 677. Virgin, life of: Death and Assumption; Patrons: Stowe 17, ff. 270v-271 678. Virgin, miracles of: abbess unchaste: Add. 42130, f. 104

679

680

681

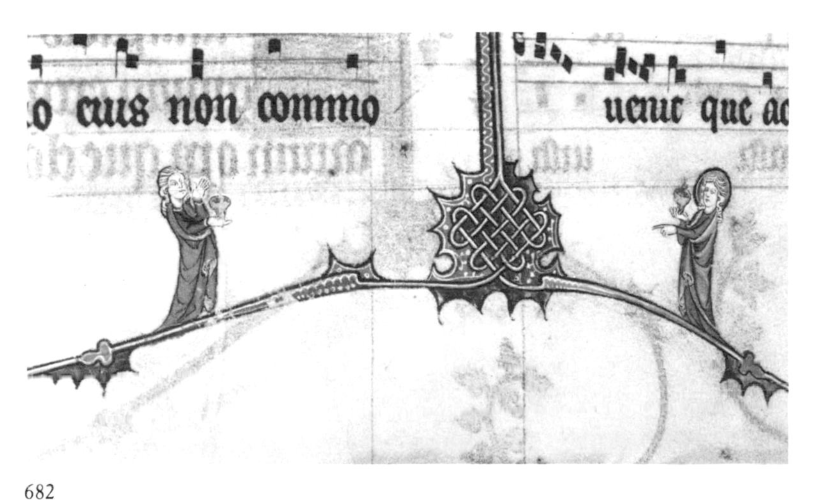

682

683

CXLIII 679. Virgin, miracles of: king's soul saved from devil: Royal 10 E.IV, f. 266 680. Virgin, miracles of: painter of the Virgin: Royal 2 B.VII, f. 211 681. Virgin, miracles of: Theophilus, deed returned by devil: Royal 2 B.VII, f. 205 682. Virgins, wise and foolish: Y.T. 8, f. 354v 683. Whale, Bestiary representation: Munich c.g. 16, f. 64

684

686

685

687

688

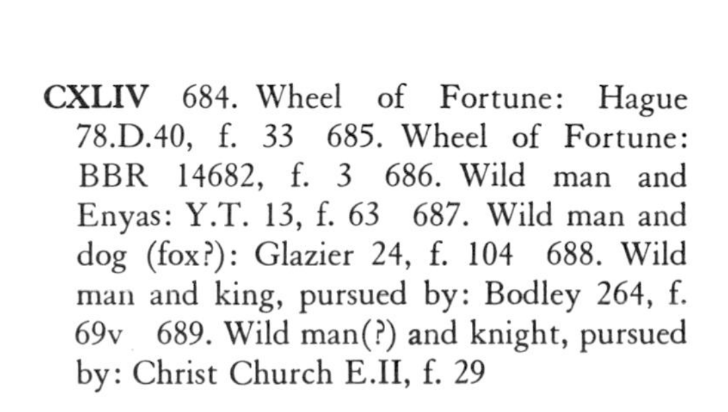

CXLIV 684. Wheel of Fortune: Hague 78.D.40, f. 33 685. Wheel of Fortune: BBR 14682, f. 3 686. Wild man and Enyas: Y.T. 13, f. 63 687. Wild man and dog (fox?): Glazier 24, f. 104 688. Wild man and king, pursued by: Bodley 264, f. 69v 689. Wild man(?) and knight, pursued by: Christ Church E.II, f. 29

689

690

692

691

693

694

695

CXLV 690. Wild man and knight, charged by: Douce 131, f. 68v 691. Wild man and knight, slain by: Douce 131, f. 81v 692. Wild man and lion: Glazier 24, f. 40v 693. Wild man with skull and bone: Cloisters 54.1.2, f. 50v 694. Wild man and wild woman: Christ Church E.II, f. 64v 695. Wild woman(?) with basket containing birds: Y.T. 8, f. 186v

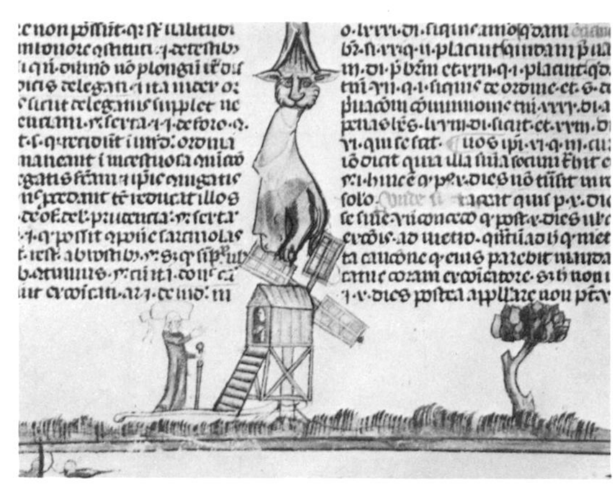

698

699

ne quem totus orb
nō capit portans pu
elle uiscera.
dix iesse iam floruit
et uirga fructū ededit
fecunda partū protu
lit et uirgo mat' per
net. Gloria tibi do
mine. qui natus est
de uirgine cum patre
et sancto spiritu in
sempiterna secula a
men. Beata mat'.

696

CXLVI 696. Windmill, man with sack on head approaching: Stowe 17, f. 89v 697. Windmill, man with whip approaching: Add. 42130, f. 158 698. Windmill, woman with sack on head approaching: Royal 10 E.IV, f. 70v 699. Windmill, man with sack and man driving ass approaching: Valenciennes 838, f. 55

obliuionis.

697

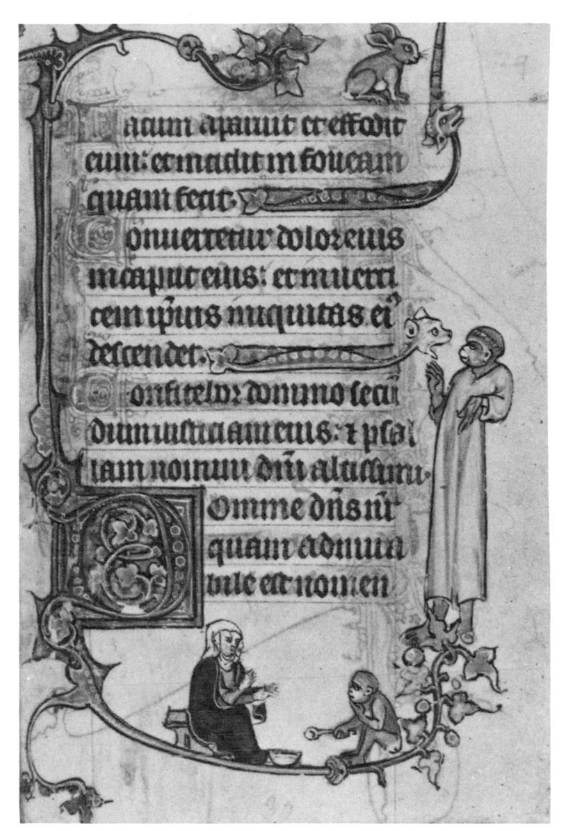

700

701

703

702

CXLVII 700. Woman and ape, observing; Ape as cleric: Douce 5, f. 29 701. Woman and chickens, feeding: Add. 42130, f. 166v 702. Woman and child by fire: Douce 6, f. 22 703. Woman and child: Glazier 24, f. 34

704

705

706

707

CXLVIII 704. Woman and child, bathing: Melbourne 1254/3, f. 10 705. Woman and Christ child, bathing: Douce 118, f. 135 706. Woman and Dominican, tilting: Yale MS., f. 100v 707. Woman and hare, hunting: BBR 329-41, f. 162

au plus priueement quil poroie

708

709

parentis p
meum uid

710

CXLIX 708. (Woman and knight) Knight and woman, charged by: fr. 95, f. 226 709. (Woman and knight) Knight and woman, charged by: Yale MS., f. 329 710. (Woman and knight) Knight and woman, charged by: Y.T. 8, f. 224

711

712

713

714

715

CL 711. (Woman and man) Man and woman, trapped by, in net; Man drinking: Douce 6, f. 83v 712. Woman and ram, baiting: Bodley 264, f. 20v 713. Woman and unicorn, baiting: Nancy 249, f. 206v 714. Woman and stag, hunting: Add. 24686, f. 13v 715. Woman and stag, hunting: Bodley 264, f. 122v

716

CLI 716. Woman as falconer; Falconer; Woman with vielle: Verdun 107, f. 12 717. Woman by fountain(?); Hybrid man and hybrid woman, bombarded with flowers by: latin 10435, f. 38v

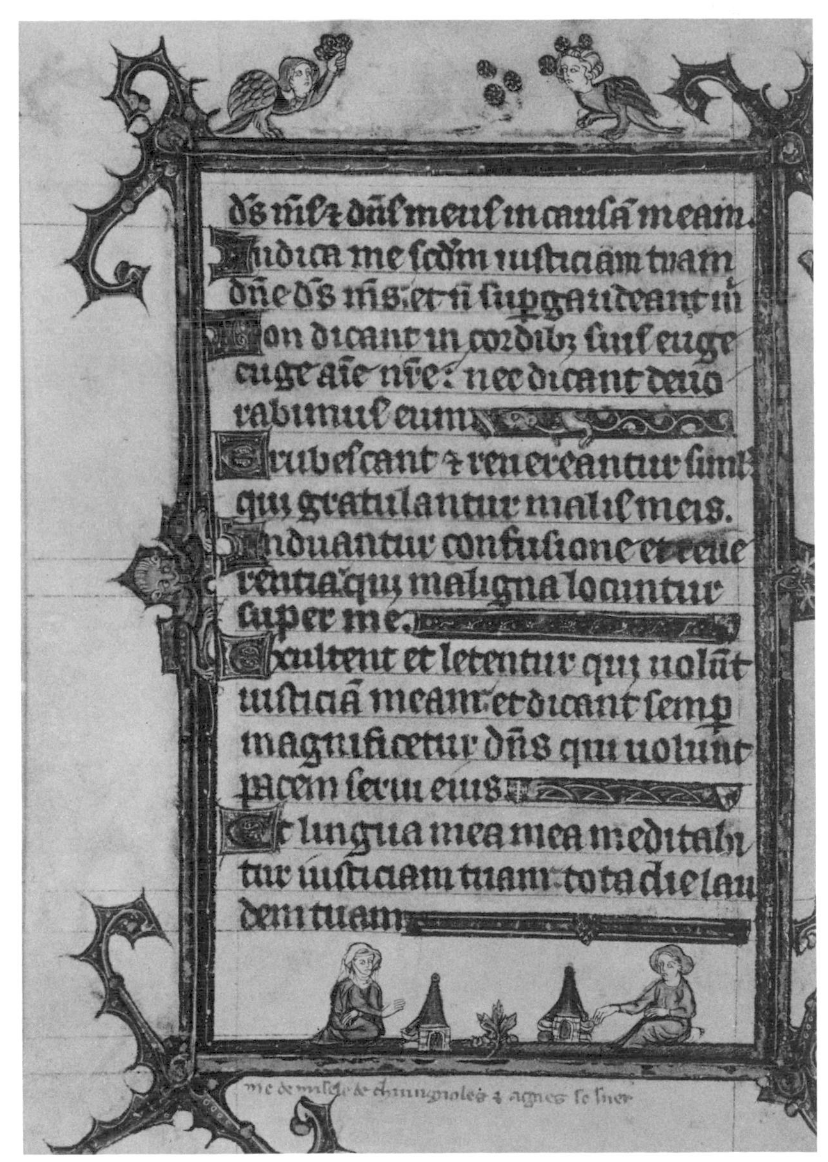

717

locutum est os meum:

718

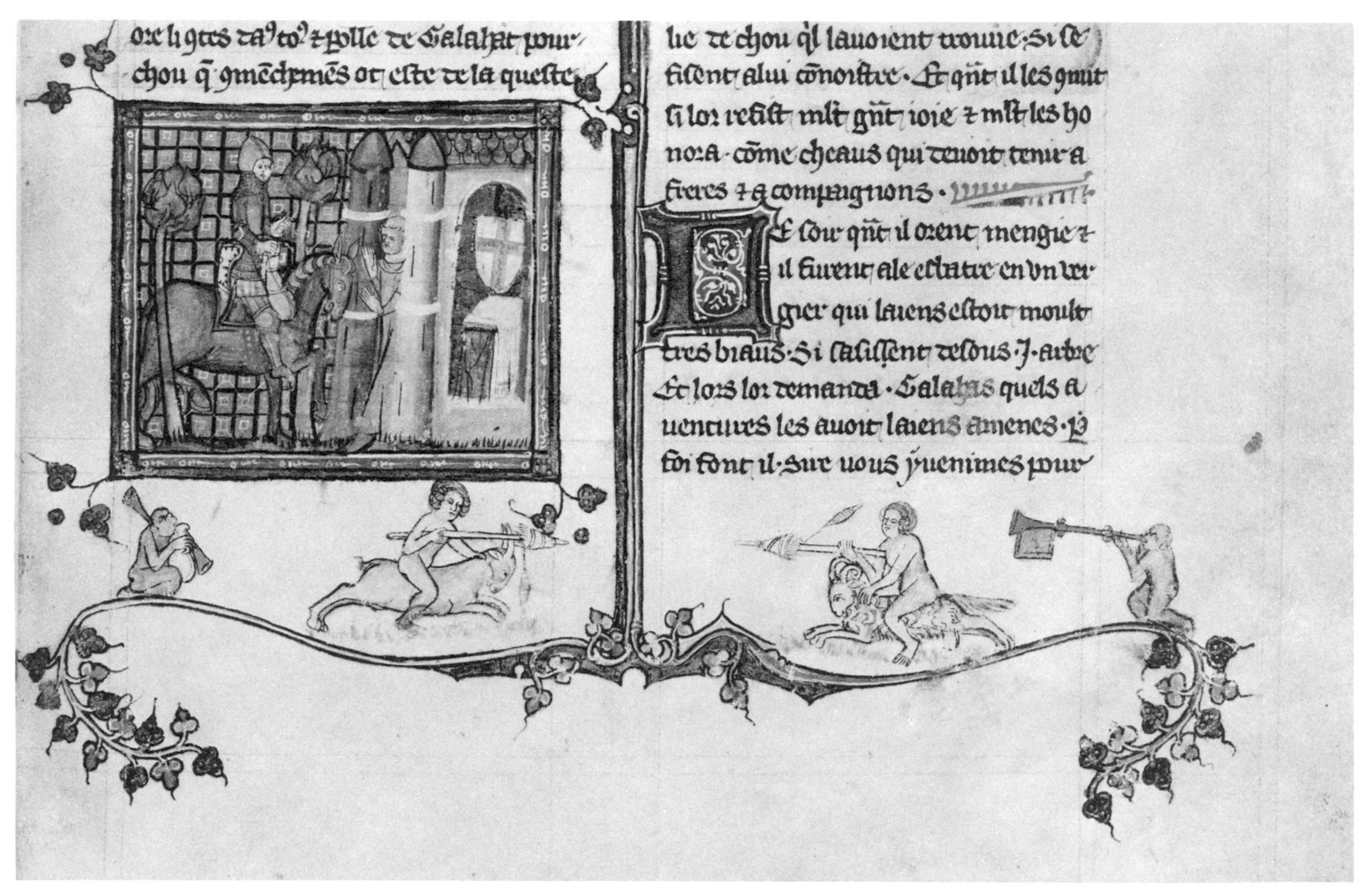

719

CLII 718. Woman balancing on hands: Rutland Ps., f. 65 719. Woman nude and goat, astride with distaff and spindle charging woman astride ram: Arsenal 5218, f. 10

CLIII 720. Woman balancing sword, man reaching for sword; Man with pipe and tabor: Cambridge Dd.5.5, f. 55
721. Woman nude and snail, fighting: Harley 6563, ff. 86v-87

720

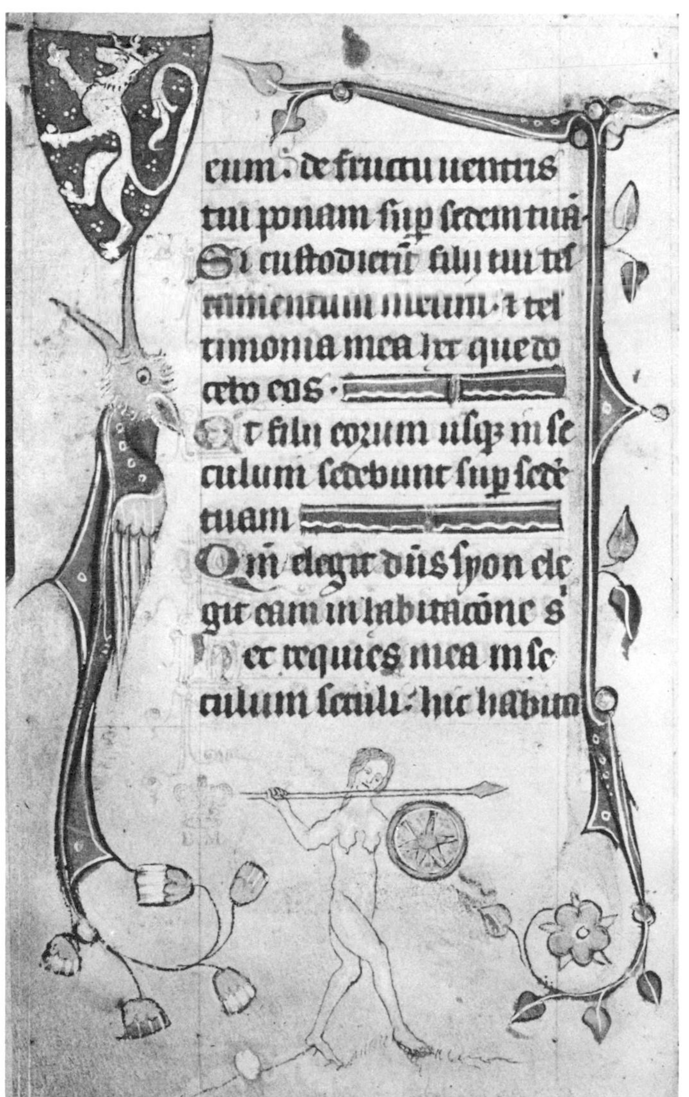

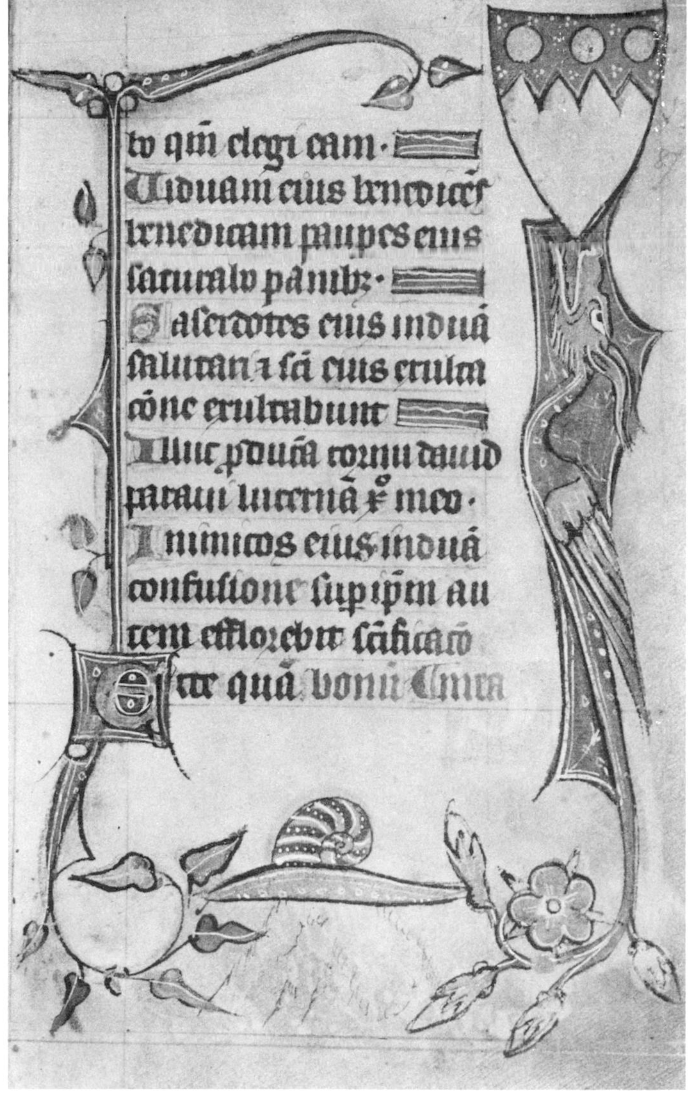

721

722

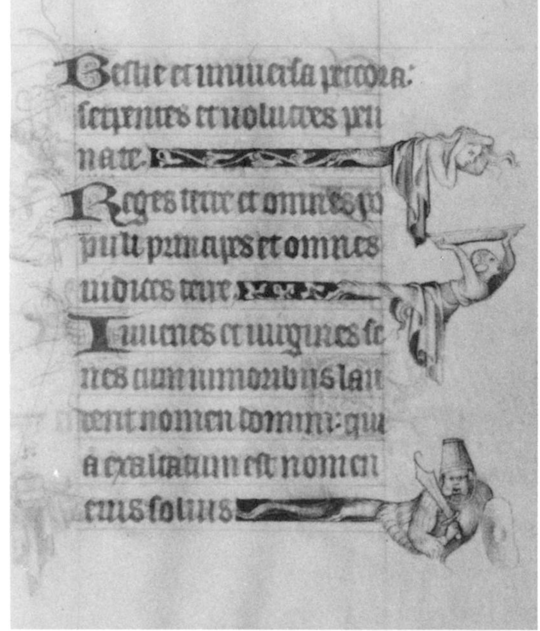

723

724

CLIV 722. Woman pulling boat containing man with bleeding neck (fabliau?): Nancy 249, f. 236 723. Woman washing hair; Saracen with falchion and shield, bucket on head: Cloisters 54.1.2, f. 45 724. Woman weaving (Naa-mah): Munich c.g. 16, f. 20v

725

726

727

728

CLV 725. Woman with basket, man with purse: Trinity B.11.22, f. 160v 726. (Proverbs) Woman with basket on head: Stowe 17, f. 67 727. Woman with basket: BBR 1175, f. 59 728. Woman with bundle on head: Fitz. 2-1954, f. 131v

729

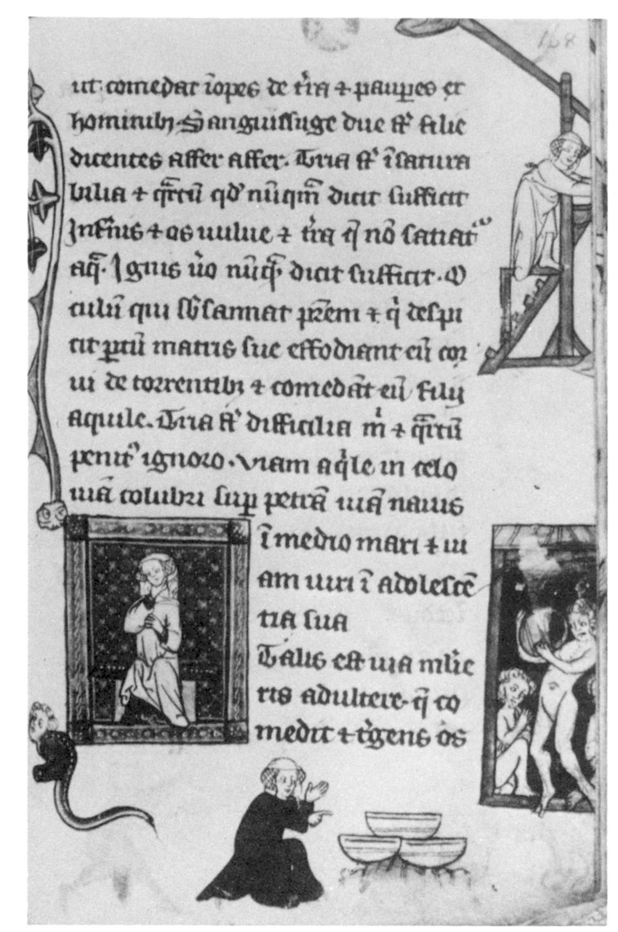

730

731

CLVI 729. Woman with birdcage: BBR 9961-62, f. 66 730. Woman with bowl(s); Woman ascending steps: Rothschild MS., f. 168 731. Woman with distaff and spindle on ducking stool (scold?): Rutland Ps., f. 86

is nomen eius in idip

732

733

CLVII 732. Woman with comb, seated, maid with mirror; (Dragon): Add. 42130, f. 63 733. Woman with distaff and spindle atop shell; Dolphin: Glazier 24, f. 107 734. Woman with distaff and spindle, dancing, knight with reel: Arras 47, f. 32 735. Woman with reel, man with distaff and spindle: Arras 47, f. 208v

autem in cordibz eorum.
scdm opera eor: et scdm neq

734

go dixi dne miserere mei: sana aiam
meam quia peccaui tibi.

735

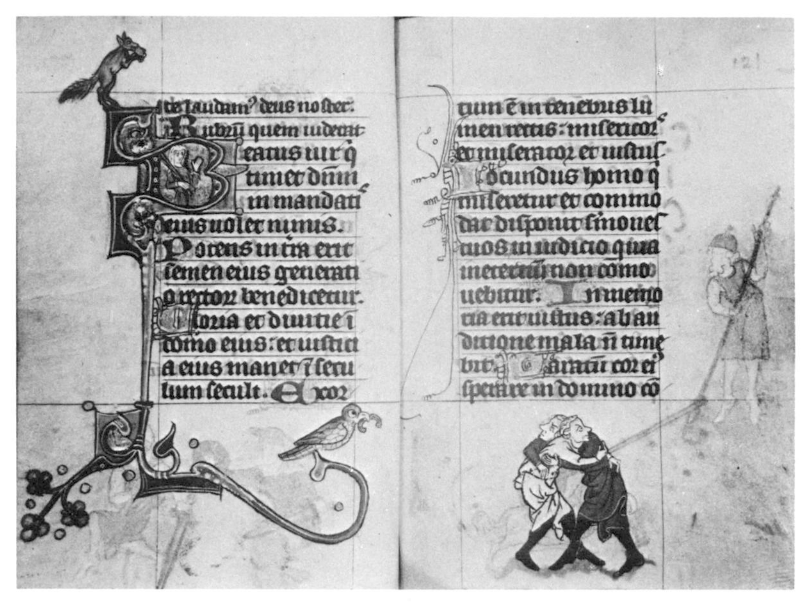

736

737

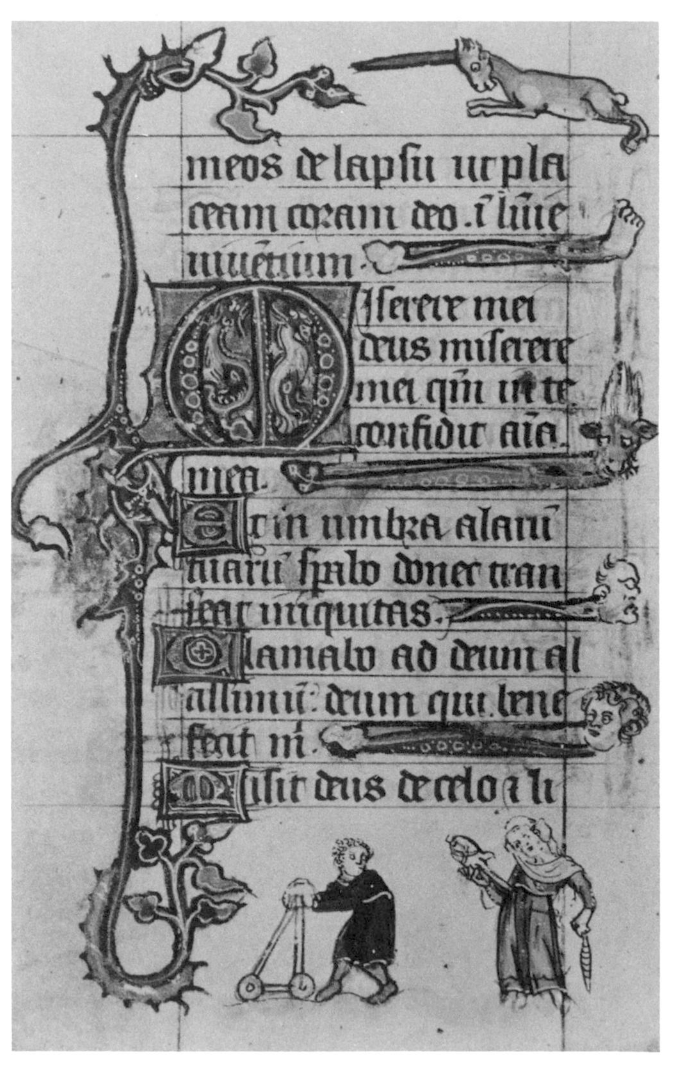

738

739

CLVIII 736. Wrestling, men; Bird with horseshoe(?); Fox with fruit: Stowe 17, ff. 120v-121 737. Woman with purse, two men bearing chest toward building: Douce 6, f. 100v 738. Woman with distaff and spindle, child with walker; Sciapode variant; Unicorn butting: G.K.S. 3384, f. 104v 739. Wrestling, men: Rutland Ps., f. 11